MW01628214

TITIAN • TINTORETTO • VERONESE

RIVALS IN RENAISSANCE VENICE

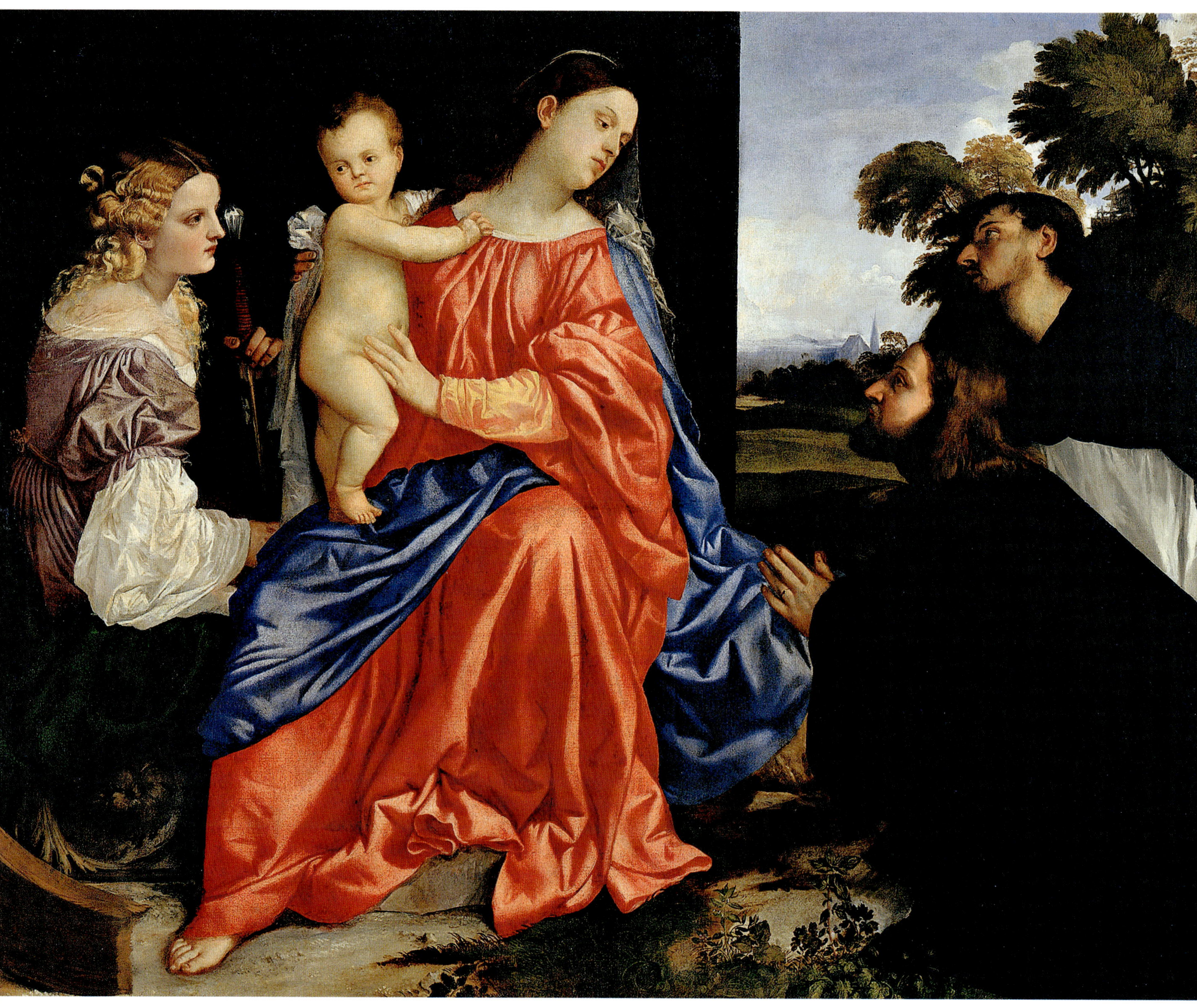

TITIAN ✦ TINTORETTO ✦ VERONESE

RIVALS IN RENAISSANCE VENICE

Frederick Ilchman

WITH CONTRIBUTIONS BY

Linda Borean, Patricia Fortini Brown, Vincent Delieuvin, Robert Echols, John Garton, Rhona MacBeth, John Marciari, David Rosand, Jonathan Unglaub, and Robert Wald

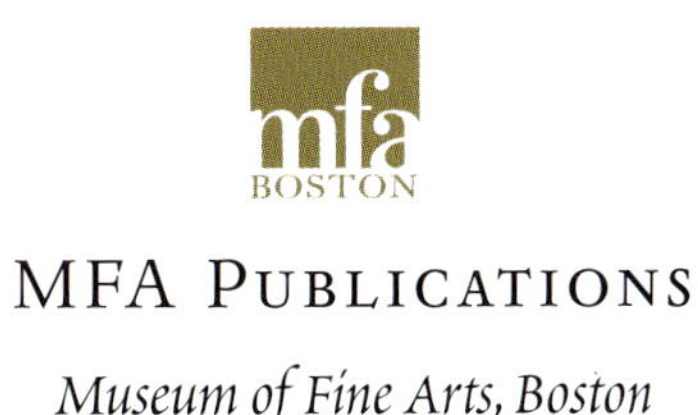

MFA Publications

Museum of Fine Arts, Boston

MFA Publications
Museum of Fine Arts, Boston
465 Huntington Avenue
Boston, Massachusetts 02115
www.mfa.org/publications

This book was published in conjunction with the exhibition "Titian, Tintoretto, Veronese: Rivals in Renaissance Venice," organized by the Museum of Fine Arts, Boston, and the Musée du Louvre, Paris.

Museum of Fine Arts, Boston
March 15, 2009–August 16, 2009

Musée du Louvre, Paris
September 14, 2009–January 4, 2010

The exhibition is sponsored by Pioneer Investments and UniCredit Group.

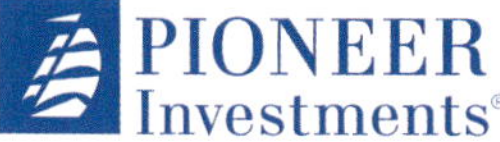

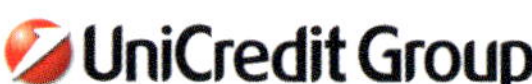

Generous support for the catalogue is provided by the Andrew W. Mellon Publications Fund and by Scott and Isabelle Black.

ISBN 978-0-87846-739-6 (hardcover)
ISBN 978-0-87846-740-2 (softcover)
Library of Congress Control Number: 2008941173

For a complete listing of MFA publications, please contact the publisher at the above address, or call 617 369 3438.

Front cover: Titian, *Venus with a Mirror*, about 1555 (detail, cat. 30)

Back cover: Tintoretto, *Tarquin and Lucretia*, 1578–80 (detail, cat. 46)

Pages 16–17: Giovanni Merlo, *Map of Venice*, 1670, published by Stefano Scolari. Courtesy of the Kunsthistorisches Institut in Florenz—Max-Planck-Institut. Site numbers and key added by Mary Reilly and MFA Publications, with permission.

Research assistance by Martha Clawson
Linda Borean's essay translated by Martha Clawson and Frederick Ilchman
Vincent Delieuvin's contribution to "Late Styles" translated by Mark Polizzotti
Edited by Matthew Battles, Mark Polizzotti, and Sarah McGaughey Tremblay
Copyedited by Dalia Geffen and Jodi M. Simpson

Designed by Cynthia Rockwell Randall
Produced by Cynthia Rockwell Randall and Jodi M. Simpson
Printed and bound at Arnoldo Mondadori Editore, Verona, Italy

Available through
D.A.P. / Distributed Art Publishers
155 Sixth Avenue, 2nd floor
New York, New York 10013
Tel.: 212 627 1999 · Fax: 212 627 9484

FIRST EDITION
Printed and bound in Italy
This book was printed on acid-free paper.

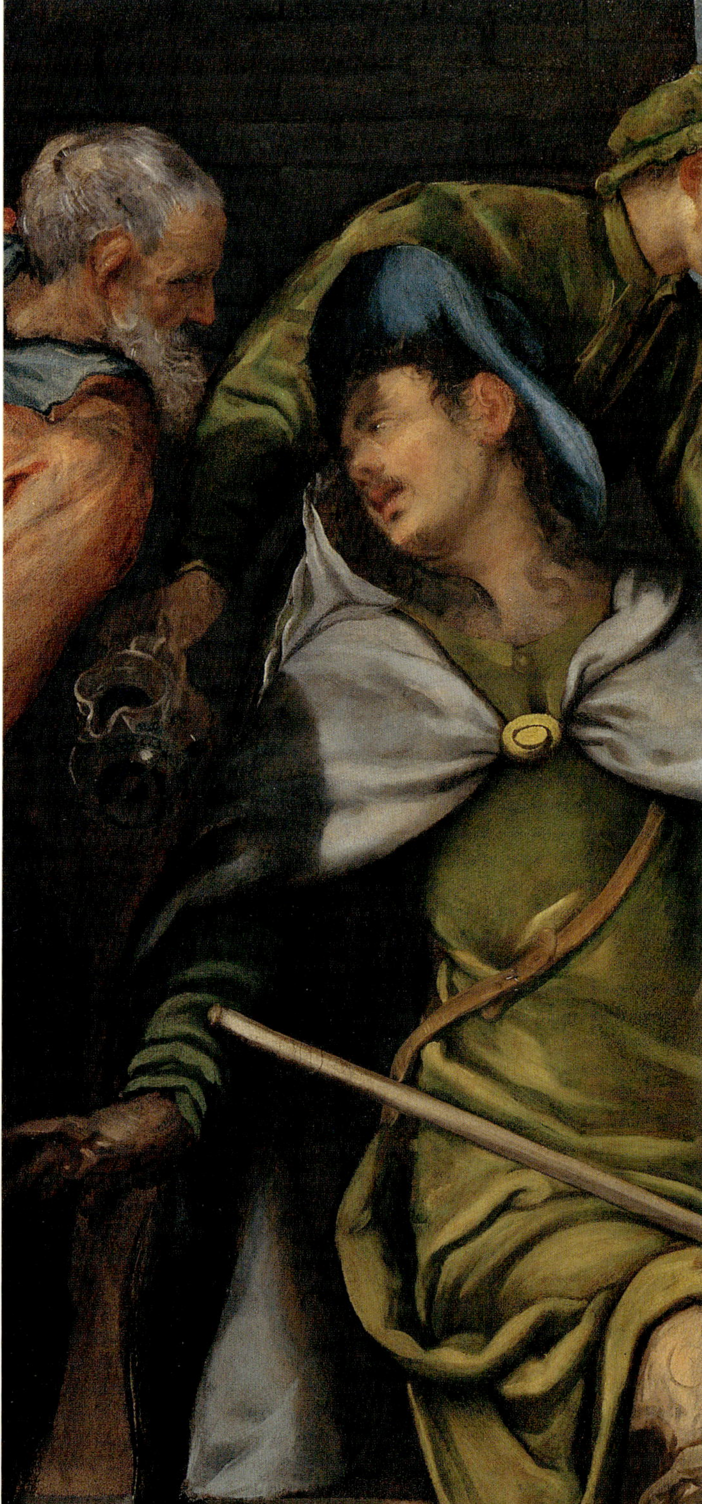

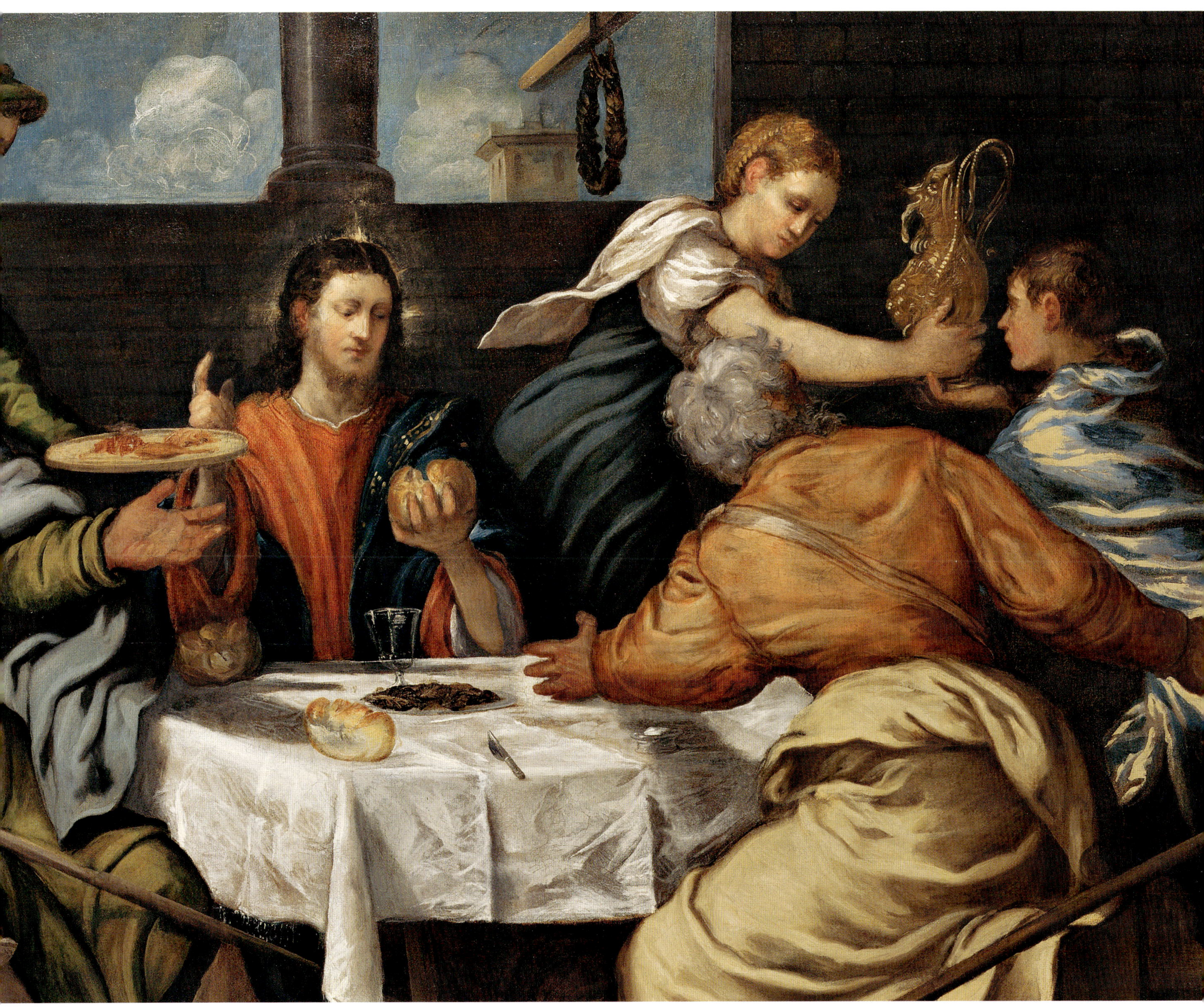

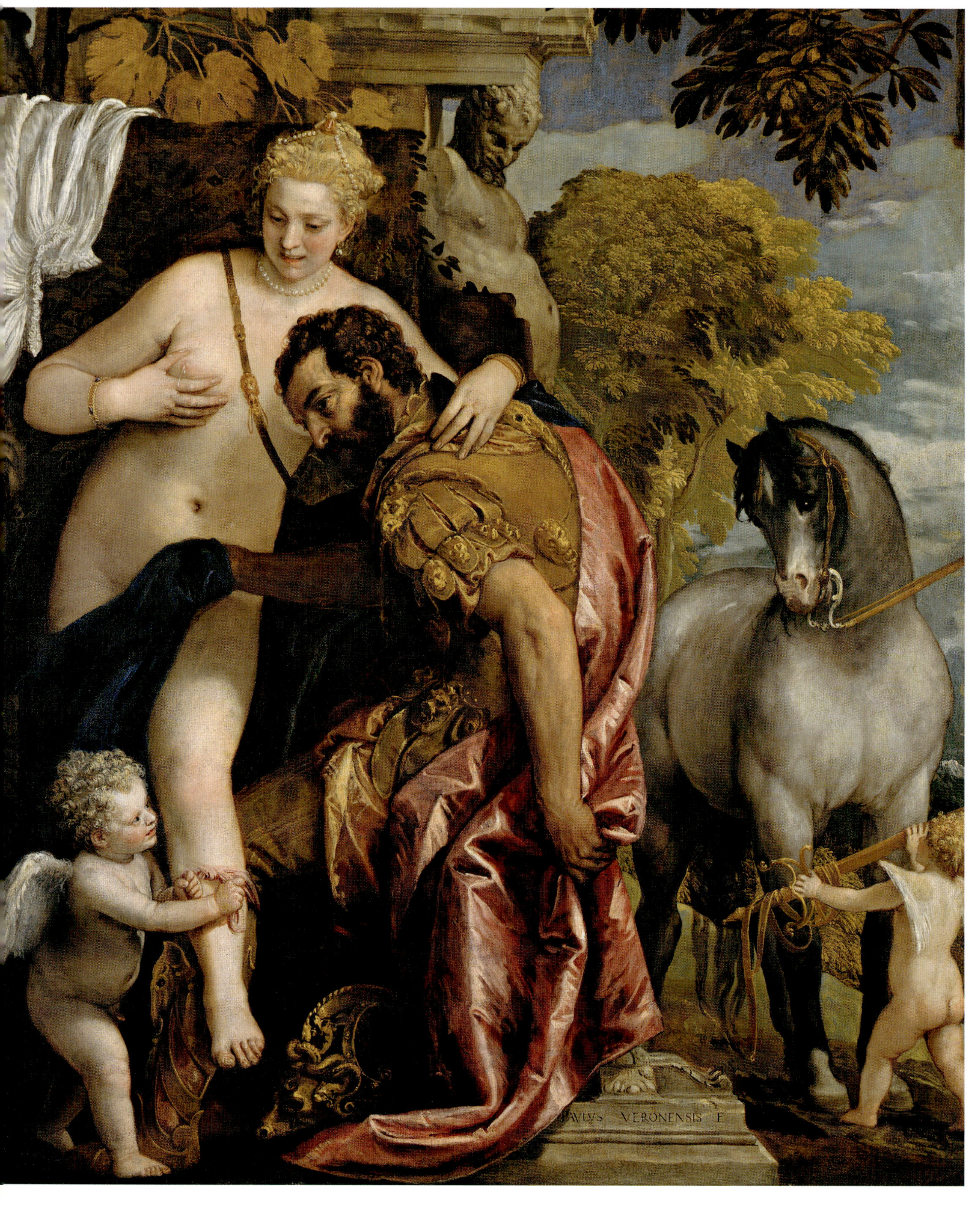
PAVLVS VERONENSIS F

CONTENTS

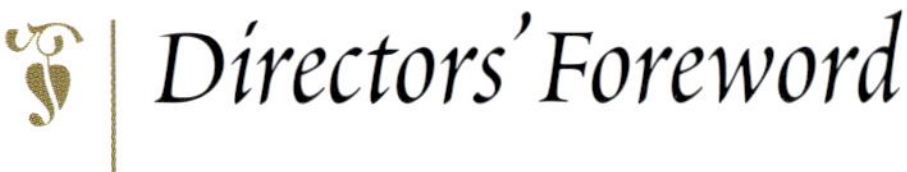

Directors' Foreword

Since their creation, the paintings of Titian, Tintoretto, and Veronese have been widely praised, coveted, and collected. Enthusiasts of these paintings have included Venetians and foreigners, kings and commoners, clerics and writers. Titian has always been particularly admired; his contemporary Ludovico Dolce claimed that "there was never a man who put painting into higher esteem." His formidable accomplishment comes into focus, however, only when set against the two greatest Venetian painters of the subsequent generation, Tintoretto and Veronese, who were both his close followers and most astute critics. The response of these two younger painters to Titian, and to each other, constitutes one of the most fascinating chapters in the history of art.

In subsequent centuries, the works of Titian, Tintoretto, and Veronese have been held up among the highest achievements in Western culture, fully representative of a Golden Age of Venetian painting. The legacy of these three artists endures not just in their fame but in how, together, they created a body of work that defined a "Venetian style" through loose technique, rich coloring, and often sensual subject matter. This style perpetuated a Venetian current both in Northern Italy and in the painting of later non-Italians, through artists as varied as El Greco, Rubens, Velázquez, Delacroix, and the Abstract Expressionists of the twentieth century.

Although Titian, Tintoretto, and Veronese may today seem the ultimate Old Master artists, like any aesthetic current Renaissance painting was once contemporary art: experimental, bold, even shocking. Each of these three painters forged his own art by responding to his rivals, recognizing the demands of the market, and offering his own original ideas. The exhibition "Titian, Tintoretto, Veronese: Rivals in Renaissance Venice," organized by the Museum of Fine Arts, Boston, and the Musée du Louvre, recreates, through carefully chosen juxtapositions, the heated discussions about the art of painting in sixteenth-century Venice: significant groupings of two or three canvases demonstrate how the artists were influenced by one another or, on the contrary, how they diverged. Within this dialogue, certain works can be seen as critiques of or tributes to another painter, but each artist ultimately emerges as a distinct individual.

The achievements of Titian, Tintoretto, and Veronese have been considered individually in many books and exhibitions, while other studies have set them within the wider context of the Venetian sixteenth century. However, this is the first major exhibition ever devoted specifically to their artistic exchange and rivalry. Whereas some of the pictures presented here are well known, others have been relatively neglected, and many have been newly conserved for the exhibition. A number of the juxtapositions featured here have never been proposed or executed. "Titian, Tintoretto, Veronese" is the most ambitious exhibition of Italian Renaissance painting in Boston in fifty years and an unprecedented opportunity for the American public to compare the work of the three painters. For Paris, the show builds upon the proud tradition of important exhibitions of Venetian painting organized by the Musée du Louvre and the Réunion des Musées Nationaux, including the magnificent exhibition of 1993, "Le Siècle de Titien," and, more recently, "Le Paradis de Tintoret: Un concors pour le palais des Doges" of 2006, organized by Jean Habert.

Finally, the present exhibition, besides offering an unprecedented look at the connections among these three painters, also simultaneously presents remarkable and carefully chosen surveys of the individual artists, including, for example, the greatest group of Tintoretto paintings ever assembled in the United States or France.

This exhibition is the result of a partnership between the Museum of Fine Arts, Boston, and the Musée du Louvre. We wish to salute the curatorial team that has prepared it: Frederick Ilchman, Mrs. Russell W. Baker Assistant Curator of Paintings, Art of Europe, at the Museum of Fine Arts; and Jean Habert, Senior

Curator, and Vincent Delieuvin, Curator of Sixteenth-Century Italian Painting, in the Department of Paintings at the Musée du Louvre. The scholarly collaboration of these three specialists has enabled a truly fascinating story to be told. The work of securing loans has been aided greatly in Paris by Vincent Pomarède, Chair, Department of Paintings, at the Louvre; and in Boston by George T. M. Shackelford, Chair, Art of Europe and Arthur K. Solomon Curator of Modern Art, and Ronni Baer, William and Ann Elfers Senior Curator of Paintings, both at the MFA.

The essays in this catalogue benefit from much new research and technical investigation that has taken place over the past decade. We are particularly indebted to Frederick Ilchman for conceiving, organizing, and bringing to publication these groundbreaking texts. We would also like to thank Patricia Fortini Brown, Linda Borean, and Robert Wald for their illuminating essays; and Vincent Delieuvin, Robert Echols, John Garton, Rhona MacBeth (Eijk and Rose-Marie van Otterloo Conservator of Paintings, Head of Paintings Conservation), John Marciari, David Rosand, and Jonathan Unglaub for important contributions to the catalogue. Victoria Reed, Monica S. Sadler Assistant Curator for Provenance at the MFA, reviewed and compiled the provenance information; Martha Clawson, Curatorial Research Associate, prepared the selected references, bibliography, and other aspects of this volume.

A project of this scale and complexity can only come to fruition through the financial support of generous individuals, foundations, and corporations. We are especially thankful to Pioneer Investments and UniCredit Group for sponsoring the exhibition in Boston. We are pleased that a global firm with Italian roots has found it fitting to make possible a celebration of Italian creativity in the United States. Additional support for the exhibition was provided by the Samuel H. Kress Foundation. The catalogue was made possible by generous funding from the Andrew W. Mellon Publications Fund and from Scott and Isabelle Black.

Early in the planning for this exhibition, the Museum of Fine Arts, Boston, was fortunate to receive the encouragement and assistance of a number of officials in the Ministero per i Beni e le Attività Culturali of the Republic of Italy, particularly in Rome and in the superintendencies of Naples, Florence, and, above all, Venice. In Venice, the cooperation of the Soprintendenza Speciale per il Polo Museale Veneziano and the Curia Patriarcale of the Diocese of Venice was essential. Crucial loan commitments for groups of paintings were secured in particular from the National Gallery of Art, Washington, DC; the Museo Nacional del Prado, Madrid; the Kunsthistorisches Museum, Vienna; and the Metropolitan Museum of Art, New York. The Pinacoteca di Vicenza was especially encouraging right from the start. The partnership with the Musée du Louvre not only secured remarkable loans from their holdings but also greatly aided borrowing works from a number of French institutions. We are extremely grateful to these lenders, and to all of the other public institutions and private collectors who generously allowed us to exhibit their precious paintings.

This Boston and Paris exhibition is not the first time that some of these paintings have been brought together since they left the artists' studios. For example, a number of the pictures were in the collections of King Charles I of England in the seventeenth century or the Ducs d'Orléans in the eighteenth. We would wager, however, that the selection in the present display revives the artistic dialogue and rivalry of Titian, Tintoretto, and Veronese in a way that the painters themselves would recognize and admire.

MALCOLM ROGERS
Ann and Graham Gund Director
Museum of Fine Arts, Boston

HENRI LOYRETTE
Président-directeur
Musée du Louvre

Curator's Introduction and Acknowledgments

"Titian, Tintoretto, Veronese: Rivals in Renaissance Venice" was conceived in Boston as an attempt to provide a new lens on sixteenth-century Venetian painting. Many past exhibitions dedicated to Venice's Golden Age, while brilliantly organized and extremely satisfying to visit, may not have been able to plumb certain aspects of the creation of a work of art with the depth or focus they deserved. While shows devoted to a single artist, such as the exemplary surveys of Titian (Venice and Washington, 1990; London and Madrid, 2003), Veronese (Washington, 1988), or Tintoretto (Madrid, 2007), might thoroughly address the artistic development of a painter and help us understand the arc of his career, such concentration can neglect the big picture, promoting the sense that a painter developed in a vacuum, without regard to the work of predecessors and contemporaries. Conversely, the great surveys in London (1983), Paris (1993), and Washington and Vienna (2006), among others, presented the rich milieu of Venetian Renaissance painting in its full context, displaying the variety of themes, individuals, and media that made up this flourishing school (and, along the way, introducing the wider public to relatively under-appreciated artists, as was likely the case with Lorenzo Lotto, thirteen paintings by whom were included in the 1983 London exhibition "Genius of Venice"). By their very breadth, however, these surveys were necessarily limited in focus, and the contributions of the individual artists often became lost in the sheer range of material.

"Titian, Tintoretto, Veronese" intends a middle ground between the monographic retrospective and the presentation of an entire school, centering on a limited number of personalities while including enough relevant context that the growth of each painter reflects the contributions made by the others. As such, the exhibition in Boston, apart from two paintings at the start of the show, includes only works by the three principals, often referred to as the "Big Three" of Venetian Renaissance painting. My thesis is that a re-creation of the artistic dialogue and rivalry among the era's three greatest painters sheds new light on this well-studied period. Although Titian was born thirty years before Tintoretto and forty years before Veronese, his extremely long life meant that the three painters overlapped creatively and professionally for nearly four decades. Their art is one of response, critique, and emulation. Furthermore, while the careers of Tintoretto and Veronese can be seen largely as accommodations and reactions to the example of Titian, the influence did not pass in one direction only: indeed, much of Titian's later career was informed by his response to the two younger painters, who affected his choice of commissions, his treatment of iconography, and even his manner of applying paint. Most of the grand surveys of Venetian painting have concentrated on the early decades of the sixteenth century, particularly on the exciting overlap of Giovanni Bellini, the mysterious Giorgione, and the initial development of Titian and Sebastiano. Those exhibitions that progressed to the second half of the Cinquecento paid less attention to the later painters and generally gave short shrift to Veronese and Tintoretto. An overriding aim of the present exhibition is to concentrate on the period after 1545, showcasing the two younger artists at their best and highlighting the "late styles" of all three. In this context, the individual contributions to the remarkable loosening of paint handling, visionary expression, and development of the oil-on-canvas easel format in sixteenth-century Venetian painting can be discerned.

One might well wonder at the absence of Jacopo Bassano, also justly considered one of the truly great painters of the sixteenth century. After all, Bassano's own experiments with loose brushwork are arguably as innovative as the late styles of the Big Three, and Veronese (and quite likely the other two as well) seems to have admired him greatly. But Bassano, while closely aware of developments in Venice, executed few public commissions for the city and largely had a more provincial clientele than the Big Three. He also developed specialties with subjects, such as pastoral topics or biblical stories within genre scenes, that had little in common with the work of Titian, Tintoretto, and Veronese. More to the point, Bassano did not significantly participate in the rivalry among these three titans, and therefore stands outside the story being told here.

The concept for an exhibition about the rivalry between Titian, Tintoretto, and Veronese, begun in Boston, was greatly refined and improved when a collaboration was initiated between the Museum of Fine Arts and the Musée du Louvre in 2007. My co-curators at the Louvre, Jean Habert, Senior Curator in the Department of Paintings, a distinguished scholar on Venetian painting and curator of several important exhibitions, and Vincent Delieuvin, Curator of Sixteenth-Century Italian Painting, made the exhibition plan far more complex and sophisticated than first envisioned. Certain key themes and a number of ingenious pairings, such as the group of beautiful women and mirrors, should be credited to them. In addition, the eminent reputations of my colleagues, the prestige of the Louvre, and its track record in organizing great exhibitions of Renaissance painting aided us greatly in securing loans of the highest quality. The shaping of the exhibition and its themes were much improved as a result of my discussions with Jean and Vincent, and it has been a pleasure working with them.

Scholars of the period are familiar with the abundance of biographies, dialogues, letters, and commentaries about Italian art of the sixteenth and seventeenth centuries. From such texts, one can begin to reconstruct contemporary discussions about painting, style, and subject matter, including the crucial debate over *disegno* and *colorito*, and the present catalogue makes full use of this rich source material. The most eloquent documents about Renaissance art, however, are the paintings themselves. When arranged in groupings of similar subject matter or composition—for example, Saint Jeromes by Titian, Tintoretto, and Veronese placed in juxtaposition—the paintings reveal the aesthetic priorities of each artist, demonstrating how an earlier work might well have provided the impetus for a pointed response. In most cases, there is no written evidence that one artist's painting was a corrective of another's, making the visual similarities and differences suggested by such juxtapositions, and the conclusions we can draw from them, all the more evocative.

Moreover, as the map of Venice makes clear, these artists were quite aware of their rivals' works, and often found themselves angling for pubic commissions just around the corner from one another, sometimes even in the same building. What they were competing for, however, was not just employment but their place in posterity, and each one cared deeply about how other artists perceived his creations. In this context, it is important to stress that a goal of this show is not simply iconographic comparisons, for which copies or workshop paintings would be sufficient, but rather a profound display of the individual handling, brushwork, and touch of the artist. The distinctive way each of these three painters manipulated the brush helps account for the general disappearance by the 1520s of signatures in Venetian painting: if one can tell a Titian, a Tintoretto, or a Veronese by its brushwork, a signature becomes superfluous. Making such comparisons, of course, requires autograph works of the highest quality and in good condition, and I am extremely grateful to the lenders who have generously allowed us to borrow many masterpieces by these artists and display them together.

Indeed, if this exhibition proposes to reconstruct the rivalry and dialogue of these artists accurately, the works included must be by the masters themselves and should be dated securely, since an argument of artistic influence necessitates determining precedence. Of the three painters, Titian is surely the most studied, and most scholars would agree on the central questions of authorship and chronology, even if some controversies remain. Thus the greatest challenge was not so much choosing autograph examples by Titian, but obtaining loans of pertinent Tintoretto and Veronese works that had not traveled too much to recent exhibitions. Tintoretto, however, presented another test, as his oeuvre continues to be misunderstood: many of the paintings accorded autograph status, and even great importance, in the standard catalogue raisonné are actually by his workshop or imitators. To this end, research by Miguel Falomir and Robert Echols, as well as my own work, has begun to clarify Tintoretto's output and chronology, reflected notably in the 2007 Tintoretto exhibition at the Museo Nacional del Prado, in Madrid. The paintings by Tintoretto included in Boston thus follow this stricter view of attribution and chronology, sometimes differing dramatically from the opinions in the older literature. Alas, Veronese connoisseurship and chronology remain more problematic, and much work is still to be done. The more approximate dates given for his paintings in this catalogue reflect this uncertainty.

No exhibition of Venetian painting can replace a visit to Venice, and even the remarkable selection of paintings assembled here loses some of its meaning when the works are removed from their original context—whether the specific buildings for which some were commissioned (where the painters may have taken into account existing architecture, other paintings, and the available light sources) or even the city itself, with its mosaics and gilded polyptychs, the sun flickering off moving water, and the moist air coming off its lagoon. To take one example, this show contains a number of important altarpieces by Tintoretto and Veronese, which cannot be hung as high in a museum as they were in their ecclesiastical settings. By way of compensation, however, an exhibition offers the opportunity to compare in the same gallery paintings clearly created in the spirit of dialogue that now hang in different churches and museums, often an ocean apart. Bringing together these selected works allows us to revive the conversations about art that made the era of Titian, Tintoretto, and Veronese so exciting for contemporaries and later generations alike. An exhibition also gives us the opportunity to view the surfaces of the paintings from the vantage point of the artist, something few contemporary Venetians were able to do—to see them, as the scholar David Rosand put it when asked how far one should stand from a Renaissance painting, at an arm's length, plus one brush.

This project has found inspiration in numerous sources, including previous exhibitions of both Renaissance and modern art; the writings of Roger Rearick; Rona Goffen's brilliant book *Renaissance Rivals*; and the delightful guide to the Budapest Museum of Fine Arts, *A Dialogue of Paintings* by Vilmos Tátrai. In addition, I am indebted to the many colleagues who provided invaluable help in preparing this exhibition and catalogue—first and foremost, my esteemed partners at the Musée du Louvre: the museum's director, Henri Loyrette; Vincent Pomarède; Jean Habert; Vincent Delieuvin; Sixtine de-Saint-Leger; Pascal Perinel; and Violaine Bouvet-Lanselle.

I would also like to express my gratitude to the following individuals and lending institutions: Karl Schütz, Sylvia Ferino-Pagden, Elke Oberthaler, and Robert Wald at the Kunsthistorisches Museum in Vienna; Olivier Le Bihan at the Musée des Beaux-Arts de Bordeaux; Patrick Ramade at the Musée des Beaux-Arts de Caen; Sylvie Ramon and Isabelle Dubois at the Musée des Beaux-Arts de Lyon; Francis Ribemont and Anne-Laure le Guen at the Musée des Beaux-Arts de Rennes; Reinhold Baumstark, Cornelia Syre, and Jan Schmidt at the Alte Pinakothek in Munich; László Baán, Ildikó Ember, Vilmos Tátrai, and Axel Vécsey at the Szépmıvészeti Múzeum in Budapest; Cristina Acidini, Antonio Natali, Serena Padovani, Rosanna Morozzi, and Marino Marini at the Soprintendenza Speciale per il Polo Museale Fiorentino, the Galleria degli Uffizi, the Galleria Palatina, and the Donazione Contini Bonacossi in Florence; Manfredo Manfredi, Simona Tosini Pizzetti, and Stefano Roffi at the Fondazione Magnani Rocca in Mamiano di Traversetolo; Serenita Papaldo, Maria Grazia Bernardini, Mario Scalini, and Angelo Mazza at the Soprintendenza per i Beni storici, artistici ed etnoantropologici di Modena e Reggio Emilia and the Galleria Estense in Modena; Nicola Spinosa and Brigitte Daprà at the Soprintendenza Speciale per il Polo Museale Napoletano and the Museo di Capodimonte in Naples; Giovanna Nepi Scirè, Giulio Manieri Elia, Roberto Fontanari, Sandra Rossi, Luca Caburlotto, Alfeo Michieletto, and Giulio Bono at the Soprintendenza Speciale per il Polo Museale Veneziano and the Gallerie dell'Accademia in Venice; Monsignor Antonio Meneguolo, Don Gianmatteo Caputo, Irene Galifi, and Elisabetta Venturini at the Curia Patriarcale di Venezia and the Ufficio Beni Culturali del Patriarcato di Venezia in Venice; Maria Elisa Avagnina and Iole Adami at the Musei Civici, Pinacoteca di Palazzo Chiericati in Vicenza; Miguel Zugaza Miranda, Gabriele Finaldi, Miguel Falomir, Ana González Mozo, and Lorena Casas at the Museo Nacional del Prado in Madrid; Carlos

Fernández de Henestrosa y Argüelles and Guillermo Solana Diez at the Museo Thyssen-Bornemisza in Madrid; Evert J. van Straaten at the Kröller-Müller Museum in Otterlo; Sjarel Ex and Jeroen Giltaij at the Museum Boijmans Van Beuningen in Rotterdam; Michael Clarke, Christopher Baker, and Aidan Weston-Lewis at the National Gallery of Scotland in Edinburgh; Nicholas Penny, David Jaffé, Carol Plazzotta, and Claire Hallinan at the National Gallery in London; Her Majesty, Queen Elizabeth II, Desmond Shawe-Taylor, Lucy Whitaker, and Jennifer Scott at the Royal Collection in London; Gary Vikan, Joaneath Spicer, and Danielle Hall Bennett at the Walters Art Museum in Baltimore; Anne Hawley, Alan Chong, and Gianfranco Pocobene at the Isabella Stewart Gardner Museum in Boston;: James Cuno, Douglas W. Druick, and Martha Wolff at the Art Institute of Chicago; Timothy Rub and Jon L. Seydl at the Cleveland Museum of Art; Susan Lubowsky Talbott, Coleman H. Casey, Eric Zafran, Linda H. Roth, and Ulrich Birkmaier at the Wadsworth Atheneum Museum of Art in Hartford; Michael Brand, David Bomford, Scott Schaefer, Mark Leonard, and Peter Björn Kerber at the J. Paul Getty Museum in Los Angeles; Sarane H. Ross, Jock Reynolds, Laurence B. Kanter, and John Marciari at the Yale University Art Gallery in New Haven and the Barker Welfare Foundation; Philippe de Montebello, Everett Fahy, Keith Christiansen, Andrea Bayer, George Bisacca, Charlotte Hale, and Cynthia Chin at the Metropolitan Museum of Art in New York; William J. Hennessey, Catherine Jordan Wass, Jefferson C. Harrison, and Mark Lewis at the Chrysler Museum of Art in Norfolk; J. Brooks Joyner, Anne El-Omami, John Wilson, and Deborah Long at the Joslyn Art Museum in Omaha; the late Anne d'Harnoncourt, Joseph Rishel, and Carl Brandon Strehlke at the Philadelphia Museum of Art; Earl A. Powell III, Franklin Kelly, and David Alan Brown, who was particularly helpful and encouraging, at the National Gallery of Art in Washington, DC. I also thank those lenders who wish to remain anonymous.

I salute the special relationship between the Republic of Italy and the Museum of Fine Arts, Boston, and the benefits of this ongoing cultural collaboration. The MFA is grateful to the Ambassador of Italy to the United States of America, Giovanni Castellaneta; the Consul General of Italy in Boston, Liborio Stellino, who has been a tireless supporter of the Museum and this exhibition; and the Director of the Italian Cultural Institute in New York, Renato Miracco. Our colleagues Sandro Bondi, Francesco Rutelli, Giuseppe Proietti, Rosanna Binacchi, and Mariateresa Di Dedda in the Ministero per i Beni e le Attività Culturali in Rome deserve great thanks for advice, coordination, and support on all aspects of loans from Italy.

At the Museum of Fine Arts, Boston, many colleagues have contributed, foremost among them Malcolm Rogers, Ann and Graham Gund Director; Katie Getchell, Deputy Director; and members of the Art of Europe department, beginning with George T. M. Shackelford, Chair, Art of Europe and Arthur K. Solomon Curator of Modern Art, and Ronni Baer, William and Ann Elfers Senior Curator of Paintings, who were essential in shaping the exhibition's themes and securing loans. Victoria Reed, Monica S. Sadler Assistant Curator for Provenance, compiled the provenance information. I also thank Marietta Cambareri, Deanna Griffin, Sabrina Abron, Kathleen Drea, Xiomara Murray, John Steigerwald, Leah Whiteside, Susie Wager, Brooks Rich, Nicole Bensoussan, Catherine Walsh, and Mari Yoko Hara. The members of the MFA's paintings conservation laboratory deserve special recognition, notably Rhona MacBeth (Eijk and Rose-Marie van Otterloo Conservator of Paintings, Head of Paintings Conservation), Lydia Vagts, Meta Chavannes (Andrew W. Mellon Fellow for Advanced Training in Paintings Conservation), Sandra Kelberlau (Cunningham Assistant Conservator of Paintings), Richard Newman, and Andrew Haines, who painstakingly framed the paintings. I would also like to recognize the staff of MFA Publications for their efforts in creating the present handsome volume, including Mark Polizzotti, Cynthia Randall, Matthew Battles, Jodi Simpson, Terry McAweeney, and especially Sarah Tremblay. Thanks to Thomas Rassieur, Pamela and Peter Voss Curator of Prints and Drawings, for his support at the start of the project, as well as to Matthew Siegal and Patricia Loiko of Conservation and Collections

Management. Helen Connor worked tirelessly to ensure the safe arrival of the borrowed paintings. The Exhibitions and Design team, notably Patrick McMahon, Keith Crippen, Leila Simon Hayes, and Neal Johnson, created a beautiful installation. For research help, I thank Maureen Melton (Susan Morse Hilles Director of Libraries and Archives and Museum Historian), Julia McCarthy, Catherine O'Reilly, Shirin Fozi, Justine De Young, Ethel Cohen, and the staff at the MFA library. I am grateful to the following for promoting and publicizing the exhibition and obtaining image permissions: Kim French, Janet O'Donoghue, Jennifer Weissman, Dawn Griffin, Kelly Gifford, Jennifer Gillespie, Mary Keith, and Sionan Burke; and to colleagues in the Museum's Education, New Media, and MFA Programs departments: Barbara Martin (Barbara and Theodore Alfond Curator of Education), Benjamin Weiss, Philip Getchell, Jenna Fleming, and Lois Solomon. My thanks to William McAvoy, Erika Field, Laura Mercury, Sara Cofrin, and Heidi Rosenfeld for raising funds and securing grants, and to Mark Kerwin and his team for financial support. The installation would not have been possible without the efforts of David Geldart, Alton Davis, Ralph LaVoie, and the entire Facilities crew. Finally, Martha H. Clawson, Curatorial Research Associate, has helped coordinate all aspects of the exhibition with exemplary energy and professionalism.

The following scholars have helped on a variety of topics: Lilian Armstrong, Victoria Avery, William Barcham, Fabio Barry, Jane Bridgeman, Giorgio Bonsanti, Caroline Campbell, Roberto Contini, Carlo Corsato, Jodi Cranston, Una Roman D'Elia, C. D. Dickerson, Mary Frank, Peter Fergusson, Augusto Gentili, Diana Gisolfi, Michel Hochmann, Holly S. Hurlburt, Peter Humfrey, Paul Joannides, Ian Kennedy, Blake de Maria, Gino Marin, Stefania Mason, Benjamin Paul, Giuseppe Pavanello, Giandomenico Romanelli, Philip Rylands, Philip Sohm, Xavier Salomon, Kurt Sundstrom, Leo Steinberg, Giorgio Tagliaferro, Gennaro Toscano, and Stephan Wolohojian.

A group of art historians and conservators explored some of the themes of the exhibition in a conference, generously sponsored by Scott and Isabelle Black, held at the MFA in May 2007. The presenters included Linda Borean, Patricia Fortini Brown, Tracy Cooper, Robert Echols, Miguel Falomir, Rhona MacBeth, and Robert Wald. These experts have constituted an informal "comitato scientifico" for the present exhibition, and their advice has been invaluable. In addition, I thank the contributors to the catalogue, both those named above and Vincent Delieuvin, John Garton, John Marciari, David Rosand, and Jonathan Unglaub. Robert Echols and Holly S. Hurlburt read the manuscript and provided crucial advice.

Christopher Apostle, Anthony Crichton-Stuart, and, above all, Marco Grassi deserve my deepest gratitude for their assistance in completing the indemnity application.

It is a pleasure to acknowledge those in Venice or with a special link to that city. These must include, but are not limited to, the staff and supporters of Save Venice Inc., especially Melissa Conn for countless favors and valuable guidance, Jill Weinreich, Leslie Contarini, and the Save Venice office in Venice. I am grateful to Beatrice and Randolph Guthrie, and especially Daniela Chiara and Christopher Mason, my hosts in Venice. Peter Freeman's generosity in honor of his father, Donald Freeman, through a gift to the Boston Chapter of Save Venice Inc., has made possible the restoration of Tintoretto's *Deposition*, without which the painting could not travel to this exhibition or eventually take its rightful place in the renovated Gallerie dell'Accademia.

This exhibition and catalogue were made possible by generous support from Pioneer Investments, UniCredit Group, the Samuel H. Kress Foundation, the Andrew W. Mellon Publications Fund, and Scott and Isabelle Black. I thank them all.

FREDERICK ILCHMAN
Mrs. Russell W. Baker Assistant Curator of Paintings
Museum of Fine Arts, Boston

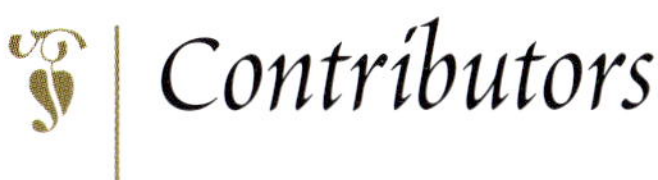

Contributors

FREDERICK ILCHMAN is the Mrs. Russell W. Baker Assistant Curator of Paintings at the Museum of Fine Arts, Boston. He was part of the curatorial team that prepared the 2007 Tintoretto exhibition at the Museo Nacional del Prado, and a contributor to its catalogue.

LINDA BOREAN is Associate Professor of Art History at the University of Udine. Her research focuses on the history of collecting, particularly in Venice and the Veneto. She has published several books and many articles on these subjects.

PATRICIA FORTINI BROWN is Professor of Art and Archaeology at Princeton University. Her writings include *Private Lives in Renaissance Venice: Art, Architecture, and the Family* (Yale University Press), *Art and Life in Renaissance Venice* (Harry N. Abrams), *Venetian Narrative Painting in the Age of Carpaccio* (Yale University Press), and many articles.

VINCENT DELIEUVIN began his curatorial career at the Musée National du Château de Compiègne. A specialist in the work of Federico Barocci, since 2007 he has been the curator in charge of sixteenth-century Italian painting in the Department of Paintings at the Musée du Louvre.

ROBERT ECHOLS is an independent scholar who specializes in fifteenth- and sixteenth-century Venetian painting. He contributed to the catalogue of the 1990 Titian exhibition at the National Gallery of Art, *Titian: Prince of Painters*. More recently, he was part of the curatorial team at the Museo Nacional del Prado for the 2007 Tintoretto exhibition, and contributed to its catalogue.

JOHN GARTON is Assistant Professor, Department of Visual and Performing Arts, at Clark University and the author of, among others, *Grace and Grandeur: The Portraiture of Paolo Veronese* (Harvey Miller Publishers).

RHONA MACBETH is the Eijk and Rose-Marie van Otterloo Conservator of Paintings, Head of Paintings Conservation at the Museum of Fine Arts, Boston. She trained at the Courtauld Institute in London and has also worked for the Royal Collection.

JOHN MARCIARI is Curator of Italian and Spanish Paintings at the San Diego Museum of Art. His publications include, most recently, *Master Drawings from the Yale University Art Gallery* (Yale University Press), for which he was co-editor and an author.

DAVID ROSAND, the Meyer Schapiro Professor of Art History at Columbia University, is the author of *Myths of Venice: The Figuration of a State* (University of North Carolina Press), *Painting in Sixteenth-Century Venice: Titian, Veronese, Tintoretto* (Cambridge University Press), *The Invention of Painting in America* (Columbia University Press), and others.

JONATHAN UNGLAUB is Associate Professor of Fine Arts at Brandeis University. He is the author of *Poussin and the Poetics of Painting: Pictorial Narrative and the Legacy of Tasso* (Cambridge University Press), as well as articles on Baroque art and Venetian Renaissance painting in the *Art Bulletin*, *Burlington Magazine*, and elsewhere.

ROBERT WALD is conservator of paintings at the Kunsthistorisches Museum in Vienna, as well as chief conservator for the Liechtenstein Princely Collections. His research is particularly connected with Italian paintings, and he has lectured and published on a variety of artists including Tintoretto and Titian.

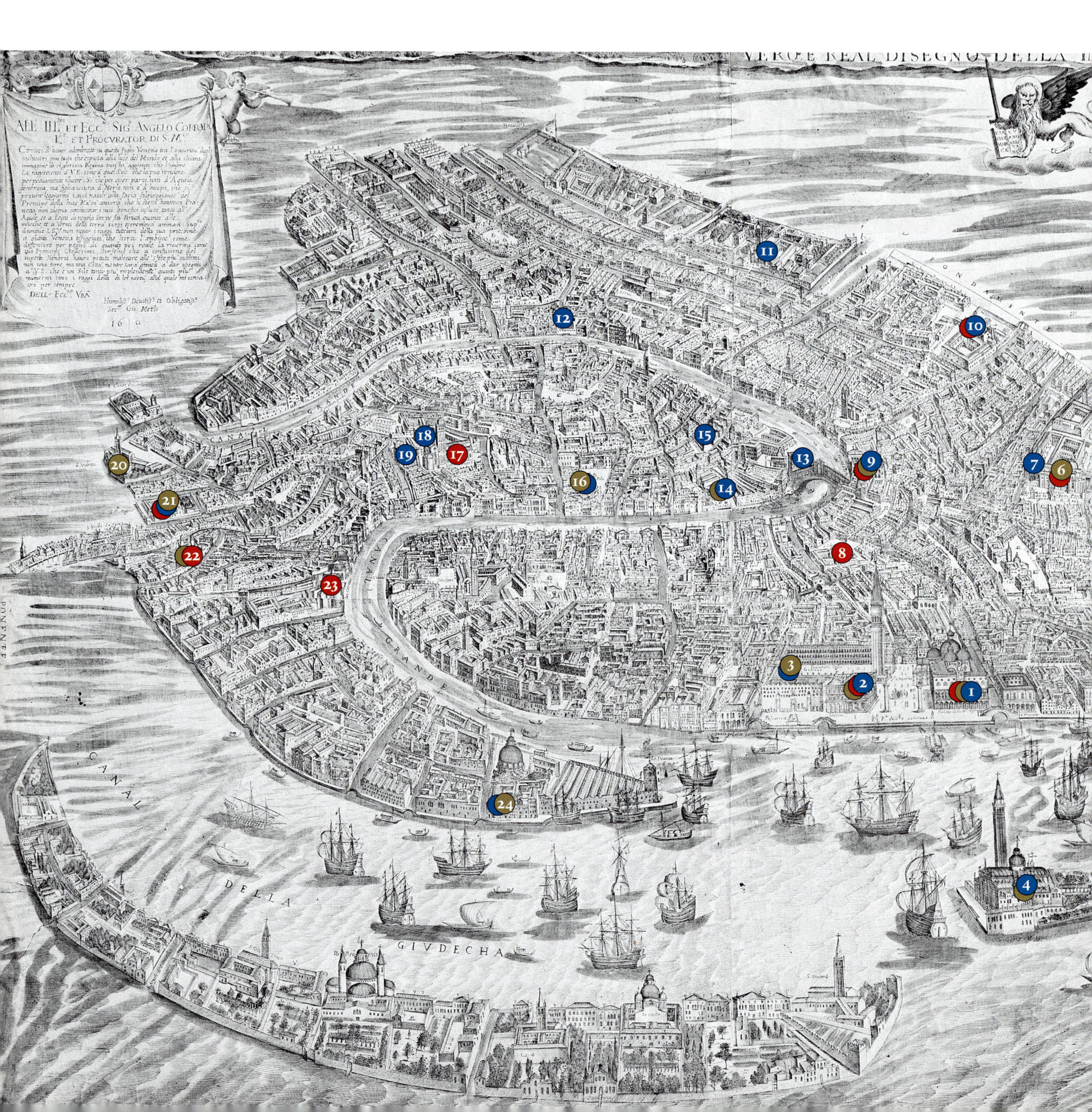
VERO E REAL DISEGNO DELLA
CANAL DELLA GIUDECHA
1
2
3
4
6
7
8
9
10
11
12
13
14
15
16
17
18
19
20
21
22
23
24

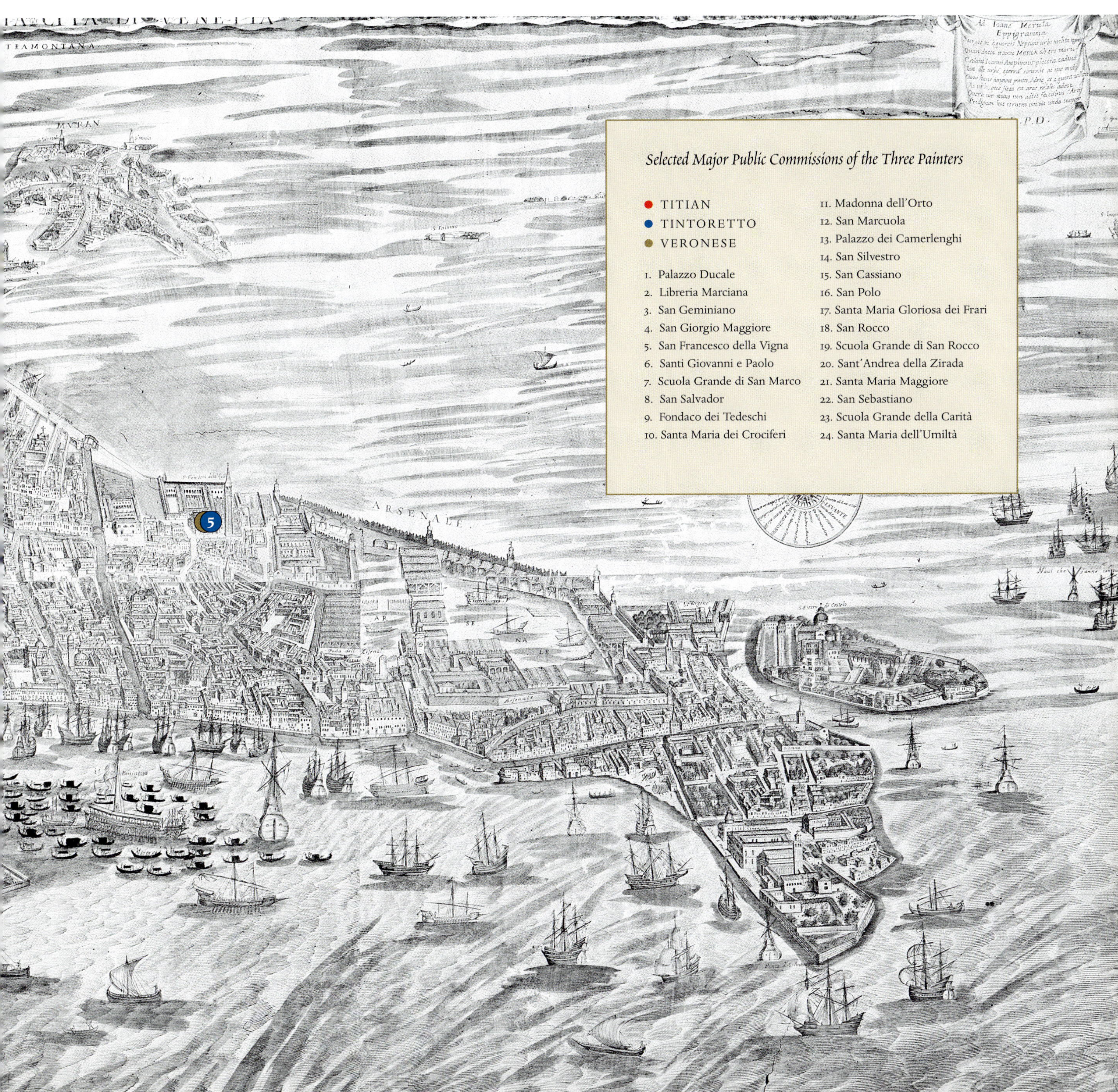
TRAMONTANA
ARSENALE
5
Selected Major Public Commissions of the Three Painters
TITIAN
TINTORETTO
VERONESE
1. Palazzo Ducale
2. Libreria Marciana
3. San Geminiano
4. San Giorgio Maggiore
5. San Francesco della Vigna
6. Santi Giovanni e Paolo
7. Scuola Grande di San Marco
8. San Salvador
9. Fondaco dei Tedeschi
10. Santa Maria dei Crociferi
11. Madonna dell'Orto
12. San Marcuola
13. Palazzo dei Camerlenghi
14. San Silvestro
15. San Cassiano
16. San Polo
17. Santa Maria Gloriosa dei Frari
18. San Rocco
19. Scuola Grande di San Rocco
20. Sant'Andrea della Zirada
21. Santa Maria Maggiore
22. San Sebastiano
23. Scuola Grande della Carità
24. Santa Maria dell'Umiltà

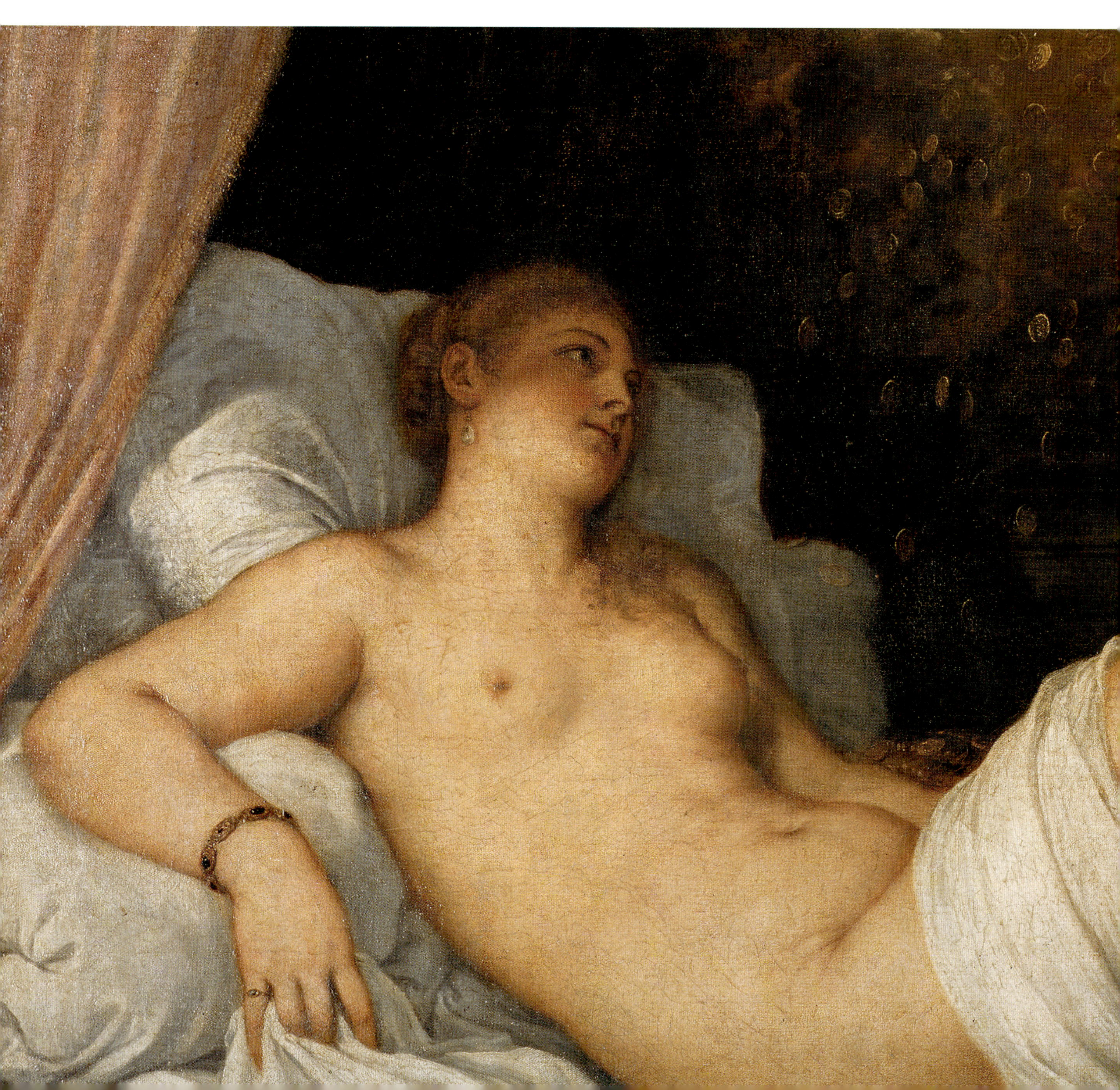

TITIAN · TINTORETTO · VERONESE

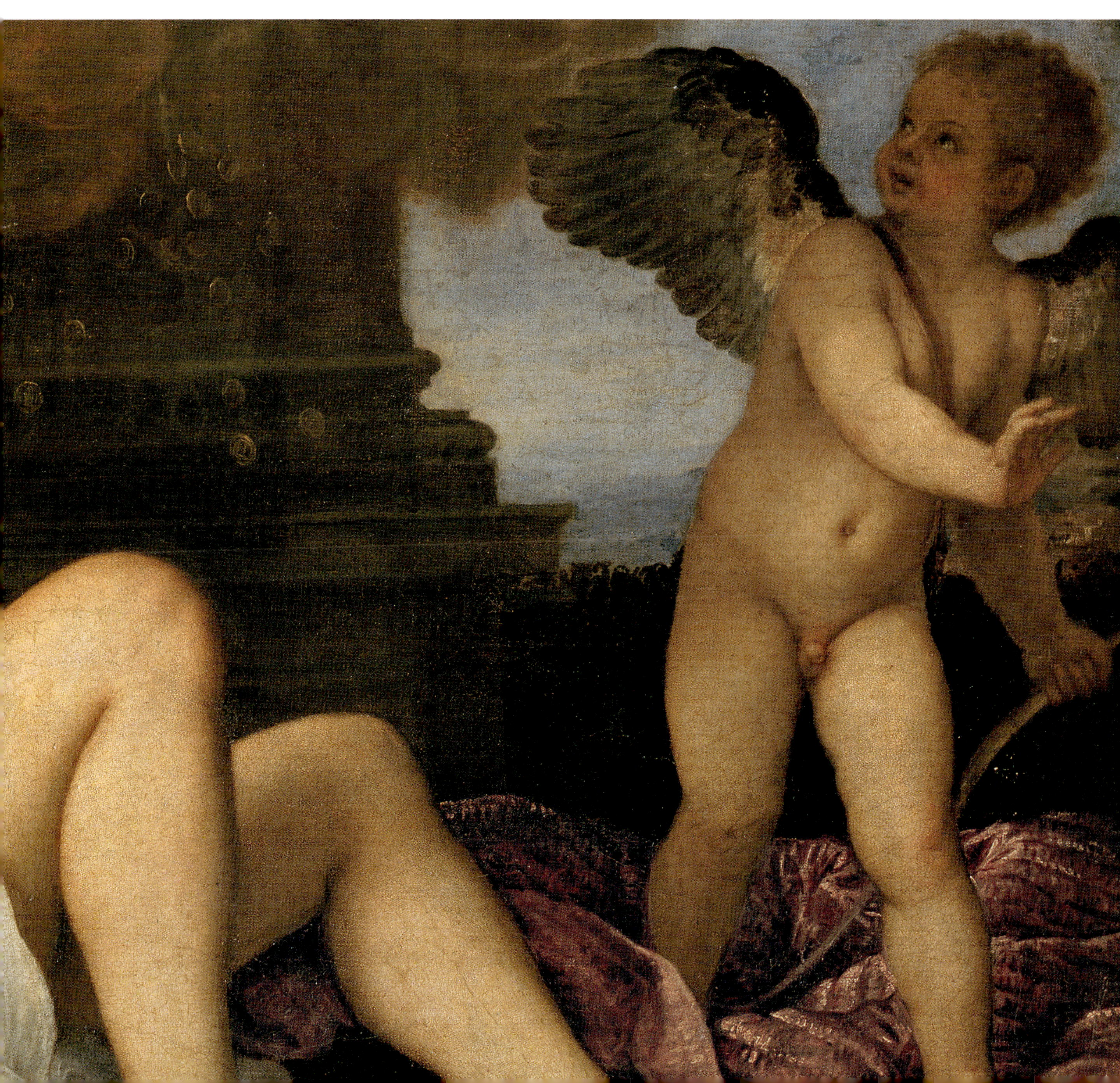

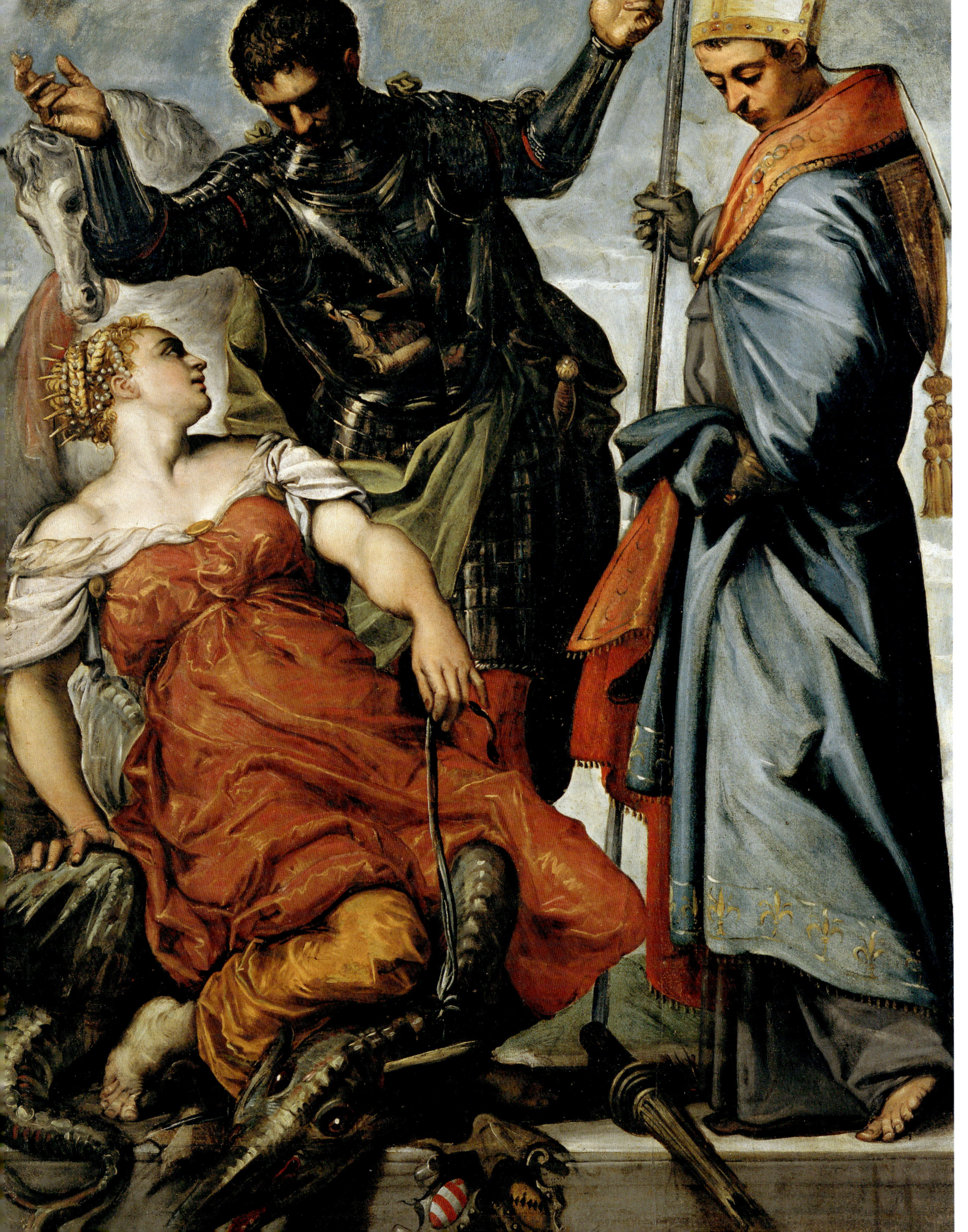

Venetian Painting in an Age of Rivals

FREDERICK ILCHMAN

Having Veronese as a competitor caused Tintoretto to put greater effort into these paintings, for rivalry sometimes serves as a spur, making the artist more attentive so as not to fall behind his competitor.

Carlo Ridolfi, 1642

The Cinquecento, or sixteenth century, was an era of artistic rivalry in Venice. The best painters thrived in this context of ambition, envy, and pressure. The history of the time is littered with anecdotes and turns of phrase that make clear that painters, their patrons, and their audiences all understood that competition, and a flourishing demand for pictures, often brought out the best in artists, making Venice a hub not only of commerce but also of painting.[1] Artists who made a strong impression were off to a good start, but in Venice's competitive climate it was not easy to keep up. Written sources frequently describe how a certain painting was executed "in competition with" another artist, how fame and jealousy were constant spurs to redoubled effort, and how painters who could not sway public opinion were forced to abandon the field ignominiously.[2]

Venetian museums, churches, and *scuole* (lay confraternities) abound in paintings by scores of talented artists, who clearly learned from one another and challenged each other in their work. Three painters from the second half of the sixteenth century, however, stand above the others in their artistic capacity, distinctive styles, and awareness of their most important rivals. To be sure, Titian, Tintoretto, and Veronese have received substantial attention from art historians. They have often been discussed together, their distinctive styles, subject matter, and patronage patterns compared and contrasted; or, conversely, they have been the subject of in-depth monographic treatments focusing on one or the other's output alone. But whether treated as a group, within the broad context of Venetian Renaissance art, or severally, the artistic dialogue and interchange between these three painters have been relatively neglected. The lens of rivalry—in particular, how these artists promoted their own art and careers, and how they responded in paint to the challenges posed by their competitors—will help illuminate the history of Venetian painting by elucidating largely overlooked visual sources and motivations.[3] When examined side by side, many works by Titian, Tintoretto, or Veronese can be seen as responses to and, at least in part, critiques of paintings by the other two artists, providing a richer understanding of all three and their fundamental role in the development of painting in Cinquecento Venice. Period sources, such as letters, biographies, and treatises, make clear how often contemporary writers (frequently painters themselves) regarded artistic rivalry as a prime motivation for the creation of the three artists' pictures. Considering these written sources along with juxtapositions of selected paintings—the most eloquent statements of their artistic dialogue—demonstrates how Titian, Tintoretto, and Veronese calibrated their styles and sought commissions in response to each other.

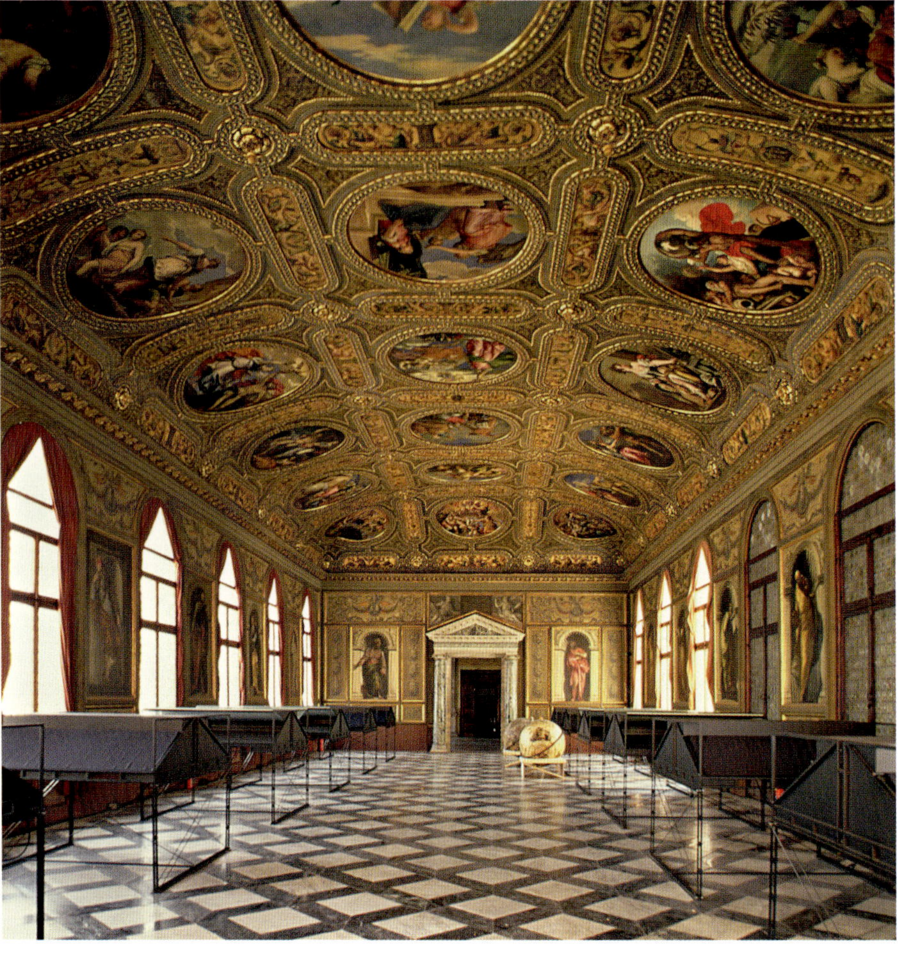

Fig. 1
Jacopo Sansovino (about 1486–1570)
Interior of the Reading Room
Libreria Marciana, Venice

Titian (Tiziano Vecellio) was born about 1488 in Pieve di Cadore, a town in the Dolomite Mountains north of Venice. He moved to Venice as a child and in the first decade of the sixteenth century was trained by a sequence of notable painters, including the brothers Gentile and Giovanni Bellini and Giorgione. He rapidly absorbed the lessons of his teachers, soon even leaving Giorgione "countless miles behind," according to Ludovico Dolce in 1557.[4] After remarkable artistic success both in Venice and for foreign clients, by the end of the second decade of the sixteenth century Titian had risen to become by far the most famous painter in the city, and within a few years would be among the most eminent in Italy.

Jacopo Tintoretto (born Robusti, but called Tintoretto after the profession of his father, a *tintore*, or cloth dyer) was born around 1518 in Venice, and would have trained a full generation after Titian. According to early sources, Tintoretto was briefly apprenticed to Titian, but did not remain long in his studio, either driven out by the jealous older artist—as recounted by the Venetian biographer Carlo Ridolfi and the seventeenth-century critic Marco Boschini—or possibly leaving of his own accord when he realized what a poor mentor Titian could be to his pupils.[5] Whatever the cause, a strong personal antipathy seems to have developed between the two painters, and numerous commissions or pledges appear to be attempts by one to outdo or block the other.

Paolo Veronese (also known later in his career as Paolo Caliari) was born in 1528, a decade after Tintoretto, in the city of Verona, as his last name suggests. Veronese moved definitively to Venice in the early 1550s and challenged Tintoretto's newfound status with a string of impressive commissions in a number of churches, as well as in the Palazzo Ducale, the seat of government.

Titian seems to have regarded Veronese as a protégé, or perhaps more accurately a pawn, in these rivalries. He used his position and prestige in Venice to boost Veronese at the expense of Tintoretto, notably in the decoration of the ceiling of the Libreria Marciana, the state library, in 1556–57 with twenty-one circular canvases (fig. 1). In this case, not only was Tintoretto excluded from the commission in favor of seven other painters, some decidedly minor, but his rival Veronese was also awarded a gold chain for the best contribution to the cycle, an accomplished *Allegory of Music* (fig. 2). Ridolfi adds that the judges for this competition were Titian and the library's architect, Jacopo Sansovino. Tintoretto undoubtedly read his absence in this episode as indicative of his precarious position in official Venice.[6]

Although Titian was born thirty years before Tintoretto and forty years before Veronese, he lived until 1576, when he was in his late eighties—the result being that the three painters' careers overlapped for nearly four decades. After Titian's death, the rivalry between Veronese and Tintoretto continued for another dozen years (Veronese lived until 1588, Tintoretto until 1594), with Titian's achievement continuing to loom over Venetian painting. Moreover, the younger two did not merely follow Titian's example but, on occasion, influenced his artistic development, as they did each other's: examples in many different genres—church altarpieces and narrative paintings, devotional pictures for private collectors, mythologies, and portraits—attest that each artist often seems to have felt the work of the others as a prod demanding a response.

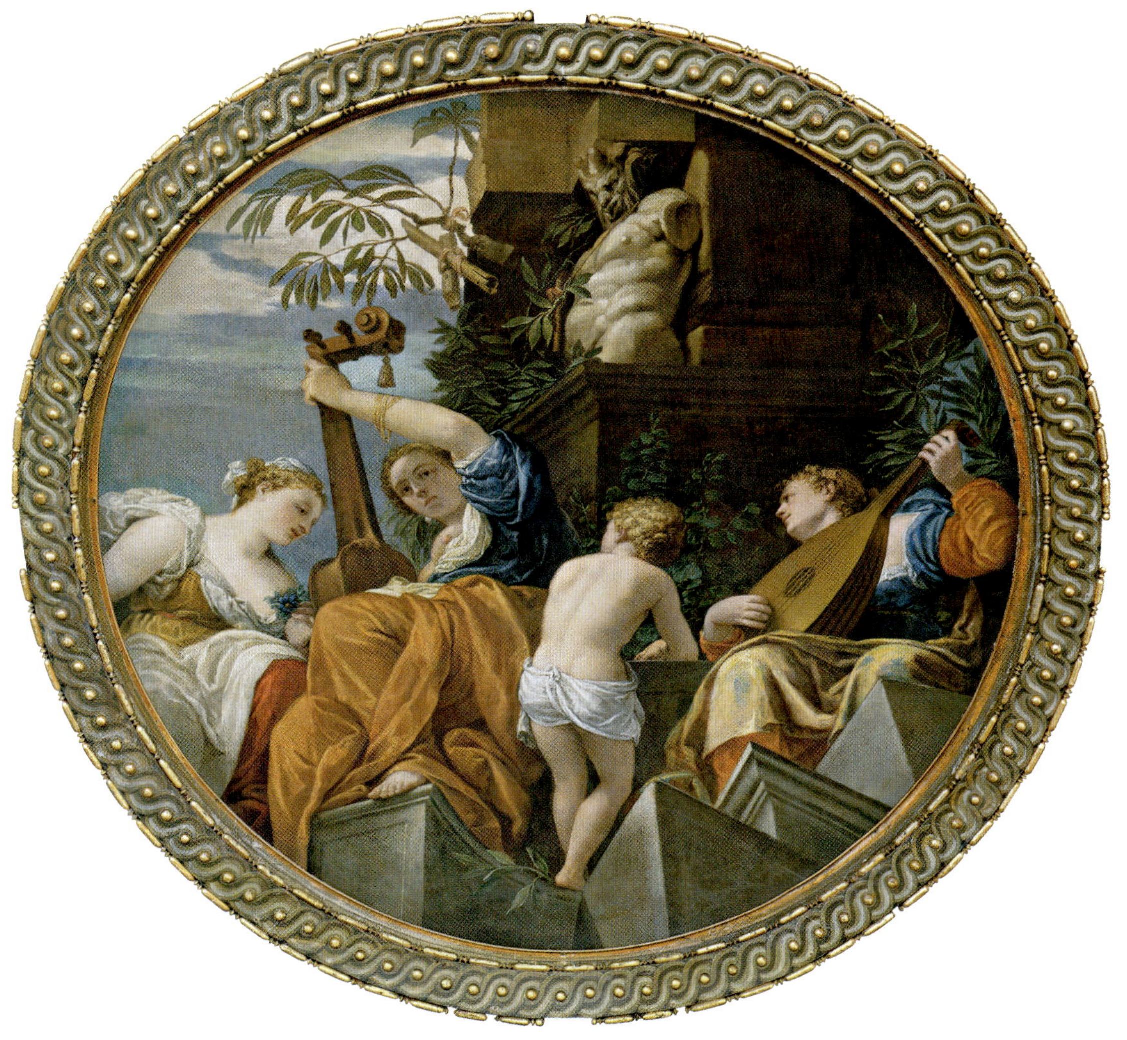

Fig. 2
Veronese
Allegory of Music, 1556–57
Oil on canvas
Libreria Marciana, Venice

Titian, Tintoretto, and Veronese also helped transform for later artists and patrons the very essence of the painter's product. Although Titian was trained to paint with tempera and oil on panel, he soon abandoned this technique in favor of the new possibilities of oil on canvas. Following Titian's lead, the two younger painters employed canvas as a textured surface upon which to define form through patches of color and layers of expressive brushstrokes, rather than by the sharp contours that characterized much Italian painting before this. The emphasis on *colorito* (coloring) rather than *disegno* (drawing or contour) was heralded by contemporaries such as Ludovico Dolce as allowing the depiction of human flesh with unprecedented verisimilitude, and came to be seen as a particularly Venetian approach.[7] The competition between the three painters was a major factor in both the development of Venetian *colorito* and the promotion and eventual triumph of a new pictorial format, the oil-on-canvas easel picture—a format that transformed not only Venetian painting but, following its thorough exploration by Titian, Tintoretto, and Veronese in the second half of the sixteenth century, European art as a whole.

Venice was, of course, not the only artistic center in the Cinquecento with cut-throat competition. Giovanni Battista Armenini's 1587 treatise on painting, for example, bemoaned the jealousy and greed of established painters in Rome several decades earlier that had made lives miserable for young artists, hindering their progress at the start of their careers and leading to aesthetic degradation.[8] But the context in Venice was fundamentally different from that in Rome, Florence, and other major cities. At the time, Venice was one of the largest cities in Europe, and perhaps the wealthiest, boasting a pronounced commercial mentality distinct from royal or imperial capitals. Rather than artistic taste (and prices) being dictated by a single ruling family or court, art patronage in Venice was broadly based. Commissions streamed from a host of private, ecclesiastic, and civic sources, not to mention many foreign clients, and this thriving market supported numerous painters of varying reputation and specialization. Venetian society did not patronize a single court artist or favorite, and indeed preferred to ensure harmony by spreading official commissions over a range of candidates. This steady patronage encouraged an unparalleled concentration of painters in Venice and a growing, often international, market for their products.

At the top of this pyramid stood Titian, Tintoretto, and Veronese, whose shared dominance of the Venetian market is indicated by both the prestige of their commissions and their acclaim in writings of the sixteenth and seventeenth centuries. The long careers of the three painters—extremely long in the case of Titian—and the sustained period during which their activity overlapped lent stability to the Venetian artistic scene and allowed viewers to make frequent comparisons of their work and ongoing development. Moreover, the huge volume of canvases produced in their bustling workshops meant that the distinctive styles of the three artists were a continued presence, not only in Venice but wherever their pictures were appreciated, and not just for several years but for decades.

The transition to canvas had profound consequences for the evolution of this dynamic and the fame Titian, Tintoretto, and Veronese were able to enjoy. Artists specializing in fresco decoration, for example, were forced to paint in situ. Canvas paintings, on the other hand, could be produced in workshops and then easily delivered to their eventual destinations. This portability automatically made the milieu more competitive, since painters were now able to work in Venice without having to travel to their clients, and, equally important, collectors could live far from the sites of production. Titian, in fact, became perhaps the first nonresident court artist, serving two successive Spanish monarchs, Charles V and his son Philip II, for over twenty years each, all the while based at home.[9] Nor were fresco paintings—arguably the glory of the Central Italian school—collectible in any meaningful way. The fact that Titian, Tintoretto, and Veronese painted the majority of their pictures on canvas greatly facilitated and encouraged the collecting of their work, and with it the comparison of (and thus publicity for) their accomplishments. In return, the determined rivalry of these three painters did much to promote the spread of canvas painting as a format, even as it reinforced Venice's reputation as a supremely active and competitive market. This reputation was further enhanced by Venice's prominent publishing industry, which disseminated the opinions of a community of critics. Faced with commentary in the forms of treatises, dialogues, guidebooks, and even published letters, artists felt a new challenge to stay on top of the conversations of the day, and on the right side of posterity.

The most influential of these writers, Giorgio Vasari, the sixteenth-century Tuscan artist and biographer (who was not known for his sympathy to Venetian artists in general), noted a particular intensity in artistic rivalry in Venice, where enmity not only motivated artists to do their best, but even apparently dictated where they should seek commissions. The painter Pordenone, for instance, according to Vasari's *Lives of the Artists* (1568), "out of rivalry ... always sought out to do work in places where Tiziano had also worked."[10] The opportunity to execute a painting for a prominent place could be a powerful motivator: a commission to paint in the Sala del Maggior Consiglio, the great council hall in the Palazzo Ducale, presented Tintoretto with the chance to "equal if not vanquish and surpass, his rivals who had worked in that place," the rivals in question including both Titian and Veronese. Even frescoes on the exteriors of buildings, while not long lasting (and considerably cheaper than covering a facade in stone), were especially noticed and were generally assigned to qualified painters. According to Vasari, sometime after 1505 Giorgione was awarded the commission to fresco the facades of the Fondaco dei Tedeschi, the warehouse and headquarters of the German merchants in Venice on the Grand Canal at the Rialto Bridge, because the setting was recognized as "the most beautiful place and the most conspicuous site in the city." The resulting frescoes, said Vasari, indeed allowed Giorgione to "display his art,"[11] but the public acclaim that greeted the paintings on the building's side facade turned into a public humiliation. Indeed, while most viewers assumed that Giorgione had painted the entire warehouse himself, and congratulated him on saving his best for the side section, in reality these latter paintings had been executed by his protégé, the very young Titian. Giorgione's embarrassment at being bested by his junior rival permanently severed the two men's professional and personal relations, and showed that the opportunity to work in a prominent setting could sometimes backfire. Although the chronology of Giorgione's work is notoriously convoluted, it is telling that in his later work he seems to have specialized in recondite pictures for private collectors, a strategy that kept hostile viewers at bay. By contrast, first Titian, then Tintoretto and Veronese, made a point of proving themselves in the public arena through major church and civic commissions.

Tintoretto used exterior frescoes, among other giant paintings, to advertise his art on a grand scale. He even worked without pay in order to secure commissions for facade frescoes of private homes, creating his own opportunities to—as Ridolfi put it—"give full play to his talent" and advertise his work. Ridolfi, a far more supportive biographer than Vasari, wrote in 1642 that Tintoretto had frescoed a house near the bridge of Sant'Angelo, charging only for materials. The range of imagery (a battle of mounted knights, a "cornice held up by simulated bronze hands and feet," a variety of beautiful women), apparently chosen by the artist himself, impressed the most important critics: other painters. Even more audaciously, Tintoretto proposed, in about 1559–60, to undertake at his own expense a pair of gigantic paintings in the church of the Madonna dell'Orto, the tallest canvases of the Renaissance, precisely to (in Ridolfi's words) "make himself known as the most daring painter in the world." Tintoretto's bold gambit—a self-generated commission, offered at a bargain price—"had appropriated the most conspicuous commission in the city" and infuriated his established rivals, who would have included Titian and Veronese.[12]

These examples reveal how Venetian painters angled for prominent opportunities to show off their styles and shore up their brands. Early written sources suggest that entwined with this ambition was a certain leverage that the artists had obtained over the choice of subject matter. And indeed, Venetian painters in the sixteenth century enjoyed a degree of artistic freedom impossible a century earlier, an arrangement that allowed them to assert their own manner and compositional ideas, and critique, or even humble, the products of their competitors. Success in artistic rivalry often came at a price, however: a recently discovered document of May 30, 1577, shows Tintoretto begging the Venetian Senate for a reduction of his taxes, which had been incorrectly applied "owing to lies spread by those of my profession who hate me."[13] This testimony underscores the intensity of artistic rivalry in Venice—not so much because it portrays an ambitious painter having enemies, but because it shows him having no qualms about playing his controversial fame for sympathy.

Aggressive tactics

Given the high stakes involved, it is not surprising that rivalries could turn acrimonious and tactics deceitful. There exists no more famous example of scheming by a Venetian Renaissance artist than the 1564 competition for the ceiling painting of the Sala dell'Albergo (boardroom) in the Scuola Grande di San Rocco, a prestigious, if patently nouveau riche, confraternity. The commission was a plum opportunity, which, if successfully executed, might lead to further assignments within the vast, as yet undecorated building. When four eager painters—Giuseppe Porta Salviati, Federico Zuccaro, Veronese, and Tintoretto—approached the Scuola one morning in early June 1564 to have their designs judged by the Scuola's governing board (*banca e zonta*), the hostility between them must have been palpable. Just two weeks earlier, on May 22, Gian Maria di Zignoni, a member of the confraternity, had pledged the sum of 15 ducats toward the painting (rather than the 2 or 5 ducats offered by most other members), on condition that the job go to someone other than Tintoretto—showing that factions in favor or against various artists had already emerged within the membership of the Scuola, and that at least one patron had decided to put his money where his mouth was. On May 31, the governing board approved the proposal to choose "three or four of the most excellent painters now found in Venice," and to select from these an artist who would execute an oval canvas for the ceiling. Tintoretto was the only native Venetian on the short list, and this may have helped his cause. But at forty-six years old, he was also the senior competitor of the four artists—the youngest, Zuccaro, was a full twenty-two years his junior—and therefore had the most to lose.[14]

Piecing together the accounts of Vasari and Ridolfi, it seems that the four painters stood before the governing board, each awaiting his chance to present the requested drawing. These drawings were meant to illustrate their plans for the ceiling canvas, the subject of which was Saint Roch received in heaven by God the Father. Tintoretto, however, had arrived without a drawing, and this must have prompted the suspicion, not to say the alarm, of the other three. And with good reason: when it came time for Tintoretto to present his design to the leaders of the Scuola, he removed a large piece of cardboard on the ceiling to reveal, not a drawing, but a completed canvas painting, installed in the intended position (fig. 3). The other painters were

Fig. 3
Tintoretto
Saint Roch in Glory, 1564
Oil on canvas
Sala dell'Albergo, Scuola Grande di San Rocco, Venice

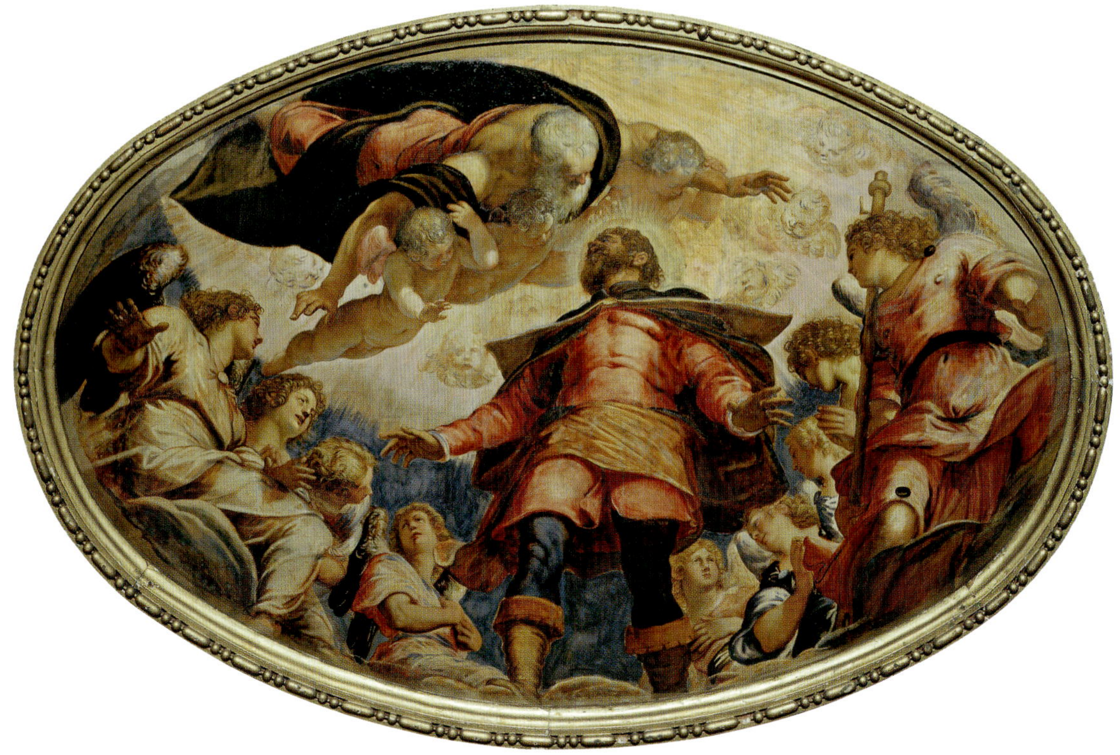

understandably flabbergasted, and the board of the Scuola furious, at this breach of protocol. Not only had Tintoretto refused to produce the required sketch, but he clearly had been aided by at least one member of the Scuola in order to measure the space and install the finished canvas. Tintoretto answered their charges by insisting that they should be judging actual pictures rather than preparatory drawings, "so as to deceive no one," and that if they did not want to pay for his work, he was happy to make a gift of it to Saint Roch. The gesture was not as altruistic as it might seem: Tintoretto knew full well that the Scuola was obligated to accept all donations, as indeed they accepted this one, and therefore that he was simultaneously thwarting his rivals and getting his foot in the door at the Scuola Grande di San Rocco. Tintoretto's coup temporarily stalled Veronese's ascent, and not surprisingly turned Zuccaro from a rival into an out-and-out enemy—all the more so given that, within a few years, Tintoretto received further commissions for paintings in the same room, and even membership in the Scuola.[15]

Still, however underhanded it might appear, when viewed in the context of the heated competition among these painters, Tintoretto's maneuver begins to look understandable, even necessary—less an outlandish gesture than a justifiable self-promotional tactic. While all the competitors would have coveted the opportunity to paint in the Scuola Grande di San Rocco, Tintoretto, the only Venetian on the short list, must have particularly yearned for the chance. The Scuola had been under construction for most of his life: the building was begun in 1517, about a year before his birth, but was completed only in late 1540s, around the time he established himself as a mature painter with his breakthrough *Miracle of the Slave* of 1548 (fig. 5). The huge structure of the Scuola seemed to cry out for decoration by an ambitious painter, and Tintoretto must have seemed a perfect choice. But in the early 1550s, Titian—who had spent the previous years away from Venice or otherwise working for foreign clients—reasserted himself on the Venetian stage in that very institution. His name suddenly appeared on the Scuola membership roster in 1552, after a long lapse, and the following year he made a bold offer to paint "that big picture for the Albergo to go over the members of the Banca"—the very spot that Tintoretto eventually filled with his *Crucifixion* (fig. 110). Although Titian's proposal was easily accepted and the funds were readily available, no picture was ever produced, suggesting that Titian's main goal was less to decorate the meetinghouse of his *scuola* than to crowd Tintoretto out (a gambit that ultimately failed). Titian may also have quietly supported the candidacy of Veronese, an obvious front runner, given his notable successes in the previous decade in both religious and civic settings, for this commission. Furthermore, Tintoretto must have known that in a competition to produce the "best and most beautiful drawing,"[16] he would not stand a chance against the other three artists, all accomplished draftsmen known for the finish of their renderings. Indeed, the surviving presentation sheets for the competition by Zuccaro (British Museum, London) and Veronese (Isabella Stewart Gardner Museum, Boston) make the abbreviated notations of Tintoretto's own drawings seem modest. Given this disadvantage, Tintoretto must have recognized that his only chance was to submit a completed canvas—which means that the most famous drawing in his career was one he didn't actually make.

The constraint of tradition

While the rivalry between artists helped foster the kind of grandstanding to which Tintoretto resorted for the *Saint Roch* commission, the circumstances of Venetian painting had not always favored such conspicuous contention. Earlier painters and their patrons had prized harmony and concord above all. The aesthetics of Venetian art were in large part determined by precedents and predilections inherent in the city's geography, aesthetic traditions, and institutions. From its physical setting alone—a grouping of islands set in a tidal saltwater lagoon, with dual systems of navigation on water and land—Venice has always been seen as an anomaly among cities, and has often been described as unique. The city lacked the fortifications and walls that characterized most medieval and Renaissance urban centers, relying instead upon its watery borders and strong navy for protection. The Venetian diarist (and unabashed chauvinist) Marin Sanudo marveled that his city "has no surrounding walls, no gates which are locked at night . . . no one can attack or frighten it."[17] Venice's stability and prosperity merited the appellation *La Serenissima,* the Most Serene Republic, and was envied the world over. Travelers continually remarked on the paradox of a city of such concentrated riches in this improbable situation. Implicit in their praise was an acknowledgment that nearly all building materials, foodstuffs, and art supplies were imported at great cost. In the mid-fourteenth century, long before many of Venice's Renaissance monuments were created, Petrarch noted that the city was "rich in gold, but richer in fame, mighty in resources but mightier in virtue." In 1494, the French ambassador Philippe de Commynes declared it "the most sumptuous city which I have ever seen."[18]

Any visitor to Venice, and any painter practicing there, would have found constant reminders of the city's singular nature and unlikely military and commercial superiority. Venetian leaders cultivated civic unity and stability over individuality and diversity, and this mentality must have been encouraged by the city's precarious setting. The emphasis on order and conformity took visible form in the confident arcades and impressive buildings constituting the complex of civic and religious structures at the Piazza San Marco. It played out as well in a preoccupation with intricate governmental procedure and public spectacle, such as the one so memorably depicted in Gentile Bellini's *Procession in Piazza San Marco* of 1496 (fig. 49). Venice's fixation with lavish display and outward appearance encouraged a projection of how things should be, rather than how they may have been.[19]

Venice also stood apart from other centers by being the only large city on the east coast of Italy, oriented to the Eastern Mediterranean and, for its time, home to unusually large ethnic communities, including Greeks, Slavs, Germans, Turks, and Jews. It welcomed the trade that foreigners brought, but closely regulated their commerce and, indeed, behavior. The pro-business attitude of the Venetian government is encapsulated in the Fondaco dei Tedeschi, the aforementioned headquarters and exchange house of German merchants located at the commercial heart of the city. After the Fondaco was consumed by fire in 1505, it was rebuilt quickly at government insistence and subsidy to ensure a minimal interruption of trade with merchants from north of the Alps, and also to concentrate their activity and keep this foreign population under supervision.[20] The Venetian government's willingness to support German trade speaks to an approval for business echoed in Shakespeare's *The Merchant of Venice*: "the trade and profit of the city / Consisteth of all nations."[21]

The commercial hum and variety of humanity of this neighborhood off the Grand Canal is captured in Carpaccio's *Healing of a Possessed Man at Rialto* (fig. 51) of about 1496. This large canvas makes clear the urban density of the city, the importance of water transportation in daily life, the variety of texture and color in architecture and costume, and the attentiveness of painters to the particular characteristics of light in Venice. These characteristics are part of what defines Venetian visual culture. The maritime setting and constant presence of water throughout the center of the city make the experience of space and light fundamentally different from that in any other place. The presence of fog and haze mediates solid objects, bathing them in the palpable atmosphere of heavy air. Forms might be crisply reflected in still water or shattered into infinite facets when wavelets lap across the surface. The pleasure taken in the active play of light, enhanced by candlelight on mosaics, gilded altarpieces, or Murano glass, has been a constant of Venetian taste.[22] Such effects could be unplanned: the reflections of sunlight or torchlight on the underside of a bridge suddenly transform that surface into a mosaic dome; the late afternoon sun turns the whole lagoon into a shimmering golden realm. Nature and culture collaborate to make the city of Venice itself the world's greatest work of art. This embrace of the momentary and the palpable, the attentiveness to luminosity and meteorological conditions, prepared Venetian painters for their explorations of light and form through paint.

While Venice's cosmopolitan society adopted a variety of new ideas and artistic influences, the city was fundamentally conservative. The culture had a deep respect for tradition. Venice was a gerontocracy; elderly men occupied the most important roles of government, and older artists—from Giovanni Bellini to Titian to Tintoretto—continued to garner respect even as their production slowed and younger artists appeared on the scene. This conservative bent extended to Venetian visual culture, which, combined with cues from the environment, helps account for the local penchant for rich colors and expensive materials, and the persistence of the mosaic aesthetic. Venetian taste encompasses preciousness in its materials, such as the interior of the church of San Marco, covered with mosaics and costly marbles, and also replications of such lavish settings in paintings. This simulacrum of reality, visible in the most innovative altarpieces of their day, elucidates the appeal of grounding religious painting in venerable Venetian convention. Traditional chapel decoration materials such as mosaic and stone are invoked in paintings as different as Giovanni Bellini's altarpiece in the church of San Zaccaria of 1505 (fig. 36) and Titian's last work, the *Pietà* (fig. 109) of the 1570s. The continued validity of the mosaic tradition may be surprising in an era of oil on canvas, yet important Cinquecento painters—notably Tintoretto—supplied cartoons (same-scale preparatory drawings) for mosaics in San Marco, and Titian, Tintoretto, and Veronese all served as expert witnesses in a 1563 dispute over mosaics executed by the Zuccati family.[23] In Venice, the past could be unusually dominant for a culture that was in many ways so advanced.

A somewhat paradoxical result of this reverence for the past is that Venetian artistic innovations occurred within institutions that, by nature, were least favorable to such tendencies. Most successful painters ran large family workshops, and these determined the training of young artists, the production of a consistent product, and an inherent caution or reluctance to discard a successful formula. In a painter's *bottega*, or workshop, individuality and self-expression were discouraged in favor of maintaining a "house style" dictated by the master. Certainly painters' workshops flourished elsewhere throughout this period as well. In Venice, however, the family *bottega* possessed a particular tenacity. Not only Titian, but also Tintoretto and Veronese in his wake, directed large workshops stocked with family members—despite the changes that all three wrought on the culture of painting in Venice.

Moreover, each of the three took special pains to maintain continuity across generations, and indeed to keep matters in the family. Veronese married the daughter of his teacher Antonio Badile; and after Paolo's death, his brother Benedetto, sons Carletto and Gabriele, and a nephew continued to produce paintings under the signature of the "Haeredes Pauli," the "heirs of Paolo" (the assumption being that the next of kin was the next best thing).[24] Jacopo Tintoretto employed two sons, Domenico and Marco, and a daughter Marietta, nicknamed Tintoretta, in his workshop. He also made unambiguous his expectations that his descendants would perpetuate the family business—in consequence of which another daughter, Ottavia, while not an artist herself, agreed to marry a much younger painter, the German Sebastian Casser, in order to sustain the enterprise for a third generation. Ottavia's will of 1645, a half-century after her father's death, reveals the powerful influence of familial and institutional obligation: "I find myself bound in matrimony to Messer Sebastian Casser . . . by the order and command of my brothers Domenico and Marco, who, before they died, made me promise that if the said Sebastian proved to be an able painter I should take him for my husband; in this way, by virtue of his talent, the Tintoretto name would be maintained." In turn, Casser was required by Ottavia to adopt her family name.[25]

The constraint on artistic individuality represented by the Venetian workshop was reinforced by traditional Venetian structures of patronage, which carried over into the first part of the Cinquecento. In Florence in 1503–4, Leonardo and Michelangelo were famously assigned murals in the same room in the Palazzo della Signoria, in order that they would produce greater works through competition with each other. Such a pointed strategy would have been frowned upon in fifteenth-century Venice. According to practices current through the end of that century and the first half of the next, those responsible in Venice for assigning commissions in major government buildings and important confraternities, the so-called *Scuole Grandi*, made a point of spreading the work among different workshops, so as not to elevate any one artist at the expense of others and thus disturb social harmony. Official government policy promoted the continuity of institutions over the glorification of individuals, curbing attempts to enable a cult of personality through such means as restricting the movements and communications of the doge, the elected leader for life of the Venetian Republic, or by resisting proposals to erect statues of rulers and military heroes in public squares. Moreover, no artist was allowed to dominate with his paintings the decoration of the most prominent meeting rooms, thus precluding a painter from creating a personal monument in an institutional setting. To this end, the petition of Alvise Vivarini in 1488 to paint in the Sala del Maggior Consiglio alongside both Gentile and Giovanni Bellini was easily approved.[26] Similarly, the Sala dell'Albergo of the Scuola di San Giovanni Evangelista was decorated with narrative canvases in the 1490s and first decade of the Cinque-cento by six different painters. Even today, viewing the surviving paintings from the Sala dell'Albergo, it is hard to tell the hands of the artists apart, so much did each painter work to create a consistent style, honoring the miracles depicted and the harmony of the Scuola above any opportunities for self-advancement. That Titian, who grew up in the artistic world of Gentile Bellini and Carpaccio, was able to break free from the strictures of Venetian tradition to build a strong individual artistic identity, thereby creating the context for an artistic dialogue with both Tintoretto and Veronese based on highly personalized styles, is all the more impressive in light of their culture's inherent conservatism and insistence on preserving communal tranquility.

The brushstroke as signature

One could say that the development of new kinds of paint handling in the sixteenth century led to a new self-consciousness and creative independence among Venetian artists, shattering the old constraints of social and aesthetic expectations. Throughout much of the Quattrocento (fifteenth century), painters across Italy employed an egg tempera medium on a wooden panel support, materials in widespread use since at least the thirteenth century. This combination tended to produce a style of sharp contours and bright tonalities, and required minute brushstrokes, with an application of the medium in thin layers so that it would dry. Thick paint application was impossible with tempera, and thus distinctive brushwork was not even a consideration. In the last third of the Quattrocento, painting in Venice slowly began to break away from the styles in other parts of Italy. The primary cause seems to have been technical. In the 1470s, the Venetian painters—led by Giovanni Bellini and then much encouraged by the arrival of Antonello da Messina in 1475—began gradually to switch to oil instead of tempera as their preferred medium, since it allowed for layered colors, subtle tonal gradations, and new effects of light. They also began to favor canvas rather than the traditional wood support: its portability and resilience in the humid environment of Venice made it an appropriate substitute for mural paintings in fresco. Painters tended to apply a thick coating of gesso as a ground to these canvases, rendering the surface nearly as smooth as a panel and affording a similar level of detail in paint handling. But even before the century was over, certain Venetian painters made an extraordinary conceptual leap by reducing the thickness of this preparation layer, thus revealing the weave of the cloth as a textured surface to exploit.[27]

The decisive moment in Venetian pictorial technique arrived in the first decade of the new century, however, as painters began to understand the expressive implications of this combination of oil binder and supple canvas support. Instead of creating forms through taut contours—confident draftsmanship being the basis of Florentine *disegno*, an artistic conception and idea championed by Vasari—Venetian artists, beginning with Giorgione and Sebastiano, then more fully with Titian, pioneered the idea of the brushstroke as caress, layering opaque tones to produce a seductive naturalism that proved particularly effective in the depiction of flesh. Unlike tempera, oil paint could also be thickly applied, projecting in relief and preserving the vector of the brush. David Rosand, examining the expressive implications of visible brushwork in American painting, makes an assertion equally applicable to the technique's genesis in Venetian painting: "The brush stroke—the directed application of pigment to the surface of the painting, the touch that retains its independence as a mark, resisting sacrifice of its own reality in the service of illusion—asserts the

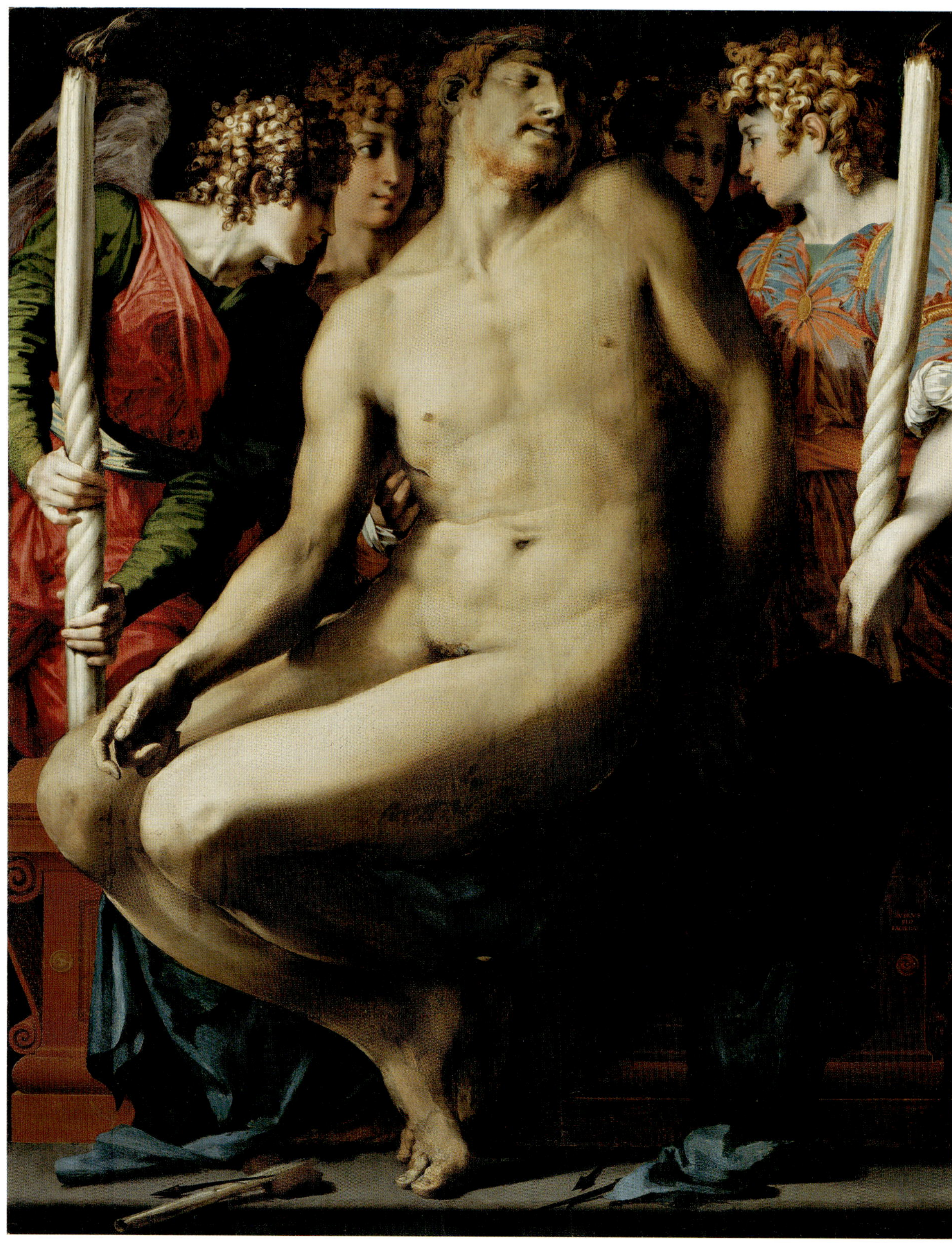

Fig. 4
Rosso Fiorentino (Giovanni Battista di Jacopo) (Italian, 1494–1540)
Dead Christ with Angels, about 1524–27
Oil on panel
Museum of Fine Arts, Boston

claims of Art over Nature. His own unique mark, it stands for the artist; it is his trace."[28] A new kind of paint application and a new format, the oil-on-canvas easel picture, marked a break with the past and a way for the future.

In turn, this emphasis on the process of coloring, or *colorito*, became the dominant mode in Venice, in contrast to the Florentine emphasis on *disegno*—resulting in two markedly divergent approaches: a characteristic Florentine manner of strong contours and a distinct Venetian one with broadly applied strokes and patches of warm coloring. The pronounced differences between these two ideals are exemplified by a pair of paintings, each featuring a prominent nude figure in the foreground, and created within a dozen years of each other: Rosso Fiorentino's *Dead Christ with Angels* of about 1524–27 (fig. 4) and Titian's *Venus of Urbino* of about 1538 (fig. 76). While both are painted in oil and reveal the mastery of subtle gradations of light allowed by that medium, Rosso's painting employs a panel support, lending a sheen to his surfaces and a tightness to the lines that constitute the figures. Rosso's Christ is remarkably sculptural and preternaturally smooth, apparently citing both Michelangelo's marble sculpture and the *ignudi* of the ceiling frescoes of the Sistine Chapel. The perfection of the body was doubtlessly assured through numerous preparatory drawings. By contrast, Titian's sensuous painting, evoking all the visual delights of an unperturbed nude woman on a soft bed, reveals the expressive possibilities allowed by painting on canvas. Here preparatory drawings were minimal, if any. Instead, Titian constructed his figure on the canvas itself, employing a variety of visible brushstrokes and profiting from the broken line generated when he dragged a brush across the canvas's rough surface. These broken lines and soft gradations of shading create a believable figure without hard contours, setting this nude in a palpable atmosphere. Thus, even before Titian's paint handling broadened dramatically in the 1540s, the differences between Venetian *colorito* and Florentine *disegno* were well established.

In Titian's paintings after the early 1540s, such as his *Danaë* of 1544–46 (cat. 27) and several variations on the subject of *Venus and Adonis* (see cat. 33), the artist took full advantage of the possibility of painting thickly, allowing his brushstrokes to possess direction and energy, whether in rendering the golden cloud above Danaë or the red velvet under Venus. According to Vasari, Michelangelo, who viewed *Danaë* in Rome, admired Titian's "coloring and manner" but criticized the faulty *disegno*, the weakness of Venetian artists who "did not learn to draw well in the first place."[29] The apparent opposition of *disegno* and *colorito* as artistic ideals, and their relative merits, engendered extensive argument in the conversations between artists and the published art criticism of the sixteenth and seventeenth centuries.

Not everyone considered these two ideals mutually exclusive, however: soon after Titian began to produce works such as *Danaë*, the Venetian critic Paolo Pino declared that a painter might reach perfection by uniting them: "If Titian and Michelangelo were just one body, that is with the drawing [*disegno*] of Michelangelo joined to the color of Titian, he could be called the god of painting."[30] Pino's proclamation was published in the same year as Tintoretto's signal success, the *Miracle of the Slave*. The picture displays a variety of coloring and strength of drawing absent from Tintoretto's earlier works, as if a conscious fusion of *colorito* and *disegno* had been intended and achieved for the first time. Bravura brush effects worthy of Titian maintain a lively paint surface, particularly in the rendering of cloth folds and the glint of metal, while firm contours render anatomy of the human body confidently.

According to Tintoretto's biographer Ridolfi, writing in 1642, this union of Michelangelo and Titian was more than an unstated goal; indeed, the young painter inscribed the following motto on the wall of his studio: "The draftsmanship of Michelangelo and the coloring of Titian."[31] Certainly, the younger painter often seems to give a nod to Michelangelo (see cat. 14), or to Titian (see cat. 36), or even to both (see cat. 53). It is worth noting that Tintoretto, who never traveled to Florence or Rome, still managed to engage in rivalry with Michelangelo, an artist he had never met and whose works he knew mostly at second hand, through copies, drawings, and prints. New kinds of expressive paint handling allowed Tintoretto to put his models in their place.

Indeed, while the *disegno-colorito* controversy would have informed many discussions of painting in Cinquecento Venice (as would the debate over the *paragone* between painting and sculpture: see page 137), it may well be that the expressive brushstroke, set in motion by the combination of oil and canvas, was the most profound artistic innovation of the mid-sixteenth century. In the crucial decades covered in this book, 1540–80, all three artists, celebrating the handling of paint as paint, and not just as a medium for depicting forms from the natural world, embarked on a journey that has had significant repercussions for all painting in their wake. Titian perfected a new kind of delicate layering of strokes, after which Tintoretto and Veronese, each in his own way, pursued different directions in exploring the expressive possibilities of oil paint on canvas—a pursuit that continued, in a variety of forms, at least as far as Abstract Expressionism in the 1950s.

Both younger artists declared their presence with visible, even conspicuous brushwork, reveling in impasto, thickly applied paint that stands in relief. Tintoretto's brushstrokes tend to be self-assured and defiant, whether describing forms of cloth or skin or shiny metal. The seventeenth-century critic Boschini was probably thinking of Tintoretto when he declared the bold stroke (*il colpo sprezzante*) a finishing touch to the careful process of creating forms through coloring.[32] This is not to say that Tintoretto eschewed contours. Indeed, he creates his human figures through powerful, elongated contours, drawing in paint in a manner similar to his abbreviated and efficient black chalk and charcoal drawings on paper. He conveys folds of drapery with energetic zigzags; his strokes emphasize their existence as paint, thus drawing attention, often brazenly, to the surface of the canvas as well. With few exceptions, it was not until considerably later in the century—and with the example of Venetian brushwork firmly in sight—that Florentine painting would obtain a similar freedom of execution.

By contrast with Tintoretto, Veronese's brushwork possesses a certain restraint. His strokes are also designed to be appreciated for their own sake, not just for their mimetic functions, but, in Rosand's words, they "are more flexible and inflected than Tintoretto's," displaying a "calligraphic quality."[33] In addition, Veronese, more than any of his Venetian contemporaries, seems to have most fully exploited the weave of the canvas for expressive ends—such as his remarkable utilization of the herringbone cloth in his *Saint Jerome in the Wilderness* (cat. 52), whereby the paint from a dry brush catches only the higher threads and leaves the lower ones untouched. This technique produces a regularly interrupted line and conveys the impression of light catching the thick pile of the saint's velvet drapery. By such details, these painters personalized their stroke, and revealed themselves not just in their palette, figure types, and compositions, but also through the minute, characteristic motions of the hand that wielded the brush.

Perhaps it is significant that the prominent signatures typical of Venetian paintings around 1500—for example, in Bellini's *Virgin and Child with Saints* of about 1505–8 (cat. 1)—had generally dropped out of use by the time Tintoretto and Veronese appeared on the scene. It is not so much that these painters were abandoning signatures as making them redundant through distinctive handling—the soft caress of Titian, the brash zigzag of Tintoretto, the elegant stutter of Veronese—precluding the need for any written name.[34] Apart from works for some foreign clients, who might have insisted on a more literal attribution, signatures largely fell out of use. Venetian painters had inscribed their personality not just in the narrative or syntax of their visual language, but even in the very alphabet of forms. Given this individual investment in the expressive act of painting, it follows that artists such as Titian, Tintoretto, and Veronese no doubt chafed at the traditional restrictions against self-aggrandizement assumed by Venetian patrons, as this new self-assurance would have encouraged each one to pit his art against that of his colleagues. Perhaps most interesting is that, unlike in other cities where competition was stoked by patrons, in Venice it seems to have been generated largely by the painters themselves.

Artistic license

Examples of artist-generated rivalry were not new, of course, and go back to the earliest surviving history of art, Pliny the Elder's *Natural History*, compiled in the first century AD. Pliny's was also one of the first ancient texts to be published, in Venice in 1469, with many subsequent editions. The last six books of *Natural History*, which survey the history of ancient art by medium, provided Renaissance audiences with numerous influential anecdotes about the progress of art and individual artists. Some of Pliny's most vivid examples focus on the role that the personal mark of the artist played in artistic competitiveness. In book thirty-five, he recounts how the Greek painter Apelles sailed to Rhodes to view works by the renowned artist Protogenes. Told by the housekeeper that Protogenes had left for the day, Apelles recorded his visit by drawing a single fine line across a blank panel. Upon his return, Protogenes immediately guessed the identity of his visitor, since only Apelles was capable of such perfection. Not about to be upstaged, Protogenes painted a finer line in a different color along the length of the first, and left home again, instructing his housekeeper to display this to Apelles should he come back.

> It fell out as he expected; Apelles did return, and, ashamed to be beaten, drew a third line of another colour cutting the first two down their length and leaving no room for any further refinement. Protogenes owned himself beaten and hurried down to the harbor to find his visitor; they agreed to hand down the painting just as it was to posterity, a marvel to all, but especially to artists.[35]

Like the personalized brushstrokes of Titian, Tintoretto, and Veronese in the sixteenth century, the lines of Apelles and Protogenes served as a form of signature. This anecdote also suggests that while patrons footed the bills, as far as the artists were concerned their most important audience, whether in the ancient world or Cinquecento Venice, was their peers.

For Titian, Tintoretto, and Veronese to engage in this kind of one-upmanship, a measure of artistic freedom to choose what they painted and how they interpreted the subject was essential. Certainly, painters could refuse certain commissions and vie particularly for others. In his mature career, for instance, Titian seems to have operated at an unprecedented level of artistic self-determination even when dealing with the most powerful patrons: the ongoing series of pictures he executed for Philip II starting in 1550, to take perhaps the most notable example, depicted subjects of his own choosing and was delivered on his own schedule. Even less renowned sixteenth-century painters had far more agency than is generally assumed. In fact, there is little evidence in Italian Renaissance art that patrons typically gave specific and thorough instructions to painters beyond the subjects, or that subtleties within a composition—costumes, gestures, props—should necessarily be assigned to the client rather than the painter.[36] On the other hand, there are many examples from the Cinquecento of clients deferring to the greater experience and knowledge of the artist, even allowing the painter to pick the subjects. For example, in a 1539 document, the governing board of the Scuola Grande della Carità summarized a meeting with the painter Pordenone about continuing the cycle of paintings for their Sala dell'Albergo, which had just been enriched by Titian's *Presentation of the Virgin in the Temple* (1534–38; fig. 13). The document recounts that when Pordenone asked which subject the board desired, one of the Scuola's members suggested the Assumption of the Virgin. Pordenone was reluctant, however, arguing that the proposed location and format of the projected work, as well as its proximity to a canvas of the same subject by "the excellent master Titian," made it more suited to a Marriage of the Virgin. Convinced by the artist's expertise, the clients changed their minds.[37]

Many other examples also exist in the literature. The account book of the Bassano workshop includes three cases where clients left the entire choice of subject to the painter, the desired product evidently being not so much a specific topic as a "Bassano." Similarly, even a patron as important and sophisticated as Isabella d'Este, the Marchesa of Mantua, eventually ceded all leverage to certain artists in her quest for paintings, agreeing, for example, to buy a picture by Leonardo, regardless of subject. Meanwhile, her attempts to dictate the subject of a painting to Giovanni Bellini in 1506 met with a gentle reprimand from an intermediary, the writer Pietro Bembo, who advised her that the painter was not keen on detailed instructions and preferred to do things his way.[38]

The concept of acquiring already-completed pictures (and often from someone other than the artist, such as a patron) meant, in some cases, that paintings originally made for religious devotion were now collected as characteristic examples of a certain master's hand. In turn, this new channel of acquisition—akin to the current "secondary market"—also required a new standard, that of connoisseurship, by which to judge potential purchases.[39] Thus, by the start of the sixteenth century, around the time of Titian's emergence, not only paintings were being collected but also painters. This changing attitude to collecting heightened the influence prestigious painters sometimes enjoyed with patrons, enabling the artist to make suggestions both large and small. One might imagine, for instance, that the heavy lynx fur coat and leather gloves worn by the sitter in Tintoretto's *Portrait of a Man Aged Twenty-Six* (cat. 36)—painted in the sweltering heat of June—was not the client's choice. Rather, Tintoretto may have insisted on this outfit the better to challenge his rival Titian, who was known for his skill at rendering fur and gloves (see cat. 35 and fig. 91). Tintoretto's portrait, in other words, is as much a depiction of his response to Titian as it is of his wealthy client.

Both Tintoretto and his handsome sitter must have thought that expanding the format of the picture from half length to three-quarter length was an improvement. In turn, Veronese's *Portrait of a Man*, now in Budapest (cat. 37), adds further elements of a suave pose, vine-covered wall, red curtain, landscape with ruins, and a pale blue sky (is it always a sunny day with Veronese?), as if more were necessarily more.

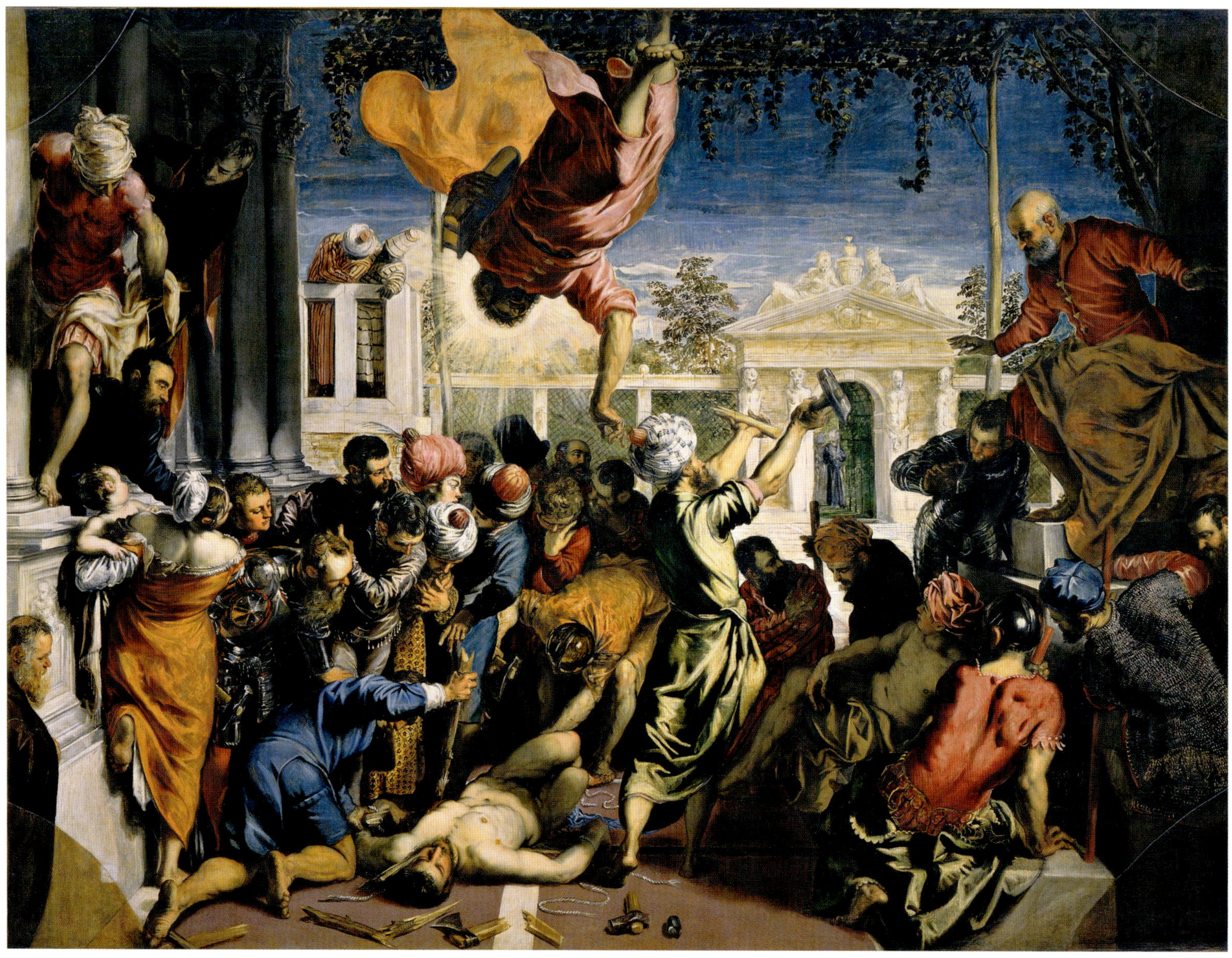

Fig. 5
Tintoretto
Miracle of the Slave, 1548
Oil on canvas
Gallerie dell'Accademia, Venice

Again, it seems likely that Veronese's departures from Venetian portrait tradition were prompted by the painter's desire to show off rather than by the patron. In other cases, such as three versions of the *Supper at Emmaus*, one by each painter (cats. 21–23), the elements in common—Christ seated at the center of a table with a prominent white tablecloth, his importance emphasized by the looming column and clouds in the background—suggest once again that the artists were reacting not just to a broader iconographic tradition but to specific works by their close rivals. Indeed, in order to imitate (and surpass) a rival most effectively, an artist must acknowledge his source. Tintoretto's declaration of his artistic arrival, the *Miracle of the Slave* (fig. 5), prominently cites Michelangelo, Raphael, Titian, and even Sansovino. As Robert Echols notes, these many allusions serve not so much to demonstrate his knowledge of preceding artists as to announce "that the name of Tintoretto now belonged among theirs."[40] Tintoretto's deliberate reinvention of large-scale narrative painting was so successful that Titian essentially abandoned this category to younger artists.

Moreover, for a critique to be successful, the gesture has to be understandable, and many examples by all three painters make their points of departure clear: Titian critiques Michelangelo (see cat. 27), Tintoretto in turn parodies Titian and Michelangelo (see fig. 81), and Veronese takes on both Tintoretto (successfully: see cat. 16) and Titian (less successfully: see cat. 32). In certain cases, it is unclear from the chronology who initiated an idea and who followed, such as with Tintoretto's *Tarquin and Lucretia* (cat. 46) and Veronese's *Perseus and Andromeda* (cat. 47), both datable to the late 1570s. The questions are even more fraught when considering technique. Veronese's pastel palette—often employing lime green, robin's egg blue, and salmon pink—stands apart from Tintoretto's consistent use of earth tones, and each artist may have hewn to a particular spectrum of colors to reinforce his signature "look." It is not clear, however, if this development was a reaction of one painter to another or if the ongoing rivalry hardened innate chromatic tendencies. Similarly, it is difficult to attribute innovations in brushwork. In two contemporaneous paintings as close in handling as Titian's *Pietro Aretino* (fig. 44) and Tintoretto's *Self-Portrait* (cat. 9), who was looking at whom? And was the new freedom of brushwork in Titian's portrait prompted by works such as Tintoretto's earlier ceiling canvas, the *Contest between Apollo and Marsyas* (cat. 8), painted for the same patron?

A culture of rivals

Besides the infamous case of the ceiling painting for the Scuola Grande di San Rocco, or the more loosely defined competition to select the best painter from among the ceiling canvases of the Libreria Marciana in 1556, Titian, Tintoretto, and Veronese also took part in some of the official competitions that occurred in sixteenth-century Venice. Ridolfi and others have claimed that in 1530, some three decades before the Scuola Grande di San Rocco competition, Titian had won a contest for an altarpiece for the Scuola di San Pietro Martire in the church of Santi Giovanni e Paolo, beating both Palma Vecchio and Pordenone, and producing his revolutionary *Saint Peter Martyr* altarpiece (lost and known only from copies and engravings; see fig. 23). Other accounts, however, suggest that no such competition occurred, and that the Scuola merely settled on Titian as the best painter.[41] A better-documented competition is the one held to replace Guariento's badly deteriorated and damaged fresco *Coronation of the Virgin* in the Palazzo Ducale with a huge canvas painting. In 1582, Tintoretto, Veronese, and probably Federico Zuccaro (all veterans of the Scuola Grande di San Rocco competition), as well as two painters of a younger generation, Palma Giovane and Francesco Bassano, entered large *modelli* and drawings for selection by a small committee of patricians. Although the commission was jointly awarded to Veronese and Francesco Bassano—presumably another case of preserving social harmony—by the time Veronese died in 1588, little progress had been made because of differences in their styles, according to Ridolfi. Faced with another chance, Tintoretto's second *modello* (fig. 102) finally carried the day. The resulting mural in the Palazzo Ducale, the *Paradiso* (fig. 6), is both a monument to his ambition and the capstone to his career—even if the final painting was executed largely by his son Domenico.[42] The fact that it took Tintoretto two attempts to win the competition suggests the depth of talent among Venetian painters in those years, and also that Tintoretto's success and ambition could occasionally work against him.

Far more interesting, however, are the informal competitions frequently held during the decades when Titian, Tintoretto, and Veronese were all active. Both Veronese and Tintoretto painted head-to-head in a second cycle for the Libreria Marciana, depicting a series of large *Philosophers*; one of Tintoretto's works, a massive figure with crossed legs, the so-called *Diogenes*, seemingly taken straight from Michelangelo's Sistine

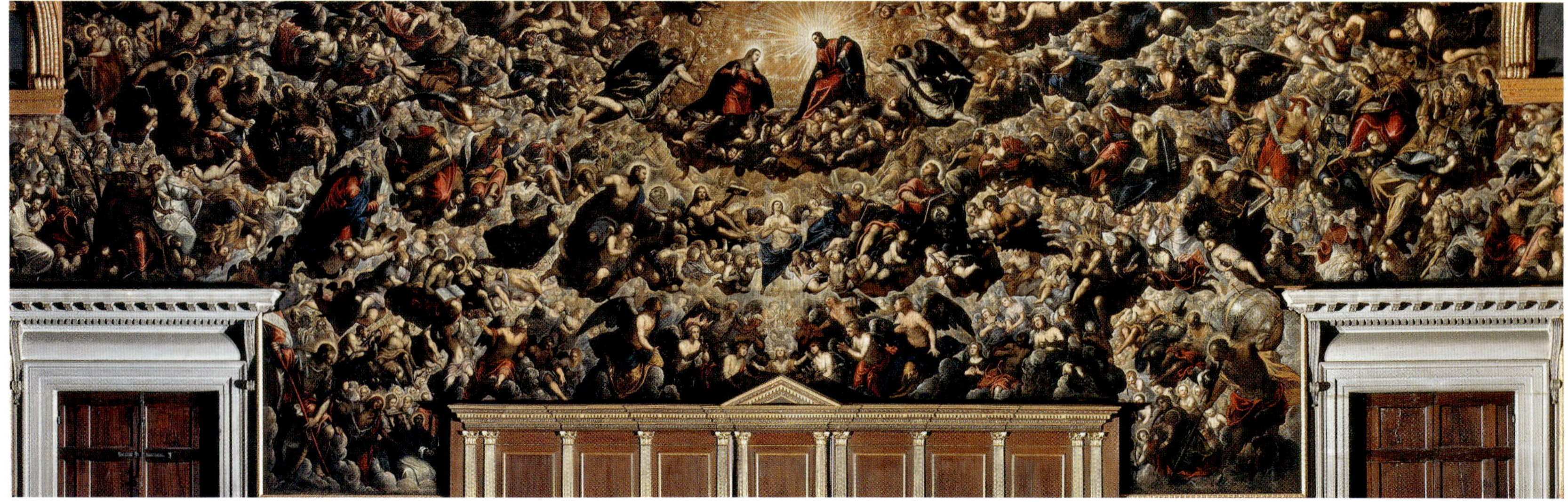

Fig. 6
Domenico Tintoretto and Workshop, following designs by Jacopo Tintoretto
Paradiso, 1588–92
Oil on canvas
Sala del Maggior Consiglio, Palazzo Ducale, Venice

Chapel, was recognized by Ridolfi as not just countering Veronese's new contributions to this setting, but as getting back at Veronese's mentor, Titian: "By the excellence of this painting Tintoretto avenged the wrong that Titian had done him and showed how clearly unfair he had been."[43] Veronese and Tintoretto also executed works side by side in more than one room for the Palazzo Ducale; the churches of Santa Maria dell'Umiltà, San Silvestro, Santa Maria Maggiore, and the Redentore; and the Scuola dei Mercanti, among others, the last being very much in Tintoretto's neighborhood, adjacent to the church of the Madonna dell'Orto. In each of these instances, the painter would have been well aware that his effort would be compared to that of his rival only a short distance away. Examining the relationships between paintings executed by artistic competitors for the same site can offer new insights into these works, and remind us that art history not only is about setting, patronage, and technique, but also stems from such basic human passions as jealousy, competitiveness, and pride.

In certain cases, the very reason for executing a work in the first place can be attributed to the presence of works by a rival. About 1563, Titian painted a minor altarpiece, a *tavoletta*, depicting Saint Nicholas, long after the artist had abandoned such relatively unimportant commissions. The location provides a clue as to the reason: the church of San Sebastiano, which in the previous decade had become something of a showpiece for Veronese's art as he covered the ceilings and walls (fig. 15). One eighteenth-century critic understood how central this decorative cycle was to Veronese's achievement, concluding that the church of San Sebastiano contained "sufficient paintings to understand the principles, the advancements, and the sublimity of Paolo's style."[44] In light of Veronese's growing accomplishment, Titian likely accepted the commission—or perhaps even suggested it—in order to insert himself into Veronese's personal church, reminding both the average viewer and Veronese who still was the top painter in Venice. A telling passage can be found in Vasari's *Lives*: although Vasari mentions that Veronese had painted the massive paintings on the ceiling, high altar, and elsewhere in the church, not a single subject or title is specified, whereas he indicates precisely the subject, composition, and patron of Titian's *tavoletta*. This detailed information had likely come from Titian himself, and suggests that the aging artist wanted to ensure that his incursion into Veronese's church be recorded for posterity.[45]

The greatest examples of the three painters' rivalry, however, are not so much the paintings they executed in proximity to the others, but rather the cases where they created unprecedented personal monuments to their art, transforming interiors with altarpieces and huge canvases. Titian may have started the trend in the church of Santa Maria Gloriosa dei Frari with his great altarpieces the *Assumption of the Virgin (Assunta)* of 1516–18 (fig. 50) and the *Madonna di Ca' Pesaro* of 1519–26 (fig. 47), two pioneering works that were later to be crowned with a third altarpiece, the *Pietà* (fig. 109), for his own tomb. By precisely calibrat-

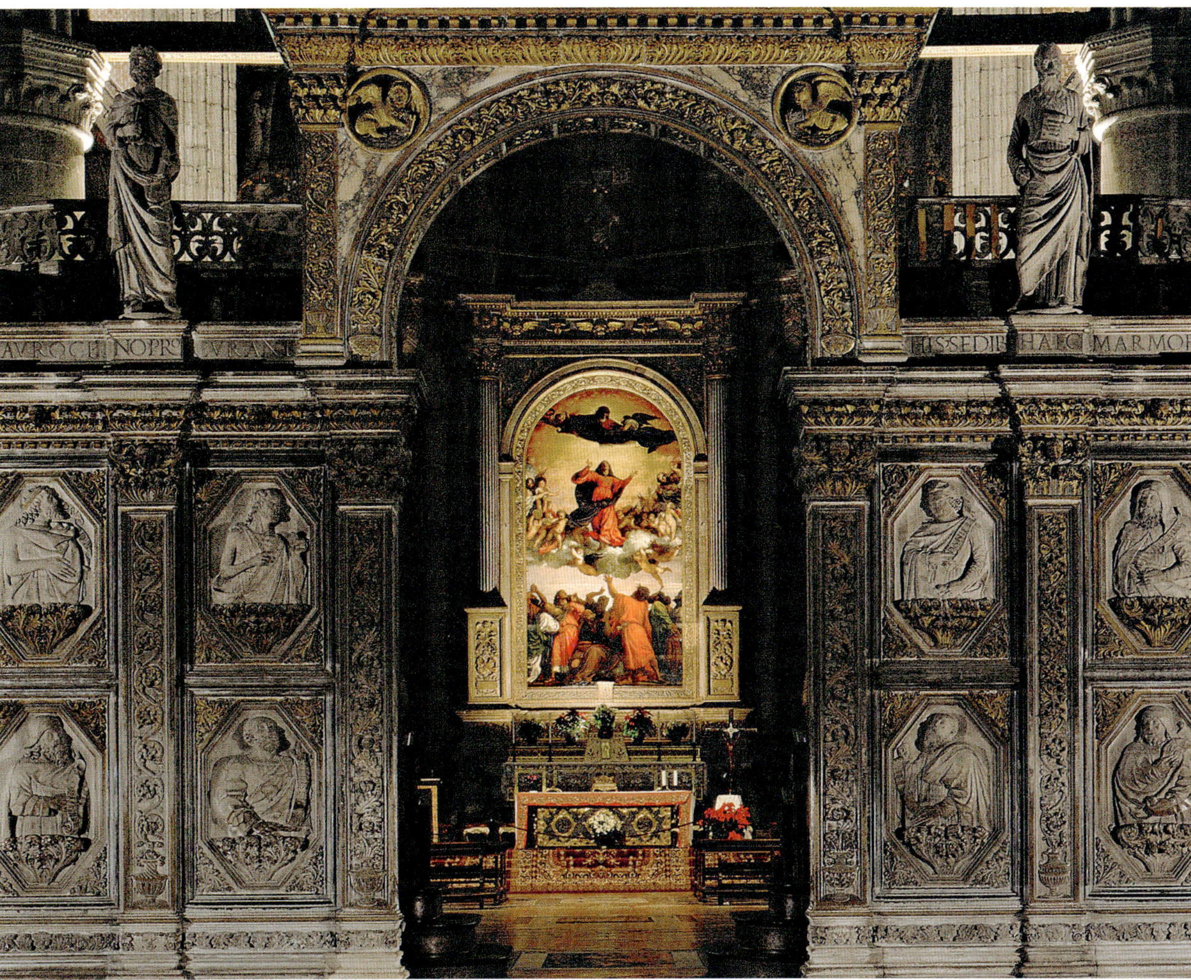

Fig. 7
Church of Santa Maria Gloriosa dei Frari, Venice, with the high altar and Titian's *Assumption of the Virgin (Assunta)* (1516–18) seen through the arch of the choir

ing the *Assumption* for its setting, taking into account both existing architecture and the positions of viewers, Titian had in effect made the entire building seem to react to his altarpiece (fig. 7).[46] Similarly, the *Madonna di Ca' Pesaro* was designed to be viewed both head-on and from an angle, thus involving observers in new ways and transforming the spatial relations in the nave of the church. Veronese, beginning in 1555, covered the ceilings and walls of San Sebastiano, the church where he himself would eventually be buried. And at around the same time, Tintoretto painted, as the organ shutters for Madonna dell'Orto, a *Presentation of the Virgin in the Temple* (fig. 8), responding in a more dramatic vein to Titian's famous prototype of two decades earlier while simultaneously staking his own claim to a building. Within a few years, and undoubtedly in response to Veronese's continued success, Tintoretto used his self-generated commissions for the enormous paintings the *Last Judgment* and the *Making of the Golden Calf* to take over the vast choir area of this church right in his neighborhood, a building that he knew would be the site of his own grave, in the vault of his father-in-law.[47]

But Tintoretto's indisputable triumph was the decoration of the Scuola Grande di San Rocco (fig. 9). As noted above, his devious ploy for the Scuola's *albergo* eventually led to his decoration of most of the surfaces of the building with large narrative canvases, making the spaces of the huge confraternity a vehicle for his own attempts to surpass Titian and Veronese.[48] Painting the majority of pictures in a building provided a memorial to a painter's art without any distractions from competitors. Moreover, the proximity of San Rocco to the church of the Frari, the site of Titian's breakthrough altarpieces, must have made his unique achievement even more satisfying for Tintoretto.

That Tintoretto in the Scuola Grande di San Rocco and Veronese in the church of San Sebastiano could essentially undertake the entire decoration of a

Fig. 8
Tintoretto
Presentation of the Virgin in the Temple, about 1556
Oil on canvas
Church of the Madonna dell'Orto, Venice

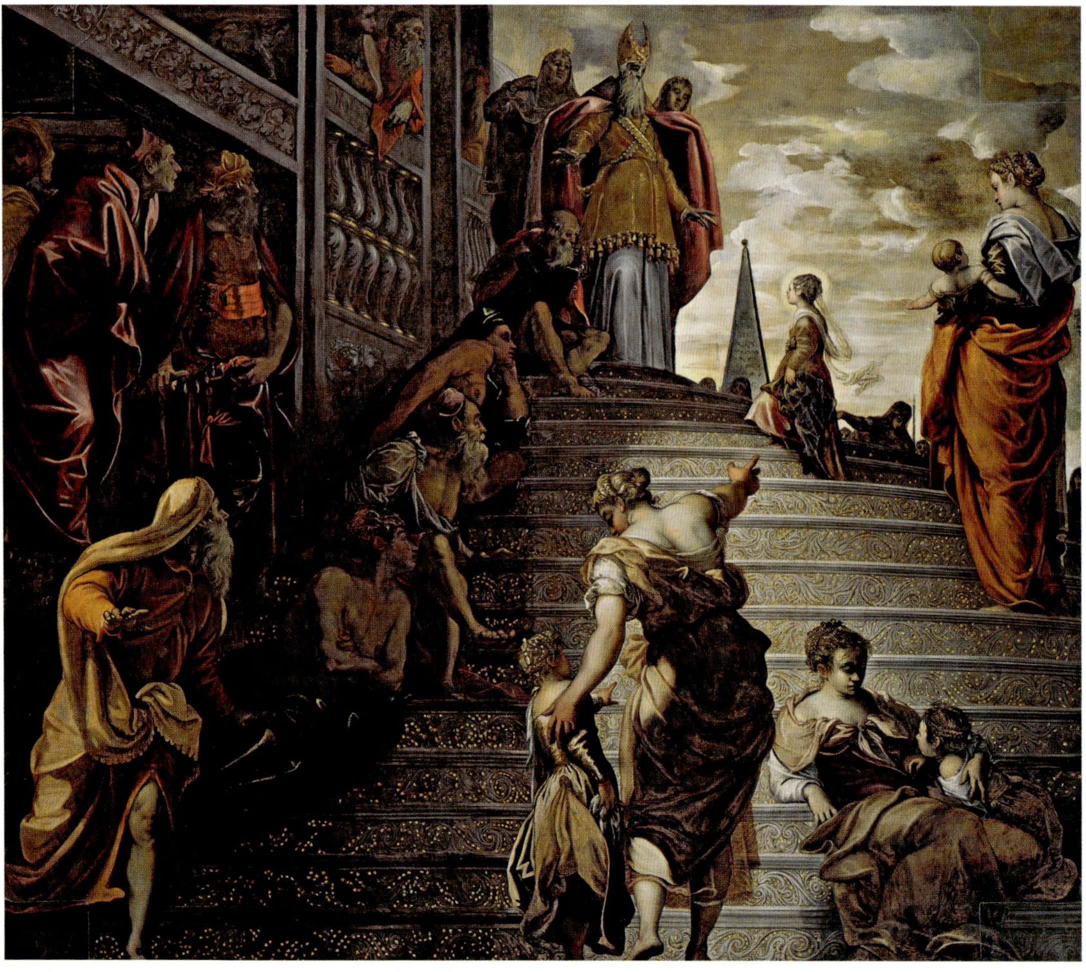

large building was a testimony not just to their ambition and competitiveness, but also to a new approach to painting, one that relied less on careful sequences of preparatory drawings and more on inventing forms directly on the canvas. The oil medium allowed painters to cover large surfaces with a rapidity and economy of means that would have astonished the painters of Giovanni Bellini's generation, who were accustomed to a deliberate, unhurried creative process, and an assumption that major cycles would always be divided up among various workshops. More than this, Titian, Tintoretto, and Veronese found eloquent expression for their visionary ideas in the unprecedented freedom and personality of their brushwork, pioneering the notion that an artist's identity could be one and the same with his distinctive paint handling. Such handling, along with the new format of the oil-on-canvas easel picture that they helped establish, allowed them a greater degree of creative freedom in their quest to cover the walls of their city and spread Venetian *colorito* far from the shores of the lagoon. In many of its aspects, our modern concept of painting, and the artistic self-determination it assumes, owes much to the rivalry between Titian, Tintoretto, and Veronese in Cinquecento Venice.

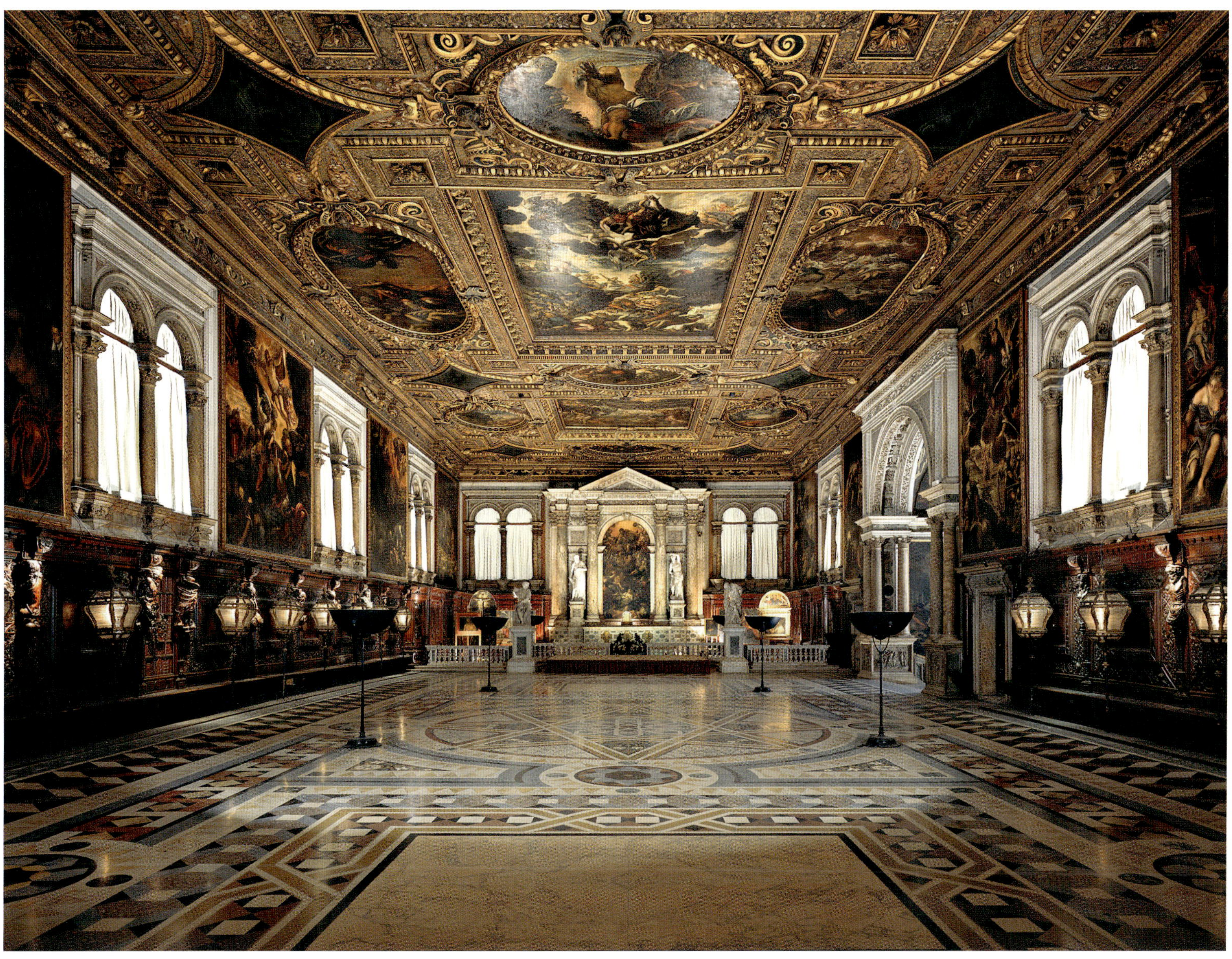

Fig. 9
View of the Sala Superiore, with paintings by Tintoretto, 1576–81
Scuola Grande di San Rocco, Venice

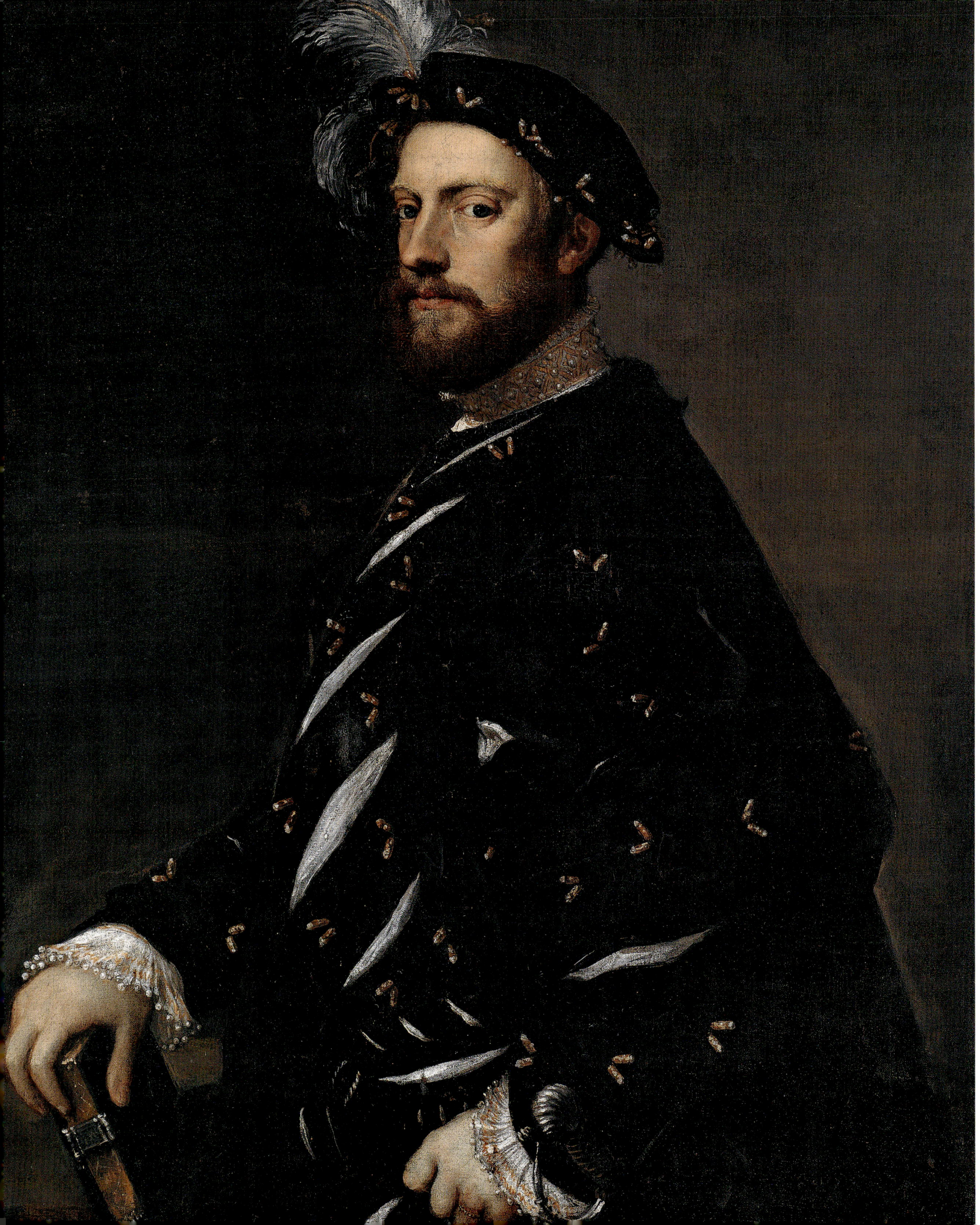

Where the Money Flows: Art Patronage in Sixteenth-Century Venice

PATRICIA FORTINI BROWN

> VENETIAN: *Have you noticed that in Venice there are more paintings than in all the rest of Italy?*
> FOREIGNER: *It is right and proper that you, being the richest men in Italy, should also have more beautiful things than the others, because craftsmen go where the money flows and where the people are soft-living and well fed.*
>
> Francesco Sansovino, 1561

By the middle of the sixteenth century, Tintoretto and Veronese had begun to fashion their career trajectories in response to one another and to the reigning master, Titian. The clients who made the money flow were key players in the drama: state officials, confraternities, the clergy, private patrons in and around the city, and foreign princes.[1]

Three features distinguished art patronage in Venice from that in other major cities. First, in the absence of a court culture, opportunities for artists were shaped by a legally defined caste structure that was over two centuries old: a top tier of patricians or nobles who filled all the political offices on a rotating basis; a middle tier of nonnoble *cittadini*, most of them bureaucrats or merchants; and a large lower tier of *popolani*, embracing a broad range of occupations, from artisans and small shopkeepers to the indigent. While great wealth was concentrated primarily in the noble caste, the two lower orders also included families of substantial means, and art patronage was one way to show it. A second peculiarity, often noted by visitors to the city, was the vast network of lay confraternities, or *scuole*, which accounted for an impressive number of artistic initiatives. These two features determined a third important characteristic of Venetian patronage: a significant portion was corporate in nature. Decisions on projects for government buildings and confraternities were made by committee, often over a prolonged period of time. And yet, whether a project was sponsored by an individual or by a group, personal connections were the dominant factor in an artist's success. One important patron led to another, and sponsorship by the wealthy and the powerful could sway the decisions of a governing board or committee.[2]

Titian was a skillful master of the game, both suavely diplomatic and shrewdly competitive. On the one hand, he adroitly cultivated influential clients, often making gifts of paintings with an eye to future commissions and other benefits; on the other, he did not hesitate to elbow aside rivals and to work for modest fees on prestigious projects that would enhance his reputation, a practice with a long tradition in Venice. But he was a sharp businessman and not averse to haggling over the price after a work was completed. During his long relationship with Philip II of Spain, Titian withheld works on occasion until payments on his pension came through, although their relationship remained cordial.[3]

Tintoretto and Veronese drew upon differing lessons from the old master. Tintoretto, with an aggressive personality and the need to support a large family, followed Titian's lead in undercutting the competition on price, but he did it across the board and not only for high-profile commissions. His business ethic was sometimes questionable. In a well-known incident at the Scuola Grande di San Rocco, he made a mockery of a competition called by the confraternity by secretly installing his completed *Saint Roch in Glory* (fig. 3) on the ceiling of the Sala dell'Albergo, whereas the other contenders had made only the requested sketches. The strategy worked, although not without opposition; the painting was accepted by a split vote of 31 to 20, even though it was offered as a gift.[4] Producing canvas after canvas at bargain prices, Tintoretto offered quick results to entice clients who wanted a project finished. With his large workshop, he produced far more paintings each year than did Titian, and as much as double that of any other artist.[5]

Veronese, endowed with a more diplomatic disposition, moved easily among the patriciate. He was, Carlo Ridolfi reported (not without an implicit jab at Tintoretto), "always without guile in his contractual agreements; he never exerted himself to obtain any commission; nor did he degrade himself with low dealings; he always kept his promises and earned praise for all his actions."[6]

For the honor of the state

Government projects had the highest visibility and were arguably the most prestigious—if not always the most lucrative—commissions available to painters within the city.[7] The corporate mentality that underwrote the patrician ethos of solidarity and consensus, coupled with the suppression of individual glory, carried through in the commissioning of art for the state. Decisions were made by committee; large decorative programs in the Palazzo Ducale often called for artists to work as a team; and no single artist—however eminent—was allowed to monopolize a major project. It was a matter of practicality as well as fairness; distributing the work among several workshops spurred competition and got the job done more quickly. With the Senate exerting control over the iconography of the programs, financial arrangements were subject to approval by the Council of Ten, the most important governing body of the state, consisting of ten noble *primi di la terra* (first ones of the city). The Ten were elected for one-year terms by the Great Council and met with the doge and his six councillors. They had wide-reaching powers, including foreign relations and the investigation of criminal, moral, religious, and political offenses, as well as state finances.[8] The choice of artists and subject matter might be delegated to *Provveditori sopra la fabbrica del Palazzo* (surveyors of works in the palace), patricians appointed by the Senate from time to time to supervise large-scale projects.[9] The close scrutiny of state-sponsored art by both the Senate and the Council of Ten attests to its importance as an expression of the Republic's ideology and magnificence. Curiously, these programs of splendor were financed by a mundane commodity; bills were paid by the Magistrato del Sal (Salt Office) from a tax on salt that brought in thousands of ducats a year.[10]

Two devastating fires, in 1574 and 1577, destroyed nearly all of Titian's canvases in the Palazzo Ducale, along with works by Tintoretto and Veronese and other major artists of the time. And yet, allowing that our understanding of the palace decoration before the fires will always remain incomplete without the objects, surviving documents give us a good sense of the patronage practices of the patrician clients.[11]

The cycle of twenty-two monumental paintings in the Sala del Maggior Consiglio depicting the Peace of Venice of 1177 was the most important state painting program of the first half of the sixteenth century. A showcase of more than three generations of the city's best artists, from Gentile and Giovanni Bellini to Titian, Tintoretto, and Veronese (among others), it was completed in 1564 after a ninety-year campaign. The cycle survived intact for only thirteen years before its destruction in the fire of 1577.

Titian had inserted himself in the program in 1513, by offering to paint "that battle piece [*Battle of Spoleto*, see fig. 10], a task which no other painter, until now, has wished to undertake."[12] He proposed to work without pay with the understanding that he would receive the next available *senseria* (a pension paying around 100 ducats per year) even though other artists were ahead of him in the queue. The Council of Ten initially agreed, but in a chain of events demonstrating the hazards of patronage by committees that changed each year, the contract was revoked by a subsequent council, which found the preferential treatment unfair, only to be reinstated by a later one in 1516 with a 300-ducat contract for the painting. More important, a few months after Giovanni Bellini's death, Titian was given his *senseria*, a sinecure that brought him official recognition and a modest steady income for the rest of his life. A "payment in effect for existing," as Paul Joannides put it, the

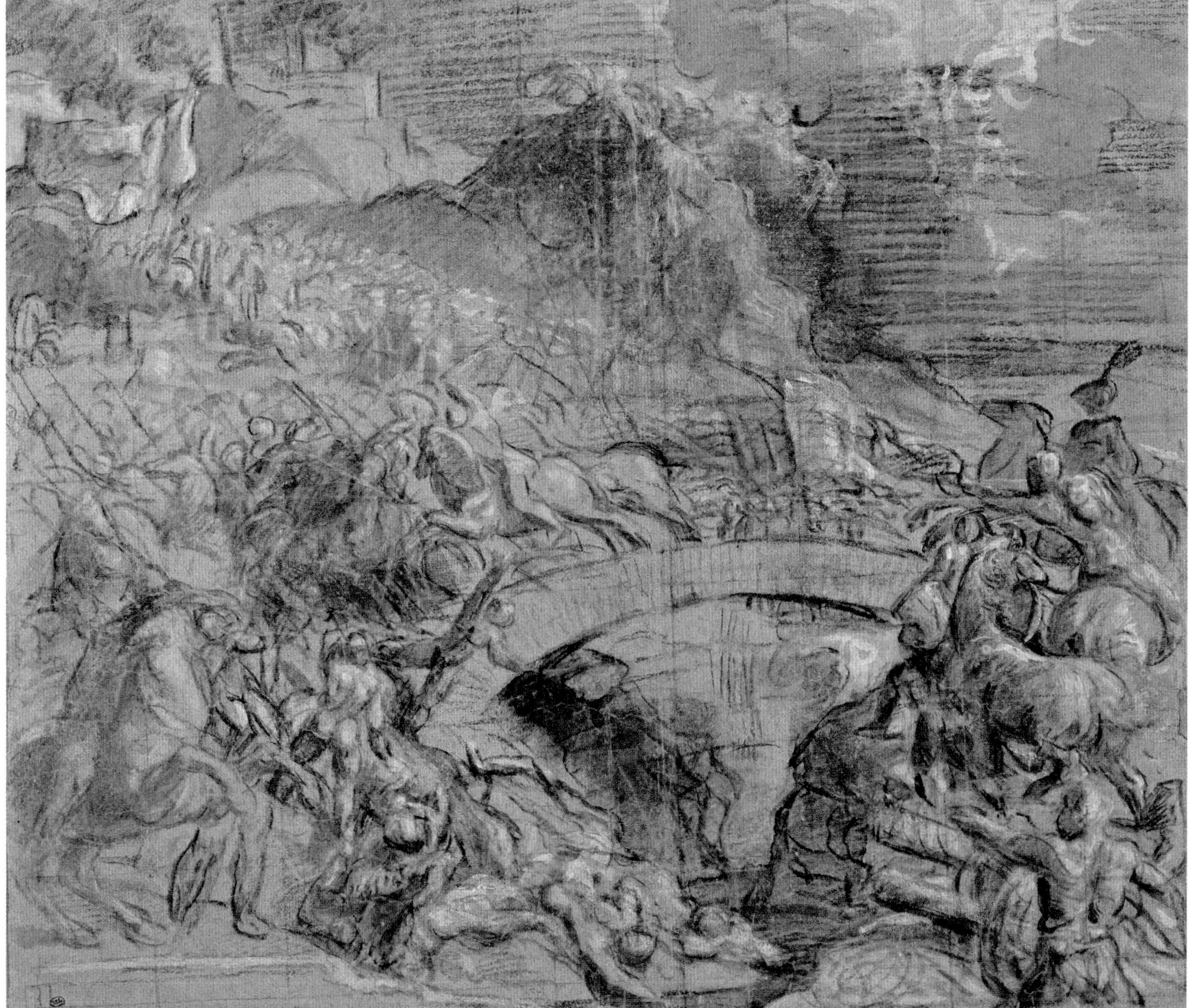

Fig. 10
Titian
Drawing for Battle of Spoleto, about 1538
Charcoal and black chalk on paper
Musée de Louvre, Paris

senseria required only that he paint a succession portrait of each doge for the Sala del Maggior Consiglio for a fee of 25 ducats.[13] In practice, he would also produce a votive painting, paid for by the doge himself, for one of the other council chambers.[14]

Titian's relationship with his patrician employers on the Council of Ten was often contentious. He completed two paintings in the Sala del Maggior Consiglio—the *Submission of Frederick Barbarossa before the Pope* (1523) and the *Battle of Spoleto* (1538)—but only after being threatened with the loss of his *senseria* and the reimbursement of all funds paid him to date. In the latter instance, he was probably also moved by the implicit threat that his commission for the *Battle* would be transferred to Pordenone, a young rival. Although Pordenone did complete at least one canvas, installed to the left of Titian's *Battle of Spoleto*, before his death in 1539, subsequent Councils of Ten were in no hurry to complete the room, and it remained untouched for another decade. Aside from the portraits and votive paintings of the doges, Titian took on no more projects in the Palazzo Ducale after the *Battle of Spoleto*. The way was open for Veronese and Tintoretto.[15]

Given the policy of distributing commissions among several artists, it may be no coincidence that Tintoretto and Veronese obtained their first important assignments in the Palazzo Ducale around the same time, during Vettor Grimani's tenure as *Provveditore sopra la fabbrica*. Tintoretto's *Excommunication of Barbarossa by Alexander III* (now lost) was installed in the Sala del Maggior Consiglio to the right of (and inviting comparison with) Titian's *Battle of Spoleto* in 1553.[16] Veronese

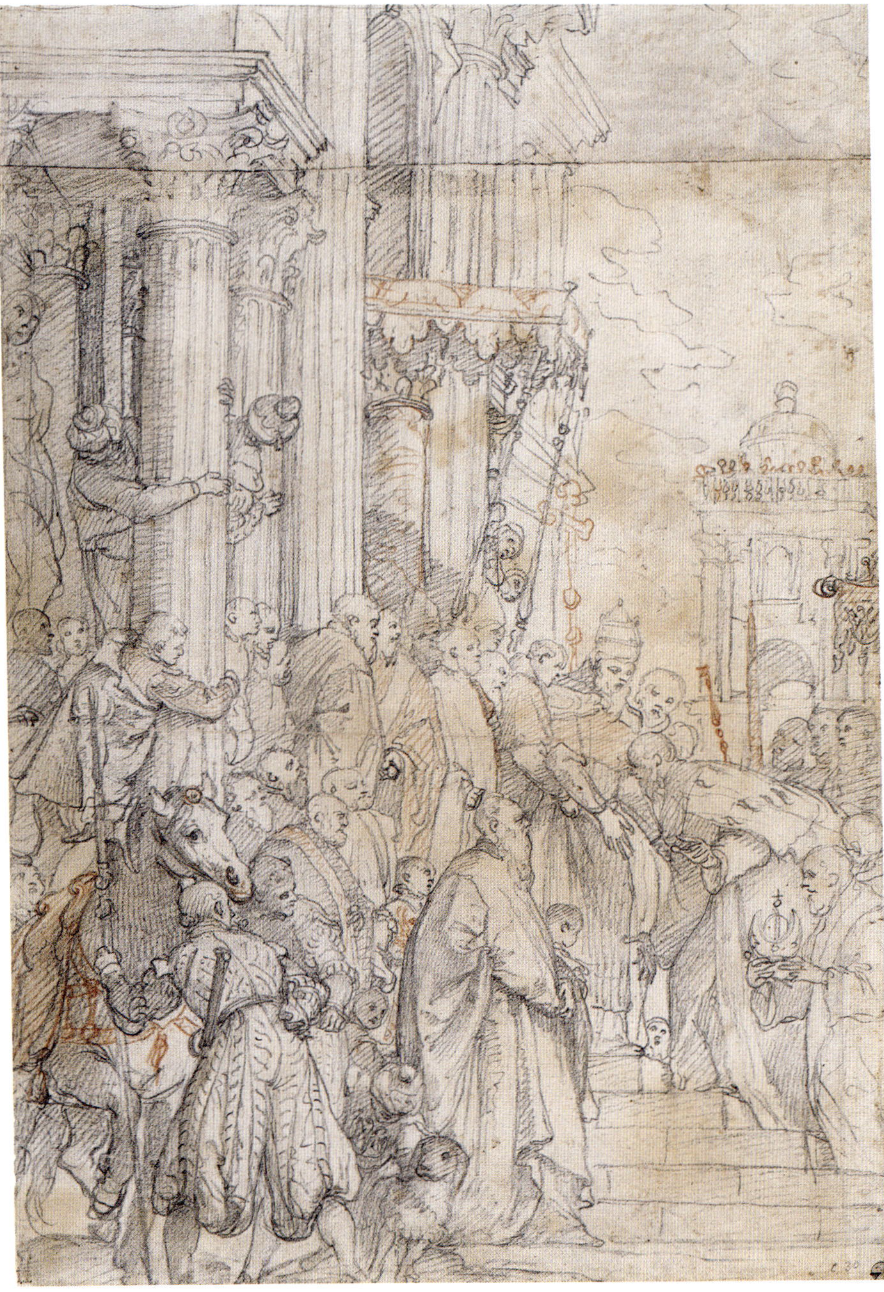

Fig. 11
Federico Zuccaro (Italian, about 1540–1609), study after Veronese *Frederick Barbarossa Kisses the Hand of the Schismatic Pope Victor IV*, 1563–65
Black and red chalk on paper
The Pierpont Morgan Library, New York

began work the same year on ceiling paintings for the newly constructed rooms of the Council of Ten—the Sale del Consiglio dei Dieci—and soon overshadowed the two other artists working on the project. Vettor Grimani, as Provveditore, and Daniele Barbaro, Patriarch-elect of Aquileia, who invented the allegorical program, oversaw the campaign. Both had classicizing tastes with connections to the papal circle in Rome. Grimani initially selected Giovanni Battista Ponchino, a priest of modest artistic talents, as lead artist, but it soon became apparent that he was not up to the task. According to Giorgio Vasari, Ponchino then brought in Veronese and Giovanni Battista Zelotti, whom he would have known through their fresco decoration of Villa La Soranza near his home town of Castelfranco Veneto, to work with him.[17] Veronese seems also to have been favored by Barbaro, who was connected by marriage to Lorenzo and Antonio Giustiniani, the artist's early patrons at San Francesco della Vigna (see fig. 48). Veronese's *Jupiter Expelling the Vices* (fig. 42), as well as other ceiling paintings in the Sale del Consiglio dei Dieci, created a sensation, a positive counterpoint to that of Tintoretto's *Miracle of the Slave* (fig. 5) in the Scuola Grande di San Marco a few years earlier, and his reputation in the city was made.[18]

Rivalries among artists played a role in Veronese's next state commission. The architect Jacopo Sansovino was allowed to choose the artists for the ceiling paintings of the main hall of his newly completed Biblioteca Marciana—the most visible public project outside the Palazzo Ducale. Although Tintoretto had identified himself as *eius amicissimus* (his very good friend) on his portrait of Sansovino (about 1548), Titian was able to persuade the architect to exclude the painter from the campaign. By contrast, Veronese had Titian's support and was hired, with Zelotti and five other artists, to paint three ceiling roundels each. When the program was completed (1557), Sansovino and Titian presented Veronese with a prestigious gold chain as a prize for his *Allegory of Music* (fig. 2), judged to be the best roundel out of twenty-one.[19] Titian, reaffirming his preeminence in Venetian public art, then claimed for himself the most prominent space in the library: the ceiling of the vestibule, which he filled with his *Sapienza* (1560), the personification of Wisdom. Tintoretto obtained commissions for six wall paintings of philosophers only in the second phase of the program (1571–72).[20]

In 1562 the Council of Ten returned to the unfinished cycle in the Sala del Maggior Consiglio. Observing that three paintings were needed to complete the cycle, the council assigned one to Veronese (known through a copy by Federico Zuccaro (fig. 11), another to Tintoretto, and the third to Titian's son, Orazio Vecellio (probably representing his father and, according to Vasari, assisted by him). The criteria of selection were the lowest price (100 ducats for each canvas) and the reputation of the artists. Although the desire to finish the program speedily and the long-standing policy of artistic diversification must have been major considerations, the choice of these artists set up an implicit (and enduring) competition.[21]

The inclusion of a host of contemporary witnesses to the historical events in nearly every scene, moreover, encouraged close examination. Sansovino's citation of over 130 portraits in the cycle documents a long-standing tradition in Venetian narrative painting. The forty-four *primi di la terra* identified by Francesco Sansovino in the final three paintings by Tintoretto and Veronese (none was listed for Titian's or Orazio's battle scenes) reads like a *Who's Who* of mid-sixteenth-century political and cultural life. It is here that we catch a glimpse of the decision makers for art campaigns in the Palazzo Ducale and get a sense of the overlapping worlds of public and private patronage in that period. For example, Tintoretto's *Excommunication* included portraits of one of his best patrons, the Procurator Jacopo Soranzo, as well as Veronese's advocates Daniele Barbaro and Vettor Grimani. Veronese's *Frederick Barbarossa Kisses the Hand of the Schismatic Pope Victor IV* portrayed his own patrons Lorenzo and Antonio Giustiniani, along with Daniele Barbaro's brother Marcantonio.[22] The cycle in the Sala offered an incomparable opportunity to compare the narrative skills of a century of Venice's leading artists and to appraise the characteristically Venetian search for balance between the quest for individual glory and collaboration toward a common goal.

The fires of 1574 and 1577, although disastrous, brought new opportunities, and major commissions were distributed with a remarkably even hand. After the fires, Veronese was assigned the ceilings of the Sala dell'Anticollegio (about 1576) and the Sala del Collegio (1575–81), and Tintoretto was given the ceilings of the Antipregadi (Sala delle Quattro Porte; 1577–81) and the Pregadi (Sala del Senato; 1581–84). But except for Veronese's votive painting of Doge Sebastiano Venier (about 1578), the walls of the Collegio and Pregadi virtually belonged to Tintoretto, who replaced the lost votive paintings of the doges (seven by Titian and one by Parrasio Michiel) and continued with those who served after 1574.[23]

The awarding of commissions after the fire of 1577 was likewise deliberately diversified. With the major ceiling paintings of the Sala del Maggior Consiglio assigned to Veronese, Tintoretto, and the rising star Jacopo Palma il Giovane, the walls became once more a gallery of the most important artists of the day, including (among others) Jacopo Tintoretto and his son Domenico; the "Haeredes Pauli" (Carletto and Gabriele Caliari); Palma Giovane; Federico Zuccaro; Andrea Vicentino; and Francesco and Leandro Bassano.[24]

Even the competition to replace Guariento's badly charred fresco of the Coronation of the Virgin on the end wall of the Sala became an exercise in collaboration. Veronese and Francesco Bassano were jointly awarded the job over competing submissions from Tintoretto, Palma Giovane, Francesco Bassano, and Federico Zuccaro. But the winners, forced to work together despite incompatible styles, failed to produce a final *modello* by the time of Veronese's death in 1588. The triumph was Tintoretto's, who was then granted the commission for the *Paradiso*, although the painting was executed largely by his son Domenico and the workshop.[25] According to Ridolfi, "the very senators congratulated [Jacopo] and affectionately embraced him for having brought to conclusion that great piece of work to the enormous satisfaction of the Senate."[26]

Indeed, Tintoretto, with his workshop, produced more paintings for the Venetian state than any other artist. From the 1550s on, he was also responsible for most of the votive paintings in the Palazzo dei Camerlenghi, the third major site of state patronage. Rebuilt and enlarged after the Rialto fire of 1514 to house eighteen departments relating to state finance and commerce, the building was completed in 1529 and a decoration program begun under the direction of the Magistrato del Sal. The project was intended to unfold over a long period of time, with the walls of each room lined with paintings paid for by the patrician officeholders themselves. Elected every sixteen months, two or three magistrates of a given office were required jointly to commission a work commemorating their service from a painter chosen by the state. The Veronese artist Bonifazio de' Pitati was put in charge, painting many of the works himself and farming out the remainder to a stable of reliable young painters. Seeking to mimic Titian's style to ensure stylistic continuity, he developed a formula of narrative scenes flanked by saints or virtues. The patrons were accorded subtle recognition by the inclusion of their

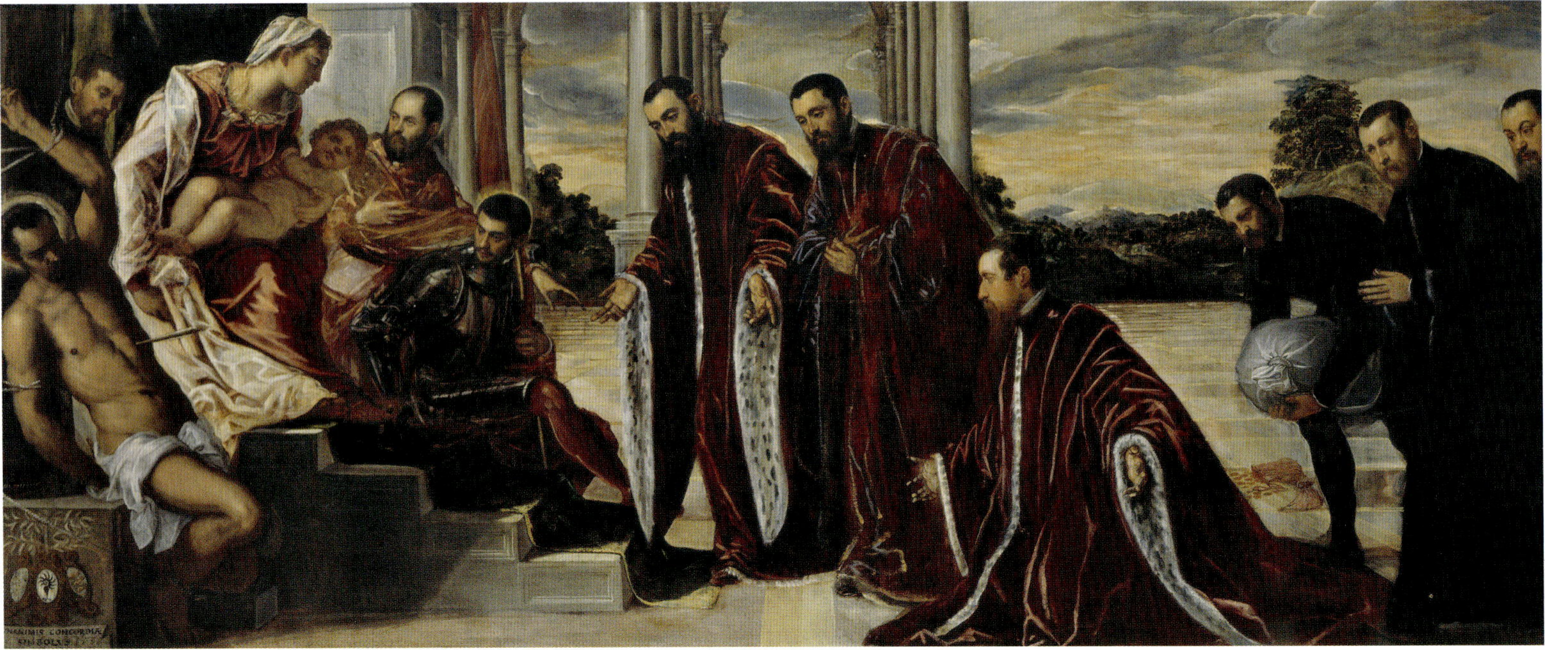

Fig. 12
Tintoretto
Madonna of the Treasurers, about 1567
Oil on canvas
Gallerie dell'Accademia, Venice

name saints and their coats of arms. As with the Palazzo Ducale, the rooms were decorated in a piecemeal fashion, with empty spaces remaining for future officeholders. According to Philip Cottrell, who analyzed the full program, what might seem like a haphazard process was a deliberate strategy proclaiming "the virtue of a sustained, cumulative contribution to the republic's status quo on the part of its ruling classes."[27]

Bonifazio's health (and the quality of the paintings) declined in the late 1540s, and around 1551, the Magistrato del Sal called in Tintoretto to continue the decoration of their rooms. If they had intended to reinvigorate the program, Tintoretto did not disappoint. The dramatic narrative action of his first two paintings—*Saint George, Saint Louis, and the Princess* (cat. 15) and *Saint Jerome and Saint Andrew*—which drew attention to the virtuosity of the artist, represented a radical break with tradition.[28] But Tintoretto was nonetheless commissioned to paint a third work for the room; it too was revolutionary, but in a different way. His *Virgin and Child with Four Provveditori* (1553) included portraits of the patrons instead of simply their coats of arms.[29] The first such painting in the program, it may be seen as a provocative challenge to Titian's votive paintings of the doges then in the Palazzo Ducale. Although the extension of the genre to the magistrates might seem a breach of Venetian values in regard to individual glory, the reverential attitudes of the officeholders reaffirmed their corporate identity and their subservience to the state. Offering an officially sanctioned vehicle for them to stand out among their peers, the votive paintings became a formula that Tintoretto pursued with success. Along with his son Domenico and the workshop, he continued to produce works for the Camerlenghi; his *Madonna of the Treasurers* (about 1567; fig. 12) is a graphic illustration of the Venetian body politic, with patrician magistrates, commemorated both in visage and coats of arms, paying homage to the Virgin and a group of saints and escorted by their (subordinate) *cittadini* secretaries.[30] Through subtle manipulation by the state, the money flowing from the pockets of the magistrates was regarded an honor, as well as an obligation.[31]

Collective piety

The Venetian *scuole* were the second most important category of corporate patrons of the arts in Venice. Similar to lay confraternities elsewhere in their focus on religious devotion and spiritual brotherhood, the *Scuole Grandi* and *scuole piccole* were uniquely Venetian in their sworn allegiance to the doge and in the extent of their charitable activities. The five Scuole Grandi (with a sixth approved in 1552) offered the nonnoble castes the opportunity to participate in public life. With all-male memberships of five to six hundred drawn from throughout the city, each group sought to maintain the right balance of rich and poor. The rich supported the poor with material benefits, such as hospices, dowries, and housing; the poor prayed for the souls of the rich and marched in their funeral processions. Under the direct control of the Council of Ten, the Scuole Grandi were run by laymen, independent of clerical supervision. Each had a large cadre of patrician members, but office holding was restricted to *cittadini originari*, who served limited terms on the model of patrician magistrates in government offices. The *banca* (governing board) of a Scuola Grande was elected by the membership and consisted of a Guardian Grande and fifteen regular officers. The Scuole Grandi enjoyed considerable financial resources and conducted ambitious building campaigns throughout the sixteenth century.[32]

The scuole piccole also had broadly based memberships in terms of social caste, occupation, and place of residence, but they differed from the Grandi in their smaller size, inclusion of women, and narrower focus of their devotional and charitable activities. The governance of the scuole piccole followed the model established by the Scuole Grandi, but with the chief executive usually called a *gastaldo*. Numbering over two hundred by the mid-sixteenth century, most were called simply *scuole di devozione* or *scuole comuni*, with some catering to specific national groups, such as the Albanians and the Dalmatians, and others linked to specific *arti* (trade guilds). The *scuole del Sacramento*, devoted to the cult of the Eucharist, proliferated during the Counter-Reformation and were found in nearly all the parishes of the city by the mid-sixteenth century.[33]

Although group devotion and mutual support were initially their stated goals, the scuole "had to decide how far to praise God through splendid architecture and elaborate ceremony, and how far to minister to Christ in his own image, the poor man."[34] At the very least, each scuola maintained an altar in a parish or monastic church, but the Scuole Grandi and the wealthier scuole piccole had their own meetinghouses, typically decorated with altarpieces, ceiling paintings, and cycles of narrative paintings. While the decision to launch a major decorative campaign was often made by a vote of the full chapter, final arrangements were made by the banca. As with museum boards today, service on the banca of a scuola brought not only honor, but also obligation, with each officeholder expected to contribute his share to decoration campaigns. Additional funds might come from the membership at large, both living and dead, since programs were often underwritten by testamentary bequests.[35]

Among the three protagonists of this volume, scuola patronage is essentially the story of two artists, Titian and Tintoretto, with Veronese virtually out of the running. Titian produced major works for two Scuole Grandi and several scuole piccole, and Veronese painted an expansive *Annunciation* for the affluent Scuola dei Mercanti, but Tintoretto dominated the field.[36] His cycles for the meetinghouses of the Scuola Grande di San Marco and the Scuola Grande di San Rocco are among the masterpieces of the Venetian Renaissance. He was, as well, the painter of choice of the scuole del Sacramento and many of the piccole.

An element of competition, not so obvious among the piccole, is evident in the commissions of the Grandi. In 1534 the officers of the Scuola Grande della Carità voted to commission "such painting and decoration as are required for the dignity of our *albergo* [boardroom] and as are to be seen in the other *alberghi* of the scuole grandi of this most illustrious city." Consulting with "sufficient and famous painters," the board engaged Titian, probably without holding a competition.[37] By 1538 his *Presentation of the Virgin in the Temple* (fig. 13), complete with portraits of officers of the confraternity, was installed in the *albergo*. A new slate of officers voted to continue with the decoration. Following the model of the state in distributing commissions among more than one artist, it settled on Pordenone, a "most ingenious and prudent man" (and Titian's rival of the moment). One member suggested that he paint an Assumption of the Virgin, but Pordenone disagreed, observing that the Scuola already had a painting of that subject in its chapter hall. He argued further that the horizontal space available was inappropriate for the subject, which, in any case, did not follow the *Presentation* in the narrative sequence. Deferring to his expertise in matters of iconography and decorum, the board accepted his proposal to paint the Marriage of the Virgin instead. When Pordenone died in 1539 without completing the painting, a competition was held to replace him. The contenders were second- and third-tier artists; Tintoretto, who had just become an independent master, with an oeuvre consisting primarily of devotional paintings for the home, was not among them.[38]

Although patricians did not play an official role in the governance, and art patronage, of the Scuole Grandi, in at least one instance their influence is apparent behind the scenes. Titian's *Vendramin Family, Venerating a Relic of the True Cross* (fig. 100) depicts a patrician family with a long history in the Scuola

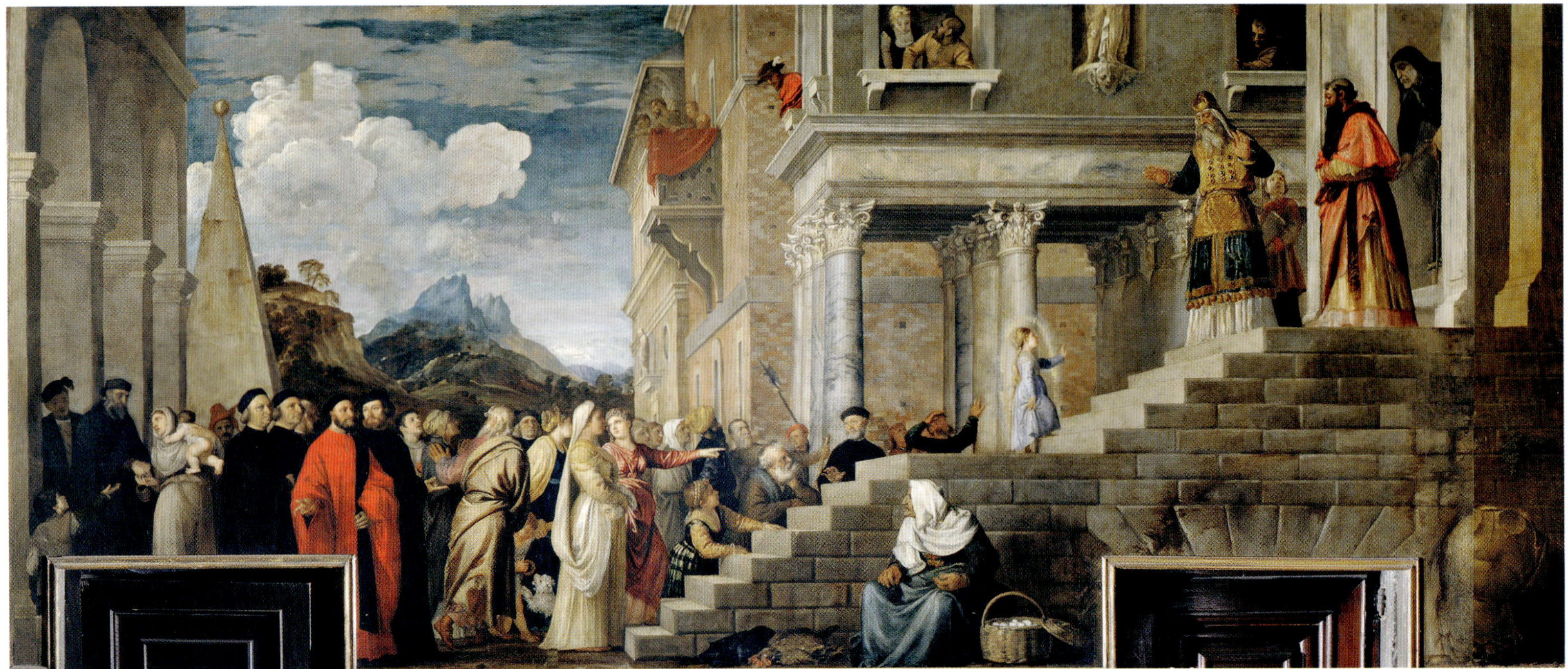

Fig. 13
Titian
Presentation of the Virgin in the Temple, 1534–38
Oil on canvas
Gallerie dell'Accademia, Venice

Grande di San Giovanni Evangelista. Their ancestor Andrea Vendramin, Guardian Grande in 1369 when the relic of the True Cross was given to the Scuola, was admitted to the patriciate in 1381. His grandson of the same name was elected doge in 1476, and his great-nephew, again of the same name, is depicted in the painting with his seven sons and probably his brother Gabriele.[39] The painting, undoubtedly intended for the *portego* (main hall on the piano nobile) of the family palace, would have been under way in 1544 when the board of the Scuola sought Titian's counsel.[40] They asked him whether certain paintings in their old *albergo*, the Sala della Croce, should be cut into to provide for a doorway to the recently constructed Albergo Nuovo. The artist did not hesitate to approve of a large cutout in the lower edge of Carpaccio's *Healing of a Possessed Man at Rialto* (fig. 51). Titian was then awarded a commission to decorate the ceiling of the new *albergo* with a canvas titled *Vision of Saint John the Evangelist on Patmos* (about 1544–48), framed by symbols of the four evangelists.[41]

Some years later, Titian's *Presentation of the Virgin* in the Scuola Grande della Carità suffered a fate similar to that of Carpaccio's painting. In 1572 the governing board of the Carità voted 17 to 9 to create a second doorway into their *albergo*, "with the adornment necessary to bring honor to our scuola." The dissenting votes presumably came from those who hesitated to mutilate a masterpiece, but as with the Scuola di San Giovanni Evangelista, convenience of access (and the passage of time) triumphed over aesthetics. A rectangle was cut from the lower left corner, thus truncating the bodies of the confraternity officers honored only a generation earlier.[42]

Tintoretto's commissions for the Scuole Grandi were often fraught with controversy. The furor created by his *Miracle of the Slave* for the Scuola Grande di San Marco in 1548 was only a prelude to the outrage that met the three paintings that he delivered to the confraternity in 1566. In each scene, he depicted the Guardian Grande Tommaso Rangone as a major protagonist, seemingly the only member of the confraternity to be so honored. Admittedly, Rangone had commissioned the works at his expense, but this was a clear breach of decorum, and Tintoretto was forced to take the works back to his studio for a time. A wealthy and learned immigrant, Rangone did not consider himself subject to the unwritten rules against self-aggrandizement, which constrained the patrician caste. Theirs was a good matchup of personalities, and he was probably Tintoretto's most important individual patron.[43]

In the meantime, the officers of the Scuola Grande di San Rocco, ever mindful of the importance of keeping up with the other Scuole Grandi, finally decided in 1564 to go ahead with the decoration of their *albergo*. Tintoretto's sharp dealing in obtaining the commission is mentioned above. With his foot in the door, he joined the Scuola the following year. As Tom Nichols put it, in "a famous sequence of donations and discounts," Tintoretto went on to fill the meetinghouse with his paintings over the next two decades. Producing three pictures yearly in return for a modest annuity of 100 ducats plus the cost of materials, he had become, in a sense, court painter for the Scuola and provided himself with a steady income while taking on numerous commissions elsewhere. The sum total over time added up to around 2,200 ducats.[44]

By midcentury those few scuole piccole with their own meetinghouses had already decorated them with narrative paintings, and new commissions were largely confined to churches where the various confraternities maintained an altar.[45] The proliferation of the scuole del Sacramento created an important new client group in each parish church. They assumed the responsibility of maintaining the chapel of the Holy Sacrament, of carrying the Host to the houses of sick parishioners, and of marching in procession following the feast day of Corpus Christi. Their art patronage focused on two types of painting for two distinctly different sites in the church: an altarpiece and *laterali* (side wall paintings) for the Sacrament chapel; and a *laterale*—typically a Last Supper—for the wall above the *banco*, a bench for the officers on the model of those in the *alberghi* of the Scuole Grandi, situated at the side of the nave.[46]

Tintoretto made *laterali* a specialty and became one of the painters of choice for these scuole. The ensemble that he created for San Cassiano attests to a moment of post-Tridentine piety and spiritual renewal that afforded the popular classes the opportunity to become patrons of the arts (fig. 14). In 1565 the *gastaldo* Zuanpiero Mazzolenghi commissioned an altarpiece for the main chapel, with the stipulation that it include the scuola's titular saints, Cassian and Cecilia. Responding to the challenge of maintaining a Eucharistic presence while incorporating two saints, Tintoretto created a "hybrid iconography," with Christ floating in the air, as in a Resurrection, and the two saints below. Paul Hills writes: "We could not wish for a clearer instance of diverse patronal imperatives accounting for a painter's unorthodox combination of subjects."[47] Three years later, a new *gastaldo*, Cristoforo de Gozzi, probably a rope merchant, commissioned the two *laterali*—the *Crucifixion* and *Descent into Limbo*—with benches beneath them for the officers, who are portrayed at the

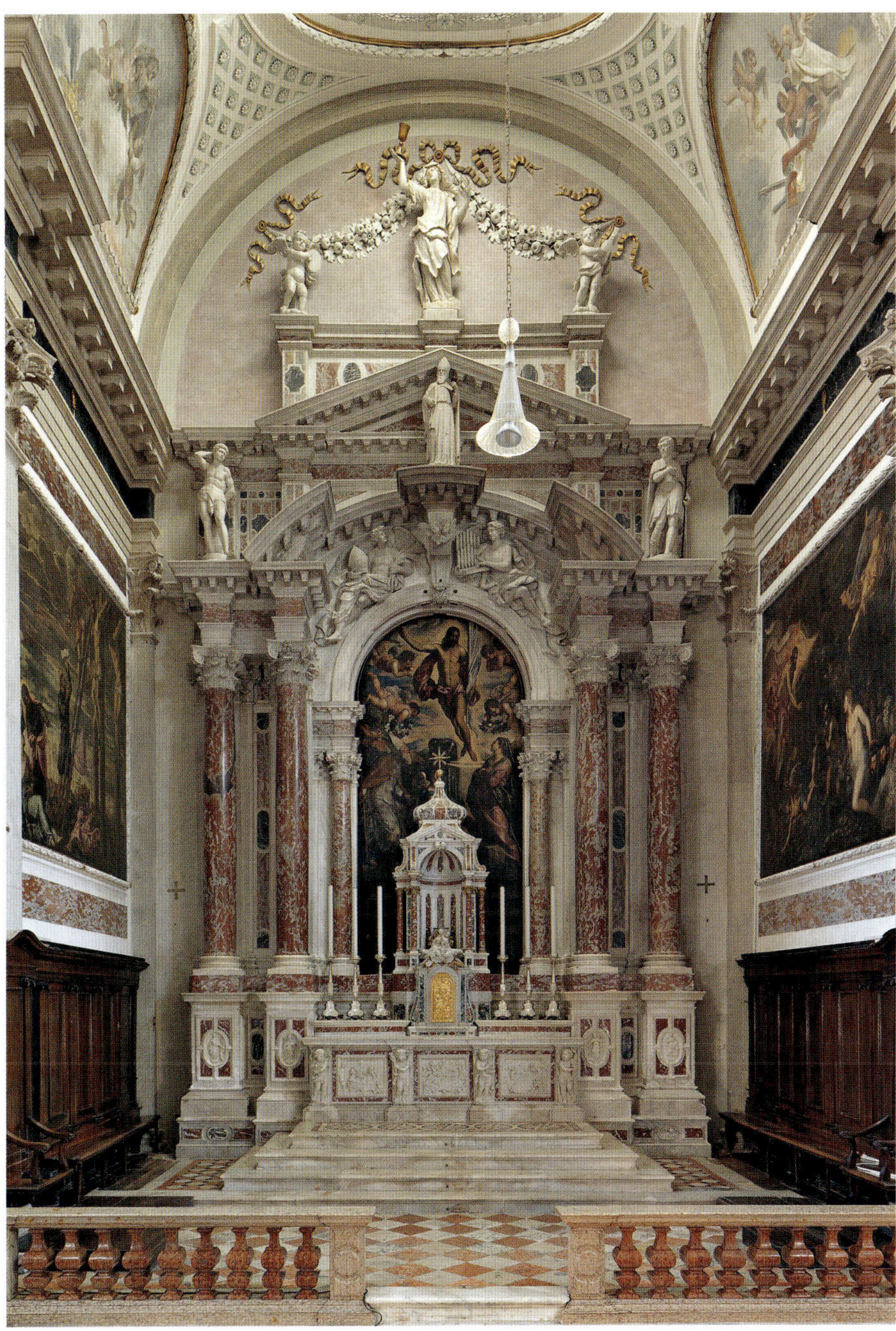

Fig. 14
High altar of the church of San Cassiano, Venice, with Tintoretto's *Resurrection of Christ with Saints Cassian and Cecilia*, 1565 (center); *Crucifixion*, 1568 (left); and *Descent into Limbo*, 1568 (right)

right edge of the latter canvas. As with the votive paintings of doges in the Palazzo Ducale, and the earlier narrative paintings of the Scuole Grandi, their personal piety stood in for the piety of the group.[48] In a sense, their custody of the main chapel made it their *albergo* and the entire church their meetinghouse.[49] And yet, in contrast to paintings in government buildings and the meetinghalls of the Scuole Grandi (which had a select audience of males, primarily patricians and diplomats in the first instance and confraternity brothers in the second), artwork in churches was available to everyone.

Places of worship

Churches and monasteries provided ample opportunities for patronage, ranging from the ecclesiastical (monastic orders and parish clergy) to the lay (private individuals and scuole), with considerable overlap between the categories. On the one hand, commissions initiated by clerics were often funded by lay donations. On the other, under the system of *juspatronatus*, the clergy sold the rights of each altar to lay patrons, who bore the responsibility of furnishing it, usually with an altar and altarpiece and other accoutrements. And yet, here too the clergy may have suggested the format, subject, choice of saints, medium, and artist. Moreover, donors often commissioned altarpieces in their wills, and their execution was carried out posthumously under clerical supervision.[50]

By the 1530s Titian was probably best known by the public at large for his altarpieces in the city's two most important monastic churches: the *Assumption of the Virgin (Assunta)* (fig. 50), commissioned by the prior Fra Germano, and the *Madonna di Ca' Pesaro* (fig. 47), made for a patrician family, in Santa Maria Gloriosa dei Frari; and the *Saint Peter Martyr* altarpiece (fig. 23), made for a scuola, in Santi Giovanni e Paolo. During the decades that followed, Titian painted altarpieces for around a dozen Venetian churches. But with his major energies increasingly directed outside the city, most were made for patrons who were friends or business acquaintances, and these included commoners as well as patricians. The personal network was in play, for example, when he accepted a commission from his friend Lorenzo Massolo to paint the *Martyrdom of Saint Lawrence* (1546–48; now in the church of the Gesuiti) for the family tomb in the church of Santa Maria dei Crociferi. Titian had already painted two portraits (now lost) of Massolo's patrician wife, Elisabetta Querini, renowned for her beauty and erudition, and had gone to Rome in 1546 at the behest of her uncle Gerolamo Querini—a friend of Pietro Bembo's, who was also a friend of Titian's. Busy with Hapsburg commissions, the artist completed the altarpiece only after the patron's death in 1557.[51]

Likewise, Titian's acceptance two years later of no fewer than three commissions for altarpieces in the church of San Salvador can be explained only by personal ties. The project was conceived by two wealthy *cittadino* merchants, Zuanne d'Anna and Antonio Cornovì della Vecchia, who had made fortunes in the textile trade. Well aware that they could never attain noble status, they sought to establish themselves in the upper tier of Venetian society. What better way to assert family honor than to acquire *juspatronatus* of altars in the newly restructured church of San Salvador?[52] And what better artist to express their piety than the famous Titian, with whom they were well acquainted as *confratelli* in the Scuola Grande di San Rocco? Titian had already painted three works for the d'Anna family palace, including the *Christ before Pilate* (1543, Kunsthistorisches Museum, Vienna), and was godfather to Zuanne d'Anna's son. The artist had also recently completed a *Crucifixion* (1558) for Antonio Cornovì della Vecchia's first cousin Pietro in the church of San Domenico in Ancona.[53]

The program for San Salvador consisted of a *Crucifixion* for a newly acquired d'Anna family chapel on the left wall of the church, an *Annunciation* for the family chapel of Antonio Cornovì della Vecchia directly across the nave, and a *Transfiguration* for the high altar.[54] The last commission is undocumented, but was probably underwritten by the Augustinian canons to complete the campaign. Whether or not the commissions added up to a coordinated altarpiece program—a rarity in Venice—the ensemble would have formed a powerful spiritual triad, illustrating the human and divine nature of Christ in a church that had particular civic resonance.[55] Although Titian finished all three paintings for San Salvador, the d'Anna family fell on hard times and failed to complete the construction of their altar; the *Crucifixion* went elsewhere.[56] The other two paintings ended up in the church, but the great scheme by which the Cornovì della Vecchia and d'Anna families may have "hoped to insert themselves into the renewable sequence of Venice's sacred, and infinite, history" was never fully realized.[57]

Veronese made his debut in Venetian ecclesiastical space in San Francesco della Vigna in 1551. He could not have had more auspicious beginnings. The newly rebuilt church featured a cornerstone laid by

Doge Andrea Gritti and chapels purchased by some of Venice's wealthiest *primi di la terra*. Commissioned to paint an altarpiece by Lorenzo and Antonio Giustiniani, Veronese quickly established his Venetian credentials by modeling his *Holy Family with Saint John the Baptist, Saint Anthony Abbot, and Saint Catherine* (fig. 48) after Titian's *Madonna di Ca' Pesaro*. The Giustiniani brothers, who were related to both Doge Gritti and Daniele Barbaro, provided Veronese an entrée into patrician circles, where he encountered his most generous clients.[58]

Veronese's connections in Verona continued to bring in commissions from numerous patrons on the mainland, but they also played a role in Venice. In 1555 he was commissioned by Bernardo Torlioni, a fellow Veronese and the prior of the monastery of San Sebastiano, to paint the ceilings of the church's sacristy and nave with a series of Old and New Testament paintings (fig.15).[59] His commission for the organ shutters around 1558 seems to have led to a call from the parish priest in San Geminiano to do the same for his church at the end of Piazza San Marco (cat. 16).[60] Veronese continued to work in San Sebastiano over the next twelve years, the campaign culminating in 1570 with the altarpiece and scenes from the life of Saint Sebastian in the presbytery.[61] Despite the monastic setting, in a typical amalgam of lay and ecclesiastical interests, the latter space served as a burial chapel for the wealthy Soranzo family. In 1559 the patrician noblewoman Lise Querini, acting as the executor of her deceased husband, Zuane Soranzo, signed a contract with the stonemason, a certain Salvador of San Maurizio, who promised to complete the "altar, pavement, sepulchre, benches and the renovation of the windows in the Cappella Maggiore" within two years for 380 ducats. The document also specified that "the altar should be made of white stone . . . according to the drawing made by messer Paulo Veronese."[62] The church as a whole, crowned by Veronese's altarpiece the *Virgin and Child in Glory with Saints* in the apse, is a tour de force, perhaps comparable to Tintoretto's achievement in the Scuola Grande di San Rocco.[63]

Veronese was also favored by the Benedictines. Commissions from the order included three large altarpieces for the monastery of San Benedetto Po near Mantua in 1561 (see cat. 19), probably on the recommendation of Daniele Barbaro, to be followed the next year by orders for two altarpieces for the abbey in Praglia[64] and a contract with the Benedictine monks of San Giorgio Maggiore to paint the *Wedding Feast at Cana* in their new refectory designed by Palladio:

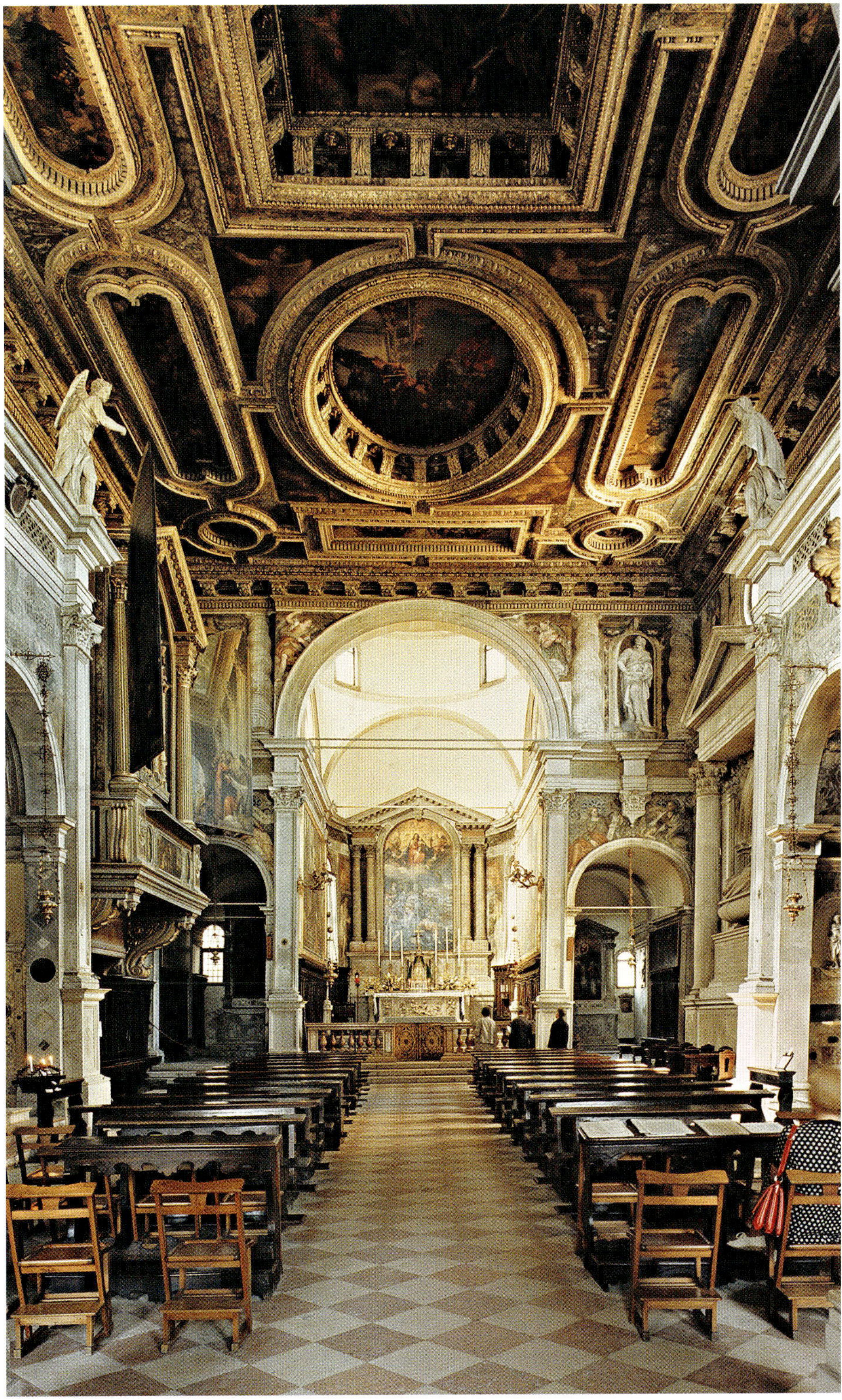

Fig. 15
Nave of the church of San Sebastiano, Venice, with paintings by Veronese

It is to be as wide and high as the wall and is to cover it completely. He is to represent the story of the Supper or Miracle worked by Christ at Cana in Galilee. He is to paint that number of figures which will go into it comfortably, and which are necessary for the story. Master Paulo will paint the work and also provide all kinds of pigments at his own expense, and he will order the preparation of the canvas and bear the cost of anything else concerning it . . . and the said Master Paulo will be obliged to use the highest quality pigments in the work, of the kind that are approved by all experts. . . . And for his payment for the work we promise 324 ducats . . . to be given him from day to day according to his need, and for earnest money we have given him 50 ducats. Master Paulo promises to finish the work by the Feast of the Madonna in September 1563, and in addition to the fee we promise him a cask of wine, to be brought by us to Venice and consigned to him, and the monastery will pay for his food during the period that he is working on the said picture, and will bear the cost of the meals which he eats in the refectory.[65]

Like Titian and Veronese, Tintoretto completed a variety of assignments in Venetian churches for both ecclesiastical and secular patrons. The organ doors for the monastery church of Madonna dell'Orto, for which he signed a contract in 1548 (revised in 1551), were among his most important early commissions. They were ordered by the Secular Canons of San Giorgio in Alga, an elite congregation of Venetian patricians, as part of a campaign to renovate the church. Tintoretto's response was characteristic. Instead of emulating Titian, as Veronese had done in San Francesco della Vigna, he critiqued the old master's *Presentation of the Virgin* in the Scuola Grande della Carità, creating his own version in vertical format (fig. 8).[66] A few years later, Tintoretto saw an opportunity to comment on Michelangelo in the same church and offered to fill two bays of the Gothic choir with a *Last Judgment* and the *Making of the Golden Calf*. According to Ridolfi, he promised the canons "to make them a gift of his labor," requesting only a modest payment for materials. The prior accepted and agreed to pay just 100 ducats for two enormous paintings—around 14.5 meters (about 47 feet 7 inches) high—containing numerous figures. The unusual iconography was probably Tintoretto's own, intended to distinguish him from Michelangelo and to confirm his own (more) Catholic orthodoxy.[67]

Tintoretto had yet another occasion to make a statement of faith in the church with his *Saint Agnes Cures Licinius*, an altarpiece commissioned by Procurator Tommaso Contarini for his family chapel. Tommaso had purchased the chapel in 1557 as a burial site for his brother, Cardinal Gasparo Contarini, a distinguished scholar whose religious writings on justification by faith had been censored after his death in 1542 by the Council of Trent. Tintoretto's unique treatment of Saint Agnes and Licinius in the altarpiece, probably completed in the 1570s, has been interpreted "to conform to the beginning and the end of the process of justification, as codified by the Council of Trent." It thus rehabilitated Gasparo in the eyes of the church and confirmed his orthodox credentials.[68] Tintoretto moved to a house nearby on Fondamenta de' Mori in 1574. Ridolfi would later write that Madonna dell'Orto was the artist's favorite church in all of Venice, where "he spent much time in pious meditation . . . in conversation on moral themes with those Fathers who were his intimates."[69] He was buried there in 1594 in the family tomb of the Episcopi (his wife's) family.

Aristocratic spaces

The private space of the aristocratic palace rivaled the Palazzo Ducale and the Scuole Grandi in the splendor of its pictorial decorations. As Francesco Sansovino put it, "There are countless buildings with ceilings of bedchambers and other rooms decorated in gold and other colors and with histories painted by celebrated artists."[70] But most private commissions were for portraits and small-scale devotional paintings; monumental murals and ceiling decoration were conspicuous exceptions. Titian, the preeminent portraitist in the city until the Hapsburgs consumed his energies, painted the intellectual, social, and political elite of his day, capturing the character and personality of commoner and noble, churchman and merchant, men, women, and children alike. Nearly half of his some two hundred documented portraits were of identifiable Venetian sitters, many of them friends, often painted more than once.

Titian's oeuvre as a portraitist reads like a roll call of the city's most influential thinkers and writers: Pietro Aretino (fig. 44, self-styled "Scourge of Princes," prolific writer, and tireless promoter of Titian); Grand Chancellor Andrea de Franceschi; the humanist Daniele Barbaro (fig. 92, patron of Palladio and editor of Vitruvius's *Ten Books on Architecture*); the Paduan humanist Sperone Speroni (author of dialogues on rhetoric, love, and the status of women); the Florentine poet Benedetto Varchi; and the Venetian patrician Nicolo Zen (historian and high government official), to name a few.[71] Ludovico Dolce wrote in his *Dialogo della pittura, intitolato l'Aretino* (Venice, 1557): "Nor was there ever a cardinal or other grandee in Venice who did not visit Titian's establishment to see his creations and have his own portrait painted."[72] Some portraits were gifts from Titian himself. Pietro Bembo wrote to the patrician Girolamo Querini from Rome in 1540, asking him to "thank Titian for the gift of my second portrait, which I had intended to write you that I had seen, so that it should be properly paid for. Now that he is so kind as to wish to do me this favor, let it be so and I will some day do something for him in return."[73]

Titian was also the painter of doges, in both official and personal commissions. At a time when aristocrats typically displayed portraits of male members of the family in the *porteghi* of the family palace, doges or their families usually commissioned versions of their official portraits in the Palazzo Ducale for private space. For example, a 1557 inventory of Doge Andrea Gritti's cousin Piero Gritti's palace at San Salvador listed "uno retratto del Serenissimo Principe Grittj in tella con marche d'oro" (a portrait of the Most Serene Prince Gritti on canvas with seals of gold), valued at 5 ducats, in the *camera d'oro*.[74] The modest valuation suggests perhaps a copy of Titian's portrait of the doge in Washington, DC, of which several variants are known. Titian must have painted his superb portrait of Doge Francesco Venier (1489–1556; fig. 16) around the same time as the state portrait that he made for the Sala del Maggior Consiglio (1555).[75] In poor health, the doge died the following year; his frail visage is an ironic reminder that he was roughly the same age as Titian, who had yet to paint another 150 or so works before his death.[76]

Aside from his portraits, however, Titian was not a decorator of the Venetian palace. Few of his paintings of religious subjects can be documented in Venetian homes, and most of these predate 1530. His *Christ before Pilate*, painted for the merchant Giovanni d'Anna in 1543, is a singular example of a large-scale work painted by him for a private setting in Venice.[77] The same is true of Titian's secular works. His *Sacred and Profane Love* (fig. 87), commissioned by Nicolo Aurelio, secretary of the Council of Ten, to celebrate his marriage in 1514, and Giorgione's *Sleeping Venus* (fig. 84), completed by Titian around 1510 for Girolamo Marcello, are notable exceptions. Except for the half-length paintings of beauties made in the second decade of the sixteenth century, probably for Venetian clients, his mythologies seemed to fly out of the city to foreign patrons.

There is little evidence to conclude, as some have argued, that Tintoretto was less successful than Veronese in obtaining commissions from the leading families of the patriciate. It is a question of genres. Although Tintoretto painted few large decorative schemes for Venetian palace interiors after his ceiling allegories of the 1540s for Vettor Pisani, Pietro Aretino, and the Barbo family, he frescoed as many as ten patrician palace facades after the death of Pordenone—more than any other artist.[78]

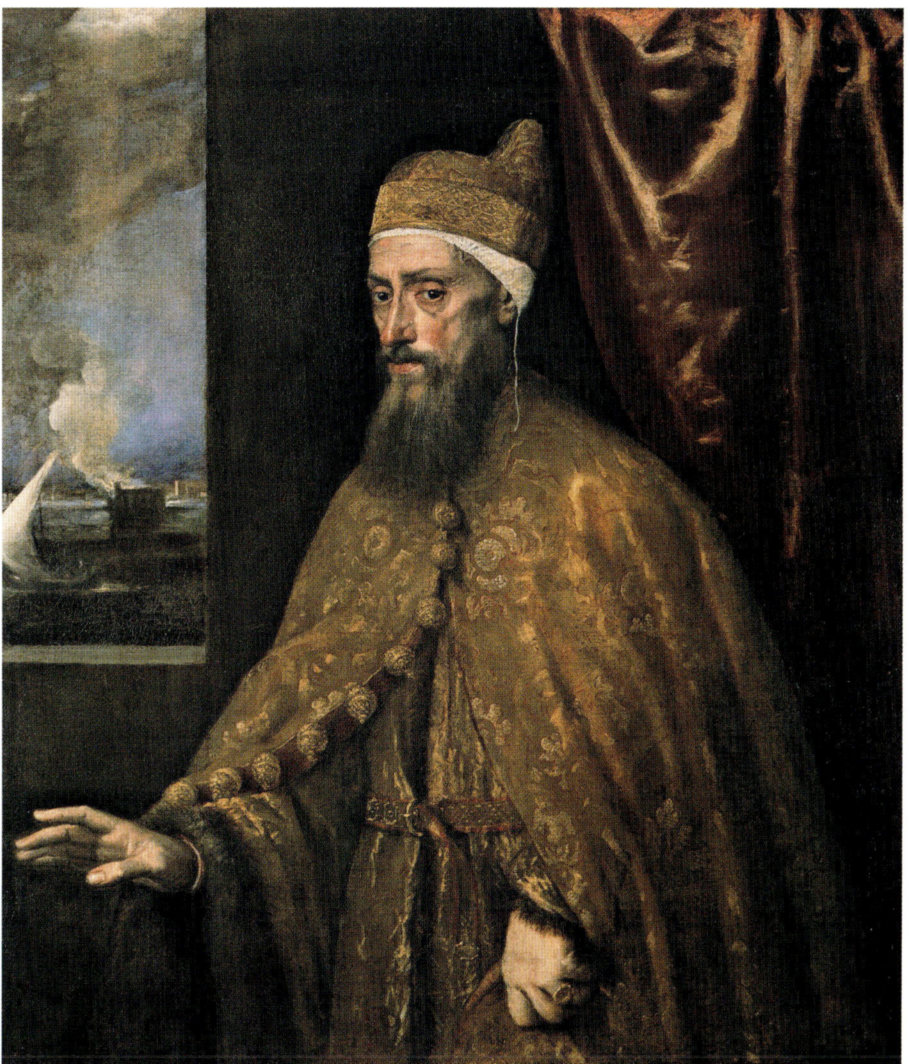

Fig. 16
Titian
Doge Francesco Venier, 1554–56
Oil on canvas
Museo Thyssen-Bornemisza, Madrid

He also counted many more patricians among his clients for portraits than did Veronese. As Titian decreased his production of portraits in the 1550s, Tintoretto took up the slack, with official commissions spilling over into the private realm.[79] The surnames of identifiable sitters constitute a roster of the political elite: Soranzo, Priuli, Grimani, Capello, Morosini, Emo, Da Lezze, Contarini, Venier, Mocenigo, Loredan, Barbarigo, and so on. The *dal banco* branch of the Soranzo family, whose late-Gothic palace still stands on Campo San Polo, commissioned portraits (both official and private) of Procurator

Fig. 17
Tintoretto
Jacopo Soranzo, about 1550
Oil on canvas
Civica Pinacoteca del Castello
Sforzesco, Milan

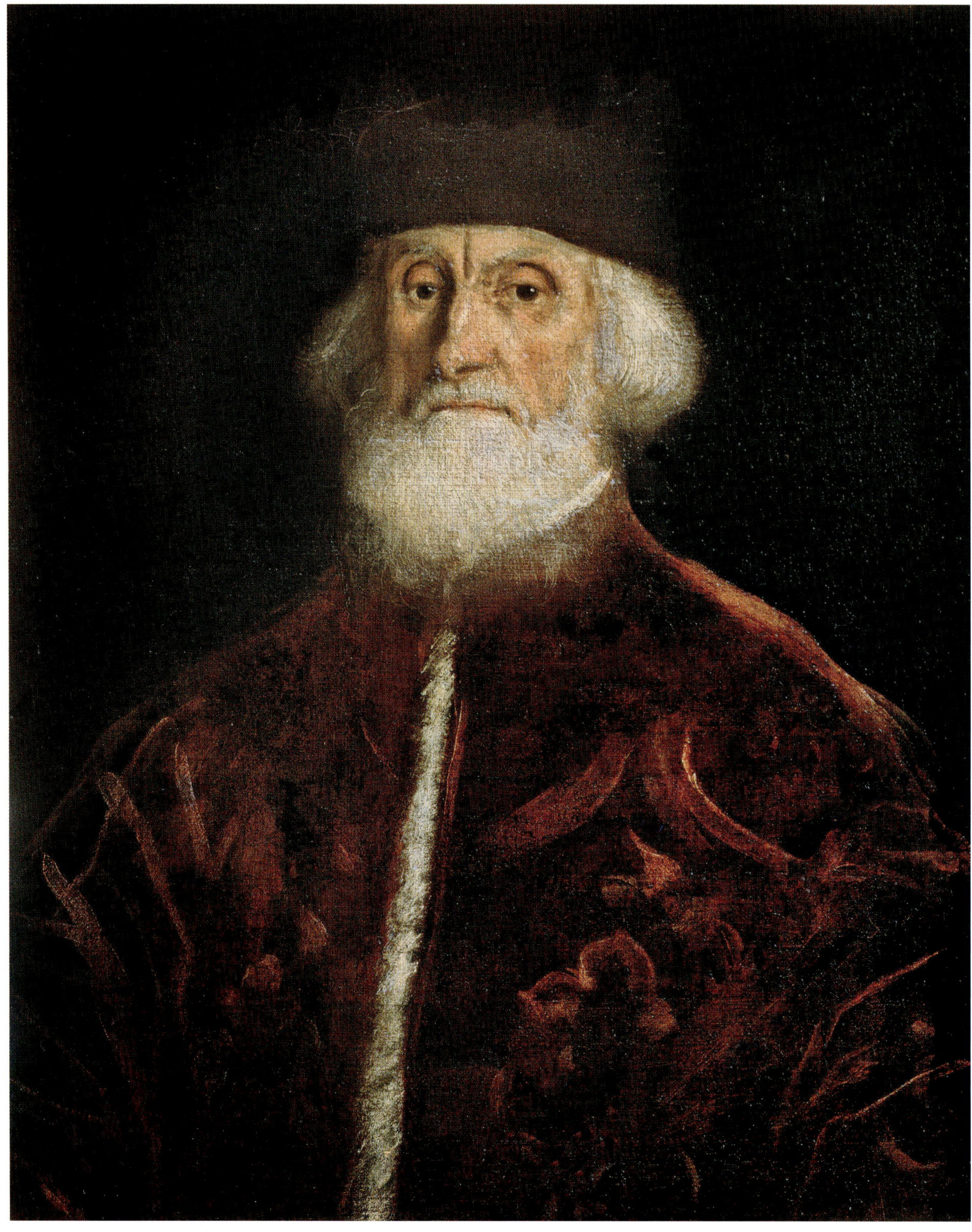

Jacopo Soranzo (fig. 17) and several members of his family in the early 1550s. Among these works is an extraordinary group portrait—a *unicum* in Venice—of three generations of the clan, both men and women, executed by the workshop over several years.[80]

Ridolfi claimed that Tintoretto "was honored with visits of prelates, cardinals, and princes, who from time to time came to Venice, desirous of seeing their faces eternalized by his sublime brush, and besides the kings of France and Poland . . . he also portrayed many dukes and lords of Italy and other northern princes and barons, and in particular all the doges of Venice . . . who lived in his time, the effigies of whom are kept in the houses of their families."[81] Ridolfi was correct about the doges, but a survey of Tintoretto's surviving and documented works yields few identifiable foreign sitters. He allowed furthermore that Tintoretto's lost portrait of Henri III, king of France, was the product of the artist's initiative and not a royal commission. In an episode reminiscent of Tintoretto's preemptive strike at San Rocco, the artist was said to have disguised himself as a squire of the doge and sketched the king surreptitiously on board the *Bucentauro*. Transferring the sketch to canvas, Tintoretto presented it to the king, thus earning praise and an offer of knighthood, which he purportedly declined out of modesty—a claim that Miguel Falomir rightly finds "hard to believe."[82]

While Veronese painted far fewer individual portraits than Titian or Tintoretto, he was the decorator (in the best sense) of private space par excellence. He seems to have received his first important assignment in 1545 at the age of seventeen when the architect Michele Sanmicheli, also from Verona, hired him along with a stuccoist to create the frescoed ceiling decoration of the newly built Palazzo Canossa in Verona with mythological and Old Testament scenes. In 1551 Sanmicheli brought Veronese into one of his projects again, this time with Giambattista Zelotti, to decorate Villa Soranza near Treviso (destroyed 1817). The fresco campaign, an early announcement of the grand illusionistic allegorical schemes for which Veronese would become famous, introduced the artist to the Venetian patriciate and probably landed him the commission to paint in the Sale dei Consiglio dei Dieci in the Palazzo Ducale. The owners of the villa were second cousins to the Soranzo family, who was employing Tintoretto at around the same time to paint their portraits in Venice.[83] Veronese also caught the eye of the wealthy Vicentine nobleman Iseppo da Porto, who commissioned him to paint some small frescoes for his new palace, which was being completed in Vicenza by Andrea Palladio, along with full-length portraits of himself and his wife with two of their children (cats. 43–44).[84]

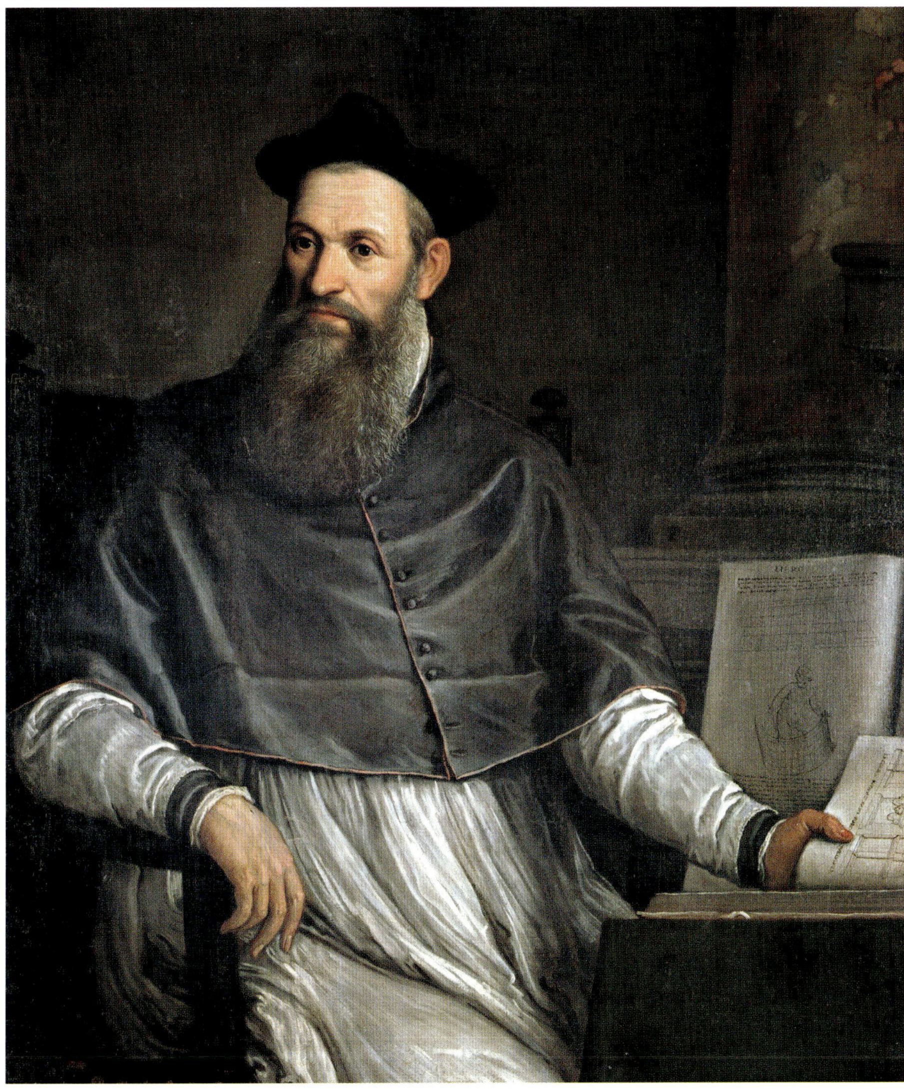

Fig. 18
Veronese
Daniele Barbaro, about 1567
Oil on canvas
Rijksmuseum, Amsterdam

Daniele Barbaro was undoubtedly Veronese's most significant private patron, not only commissioning the fresco decoration of his villa at Maser around 1561 (e.g., fig. 86), as well as his own portrait (fig. 18), but also backing him for other major projects, such as the rooms of the Council of Ten and Palazzo Trevisan at Murano.[85] Like Titian, Veronese was also a favorite of the wealthy Cuccina family and produced an extraordinary suite of four paintings for the *portego* of the family palace. The *Madonna of the Cuccina Family* (Staatliche Kunstsammlungen, Dresden), a votive portrait modeled on those in the Palazzo Ducale and Palazzo dei Camerlenghi, was exceptional in its inclusion of the entire family.[86]

Painters of princes

In his *Dialogo della pittura,* Ludovico Dolce put words into the mouth of Pietro Aretino: "Titian's fame did not confine itself within the bounds of Venice, but spread far and wide through Italy, and made many nobles eager to have him work for them. . . . His fame passed into France as well, and King Francis the First did not fail to importune Titian with every sort of lofty stipulation, in order to attract the artist to him; but Titian never wanted to give up Venice, having come there as a small boy and chosen it for his home."[87]

Titian built his international clientele through personal referrals within the family networks of titled nobility, the advocacy of writers such as Aretino and Dolce, and an ability to charm the rich and powerful.[88] Alfonso d'Este, Duke of Ferrara, recommended him to his nephew Federico II Gonzaga, Marquis (later Duke) of Mantua, who introduced the artist to Emperor Charles V in 1529 and became Titian's major foreign patron of the 1530s. After Titian painted the emperor's portrait in 1532, according to Ridolfi, a delighted Charles paid the artist 500 scudi, praising him as "huius saeculi Apelles" (the Apelles of our times), and named him a Count Palatine and Knight of the Golden Spur.[89] Titian painted his way through the following decade with a succession of princely patrons in courts large and small, including (among others) not only Gonzaga and Francis I, but also Francesco Maria della Rovere, Duke of Urbino, and Alfonso d'Avalos, the Marchese del Vasto, captain general of the emperor's infantry in Italy (fig. 94).[90]

In 1539, with the major Hapsburg commissions yet to come, Aretino let it be known that Titian was ready to paint the "principi de la celeberrima stirpe farnese" (the princes of the most celebrated Farnese line).[91] He got his opportunity three years later with a commission to portray Ranuccio Farnese, the twelve-year-old grandson of Pope Paul III (cat. 42). The humanist Gian Francesco Leoni wrote to the boy's brother, Cardinal Alessandro Farnese: "You can count on acquiring this man, whenever you think fit. Quite apart from his ability [*virtù*], Titian has appeared to everyone to be a reasonable, charming and obliging person, which is a consideration in such rare men."[92] An enthusiastically received (and much copied) *Pope Paul III* (cat. 7), painted the following year, brought praise from Aretino as "the miracle wrought by your brush" and an offer from the pope of the office of Keeper of the Papal Seal. Although it carried a yearly stipend of 80 ducats, Titian declined the honor, ostensibly because it was still held by his friends Sebastiano del Piombo and Giovanni da Udine, a diplomatic way of saying that he "never wanted to give up Venice."[93]

But Titian was not through with the Farnese. Only the next year, Giovanni della Casa reiterated Titian's earlier offer in a letter to Alessandro, writing that the artist, in pursuit of a benefice for his son Pomponio, "is ready to paint the portrait of the Illustrious House of Your Most Reverend Lord *in solidum*, everyone including the cats."[94] He did just that during his visit to Rome in 1545–46, memorializing the Farnese dynasty with portraits of Ranuccio's brothers Alessandro (fig. 19) and Ottavio, their father, Pier Luigi, their grandfather Paul III (probably twice), and the group portrait *Paul III with Alessandro and Ottavio Farnese* (Museo Nazionale di Capodimonte, Naples).[95] Cardinal Alessandro also had a taste for the sensual. Della Casa commented on the *Danaë* that the cardinal had commissioned from Titian, judging that the *Venus of Urbino* appeared to be "a Theatine nun next to this one."[96] These paintings brought fame but not riches; in 1567 Titian, still unpaid, was seeking the promised benefice, but without success.[97]

In October 1547 Charles V summoned Titian to the imperial court at Augsburg, and the Hapsburgs swiftly replaced the Farnese as the artist's most illustrious clients. The story is well known. After crossing the Alps the following January, in the dead of winter, Titian remained in Augsburg for eight months and painted the portraits of Charles and other members of the court. In a relationship suggesting that of Alexander the Great to Apelles, Titian was lodged in an apartment next to the emperor's chambers, "so that one could go to the other without being seen."[98] He had become the Hapsburg court painter *extra muros*. Aside from a soaring international reputation, what did Titian gain from his position in a monetary sense? Not much from Charles until after the emperor's death: a concession to export corn from the kingdom of Naples in 1536 and the promise of an annual pension of 100 scudi from the nearly bankrupt imperial treasury in Milan in 1541, a sum that was doubled in 1548 but remained unpaid for a decade.[99]

Titian fared better financially with Charles's son Philip II. Their quarter-century-long relationship began with a meeting in Milan in late December 1549, a two-week sojourn that brought an order for "certain portraits" with a price tag of 1,000 scudi. Called to Augsburg again in 1551, Titian painted *Philip II* (fig. 97) for 260 gold scudi, plus an additional 30 for colors.

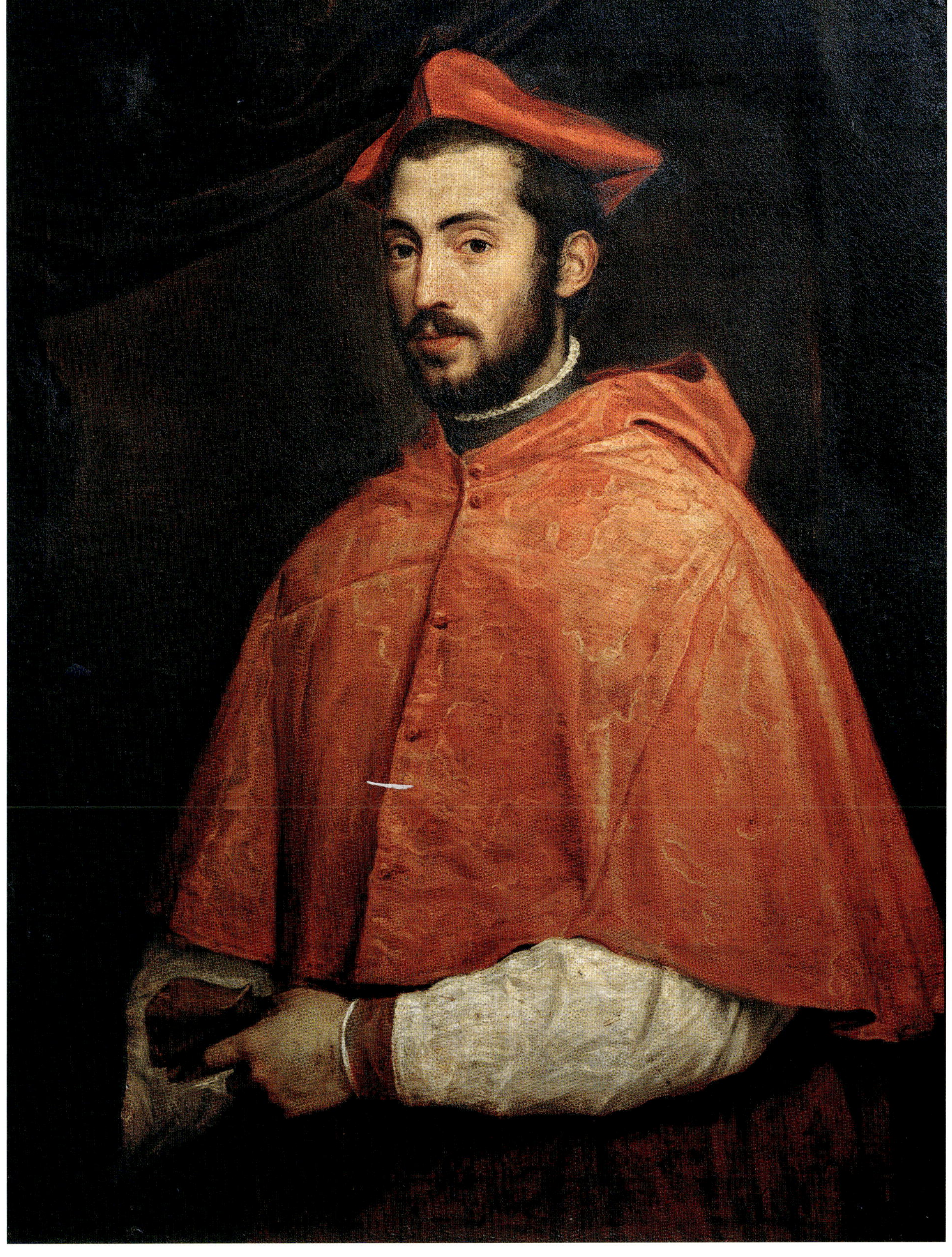

Fig. 19
Titian
Cardinal Alessandro Farnese, 1545–46
Oil on canvas
Museo Nazionale di Capodimonte, Naples

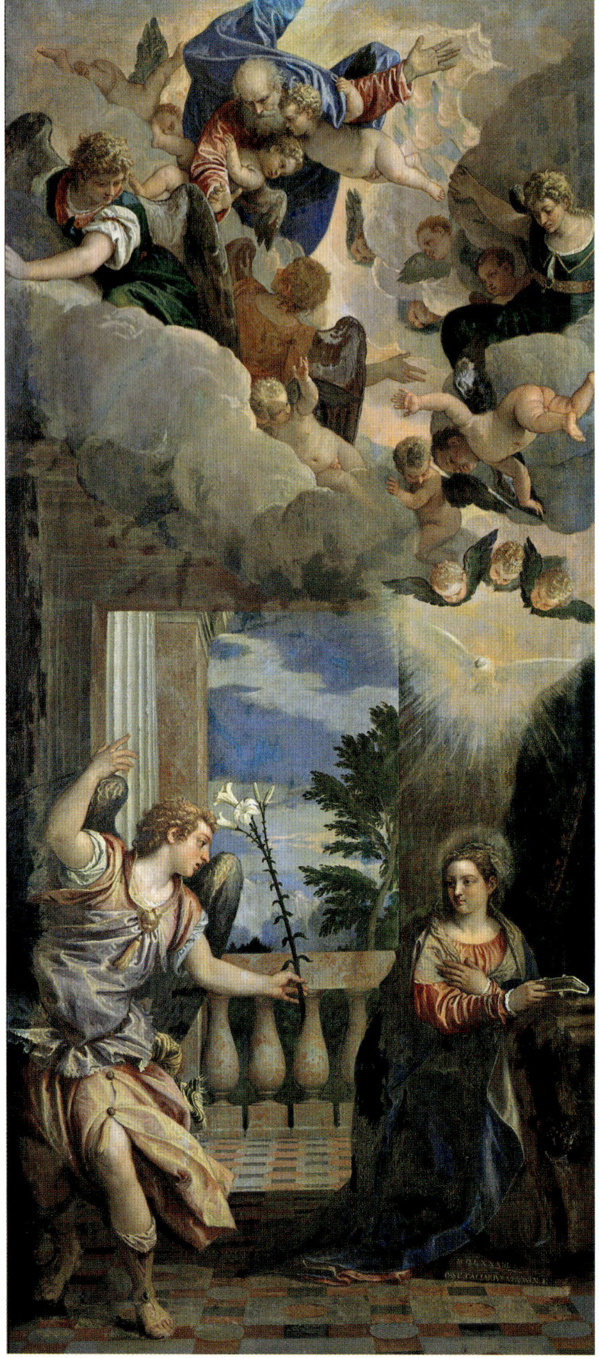

Fig. 20
Veronese
Annunciation, 1583
Oil on canvas
Patrimonio Nacional, Real Monasterio de San Lorenzo de El Escorial

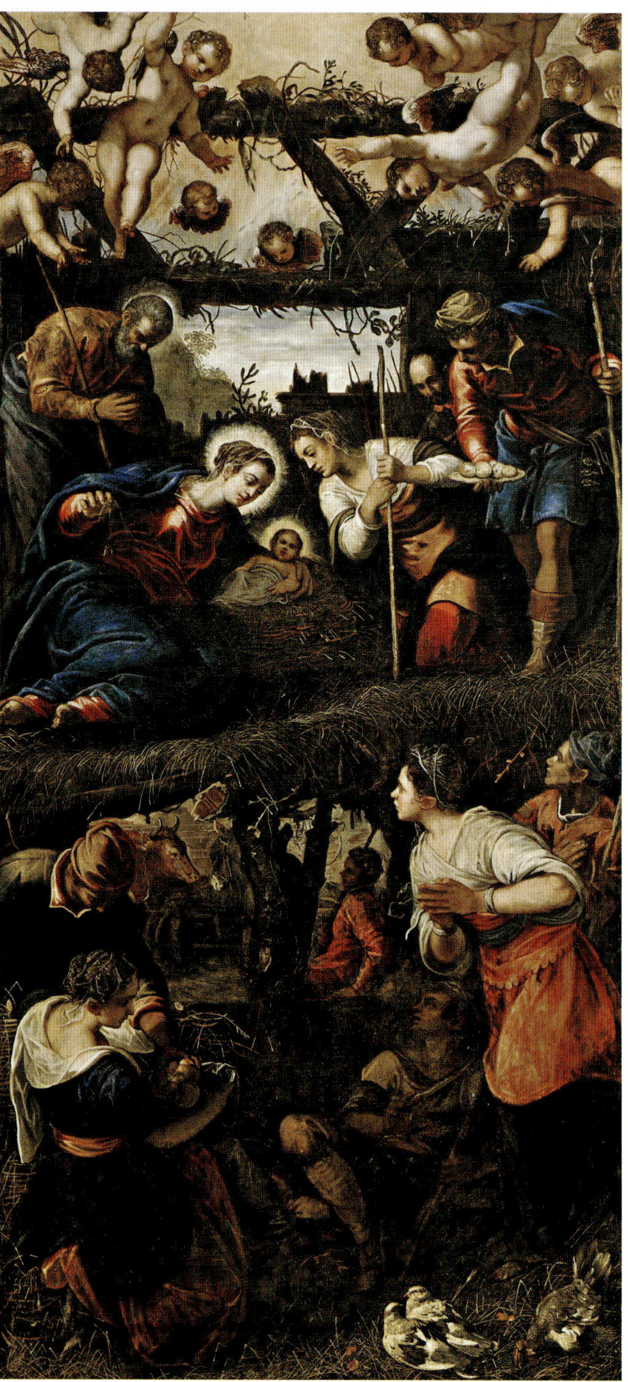

Fig. 21
Jacopo and Domenico Tintoretto
Adoration of the Shepherds, 1583
Oil on canvas
Patrimonio Nacional, Real Monasterio de San Lorenzo de El Escorial

Although the prince sent the painting to his aunt, Mary of Hungary, with a note complaining that "it is easy to see the haste with which it has been made and if there were time it would have been done over again," Philip commissioned ten large paintings, including the six *poesie*, plus some smaller works, to be delivered over the next decade. Titian was paid 1,000 scudi, plus 200 for his son Orazio, and promised an additional pension from the Spanish treasury of 200 scudi per year. During this visit Titian was also commissioned to paint the *Gloria* (*Adoration of the Trinity*), a monumental painting completed in 1554 (now in the Museo Nacional del Prado, Madrid), which Charles took with him to the monastery at Yuste, Spain, when he retired in 1555.[100] On Christmas Day in 1558 Philip II finally set the accounts straight, ordering the Duke of Sesa, the new governor in Milan, to pay Titian the accrued pension promised by his father, a sum amounting to 2,000 scudi. Although his pensions were often in arrears, Titian would deliver twenty-five major works to Philip before his death in 1576.[101]

In late 1568 Veit von Dornberg, the imperial envoy in Venice, had written to Emperor Maximilian II that Titian was willing to supply seven "fables," six of them versions of Philip's *poesie*. The emperor expressed an interest but was concerned that the aging Titian could no longer paint as he once did.[102] Nothing seems to have come of the offer, but Maximilian's son Rudolf II inherited his passion for art. He succeeded to the imperial throne in 1576, the same year that Titian died, and opportunities finally opened up for both Tintoretto and Veronese.

In 1578–79 Guglielmo Gonzaga, Duke of Mantua, commissioned from Tintoretto a cycle of eight large narrative canvases depicting the deeds of the Gonzaga for the Palazzo Ducale in Mantua. He prescribed a specific iconographic program and oversaw Tintoretto's progress so closely that the paintings were completed in only eight months. As so often with princely commissions, it yielded more prestige than profit. The fee of only 234 ducats, a modest sum for a campaign of this dimension, also points to the trade-off made when paintings were largely executed by the workshop, with little work done by Jacopo himself other than some designs. Characteristically, after installing the works on his first recorded trip outside Venice, Tintoretto sought (without success) to replace the court artist Ippolito Andreasi with himself.[103]

Although documentation is lacking, Rudolf II seems to have acquired a number of Veronese's magnificent allegorical paintings through Jacopo Strada, his agent in Venice. These included a suite of four ceiling canvases, *Allegories of Love* (National Gallery, London), and a succession of five mythologies celebrating virtue and honor, culminating in *Mars and Venus United by Love* (cat. 34). It is unknown whether any or all of these works were commissioned by the emperor or painted for a palace in Venice and then resold.[104] Rudolf also acquired four scenes from the life of Hercules from Tintoretto, one of which was the *Origin of the Milky Way* (fig. 85). As Nichols suggests, the high degree of finish and refined eroticism are Tintoretto's response to Rudolfine tastes for esoteric subject matter packaged in a late-mannerist style.[105] Veronese added another royal patron to his clientele in 1582, when Duke Carlo Emanuele I of Savoy, grandson of Francis I, commissioned four large paintings of the Old Testament, probably for his palace in Turin.[106]

In 1583 Philip II invited Veronese and Tintoretto to paint a canvas each for the high altar of the Escorial, an *Annunciation* and an *Adoration of the Shepherds*, respectively, at 400 ducats apiece (figs. 20–21). As it happened, Philip found the paintings not to his taste and had them removed. But if he had intended the invitation to be a competition, then Veronese was the victor, for two years later Philip offered him the considerable sum of 9,000 ducats to move to Spain. And yet, like Titian, Veronese was loath to leave Venice to take a position as court painter, no matter how prestigious, and turned the emperor down.[107]

Neither Veronese nor Tintoretto could match Titian's success as painter to the crowned heads of Europe during their lifetimes, but in the centuries that followed, many of their works found their way into royal collections. Ridolfi observed: "In the gallery of the King of England there are many of Tintoretto's paintings collected at great expense by that magnificent monarch. . . . And in that of the Grand Duke of Tuscany is conserved a portrait of Jacopo Sansovino, famous Florentine sculptor, painted in majesty with a compass in his hand, and a beautiful picture of the Agony in the Garden."[108] As to Veronese, "his paintings spread in the most famous Galleries of Europe . . . no Palace does in fact appear adorned if there is no work by this hand."[109]

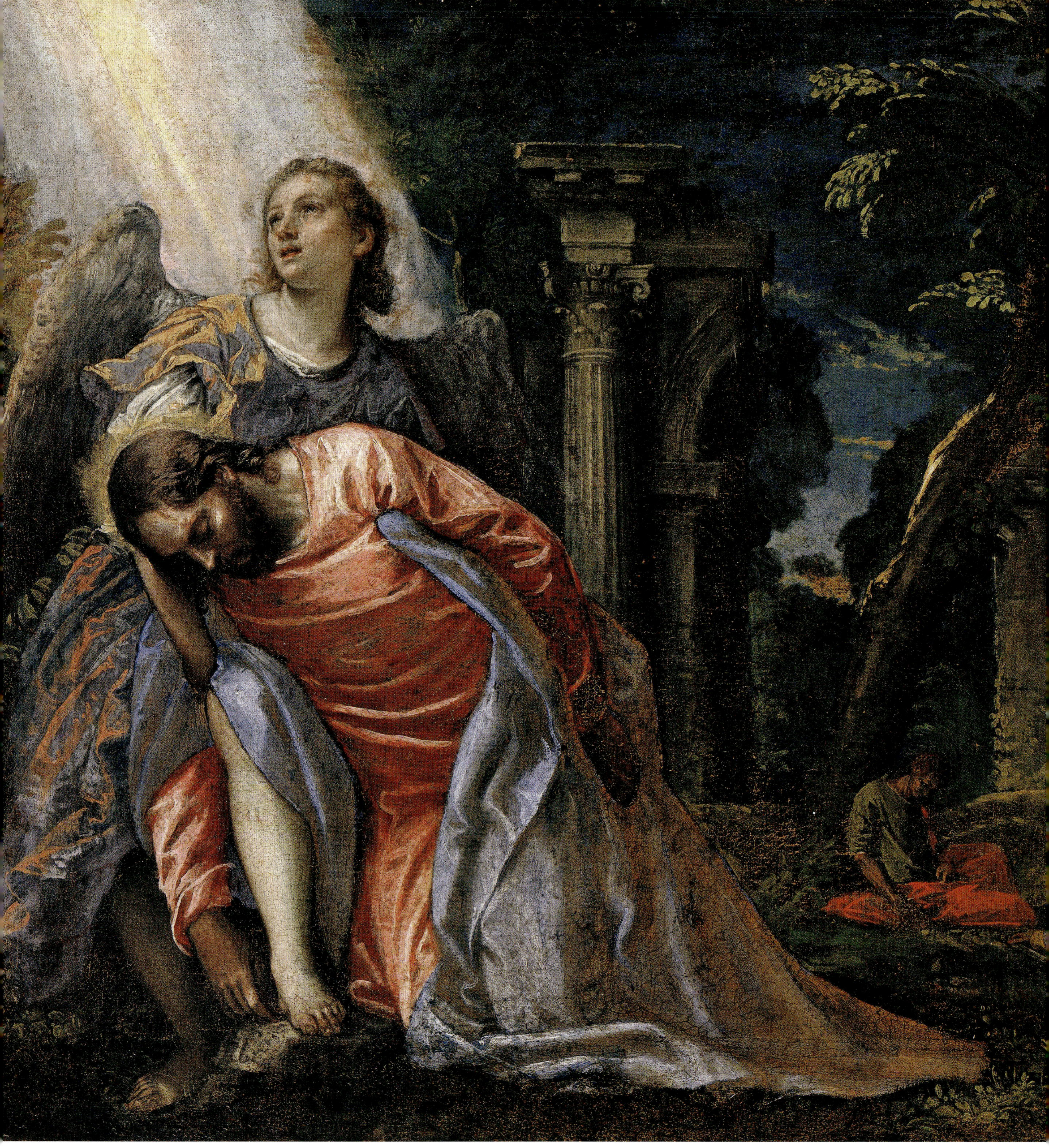

Collecting in Sixteenth- and Seventeenth-Century Venice: Originals, Copies, and "Maniera di"

LINDA BOREAN

In a famous letter sent to Jean-Pierre Mariette from Potsdam on February 13, 1751, the Venetian writer and art dealer Francesco Algarotti affirmed that "when acquiring old paintings I would always proceed, as I have done, with the greatest caution. It is not enough that a painting be a Titian; it should be well preserved, beautiful, and demonstrating his most *bella maniera*. Otherwise one runs the risk of admiring only names."[1]

Algarotti's reaction reveals an attitude common among art collectors of the era, that is, appreciation for works of art based solely on the artist's *name* rather than on the quality of execution. In this context originals by the great masters of the Renaissance, including Titian, Tintoretto, and Veronese, were truly rare and for the most part lacked signatures.[2] This last point encouraged connoisseurs to consider not only style and manner, but also—under the pressure of new collecting patterns and the business of art dealing, forces in rapid expansion by the middle of the sixteenth century—to practice a certain nonchalance regarding attribution, which caused paintings from the workshop or from able copyists to be identified as autograph works. It is possible to consider the rivalry between Titian, Tintoretto, and Veronese by reexamining the critical fortunes of their works in precisely this context of early collections and the art market through a purely quantitative approach to the popularity of replicas and copies—naturally taking into consideration the different trajectories and conclusions of the careers of Titian, Tintoretto, and Veronese and their respective workshops as they sought to meet the demands of a growing client base.[3]

Sixteenth- and early-seventeenth-century writers on art from Marcantonio Michiel and Francesco Sansovino to Vincenzo Scamozzi[4] noted the expansion of art collections in Venice, above all the shift from heterogeneous "cabinet" collections to galleries often dedicated exclusively to paintings, some with a preference for a single artist. One famous example was the group of Veronese canvases owned by the ducal secretary Simone Lando and donated by him in 1584 to the church of Santa Maria Maggiore, including an *Agony in the Garden*, the painting now housed in the Pinacoteca di Brera, Milan (fig. 112). The collection owned by Gabriele Vendramin, on the other hand, renowned for its Titians, was appraised by Tintoretto during the compilation of the inventory of the collection in 1567.[5] At the end of the century, Cristoforo Barbarigo, who in 1581 had bought Titian's house in the neighborhood of Biri grande from Titian's son Pomponio Vecellio, boasted that he possessed at least four autograph works by Titian, diligently enumerated in his will of 1600.[6]

Literary sources, however helpful, only offer a starting point: the cited sources, Michiel, Sansovino, and Scamozzi, followed in the mid-seventeenth century by Carlo Ridolfi and Marco Boschini,[7] constitute precious guides to Venetian collecting practices. Their objective, however, was not to offer a systematic summary or to detail the ways in which collectors judged the works of Titian, Tintoretto, and Veronese, but to demonstrate these artists' fame through examples, thus placing them at the top of the aesthetic canon while simultaneously promoting the value of good taste. Regarding Veronese, Ridolfi remarked that "important princes and gentlemen . . . through excessive spending" were purchasing many paintings by the artist, and furthermore, that a palazzo was not considered properly adorned "without a work by his hand."[8] Particularly desirable were his Last Suppers and other paintings of religious feasts (upon which, according to Ridolfi, Paolo's fame was based), with their sumptuous settings "in the manner of royal banquets."[9] Titian, on the other hand, was acclaimed by Boschini as the unsurpassable "Dio dela Pitura" (God of Painting), to whom every artist must subordinate himself as a "servant" and an admirer.[10]

As a juicy anecdote reported by Ridolfi suggests, however, Tintoretto would not have agreed with that view. The enfant terrible of the trio, Tintoretto was disturbed by the praise bestowed upon Titian's portrait of a woman by many artists and connoisseurs who were gathered in the house of Giacomo Contarini (the influential nobleman responsible for the selection of painters for the redecoration of the Palazzo Ducale after the fires of 1574 and 1577). One of these connoisseurs declared in Tintoretto's presence that "one must paint" as Titian does—a comment particularly galling given Tintoretto's success in portraiture. To get even, Tintoretto forged a "Titian" and submitted it for judgment to the same so-called experts, who commended this portrait as a singular work by Titian, not recognizing Tintoretto's hand. Thus, Tintoretto had the last laugh, exclaiming, "Now, gentlemen, you see the value of authority and opinion in judgment, and how few people truly understand painting."[11] These hapless connoisseurs were not the only contemporaries to confuse the portraits of Titian and Tintoretto; Raffaello Borghini noted in 1584 that "in his coloring Tintoretto has truly imitated nature, and then especially Titian, so much so that many portraits by him are held to be by the hand of Titian."[12]

The situation presented in the printed sources is largely confirmed by archival documents, including inventories (more than four hundred dating from 1560 to 1750 were sampled for this essay; see note 1) and wills. These documents shed light on a wide variety of issues relevant to Venetian private collections beginning in the sixteenth century: the formation of an artistic canon; supply and demand; and the varying appeal of autograph works, copies, and paintings "in the style of" (*in maniera di*) the most highly esteemed artists. Titian's popularity, for instance, was pronounced among aristocratic patrons (particularly non-Venetians) who wished to be immortalized through proud portraits; it is clear that for an owner or heirs, the value of a painting increased if it could be attributed to Titian by school or manner. Such clients would also permit Titian to experiment with sensual mythological subjects with minimal interference. The Spanish monarchy monopolized this aspect of the artist's production, deeming only Veronese a worthy substitute after Titian's death.[13] For the Venetian market, however, Titian generally preferred to make available canvases produced by his workshop from prototypes, now and then adding finishing touches of his own.[14] Yet Venetian collectors continued to seek paintings by Titian (and his workshop) with tenacity, a process that began to accelerate at midcentury. These collectors included fellow artists and competitors; it seems that Jacopo Tintoretto owned several paintings by Titian, including the *Crowning with Thorns* (fig. 22), a masterpiece either unfinished or in Titian's least finished style.[15] The mosaicist Valerio Zuccato, a member of Titian's circle, had to be content with copying or reworking a "Christ in the garden which came from Titian," probably based on a replica of that subject kept in Titian's studio following the shipment to Spain of two versions of the *Agony in the Garden* prior to 1574 (Museo Nacional del Prado, Madrid, and El Escorial). In his will of March 14, 1576, Zuccato bequeathed the painting to his wife, Apollonia, the celebrated actress, along with a *Saint Catherine* by Veronese.[16]

Titian's name was specified in inventories even when other paintings were listed anonymously, and in the period between 1560 and 1650 the few works that were noted were all considered "of the hand of Titian."[17] These documents, however, do not specify whether canvases date from the painter's youth or his old age (a situation similar to the listings of Tintoretto and Veronese); for example, *sacre conversazioni* in the manner of the "Madonna et San Iseppo schietto de man de Titian" (Virgin and Saint Joseph, a genuine Titian) in the house of Lorenzo Donà in 1589,[18] but also paintings with improbable attributions, such as "Saint Cosmas done in part by Titian and in part by Tintoretto," owned by the Widmann family and valued by the painter Nicolas Régnier in 1659 at 120 ducats.[19]

Only in the second half of the seventeenth century, by which time many kinds of people—artisans, merchants, nobles, ecclesiastics—had dedicated themselves to collecting art,[20] does one observe the distinction between originals and paintings described as being done in Titian's "*maniera*," assigned to his "*scuola*," or which "came from him," meaning copies—a distinction that

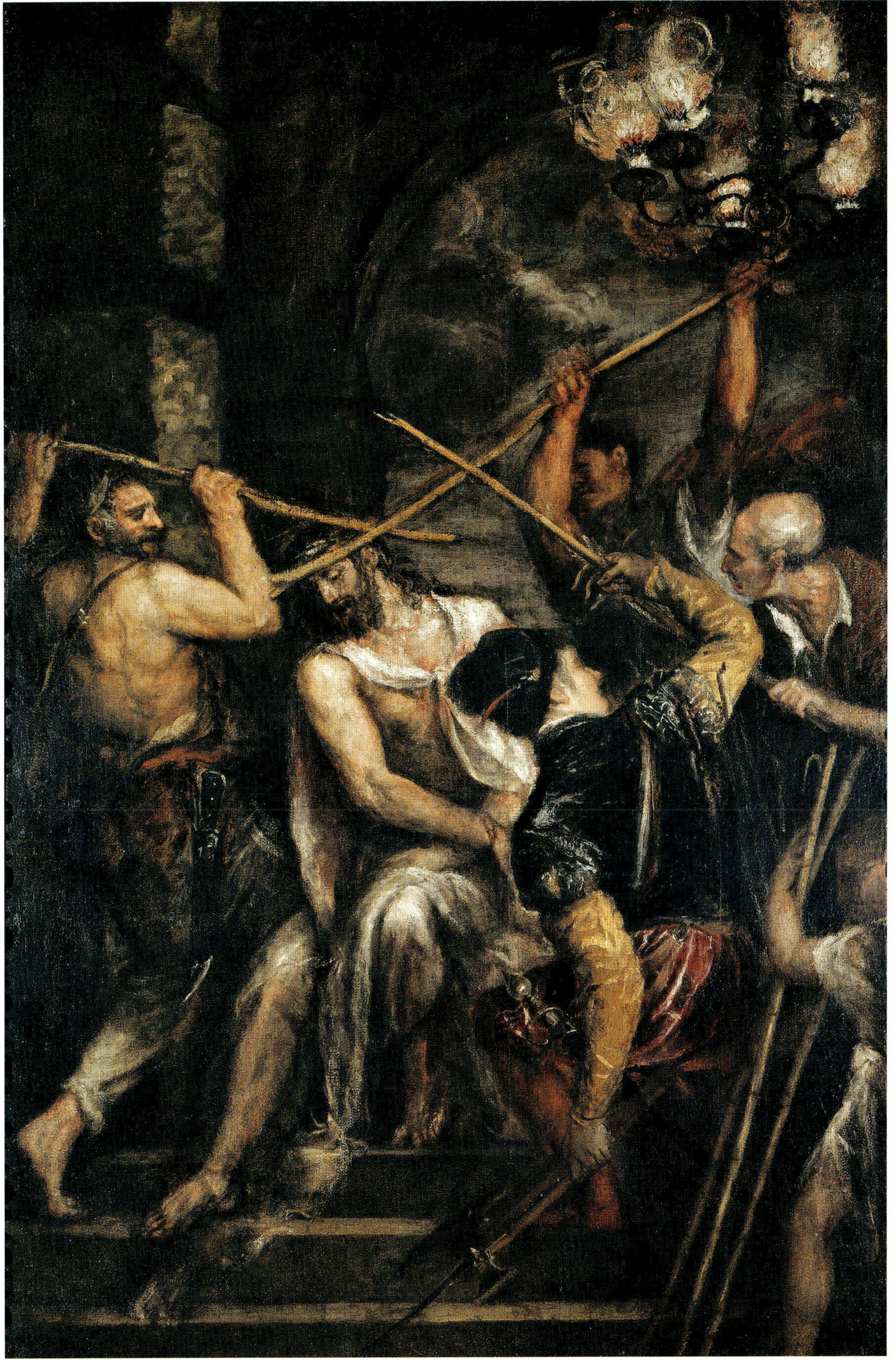

Fig. 22
Titian
Crowning with Thorns, about 1570–76
Oil on canvas
Bayerische
Staatsgemäldesammlungen,
Alte Pinakothek, Munich

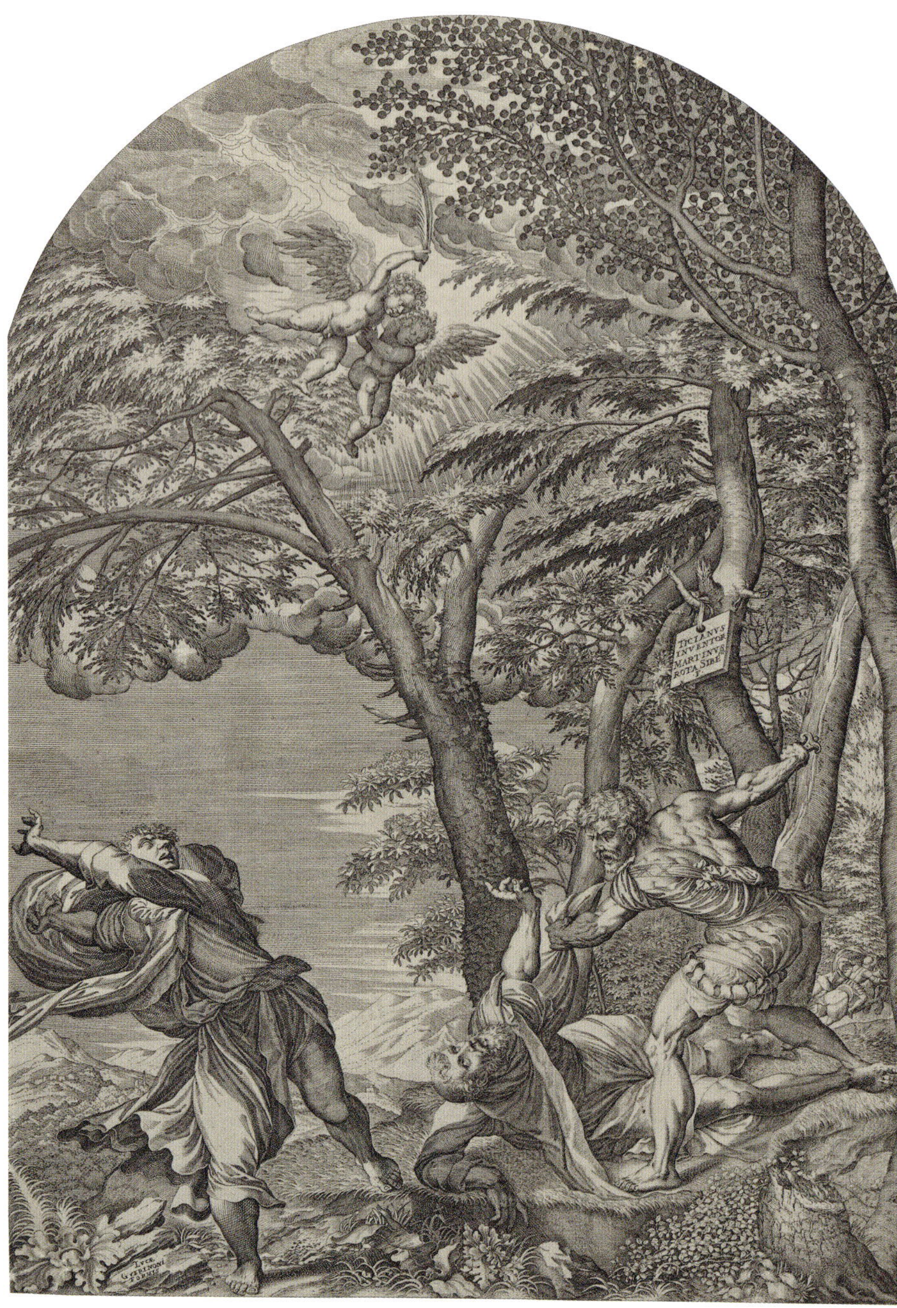

Fig. 23
Martino Rota (Croatian, about 1520–1583), after Titian's lost original of 1530
Saint Peter Martyr, about 1560
Etching and engraving
The Metropolitan Museum of Art, New York

emerges in parallel with a growth in the number of paintings attributable to Titian and his circle.[21] As originals were always extremely scarce, the hunt for paintings shifted to works found in churches on the mainland, for example the altarpiece from the Duomo of Santa Maria at Serravalle or the *Assumption of the Virgin* from the cathedral of Verona. Nor did collectors hesitate to remove Titian's works from their original architectural settings (such was the case with canvases of Tintoretto and Veronese as well).[22] These copies and imitations won approval among collectors and critics, so much so that these paintings were even in competition with originals and were defined as "delights among paintings" or "laudable deceits"[23] because they were the fruit of two arts, that of the inventor and that of the copyist (one example among many would be the *Venus and Adonis*, an "extremely beautiful copy of Titian"[24] purchased for only 3 ducats in 1667 by Giovan Donato Correggio, the owner of many Titian replicas executed by his painter of choice, Antonio Cecchini).

The derivations from original Titians had, for some time, not been limited to his own workshop's production (an analogous argument can also be made for Tintoretto and Veronese).[25] Artists of modest ability such as Rocco da San Silvestro had sniffed out the available opportunities and set up businesses based on creating copies of the works of famous painters. This market made use primarily of Flemish artists such as Gasparetto Piterman, who is recorded as having made a copy of a Titian Magdalen that was "ritocata dal Rotenhamer," that is, retouched by Hans Rottenhammer and acquired by Gaspare Chechel, consul of the Fondaco dei Tedeschi in the first half of the seventeenth century.[26] Even in the workshop of the fourth protagonist of the Venetian Renaissance, namely Jacopo Bassano, there were numerous replicas of original paintings by other artists, including Titian. For example, a "Magdalen, copy of Titian, finished by the hand of signor Geronimo [Gerolamo]," together with a "Magdalen derived from Titian, finished by the hand of signore Geronimo," was listed in the 1621 inventory of the painter's son Gerolamo Bassano, himself a painter.[27] In this context, where illustrious *imitatori* operated—one thinks of Pietro Vecchia—doubts about attributions increased, and the connoisseurship skills of the experts were continually put to the test when confronted with accurate replicas, imitations, and pastiches "in the manner of."

One interesting case is the perplexity the painters Stefano Rubini and Nicolò Rossi expressed in 1709 when challenged to confirm the authenticity of the eight (!) Titians owned by Giorgio Bergonzi. A refined collector, Bergonzi had inherited a rich picture gallery of sixteenth-century masters from his father, Francesco, a friend of the writer Carlo Ridolfi; Giorgio subsequently added to this collection.[28] If the two appraisers, Rubini and Rossi, could be forgiven for mistaking a Polidoro da Lanciano for a Titian, it is astonishing that they would confuse Perino del Vaga with Titian. The best Titians in the Bergonzi collection were two portraits, one of a jeweler and the other, from the Marcello family, of a woman "painted with great freshness" and recorded also by Ridolfi. Each portrait was assigned the high value of 500 ducats, well above the market at the time.[29]

Descendants of the first owners of autograph portraits by Titian tended to hold on to them as family heirlooms or because this had been stipulated in a will, and portraits constitute one of the more common categories found in Venetian inventories. For example, Andrea de Franceschi (1473–1551), of the Leone branch of the family, occupied the important government post of grand chancellor from 1529 until the time of his death.[30] Titian painted two versions of his portrait; Andrea's will of March 1, 1535, left "my first portrait painted by the hand of Titian" to one of his nephews, Pietro de Franceschi, and "my second portrait by the hand of Titian" to another nephew, Girolamo de Franceschi.[31] Pietro was the secretary to the Council of Ten,[32] and on June 28, 1581, his property was divided. Among Pietro's goods was a portrait of Andrea by Titian, made when the sitter was "sixty years old."[33] To the de Franceschi family, then, information about the priority (and thus perhaps the quality) of the two portraits, as well as the age of the sitter, seems to have been confirmation of value important enough to pass on to the next generation.

Besides portraiture, the most popular subject by Titian in Venetian collections was without doubt that of the Magdalen. The theme, which combines piety with female beauty, was thought to be very dear to Titian—so much so that Giovanni Battista Cavalcaselle noted in the middle of the nineteenth century in the margin of his drawing after the Barbarigo *Magdalen*, "They say [Titian] died holding this [painting]."[34] The oldest document from an inventory concerning this subject is the 1563 division of property belonging to Antonio Grimani of San Polo among his sons, Giovanni, Alvise, and Girolamo. Girolamo received a *Magdalen* by Titian, which can probably be connected with a "document of messer Titian on the 20th day of July 1557," corroborated in the 1563 family inventory.[35]

Certain other themes appeared frequently, corresponding to high points in Titian's oeuvre, such as the *Saint Peter Martyr* altarpiece (fig. 23) installed in 1530 in the church of Santi Giovanni e Paolo. The astute dealer Daniel Nijs offered the amazing sum of 18,000 scudi for the original.[36] The "Bacanal copy of Titian in Padovanino's hand," listed by Boschini in a posthumous inventory of Paolo del Sera in 1680,[37] brings to mind what may be another set of replicas, now in Bergamo, made by Padovanino (1588–1649) after the celebrated mythologies by Titian for the *camerino* of Alfonso I d'Este.[38] By 1598 Titian's paintings from the camerino could be found in the Aldobrandini collection in Rome, where Padovanino, of a generation that sought inspiration from the masters of sixteenth-century Venice, hastened for the express purpose of copying these masterpieces. Padovanino was evidently able to meet the demand for paintings in a market continually being depleted of original Titians, so much so that one begins to wonder if his choice to take over Titian's seat (the "sedia di Tician," in Boschini's words)[39] had been influenced by commercial motivations and perhaps the prodding of Boschini, who as a successful dealer intended to satisfy his clientele, guaranteeing also the success of painters of his own era.[40] As many documents attest, Padovanino made a career of imitating Titian;[41] one such document describes a work in the paintings gallery of Cecilia Corner (of the San Maurizio branch, widow of the Procurator of San Marco "*de supra*" Daniele Bragadin) as a "Lord in Emmaus, three figures in a black frame with a gold band, copied from a Titian by Padovanino."[42] The painting may be related to the version (fig. 24), once located in the Palazzo Ducale, that the Contarini family gave to the Republic in the sixteenth century, having judged the work more appropriate for a public building than a private residence.[43] The fortunes of collecting, however, returned Titian's *Supper at Emmaus* to a private home (Brocklesby Park in Lincolnshire, seat of the Count of Yarborough) thanks to the well-timed efforts of Sir Richard Worsley, the last British diplomatic resident in Venice and ancestor of the painting's current owner, who seems to have purchased the celebrated work from French authorities in 1797. Another version of this composition by Titian, made for Count Nicola Maffei, an official in Mantua, was later sold to the ruling Gonzaga family (cat. 21).

If the popularity of Titian paintings in Venetian collections rested principally on works executed for private patrons, in Tintoretto's case, besides portraiture, commissions for government or religious buildings played a significant role, providing the foundation of the artist's fame.[44] Regarding princely patrons, Tintoretto did receive requests from the Gonzaga family as well as

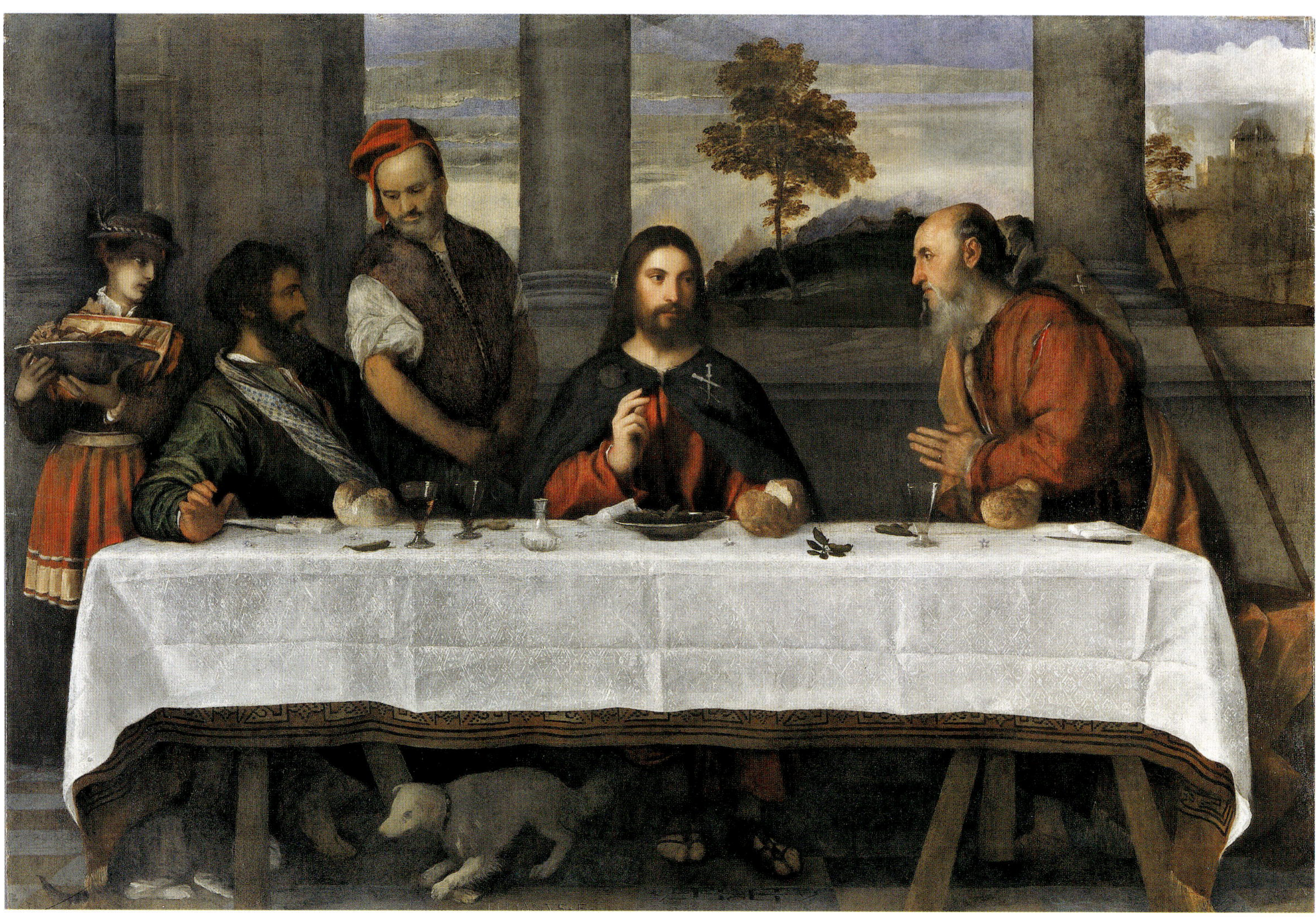

Fig. 24
Titian
Supper at Emmaus, about 1530–34, possibly earlier
Oil on panel
Brocklesby Park, Lincolnshire, Earl of Yarborough, on loan to Walker Art Gallery, Liverpool

Rudolf II, the Holy Roman Emperor, but he did not gain more than a foothold in the Spanish court. They preferred Parrasio Michiel, and even after Michiel's death in 1578, Tintoretto was largely shut out. His plan in 1587 to give Philip II a "beautiful painting of the Last Judgment" made little difference.[45]

In his *Breve istruzione* inserted in the 1674 publication of *Ricche minere della pittura veneziana*, Boschini expressed his opinions on Robusti's huge canvases in the church of the Madonna dell'Orto this way: "Tintoretto painted them for 50 ducats each. Now, if one had to sell them, and I know who you would be, I estimate that to the two numerals that make up the number 50, you would add another three zeros, and not lettering of a pen, but in lettering of gold."[46] Boschini's observation justifies his conclusion that great painting was more valuable than gold—"più vale la pittura che l'oro"—and also emphasizes the high commercial value that Tintoretto had reached. Less than a century after his death, Tintoretto's enduring position within local taste was documented also in a literary appreciation, when he was celebrated in a collection of verses published in 1677 by the painter and man of letters Giovanni Prati. Prati devoted a sonnet to a *Last Judgment* by "Robusti immortal opra sublime." Tintoretto was the only Venetian painter of the sixteenth century to be included in this collection of poems.[47] An examination of the inventories of the second half of the sixteenth century through the seventeenth century has revealed that above all, starting from the middle of the seventeenth century, there was a growing circulation of replicas and works classified as "scuola di" or "si dice di" (said to be by), but with a clear distinction, however, between Tintoretto *vecchio* and Tintoretto *giovane*, which is to say between Jacopo and his son Domenico. Despite the fact that his father had bequeathed him the workshop, with the obligation to complete all of the paintings left unfinished at the time of his own death with "diligence," accuracy, and patience,[48] Domenico, in fact, developed his own personal style, a distinction that did not escape the expert's eye.

References to portraits dominate the documents and early sources on Tintoretto. Indeed, the painter earned great fame in this category in his early maturity. In 1551 the publisher Francesco Marcolini, who considered Tintoretto something of a protégé, declared to Pietro Aretino, the referee of the Venetian artistic scene, how skilled this artist was at making a sitter appear alive.[49] That the personality of the sitter could constitute some of the appeal for a collector is shown by an interesting portrait dated 1561 of Giovanni Paolo Cornaro (or Corner), nicknamed dalle Anticaglie (of the antiquities) because he was a famed accumulator of antiquities from the classical world (fig. 25).[50] Tintoretto portrays precisely this aspect of the sitter, showing him with his forearm resting on top of a presumably ancient statue. Ridolfi mentions that the portrait is in the possession of the Zaguri family,[51] who seemed to have owned it after 1618, thanks to the inheritance of Pietro Pellegrini. Pellegrini, the illustrious secretary of the Council of Ten, was known above all as an antiquities expert, a passion that may have encouraged a marriage of convenience to Samaritana Corner, the daughter of Giovanni Paolo. Pietro came to possess, in fact, his father-in-law's collection, including the portrait by Tintoretto, which would have been particularly appealing to a collector of antiquities such as Pellegrini.[52]

The appreciation, commercial or otherwise, for Tintoretto's portraiture among seventeenth-century collectors is exemplified by the efforts Paolo del Sera made to track down portraits by Tintoretto. Del Sera, a great admirer of the painter, seems to have been inspired in this category of painting by the enthusiasm of his employer, Cardinal Leopoldo de' Medici. In May 1657 del Sera found in the house of the collector Stefano Celesti

> a portrait by Tintoretto the Elder of a man armed from the knees up and with a spirited attitude, with a colonnade behind and a window through which one sees the distant sea with a galleon, in the most exquisite manner of this artist, with the armor being both so beautiful and awesome, that if one did not know the sitter's face, which shows Tintoretto's hand, any one of us would believe that the painting had been done by Titian. The portrait depicts Venier, who would later become the Capitano Generale da Mar of the Venetian fleet in 1571 but was, at the time this portrait was painted, forty years old and the Capitano di Golfo.[53]

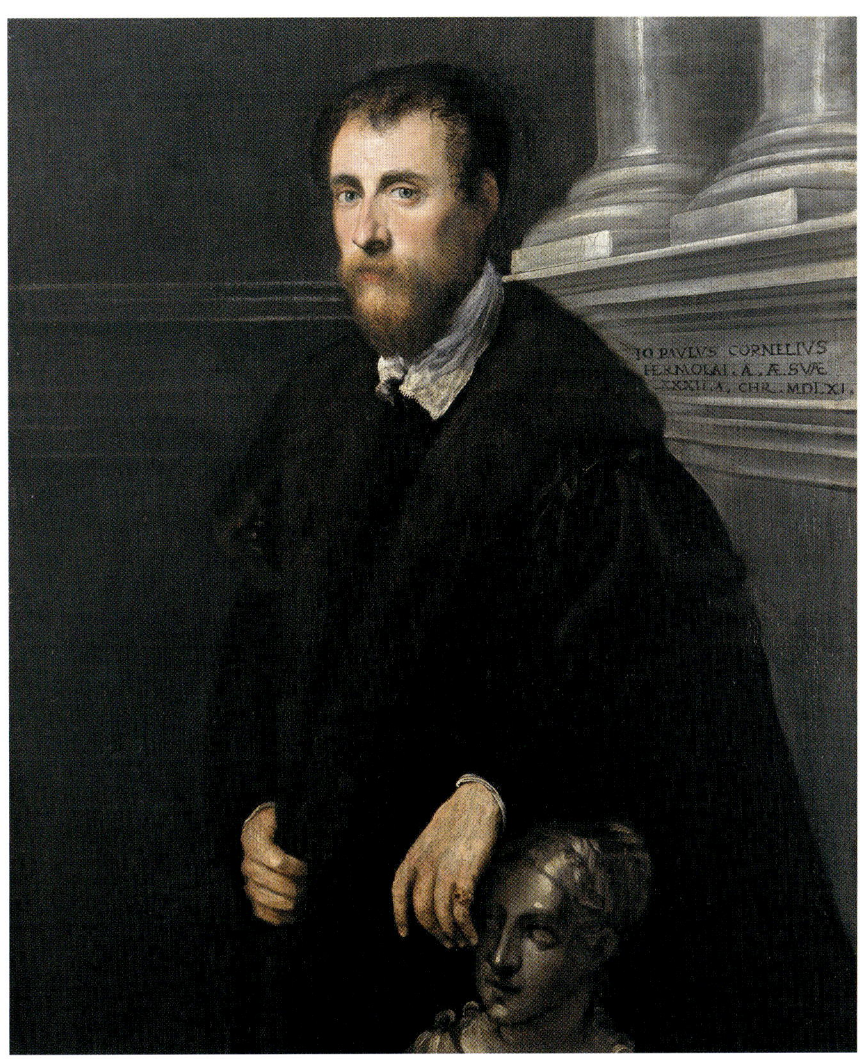

Fig. 25
Tintoretto
Giovanni Paolo Cornaro, 1561
Oil on canvas
Museum voor Schone Kunsten, Ghent

Del Sera concludes his letter by remarking that the painting "could stand alongside any portrait by Titian," the painter evidently considered supreme in portraiture.

Many of the faces immortalized by Tintoretto remain unidentified; one example is the *Portrait of a Man Aged Twenty-Six* (cat. 36), which has a coat of arms on its reverse side, identified according to one hypothesis as that of the Giustinian-Lolin family of Venice; on the frame one can also read the inscription "C. Giusti," while a second inscription states "Count Balbi Venezia," suggesting that the painting passed through an English collection.[54]

Compared with his portraits, Tintoretto's religious works appeared less frequently in private collections. Among these paintings, some themes are common and others are quite rare—as is the case with the *Supper at Emmaus* attributed to him. This work is mentioned in the 1654 inventory of the possessions of Lorenzo Gabrieli, the Procurator of San Marco starting in 1651 and the son of Zaccaria Gabrieli, who had been one of the candidates for doge in 1623.[55] So far, this record constitutes the only mention in the Venetian context of a work by Robusti of that subject,[56] and can perhaps cast new light on the provenance of the Budapest *Supper at Emmaus* (cat. 22), which was purchased in Paris in 1821 with the attribution of Andrea Schiavone, a painter whose works were often confused with those of Tintoretto.[57]

Records of Venetian private collections attest to Tintoretto's fame in the public sphere, documenting reduced-scale copies, preparatory models, and reproductive prints. Such smaller works could serve as substitutes for immovable originals. The *Crucifixion* from the Scuola Grande di San Rocco was engraved by Agostino Carracci in 1589, and the print immediately became highly esteemed, so much so that Boschini could claim that Tintoretto considered the engraving the equal of the canvas; meanwhile, the copperplate ended up in the hands of the dealer Daniel Nijs, who took it to Flanders and purportedly faced it in gold to prevent its deterioration.[58] The *Paradiso* in the Palazzo Ducale (fig. 6), painted after a hard-fought official competition among the top painters in Venice following the calamitous fire in the Sala del Maggior Consiglio in 1577,[59] was also admired by connoisseurs, as seen in the case of one of the *modelli* related to the great canvas. The friendship between Tintoretto and Grand Chancellor Giovan Fancesco Ottobon, and the influential position of his nephew Leonardo, secretary of the Council of Ten from 1588 on,[60] meant that they were perfectly placed to acquire and to appreciate a *modello* for a famous painting in the Sala del Maggior Consiglio, as part of a conspicuous group of paintings by Robusti.[61]

Even though in the seventeenth century *modelli* were often considered superior to the finished canvas and could be obtained for modest prices, preparatory models were not enough for some demanding collectors. Indeed, written sources bear witness to numerous attempts to acquire large-scale canvases suitable for "royal salons." In 1656 Paolo del Sera tried to persuade Leopoldo de' Medici to conclude a deal for Tintoretto's *Wedding Feast at Cana* from the refectory of the brothers of the Crociferi, taking advantage of the suppression of the order by the pope to finance La Serenissima's war against the Ottoman Empire.[62] Thanks to the intervention of painters and the Venetian government, the painting remained in Venice, now housed in the church of the Salute. An outcome less fortunate for Venice befell the *Washing of the Feet* from the church of San Marcuola, which left the lagoon at a still-unknown date and has been identified by scholars with the version in the Museo Nacional del Prado (fig. 26), where it would have arrived from the collection of Charles I of England prior to 1657.[63] It is precisely in Spain, among noble families who had diplomatic posts in Italy, that an extraordinary interest in Tintoretto developed in the seventeenth century. In this period Tintoretto's popularity nearly rivaled that of Titian in Spain. The Marquis of Carpio's efforts to acquire the contents of Tintoretto's studio in 1678 provides powerful testimony of Tintoretto's appeal, as does the inventory of the Marquis's collection, crammed into his palazzo at the Piazza di Spagna in Rome, where apparently 108 works attributed to Robusti were recorded in 1682.[64] But by this time, the workshop of the celebrated painter, squalidly maintained by Sebastian Casser, Tintoretto's son-in-law, had already given up its greatest treasures; Casser's death sparked a raging debate about the fate of the remaining works of art, with chests full of pictures carried away in secret.[65]

By comparison, the descendants of Paolo Veronese demonstrated a more careful attitude to their inheritance. Upon the death of Gabriele Caliari, Paolo's son, in 1631, the contents of the workshop passed to his son Giuseppe, who then became their faithful custodian, despite never having taken up the profession himself, which his father had abandoned earlier.[66] The paintings and drawings recorded—though without specific attributions—in the famous inventory of the house of Caliari in 1682[67] would mostly have been workshop productions from the end of the Cinquecento and the start of the Seicento, though there may have been some works by Paolo himself, according to Ridolfi (1648). To take on numerous commissions, Veronese had created an enterprise characterized by the practice of what Beverly Louise Brown calls "collaborative imitation," indicated by the signature Haeredes Pauli, adopted by his heirs; the system produced "autograph" paintings with or without the direct intervention of the master, making it tricky to distinguish the hand of Paolo from that of Carletto and Benedetto, core members of the Caliari workshop.[68] The experts thus limit themselves to using terms such as "copy of" and, in rare cases, "coming from" (*viene da*) without being more specific. One pertinent example is offered by a painting of the "Virgin Annunciate with the Eternal Father carried by two angels and three cherub heads with the Holy Spirit by Carletto, retouched by Paolo Veronese," in the collection of Giovan Donato Correggio; the description furnished by the owner suggests that the painting was being circulated as an autograph work on the authority of col-

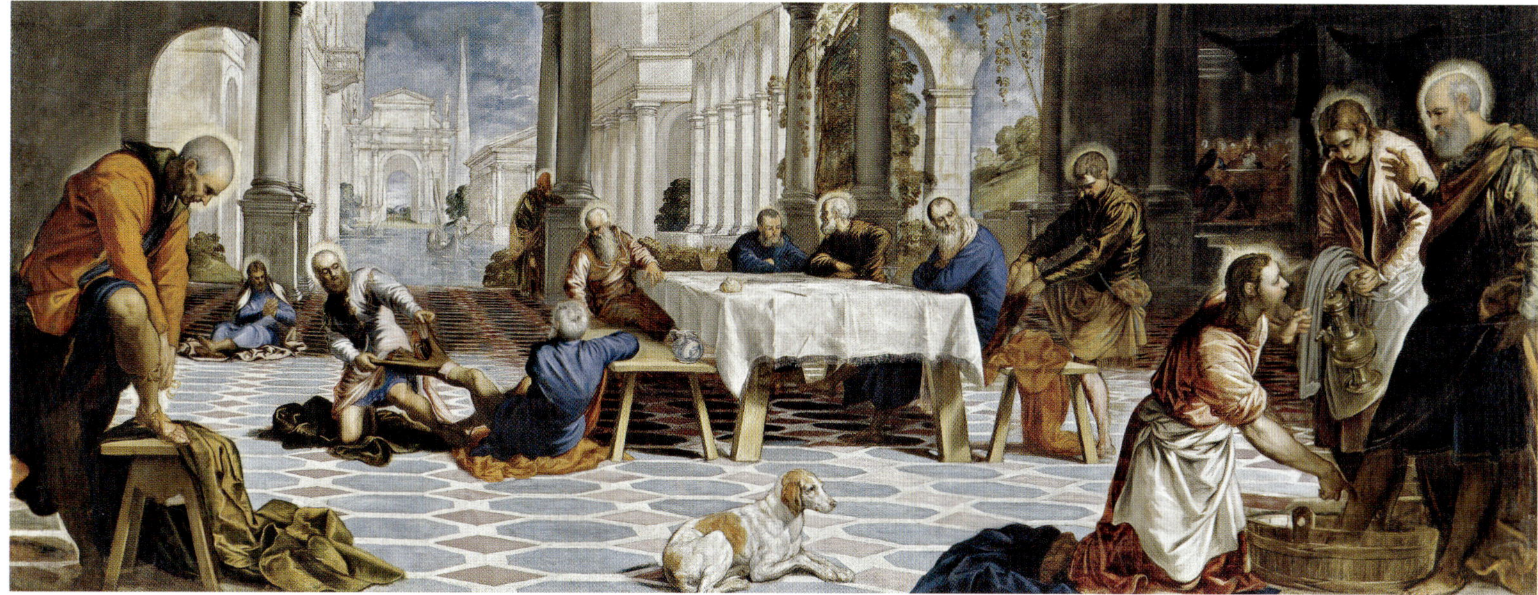

lectors and experts.[69] Similarly, one should not be surprised that collectors and agents made negative, indeed cutting, judgments about the works remaining in the Caliari studio. In 1632 Giovanni Antonio Massani, the secretary to Giovan Battista Agucchi, brought back to Cardinal Francesco Barberini, at that time searching for works by Veronese,[70] the opinion of an expert that in the Caliari house "there are many things that could have been designed by Paolo, but not colored or finished by him; and I have been assured that among the said pieces there is not even one which is worthy of being valued as a good thing by the hand of this master."[71] At this time Veronese's fame had expanded beyond the borders of La Serenissima. Already he was the undisputed protagonist of prestigious decorative campaigns sponsored by the Venetian government and religious orders; starting in the 1570s, the painter tried to bring his work to international collectors through allegorical canvases of considerable size, like *Wisdom and Strength* (The Frick Collection, New York) and *Allegory of Virtue and Vice (The Choice of Hercules)* (fig. 27). The goal would have been to impress (with the help of influential dealer Jacopo Strada) princes from Northern Europe such as Albert of Bavaria and Maximillian II Hapsburg, who in 1571 came into contact with the artist through his ambassador in Venice, Viet von Dornberg.[72] Particularly after Veronese's death, his critical reputation and the prices for his works grew; the aforementioned Massani specifies that "the works by this Master were not very esteemed here in the past, but today their worth is much appreciated, and anyone who owns something of his deems it to be of great worth (as if it were by Titian himself, who has always been regarded as divinity itself in this country), judging that Paolo was perfect in *disegno*, beautiful in *colorito* . . . and skillful in inventions."[73] Veronese, therefore, was admired as being capable of eclipsing Titian, reflected in "the universal taste of great princes and lords for this eminent painter."[74]

According to the documentary record, those in Venice who had the good fortune to own original works by Veronese (or were capable of recognizing them) were mostly patricians; merchants and citizens possessed predominantly replicas and derivative works.[75] These patrician collectors were loath to relinquish paintings by Veronese, and they even attempted to prevent their being copied. This is exemplified by the negotiations in 1664 between Pietro Basadonna, the Venetian ambassador to Rome, and the agents of Queen Christina of Sweden on the matter of a picture much admired before the nineteenth century, the *Family of Darius before Alexander*, then owned by the Pisani Moretta and now in the National Gallery, London. This esteemed picture inspired the appetites of the wealthiest collectors, but the asking price was astronomical, over 5,000 ducats,[76] and no one dared spend that much. Perhaps the hope for a similar price inspired stipulations in the wills of the family's ancestors that prohibited its sale and forbade its copying, presumably to preserve the uniqueness of the work.[77] In fact, replicas did exist, as did workshops that specialized in them, such as the dealer-restorer Michele Spietra (d. 1656). Such work-

Fig. 26
Tintoretto
Washing of the Feet, 1548–49
Oil on canvas
Museo Nacional del Prado, Madrid

Fig. 27
Veronese
Allegory of Virtue and Vice
(The Choice of Hercules), about 1565
Oil on canvas
The Frick Collection, New York

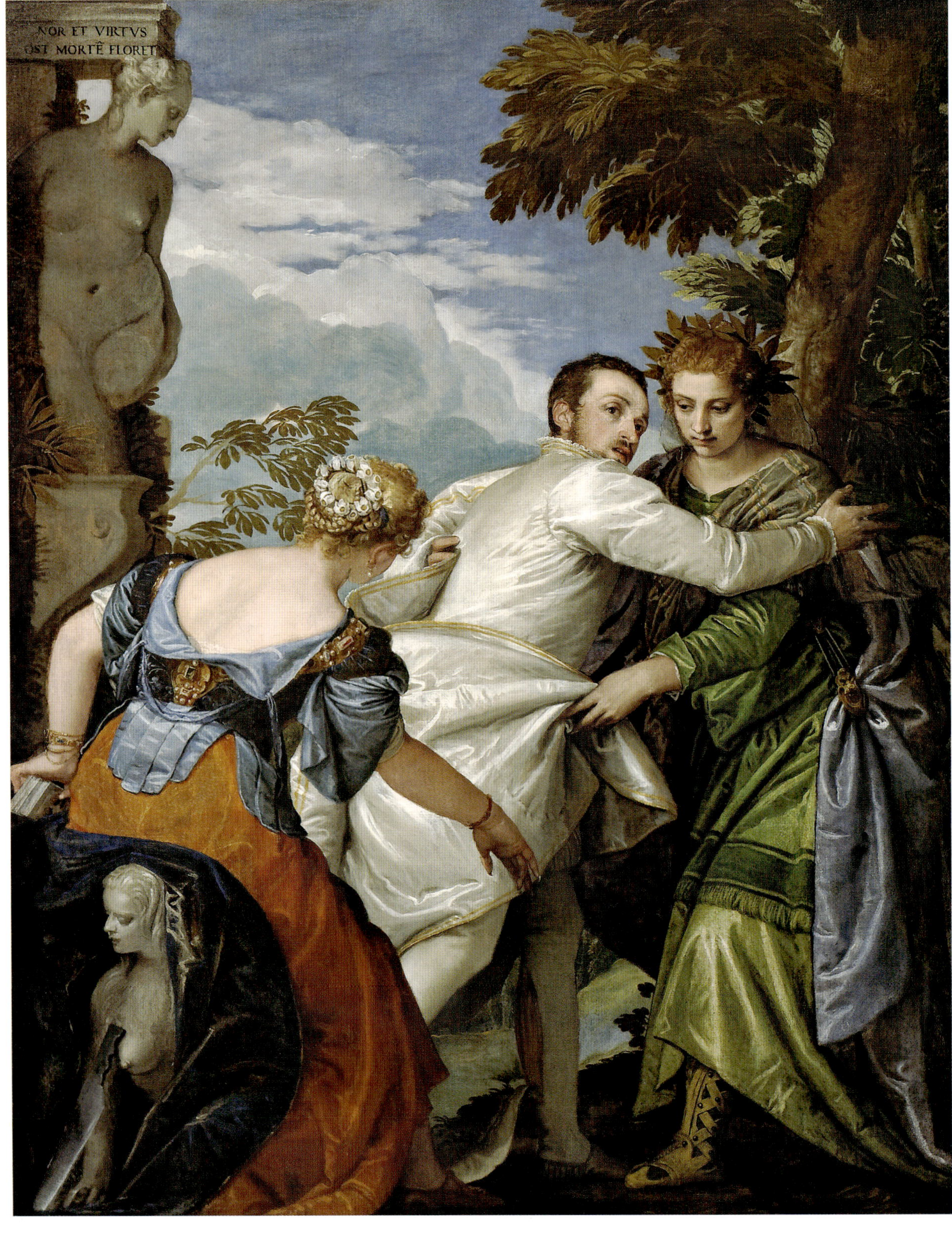

shops offered copies at reasonable prices, after popular themes such as the Adoration of the Magi, Christ and the Centurion, and the Finding of Moses—religious subjects that Veronese interpreted in an elegantly secular manner.[78] Returning to the *Family of Darius before Alexander*, the derivatives made by the French artist Valentin Lefèvre, one of the painters most influenced by the language of Caliari in the seventeenth century, satisfied impassioned admirers of Veronese; Giorgio Bergonzi valued his copy of the Pisani Moretta painting, in fact, at 80 ducats,[79] a rather high price if we consider that the same collector valued at only 100 ducats the "portrait done by the hand of Paolo Veronese of the famous Agostin Barbarigo, with the arrow in one hand, dressed in armor, with a baton in the other," hanging in the *portego* of his palace. This most probably relates to the same version Pietro Edwards recorded later in an unpublished manuscript catalogue he compiled in 1794 of the Gerolamo Manfrin Gallery, which probably included the portrait of Agostino Barbarigo, now in the Cleveland Museum of Art (cat. 41),[80] a painting whose commemorative character one would associate with a public setting or a residence of the Barbarigo family.[81] Bergonzi had ordered that his painting be transferred to the church of Sant'Andrea della Certosa "so that it hangs in the chapel above the chest wherein lie the illustrious remains," that is, those of the admiral Agostino Barbarigo.[82] As far as we know, the portrait was never conveyed to this location.

The Venetian state wholeheartedly supported Veronese during his lifetime by involving him in the prestigious decorations of the Palazzo Ducale. A little less than a century after his death, however, the government decided to remove from Venice one of his major works and send it abroad for political ends. In 1664, at the suggestion of the able diplomat Alvise Molin, the Venetian government donated the enormous *Feast in the House of Simon* from the refectory of the Servite monastery to Louis XIV (now at the Musée National du Château, Versailles), thus sealing the artist's international reputation and his fame among collectors.[83] The removal of the painting to Versailles fueled the trade in replicas and derivatives and provided a destination for endless visits by princes and collectors who would never have let the picture return to the lagoon, since it had so fed the taste for the Venetian master within France. The episode, which mobilized all of the ambassadors and principal agents of the city between 1650 and 1660, was a fascinating struggle among rival princely collectors—Leopoldo de' Medici, the Duke of Mantua, Alfonso IV d'Este, the Marchese Spinola, and Louis XIV. Undoubtedly *the* event in the art market at the middle of the Seicento, the struggle has been recently reconstructed.[84] Such episodes were fueled by heated competition between collectors and dealers, since all princes and sovereigns hoped to acquire a *Supper* by Veronese for their own salons, for which the sumptuous costume banquets of the biblical episodes were well adapted as decoration.

Fortunately many attempts to remove paintings by Veronese from Venice failed. In 1666 Paolo del Sera wrote to Cardinal Leopoldo de' Medici and recommended the purchase of a *Rape of Europa*, since at that time there were no other large works by Veronese in private hands, with the exception of the *Family of Darius before Alexander* of the Pisani Moretta. Leopoldo's nephew Cosimo III, Grand Duke of Tuscany, later considered acquiring the painting from del Sera. The tale of Europa was one of the subjects most beloved by connoisseurs, a fad that began when Giacomo Contarini commissioned from Veronese the famous version in which the mythological episode was transformed into a kind of marriage feast (Sala dell'Anticollegio, Palazzo Ducale).[85] It has recently been proposed that the painting in the Dresden Gemäldegalerie (attributed to the workshop) be recognized as the one owned by del Sera.[86] Indeed, the information del Sera supplied in the letter to Leopoldo of March 13, 1666, corresponds with the example at the German museum ("the Story of Europa seated on a white bull, with maidens who serve her, little cupids, and additional little figures and animals, with a countryside and beautiful trees"),[87] down to the measurements expressed in "braccia fiorentine." Boschini records that del Sera had claimed the painting was worth the enormous sum of 3,000 ducats.[88] Perhaps that high price caused the negotiation with Cosimo III to fail, even though experts had judged the painting "the sweetest work created by that famous brush."[89]

With another acquisition in mind, the Grand Duke later sent his architect, Pier Maria Baldi, to Serravalle (Vittorio Veneto) to evaluate the quality of Titian's large altarpiece in Santa Maria Nuova.[90] The architect did not acquire that altarpiece, deciding that it was in poor condition, nor did he bring back any canvases from Venice. Baldi visited a Venice awash in copies, workshop productions, and works "in the manner of" Titian, Tintoretto, and Veronese. But paintings by the very hands of these three equally supreme artists so astounded the architect that although unsuccessful in his mission, he was consoled by what his eyes had enjoyed. In 1677 Baldi returned to Florence empty-handed but "with his head full of paintings . . . of extraordinary beauty by the most famous artists."[91]

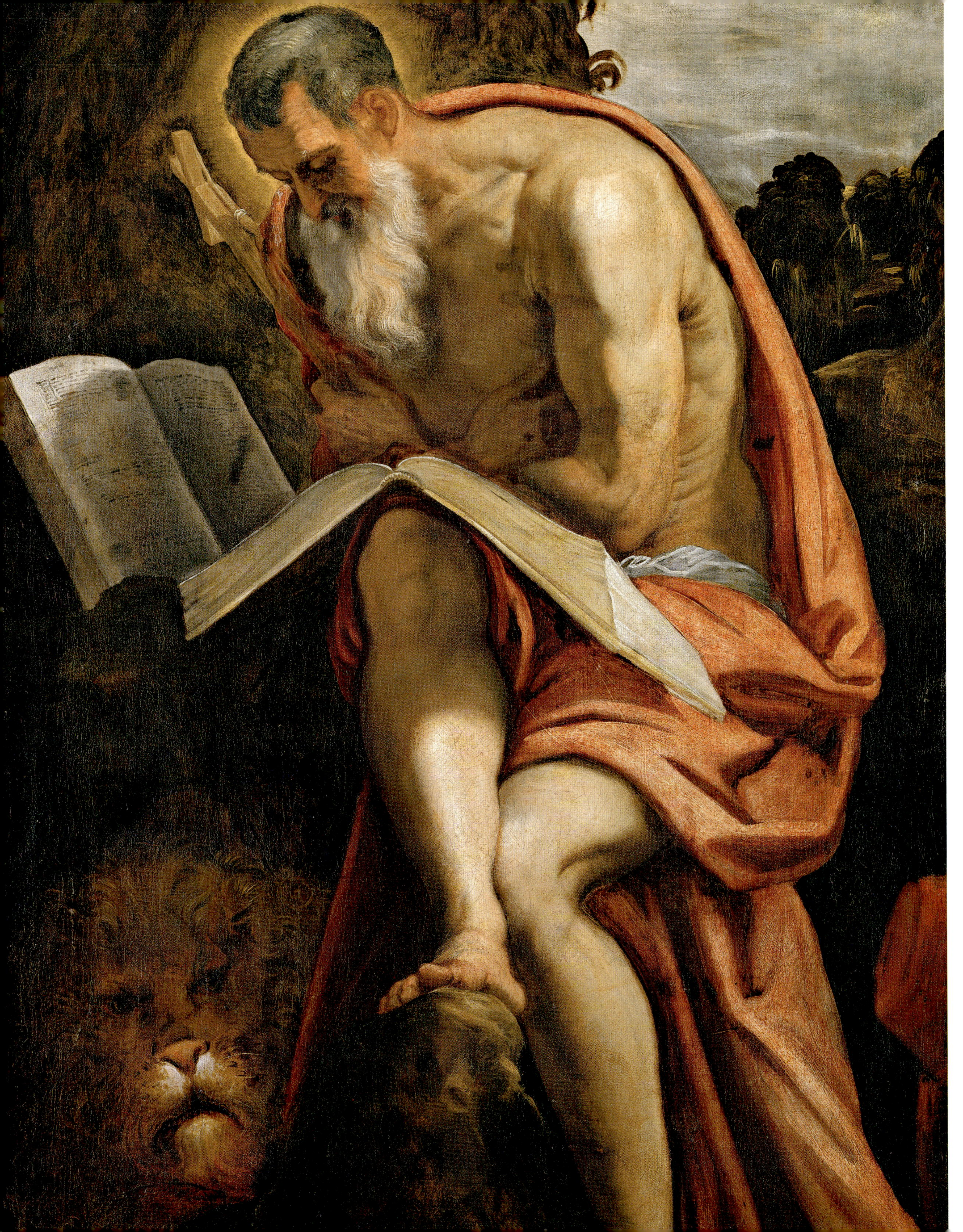

Materials and Techniques of Painters in Sixteenth-Century Venice

ROBERT WALD

A crossroads of materials, culture, and human populations in the Mediterranean world, Venice in the sixteenth century was a remarkable place to be an artist. Renowned for its economic power and its cosmopolitan blending of Christian, Jewish, and Islamic cultures, the city controlled the import markets for spices, valuable textiles, and rare raw materials in addition to luxury and collectible goods such as ceramics, Greek antiquities, and Byzantine literature.[1] Also a major center of expertise in glass, dyes, printing, weaving, and metalworking, Venice offered its artists an abundance of materials and the trained manpower to manipulate them. The city's economic advantages gave its elite leverage in the flourishing art market and encouraged keen competition among painters.

Venice's unique conditions drove artists in other ways as well. The island city was not congenial to fresco painting, although the medium was practiced there as it was elsewhere during the Renaissance. Despite modified techniques for wall-painting preparation in Venice, namely the *pastallone* surface of absorbent crushed brick,[2] the problems associated with moisture in the Venetian Lagoon were fatal, and in fact the frescoes in the Palazzo Ducale needed restoration by 1409, less than fifty years after they were painted. Tintoretto alone frescoed eleven documented facades in Venice (of which only meager fragments survive);[3] of Titian's and Veronese's frescoes, not much more survives in Venice. Due to climate and other factors, Venetian painters increasingly expressed themselves on canvas supports rather than plaster-prepared walls.

Supports

Venice was a major center for weavers of luxury fabrics in silk and wool, as well as those who worked in the cotton and flax that were vital for everyday wares and sails.[4] For canvas supports, Venetian painters most often turned to linen, hemp, and jute, sometimes in blended fabrics. Some fabrics were made of simple weaves (tabby and twill), while others incorporated more decorative designs (herringbone and damask). Fabrics were available in various thread densities and thicknesses. Little research has been carried out on the trade of canvas at this time; weavers' stamps, however, show that canvases produced in the Low Countries were being used by Italian artists by about 1600 (and probably quite a bit earlier) (fig. 28).[5]

There were aesthetic as well as practical reasons for the favoring of canvas supports over fresco and panel painting (also sensitive to excessive moisture levels) in Venice. The limited palette and saturation of fresco made it hard to challenge the emergence of new oil-based paint media; and as tastes moved away from heavily decorated and gilded backgrounds for panel paintings toward more illusionistic settings, the solid supports that gilding called for

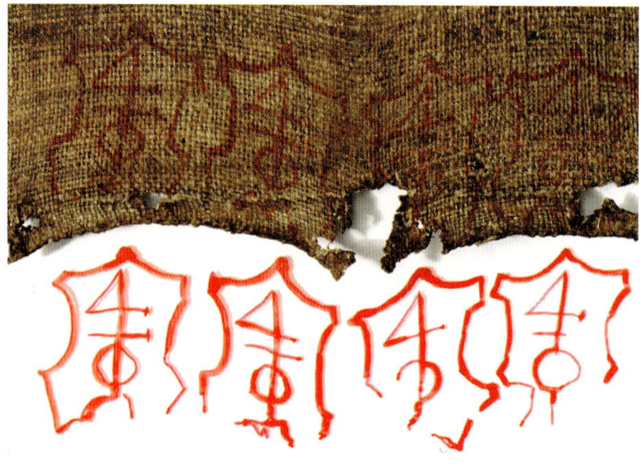

Fig. 28
Weaver's stamp on reverse of canvas.
Orazio Gentileschi, *Road to Calvary*, about 1603
Kunsthistorisches Museum, Vienna

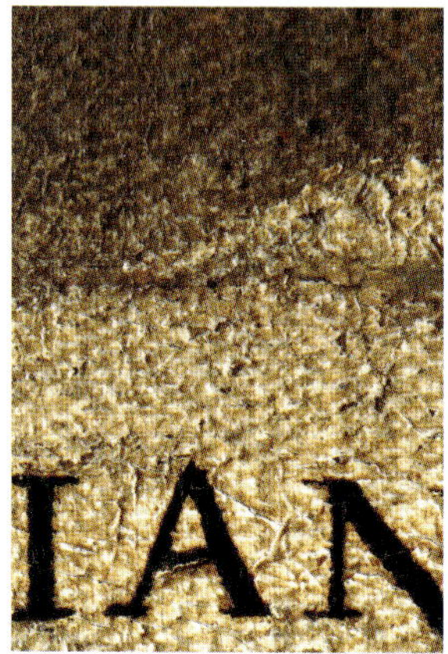

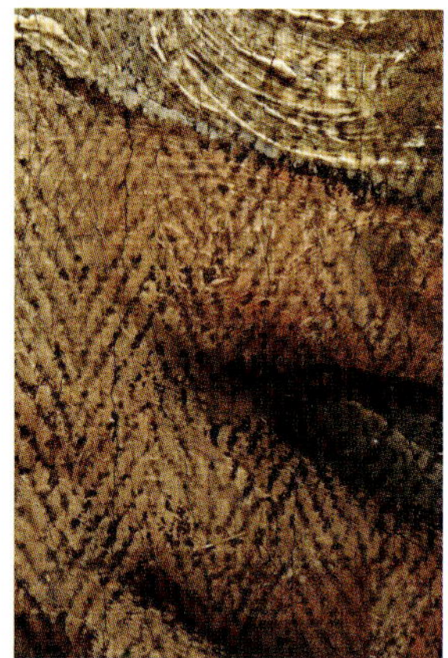

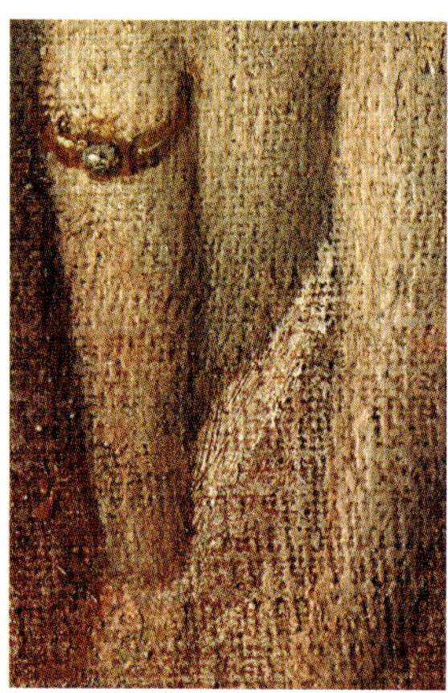

Fig. 29
Examples of canvas weaves.
Left: twill weave
Center: herringbone weave
Right: tabby weave

were no longer necessary. Painting on canvas also allowed artists to execute large works in their studios instead of on-site. Furthermore, substantial numbers of paintings were being exported from the city and often needed to be rolled for efficient transport.

Although small paintings would sometimes be stretched over a wood panel system,[6] large canvases could be rolled and shipped to their site of installation and either mounted to a wooden strainer or fixed directly to the wall.[7] From documents concerning the shipment, largely by river, of Archduke Leopold Wilhelm of Austria's collection of paintings from Brussels to Vienna in the mid-seventeenth century, we know that many medium-sized paintings were removed from their stretchers and rolled around one another with straw cushioning.[8] Numerous paintings would fit in one vessel, and upon arrival new stretchers and frames would be fabricated for them. Presumably this is how many paintings left Venice.

For large works, thicker twill and herringbone canvases often were chosen for their durability and strength; to keep them flexible for transport, the Venetians laid out thin gesso grounds. This mixture of a heavier canvas and a thinner ground created a unique surface for many Venetian paintings; it was this rough and textured surface to which painters had to adapt their application of paint (fig. 29).[9] Some larger works by Tintoretto (*Archangel Michael in Combat with Lucifer*, at the Gemäldegalerie, Staatliche Kunstsammlungen, Dresden) and Titian (*Pietà*, fig. 109) display a mixture of canvas sections having different canvas weaves within the same painting support. This is not to say that the oft-discussed vaporous quality of the "broken" Venetian brushwork was born exclusively of canvas constraints—although it cannot have been solely an aesthetic decision either.

Looms in sixteenth-century Italy were generally between 60 and 100 cm (23⅝ and 39⅜ in.) wide, although open tabby weaves and heavier twills were available up to 120 cm (47¼ in.) in width. A typical, economically minded way to bring together a medium-sized easel-painting support (about 170 x 140 cm [66⅞ x 55⅛ in.]) would be to take a full width of canvas from the loom (about 90 cm [35⅜ in.] wide and 240 cm [94½ in.] long) and cut one-third of the length from one end. This extra third (about 80 cm [31½ in.]) would then be cut again in half and the two pieces added one next to the other on top of the larger section, resulting in a support of adequate size and pleasing proportions with no loss of material. It is the method that was used for Veronese's *Wisdom and Strength* (about 1580, The Frick Collection, New York) in a vertical format and Titian's *Danaë* (1560–65, Kunsthistorisches Museum, Vienna) in the horizontal format (fig. 30).[10]

The format could be extended horizontally in the same manner to provide supports such as that found in Tintoretto's *Washing of the Feet* (fig. 73). Fuller, square-shaped formats would normally employ a single seam in the middle of the composition (for instance, Titian's Ferrara-cycle paintings and most of those for Philip II's *poesie*).[11] Still larger square-format works would use several full loom widths sewn together, as in Tintoretto's Gonzaga Cycle.[12]

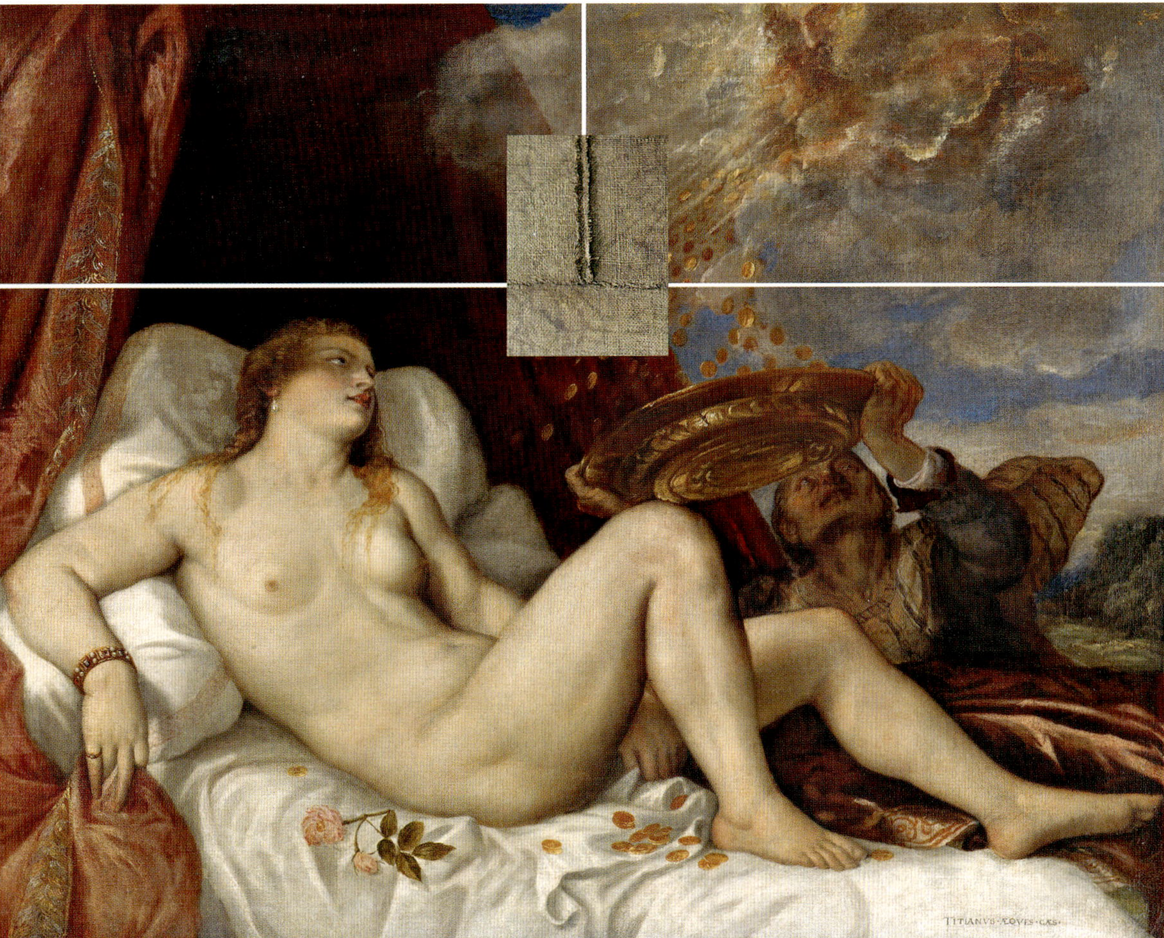

Fig. 30
Canvas support construction with detail from reverse side of canvas (inserted) showing seams.
Titian, *Danaë*, about 1560–65, Kunsthistorisches Museum, Vienna

Preparation

Titian and Tintoretto frequently followed established practice in using light-colored gesso grounds composed of calcium sulfate derived from gypsum.[13] These reflective ground layers would be modified with colored underpainting, depending on the passages to be executed. Veronese, who arrived in Venice right after midcentury, also used white gesso grounds, but apparently with additional toning layers or *imprimatura* in a warm pink-gray color, not unlike the tone described by Armenini in his treatise of 1586.[14] The light, more highly reflective ground had helped bring to life the very fine applications of egg-tempera passages, often made with clearly separated or hatched strokes of paint, of artists of the previous century.[15] Within these earlier works, the color of the ground layer was an integral part of the paint-layering process. As paint became richer in color and its application more dense, homogeneous, and fluid through the transition to ever more oil-rich tempera mixtures (*tempera grassa*), the function of the ground also changed. Having retained an optical function within the overall color scheme, it now helped to lighten the density of paint application by selectively acting as a middle tone between shadow and highlight.[16]

In this sense, many painters were drawing on the techniques used in preparing colored wash studies on toned paper (a common practice of northern artists by the sixteenth century, found in many of Veronese's drawings as well). The toned ground also aided painters with relative color matching when composing directly on the prepared canvas support. In addition, the reduced reflective quality of the ground freed the artists to rework passages to a greater extent without creating a technical or optical imbalance. This technical shift in the second quarter of the sixteenth century

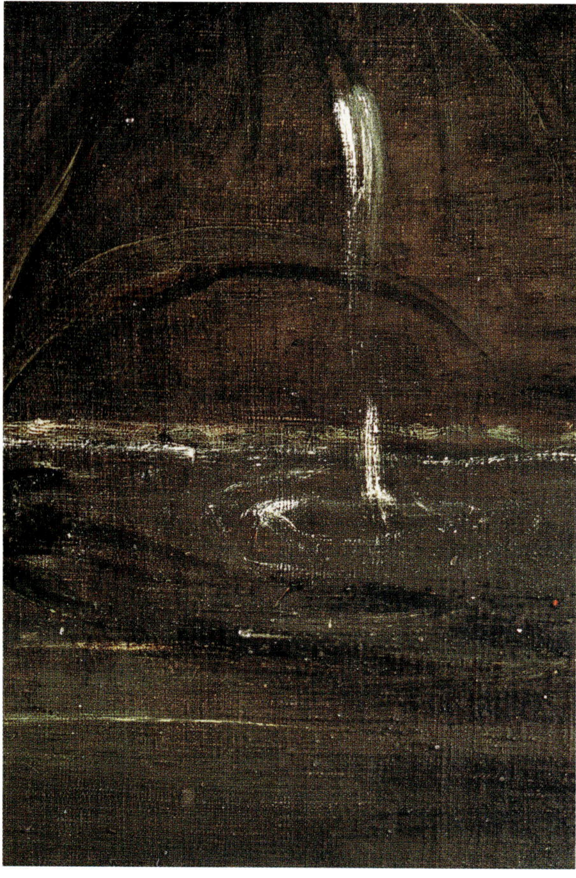

Fig. 31
Detail showing warm medium-brown tone of *imprimatura*. Jacopo Tintoretto, *Susannah and the Elders*, about 1555–56 (cat. 31), Kunsthistorisches Museum, Vienna

allowed artists to experiment more with improvised compositions and to be less dependent on fixed, preconceived designs.

Titian in his later career worked with slightly warm, medium-gray-colored coatings on top of traditional gesso grounds,[17] employing selective underpainting to predetermined areas of the composition (cooler layers under the skin tones, for example). Titian also used gesso-based grounds throughout his career—perhaps due to his copious use of glazing, which would have required a more absorbent ground to dry within a practical time frame.[18]

Tintoretto's early works, too, were constructed on white gesso grounds; by the late 1550s he was using toned grounds and underpaintings of various colors.[19] This shift is most likely in response to the large canvases he needed to complete. The darker ground allowed him to be more efficient with the larger scale of his commissions, saving him time in overall image construction. Darker grounds also afforded a more efficient use of materials, as their base tone could be made by bulking the mixture with old palette scrapings. They could, however, prove troublesome over time, as they tend to show through overlying oil-based paint films that become more transparent with age. Tintoretto's smaller and more refined midcentury works, for example *Saint George and the Dragon* (about 1553, National Gallery, London) and *Susannah and the Elders* (cat. 31), are painted in a more traditional manner using fine-weave canvases and lighter colored grounds (fig. 31), selected underpainting, and more fully modeled and refined forms.

With few exceptions, Veronese retained light-colored grounds in his works. The omissions appear to be the very-large-format works that show no signs of a colored *imprimatura*, with paint layers applied directly over the white gesso preparation. Calcium carbonate (instead of the usual calcium sulfate from south of the Alps) has been identified as the ground material of the *Adoration of the Kings* (1573, National Gallery, London).[20]

Artists discovered that certain adjustments needed to be made when constructing paintings that were to be rolled for transport. Tintoretto experienced delamination, or separation of paint layers, with the transport of the Gonzaga pictures.[21] Titian also had difficulties with the transport of his paintings, in particular a *Venus and Adonis* and most likely *La Bella* (underlying the composition of the *Girl with a Fur Wrap*, in the Kunsthistorisches Museum, Vienna), which appears to have been sent back to his studio in Venice.[22] In 1550–51, in Augsburg, he learned of seemingly irreparable damages to paintings that he had sent to Nicola Granvelle in Brussels in 1548; the problems were associated with the fresh state of the works. As a result, it seems, the portrait *Johann Friedrich von Sachsen* (1550–51, Kunsthistorisches Museum, Vienna), sent later from Augsburg, was executed on an unusual pure lead-white and walnut-oil ground in an attempt to increase the flexibility of the paint films and reduce the further chances of damage during shipment.[23] Indeed, the concern over damage to canvases during transport may best be supported by Vasari's ninth chapter in his reworked 1568 treatise on technique, where he suggests avoiding a traditional gesso preparation, which would prove too brittle, and to adopt a mixture of flour, walnut oil, and lead white applied with a priming knife.[24]

Underdrawing

Increased interest in Venetian painting technique and the vast improvements made in investigative instrumentation in the last decade or so have changed how we view Venetian painters as draftsmen.[25] The traditional understanding upheld the dichotomy of *disegno* and *colorito*, according to which, Venetian paintings were believed to be executed largely without the aid of preconceived underdrawings. There is now enough evidence, however, to demonstrate that underdrawing played a much more active role in Venice (fig. 32).

Recent comparisons of panel paintings by Giovanni Bellini (in 1510) and Titian (in 1515) demonstrate the older artist's more calculated approach to underdrawing and Titian's increasing willingness to make freehand changes to predetermined and already-transferred compositions.[26] We know that Titian, Tintoretto, and Veronese received conventional training; Titian also studied mosaic, an art that requires precise measurements in design and production.[27] It is also known that all three artists used various methods of recording and transferring designs for further use. All have left their marks behind in fresco paintings, in the form of incised lines for design transfers; Titian's *Saint Christopher* (Palazzo Ducale, Venice), Tintoretto's work at Ca' Soranzo, and Veronese's decoration of the Villa Barbaro in Maser are prime examples. Vasari also mentions that Titian had received a pricked cartoon for a painting he was to make for Emperor Charles V.[28] In addition, all three painters were known to have enlarged smaller-scale drawings of complete compositions, whole or in part, for use in larger canvases.[29] Small drawings were enlarged through a grid system for Titian's portrait of Francesco Maria della Rovere (1537, Galleria degli Uffizi, Florence). Similar drawings must have been used for Tintoretto's *Susannah and the Elders* and *Saint Jerome in the Wilderness* (cat. 50).[30]

The repetition (often with modifications) of sought-after compositions proved to be very popular and lucrative for painters of this time, Titian in particular.[31] This was largely made possible through reliable copies, or *ricordi*, that would be made after a completed full-size work. These replicas were kept in studios for later reference to color scheme, to secure the likeness of a specific person, or to capture the gestures and proportions of a figure or group of figures.[32] Titian's paintings of Venus and a Musician (see cat. 28, fig. 79), Venus and Adonis (see cat. 33, fig. 83), and Mary Magdalen are excellent examples of this type of recording, all existing in more than six variations apiece.

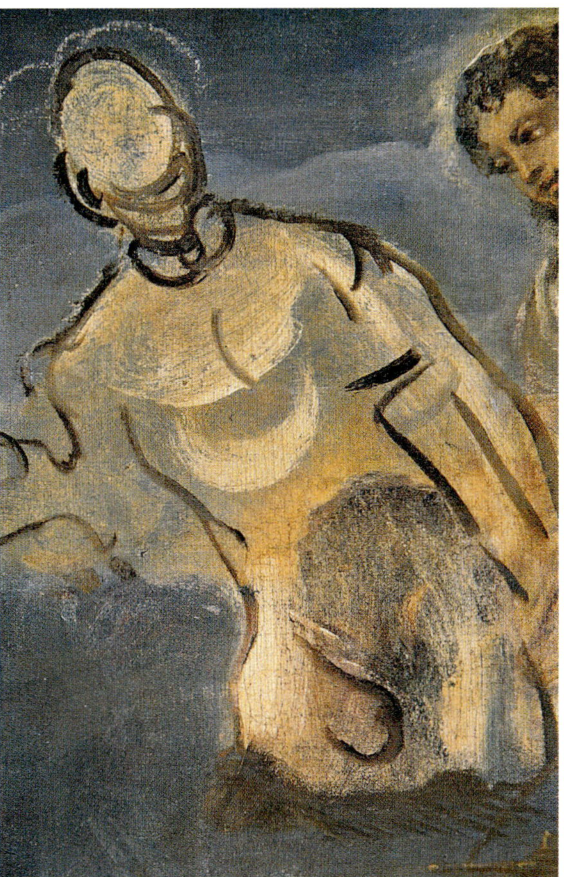

Fig. 32
Detail showing underdrawing in black paint within unfinished passage. Jacopo Tintoretto, *Doge Alvise Mocenigo Presented to the Redeemer*, about 1571–74, Metropolitan Museum of Art, New York

One painting that Titian realized would be appealing and could be easily modified for more than one client was the *Danaë*. The first rendition of this theme was for Cardinal Alessandro Farnese of Rome; from this composition, Titian prepared seven more works with modifications over the course of the following decades for several very important clients, including Philip II of Spain. The artist appears to have used 1:1 cartoons for the central figure, which, as research has suggested, would be only slightly modified from one version to the next.[33] The similar use of cartoons to transfer key compositional elements from one painting support to the next have also been detected in Tintoretto's portrait work. Recurring compositions also appear in the oeuvre of Veronese—for instance, multiple versions of *Europa* and the *Finding of Moses*. The separate versions of *Europa* exhibit considerable variation, suggesting that, while Veronese

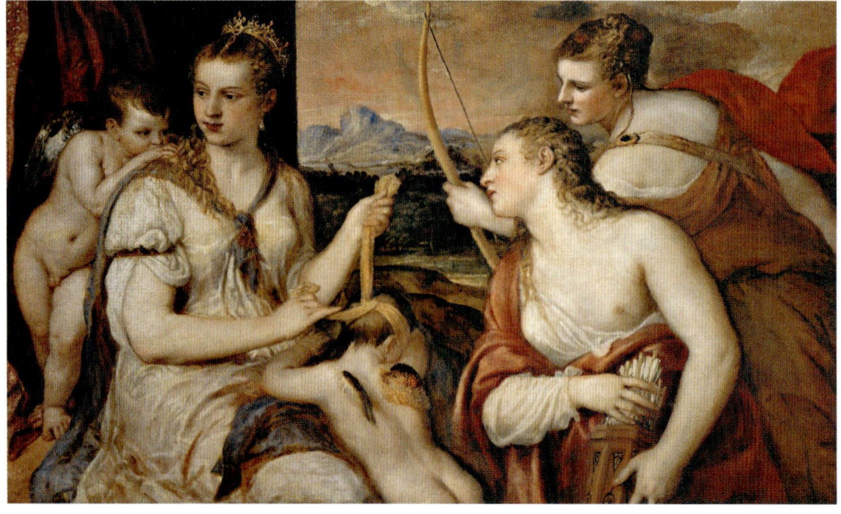

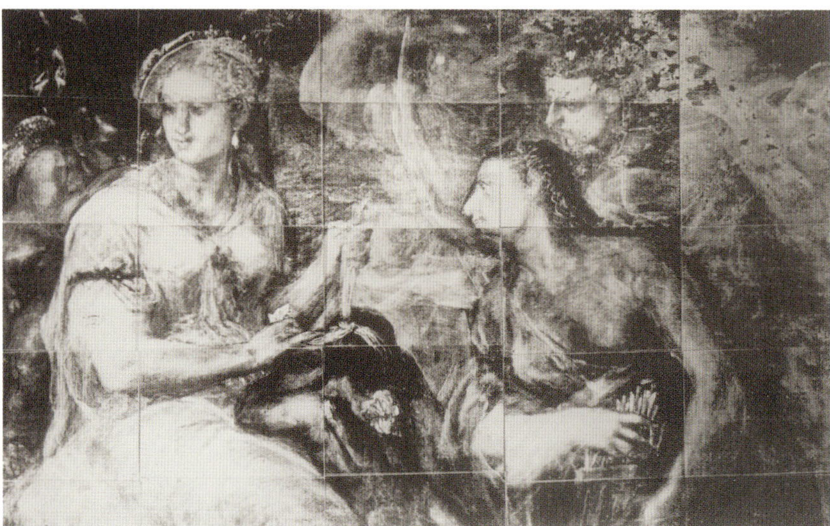

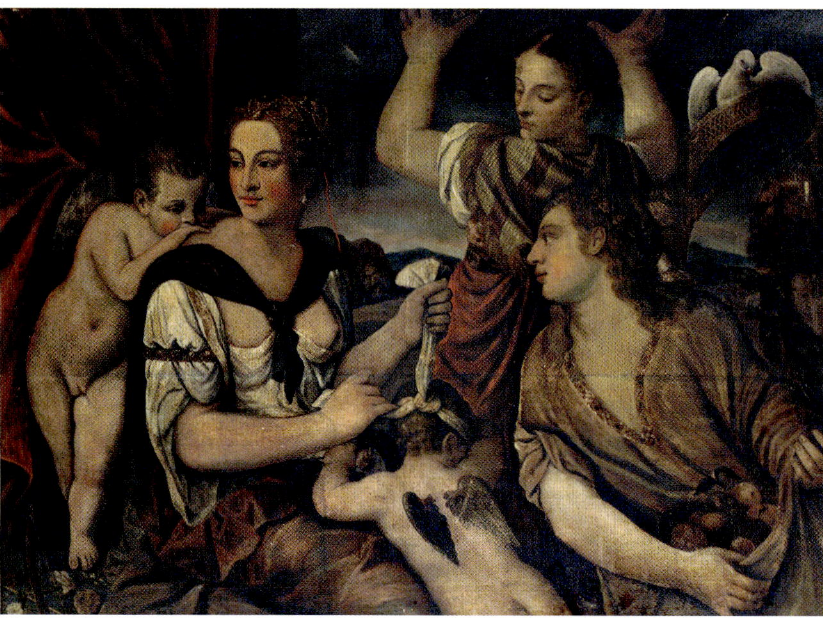

would have had a master record of the subject, he allowed for comparatively more freedom than with the *Finding of Moses*, which, excluding the background, is very consistent in both canvases.

Venetian artists made use of three-dimensional models as well, particularly scaled-down wax, plaster, and bronze reproductions of antique statues and relief works in addition to contemporary sculptures by leading artists of the day.[34] Carlo Ridolfi noted Tintoretto's fabrication of small figurines (by a specialist in his studio rather than by his own hand) and Raffaele Soprani mentioned his purchase and commission of small-scale bronzes from Nicolò Roccatagliata and possibly Barthélemy Preiur in the 1560s.[35] The *Flagellation of Christ* (1585–90, Kunsthistorisches Museum, Vienna) is an example of the use of such specialized figurines in developing painted compositions.[36] Tintoretto also collected (as did Lorenzo Lotto) antique sculpture and casts as well as prints of other artists' works.[37] Venice also boasted one of the most important collections of ancient Greek sculpture, that of the Grimani family, inhabitants of Venice since the tenth century, who had ties to Crete and imported spices, slaves, and antiques. Their collection was moved from Rome to Venice in 1523 and was partially displayed in the Sala della Testa in the Palazzo Ducale from 1524, and also in the family residence in Santa Maria Formosa. This collection was accessible to prominent artists from Venice and the region, as numerous paintings can confirm.[38]

Painting technique

It often has been asserted that tempera painting lasted in Italy until the last quarter of the fifteenth century, and that the gradual shift to oil stems from an earlier generation of painters, notably Jan van Eyck, coming from Flanders and the Netherlands. Recent research complicates this understanding, however, showing that oil-based media were in use in Italy by around 1428,[39] while Flemish treatises on painting techniques from the mid-seventeenth century still suggest the use of aqueous vehicles for applications of blue and other light-tinted passages to prevent their being yellowed by oil-based paints.[40]

Venice was the center for dyestuffs and pigments in the first half of the sixteenth century and one of Europe's oldest sites for processed chemicals and apothecary wares. The city produced, imported, and exported pigments to serve a wide-ranging clientele from numerous vocations directly and indirectly associated with the field of painting. The glass-making and dyeing industries of Venice aided in the development of pigment manufacturing, bolstering the local market for the pigment merchants, or *vendecolori*. Numerous mineral pigments sold in Venice came from northern Europe; Germany and Hungary were sources for azurite blue, Poland provided carmine red, and the Netherlands supplied verdigris green. These materials were collected and shipped to Venice through dealers stationed in Nuremberg. Other minerals such as natural ultramarine blue were imported from what today is Afghanistan, and various other plant and insect extracts were brought in from neighboring eastern regions. Greece supplied certain green earths, and further exotic colorants such as indigo and woad (from which a blue dye was produced) and brazilwood (used in a red dye) would be shipped from the New World.[41] Shops specializing in art supplies—not only pigments, but canvases, solvents, and other materials—seem to have surfaced in Venice around 1500.[42]

Early attempts to integrate oil into paintings resulted in varying degrees of adaptation and modification. Painters in Rome and Florence were quite comfortable with the multicolored modeling techniques demanded by tempera and fresco; in this region, painters such as Botticelli and Ghirlandaio first attempted to increase the range of modeling through oil glazes by applying transparent layers over an already-prepared design executed in tempera. Elsewhere, painters—Carlo Crivelli and the young Michelangelo, in particular—prepared mixtures of tempera and oil known as *tempera grassa*, using egg yolk to suspend a higher concentration of oil in water. In some instances, such as in works by Mantegna and Raphael, multiple techniques—egg tempera, *tempera grassa*, and pure oil paint—are divided among specific passages and integrated into a single work. Technical examination of Giovanni Bellini's paintings has shown that he was confident in oil glazing by 1475, although he, like several of his contemporaries, was applying underpainting in tempera with modeling produced through hatched brushstrokes.[43] It is in the works of Giorgione and early paintings by Titian from the first decade of the sixteenth century that we see a departure from such hatched modeling. Additionally, these artists further divorced themselves from a constricting dependance on cartoon/transfer underdrawing, and so freed themselves for a mode of painting affording more expression and individuality. These adaptations in materials and techniques lay the foundation for Venetian painting of the sixteenth century. A more integrated and fluid use of underdrawing and the increasing use of color within the underlayers tended to diffuse the boundary between the various elements in the composition. The separation of compositional elements within space is increasingly characterized through color rather than line—the approach known today as atmospheric perspective or tonal painting.

The Venetian approach to materials and technique produced a particular form of color mixing—one associated with the eyes' propensity to resolve and fuse differences in hue from separate, however superimposed passages of distinct colors, rather than through the actual mixing of paint on the palette to be subsequently applied in a single, blended layer. This approach, sometimes referred to as *broken color*, creates variations in color, texture, and focus, depending on the viewer's distance from the painting.[44]

While Venetian painters worked within the framework of constraints described above—local conditions, the availability of materials, and the sensibilities of their patrons—individual artists reveal their genius in their selection of materials and themes, their working methods, and their approach to audience. Taken together, these constitute the artists' unique responses to particularities of time, place, and materials.

Titian, unlike Tintoretto and Veronese, was born in the fifteenth century and lived to be around eighty-eight years old. His career was comparatively long and his development in terms of technique and approach in painting was more self-reflective than appropriative. Although stylistically his works develop from a more precise and naturalistic formula based on the studio of the Bellini, he was able to forge his position as an impeccable portrait painter in the 1530s to 1550s. His keen understanding of his clients' tastes and wishes (from various regions) sometimes required that he modify his technique, and selectively return to an earlier mode of execution to satisfy their demands. However, there is a clear and consistent undercurrent in his approach to his paintings that follows him throughout his career: his compulsion to rework and modify his compositions within the painting process itself (fig. 33). Much technical research has been carried out on works of Titian in the last decade or so and it can be made evident, primarily through X-radiography, that the artist often did not start to paint with a clear end in sight. According to contemporary descriptions of his working habits, he often had several paintings in progress and selectively revised them after a brief study, only to return to them at a later date.[45] By contrast with many of his colleagues, this is a quite per-

Fig. 33
Top: Titian, *Venus Blindfolding Cupid*, about 1565, Galleria Borghese, Rome.
Middle: X-radiograph revealing the artist's changes to the composition during execution.
Bottom: Unknown (18th-century?) artist's copy of Titian's earlier composition for the Borghese canvas, possibly copied from a version (now reduced in size) in the National Gallery of Art, Washington, DC.

Fig. 34
Detail illustrating Tintoretto's construction of form through line. Jacopo Tintoretto, *Baptism of Christ*, 1579–81
Scuola Grande di San Rocco, Venice

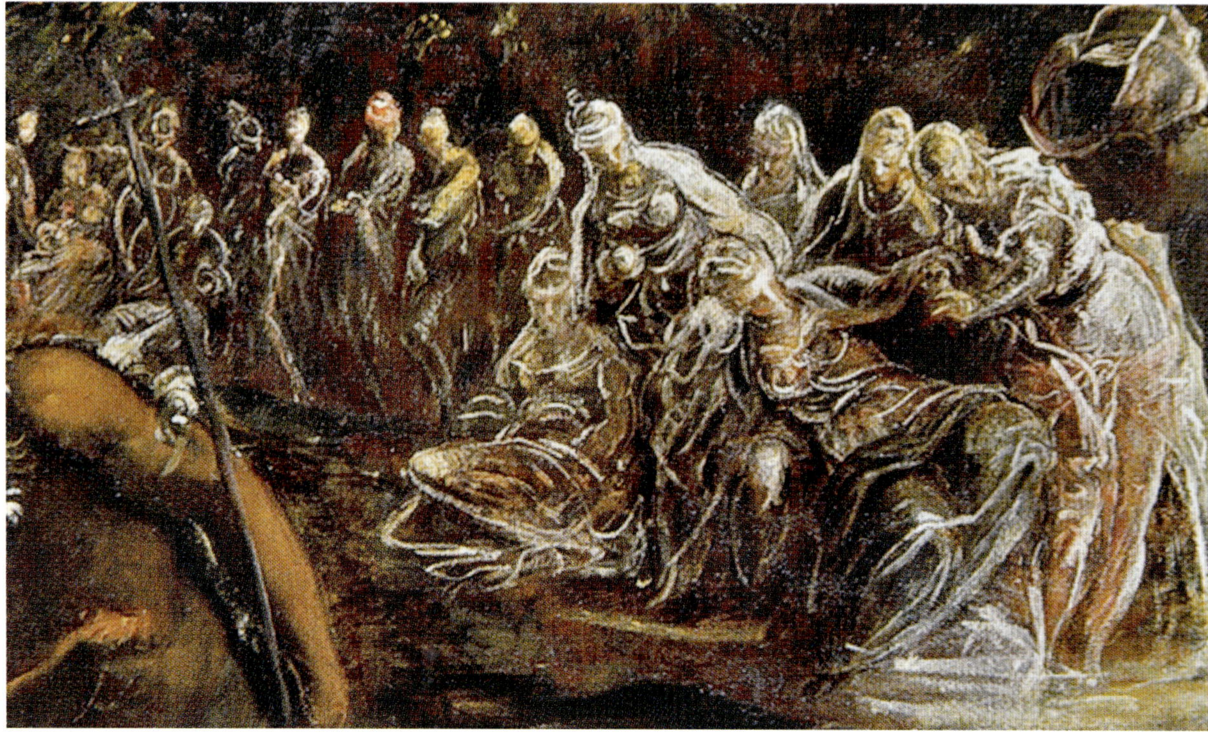

sonal and more "modern" approach to making art; however, it was not an approach that lent itself to efficient division of labor in a larger studio. This is why Titian's legacy as an artist and practitioner is not to be found within the larger projects for which Tintoretto and Veronese were better suited, but rather in the very personal and technically far-reaching images of his last years.[46]

Tintoretto was very industrious and capable as a painter, and he did not shy away from the most daunting tasks. He was calculating, however, in how he chose to spend his energies, concentrating on large-format cycles and portraiture, two modes of painting that Titian steered away from after midcentury.[47] Titian's *Assunta* for Santa Maria Gloriosa dei Frari (1516–18, fig. 50) was a landmark work that inspired numerous Venetian painters, as did the works that closely followed in San Giovanni e Paolo, and the altarpieces in Ancona and Verona. After his *Presentation of the Virgin in the Temple* (about 1534–38, fig. 13), however, he produced fewer large-scale commissions. It has also been pointed out that Titian may have exhausted much of his artistic interest, as well as clientele, in portraiture by midcentury, and focused instead on his mythologies, which seem to have fed him with more inspiration and income.

Boschini writes that when Tintoretto received a commission for a public space he would visit the location to estimate the volume and distance in which the image would be placed, and would construct the design and composition independently from aspects of color. This reinforces one of the differences between Tintoretto's approach and that of his rivals, Titian and Veronese: the sculptural or volumetric perspective in which he formulated his works. Infrared reflectography and X-radiography help show that Tintoretto's development of forms and figures from underdrawing to final painting was not divided into rigid steps, as was the case with many of his contemporaries. Often starting as quite fluid underdrawings, his contours transform into drawn paint strokes that tend to metamorphose into three-dimensional models seemingly made from looping spools of wire (fig. 34).[48] Not only did Tintoretto have an uncanny ability to design his forms as if in the round, but he also understood how to imbue his figures with a sense of gesture and dynamics in relation to the often large formats of his works (an approach later to be taken up by Tiepolo). With his higher levels of contrast and his decreased adherence to local color, he stands apart from Titian and Veronese and anticipates Caravaggio, just several decades away.

Veronese's approach to oil painting was influenced by his early training as a fresco painter, in which a systematic approach to applying color passages was necessary. This same technique can be seen in many of his wash drawings (preliminary designs), which echo his ability to systematically deconstruct his coloring process. Veronese painted with a sense of strong local color, often set within a clear and cooler (neutral) atmosphere, and there is often a notable definition between color passages, the sharpness of which the artist regulated with light applications of glazes. Although he is effectively a tonal painter in the Venetian sense, there are aspects of his technique that dip into the reserves of Central Italian chromatic theories.[49] This becomes particularly apparent in his systematic approach to depicting drapery, in which he juxtaposes colors, adjusting values of lightness and darkness to achieve a sense of form. This method of color juxtaposition tends to evoke a more abrupt chromatic separation than true tonal painting, which involves more fluid transitions. Ultimately, Veronese's method has roots in the ancient color-theory treatises of Aristotle and Pliny. Although he could often be comparatively subtle in his fusion of colors, Veronese appears to have been much more absorbed with the primary attributes of his painting materials—their vibrancy and their capacity to entice the viewer. An important aspect of his technique is the often sharp juxtaposition of contrasting colors for highlights (*cangianti*), a form of optical distortion sometimes used by fresco painters (most famously by Michelangelo on the ceiling of the Sistine Chapel, 1508–12) to achieve well-defined modeling that could be seen even at great distances (fig. 35). This was also a concept that was present in the work of northern masters from the early sixteenth century.

In execution, Veronese reveals a more systematic approach than either Titian or Tintoretto. This was indeed necessary for an artist working on his scale and with the number of assistants he needed to coordinate. In this respect, Veronese influenced Rubens and other Northern artists, who, like him, would break the painting process down into more clearly defined stages to be followed by numerous assistants, producing extensive passages that could be integrated into a seamlessly balanced whole. In working methods, as in materials and commissions, Veronese and his fellow Venetian painters reached beyond the Lagoon to engage not only one another but their fellow artists throughout the continent in dialogue, emulation, and competition.

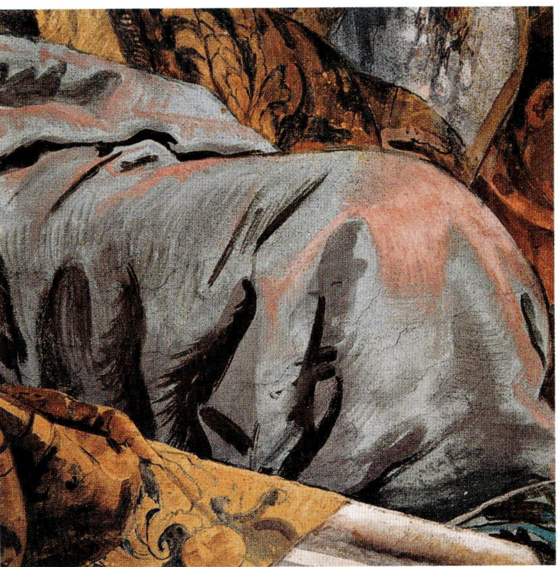

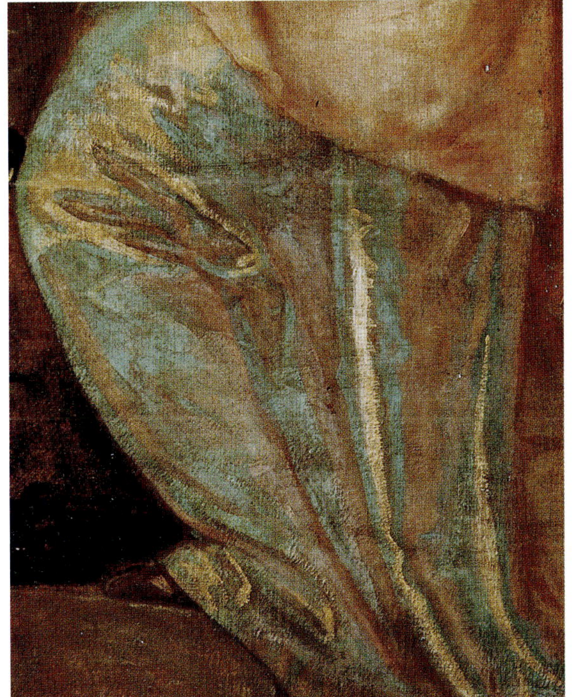

Fig. 35
Top: Detail of color separation (*cangianti*) in Tiepolo's figure of Europa, 1751–53, Würzburg Residenz. Bottom: Detail of color separation in Veronese's *Christ and the Samaritan*, about 1580, Kunsthistorisches Museum, Vienna.

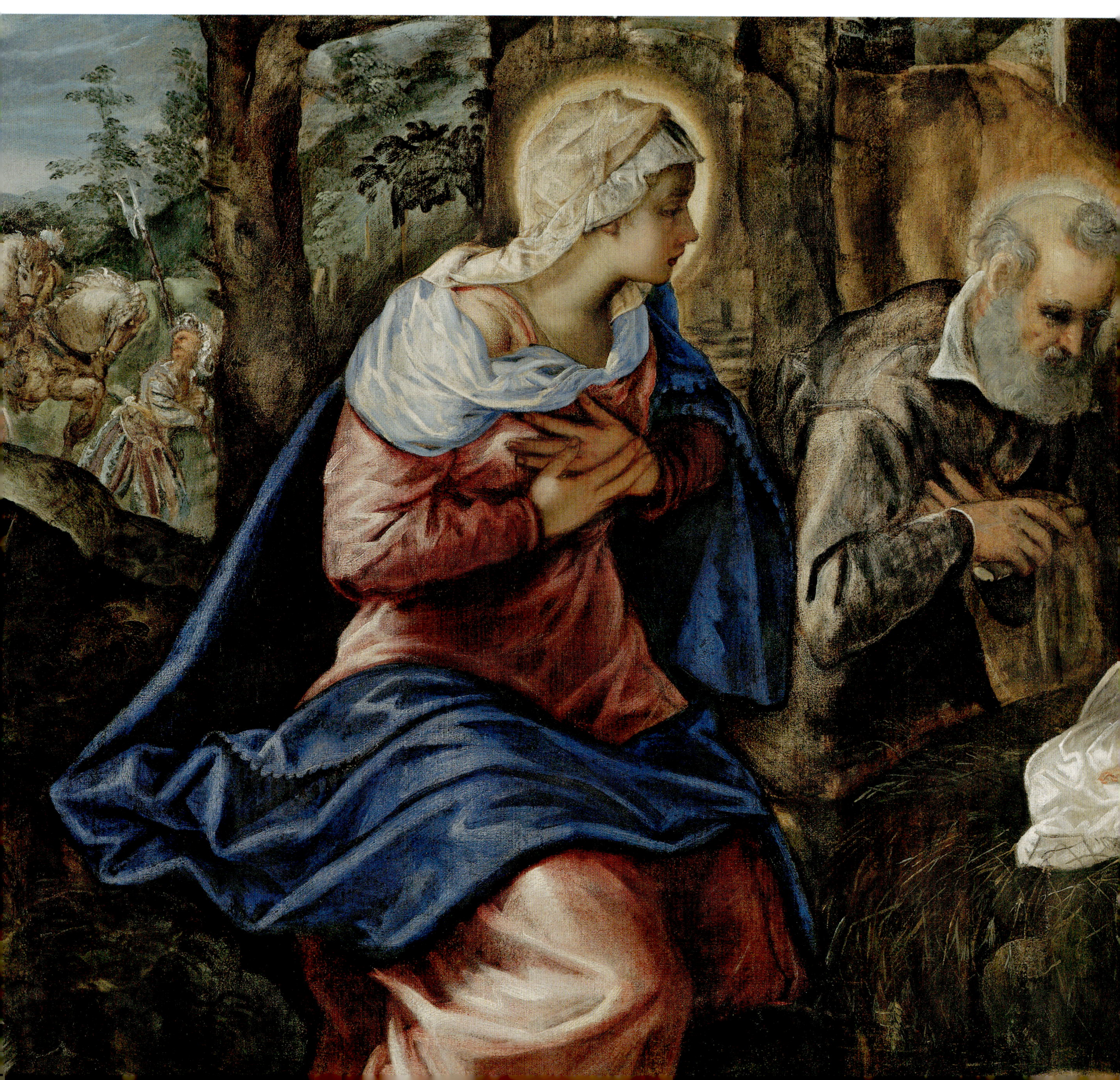

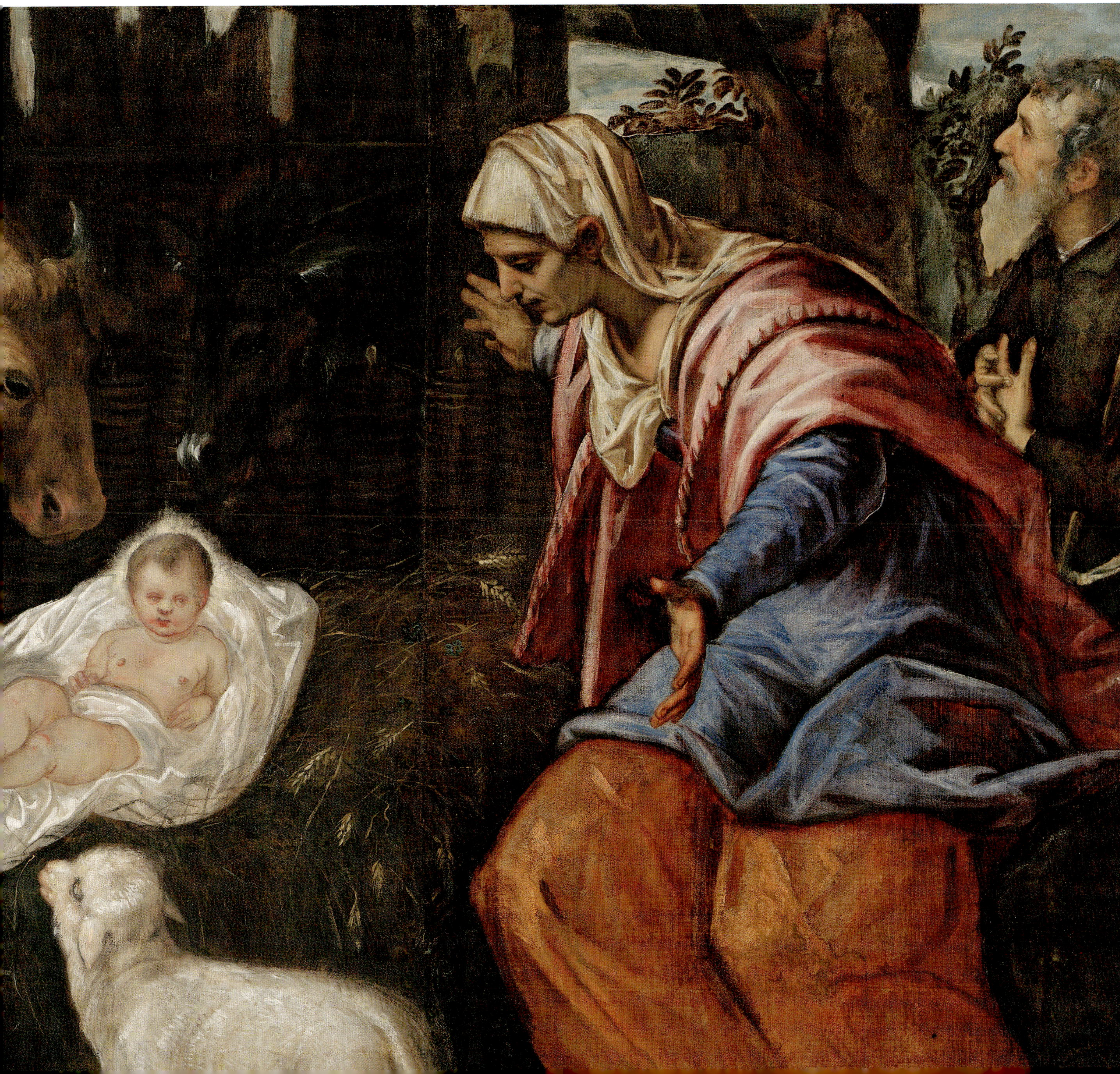

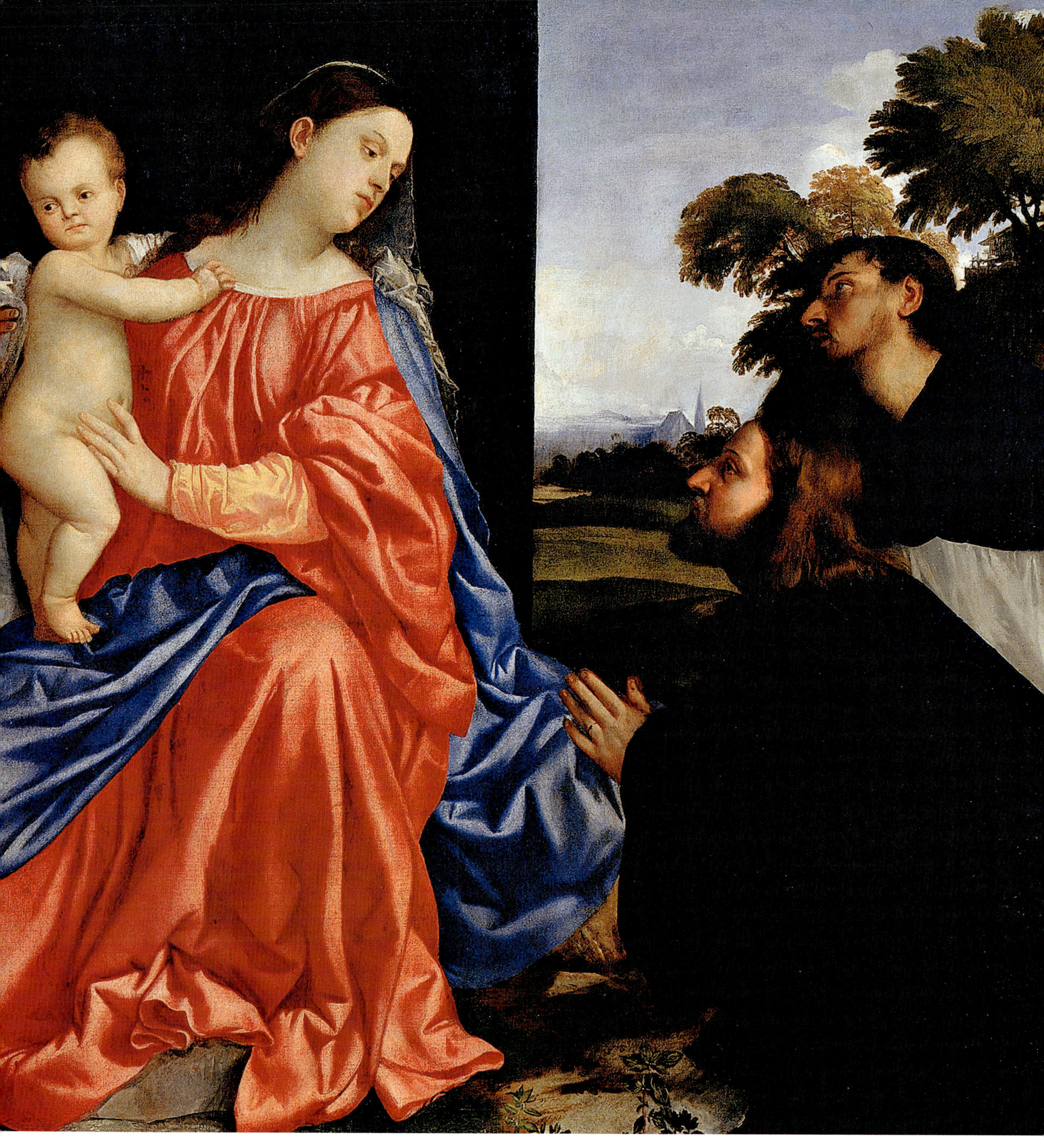

Prologue: The Transformation of Venetian Painting around 1500

Venetian artists and patrons transformed the conception of painting in the final years of the fifteenth century and the first two decades of the sixteenth. In this brief period, the materials, style, and subject matter of paintings changed fundamentally.[1] The greatest revolution came in the very substance of the painting: canvas became the standard support and oil the universal medium, replacing wooden panels and egg tempera. These materials permitted a style of softer contours, complex sequences of paint layers, and expressive brushstrokes. New approaches to the rendering of light and atmosphere, and new subjects such as landscape, innovative portraits, and the erotic nude—at first appreciated only by a small circle of clients and artists—soon became widespread in Venice. Demand for the services of specific painters gave these artists new status and a level of self-determination impossible only a generation earlier. Individuals began to acquire pictures not simply as aids to religious devotion but for their beauty. Often they purchased these paintings from sources other than the artists who had produced them. Thus the collector of paintings and the secondary art market, in a form we would recognize today, made their appearance.

One document linked to a lost picture sums up much of what is fascinating about Venetian painting in this period. A letter of October 25, 1510, from Isabella d'Este in Mantua to her agent in Venice instructs him to purchase a painting of "una nocte" ("night," meaning the Nativity) from the estate of the painter Giorgione. Within two weeks, the agent is forced to reply with the disappointing news that Giorgione had died of the plague and the painting was not found in his estate. The painter had in fact executed two treatments of the theme for private individuals, but neither would sell, even at an inflated price, since they had commissioned the pictures for their enjoyment.[2] This episode illustrates that Giorgione's pictures were rare and desirable, that private owners constituted his clientele, and that by the time of his early death his reputation had spread far beyond Venice. His paintings looked different from the Venetian art that had come immediately before, and this encouraged a new attitude to collecting.

These radical changes coincided with the last twenty years of Giovanni Bellini's career before his death in 1516, as well as with his pupil Titian's training, emergence as an independent artist, and triumph on the Italian stage. The overlap and exchange between two extremely talented generations—Bellini's and Titian's—help explain the extraordinary artistic ferment around 1500 in a fundamentally conservative, and indeed self-consciously serene, society. The older generation of painters comprised such established figures as Gentile and Giovanni Bellini, Vittore Carpaccio, and Cima da Conegliano. The rising generation included Giorgione, Sebastiano (later known as Sebastiano del Piombo), and Titian—all three of them pupils of Giovanni Bellini—and Palma Vecchio. A steady stream of foreigners, such as Albrecht Dürer from Nuremberg, who worked in Venice in 1505–7, ensured further ideas and receptive audiences. The concentration of talent in Venice is arguably as astonishing as that which flourished simultaneously in Florence, where Leonardo and Michelangelo competed with monumental frescoes for the Palazzo Vecchio, as Piero di Cosimo, Fra Bartolomeo, and the young Raphael looked on.

Although the year 1500 may seem too convenient a number to mark a watershed, it has some validity as a dividing line. In 1500 Jacopo de' Barbari published his famous woodcut map of Venice seen from the air, a demonstration of both technical virtuosity and of a thriving, and previously unimaginable, commercial market for giant prints. In March of that year, Leonardo visited Venice. Although his purpose was military engineering, he made a great impression both on older artists, such as Bellini, and younger ones, such as Giorgione, who may have discussed art with him and certainly saw his drawings.[3] Later in the century, Vasari wrote of how this contact with Leonardo changed Giorgione's art, making the younger artist the Venetian proponent of the *maniera moderna* and Leonardo's counterpart for Venice as the initiator of a new age there.[4]

Striking visual differences, embodying the fundamental shift from Quattrocento to Cinquecento, can be seen by comparing paintings executed just before and just after the turn of the century.[5] These innovations were not limited to younger painters such as Giorgione and Titian but were adopted as well by the older generation, above all Giovanni Bellini.[6] Other types of visual arts changed dramatically in this period as well, with the abandonment of the polyptych altarpiece in favor of the *pala* (single-field altarpiece) and the introduction of Renaissance architecture in place of the Gothic style that had predominated for more than a century.[7] Thus, while artistic style is generally in flux in any period, the start of the Cinquecento deserves credence as a key time of transition.

These momentous artistic developments took place during a time of political uncertainty and a war that threatened to annihilate Venice.[8] Intending to check Venetian territorial expansion in Northern Italy, the leaders of the great European powers—including the Papal States, France, the Holy Roman Empire, Spain, Mantua, and Ferrara—banded together as the League of Cambrai in December 1508 to defeat Venice and carve up its territories. On May 14, 1509, the sizable Venetian mercenary army was crushed by an equally large French force at Agnadello, east of Milan. The Venetian mainland empire collapsed almost immediately as the elites of the mainland cities quickly allied themselves with Maximilian I of Germany or Louis XII of France. The Venetian government and populace, which had been optimistic about the prospects for the war, were astonished and terrified by the defeat; as the first messengers arrived at the Palazzo Ducale the following day, "there began a great weeping and lamentation, and to put it better, a sense of panic," as recorded by the Venetian diarist Marin Sanudo. In the following days, Sanudo fretted as this collective "state of gloom" persisted: "I conclude, these are bad times: we see our ruin ahead, and nobody does anything."[9] Although the League's armies ravaged the mainland and arrived right at the edge of the Venetian lagoon, the city itself was spared. Reversed alliances and new campaigning quickly restored much of the Venetian *terraferma* territory, but Venice would never again dominate Italian affairs militarily.

Titian's generation came of age in this anxious era. The departure of one of the most talented members, Sebastiano, for Rome in August 1511 should be seen not just as resulting from the invitation by Agostino Chigi, a wealthy banker, but also against the backdrop of Venetian insecurity. Certain works of art, such as Giorgione's *Tempest* (fig. 39), have been interpreted as reflecting Venice's precarious situation, though that painting may date from before the outbreak of hostilities; other works that seem to express a yearning for more placid times have been seen as reactions to a climate of pessimism and fear.[10]

Despite these crises, Venice maintained sufficient competitive advantages at the start of the sixteenth century to ensure a steady demand for paintings and support a large number of painters. It remained an important mercantile center with an enormous concentration of capital, as well as headquarters of the European printing and publishing industry. Its wealth provided a broad base of art patronage. These conditions undoubtedly played a role in generating innovations in painting. One leading circumstance, however, was related not to human activity but rather to nature: Venice's physical setting in a saltwater lagoon. The context of humidity and salinity meant that fresco paint (that is, painting in fresh or wet plaster) did not set properly and often disintegrated rapidly. Venetian artists thus turned to canvas as an alternative to fresco. Canvas was not a novel support—it had long been employed for certain functions that required a lightweight surface for painting, such as processional banners or organ shutters—but it became common in Venice only in the last quarter of the Quattrocento.

A sign of this shift came in 1474, when the Venetian Senate decreed that the fresco cycle of great events in Venetian history in the Palazzo Ducale's Sala del Maggior Consiglio would be replaced by paintings on canvas.[11] This ruling acknowledged that canvas was henceforth the standard support for large mural decorations in Venice.[12] Enormous canvas paintings, such as Gentile Bellini's *Procession in Piazza San Marco* (fig. 49) of 1496, became common.

Besides its resilience to the Venetian climate, canvas enjoyed other advantages, being transportable, economical, and relatively lightweight. Canvas also permitted a conceptual breakthrough, since a large painting could be executed in one place (a painter's studio) and conveyed to its ultimate destination, such as a wall in a church or government building. That is, unlike the traditional media of mosaic and fresco, the use of canvas meant that mural painting did not need to be executed in situ. Moreover, canvas paintings were essentially unlimited in size; an artist could expand the pictorial field simply by sewing on another section of cloth. Painters had employed large canvases in horizontal formats starting in the late fifteenth century, but it took longer for them to understand the vertical scale implications of canvas. By the middle of the sixteenth century, Tintoretto made a subsequent breakthrough with enormously tall canvas paintings.[13] Mural decoration would never be the same.

The use of oils presented the second condition for the transformation of painting. The binder favored by fifteenth-century painters—tempera, made with egg yolk—dries quickly and needs to be built up in many thin layers, precluding thick or expressive brushstrokes. As such, the medium of tempera conditioned the message, generating a consistent stiffness and crispness of forms as well as an emphasis on local color. Although Giovanni Bellini and others in Venice had employed oil experimentally in the last quarter of the fifteenth century, typically in paintings on panel, oil finally supplanted tempera by the early sixteenth century, and consistent use unlocked its many advantages.[14] Slow-drying oil paints could be blended together over a longer period of time and mixed in a range of viscosity, permitting effects from thick, opaque textures (called impasto) to thin, translucent glazes. Suddenly, new possibilities of intense colors, shading, and detail were possible. In particular, painters now could depict light with new mastery, as seen in Giovanni Bellini's San Zaccaria altarpiece of 1505 (fig. 36), a painting originally on panel but transferred to canvas after it was taken to Paris by

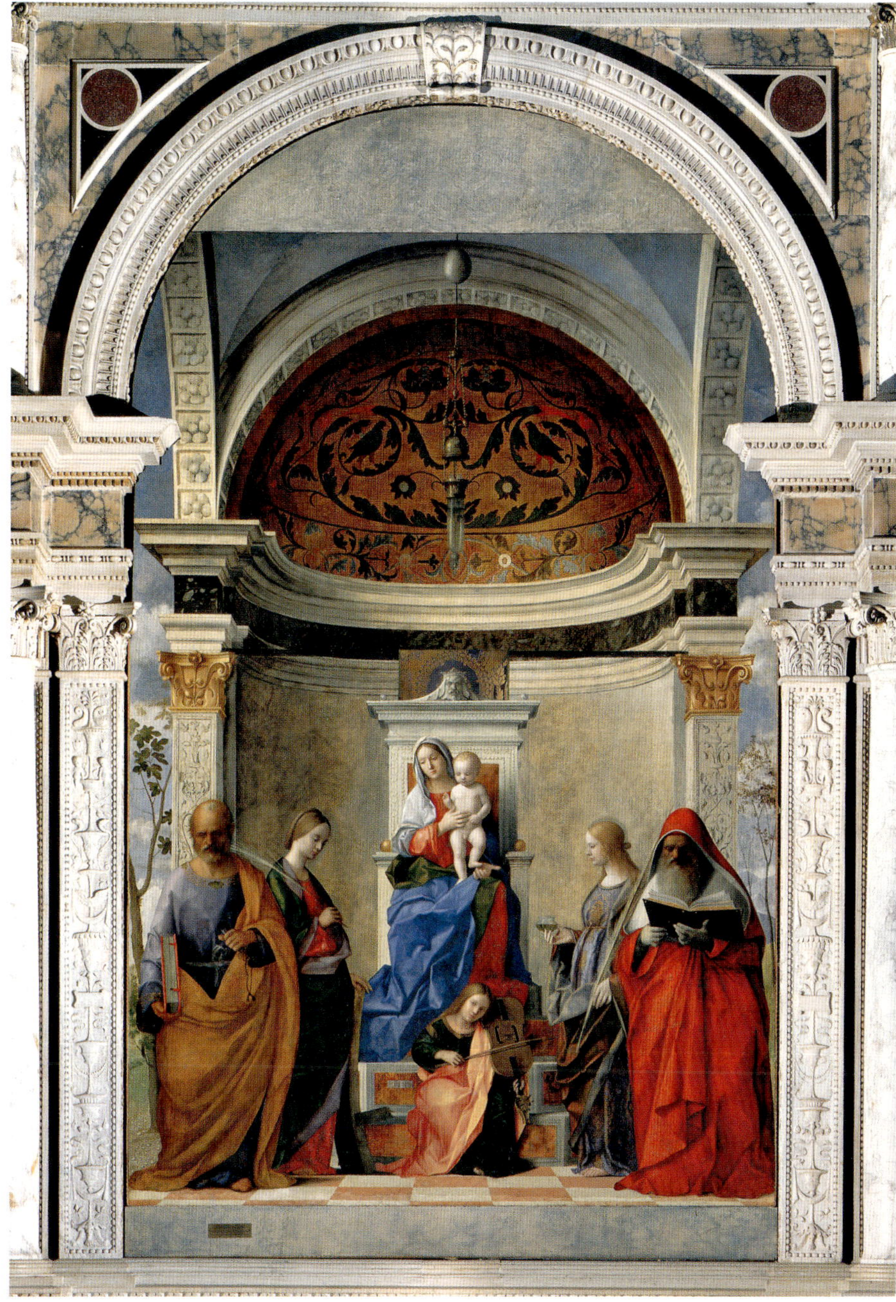

Fig. 36
Giovanni Bellini (Italian, about 1431–1516)
Virgin and Child Enthroned with Saints, 1505
Oil on canvas, transferred from panel
Church of San Zaccaria, Venice

Fig. 37
Sebastiano del Piombo (Italian, about 1485–1547)
Saint Louis of Toulouse, about 1509
Oil on canvas
Church of San Bartolomeo di Rialto, Venice (on deposit at Gallerie dell'Accademia)

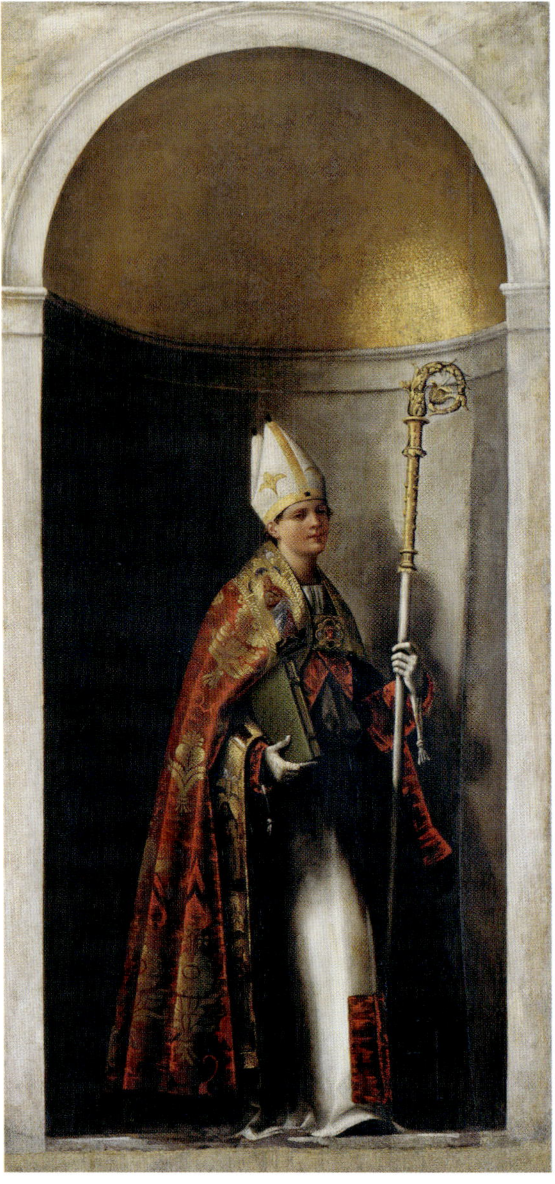

Napoleon. The effects of light visible in Bellini's altarpiece include both the soft glow in the mosaic dome and the sharp gleam of white highlights on glass. Bellini's *sacra conversazione* displays solemn figures clothed in deeply saturated colors, a careful coordination of the painted architecture with the altarpiece's frame, and a sense of atmosphere. Dürer must have had this painting in mind when he wrote from Venice to a friend in Nuremberg the next year, praising Bellini: "He is very old but he is still the best painter of all."[15] This high opinion of a seventy-year-old artist demonstrates both Bellini's continuing accomplishment and a Venetian reverence for seniority.

The real turning point in pictorial technique finally occurred soon after 1500, when Venetian artists united oil and canvas. As canvas supports became common for functions besides murals (for example, altarpieces and paintings for private devotion), Venetians seem to have been the first to understand the expressive implications of this combination. These painters, by employing a thin gesso priming, retained much of the uneven surface of the cloth and exploited this rough surface as they played with the texture of the oil medium. As David Rosand has written, "Paint stroked over the woven support left a broken, interrupted mark, lending a new vibrancy to the surface itself."[16] Forms were created not with taut contours, the mainstay of Florentine *disegno*, but through the caressing strokes of Venetian *colorito*. Moreover, thick applications of paint allowed brushstrokes to possess direction and energy. In his painting *Saint Louis of Toulouse* of about 1509 (fig. 37), Sebastiano took advantage of the tackiness of the oil medium and a variety of brushstrokes to render diverse textures far beyond his teacher Bellini's altarpiece of only a few years earlier. Sebastiano skillfully used thick paint to suggest heavy embroidery, the glow of mosaic tesserae, and the blurred sheen defining the cylindrical volume of the saint's crozier. The touch of the artist, his personality, is now evident, even immodestly so. Indeed, Sebastiano's bravura brushwork seems to have been unprecedented in Italy. He may have been more experimental and bold with his paint handling here because the *Saint Louis* was originally part of the inner shutters of the organ of San Bartolomeo di Rialto, and thus would have been placed high above and distant from most viewers. At the same time, the handsome young saint possesses a certain dreamy quality, a disposition adopted perhaps from Giorgione. The combination of extraordinary paint handling and lyrical mood demonstrates that Sebastiano was ahead of his Venetian contemporaries—and his invitation to move to Rome comes as no surprise.

Even in the conventional format of the altarpiece, Sebastiano used the oil medium with groundbreaking results. A comparison between his altarpiece in the church of San Giovanni Crisostomo (fig. 38) of about 1510 and Giovanni Bellini's San Zaccaria altarpiece, painted just five years before, shows that the young artist far surpassed Bellini in the depiction of glowing light and palpable air.[17]

Through dramatically softened contours, Sebastiano created a striking naturalism for the figures and the space they occupy. He coupled these innovations in pictorial technique with an unusual variation of the traditional *sacra conversazione* format by placing the central saint, Saint John Chrysostom, in profile and engaged in his writing. John the Baptist, in the right foreground, displays a dreamy quality similar to depictions of him in paintings by Giorgione, as well as in Sebastiano's own *Saint Louis*. His complex pose, echoed by the twisting scroll and emphasized by the flowing orange drapery, seems designed to attract attention. It would be fascinating to know if Dürer would still have regarded Bellini as the best Venetian painter had he returned to Venice in 1511 and seen Sebastiano's altarpiece.

As Sebastiano and particularly Giorgione realized, oil-on-canvas painting opened up new kinds of meteorological effects: humidity, haze, fog, dawn, dusk, as well as both stark and soft shadows. Sensitive evocations of different times of day and different levels of moisture could replace the cool, even light found in tempera painting. The proving ground for the greatest experimentation of these effects seems to have been in small pictures for private collectors. One of these, Giorgione's *Tempest* (fig. 39), offers a striking example of this new attention to the properties of air, with figures posed in a lush and moist setting; the damp air has a palpable presence. Yet the novel representation of fertile nature and coming storm is only the beginning of this picture's originality.[18] Among other things, *The Tempest* displays an emphasis on landscape previously seen only in certain religious works, such as Giovanni Bellini's *Baptism of Christ* (fig. 40). In earlier Venetian painting, landscape was a backdrop, often relegated to the edges of a composition and dominated by the saints. The diminutive scale of Giorgione's figures, in contrast, makes the enveloping atmosphere of the landscape and its deep recession all the more prominent. Moreover, the painting shows a variety of brushwork: fine stippling to craft the lighter colored foliage, thick impasto for the stark forms of white cloth. Below the surface, however, there are even more impressive innovations. X-radiography reveals that there was once a second seated female nude in the bottom left corner, beneath—and perhaps originally instead of—the man. She seems to have been later moved to the other side of the composition.

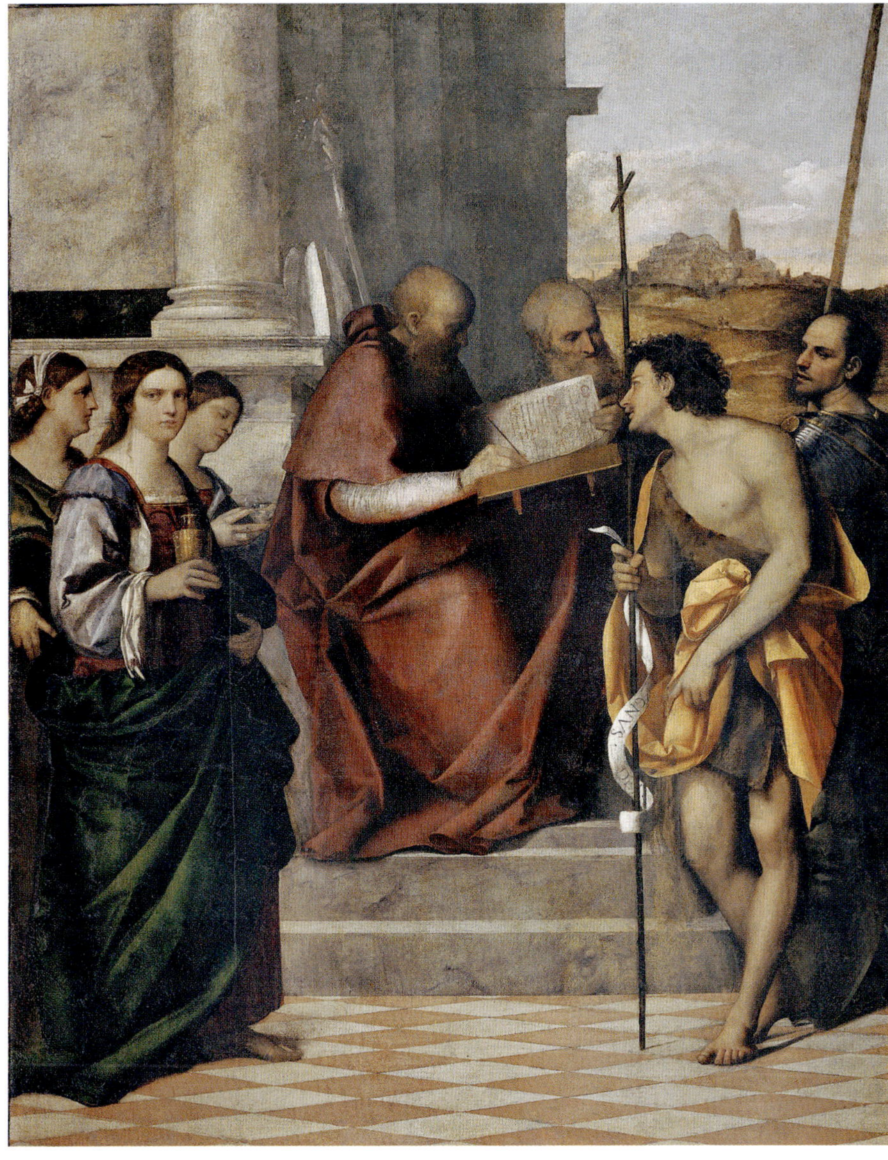

Fig. 38
Sebastiano del Piombo (Italian, about 1485–1547)
San Giovanni Crisostomo Altarpiece, about 1510
Oil on canvas
Church of San Giovanni Crisostomo, Venice

The painter also changed the costumes of both the male and the visible female, and many details of the background, including elements of the structures and foliage, were once different.[19] Rather than conforming to ideas developed in detailed preparatory drawings—characteristic of Central Italian as well as earlier Venetian artistic practice—Giorgione made major alterations during the execution of the picture. This improvisational attitude to compositions became common practice for painters in Venice, as is borne out in many dramatic modifications by Titian, Tintoretto, and Veronese as they painted their works.

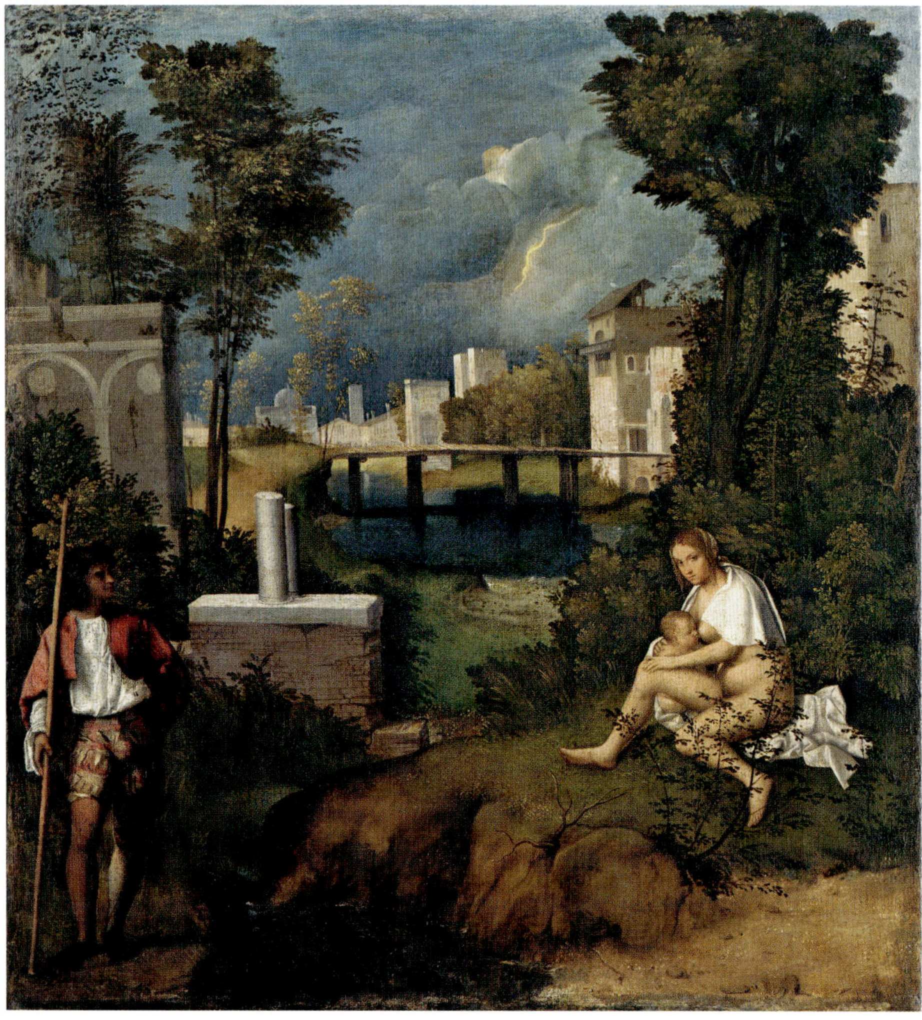

Fig. 39
Giorgione (Italian, about 1477–1510)
The Tempest, about 1506
Oil on canvas
Gallerie dell'Accademia, Venice

While *The Tempest* beguiles the viewer with its evocative setting, it confounds the scholar with its ambiguous subject. The setting has been located as the city of Padua, and the flash of lightning has been seen as a nod to the ancient Greek painter Apelles, who had painted lightning, something that according to Pliny the Elder "cannot be represented in pictures."[20] Despite numerous attempts to determine the story depicted, as an allegory or subject from classical mythology (both categories implied by the female nude), no satisfactory interpretation has been put forward.[21] In this interpretive impasse, it is worth considering whether Giorgione intended his subject to be deliberately enigmatic and known to very few, possibly just himself. *The Tempest* seems more about evoking mood than recounting a narrative, an elusive approach that is closer to poetry than conventional painting. The subtlety, not to mention complexity, of the image marks a new dynamic among painting, painter, and audience. As the public grew to appreciate these kinds of pictures, the social status of artists in Venice grew concomitantly. In 1511, the same year that Sebastiano del Piombo was lured away to Rome, a painter of the older generation, Cima, tried to increase the influence of figure painters within the guild over those artisans who painted signs, made playing cards, or designed textiles. Although Cima's attempt did not succeed—Venetians evinced a strong preference for stability and the status quo—this episode shows that even unadventurous painters were gaining a new self-confidence as artists and wanted to separate themselves from mere craftsmen.[22]

In light of innovative works such as *The Tempest*, it can be argued that while traditional categories of paintings endured, the modern concept of the painting was born in Venice in the first years of the sixteenth century. Three characteristics appeared simultaneously for the first time in European art. One, these works were oil paintings on canvas. Two, they may have been painted at the artist's initiative. Three, they were not created for a specific location. The combination of these three factors constitutes the modern easel picture, whereby a painting is understood as an independent object and not necessarily a specific commission or decoration. These modern paintings were not executed on-site but rather in the artist's private world, his studio. When the work was finished, potential buyers would come calling. Eventually, a secondary market for paintings, including even portraits, developed. This modern conception of painting eventually spread throughout Europe and, despite the range of new media employed in the twentieth and twenty-first centuries, still obtains today.

The Tempest is only the most famous example of this new kind of picture. Many paintings highlighted in the present volume may also have been created at the artist's initiative and sold to a client later, from small-scale erotic works such as Titian's *Flora* (cat. 5) and *Venus Rising from the Sea (Venus Anadyomene)* (cat. 6) to large religious canvases by Tintoretto and Veronese. Some pictures, such as Titian's late *Boy with Dogs in a Landscape* (cat. 48), seem to have perpetuated the elusive and poetic quality of some early Cinquecento paintings. Certainly, patrons continued to commission works and to exercise considerable influence over artists, and the majority of pictures were probably instigated by clients.[23] Yet even these works profited from the new expressive brushwork, treatments of light, and softer contours possible with oil-on-canvas painting. These materials, and an approach to handling that stressed coloring over drawing, gave Venetian paintings an appearance distinctive from those made elsewhere in Italy.

Moreover, Titian's career in particular demonstrates how he leveraged not just Giorgione's paint handling but also the new sense of artistic independence. Titian frequently turned down requests from the most important rulers and prelates, both in Italy and abroad. He maintained an unusual degree of artistic freedom, working in effect as a court painter for the Duke of Mantua and particularly the Hapsburg family, though he spent most of his years in Venice.[24] Even when dealing with the most prestigious patron in Europe, King Philip II of Spain, Titian had enough latitude to pick the individual subjects of paintings, work at his own pace, and change his mind, taking up new topics and abandoning pendants as the spirit moved him. This growing sense of artistic and personal independence was not limited to the Venetian artists of the younger generation. A series of letters beginning in 1496 between Isabella d'Este (who later unsuccessfully tried to acquire the Giorgione Nativity) and her agent in Venice shows how this important patron failed when she tried to instruct Giovanni Bellini to paint against his inclinations. Bellini insisted on taking his time, delaying progress for five years. Finally, in 1501, the agent advised Isabella to "give him the liberty to do what he pleases."[25] Later, a humanist friend, Pietro Bembo, recommended that she acquiesce to the painter's choices for iconography and style, "accustomed as he says always to roam at his will in paintings."[26] Isabella's desire to own a work by Bellini forced her to accept the artist's terms; as Rona Goffen puts it, Bellini had obtained "the kind of artistic license that Leonardo and even Michelangelo perhaps dreamed of but rarely achieved in commissioned works."[27] The loss of leverage by patrons as important as Isabella represented a distinct advantage for painters, and this shift accelerated in later generations.

The years around 1500 fundamentally changed Venetian and even European painting. It would be a mistake, however, to consider the age of Giorgione, Sebastiano, and the young Titian as necessarily the pinnacle of Venetian painting. It is important to remember that this period was merely the starting point of Titian's long career, one that reached fulfillment in the competitive atmosphere of the mid-Cinquecento. Just as Bellini had first guided younger painters but then learned from them, so forty years later Titian inspired Tintoretto and Veronese, only to then recalibrate his own art in response to their aesthetic challenges.

— FI

Titian Emerges

GIOVANNI BELLINI
and workshop
Virgin and Child with Saints,
about 1505–8
The Metropolitan Museum of
Art, New York
(cat. 1)

TITIAN
Virgin and Child with Saint Catherine, Saint Dominic, and a Donor, about 1513–14
Fondazione Magnani Rocca,
Mamiano di Traversetolo
(cat. 2)

In the first decade of the Cinquecento, one of the most distinctive painters in Western art emerged from the anonymity of the early Renaissance workshop. These two pictures, painted within a decade of each other, share the same subject—the *sacra conversazione*, a grouping of saints flanking the Virgin and Child—yet fundamental differences between them immediately become apparent. While the first picture is painted on panel, the second employs a canvas support. More significantly, the second shows a marked advance in conception over the first, displaying greater intensity of poses, more thoughtful interactions of the figures, and a new grandeur. Not only do these paintings illustrate the transformation of Venetian painting at the start of the sixteenth century, they chart Titian's own appearance as an independent artist.

Virgin and Child with Saints, by Giovanni Bellini and workshop, is the kind of picture—in composition, figure type, and technique—that the young Titian would have learned to paint while in Bellini's *bottega*, when it was perhaps the largest painters' workshop in Italy.[28] As such, the painting offers a plausible example of Titian's starting point, from a time before he began absorbing the innovations of Giorgione and Sebastiano. Although this panel displays signs of studio assistance, it is a large and attractive example of the high level of works coming from Bellini's workshop and, despite some lukewarm appreciations in the literature, deserves to be better known.[29] The second picture, Titian's *Virgin and Child with Saint Catherine, Saint Dominic, and a Donor*, executed perhaps as little as five years later, demonstrates Titian's remarkable arrival as a mature painter, one who now directed a workshop of his own. Titian's canvas is not mentioned in any of the period sources, and its genesis and early history remain a mystery. Only in recent decades has the painting begun to receive the attention it warrants; Paul Joannides declared it "probably the most important Titian discovery of the twentieth century."[30] The picture shows a mastery of the possibilities of oil on canvas: a dramatic range of light and shadow, modulated by delicate shading—particularly in the faces and hands of Saint Dominic and the unidentified male donor—as well as the luxurious treatment of the ample fabrics. Even in the conservative format of the *sacra conversazione*, Titian's painting confirms the emergence of a confident artistic personality.

The size of Bellini's panel and the number of figures it depicts—four standing saints flanking the seated Virgin and Child—indicate a significant commission. The patron of Bellini's painting is not known, though his name and those of his family might be reflected in the particular saints chosen: from left to right, Peter, Catherine of Alexandria (whose attribute of the spiked wheel is visible where the draperies of Peter and the Virgin part), Lucy, and John the Baptist. Both female saints carry palm branches, signifying their status as martyrs. The deep red marble parapet that runs along the lower edge of the painting provides a base to the composition and emphasizes the effect of a windowsill.[31] By serving as a boundary between the space within the painting and our world, the parapet has the curious effect of making the figures appear closer and more present. The attention paid to the texture of the stone is just one of the impressive passages in the work, while the careful treatment of fabrics, particularly the iridescent shot silk of the lining of the Virgin's cloak, also compels our admiration. The faces of John the Baptist and Lucy on the right are delicately rendered and probably the highest in quality, suggesting that they are by Bellini's own hand. Lucy's jar, one section in excellent condition, is also particularly well painted. Technical investigations reveal the care that went into the execution of this painting, including preparatory drawings underneath the paint.[32] The work also makes shrewd use of materials, such as the glaze of costly lapis lazuli layered over the cheaper azurite and white lead to create the rich blue of the Virgin's mantle. Although only a limited number of pigments were employed, the juxtapositions of the colors are harmonious and sophisticated.

Despite many competent, even beautiful, areas, however, the composition is not entirely successful.

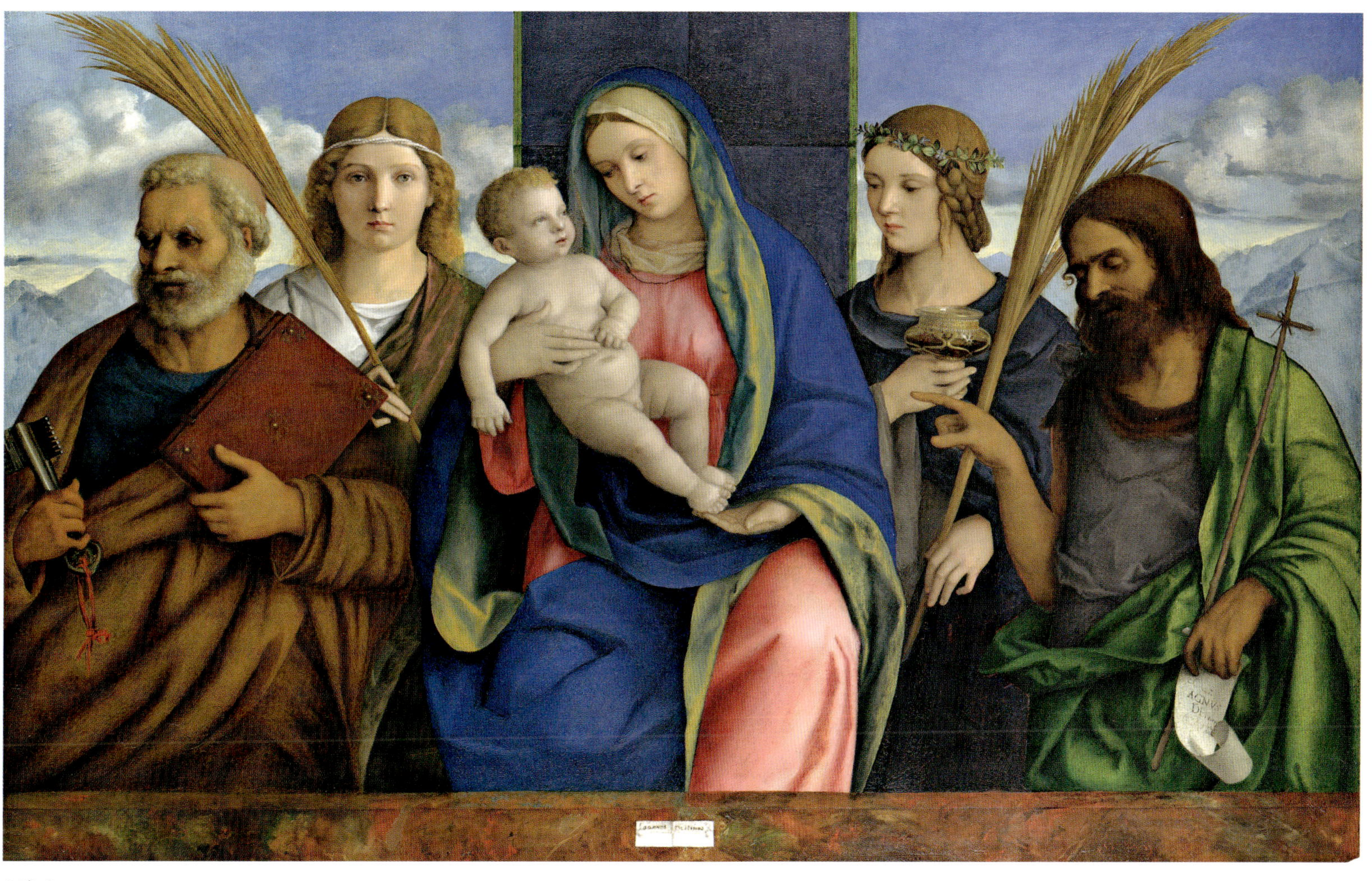

cat. 1

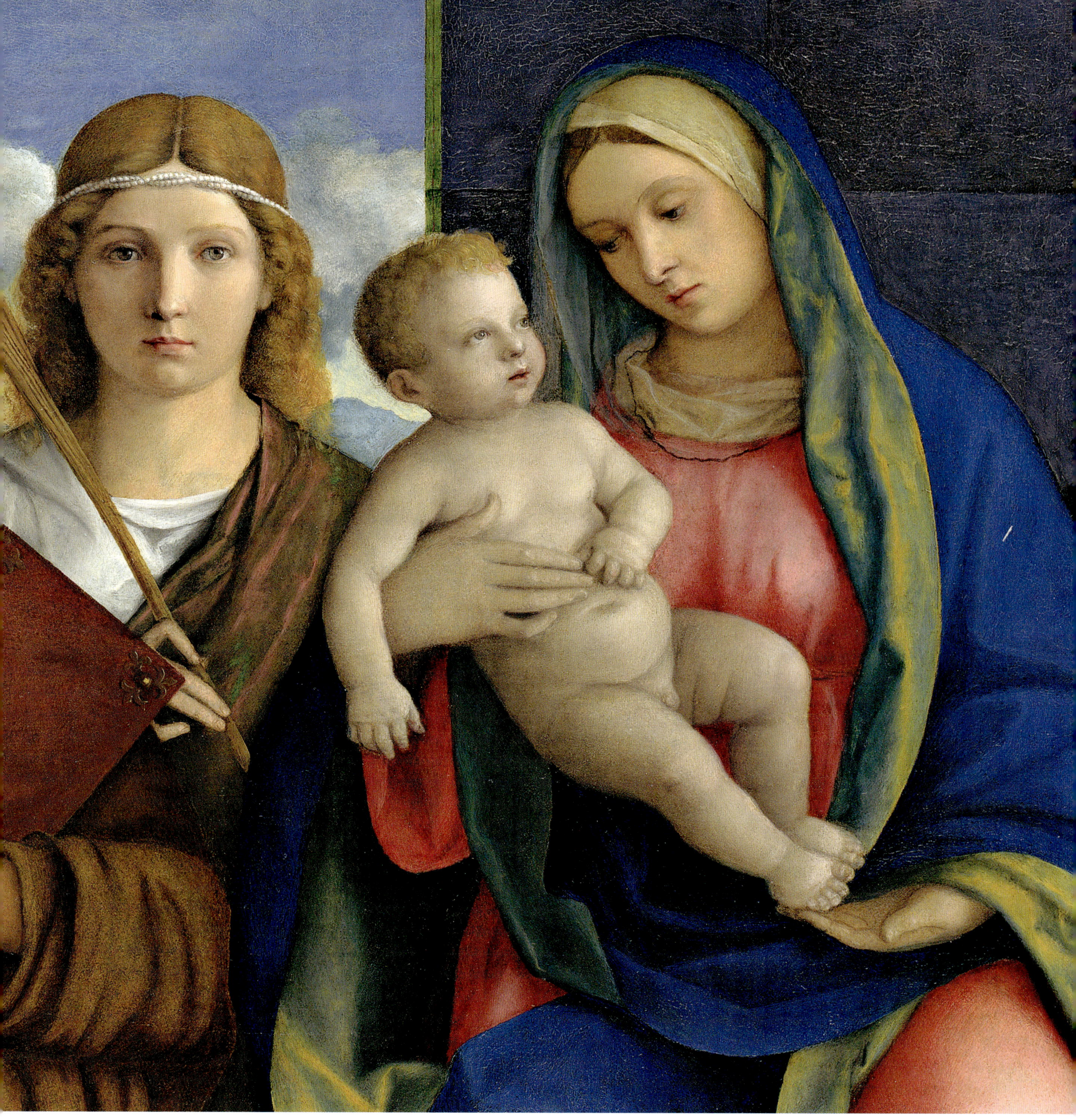

The saints seem to jockey for space. Saint Peter, rather than focusing attention on the Virgin and Child, looks to his right and out of the picture. Saint Catherine does not relate to those around her but rather gazes straight ahead; she also seems out of scale compared to those who stand before her. John the Baptist performs his role as herald of Christ by pointing, yet he does not join Lucy in looking at the infant. The overall composition seems additive, suggesting that Bellini employed figures originally used for other paintings. Thus the picture as a whole is perhaps no more than the sum of its parts.

Although the Bellini panel has sometimes been dated to 1510 or soon afterward, it seems unlikely the painting was executed that late. Probable origins of some of the figures can be traced to paintings some fifteen or twenty years earlier, including a John the Baptist from the *Baptism of Christ* in the church of Santa Corona, Vicenza (fig. 40), generally dated to 1500–1502; a Saint Peter (who closely resembles his present counterpart) on the inner shutters for the church of the Miracoli (Galleria dell' Accademia, Venice), dated to the 1490s; the reclining Christ Child, with his oddly nonchalant pose, who derives from a standing figure of Christ such as in the *Madonna of the Little Trees* of 1487 (Galleria dell'Accademia, Venice); and the Virgin herself, for whom the figure of Mary in the San Zaccaria altarpiece of 1505, with its similarly poignant expression and bulky drapery, offers an excellent point of departure. Moreover, the panel looks fundamentally different from Bellini's last works, which display the influence of Giorgione and Sebastiano. All told, a date of 1505–8, or right after the San Zaccaria altarpiece, seems most convincing—roughly the period when Titian served in Bellini's *bottega*.[33]

The signature raises another significant point. At first glance, the pastiche composition and visible disparities in quality seem to belie the prominent attribution on the *cartellino*—a fictive piece of paper, here depicted as if unfolded and adhered to the front of the parapet—that declares the painting's origin in the workshop of "Ioannes Bellinus." The signature not only announces the artist's presence but may also have underscored the Venetian pedigree, such signatures having become very common in Venice by the end of the fifteenth century. In Venetian workshop practice, the signature did not mean that the painting was necessarily executed

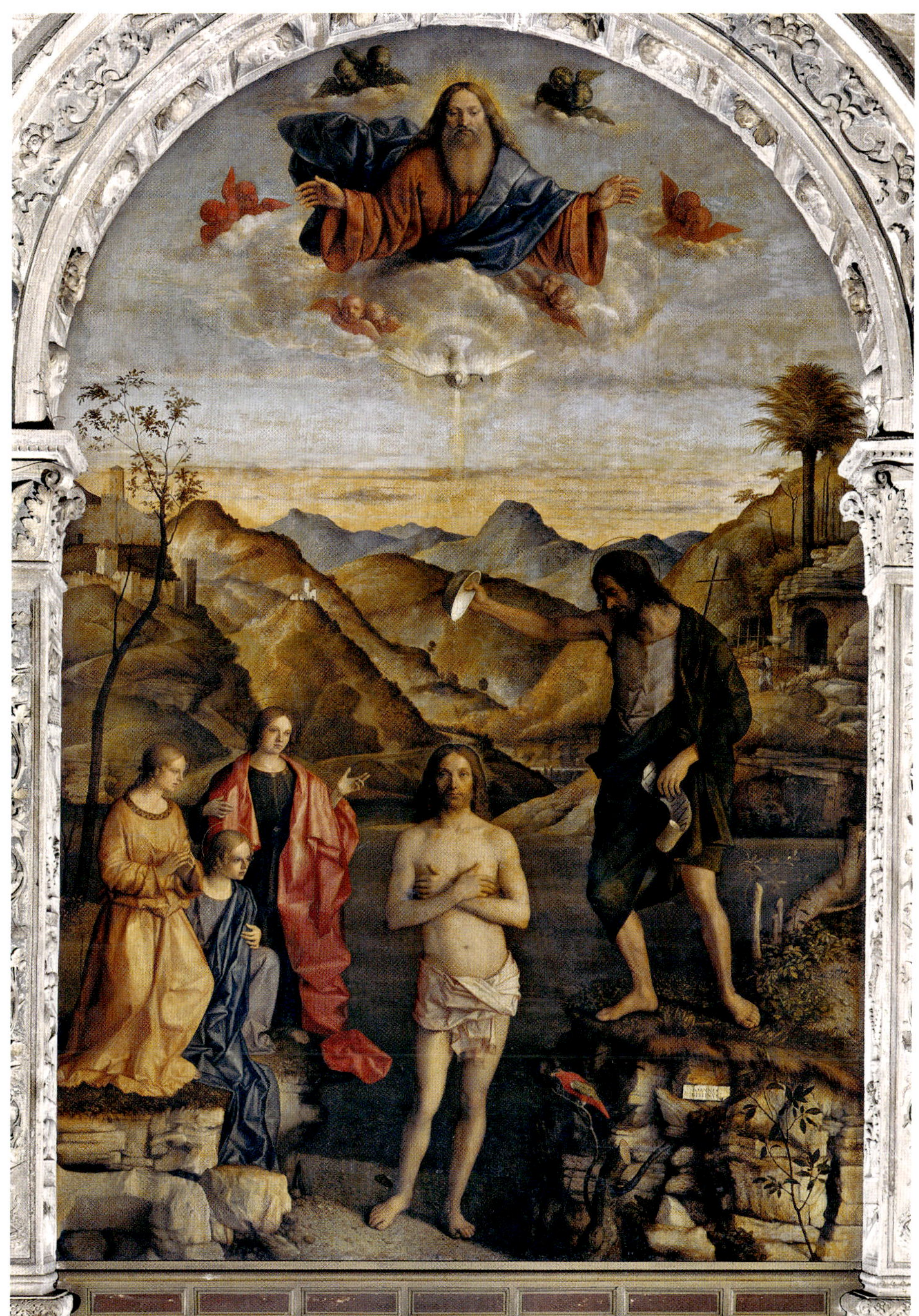

Fig. 40
Giovanni Bellini (Italian, about 1431–1516)
Baptism of Christ, 1500–1502
Oil on canvas
Church of Santa Corona, Vicenza

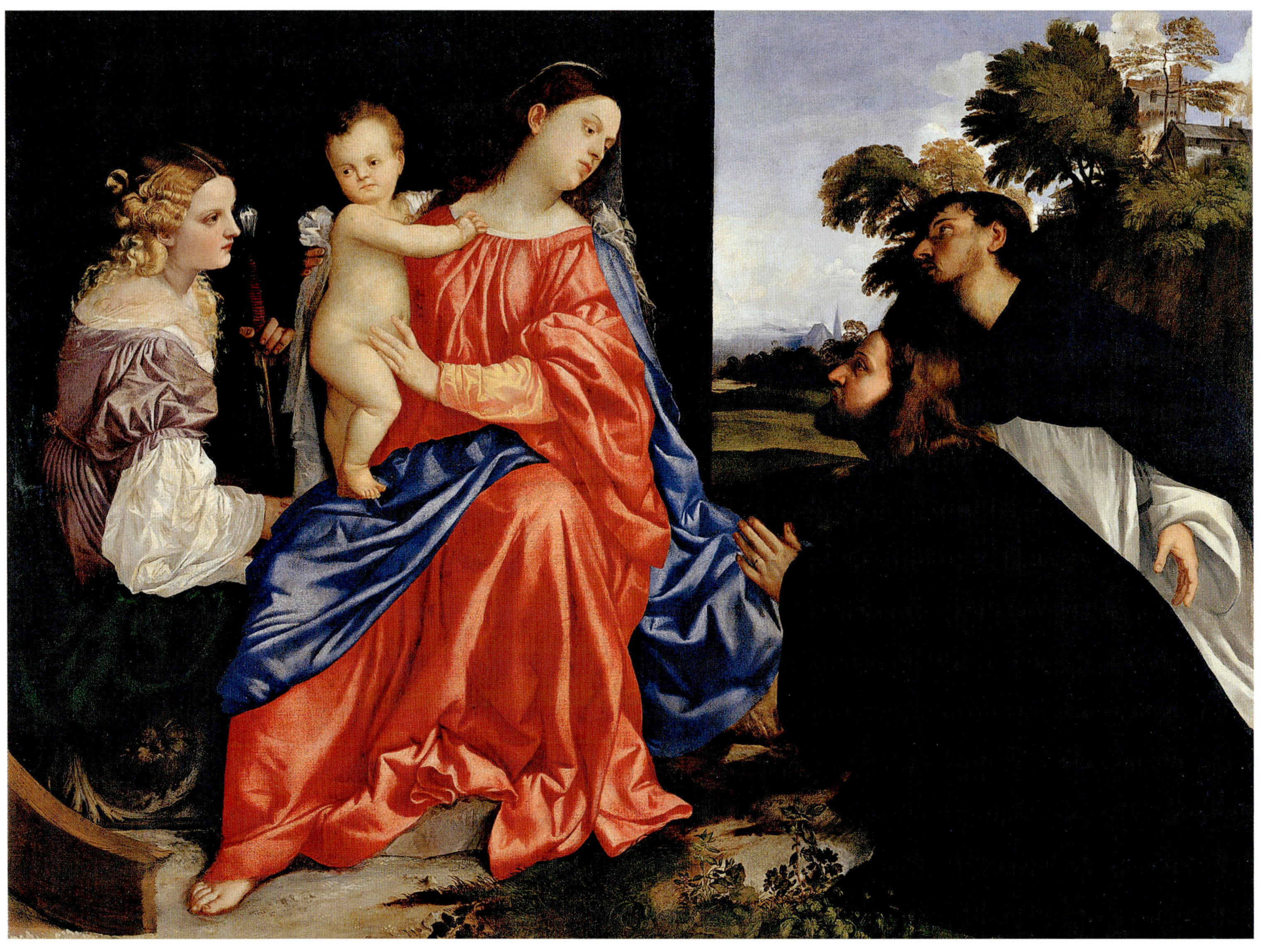

cat. 2

by Giovanni himself, however, but rather that he regarded the picture as acceptable to the high standards of his shop. As Louisa Matthew has pointed out, "A standardized signature increased the recognizability of a painter's pictures, and in the traditional fashion no differentiation would have been made by many patrons between the various hands—masters, assistants, and apprentices—within a single shop."[34] This organization of Bellini's workshop required individual members, including at one point the young Titian, to subsume their own manners to the house style. An analogy for our time might be a restaurant under the "brand" of a celebrity chef, in which the diner accepts that the chef did not necessarily prepare the meal in person. Rather, the chef devises the menu, designs the room, trains the staff to ensure certain standards, and creates "signature dishes," stressing the individual touch in a product typically (and somewhat ironically) delegated to assistants. Although the distinctive brushwork of Titian, Tintoretto, and Veronese would cause customers in Venice to become more discerning by the middle of the sixteenth century, and patrons to reject the claim that the product of the *bottega* and the master's hand were one and the same, the institution of the workshop still held sway throughout the three painters' careers.

The striking individuality of Titian's early *Virgin and Child with Saint Catherine, Saint Dominic, and a Donor* demonstrates that the young painter not only absorbed the lessons of his teachers, particularly Giovanni Bellini and Giorgione, but by this time had moved beyond them. The figures in the painting interact with each other in a mood of fervent yet graceful piety. Whereas Bellini's figures are motionless and somewhat unrelated to each other, Titian's painting includes an ingenious narrative element: from their poses, it is clear that just before this the Virgin and Child had been interacting with Saint Catherine. The donor and Saint Dominic have just arrived from the right, suddenly drawing the gazes of both women, while the Christ Child has not yet turned his head to receive them. Titian has placed these figures in a believable setting, with a view to a distant landscape in the manner of Giorgione. Bellini's panel featured the Dolomite Mountains seen through crisp air, as they appear from the lagoon after a thunderstorm. By contrast, the atmosphere in Titian's canvas displays a palpable presence. The back wall plays a similar role to Bellini's cloth of honor in emphasizing the most important figures, but here the backdrop defines the left side rather than center of the composition. There are accomplished passages throughout Titian's picture, though the artist must have wished to draw special attention to Catherine, who makes her counterpart in Bellini's panel seem bland. Titian has given his Catherine a delicate complexion and wavy locks that fall gently on her shoulders, and dressed her in shiny, crinkly fabrics. It has been noted that the roots of Catherine's hair are dark, implying that she has bleached it.[35] The beauty of a sacred figure is here grounded in the experience of daily life. Such elements of feminine allure as delicate skin, golden hair, and luxurious fabrics reappear often in Titian's work, though in some cases in a decidedly secular guise, such as the *Flora* (cat. 5) of three or four years later. A final flourish in the present picture is the sensitively treated face of the donor, an early Titian portrait of distinction, who is nevertheless literally overshadowed by the handsome, idealized Dominic. Even so, it is easy to imagine that compared to Bellini's client, Titian's patron—whoever he might have been—was the more satisfied.

— FI

The Devotional Close-Up

CIRCLE OF GIOVANNI BELLINI
Christ Carrying the Cross, about 1505–10
Isabella Stewart Gardner Museum, Boston
(cat. 3)

TITIAN
Christ Carrying the Cross, 1565–70
Museo Nacional del Prado, Madrid
(cat. 4)

Like the previous comparison of two approaches to the *sacra conversazione*, these two paintings of Christ carrying the cross contrast a picture on panel with a later one on canvas. In this case, however, the difference between them spans more than half a century and represents the extraordinary evolution of Venetian painting from an art based on hard contours to one emphasizing coloring and open brushwork—a revolution largely brought about by Titian. Although the 1505–10 panel has occasionally (and unconvincingly) been attributed to Titian himself, its real importance lies in its encapsulation of meticulous Venetian handling at the moment of Titian's training, thus offering a point of departure for his artistic development. The second picture, completed by Titian in his last decade of activity, depicts the same iconography, but here the artist exploits the expressive possibilities of the canvas surface to produce effects of loose brushwork unimaginable a half century earlier.

Both paintings show Christ bearing his cross on the way to his crucifixion at Calvary. Both feature strong geometric compositions, established by the diagonals of the cross, and highlight the eerie intensity of Christ's transfixing gaze. Although his expression is perhaps more reproachful in the panel and more fraught in the canvas, each painting emphasizes a connection with the viewer, generated through details such as the single tear that appears in both. If the first painting is timeless, the second contains enough context to pinpoint a specific moment mentioned in three of the Gospels. In these brief passages, Simon the Cyrenian, selected from the crowds following Christ, is obliged to help Jesus with his burden.[36]

Such concentrated religious images are often labeled *Andachtsbild*, or "devotional pictures," a category that flourished in the late Middle Ages and early Renaissance. These are images for private contemplation, typically in close-up, often with a single figure extracted from a narrative sequence. As in icons, the tight focus of these paintings promotes direct access for the viewer. Sixten Ringbom has discussed how the cropped compositions of fifteenth-century Northern Italian and Northern European painting and their implied window formats engaged the empathy of the beholder.[37] Ringbom cited several images, including a Milanese woodcut from about 1500 (Museum of Fine Arts, Boston) and a metalpoint drawing by Leonardo of the head of Christ, his hair grabbed by a tormentor's hand (Gallerie dell'Accademia, Venice), that served as prototypes for a whole group of paintings made in Venice and Northern Italy in the early sixteenth century. Among these are a canvas in the Scuola Grande di San Rocco, the attribution of which has been debated between Titian and Giorgione since the sixteenth century, and several paintings closely related to the present panel.[38]

The singular character of this picture, now in the Isabella Stewart Gardner Museum, has always been recognized; in the second half of the nineteenth century, while still in the possession of the Zileri dal Verme family of Vicenza, it was widely thought to be by Giorgione. When Isabella Stewart Gardner decided to acquire the work in 1896, having learned that the MFA was wavering, she enlisted the aid (as was her wont) of Bernard Berenson, who had included the painting as an early Giorgione in his *Venetian Painters of the Renaissance* two years earlier.[39] Berenson's letter to her of September 22, 1896, was curiously equivocating; he reaffirmed that the painting was "unquestionably genuine," but pointed out problems with its condition and noted that "it somehow is not the kind of thing I think of for you."[40] He nevertheless prevailed upon the Zileri family, and after prolonged negotiations Gardner acquired the painting in 1898. The Giorgione attribution has since fallen out of favor, most recent authorities assigning the picture

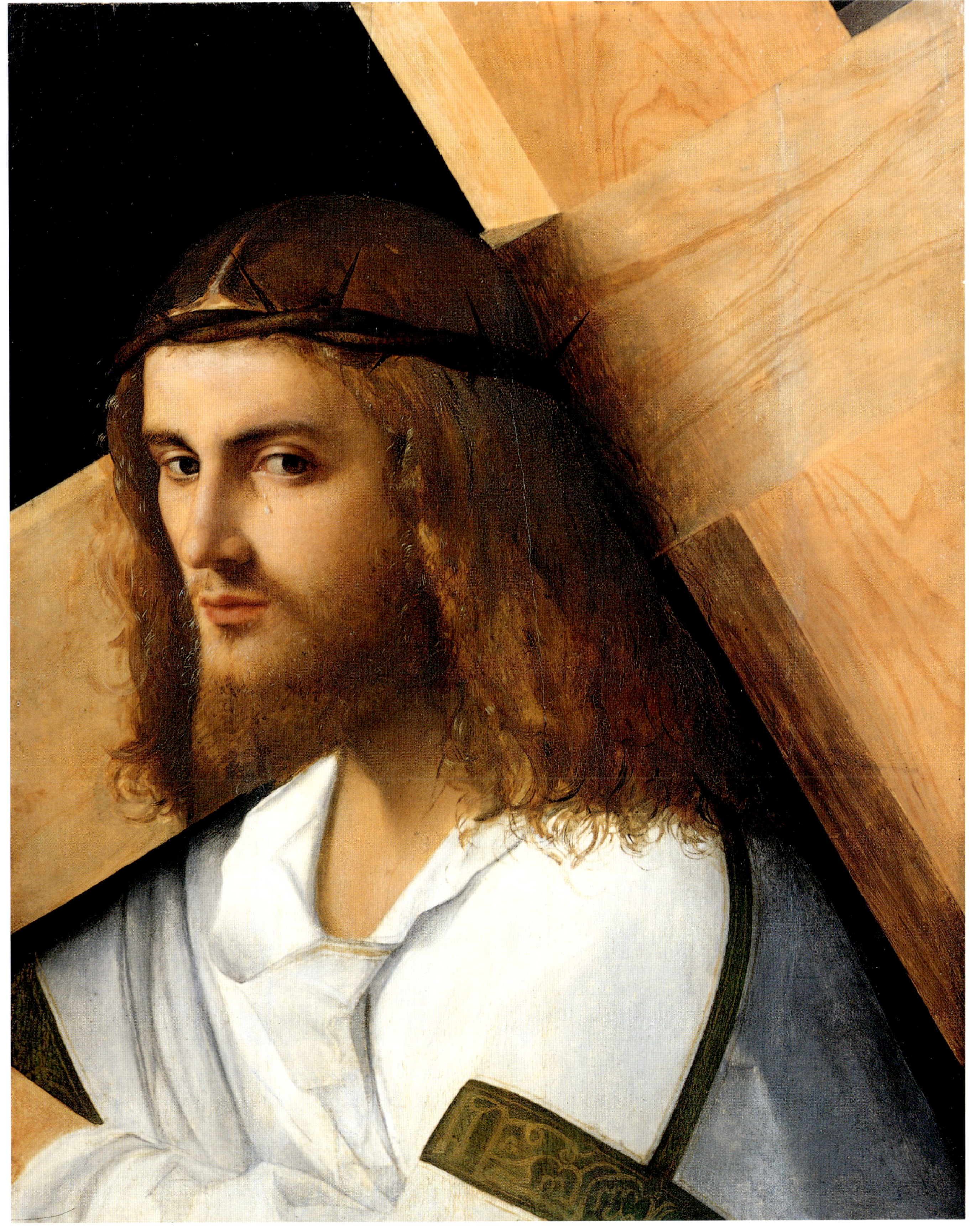

cat. 3

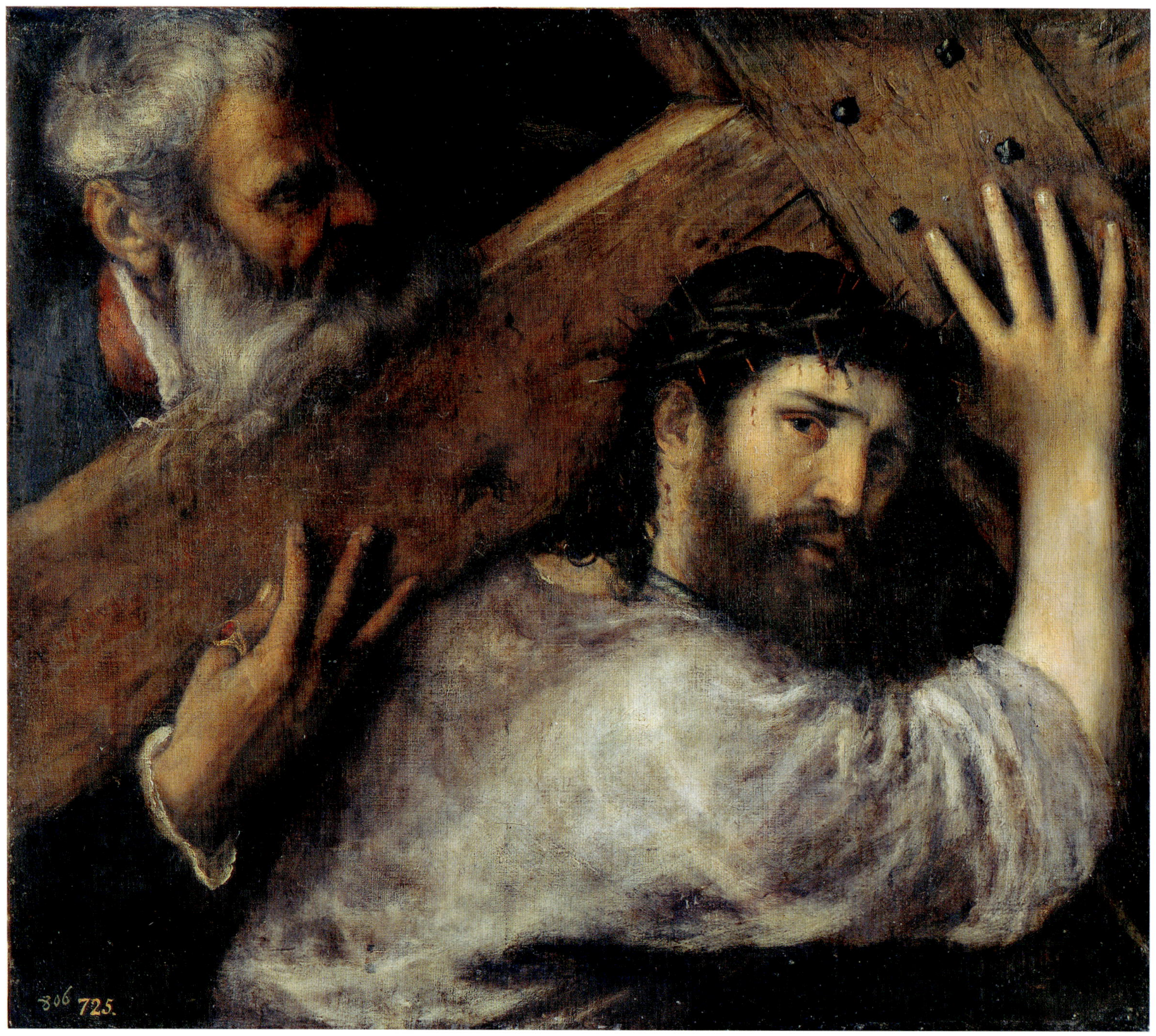

cat. 4

to the workshop of Giovanni Bellini or a close follower. The artist of the Gardner panel is clearly a painter of substantial talent, however, and not just an anonymous Bellini workshop assistant.[41]

While the author of the panel remains uncertain, there is little question who painted the 1565–70 canvas—not just because of the signature in red capital letters on the cross, at the left ("TITIANVS AEQ. CAES. F."), but also because of the unmistakable faces, hands, and brushwork of the painter's late style. Titian has structured his composition around the diagonal of the cross that bisects the pictorial field, separating Christ, who bears the greater weight, from Simon, above. Christ's right arm forms a right angle, reinforcing the lower right corner of the composition. Simon wears a ring with a red stone on his right thumb, and other touches of red—a glimpse of his shirt, Christ's bloodshot eyes, and particularly certain thorns of the crown shiny with blood—stand out amid the enveloping gloom. Although deeply in shadow, Simon has a distinct face and may be a portrait of the unidentified patron; Ridolfi's biography of Titian claimed that a painting of this subject owned by the Barbarigo family (now in the State Hermitage Museum, Saint Petersburg) included a portrait of Francesco Zuccato "holding the Cross for him."[42] Details are masterful and economical: Christ's curly hair is heavy with sweat, and skillful highlights give heft and finish to the wooden cross and the heads of the nails. By contrast, Christ's sleeve is composed of many layers of caressing strokes.

Titian's younger rivals, painters of the generation of Tintoretto and Veronese, evinced little interest in producing these dramatic close-up paintings. Their clients may have seen the format as archaic well before the middle of the century, akin to the paintings of *belle donne* (such as Titian's *Flora*) that disappeared after several decades of great popularity. Titian's return to the subject of Christ carrying the cross may have been sparked by an interest in exploring certain subjects from the time of his youth in the pictorial language of his late style.[43] The resulting work demonstrates Titian's capacity for renewal through tradition; more broadly, it shows how, in the second half of the Cinquecento, the style and touch of the artist had come to personalize every sort of painting. Here, the inherent spiritual power of the tightly cropped devotional close-up has been augmented by the distinctive hand of a great master.

— FI

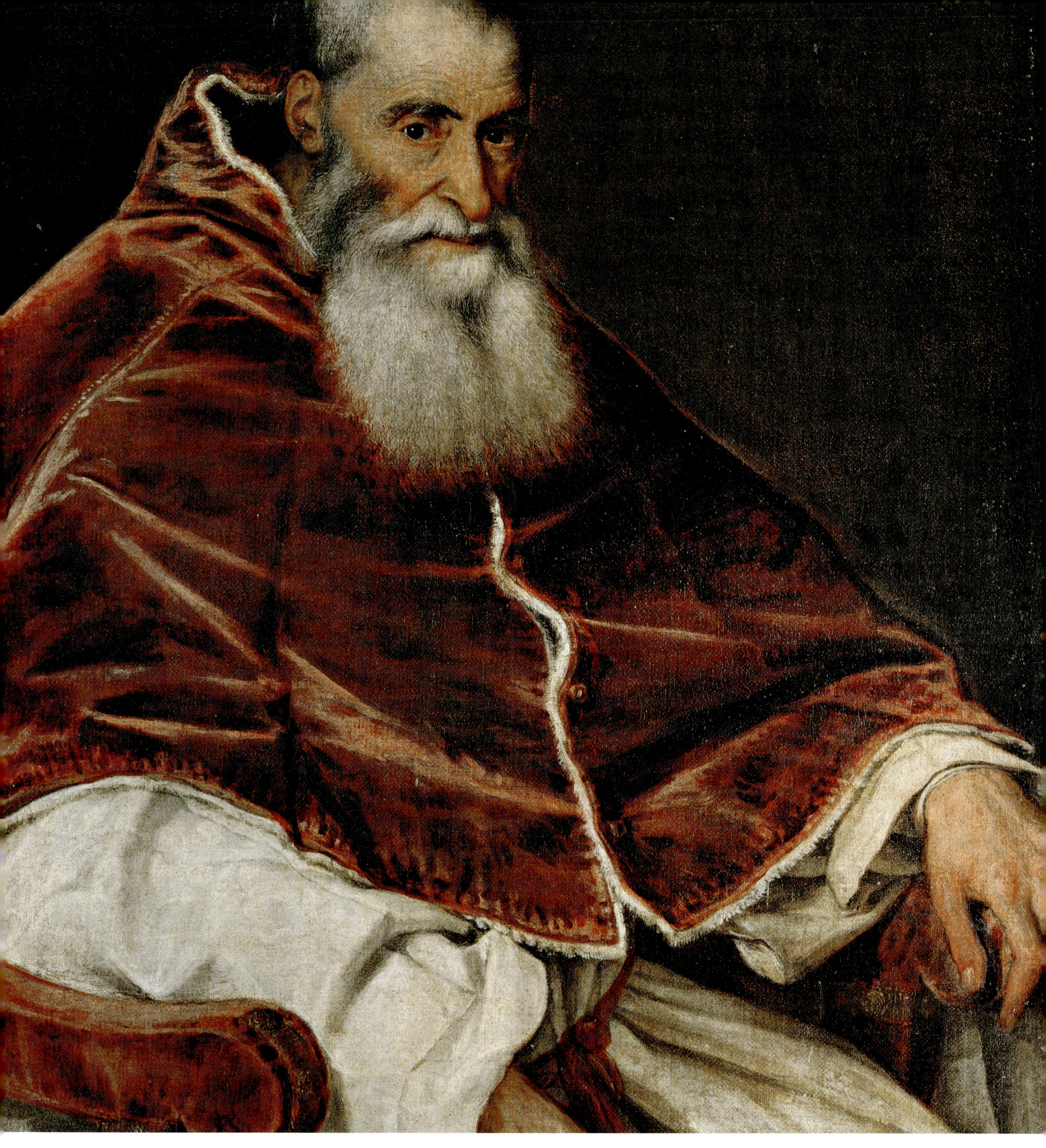

Titian to 1545

Titian was born in the mountain region of Cadore, a Venetian territory in the Dolomites, around 1488, though the date remains hazy.[1] Sent to Venice to train as a painter, he was apprenticed to Gentile Bellini but subsequently decided to move to the studio of Giovanni Bellini, the most prominent painter in the city. There he came under the spell of the slightly older Giorgione, with whom he was closely associated in his first years as an independent artist. Bellini and Giorgione represent the starting points of Titian's style: Bellini for his naturalism and mastery of oil technique to capture rich, saturated colors; Giorgione for the visible brushwork, new sense of grandeur, and heightened atmosphere he brought to Venetian painting. When in 1508 Giorgione decorated the facade of the Fondaco dei Tedeschi, the warehouse of the German merchants on the Grand Canal, Titian was assigned the frescoes facing a side street. According to early sources, some viewers initially thought Giorgione had frescoed both facades and congratulated him for the superior murals on the side. Since these had actually been painted by Titian, Giorgione, humiliated, dropped the younger painter as a colleague and friend.[2] This anecdote of punctured pride reminds us how professional jealousy could shape artistic developments. With the death of Giorgione in 1510 and the departure of Sebastiano for Rome the next year, Titian emerged as the embodiment of the new style in Venetian painting.

Even before Bellini's death in 1516, Titian successfully positioned himself to assume the old man's mantle as the heir to its great tradition. In May 1513 he petitioned the Council of Ten to award him the commission for a "large canvas" (the *Battle of Spoleto*) in the Sala del Maggior Consiglio of the Palazzo Ducale in exchange for the next available *senseria*, a government sinecure conferring a steady salary and status as an official painter. Titian's statement indicated that he considered himself ready to paint anywhere, but would prefer to offer his services to Venice: "Although I have been in the past, and also am now urgently requested by both His Holiness the Pope and by other rulers to go and serve them; yet desiring, as the faithful servant of Your Sublimity that I am, to leave some memorial in this famous city, I have decided, if it meets with your approval, to take on the task of coming to paint in the Hall of the Great Council."[3] Titian's gambit was eventually successful, providing him with regular income and blocking opportunities for other painters in perhaps the most important public site in Venice. Secure in his official position, he took his time completing the assignment, finishing the *Battle of Spoleto* only in 1538, and only under threat of losing his *senseria* and having to refund his stipend. Although Titian maintained his links with his family and community in Cadore and traveled around Europe in pursuit of patronage, he remained in Venice his entire life, despite further lucrative offers to move elsewhere.

TITIAN
Flora, about 1516–18
Galleria degli Uffizi, Florence
(cat. 5)

TITIAN
Venus Rising from the Sea (Venus Anadyomene), about 1520
National Gallery of Scotland, Edinburgh
(cat. 6)

TITIAN
Pope Paul III, 1543
Museo di Capodimonte, Naples
(cat. 7)

Titian's success derived from his technical brilliance and his versatility as a painter, coupled with self-confidence, social acumen, and personal charm. Letters of the time often refer to his ingratiating personality. In one of 1542 to Cardinal Alessandro Farnese, a contemporary extolled Titian as not only "clever" but also "mild, tractable, and easy to deal with, which is worthy of note in respect of such exceptional men as he is."[4] From the beginning of his career, Titian demonstrated an aptitude for a variety of subjects, and made major innovations in all of them. His multifarious proficiency no doubt encouraged younger painters to range widely rather than specialize in certain formats or themes. Among his earliest productions were works for private collectors, some in the new category of independent easel pictures and probably a number created at the painter's own initiative. The young Titian showed a special talent for portraits, endowing his sitters with self-assurance and sensitive expressions as well as astonishing still-life details of costume.

The most important element in establishing Titian's preeminence in Venice, however, was a sequence of altarpieces for prestigious settings. The *Assumption of the Virgin* (*Assunta*) (fig. 50), executed for the high altar of the enormous Gothic church of Santa Maria Gloriosa dei Frari and unveiled in May 1518, not only was the largest altarpiece ever painted in Venice (and the largest painting on wooden panel anywhere) but represented an entirely new conception of what an altarpiece might be: not static and contemplative but filled with high drama, motion, and energy. For the same church, in 1526, Titian created the equally innovative *Madonna di Ca' Pesaro* (fig. 47), which transformed the *sacra conversazione* painted by artists of the previous generation (such as fig. 36). Here Titian rotated the traditional composition on its axis and took advantage of the canvas support to create compelling donor portraits of the Pesaro family and masterful evocations of textures. (Two and a half decades later, Veronese was to use this altarpiece as the prototype of his first prominent painting in Venice, for the church of San Francesco della Vigna [fig. 48]). Next, Titian painted the *Saint Peter Martyr* altarpiece for the church of Santi Giovanni e Paolo—destroyed by fire in 1867, but known from an engraving by Martino Rota (fig. 23) and many painted copies. Perhaps the most admired of Titian's paintings during his lifetime, this altarpiece introduced a level of violence and intensity unprecedented in Venetian altarpieces and seemed to make the landscape itself a participant in the drama.[5]

Titian displayed equal mastery of secular subjects, particularly those with an erotic component. Two examples demonstrate his skill in this domain, both derived from types introduced by Giorgione at the beginning of the century. Among these was the *bella donna*, the idealized representation of a beautiful woman, often shown half-length and in a state of dishabille. Titian's *Flora*, recognized as the finest example of the type, can best be dated to around 1516–18, a few years after his *Sacred and Profane Love* (fig. 87), in which the same model appears. The young woman's flawless skin, fresh and delicate—indeed, flowerlike—is set off by the textures of the sheer linen chemise that falls from her shoulder and the rich brocade she gathers to her breast. The violets, jasmine, and roses she holds suggest an association with Flora, the Roman goddess of flowers and spring, and the painting has been known by that name since the earliest documented reference, an engraving by Joachim von Sandrart of 1640. How the sitter would have been understood by Titian's contemporaries, however, has been subject to debate. A long literary tradition associated the name Flora with courtesans, and many scholars have identified *Flora* and similar *belle donne* as images of the famed courtesans of sixteenth-century Venice. A more recent point of view identifies pictures such as these as wedding gifts, intended to be seen only by the married couple, at once arousing and instructive in their celebration of the ideal wife as simultaneously desirable and virtuous.[6] Unlike other examples of the type, such as Palma Vecchio's *Blonde Woman* (fig. 89), who reveals her bare breast and whose gaze brazenly confronts the viewer, Titian's *Flora* is relaxed and unselfconscious, seemingly lost in thought. A long tradition holds that the model, who appears in several of Titian's paintings, was his mistress and later wife, Cecilia, with whom he lived for years and who bore him two sons. Paul Joannides suggests that in *Flora* and similar works, Titian introduces a new range of experience to painting, animating the image with "the husband's or the lover's gaze," which combines sexual desire with an appreciation of the beloved's personality.[7] The *bella donna* format, as perfected by Titian, remained something of a specialty of the artist and his generation, and was not picked up by later Venetian painters.

Venus Rising from the Sea (Venus Anadyomene), despite the figure's total nudity, shares a similar lack of self-consciousness and seems to depict the same model. The painting shows the goddess of love ris-

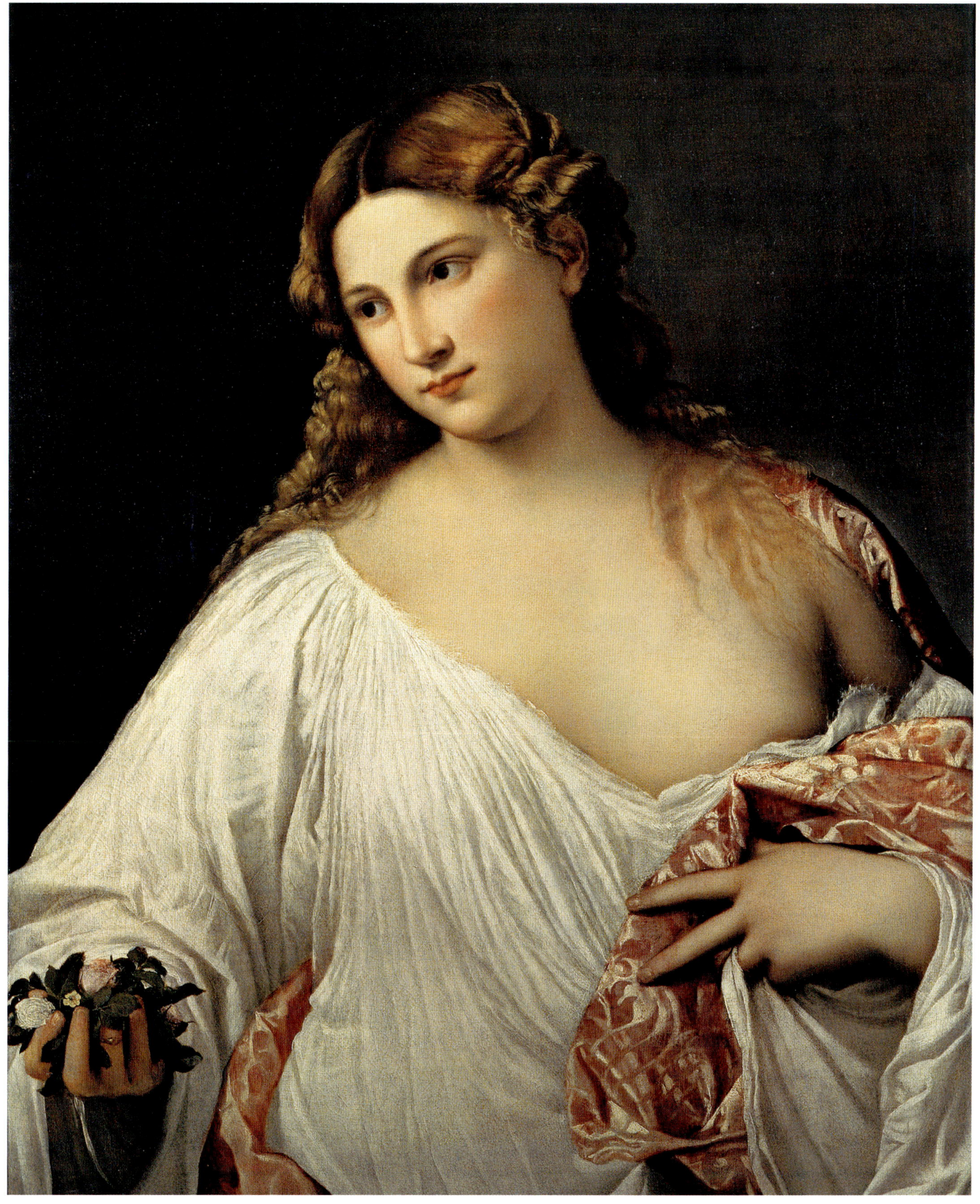

cat. 5

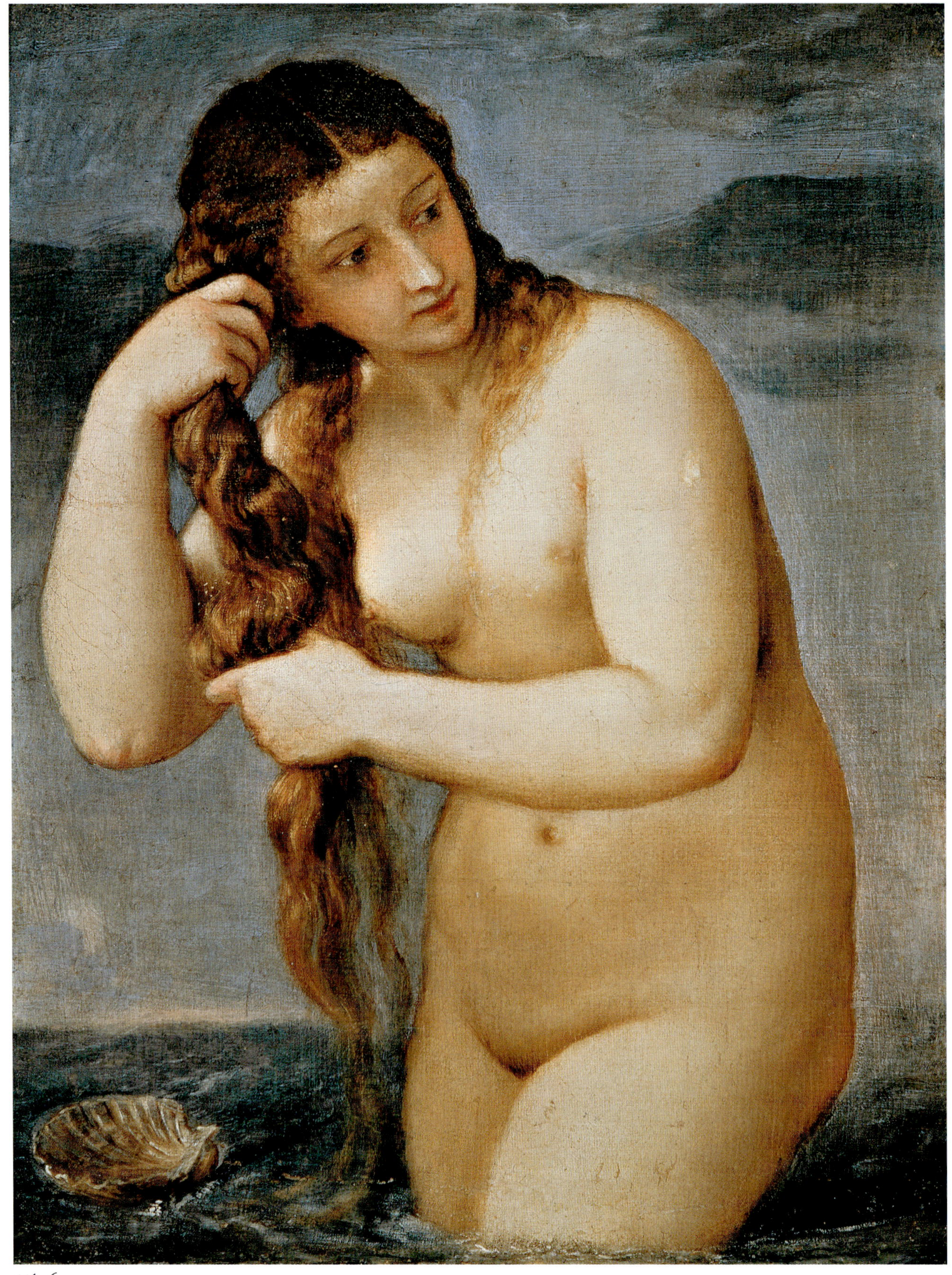

cat. 6

ing from the water, wringing out her wet hair, after her birth in the sea already fully grown. The scallop shell on which she traveled to Cyprus appears in the background. In this picture Titian is deliberately seeking to re-create a lost work of art from the ancient world, the Venus Anadyomene by Apelles, the court painter of Alexander the Great and the most famous painter of classical antiquity. According to Pliny, the emperor Augustus brought the painting to Rome, where the bottom section was later damaged—to which Titian alludes by showing Venus only from her thighs up, her lower legs hidden beneath the water.[8]

Peter Humfrey offers an intriguing argument that *Venus Rising from the Sea* was commissioned by Alfonso d'Este, Duke of Ferrara, for whom Titian painted three large bacchanals in the years 1518–23. If the duke was indeed the patron, then in re-creating the lost painting Titian compared not only himself to Apelles but also Alfonso to Alexander the Great. Arguing for Alfonso's patronage is the fact that the duke had previously commissioned a marble relief of the subject from the sculptor Antonio Lombardo. X-radiography reveals that Titian's Venus originally looked to her right, as does Antonio's. By evoking sculpture (not so much Antonio's relief of the subject as the surviving classical sculptures in the round), Titian explicitly invokes the *paragone*, the debate on the respective merits of painting and sculpture. As Humfrey writes, "The ample form and swiveling contrapposto of Titian's figure create no less convincing a sense of movement in space; yet no statue could compare with the painting in its evocation of the plump softness of the goddess's flesh, of the fall of light on her left shoulder and breasts, or of the amorphous surrounding atmosphere of air and water. Equally unlike his sculptural prototype, Titian endows his ideal figure with an inner life that transcends mere physical beauty."[9]

Alfonso d'Este was the first of numerous aristocratic clients outside of Venice whose patronage Titian pursued and obtained. Confident that he had secured his place in Venice, in the 1520s and 1530s Titian often moved beyond the lagoon for months at a time to stay at court or travel with important noblemen. In addition to Alfonso, his patrons during these years included Federico Gonzaga of Mantua and Francesco Maria della Rovere of Urbino. In 1533, in Bologna, he painted Charles V of Spain, marking the beginning of his long and fruitful relationship with the Hapsburg dynasty.

Meanwhile, in Venice, a rival had suddenly emerged: the painter known as Pordenone, after his birthplace in the Friulian region northeast of Venice.

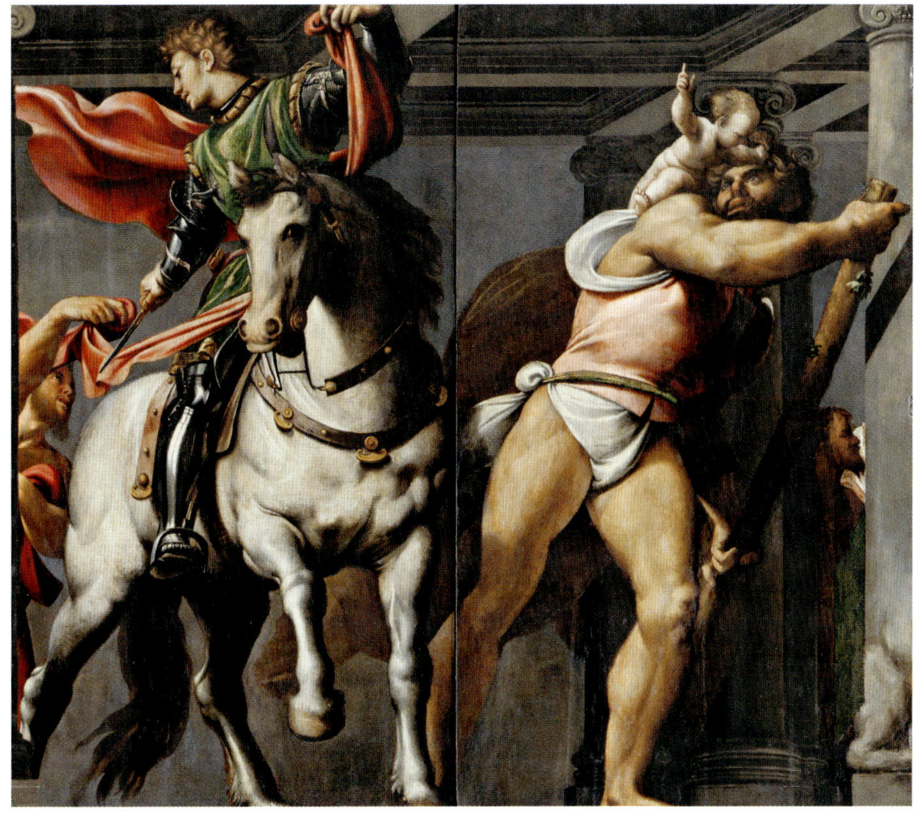

Fig. 41
Pordenone (Italian, about 1483–about 1539)
Saint Martin with the Beggar and Saint Christopher, 1528–29
Oil on panels
Church of San Rocco, Venice

Pordenone began to make a name for himself through a series of frescoes and ceiling paintings in prominent sites, characterized by their bold foreshortenings and violent energy. Some of Pordenone's work in Venice in fact predated Titian's *Saint Peter Martyr* altarpiece and may have encouraged the muscularity and violence of Titian's masterpiece. Although most of Pordenone's works for Venice are now lost or in poor condition, a sense of their impact is provided by his *Saint Martin with the Beggar and Saint Christopher* (fig. 41), where the powerful figures seem about to burst from the picture into the viewer's space. Although Pordenone's rather crude pictorial technique could not match Titian's virtuosity, his paintings were dynamic and exciting, and his pneumatic figures evoked something of the power of Michelangelo. In the mid-1530s, Pordenone moved aggressively to challenge Titian's position of leadership in Venice. According to Vasari, he deliberately sought commissions in sites where Titian had already painted: indeed, as Rona Goffen notes, "rivalry is the Leitmotif" of Vasari's biography of the painter.[10] Pordenone succeeded in obtaining coveted commissions in the Palazzo Ducale. Vasari recounts that one of these was arranged by Jacopo Soranzo, who was impressed by Pordenone's *Saint Martin with the Beggar and Saint*

Christopher. Titian was vulnerable on this front, having neglected to complete the commissioned *Battle of Spoleto* for the Palazzo Ducale for more than two decades; the threat that Pordenone might take over the commission helped spur him to action, and he finally completed the work in 1538. Destroyed in the catastrophic fire of 1577, along with Pordenone's contribution and the rest of the cycle, and known today only from an engraving and Titian's preparatory drawings (fig. 10), the *Battle of Spoleto* exerted a powerful influence on other Venetian painters. Among these was the young Tintoretto, who sought to equal—indeed, surpass—its drama in his *Conversion of Saint Paul* (National Gallery of Art, Washington, DC) a few years later.

Pordenone also tried to compete with Titian at the Scuola Grande della Carità, a prestigious confraternity (now part of the Gallerie dell'Accademia). Titian's *Presentation of the Virgin in the Temple* there (1534–38; fig. 13) conferred a new sophistication on the narrative paintings for Venetian *scuole*, invoking a High Renaissance grandeur for the processional composition but depicting it with looser and more expressive brushwork. At the same time, the emphasis on the surface plane and an abundance of quotidian detail place the picture strongly in the tradition of the murals by his teachers Giovanni and Gentile Bellini. The Scuola engaged Pordenone to paint the next canvas in the cycle, apparently relying on his rivalry with Titian to ensure the quality of his contribution. The board even deferred to the artist's judgment on the subject to be painted.[11] These commissions show that Pordenone was successfully challenging Titian in Venice at the time of his sudden death in Ferrara in 1539.

In the first half of the 1540s, his position in Venice secure once again, Titian continued to expand his international reach. In 1542 he ingratiated himself with the family of Pope Paul III, the Farneses; a letter from several years later claims the artist had promised to paint portraits of the entire Farnese family, "including the cats."[12] Titian first painted the pope's grandson, Ranuccio Farnese (cat. 42), and in 1543, in Bologna, he painted the pope himself. On the same trip, he met Charles V once again, from whom he received another portrait commission. Employed by both the pope and the emperor, Titian had reached the summit of princely patronage.

Titian's *Pope Paul III*, the first of three portraits he created of the pontiff, follows the tradition of earlier three-quarter-length portraits of seated popes, including famous examples by Raphael (Julius II) and Sebastiano del Piombo (Clement VII). In contrast to these earlier models, however, in which the sitter is aloof and lost in thought, Titian's pope looks directly at the viewer with an intimidating intensity, as though we have just come into his presence. The point of view is rather high, as though we were standing before the seated pontiff: neither the painter nor the viewer ranks high enough to be offered a chair. Although the subject was Roman by definition, the figure of the powerful older man was a familiar one in Venetian portraiture. Venice was a gerontocracy, and celebrations of the vigorous and wise elder as a military or political leader were frequent (see, for example, Tintoretto's *Sebastiano Venier* [cat. 40]). The composition of the present picture focuses attention on the pope's glittering eyes and piercing gaze: the body of the sitter is presented as a solid triangular form, with the highlights along the margins and seams of his velvet cape pointing upward and inward to the face. The fabrics are rendered with loose, painterly handling, which, along with the picture's understated colors, differs greatly from contemporary Roman painting practice. The many copies of this portrait indicate that the sitter and his family regarded it as *the* official likeness.[13]

In April 1544, back in Venice, "Titian, painter, man of experience, known to all," was invited to give his expert opinion on the renovation of the Sala dell'Albergo of the Scuola Grande di San Giovanni Evangelista, for which he would soon execute a ceiling ensemble, adding yet another work to the dozens he had provided to Venice's churches and confraternities.[14] Later that same year he embarked on another Farnese commission for a grandson of the pope, Cardinal Alessandro Farnese, the *Danaë* (cat. 27), which Titian was to take with him when he accepted an invitation to visit the papal court in Rome the next winter. These years thus find Titian not only the leading painter in Venice for both public and private patrons, but one whose works were sought by the most powerful princes in Europe as well. His only real rival in artistic fame was Michelangelo, whom he would finally meet in Rome in the winter of 1545–46. At this moment of international acclaim, Titian would certainly not have imagined that in Venice a new, wildly ambitious challenger, three decades younger, was about to burst upon the scene, followed within a few years by a second rival, and that in the coming decades the story of Venetian painting would be about not one great painter, but three.

— RE, FI

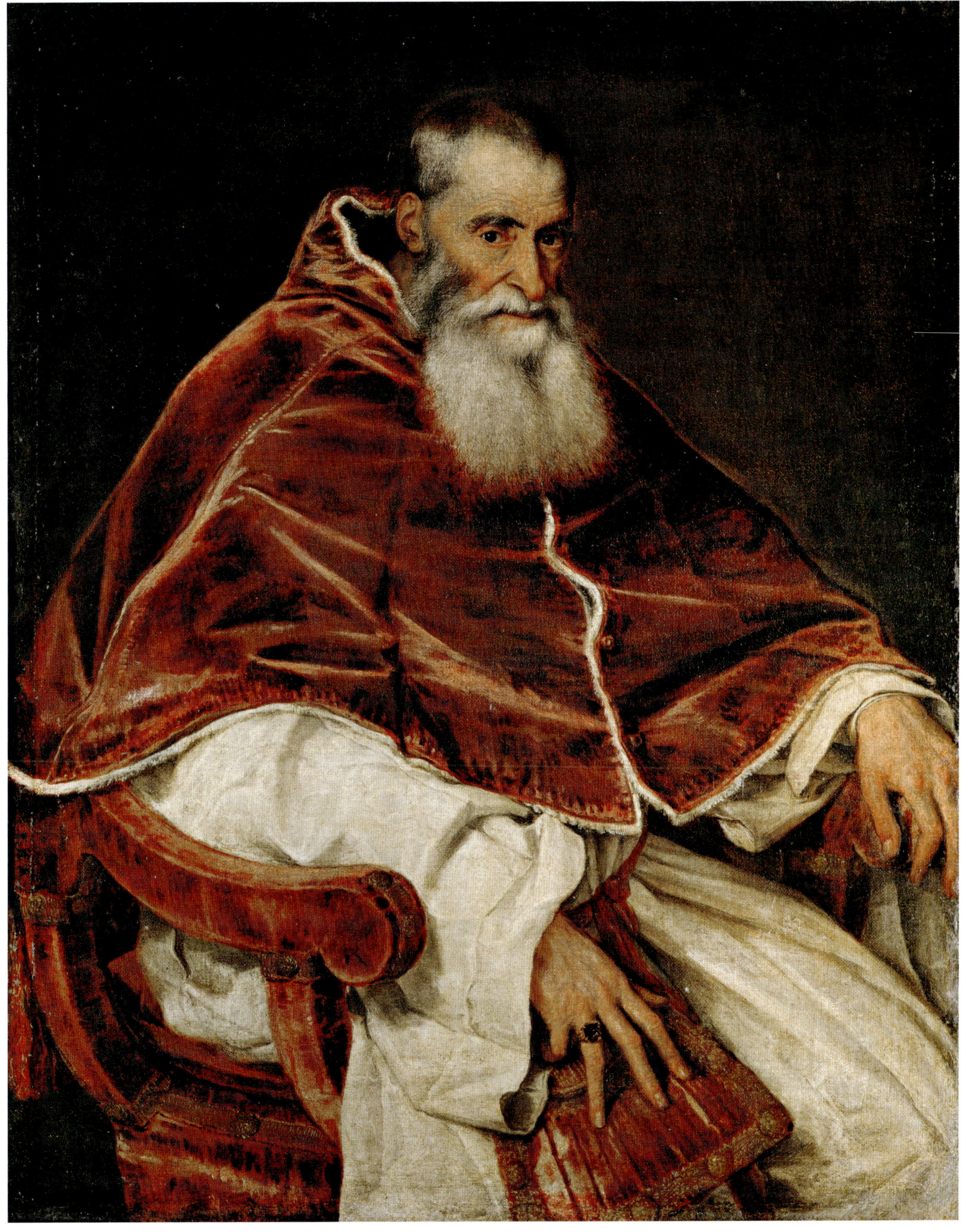

cat. 7

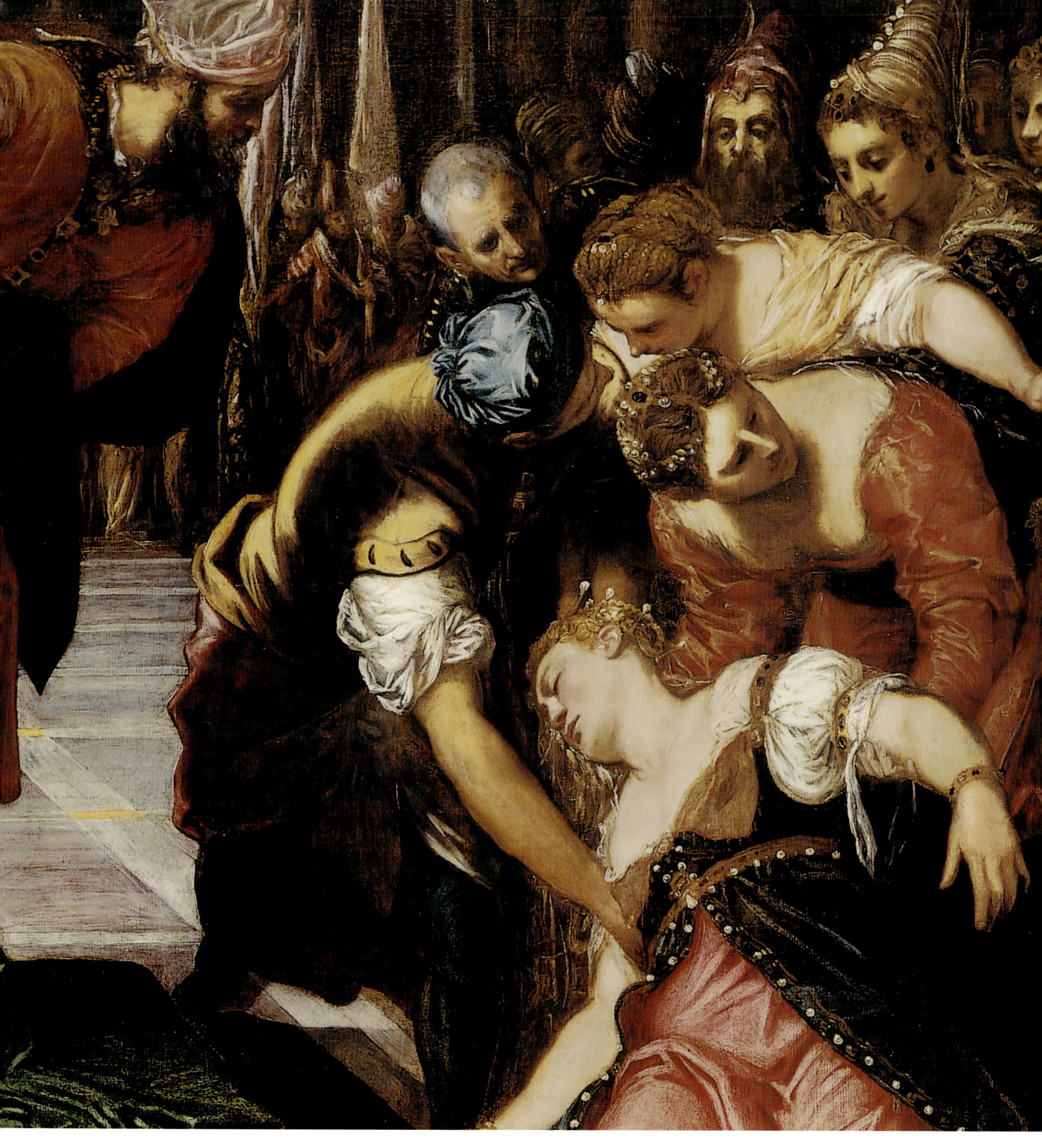

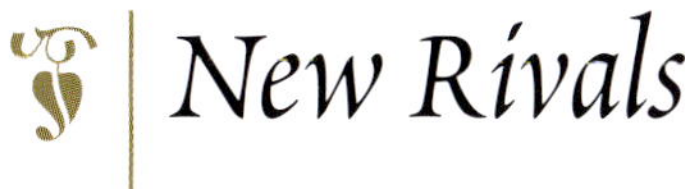

New Rivals

Titian's dominance of Venetian art went unchallenged for decades at a time in the first half of the Cinquecento. Sebastiano's departure for Rome in 1511, followed by Giovanni Bellini's death in 1516, left Titian first the most innovative painter working in Venice and then unquestionably the leading one. Pordenone's brief period of prominence in the 1530s came to an end with his unexpected death in 1539. It was not until 1548 that another rival emerged, the thirty-year-old Jacopo Tintoretto, who leapt to the forefront of Venetian painting that year with his triumphant *Miracle of the Slave* (fig. 5).

Born about 1518, Tintoretto was an independent master, making his own way, by 1538. According to his seventeenth-century biographers, he had apprenticed briefly with Titian but was ejected either for being a smart aleck ("spiritoso"), in Boschini's account, or, according to Ridolfi, because the jealous older artist recognized his precocious talent.[1] If there is any truth to the story of Tintoretto's short stay in Titian's workshop, it may well be the case that he got on Titian's nerves. Tintoretto was aggressively ambitious and his personality was intense, as contemporary descriptions make clear. A famous letter of 1548 by his friend the writer Andrea Calmo compares him to a peppercorn capable of overpowering ten bunches of poppies.[2] The later hostility between Titian and Tintoretto suggests a clash of temperament as well as professional rivalry. Alternatively, Tintoretto might have chosen to leave the studio on his own because of Titian's unwillingness to share much technical expertise with his students, just as Paris Bordone had done two decades earlier. Ridolfi reports that later in his career, Titian locked up his paintings so that his assistants could not copy them.[3] In any case, Ridolfi's biography recounts that after leaving Titian, Tintoretto embarked upon an ambitious program of self-education: copying works by other artists (especially sculpture), drawing from life, even learning anatomy by dissecting corpses, always guided by the motto "The draftsmanship of Michelangelo, the coloring of Titian" (il disegno di Michel Angelo e'l colorito di Titiano).[4]

Given the rules of the Venetian painter's guild, Ridolfi's claim that Tintoretto was self-taught is probably hyperbolic, perhaps originating with the painter himself and passed on in studio lore. It seems probable that Tintoretto completed his apprenticeship with a lesser-known master, perhaps Bonifazio de' Pitati, a reality that Tintoretto later chose to erase from his biography in favor of the more heroic tale of self-invention.[5] Nevertheless, there is a fundamental kernel of truth to the story. Although Tintoretto learned from other painters—including Andrea Schiavone, whose free handling of paint he admired; Bonifazio, with whom he clearly had some kind of association as a young man; and even the painters "of minor success" who decorated furniture—he made his own way in a highly competitive milieu, without an established master to serve as his mentor or sponsor.

As for the famous motto, the appearance of Tintoretto's early works tells a somewhat different story. Of Titian's *colorito* there is no trace in the younger artist's painting until around 1545. In Tintoretto's very early works, he paints in a bold, highly personal technique, based on his eclectic studies, very different from Titian's mature style and indeed from the mainstream of the Venetian tradition. Tintoretto's first manner is even unlike Central Italian practice; instead of surface finish, these paintings feature broad, dry brushwork that often looks like drawing in paint. In terms of *disegno*, on the other hand, from the start Tintoretto sought to identify himself with the new Central Italian mode of painting associated with Michelangelo and his followers, and to set himself up as its most daring avatar in Venice. Tintoretto borrowed voraciously from all the Central Italian sources available to him, including the sculpture of Jacopo Sansovino, who had been living in Venice since 1527; paintings executed in Venice by the visiting Tuscans Francesco Salviati (present in Venice 1539–41) and Giorgio Vasari (in Venice 1541–42); and the many prints and drawings that circulated among Venetians with advanced artistic taste. Although there is no indication that the young Tintoretto had any personal or professional relationship with Pordenone, he may have seen in Pordenone's career a strategy that he himself could emulate: setting himself up as Titian's opposite number, the embodiment of the new. Early pictures such as the *Supper at Emmaus* (cat. 22), with its wildly twisting figures, and the scenes from Ovid painted for a ceiling in the newly renovated palace of the patrician Vettor Pisani, with their broad technique and exaggerated foreshortening, seem intended to surprise, challenge, even shock.[6]

From early in his career, Tintoretto forged connections with the circle of Rome-oriented patrons, artists, and critics that gravitated around Pietro Aretino, the Tuscan writer who had settled in Venice in 1527 after the Sack of Rome. Through his letters, which he circulated widely in manuscript and collected and published at regular intervals, Aretino shamelessly advanced the careers of artists he favored. The writer also played an important role in importing the Central Italian style to Venice. In 1535, Giorgio Vasari sent Aretino his drawings after Michelangelo's Medici tomb sculptures, and Aretino's letters are filled with references to other drawings by artists working in Rome. Aretino invited Vasari to Venice and may have played a role in prompting Salviati's visit as well.[7] Among the younger artists in Venice working in the Roman vein, Aretino singled out Tintoretto as a protégé. The decorative ceiling ensemble that Tintoretto executed for him, praised by Aretino in a letter of 1545, must have been a landmark moment in the painter's career; one of the paintings, the *Contest between Apollo and Marsyas* (cat. 8), survives. The bawdy wit of *Venus and Mars Surprised by Vulcan* (fig. 81), probably painted shortly thereafter, may also reflect Aretino's taste.[8]

As much as *Venus and Mars* mocks the erotic classicism of Titian's nudes, it also shows a new effort on Tintoretto's part to exploit the ability of oil paint on canvas to capture the sensuous play of light over nude forms and luxurious fabrics. These effects suggest that Tintoretto had been looking closely at Titian's pictorial technique, and in particular at his *Danaë* (cat. 27), begun in Venice in 1544. Indeed, it is around this time, not in Tintoretto's earliest works, that the motto "Michelangelo's *disegno* and Titian's *colorito*" first becomes relevant to Tintoretto's paintings. Perhaps the young painter's growing success made him feel less impelled to shock and more inclined to please. A budding accommodation to Venetian naturalism, not to mention an acknowledgment of Titian's successful portrait formula, is also evident in Tintoretto's portraiture, which is clearly indebted to Titian's model (see, for example, cats. 36 and 39). Tintoretto's own youthful *Self-Portrait* (cat. 9), on the other hand, is more personal, brilliantly capturing his passionate, assertive personality.

Whatever personal antipathy he may have felt toward the young upstart, Titian seems to have been paying attention to the striking effects Tintoretto achieved in his pictures. When Titian turned to ceiling painting himself, for the church of Santo Spirito in Isola, he borrowed from Tintoretto's *Deucalion and Pyrrha* from the ceiling at the Pisani Palace for his own *David and Goliath*.[9] In his portrait of Aretino, painted in 1545, Titian employed passages of bold, broad brushwork similar to that used by Tintoretto. But it seems unlikely that he would have taken Tintoretto seriously as a rival at this point.

All of that was to change within a few years. In April 1548, Pietro Aretino wrote to Jacopo Sansovino that Tintoretto was nearing the finish line in the race among *virtuosi* for artistic glory. To justify Aretino's praise, Tintoretto must have recently painted other impressive paintings in addition to the just-completed

Miracle of the Slave. Surviving works from these years include several confident portraits (cats. 36, 39), the *Self-Portrait*, a *Last Supper* for the church of San Marcuola, dated August 1547, and the superlative *Esther before Ahasuerus* (cat. 10), which shares some of the impact and bravura paint handling of the far better known *Miracle of the Slave*.

The *Miracle of the Slave* marked a turning point in Tintoretto's career. Executed for the Scuola Grande di San Marco, the wealthiest and most prestigious of Venice's six *Scuole Grandi*, it was the most prominent commission that Tintoretto had yet received. As Ridolfi and Boschini tell us, the painting immediately generated controversy.[10] Some members of the confraternity argued against accepting the work, causing Tintoretto to take it back to his studio in anger. But Tintoretto and his supporters eventually triumphed, and the picture was installed in the Scuola to great acclaim. During the course of this drama, Titian was away from Venice, in Augsburg, enabling Tintoretto to stage-manage the unveiling of his important public painting and enjoy a moment of glory without interference from the older artist. Titian, conversely, must have experienced an unpleasant surprise upon his return, not simply because of Tintoretto's sudden celebrity but because he could not ignore the superb quality of the painting itself, including the pointed quotation of the figure with outstretched arms from his own breakthrough altarpiece of the *Assumption* (fig. 50). Significantly, after 1548, Titian largely abandoned large-scale narrative painting in Venice, probably unwilling to compete in a format in which his younger, more energetic rival had the advantage.[11]

After the brilliant success of *Miracle of the Slave*, Tintoretto was overwhelmed with commissions. Over the next few years, he provided important paintings for the churches of San Marziale, San Marcuola, and San Rocco and the Scuola della Trinità in Venice. With his altarpiece for the church of San Michele in Vicenza depicting *Saint Augustine Healing the Lame* (cat. 14), he sought to establish his credentials on the Venetian *terraferma* as well, here citing Michelangelo as a point of departure. He was extraordinarily busy, and some commissions went unfilled for years: a pair of organ shutters for the church of Madonna dell'Orto, for instance, commissioned in 1548, was not completed until 1556.[12] Tintoretto's activity as a portraitist also expanded in these years, including a portrait of Aretino (now

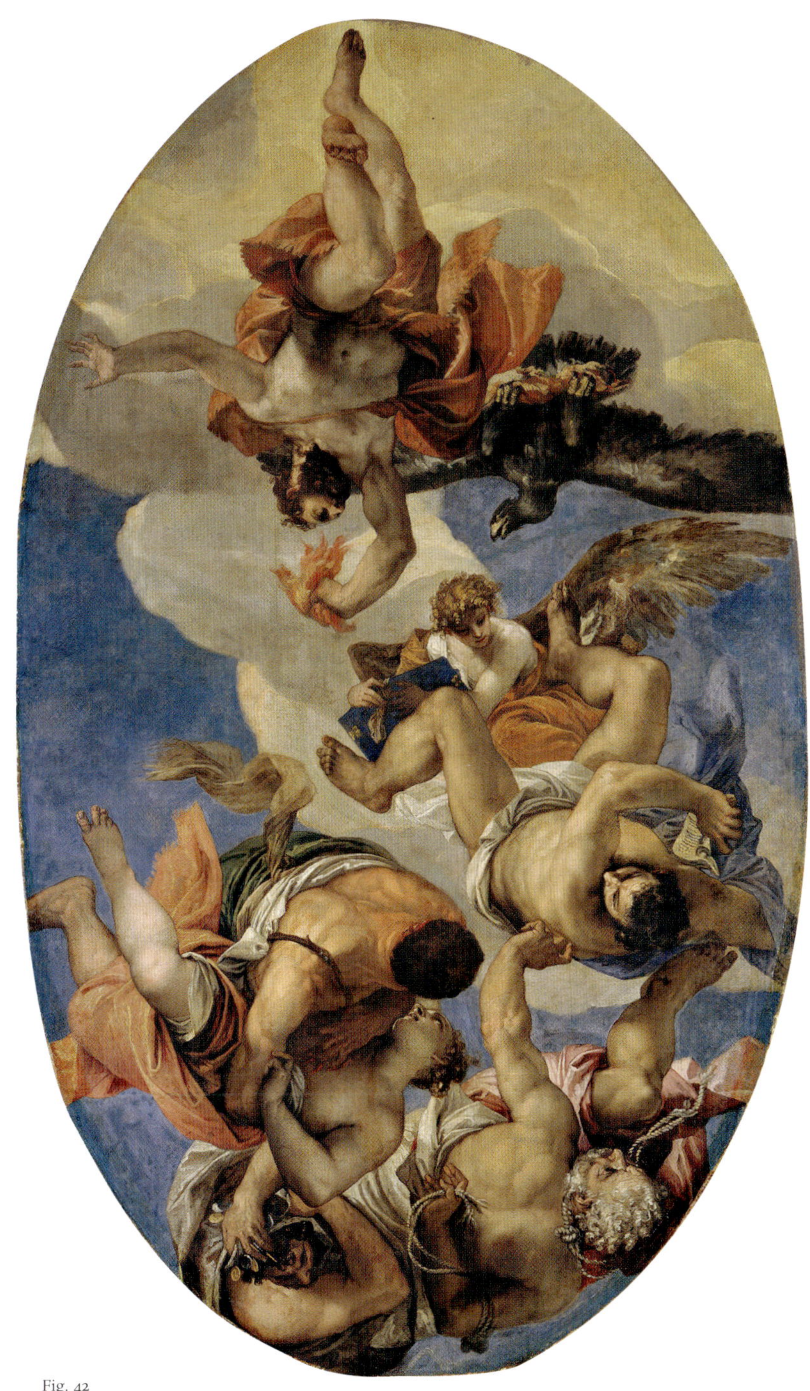

Fig. 42
Veronese
Jupiter Expelling the Vices, about 1554–55
Oil on canvas
Musée du Louvre, Paris

destroyed), mentioned in a letter of September 15, 1551, and, according to Ridolfi, painted in competition with Titian.[13] In 1551 Tintoretto received his first documented official patronage, for some unspecified pictures, probably portraits, for the Procuratia. The next year he provided two votive paintings for the Palazzo dei Camerlenghi (see cat. 15), effectively supplanting Bonifazio, in whose studio he had worked. By 1553 Tintoretto attained the summit of official Venetian patronage with a commission for a history painting for the Sala del Maggior Consiglio in the Palazzo Ducale, subsequently destroyed in the fire of 1577.[14]

Despite Tintoretto's meteoric rise, his paintings did not please all tastes. A faction of the Venetian establishment had never warmed either to his art or to his aggressive self-promotion. Titian remained implacably hostile. Indeed, Titian's enmity may have led to a breakdown of Tintoretto's relationship with Aretino. While the circumstances remain murky, Tintoretto does not appear in Aretino's letters after 1549.[15] Titian may also have successfully blocked Tintoretto from obtaining further commissions from the confraternity of San Rocco after his brilliant achievement with *Saint Roch Ministering to the Plague Victims*, executed in 1549. At that time Jacopo had sought membership in the confraternity, but no action was taken on his application. In 1553 Titian, whose membership had lapsed, suddenly offered to execute a major painting for the Sala dell'Albergo of the Scuola. Although he never followed through, Titian's offer may have been left dangling to preclude any opportunity for Tintoretto, who must have longed to decorate the still-bare walls and ceilings of the vast new building.[16]

The situation was ripe for the emergence of a rival to Tintoretto. When in the early 1550s a young painter from Verona known today as Paolo Veronese made his appearance on the Venetian scene, a prodigiously talented alternative to Tintoretto suddenly became available.

Born in Verona in 1528, Paolo trained with local masters who had little to offer beyond the fundamentals of technique and a basic visual vocabulary.[17] Although Verona was part of Venice's mainland empire, its artistic scene was provincial and not particularly oriented toward Venice. But Paolo was fortunate in finding a mentor in the architect Michele Sanmicheli, who took the young painter under his wing and, according to Vasari, treated him like a loving foster father. Through Sanmicheli, Paolo came to know the works of Giulio Romano in nearby Mantua as well as other works by artists from outside Verona. Ridolfi reports that he was granted permission to copy the painting of the Holy Family by Raphael known as *La Perla* (Museo Nacional del Prado, Madrid), then in the Palazzo Canossa in Verona.[18] The classicizing architecture of Sanmicheli himself was undoubtedly an influence as well. As a result of this wide-ranging experience and what was obviously an extremely precocious talent, at a very early age Paolo developed a style based primarily on Central Italian models, far more sophisticated than anything being achieved by his hometown colleagues.

Unlike the young Tintoretto, whose early works are filled with specific borrowings and quotations from Central Italian sources, incorporated into a highly idiosyncratic and constantly changing style, Veronese's early paintings show that he had assimilated elements from Parmigianino, Giulio Romano, Salviati, and Raphael, among others, while revealing few specific influences. Tempering the more manneristic aspects of these styles is a sense of decorum and repose that may be in part derived from the classicism of Sanmicheli but is undoubtedly intrinsic to Veronese's own temperate personality as well. Moreover, Veronese achieved this personal synthesis at an astonishingly youthful age, unlike Tintoretto, who struggled for almost a decade before attaining a similar level of consistent accomplishment. Thus Veronese's *Christ Healing a Woman with an Issue of Blood (?)* (cat. 11), painted when he was only about twenty, is comparable to Tintoretto's *Esther before Ahasuerus*, executed when Tintoretto was almost thirty. Similarly, the underlying classicism in Veronese's style enabled him to reconcile an up-to-date Central Italian style with a traditional Venetian subject from earlier in the century, the Holy Family in a landscape, as he did in the *Mystic Marriage of Saint Catherine of Alexandria* (cat. 13), based upon prototypes such as Titian's *Virgin and Child with Saint Catherine of Alexandria and a Rabbit* (cat. 12). Also present in Veronese's early works is the characteristic for which he would become especially famous, his dazzling and sophisticated color combinations.[19]

Veronese made his debut in Venice around 1551 with his altarpiece for the chapel of the influential

Giustiniani family at the church of San Francesco della Vigna, the *Holy Family with Saint John the Baptist, Saint Anthony Abbot, and Saint Catherine* (fig. 48). For his first Venetian painting, he unambiguously declared his allegiance to Titian by employing the older master's *Madonna di Ca' Pesaro* (fig. 47) as his model. With this prominent altarpiece, Veronese demonstrated his ability to work in a contemporary mode that was thoroughly grounded in the Venetian tradition, in a way that moreover would have flattered Titian and distinguished himself from the controversial Tintoretto. These tactics were so successful that with his next Venetian commission, Veronese rose directly to the highest level of patronage: in 1553, he was commissioned to participate in the decoration of the ceilings of three rooms in the Palazzo Ducale, including the great central oval titled *Jupiter Expelling the Vices* in the Sala of the Council of Ten (fig. 42). Veronese's painting combined the dramatic illusionism of Giulio Romano with a monumental classicism and radiant color and light—an up-to-date triumph that avoided the troubling lack of finish of many of Tintoretto's paintings.[20]

Beginning in 1555, Veronese began to decorate the church of the monastery of San Sebastiano, whose prior, Bernardo Torlioni, was a native of Verona. Starting with the ceiling of the sacristy, Veronese continued in 1556 with three giant canvases for the ceiling of the nave, including the *Coronation of Esther* (fig. 43), followed by further paintings and frescoes in the church.[21] Tintoretto must have watched in frustration as his rival turned San Sebastiano into exactly the kind of unified environment that he yearned to create himself—and that, later in the decade, he would succeed in achieving first at the church of Madonna dell'Orto and ultimately in his greatest monument, the Scuola Grande di San Rocco.

Thus, by the mid-1550s, with Veronese firmly established on the Venetian scene, the three rivals had assumed the roles that they would play for the remainder of their lives. Tintoretto began as a challenger to Titian and earned the older painter's lifelong enmity, although the two would continue to learn and borrow from one another throughout their careers. Veronese, whose beginnings owed as much to Central Italian influences as Tintoretto's did, nevertheless identified himself with Titian early on. Despite the inventive and innovative qualities of his art, Veronese's classical temperament and glorious coloring made him appealing to more conservative tastes, and he became the favored painter of those unmoved by Tintoretto's turbulent and unconventional canvases. Titian made his own feelings plain in 1557, when he and Sansovino awarded to Veronese a golden chain for the most distinguished contribution to the ceiling for the reading room of Jacopo Sansovino's Libreria Marciana—a commission from which Tintoretto, probably with Titian's connivance, had been excluded.[22]

— RE, FI

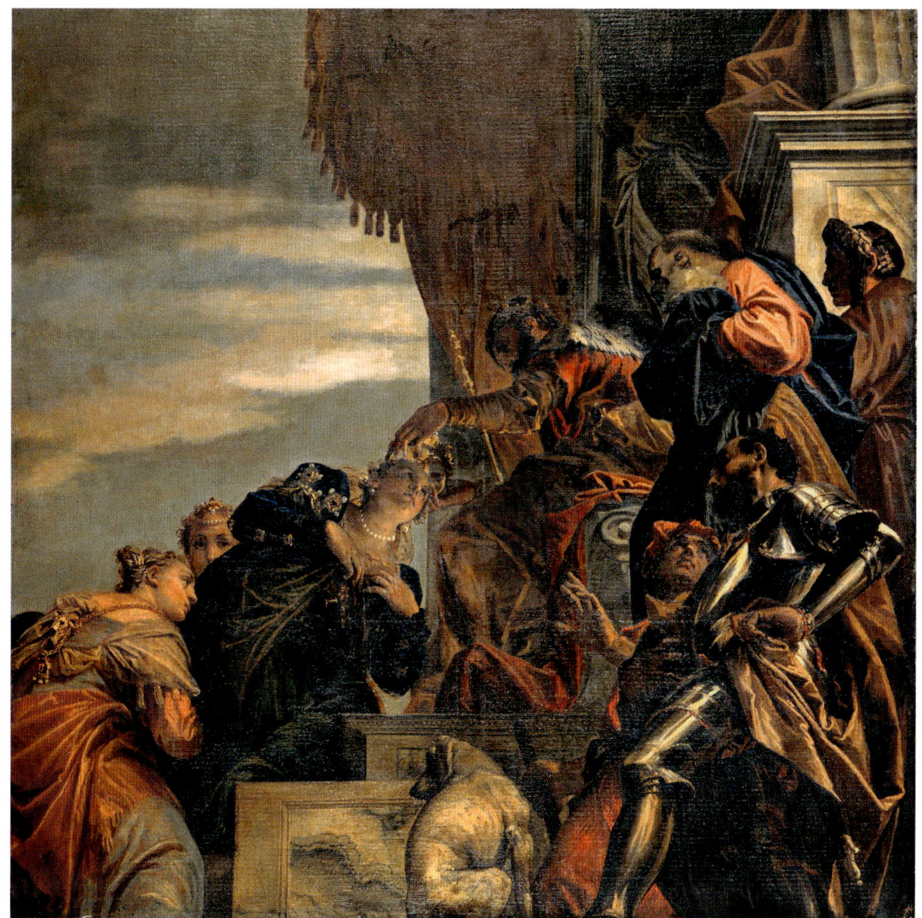

Fig. 43
Veronese
Coronation of Esther, about 1555–56
Oil on canvas
Church of San Sebastiano, Venice

The Challenge of Tintoretto

TINTORETTO
Contest between Apollo and Marsyas, 1544–45
Wadsworth Atheneum Museum of Art, Hartford, Connecticut
(cat. 8)

TINTORETTO
Self-Portrait, about 1546–47
Philadelphia Museum of Art
(cat. 9)

These two paintings are key documents from the early years of Tintoretto's career, before his triumph with the *Miracle of the Slave* in 1548, at a time when he was still struggling to establish himself as one of the leading painters in Venice. They also remind us that sixteenth-century artists promoted their fledgling careers not only with public commissions but also with paintings of very different formats and characters.

The *Contest between Apollo and Marsyas* is one of two decorative ceiling canvases that Tintoretto executed for the writer Pietro Aretino, an intimate of Titian and Sansovino and the self-appointed arbiter of Venetian aesthetic taste. Prominent painted ceiling ensembles had appeared in religious and public buildings in Venice in the 1530s, but examples in private palaces were at the cutting edge of fashion by the following decade. A few years before *Apollo and Marsyas*, Tintoretto had created a ceiling ensemble of painted wooden panels depicting scenes from Ovid for the patrician Vettor Pisani, which exploited the dramatic possibilities of the strongly foreshortened *di sotto in sù* (up from below) point of view used so effectively by Pordenone and Giulio Romano. Tintoretto's ceiling must have made a strong impression on Titian, who borrowed from it a few years later in his own ceiling painting of *David and Goliath* for the church of Santo Spirito in Isola. In the painting for Aretino, a client who preferred Central Italian artistic styles, Tintoretto employed the *quadro riportato* format, in which the picture simulates a wall painting placed on the ceiling. Although less dramatic than the illusionistic approach to which Tintoretto would return for his mature ceiling paintings, this format represented the most up-to-date Central Italian taste.[23]

This highly visible work in the latest style would have advertised Tintoretto's credentials to an influential audience, the trend-setting Aretino and his immediate circle. Tintoretto probably executed the paintings for Aretino for a low price, or even for free, a strategy that he adopted on numerous occasions to advance his career.[24] Aretino, similarly, was known for repaying gifts and favors with flattering publicity in his published letters, as he did in this instance. In a letter dated February 1545, he thanked Tintoretto for *Apollo and Marsyas* and the other painting in the ensemble (which depicted Mercury and Argus), saying, "All the connoisseurs agree that the two fables . . . are beautiful, lively, and effortless, as are the attitudes adopted by the figures therein: these you, so young, have painted to my great satisfaction and indeed to everyone else's, for the ceiling of my house, in less time than normally might have been devoted to the mere consideration of the subject."[25]

The program of the ceiling ensemble was clearly intended to celebrate Aretino's primacy over the arts. The fable of Apollo and the satyr Marsyas addresses themes of artistic innovation, competition, and judgment. As recounted by Ovid, Minerva invented the flute but then cursed it when playing the instrument caused her cheeks to puff out unbecomingly. Marsyas, who picked up the flute, learned to play with great proficiency and eventually challenged Apollo to a contest. Apollo in turn played the lyre, and the Muses naturally judged him the winner. Marsyas was hanged and flayed by the god as punishment for his presumption.[26] Both Apollo and Minerva (who also appears in the picture, identifiable by her attributes of spear and shield) are patrons of the arts; Mount Helicon, the home of the Muses, is seen in the background. Juergen Schulz, followed more recently by Philipp Fehl, has proposed that the bearded figure in green at the far right represents Aretino himself, an attractive suggestion given the client's vanity.[27] Lora Anne Palladino, by contrast, identifies the man at the right not as Aretino but as the poet Ariosto, as portrayed in the woodcut, after a drawing by Titian, on the frontispiece of the 1532 edition of his *Orlando Furioso*. She sees Ariosto's appearance in the painting as an allusion to Aretino's imitation of the older poet's courtly language.[28] The figure does appear to resemble the sharp-nosed Ariosto rather more than the bulky, thick-featured Aretino, as depicted in Titian's portrait of 1545 (fig. 44). Both identifications remain speculative, however, and no reading of the picture's iconography can be accepted as definitive. Tintoretto's companion painting for Aretino has long been lost, but this fable too—in which the god Mercury is able to slay the hundred-eyed giant Argus by using music to make him drowsy—can easily be seen as a celebration of the power of art.

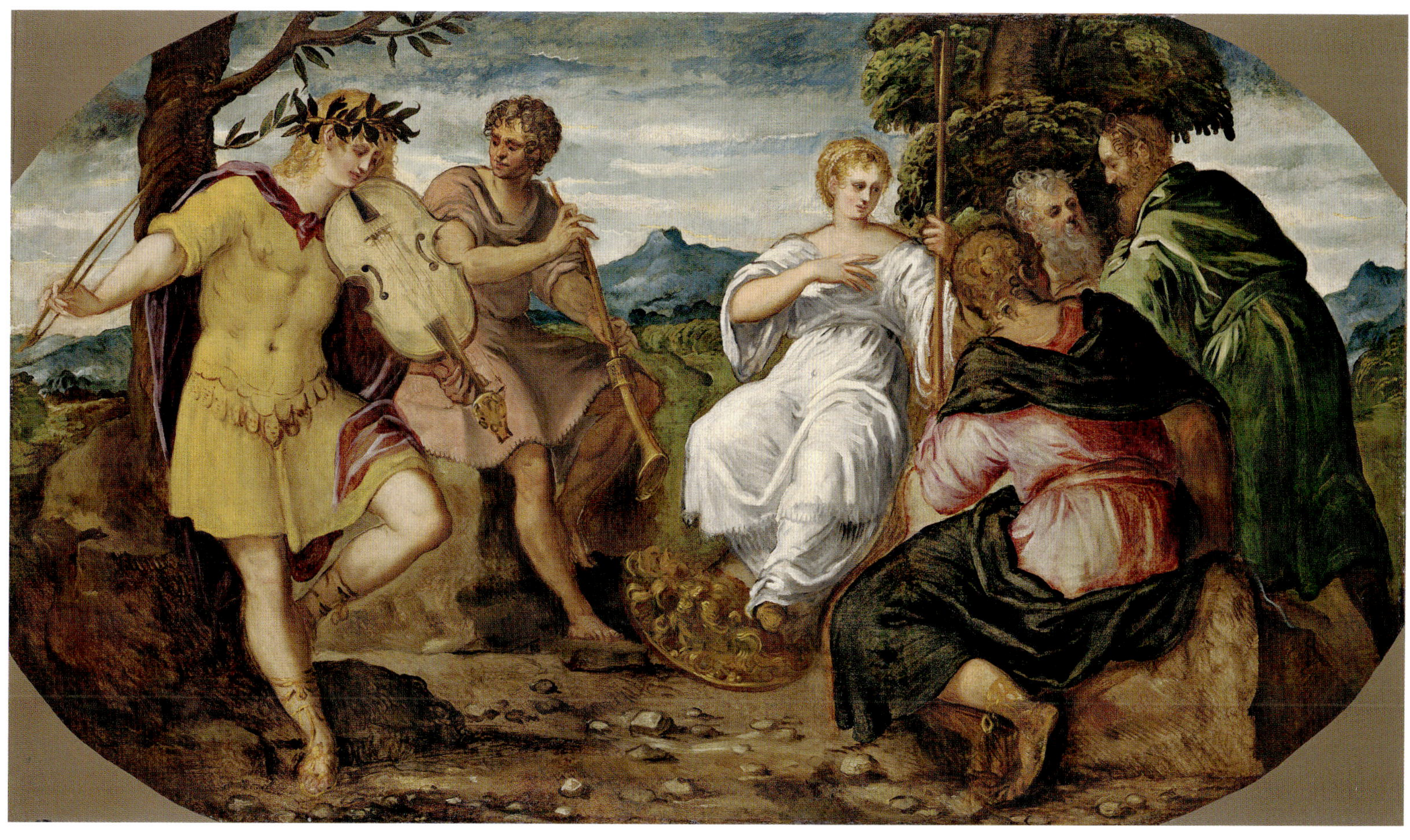

cat. 8

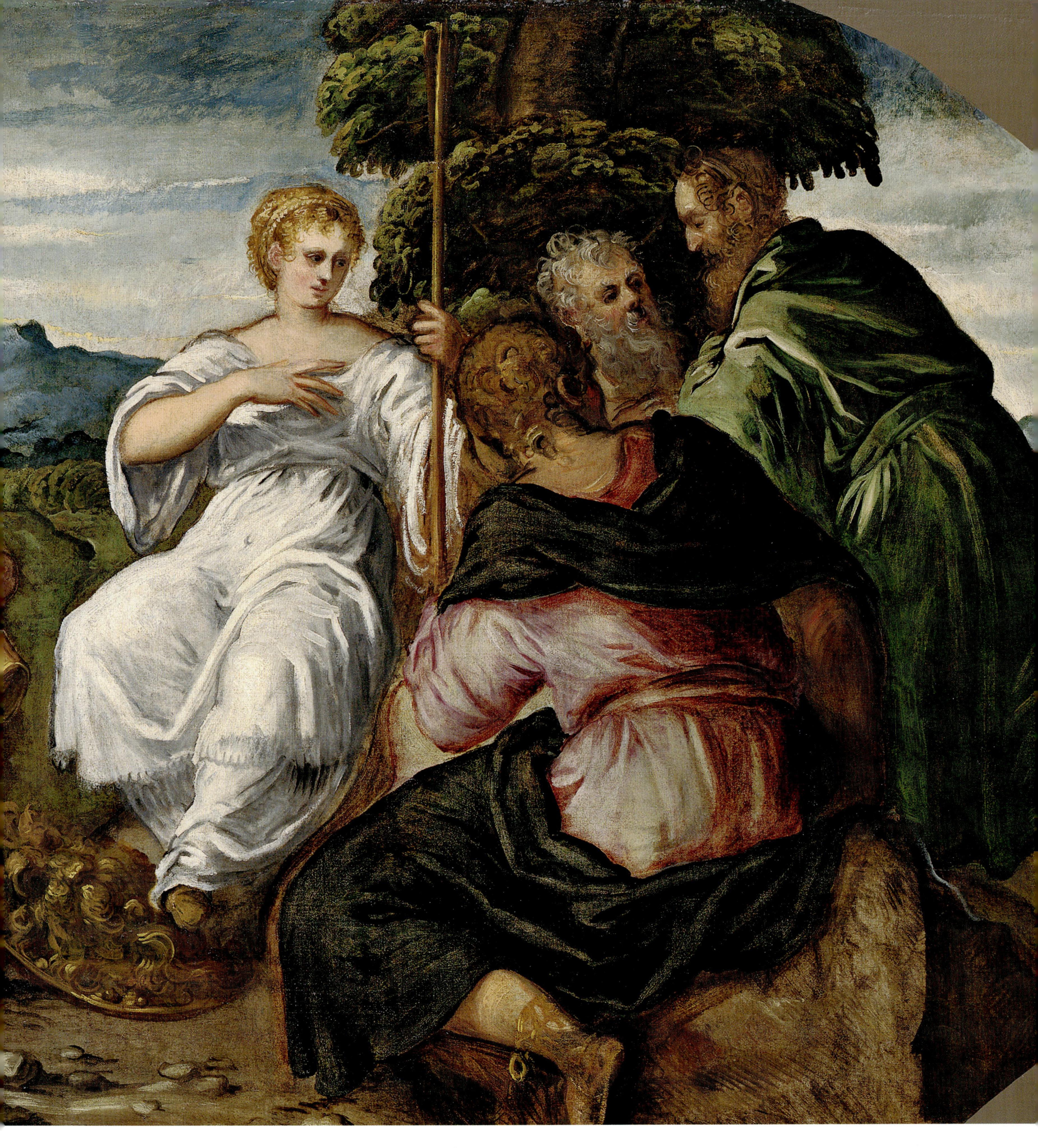

The speedy execution that Aretino's letter describes is clearly evident in the picture's loose brushwork and improvisational air—figures and faces are sketchy, some appear to have been left unfinished, and there are numerous *pentimenti*, or alterations, most prominently in Apollo's viol, the position of Minerva's right hand, and the positions of the fingers of the two protagonists on their instruments. The anatomical forms on Apollo's cuirass are executed with precisely the same kind of free drawing technique of abbreviated contours that Tintoretto used in sketching the nude figure underneath, now evident through paint layers that have become transparent with age. As a general matter, Venetian viewers were willing to accept a less finished, sketchy manner in ceiling paintings and other decorative works, and in this instance, the emphasis in Aretino's letter on the rapidity with which the work was painted suggests that Tintoretto may have painted even faster than usual, showing off his speed as a tour de force. Thus the difference in technique and quality between *Apollo and Marsyas* and the similarly painterly, but much more finished and richly textured, *Esther before Ahasuerus* of just a few years later must be attributed not entirely to Jacopo's rapid progression as an artist during this brief period, but also to the fact that audiences would have had different expectations of the two paintings.

Still, while Aretino praised Tintoretto for the speed with which he executed the ceiling paintings, he seems to have preferred pictures with a more polished character and less of the loose, expressive brushwork characteristic of *Apollo and Marsyas*. Titian's *Pietro Aretino*, for instance, was painted at almost exactly the same time as Tintoretto's ceiling and shows passages, particularly in the drapery highlights, that reflect the new, painterly techniques of Tintoretto and his fellows. Apparently the sitter did not approve; in a letter to Cosimo de' Medici, for whom Aretino had commissioned the portrait, he caustically remarked that if he had only paid Titian more, "the fabrics would have been brilliant, delicate, and stiff, like real satin, velvet and brocade."[29] To Titian himself, he complained that the portrait was more a sketch than finished ("più tosto abozzato che fornito").[30] A few years later, in his famous letter acclaiming Tintoretto's *Miracle of the Slave*, Aretino offered a similar criticism of Tintoretto's technique, tempering his praise with avuncular advice, "Blessings be on your name if you can temper haste to have done with patience in the doing."[31]

The portrait Aretino commissioned for Cosimo de' Medici was only one of many likenesses of him-

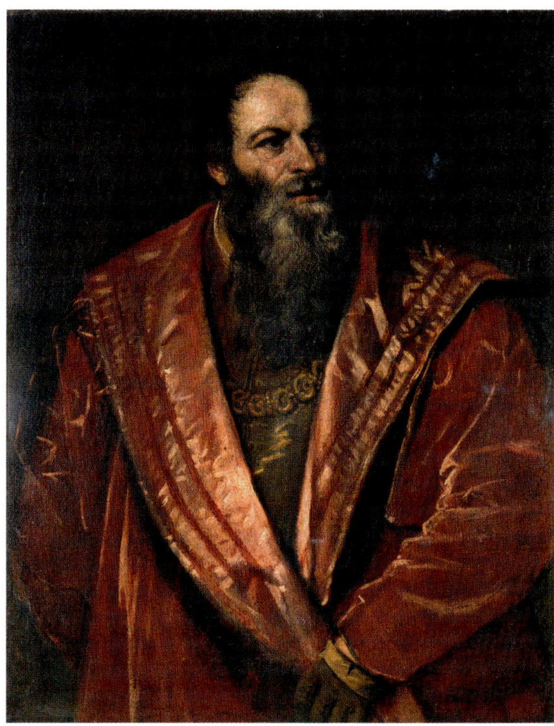

Fig. 44
Titian
Pietro Aretino, 1545
Oil on canvas
Galleria Palatina, Florence

self he ordered from various artists, demonstrating how well the writer understood the self-promoting value of portraiture. These included a total of three portraits each from Titian and Sebastiano del Piombo, one from Tintoretto (noted in a letter of 1551), and one each from Salviati, Vasari, Moretto da Brescia, and Marcantonio Raimondi, along with a half-dozen portrait medals. In two letters of 1545, Aretino boasted that his portrait had been sculpted in lead, bronze, gold, and silver; painted on wood, canvas, paper, and walls; and appeared on palace facades, comb cases, mirrors, and plates.[32] Titian, who owed much of his reputation in European courts to his gift for portraiture, also understood the power of the genre to convey status and promote the sitter's public image. Yet, despite his own growing celebrity, he seems not to have turned to himself as a subject until fairly late in his career: his first documented self-portrait is one that Vasari mentions as painted in 1545, just before the artist's trip to Rome, "to leave a record of himself for his children." After his return from Rome, Titian appeared more interested in self-portraiture; for example, in 1552, he presented the future Philip II with a small picture of himself holding a portrait of the prince. Falomir speculates that this gift should be understood in terms of Titian's desire to rival Michelangelo (spurred on by their encounter in Rome) to snare the greatest patrons on the international stage.[33]

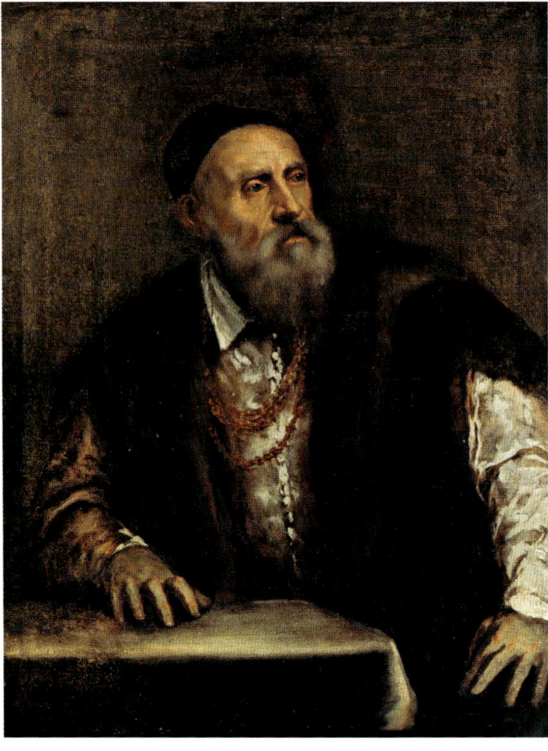

Fig. 45
Titian
Self-Portrait, about 1562
Oil on canvas
Gemäldegalerie, Staatliche Museen zu Berlin

By contrast, Tintoretto used self-portraiture to promote himself from the very beginning of his career. According to Ridolfi, one of his early works was a likeness of himself holding a piece of sculpture, a nocturne, "depicted so formidably [*con si terribile maniera*] that he astounded everyone." The painting was exhibited in the Merceria, the main shopping street between the Piazza San Marco and the Rialto, a place where, in Ridolfi's words, young artists "competitively exhibited the fruits of their labors . . . to test the reaction of their viewers." It inspired one admirer to proclaim in verse: "If Tintoret's light at night appears so fine / How shall his radiance in daylight shine?"[34] Ridolfi mentions several other youthful self-portraits by Tintoretto still present in Venetian collections in the mid-seventeenth century.

The present *Self-Portrait*, although undoubtedly executed some years later than the painting the young artist exhibited in the Merceria, conveys a sense of the "terribile maniera" of that early work. The painter's face emerges from darkness, his features brilliantly spotlit. The absence of any attributes, or indeed any color other than black, browns, and flesh tones, heightens the effect on the sitter's penetrating gaze. In his portraits of others, Tintoretto adopted the formula perfected by Titian, emphasizing the sitter's dignity and status (see cats. 38–39). That is not the case in the *Self-Portrait*, however, which seems rather to look back to paintings by Giorgione, such as the supposed *Self-Portrait as David* (Herzog Anton Ulrich Museum, Brunswick) and to focus on personality rather than status.[35] Yet there is also an element of dynamism and immediacy here that is Tintoretto's own, very different from the dreamy mood of Giorgione's portraits. Tintoretto's pose and stare make it clear that he is in the process of painting: the viewer understands that he is turning over his right shoulder to look at himself in a mirror, extending his right arm toward the very same canvas that the viewer is now seeing. (Titian's *Self-Portrait* [fig. 45], conversely, presents the artist without referring to the act of painting.) Tintoretto's direct self-confrontation in the mirror becomes a confrontation with the viewer. In it, we can read all the intensity and fiery ambition described by his contemporaries and biographers.

While the paucity of firm information about Tintoretto's youthful chronology makes it difficult to date the *Self-Portrait* with complete confidence, he appears to be in his mid-to-late twenties—certainly a number of years older than the boyish self-portrait in *Christ among the Doctors* (Museo del Duomo, Milan), datable to the early 1540s.[36] Based on its painterly handling, a date of 1546–47, shortly before the *Portrait of a Man Aged Twenty-Six* (cat. 36) and the *Last Supper* (San Marcuola, Venice), both from 1547, seems most likely.[37] This would place it soon after Titian's *Pietro Aretino*, a painting that—while very different in size and overall effect—shows some striking similarities in pictorial technique. Especially close are the brightly highlighted passages on the forehead, around the cheekbones, and on the nose, conveyed with frank, dry strokes. During the years around 1545–47, Tintoretto was paying increasingly close attention to Titian's brushwork and modeling, no longer so insistent on presenting himself as the "anti-Titian," the heir to Pordenone and a promoter of the new Central Italian style. In the older artist's *Aretino*, which Tintoretto might well have viewed in Aretino's house or elsewhere before it was sent to Florence, he could have seen handling similar to his own used to create effects of light and texture that had generally been absent from his early paintings.[38] This comparison of Titian's *Pietro Aretino* and Tintoretto's *Self-Portrait* shows how closely the techniques of the established master and his young challenger could approach in the mid-1540s—years in which they shared, as well, important ties to the same influential patron, Aretino.

— RE, FI

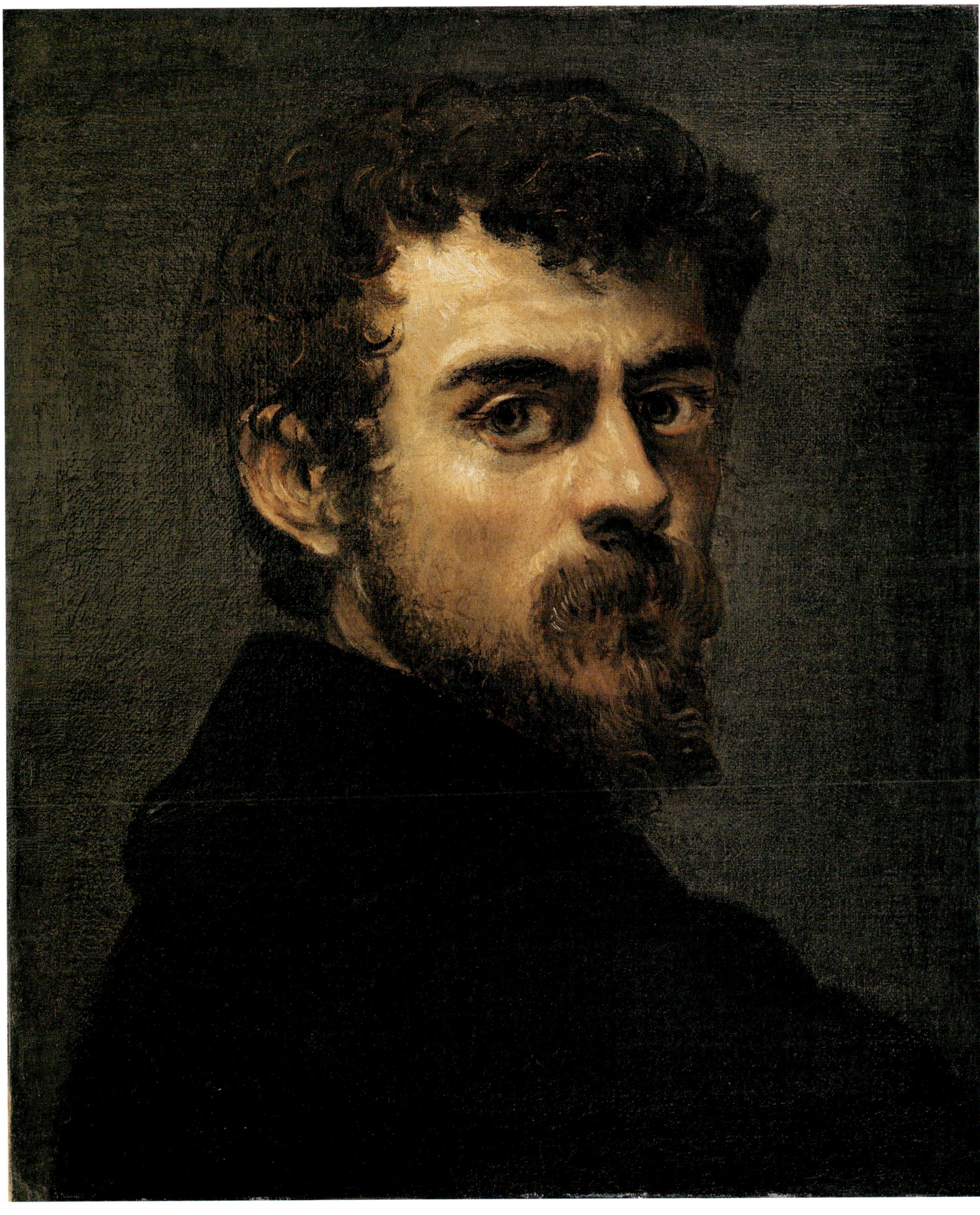

cat. 9

Veronese before Venice: Narrative Painting

TINTORETTO
Esther before Ahasuerus, about 1547–48
The Royal Collection, London
(cat. 10)

VERONESE
Christ Healing a Woman with an Issue of Blood (?), about 1548
The National Gallery, London
(cat. 11)

Produced in the early years of each artist's career, these two pictures are fascinatingly similar: horizontal narrative compositions ordered around a standing man and a kneeling or swooning woman amid a crowd of twisting bodies, turbaned men, bejeweled women, and gesticulating hands.[39] In each painting, the poses of the bystanders, their bodies advancing right up to the picture plane, add to the drama. From the perspective of five centuries, the works would appear to have been produced in competition with each other; their execution, however, is likely to have been simultaneous but independent. Moreover, Veronese was still in Verona, and there is no demonstrable proof that either artist had access to the other's studio at this time. The two pictures nonetheless illustrate the essential differences between the two artists. Veronese was also already a notable colorist, and the large pools of bright hues seen here would become a virtual trademark. Although set against shadowed columns, the scene is flooded with light, a tonality created in large part by the application of color and glazes over a light pink *imprimatura*.[40] In contrast, Tintoretto's figures emerge from the darkness, worked up in rough visible brushstrokes. Even allowing for the differences in subject matter, Tintoretto's picture is infused with a sense of energy that is absent from Veronese's more coolly mannered composition, an energy created not only through foreshortened figures but, even more, through Tintoretto's technical bravura.

Despite their fundamentally different approaches to painting, the artists shared several interests in these years, and this explains some of the compositional similarities. Both painters learned much from Central Italian art, and both pictures seem to have been designed with Raphael's cartoon the *Sacrifice at Lystra* (fig. 46) in mind.[41] As so often in his work, Veronese has framed his scene with classicizing architecture, in this case a Bramantesque stair certainly inspired by the work of his early associate, Michele Sanmicheli; even if little architecture is evident in *Esther before Ahasuerus*, Tintoretto's *Washing of the Feet* (fig. 26) and *Miracle of the Slave*, of 1548–49, have scenographic architectural backdrops of the sort that would be associated primarily with Veronese in the coming decades.

Tintoretto's painting has its source in the expanded version of the Book of Esther, which recounts the bravery of the Jewish queen of Persia who approached her husband, the king Ahasuerus, with a plea to save the Jews in his empire, who were threatened with annihilation.[42] Ahasuerus had not called for her and glared at her for her presumption. Frightened, Esther fainted, and one of her maids came to her aid. God then softened Ahasuerus's anger, and with tender concern, the king rose from his throne to comfort his queen.

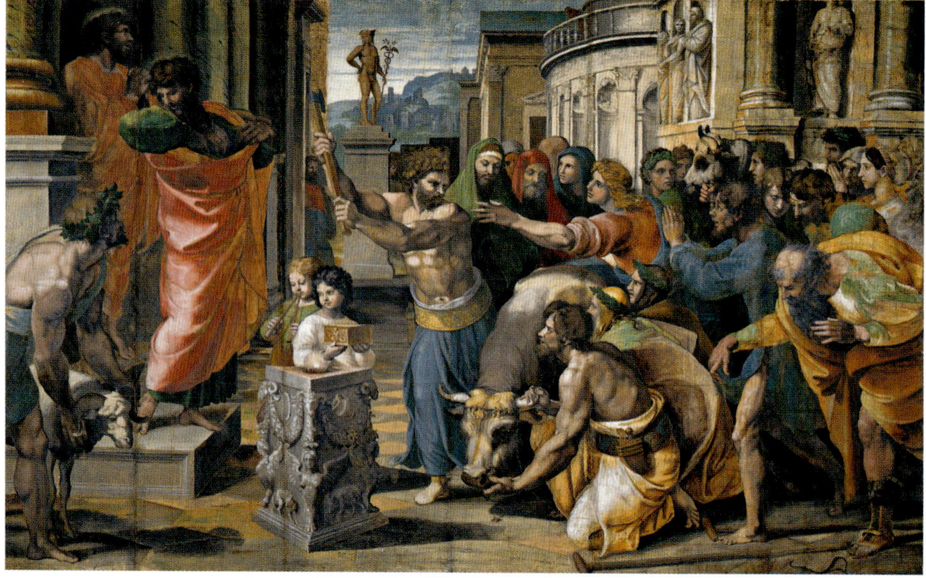

Fig. 46. Raphael (Raffaello Sanzio) (1483–1520), *Sacrifice at Lystra*, 1515–16, bodycolor on paper mounted on canvas (tapestry cartoon), Victoria and Albert Museum, London

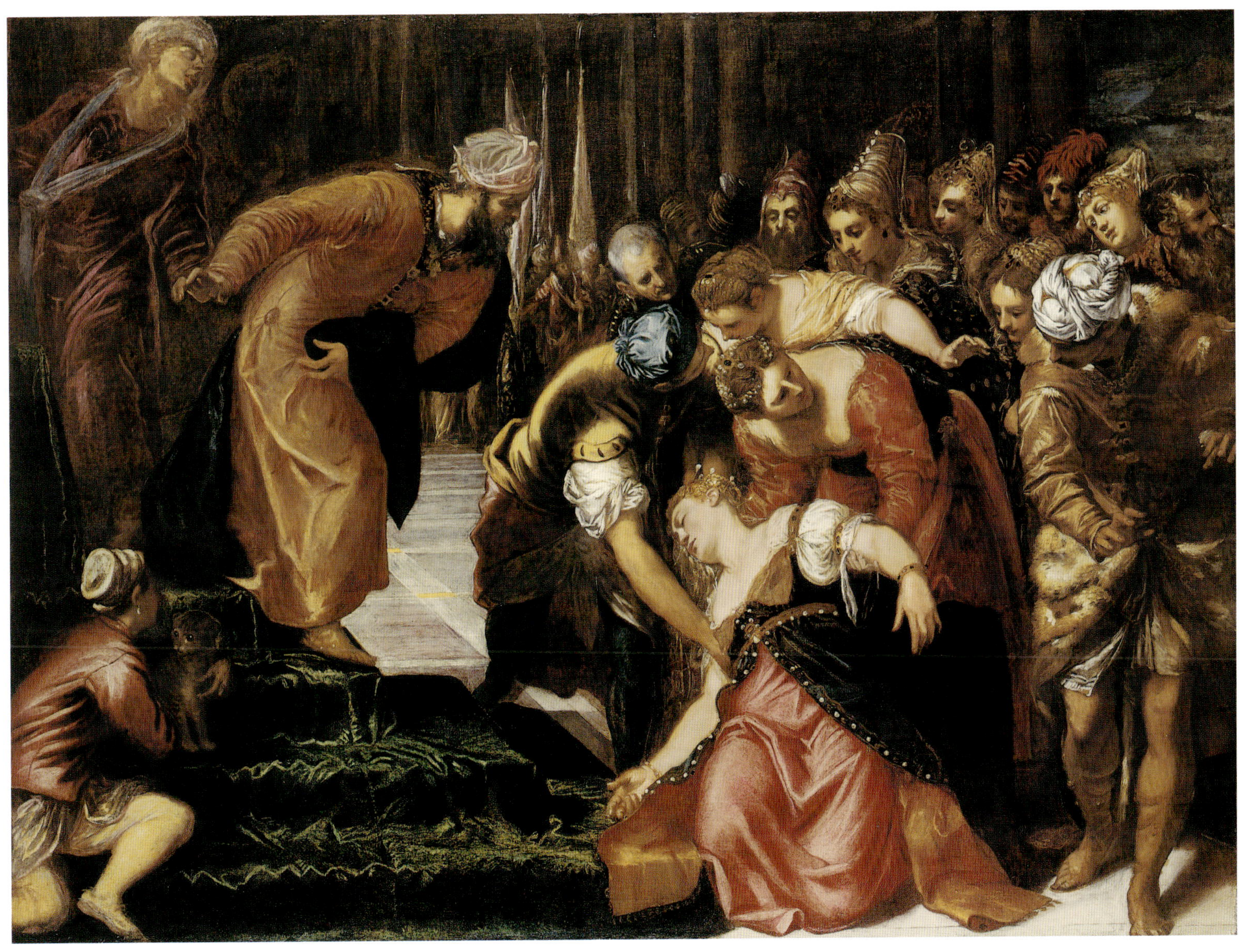

cat. 10

Although the episode's combination of richly dressed figures and human drama would seem ideally suited to the young Tintoretto, he seems to have left the *Esther before Ahasuerus* unfinished, particularly at the left edge, where the tall turbaned figure was laid in only as a sketch but never completed.[43] The circumstances of the painting's commission and the reason why Tintoretto left it incomplete are not known, but on the basis of style, the painting is dated to 1547–48, contemporary with, or just before, the *Miracle of the Slave*. Although by this time Tintoretto had been an independent master for a decade, only at this point, in the late 1540s, did he arrive at what might be deemed his own characteristic style, in contrast to earlier works that seem to be more under the influence of Schiavone, Giuseppe Porta Salviati, and Bonifazio de' Pitati (see, for example, Tintoretto's *Supper at Emmaus* of about 1542 [cat. 22]).[44]

In contrast to Tintoretto's relatively prolonged development, the precociously talented Veronese had, by the time he was eighteen or twenty years old (and well before he settled in Venice), already arrived at his individual manner.[45] Veronese's assured painting depicts an episode recounted in the Gospels in which a woman who has suffered twelve years of bleeding is cured when she touches Christ's robe. When he calls out to ask who has touched him, the embarrassed and fearful woman admits that it was she. Christ reassures her, stating, "Thy faith has made thee whole; go in peace."[46]

In assessing Veronese's development, one must revisit the chronology of his early work, for the *Christ Healing a Woman with an Issue of Blood (?)* has been variously dated between 1546 and 1556. Rather than an isolated example, this surprisingly broad window—the years in question represent the full first decade of Veronese's career—is typical of the scholarship on early Veronese, a lack of consensus that is doubly troubling if one wishes to evaluate it with respect to Tintoretto's parallel development. Despite a trend among some scholars to place *Christ Healing a Woman with an Issue of Blood (?)* in the 1550s, the London canvas is surely a painting from Veronese's time in Verona and is best dated to around 1548.[47] He would later temper the high-keyed secondary color juxtapositions seen here, and the weightless, doll-like figures are found only in his earliest pictures. It should be noted, though, that the clustered, twisted figures in this painting and the off-center composition are also found in Veronese's *Daughter of Jairus* (Musée du Louvre, Paris) of two years earlier and thus are not necessarily a response to Tintoretto's works of around 1548, as is sometimes argued. The two artists would become keen rivals in the following years, but only after each had already attained artistic maturity.
— JM

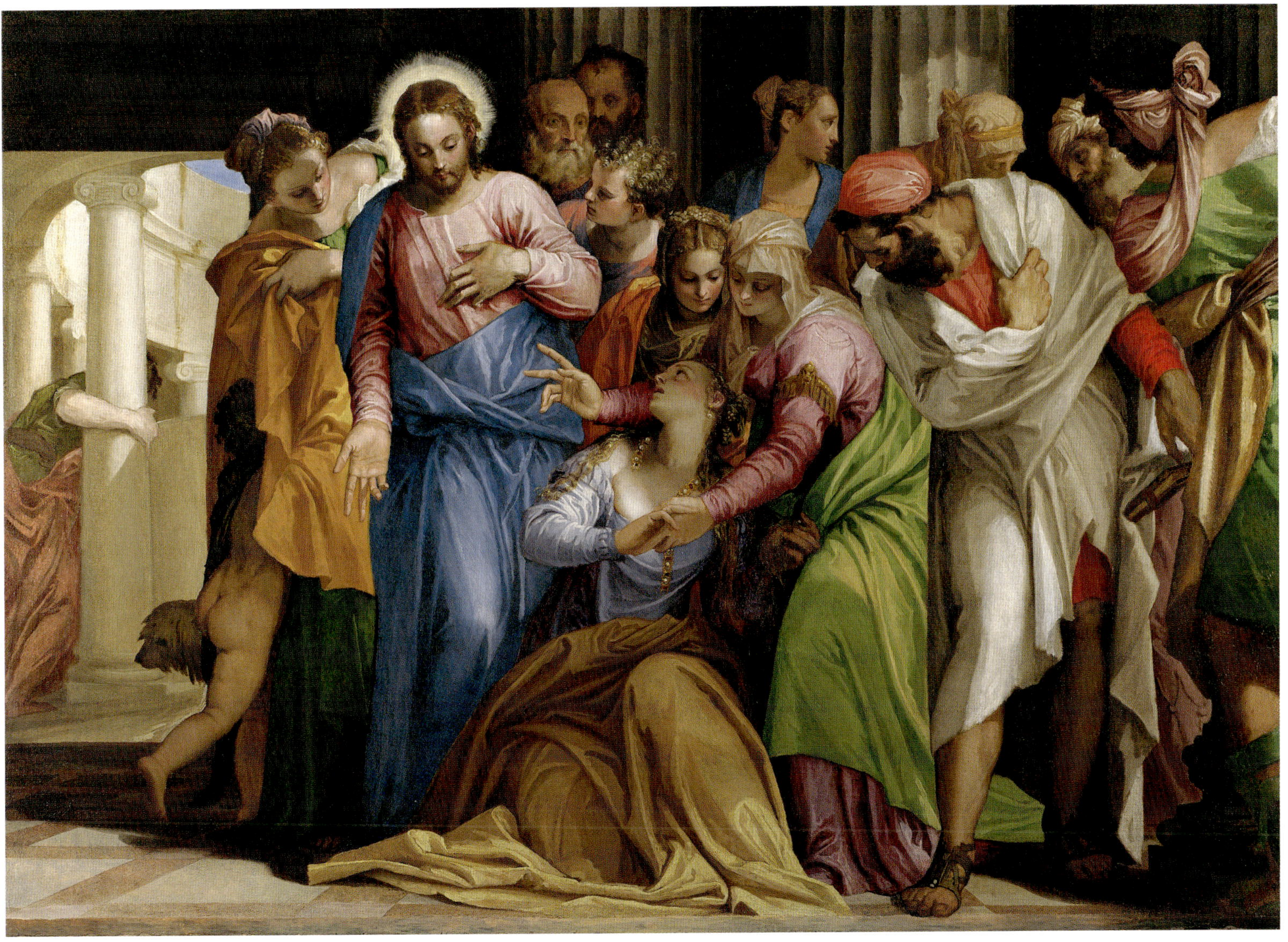

cat. 11

Veronese before Venice: Looking at Titian

TITIAN
Virgin and Child with Saint Catherine of Alexandria and a Rabbit, about 1530
Musée du Louvre, Paris
(cat. 12)

VERONESE
Mystic Marriage of Saint Catherine of Alexandria, about 1549
Yale University Art Gallery, New Haven, Connecticut
Lent by The Barker Welfare Foundation
(cat. 13)

A new pictorial type, the depiction of the Virgin and Child with saints in a landscape, should be counted among the quintessential developments of Venetian Cinquecento painting. Its evolution began when the *sacra conversazione*, as painted by Giovanni Bellini and others of his generation, came increasingly to include glimpses of a landscape background (see, for example, the *Virgin and Child with Saints* by Bellini and his workshop [cat. 1]). In the decades after 1500, especially in the work of Titian and Palma Vecchio, the Holy Family and saints were moved into the landscape. This reflected the rise of landscape painting in the secular, poetic canvases for which Giorgione is best known, and the placement of the saints in a setting other than an ecclesiastical frame shifted these hitherto iconic pictures toward narrative, making the *sacra conversazione* into something more like a real conversation.[48] The genre thus arose out of the altarpiece, and also from the Venetian votive tradition,[49] but by the time the *Virgin and Child with Saint Catherine of Alexandria and a Rabbit* (known as the *Madonna of the Rabbit)* was painted around 1530, it had become an almost secular phenomenon, as likely to be commissioned for picture galleries as for devotional function. This was the case with Titian's painting, perhaps created for Federico II Gonzaga, who is usually identified as the shepherd at right, wearing the laurel crown of a humanist poet.[50] Along with the *Aldobrandini Madonna* (National Gallery, London), probably painted for the Este court, Titian's canvas is one of the masterpieces of the type.[51]

Titian's paintings indicate that the genre became popular far beyond Venice, and it is thus unsurprising that by the late 1540s the young Veronese would produce a work like the *Mystic Marriage of Saint Catherine of Alexandria* even before he settled in Venice.[52] Its combination of broad landscape, intimate gestures, and precisely depicted details is so much like Titian's that Veronese must have had the opportunity to study a picture like the *Madonna of the Rabbit*. Indeed, the *Mystic Marriage* relies so heavily on Titian's work that initially it seems little advanced beyond Titian's picture of fifteen or twenty years earlier, although the naturalistic, pastoral mood of these pictures is likely to have had a special appeal within the humanist culture of Verona and would thus have mitigated the desire for deliberate innovation.[53]

On further examination, however, Veronese can be seen to offer a few interesting new variations on the genre. The interlocking composition of the figures is more complex than the usual disposition of the Holy Family and saints in a friezelike arrangement across the picture plane. It has often been noted that the wicker crib at left in Veronese's picture derives from the Raphael-Giulio Romano *Holy Family* known as *La Perla* (Museo Nacional del Prado, Madrid), which Veronese was able to study at Palazzo Canossa in Verona, but the overlapping figural scheme can also be linked to that important model. The manner in which the Virgin leans forward, almost puncturing the picture plane, is likewise unusual in pictures of this type, although Veronese repeatedly returned to this in the works of his Verona period.[54] Finally, the burst of glory at upper left in the *Mystic Marriage*, while familiar from many altarpieces, is an extremely uncommon, if not unprecedented, motif for the saints-in-a-landscape genre, representing an irruption of the divine into a pictorial type hitherto notable for its earthly domesticity; the orange glow also serves to set off the blues and greens of the lucid landscape at the other edge of the canvas. However persistent the example of Titian's masterpieces, the *Mystic Marriage* and other early works demonstrate the confidence of the young Veronese. In them, we find his recognizable individual style, combining Venetian and Central Italian models; these pictures also include iconographic and compositional motifs that reveal the young artist's desire to test pictorial conventions even when working within a traditional framework.[55]

—JM

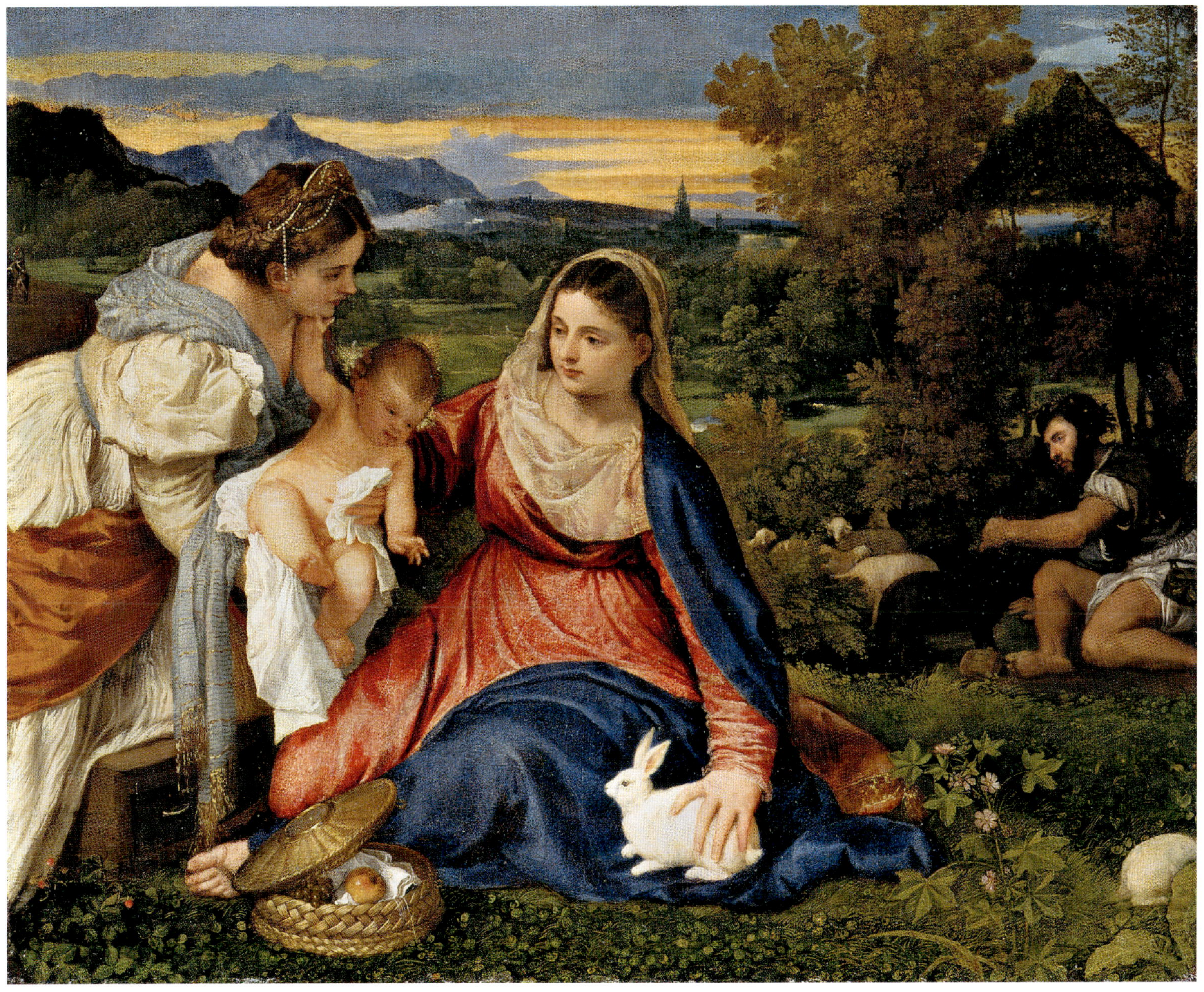

cat. 12

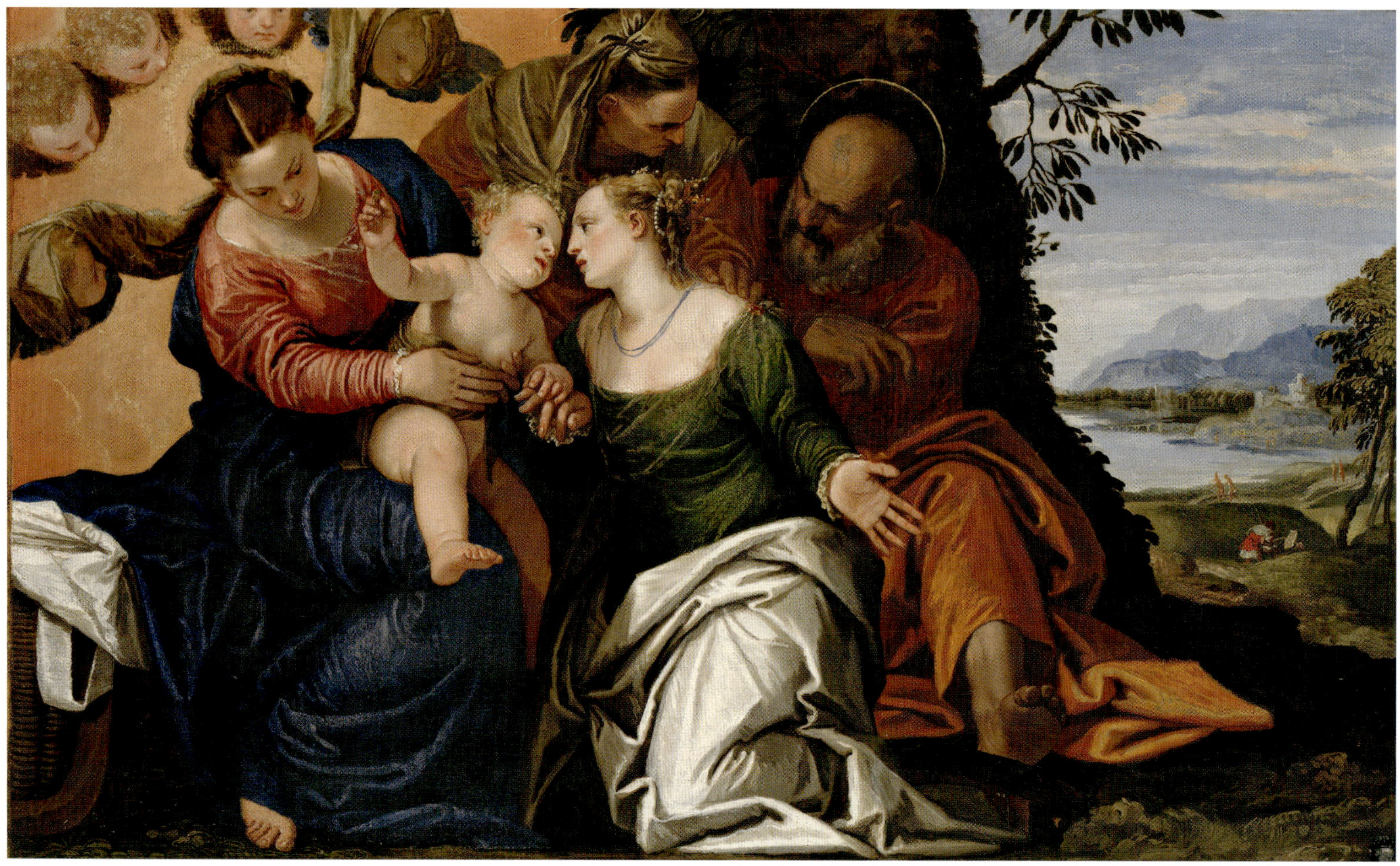

cat. 13

Tintoretto and Veronese: Declaring Allegiances

TINTORETTO
Saint Augustine Healing the Lame,
about 1549–50
Musei Civici, Pinacoteca di
Palazzo Chiericati, Vicenza
(cat. 14)

Although both Tintoretto and Veronese demonstrated, in their earliest works, a fundamental interest in Central Italian art, a comparison of the altarpiece that each painted around 1550 reveals their diverging attitudes with respect to Venetian tradition. Tintoretto's *Saint Augustine Healing the Lame*, painted for the Godi chapel in the church of San Michele, Vicenza, seems to have been the painter's first significant altarpiece commission outside of Venice. Whether he was catering to a mainland artistic culture that always seemed more responsive to Central Italian art than was the case in Venice, or whether the subject lent itself to such treatment, in this picture Tintoretto went further than any other Venetian artist in adopting the pictorial language of *michelangelismo*, even superseding his own *Saint Roch Ministering to the Plague Victims* of 1549.[56] Beyond the use of the muscular human body as a conveyor of meaning, many of the figures seem to make deliberate allusions to, if not actually quoting, works by Michelangelo. These foreshortened bodies evince Tintoretto's mastery of *disegno*, and this is combined with a virtuoso technique that can be considered a kind of drawing in paint.[57] While the increasingly loose techniques of Titian and Tintoretto approached each other in the mid-1540s, there is little in Titian to compare with the sketchy technique of the Godi altarpiece, and *Saint Augustine* seems a deliberate attempt to move beyond established Venetian conventions.

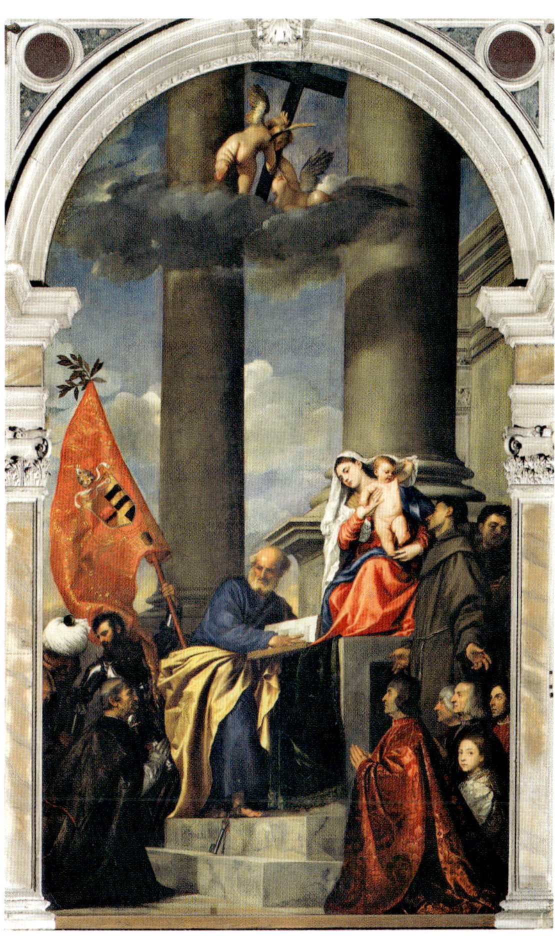

Fig. 47. Titian, *Madonna di Ca' Pesaro*, 1519–26, oil on canvas, church of Santa Maria Gloriosa dei Frari, Venice

In contrast to Tintoretto's evocations of Michelangelo, there can be no mistaking Veronese's ambition to position himself as a new Titian in adopting the *Madonna di Ca' Pesaro* (fig. 47) as the model for his first major Venetian commission, an altarpiece depicting the Holy Family with Saint John the Baptist, Saint Anthony Abbot, and Saint Catherine (fig. 48), painted for the Giustiniani chapel at San Francesco della Vigna and known as the *Pala Giustiniani*.[58] This was a clever strategy, for by then Titian's own energies were primarily turned to producing works for export. There are striking passages in the *Pala Giustiniani*—the figure of Saint Catherine with her beautifully painted draperies and the affecting figure of the young Saint John the Baptist struggling with the lamb deserve note—but the painting is perhaps less than the sum of its parts. The casual poses strike an odd note in a composition that would seem meant to aim for grandeur, and the relationships drawn between the figures could be sharper. The diagonal disposition of the scene evokes Titian's great example, but it is functionless with respect to visitors to San Francesco

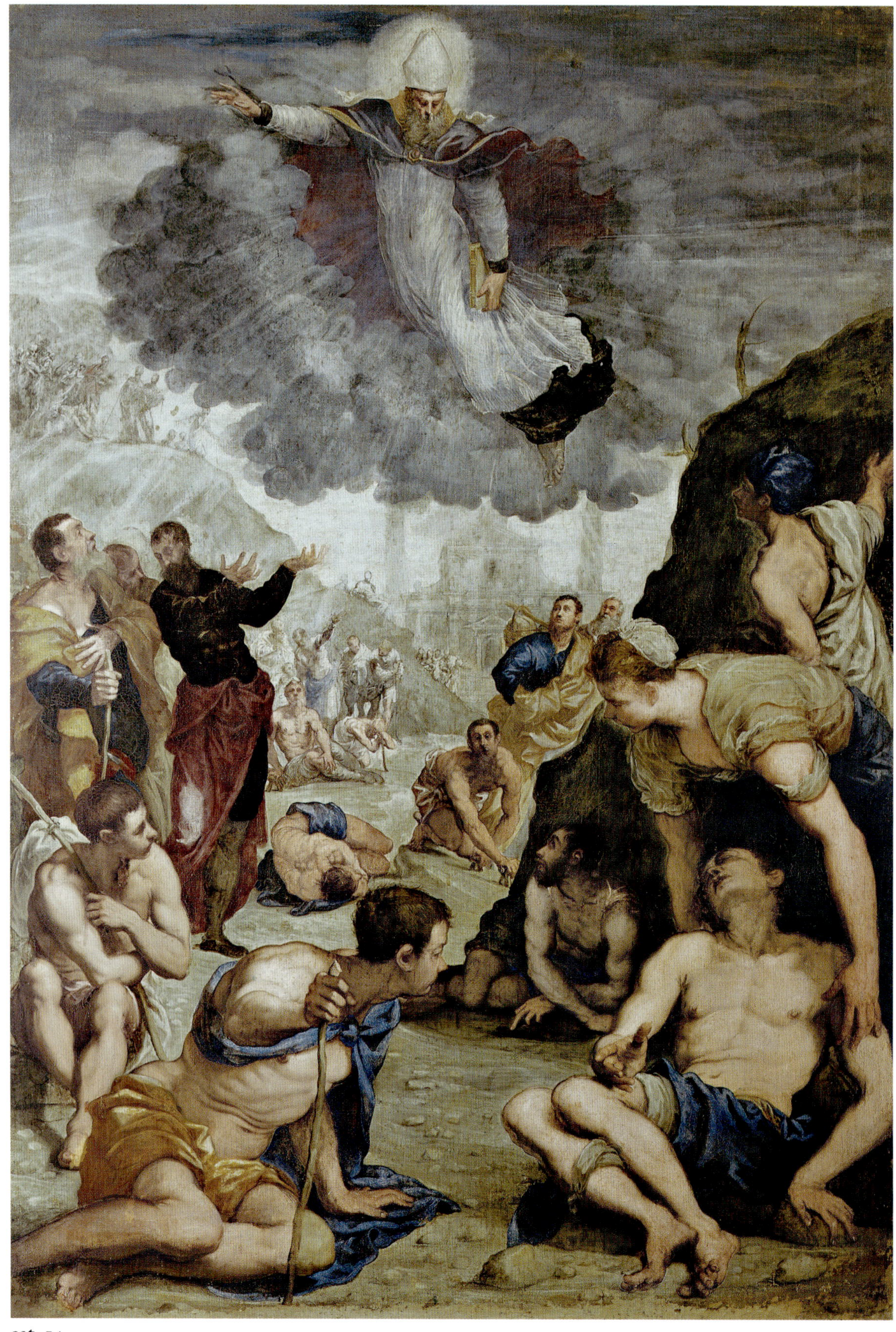

cat. 14

della Vigna: where the off-center composition of the *Madonna di Ca' Pesaro* famously accommodates the angle at which viewers approached the picture on the left wall of the church of Santa Maria Gloriosa dei Frari, the *Pala Giustiniani* sits within a deep chapel and is seen only from a position more or less in front of the canvas.[59] We are reminded that despite his precocious technical ability, Veronese was still a very young artist, as yet unaccustomed to the challenges of the altarpiece. The shortcomings of the *Pala Giustiniani* notwithstanding, the picture marks the beginning of Veronese's continual success with the Venetian establishment. Soon after, he settled in Venice, and further commissions, including the ceiling paintings of the Sala of the Council of Ten in the Palazzo Ducale, followed.

Tintoretto and Veronese would thereafter dominate the Venetian artistic scene. While Tintoretto's style signaled a more obvious break with tradition, it would be wrong to classify Veronese as an inherently traditional, conservative artist, as has sometimes been suggested. Veronese adopted the Venetian tradition, but he continually enhanced it with his own borrowings from Central Italian art—always less overt than those of Tintoretto—and rather than the tail end of a tradition, his work would offer much to artists in the years to come, something to which, for example, Agostino Carracci's impressive series of reproductive engravings after Veronese's paintings (including the *Pala Giustiniani*) would attest.[60] From the early 1550s forward, he and Tintoretto represented two widely divergent, but equally viable, paths for Venetian art.

—JM

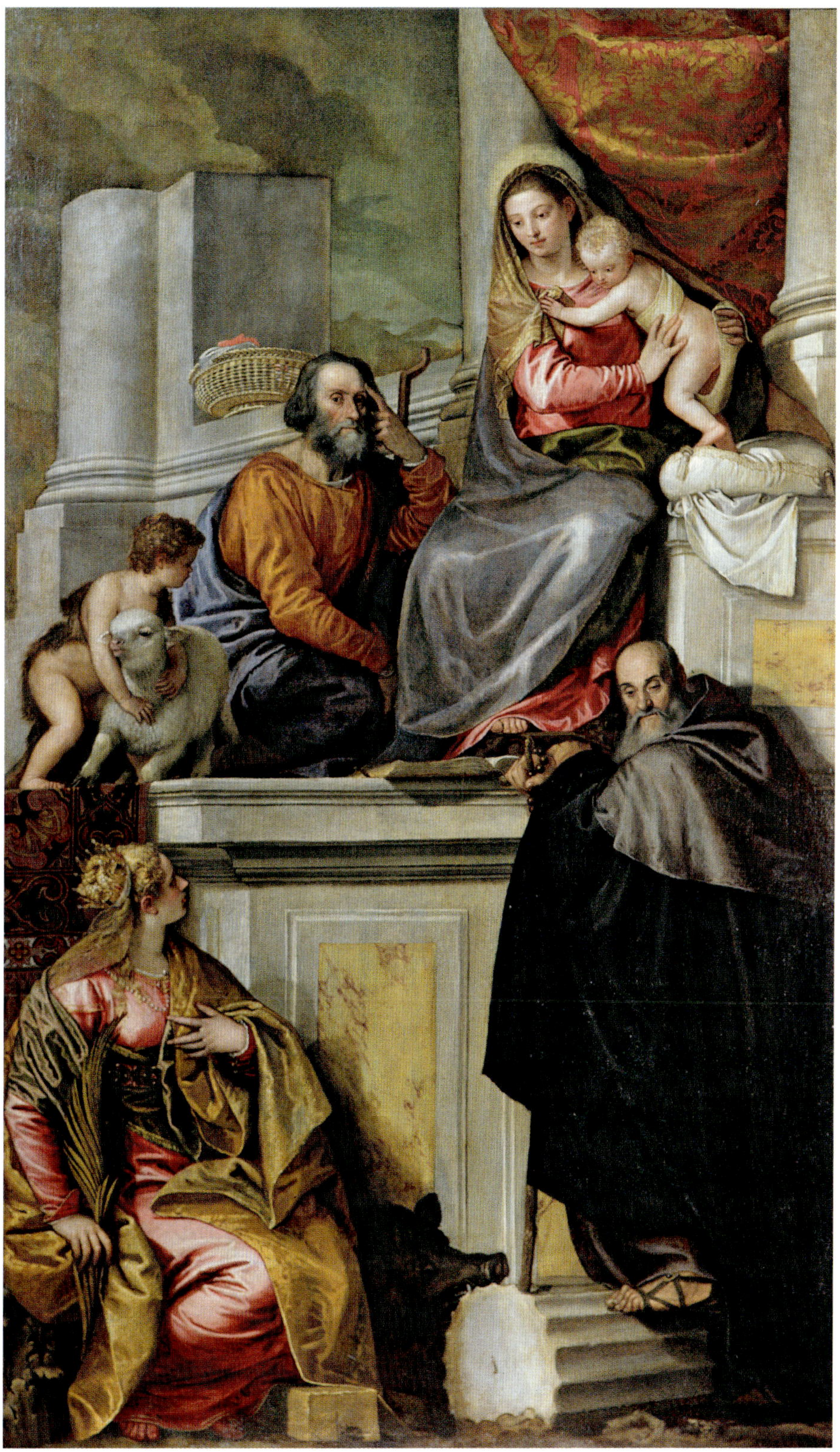

Fig. 48
Veronese
Holy Family with Saint John the Baptist, Saint Anthony Abbot, and Saint Catherine, about 1551
Oil on canvas
Church of San Francesco della Vigna, Venice

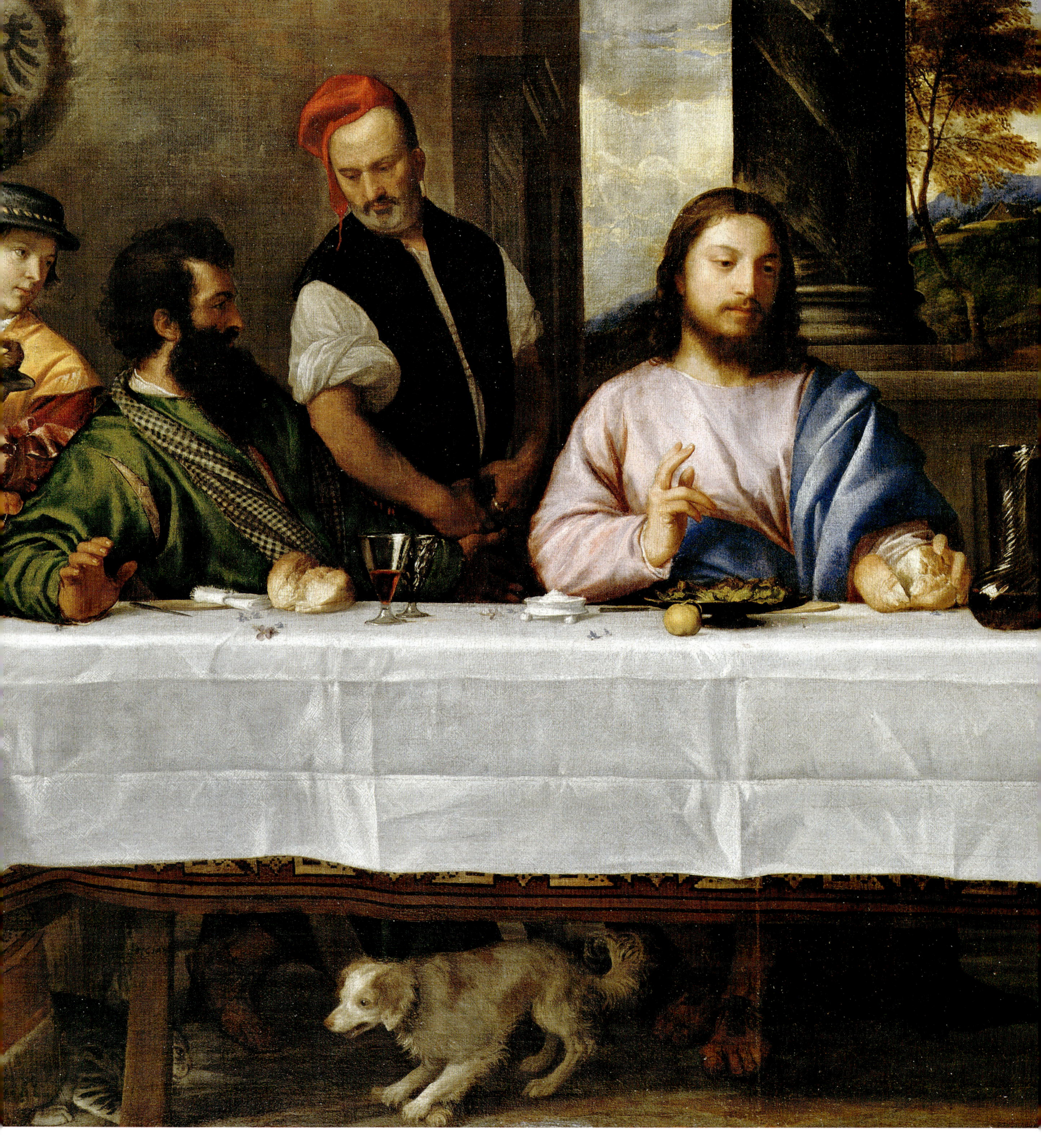

Sacred Themes

Christian belief permeated virtually every sphere of Venetian Renaissance existence, public and private. Francesco Sansovino's 1581 guidebook to Venice counted seventy parish churches and fifty-nine monasteries and convents in the city.[1] Religious sacraments marked all the major events of personal and family life. Monastic orders and religious confraternities carried out many social and charitable functions, including education and the care of the sick and the poor. Saint Mark was the special protector of the Venetian Republic, and his emblem, the winged lion, was emblazoned on the flags of its galleys and above the gates of its dominions around the eastern Mediterranean. The population of La Serenissima believed they owed their prosperity to their piety, which they celebrated publicly in frequent religious pageants and processions, such as that depicted by Gentile Bellini in the *Procession in Piazza San Marco* (fig. 49). In the words of the historian Edward Muir, "in Venice, patriotism equaled piety."[2] Miracles and faith were seen as part of daily life, and all three were completely intertwined in Venetian painting.[3]

Not surprisingly, sacred subjects constitute most of the paintings produced in Renaissance Venice. Although the newer genres of mythological pictures and portraiture flourished in the sixteenth century, they represented a relatively small part of the production of Venetian painters. In contrast, religious subject matter appears not only in pictures in churches and other religious sites but in government and private commissions as well. These range from the most prominent painting in Venice, the *Paradiso* in the Sala del Maggior Consiglio in the Palazzo Ducale, executed by Tintoretto after several competitions for the commission (fig. 6), to works used for private devotion or amassed in the collections of connoisseurs. The functions of paintings depicting sacred subjects varied widely, depending on the context for which they were produced. For some, the main function might not be devotional at all, particularly in those celebrating the Venetian state (such as Veronese's *Allegory of the Battle of Lepanto with Sebastiano Venier* [fig. 96]) or commemorating the government service of particular high-ranking officials (such as Tintoretto's *Madonna of the Treasurers*, fig. 12), often through representations of the individuals' name saints (as in Tintoretto's *Saint George, Saint Louis, and the Princess*, cat. 15).

Because of the damp climate, a strong local tradition of interior fresco painting never developed in Venice, as it did in Italy's inland cities, and most early cycles were refreshed by later artists and eventually replaced by works on canvas. As a result of the impermanence of fresco, the painted altarpiece was the primary focus of the decoration of Venetian churches and included some the most ambitious works of the great Venetian painters. High altars were usually maintained by the clergy, but the side altars and chapels were generally ceded to private patrons and confraternities, who were responsible for their decoration and upkeep.

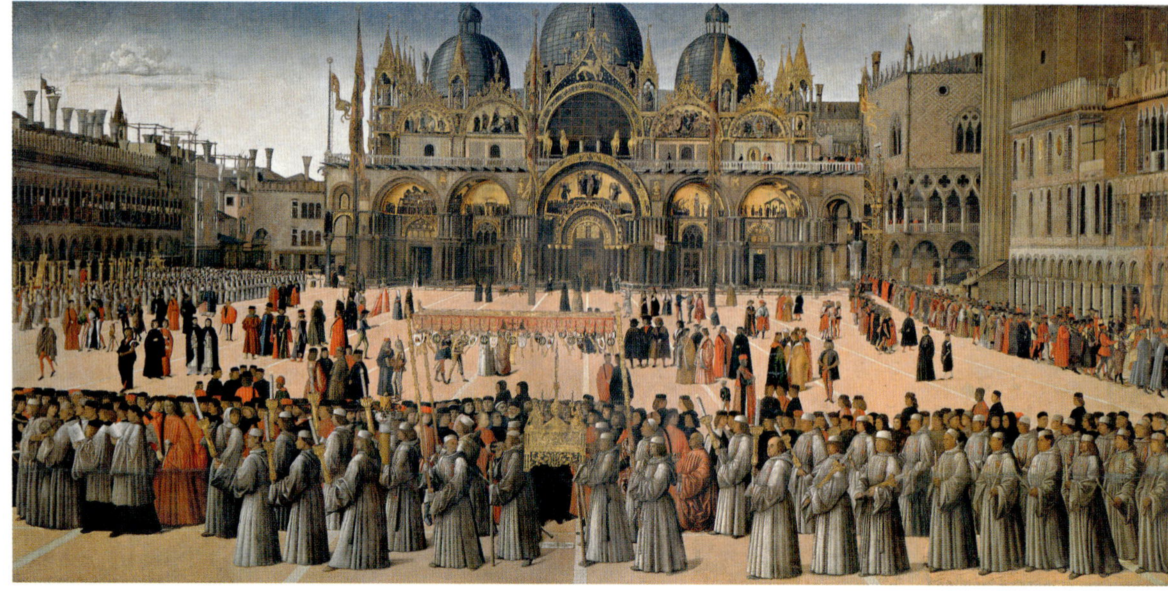

Fig. 49
Gentile Bellini (Italian, about 1429–1507)
Procession in Piazza San Marco, 1496
Oil on canvas
Gallerie dell'Accademia, Venice

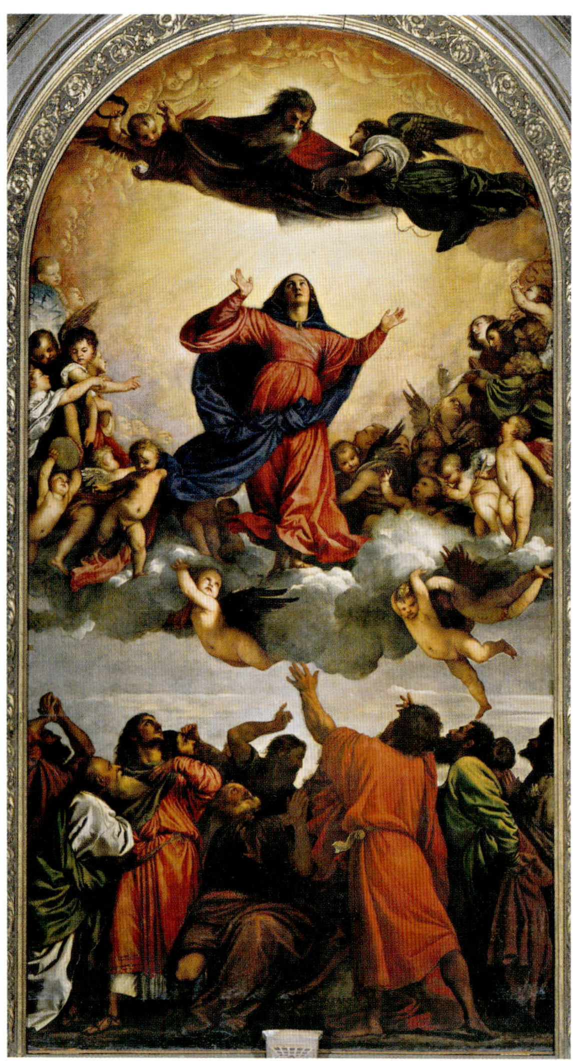

Fig. 50
Titian
Assumption of the Virgin (Assunta), 1516–18
Oil on panel
Church of Santa Maria Gloriosa dei Frari, Venice

While the most common subject for Venetian Renaissance altarpieces was the contemplative *sacra conversazione*, showing a group of saints flanking a Virgin and Child (or occasionally another saint) at the center, narrative subjects began to appear in the first half of the Cinquecento, and with them elements of drama and dynamism.[4] This transformation can be seen in the progression of Venetian altarpieces, from those by Giovanni Bellini in 1505 for San Zaccaria (fig. 36) and by Sebastiano del Piombo in about 1510 for San Giovanni Crisostomo (fig. 38) to Titian's *Assumption of the Virgin (Assunta)* of 1516–18 (fig. 50) and his *Saint Peter Martyr*, installed in 1530 (fig. 23). Titian's *Madonna di Ca' Pesaro* of 1519–26 (fig. 47) embodies another innovation, with its asymmetrical composition, reflecting both a head-on viewpoint and also that of a viewer who first sees the altarpiece while moving from the main entrance of the church toward the high altar.[5] This reminds us that altarpieces were not intended to be viewed as independent paintings but were conceived as part of an architectural and decorative whole. It is important to imagine how altarpieces would have appeared in their original context, often much higher than they can be hung in a museum, with illumination dependent on the vagaries of natural light and the flickering effects of candles.

Religious narrative painting was strongly associated with the decoration of the interiors of the *scuole*, the devotional confraternities that played such an important role in Venetian civic life. The most important of these were the *Scuole Grandi* (initially four, eventually six), each of which had five or six hundred members. In addition, there were some two hundred *scuole piccole* organized around national origin or occupation. Records of narrative painting cycles in *scuole* go back to the early fourteenth century, and they particularly flourished at the end of the fifteenth century, with many paintings surviving today.[6] Gentile Bellini's *Procession in Piazza San Marco* and Carpaccio's *Healing of a Possessed Man at Rialto* (fig. 51) both belonged to a decorative cycle in the Scuola Grande di San Giovanni Evangelista. Although they may initially appear to be secular in subject, in fact they both depict miracles worked by a fragment of the True Cross owned by the Scuola. In the later Cinquecento, the painter most associated with decoration for the *Scuole Grandi* was Tintoretto, with his cycles for the Scuola Grande di San Marco (fig. 5) and for the Scuola Grande di San Rocco, his greatest personal monument (fig. 9).

In churches, narrative paintings frequently adorned the side walls of chapels or other parts of the building (see fig. 14). Beginning in the mid-sixteenth century, such pictures were frequently commissioned by the parish's *scuola del Sacramento*, a lay confraternity dedicated to charitable work and to ensuring that the sacrament of the Eucharist was treated with appropriate reverence. The artistic aspects of this veneration included providing decoration for the altar where the Mass was celebrated and the area where the consecrated Host was stored.[7] Other kinds of religious furniture in churches were adorned with paintings as well, such as cabinet doors and organ shutters, for example Tintoretto's *Presentation of the Virgin in the Temple* for the church of Madonna dell'Orto (fig. 8, now joined together as a single painting) and Veronese's *Saint Menna* (cat. 16). In monastic buildings, the refectories, where the brothers ate, were frequently decorated with pictures of the Last Supper or similar events in the Gospels. Veronese's great series of Biblical Feast paintings were executed for refectories, for example his *Feast in the House of Levi* for the refectory of Santi Giovanni e Paolo (fig. 54). By contrast, not a single one of Tintoretto's *Last Suppers* was painted for a refectory. Instead, they were for church or scuola interiors, with nearly all of them commissioned by a Venetian *scuola del Sacramento*.[8]

Smaller-scale pictures for private patrons constituted a third major category of religious painting. Initially these were primarily images of Christ, the Virgin and Child, or saints intended to serve as a focus for the faithful in their devotions, such as *Christ Carrying the Cross* from the circle of Giovanni Bellini (cat. 3). *Sacre conversazioni*, often set in a landscape, such as Titian's *Virgin and Child with Saint Catherine, Saint Dominic, and a Donor* (cat. 2), were also popular. Over the course of the sixteenth century, as religious paintings of all types began to be appreciated for their aesthetic qualities as well as the devotional feeling they inspired, a growing market for such works developed among connoisseur-collectors. Devotional pictures began to include greater narrative content and more dynamic compositions. Private patrons began to commission and collect pictures with sacred subjects as works of art, rather than for purely devotional purposes. As more and more works of this type came into existence, pictures originally executed for private homes were sometimes presented to churches, as in the case of Veronese's *Agony in the Garden* (fig. 112).
— RE, FI

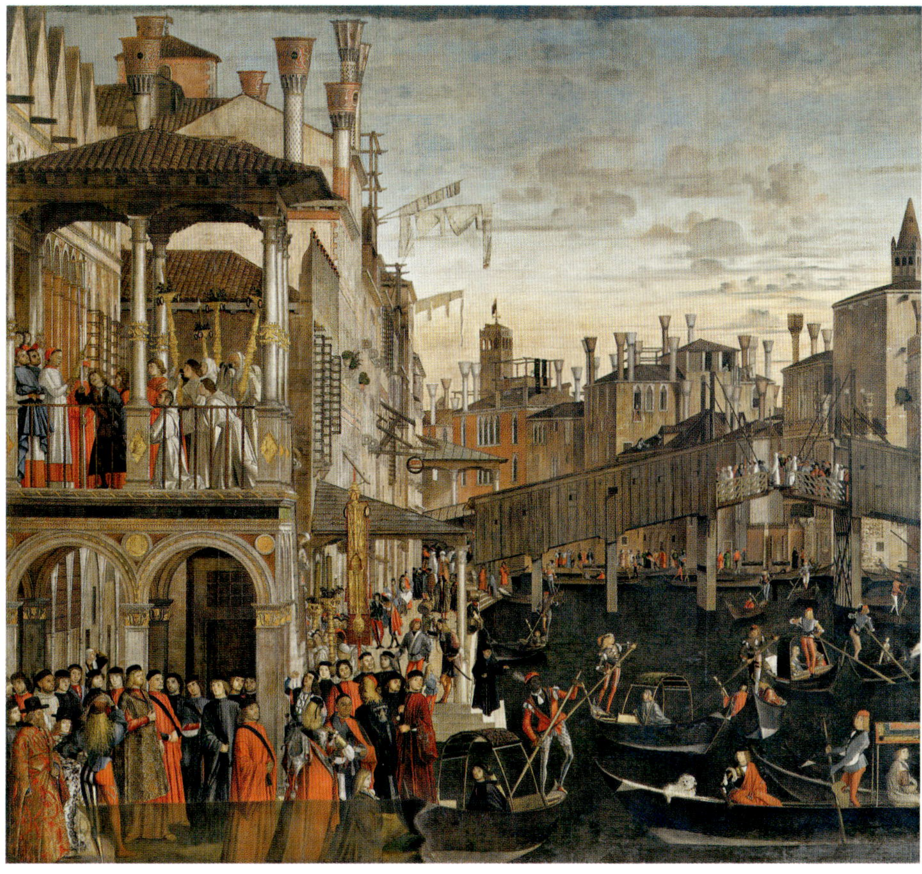

Fig. 51
Vittore Carpaccio (Italian, about 1465–about 1525)
Healing of a Possessed Man at Rialto, about 1496
Oil on canvas
Gallerie dell'Accademia, Venice

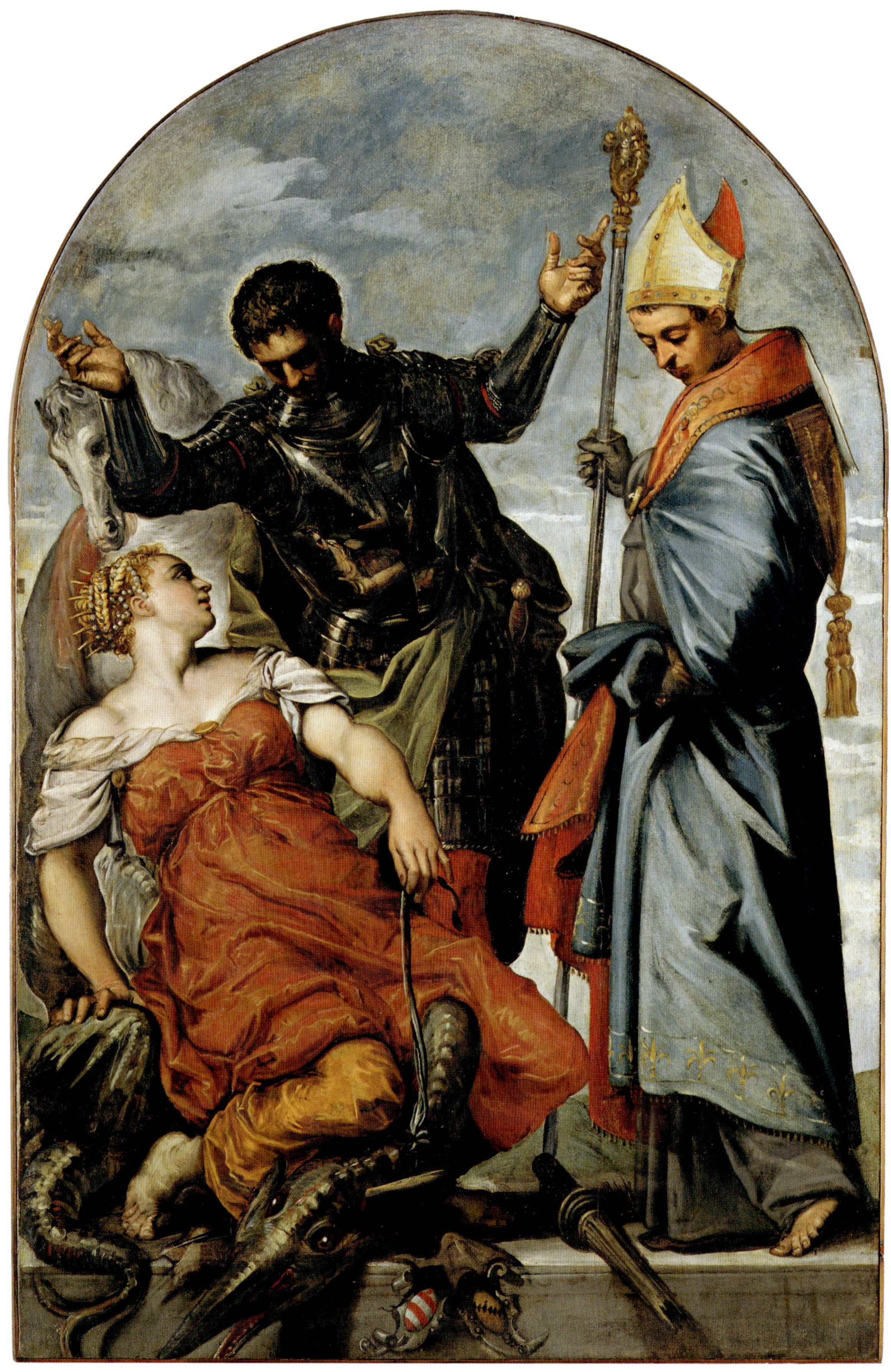

cat. 15

Armored Saints and Reflective Surfaces

TINTORETTO
Saint George, Saint Louis, and the Princess, 1552
Gallerie dell'Accademia, Venice
(cat. 15)

VERONESE
Saint Menna, about 1560
Galleria Estense, Modena
(cat. 16)

Without any knowledge of their provenance, one might suppose that these two canvases were originally altarpieces: they possess the typical tall, vertical format of Cinquecento altarpieces, and the imposing figures in both are in fact saints.[9] Yet these paintings were not designed to decorate altars. Tintoretto's *Saint George, Saint Louis, and the Princess* was painted as part of the decoration of the Palazzo dei Camerlenghi, a government office building at Rialto, while Veronese's *Saint Menna* composed half of the inner shutters embellishing the organ of the church of San Geminiano (now demolished) on the Piazza San Marco. These paintings remind us that format and subject matter do not necessarily indicate a work's original function, and, moreover, they underscore that the one-upmanship between Venetian painters was often not simply between identical subjects but could even extend to single figures within larger ensembles. In this case, in fact, the point of contention was not the figures that seem to penetrate the viewer's space but rather a particular detail: the virtuoso painting of gleaming armor.

Venetian painters seem to have relished the challenge of depicting reflections, a preoccupation reinforced by the city's watery setting and deep artistic traditions of mosaic and glass. As Venetian taste abandoned gold grounds on panels, artists used paint to evoke the reflective surface of gold, as well as other costly shiny surfaces such as marble, porphyry, mosaic, and glass.[10] The emulation of reflective surfaces through paint was a touchstone of artistic skill in Venice. Virtuoso depictions of light reflecting off armor were also recognized as hallmarks of proficiency by Venetian painters, as in Giorgione's *Castelfranco Altarpiece* (Duomo, Castelfranco Veneto) and, later, in portraits of military commanders (cats. 40–41).

A related artistic challenge involved the depiction of reflected images within paintings. The most famous Venetian Renaissance example of this no longer survives, and some have scholars have doubted if it ever existed at all. The painting, by Giorgione, is, however, described in detail in two important literary sources: Paolo Pino's *Dialogo di pittura* of 1548 and Vasari's *Lives* of 1568. According to Pino, "to the perpetual confusion of sculptors," Giorgione had depicted Saint George in armor, standing at the edge of a pool that reflected nearly his entire foreshortened body. Giorgione also included within the painting a mirror propped against a tree, reflecting the back of the saint, and another mirror opposite, showing the figure's side.[11] According to Pino, this picture proved that "a painter can make visible an entire figure at a single glance, which a sculptor cannot do." Pino is here invoking the concept of the *paragone*, the argument over the relative merits of painting and sculpture, which was highly debated in the sixteenth century. According to Pino, Giorgione's ingenious representations of mirrors and mirrored surfaces allowed the flat plane of a painting to convey a figure in the round and thus surpass sculpture. Vasari bolstered Pino's account by discussing Giorgione's painting twice in his book, both times as a particularly successful salvo in the *paragone* debate. In Vasari's report, the figure in the painting was described as a nude man, and one of the mirrors was replaced by a highly polished breastplate from a suit of armor he had just removed. Although the description of Giorgione's painting functions so well rhetorically that its existence has been doubted, the praise of Pino and Vasari proves that the depiction of mirrors as well as reflections off water and armor was central to notions of artistic merit in the mid-Cinquecento.[12]

In Venetian paintings of beautiful women, including Giovanni Bellini's *Woman with a Mirror* (fig. 82), mirrors call attention to the very act of looking; by reflecting views otherwise hidden, mirrors allow the spectator further access to the admired body.[13] Nudes by Titian, Tintoretto, and Veronese (cats. 30–32) provided opportunities for the artist to depict ravishing nudes and convincing reflections, while to some extent legitimizing the profane theme by emphasizing the self-absorption of the women, who like Narcissus are enthralled with their own beauty. Tintoretto employed mirrors in his *Venus and Mars Surprised by Vulcan* (fig. 81) to invoke not just the *paragone* with sculpture but also his own rivalry with Titian and Michelangelo; this ambitious youthful painting stakes claims to knowledge of optics even as it parodies the more serious mythologies of his predecessors.[14]

Tintoretto's *Saint George, Saint Louis, and the Princess*, especially the figure of George, should be considered within this same dual context of depicting reflections and exemplifying rivalry. In this case, the rivalry was between Tintoretto and Bonifazio de' Pitati, a contemporary of Titian. Bonifazio had a nose for business opportunities, and by offering to work for low prices, he managed to monopolize the decoration of the various financial offices housed in the Palazzo dei Camerlenghi. Thus assured of steady commissions, Bonifazio greatly expanded the size of his workshop and produced works "at what can only be described as bargain-basement prices," in the words of Philip Cottrell.[15] Government officials found Bonifazio's low cost and reliability appealing, and he was rewarded with commissions that stretched through the 1530s and 1540s. The paintings were intended to commemorate the terms of magistrates, usually overlapping terms of sixteen months; two or three officials would jointly pay for a single canvas, many of which show the patrons' name saints standing on a platform with their coats of arms below. The shape of the canvases, with arched tops, was dictated by the vaulted ceilings of the rooms in the Palazzo dei Camerlenghi, which created a series of blind arcades that ran along the walls. Bonifazio's paintings generally depicted the saints in relaxed poses like those in a *sacra conversazione* altarpiece. Cottrell notes the decline in quality of Bonifazio's paintings of saints in the late 1540s and early 1550s, as more of the execution was delegated to assistants (perhaps owing to the master's failing health in the years before his death in 1553) and the final product became "increasingly arthritic and less animated."[16]

By contrast, *Saint George,* Tintoretto's first painting for the cycle (completed in 1552), pulses with energy. George's bold gesture contrasts sharply with the sleepy poses in Bonifazio's later paintings; the princess astride the slain dragon seems about to spill out into the viewer's space; and the vigorous impasto brushstrokes defining the dragon's scaly body and the princess's shimmering dress seem designed to show up Bonifizio as predictable and old-fashioned. In Tintoretto's picture, so many elements press up against or even break through the picture plane—the head and tail of the dragon, the strongly foreshortened arm of the princess holding a leash—that the two patrons' coats of arms are marginalized. Since later officeholders commissioned further paintings by Tintoretto, the work must have been favorably received by Giorgio Venier and Alvise Foscarini, the two magistrates who commissioned it and for whom the specific saints were chosen (Alvise being the Venetian form of Louis). With his foot in the door, Tintoretto replaced Bonifazio as the primary supplier for the Camerlenghi cycle, and subsequent contributions included one of his greatest works, the *Madonna of the Treasurers* (fig. 12).[17]

It is possible, however, that Tintoretto overplayed his hand by exaggerating the prominence of the princess and the leering dragon at the expense of the name saints.[18] Indeed, this painting spurred one of the few recorded comments about Tintoretto's art from the 1550s, an opinion captured in Ludovico Dolce's dialogue *L'Aretino* (published in 1557), in which Tintoretto's painting is censured for its "lack of decorum" in having the woman "ride the dragon" in such a suggestive way.[19] Tom Nichols has written that Saint Louis standing at the right "gathers his skirts about him in a movement of instinctive pious revulsion," a reading that underscores the inappropriate sensuality that some contemporary observers noted.[20] Dolce's dialogue neglected to mention, however, the most striking passage in the painting, one perhaps designed to impress other artists more than clients or critics: the reflection of the princess in George's armor. By any standard—and particularly for a painter criticized by contemporaries for carelessness—the foreshortened and distorted image of the princess in the breastplate is a remarkable achievement. Through the power of painting, Tintoretto shows her face both in profile and frontally. Her expression emphasizes this accomplishment; she seems spellbound by her own image and possibly the talents of the painter who depicted her. Tintoretto used this dazzling detail to proclaim himself not just superior to Bonifazio but also very much part of the discourse of reflections in Venetian painting going back to Giorgione.

Veronese's painting, originally one half of the inner shutters for the organ of the church of San Geminiano, can be dated to about 1560, based on a 1558 document pledging funds for a new organ.[21] The elegant standing figure dominates the niche with a markedly sculptural effect. Although the canvases for the shutters were rectangular, Veronese may have deliberately chosen the rounded arch format as a pictorial field to emphasize the effect of statues in niches—another round in the *paragone*—and draw attention to the comparison with Tintoretto's picture. Moreover, the painter may have helped pick which saints were to be included; there are plenty of examples in Cinquecento Venice of patrons deferring to the artist's expertise and judgment.[22] Saint Menna, a soldier in the Roman imperial army who was martyred about the year 300, is almost unknown in Renaissance art. According to tradition, the church of San Geminiano originally shared a dedication to "Menna cavaliere" (Menna the Knight).[23] Choosing a figure in armor would have offered Veronese scope to challenge Tintoretto's recently criticized painting for the Camerlenghi.

All aspects of *Saint Menna* display Veronese at the top of his game. Menna's right elbow and left foot project into the viewer's space convincingly, with a believable shadow cast in the niche. The heavy folds of drapery and particularly the cold gleam of metal flaunt Veronese's skill at rendering varied textures with efficient brushwork. Above all, by refusing to engage Tintoretto in another complex reflection in armor, Veronese seems to assert that he understands the limits of mimesis in painting. That is, if the princess in Tintoretto's work can see her own reflection in the armor, then viewers should be able to see themselves as well. Veronese evidently preferred not to break the spell, depicting vague patches of reflected light rather than specific forms. The self-assured *Saint Menna* may be seen both as an explicit critique of Tintoretto and a broader claim of the painter's arrival. The pose and expression have even been read in an autobiographical key. According to Rearick, the saint's "dashing confidence suggests the self-image of the thirty-two-year-old painter, by 1560 an established figure on the Venetian scene."[24] If so, the painting would have been an even more personal riposte to Tintoretto.
— FI

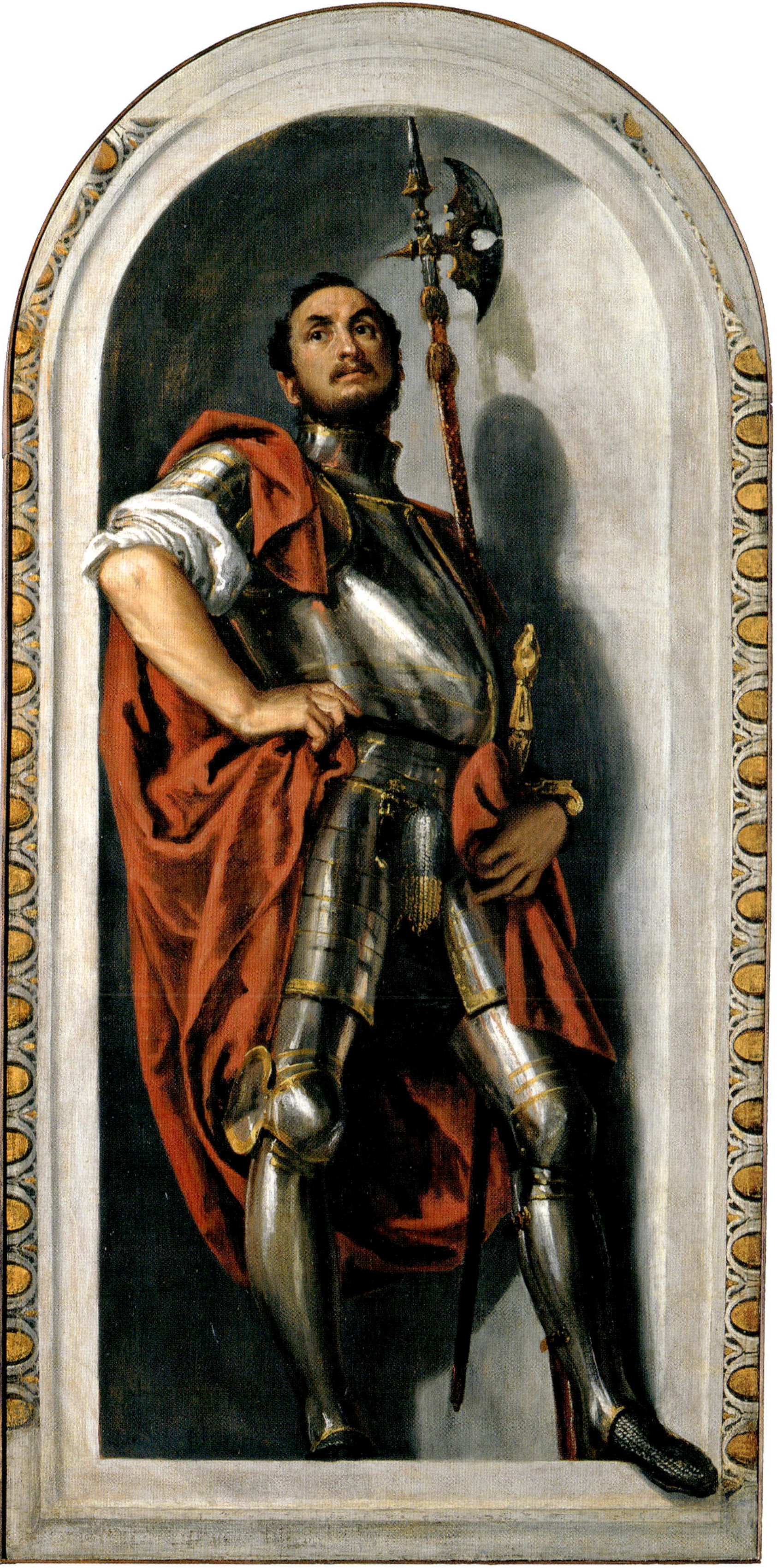

cat. 16

Paintings of the 1550s: Darkness and Torment

VERONESE
Temptation of Saint Anthony, 1552–53
Musée des Beaux-Arts, Caen (cat. 17)

TINTORETTO
Deposition of Christ, mid-1550s
Gallerie dell'Accademia, Venice (cat. 18)

The assimilation of Central Italian art that characterized the apprentice years of both Tintoretto and Veronese sometimes resulted in works by the two painters that show striking similarities despite their very different artistic personalities. Such is the case with Veronese's *Temptation of Saint Anthony* and Tintoretto's *Deposition of Christ*. Although the two works were painted for different cities—the Veronese for Mantua and the Tintoretto for Venice—they were created only a couple of years apart, and they approach their different subjects in comparable ways. Both are dark, moody, and claustrophobic, distinguished by strong chiaroscuro and a limited palette. They derive much of their power from the heroic scale of the figures in a compressed compositional field. In each picture the monumental protagonists are placed far forward, close to the picture plane, and are tightly interlocked, with the figures alone defining the compositional space. Both works are dominated by a distinctly sculptural nude male, reminding us that the period from which these paintings date can be considered the high point of Michelangelo's influence in Venice and its environs.[25]

Veronese's depiction of the torments of Saint Anthony (or Antony) evokes an atmosphere of darkness and brutality that is unique in the painter's oeuvre. Moreover, his treatment represents a clever iconographic conflation. Northern prints and paintings had generally focused on the theme of the hermit beset by demons, an episode described in the early sources whereby Anthony's resilience was tested by an attack of evil spirits who took the forms of fierce animals and grotesque insects. Afterward, when Christ finally intervenes and drives the demons away, Anthony appeals to Christ, "Where wert thou? (Ubi eras bone Jesu? ubi eras?). Christ responds by saying that he was testing Anthony and would thenceforth come to his aid.[26] Earlier Italian painting generally had treated as two distinct episodes the saint attacked by demons and a temptation by the devil in the guise of a beautiful woman.[27] Veronese powerfully combines the two moments but limits his torturers to two: a muscular male demon who strikes the old man with shocking violence and a voluptuous female devil who scratches his palm with fingers that resemble talons. Both attackers possess a bestial aspect, the female with claws like a bird of prey, and the male's monstrous facial features and thick curls akin to those of a satyr. The demon's weapon, apparently the foreleg of a horse, is similarly brutish. The female tormentor evokes a perverse sexuality that refers to Anthony's struggles in overcoming sexual temptation. No ecstatic vision appears to succor the saint (as it does, for example, in Tintoretto's painting of the same subject [cat. 20]) as Anthony desperately clutches his prayer book, crushed in the struggle, and the bell that is one of his attributes.[28]

Scholars have seen the massive form of the male demon as deriving from a number of underlying models, including the famous *Belvedere Torso* (Musei Vaticani, Vatican City) and engravings reflecting works by Michelangelo and his followers. In the female demon and the saint himself, as well as the general pictorial qualities of the painting, sources in the oeuvres of Parmigianino, Correggio, and Giulio Romano have been aptly cited.[29] Another likely source of inspiration not usually noted is Titian's *Saint Peter Martyr* altarpiece at the church of Santi Giovanni e Paolo; in many ways, Veronese's picture resembles a compressed version of the lower right quadrant of Titian's painting, with the saint prone and foreshortened at the bottom of the frame and the pictorial space dominated by the form of the executioner/demon in the act of striking, in a pose that emphasizes his bare back, shoulders, and extended arms.

Veronese's picture was one of four altarpieces Cardinal Ercole Gonzaga commissioned from painters from Verona in 1552 for the Duomo in Mantua, recently renovated after designs by Giulio Romano. A letter from the four painters to the patron in March 1553 reports that the canvases were completed.[30] The *Temptation of Saint Anthony* was thus executed just after Veronese's Giustiniani altarpiece (fig. 48), a calculated but conventional evocation of Titian's *Madonna di Ca' Pesaro*, in which Veronese sought to identify himself as an heir to the older painter. In the Mantuan picture, he responded in a much more personal way—and far more boldly—to a very different work by Titian. Veronese heightened the atmosphere of oppression and violence in the *Saint Peter Martyr* altarpiece by employing a tightly cropped composition, strong chiaroscuro, and a color scheme that features a combination of orange, gold, and plum verging on the lurid, which emerge from darkness to set off

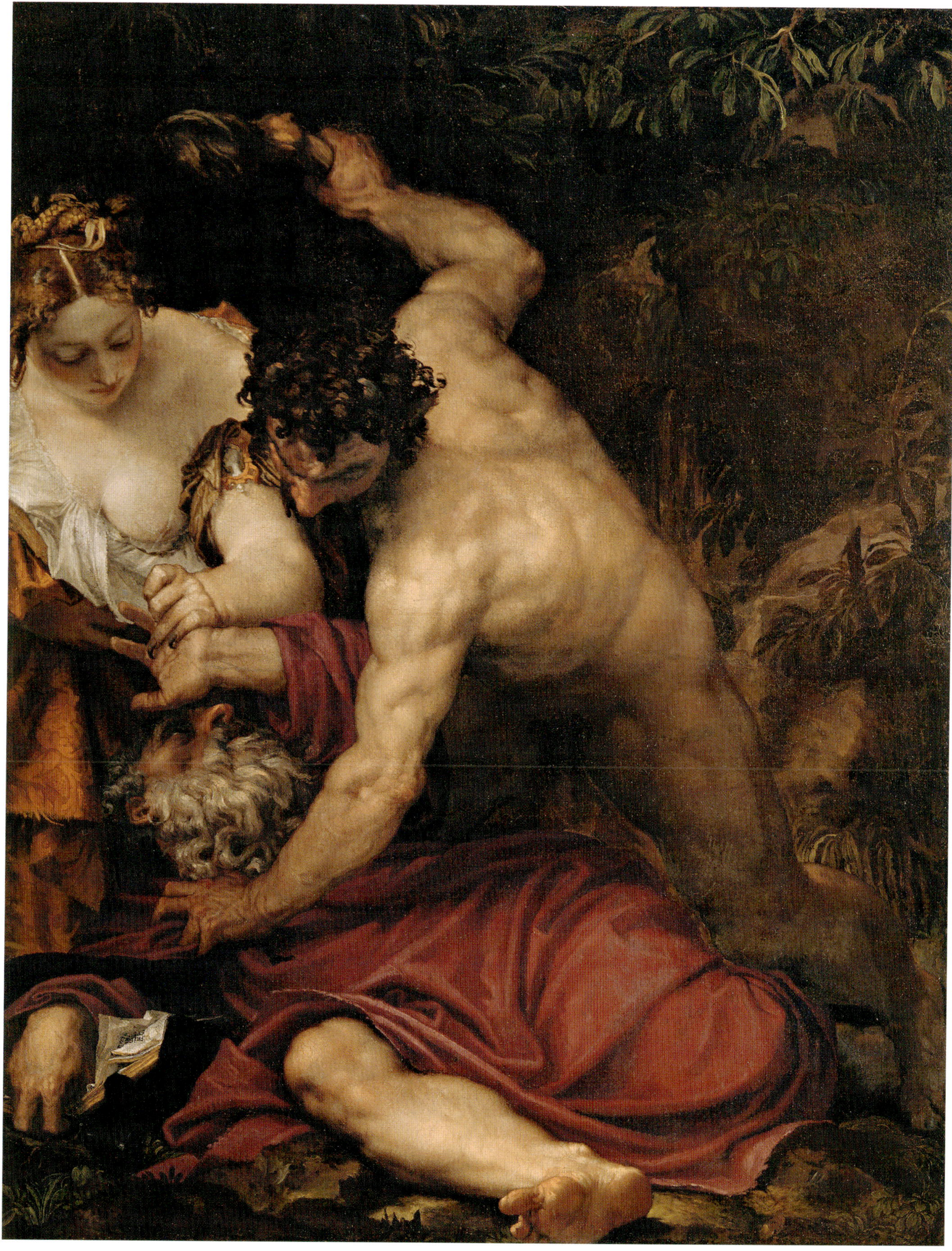

cat. 17

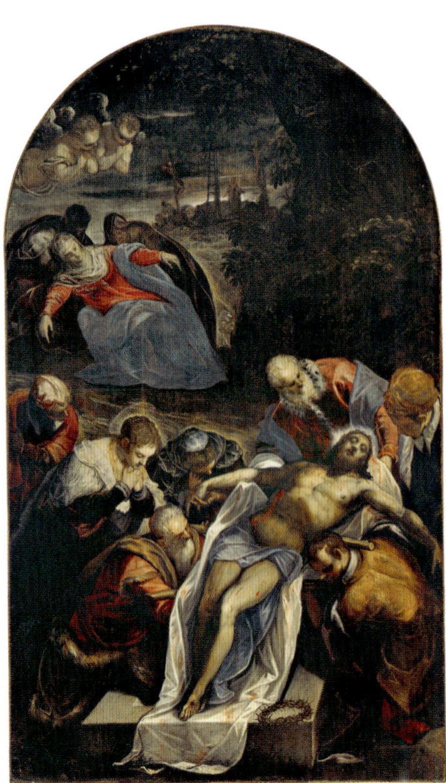

Fig. 52
Tintoretto and workshop
Entombment, 1592–94
Oil on canvas
Church of San Giorgio Maggiore, Venice

the flesh tones of the three protagonists.[31] Although the *Temptation* represents a unicum in Veronese's art, a mode he would never again pursue, it demonstrates—perhaps more than the Giustiniani altarpiece—the confidence and versatility that would enable him to surmount triumphantly the challenges posed by a commission at the very summit of Venetian patronage, in the Palazzo Ducale, just a few years later.

In Tintoretto's *Deposition of Christ*, similar artistic devices convey an equally dark mood of passionate grief and mourning. The intense chiaroscuro casts a spotlight on key passages—the sculpturesque figure of Christ, recalling a classical fallen hero, at once heroic and painfully vulnerable; the face of the swooning Virgin, with its sunken, deeply shadowed eye sockets; and Mary Magdalen's anguished gesture of lamentation. The gloom that obscures Christ's face emphasizes that his spirit has departed. The precise moment depicted is in fact between that of the active Deposition and the more static Lamentation; the body has been removed from the cross (the ladder is visible) and has been slowly lowered onto the Virgin's lap. This combination of episodes serves to emphasize the weight of the bodies and the clustering of the figures. These massive figures reflect Tintoretto's appreciation of the art of Michelangelo and his study of sculpture in general. It has often been suggested that Tintoretto was familiar with the composition of the *Deposition* fresco by Michelangelo's follower Daniele da Volterra in the church of Trinità dei Monti, Rome, which shows general similarities to Tintoretto's painting in the limp and frontally presented form of Christ and the unconscious Virgin and her attendant. Daniele's painting, however, was undoubtedly one of many models that Tintoretto would have had in mind when he began this picture.[32] Entirely his own is the tightly organized composition, in which the overlapping and interlocking figures fill up almost the entire pictorial field, to overpowering effect. (Probably the painting was originally even more densely packed, as the canvas appears to have been expanded at both edges. The landscape to the left is not in Tintoretto's style, but rather an imitation of late Titian. The original format may have been almost square.)

The *Deposition* is not mentioned in sixteenth-century guidebooks or sources, and no documentation of its commission has yet surfaced. Stylistically, the picture can best be dated to the middle or second half of the 1550s. The heroic figure types are similar to those in works such as the organ shutters for Madonna dell'Orto of around 1556 and *Christ at the Pool of Bethesda* (church of San Rocco) of 1559; the elaborate hairdress of the Magdalen is similar to that in the Vienna *Susannah and the Elders* (cat. 31).[33] The *Deposition* is first noted by Boschini in the seventeenth century in the church of the Umiltà, "sopra l'altare," over the altar, and subsequently by Zanetti in the eighteenth century, "sopra il finestrone," over the large window.[34] The church and monastery of Santa Maria dell'Umiltà was located on the Zattere, at the Rio della Salute, and demolished in 1821 following its suppression in 1806.[35] Besides this Tintoretto, its artistic treasures included three impressive ceiling paintings by Veronese.[36] While its origins are uncertain, a case can be made that the painting was executed as an altarpiece for the high altar of the church of Umiltà, commissioned soon after the Jesuits took over the church in 1549 or 1550 and replaced later in the century, during extensive renovations from 1578 until 1589. At this time the reserved Host was moved to the high altar, and a new tabernacle was built to house it. This would account for the *Deposition*'s somewhat orphaned status in the church, as described by Boschini and Zanetti.[37] The painting's monumental size certainly indicates that it was intended to be seen from a distance and to dominate a large space. The slightly horizontal format would be unusual for a canvas altarpiece, although not unprecedented.[38]

The treatment of the subject in the picture would support this provenance. The Virgin seems to be depicted as seated on the ground, in her guise as the Madonna of Humility, thus recalling the church's name.[39] Most significantly, Christ's body is offered directly to the viewer's gaze, as if presented for sacrifice, a Eucharistic image particularly suitable for placement above an altar. (In contrast, for example, in Titian's *Entombment* [cat. 55], of roughly the same date, Christ's body is seen laterally.) In two later altarpieces by Tintoretto, *Christ Carried to the Tomb* for San Francesco della Vigna (now in the National Gallery of Scotland, Edinburgh) and the *Entombment* (fig. 52), the painter similarly related the composition to the altar table. The analogy to the San Giorgio Maggiore altarpiece is particularly close.[40]

Whatever its origin, the *Deposition of Christ* is a Tintoretto masterpiece that has not received the appreciation it deserves.[41] Executed by the mature painter at the height of his powers, it embodies the deeply felt piety and pictorial genius that would distinguish his great sacred paintings of the 1560s and successive decades, and looks forward to his magnum opus, the decoration of the Scuola Grande di San Rocco.
— RE, FI

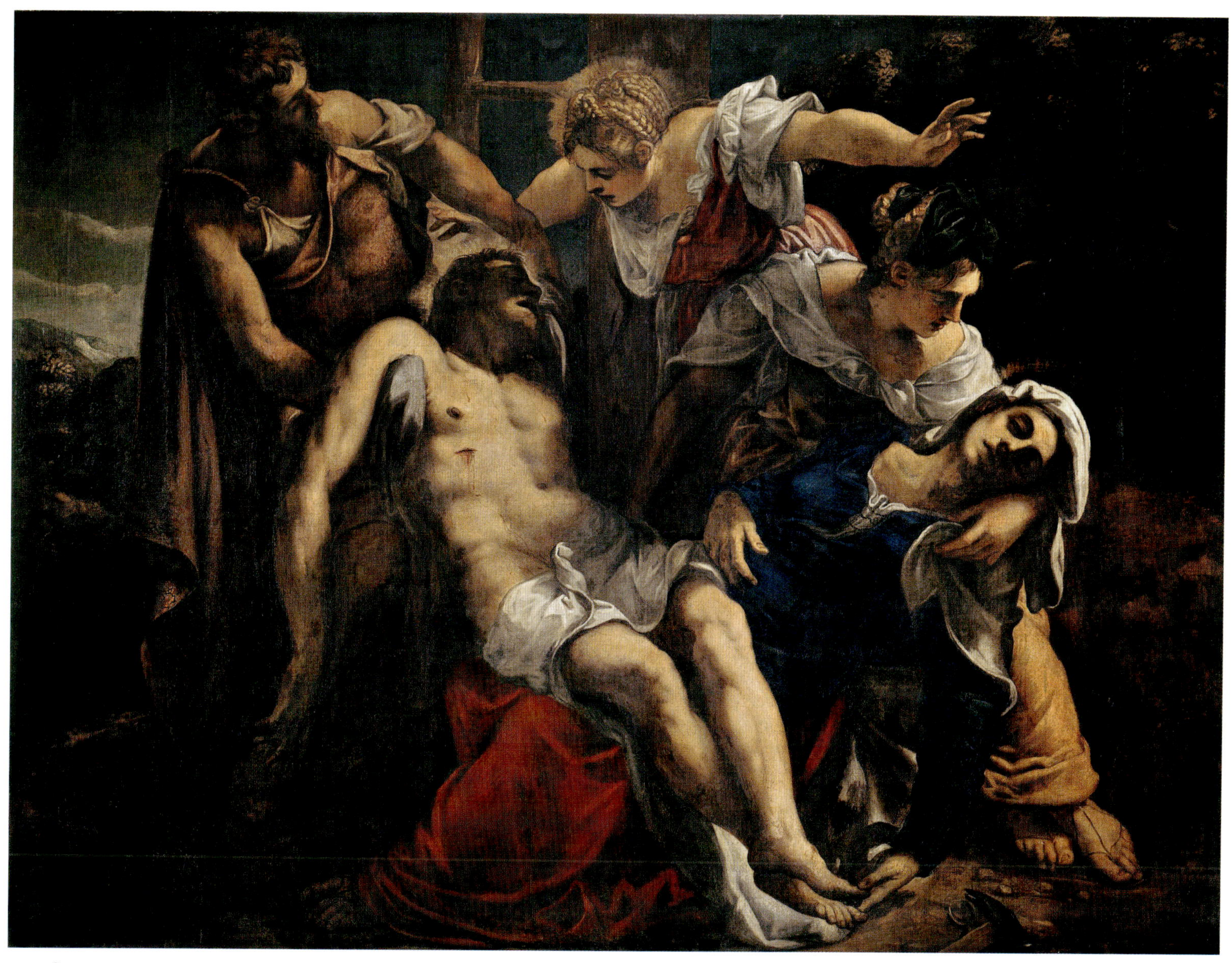

cat. **18**

Veronese and Tintoretto: Mature Altarpieces

VERONESE
Virgin and Child with Angels Appearing to Saint Anthony Abbot and Saint Paul the Hermit, 1562
The Chrysler Museum of Art, Norfolk, Virginia
(cat. 19)

TINTORETTO
Temptation of Saint Anthony, about 1577
Church of San Trovaso, Venice
(cat. 20)

According to Carlo Ridolfi, Tintoretto was able to secure the commission for the *Assumption of the Virgin* (fig. 53) over the preferred candidate, Veronese, because the painter claimed he could paint "in the manner of Veronese, so that it would be thought to be by his hand."[42] The comparison of an altarpiece by Tintoretto and one by Veronese provides an unusual opportunity to test how closely the styles of the two painters approached one another in their mature work. The two paintings make an ideal comparison; both depict Saint Anthony Abbot, and they have nearly the same dimensions. Further similarities include the upturned, foreshortened faces of Saint Anthony, the powerful and dynamic figures, the emphatically rhetorical gestures, the bold chiaroscuro, and the exploitation of the dramatic possibilities of the vertical altarpiece format. Even more striking here is the closeness of the artists' pictorial techniques, which typically are distinct from one another. Ridolfi had noted that the *Temptation of Saint Anthony* is unusually finished for Tintoretto, an example of "how well he knew how to bring his paintings to an exquisite finish when he judged it opportune and when the occasion and the quality of the place required it."[43] In this more finished mode, Tintoretto's technique, with its careful attention to detail and to the play of light over flesh and fabrics, might, in some passages—such as the face of Saint Anthony—be mistaken for that of Veronese.[44] It is as if Tintoretto's painting is a deliberate response to his rival.

The two pictures are separated by some fifteen years, but each can be securely dated. Veronese's *Virgin and Child with Angels Appearing to Saint Anthony Abbot and Saint Paul the Hermit* was one of three altarpieces he completed in 1562 for the Benedictine abbey church of San Benedetto Po (San Benedetto in Polirone), a few miles south of Mantua.[45] Although by now Veronese was well established in Venice, and remarkably busy, he frequently undertook commissions on the Venetian *terraferma*.[46] As Nicholas Penny has recently suggested, the fact that the artist was not paid much for his work at San Benedetto Po raises the possibility that he took on the job in the hope of obtaining other, major Benedictine commissions. If so, Veronese gambled correctly, for within a few months he won the commission for the enormous *Wedding Feast at Cana* for the refectory at the Benedictine Abbey at San Giorgio Maggiore in Venice, as well as two altarpiece commissions for the abbey church at Praglia, near Padua.[47]

In contrast to the San Francesco della Vigna altarpiece of a decade earlier (fig. 48), Veronese's figures here are heroic, monumental, and agitated. They fill up much more of the pictorial space than those in his first Venetian altarpiece. Although Veronese had occasionally painted bulky and dramatic figures in his early work, for example the *Temptation of Saint Anthony* altarpiece for Mantua (cat. 17), the incessant example of Tintoretto's muscular art undoubtedly inspired this development in Veronese's work.

While the meeting of the two aged hermit saints, Anthony and Paul, was a traditional subject in European art, there is no precedent for the depiction of a miraculous appearance of the Virgin and Child during their visit.[48] Undoubtedly the subject was prescribed by the Benedictines, reflecting their intention to reassure Rome of their orthodoxy by demonstrating their conformity with the Counter-Reformation's emphasis on devotion to the Virgin.[49] Veronese emphasized the newly dramatic potential of the subject by employing a very low point of view, so that the two saints would have been seen from below, strongly foreshortened, looming up above the altar. Saint Anthony is identifiably the same individual, with the same physiognomy, as in the *Temptation of Saint Anthony*, which was only a few miles away, in the Duomo in Mantua. He cranes his head back to see the vision, gesturing in surprise, his rosary beads silhouetted against the sky. Saint Paul, hand upon his chest in astonishment, almost falls backward off the rock where he has been sitting and reading his sacred text.

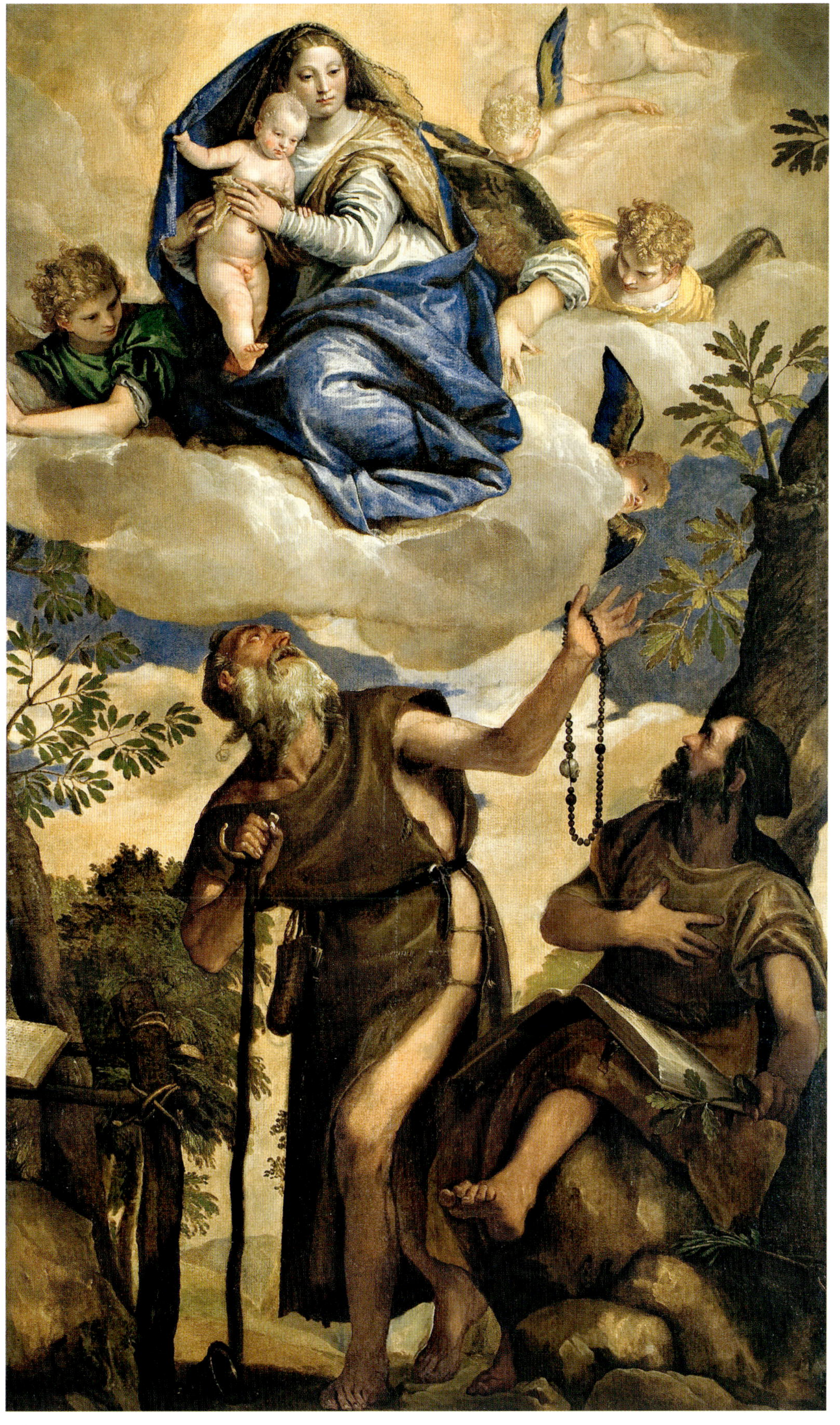

cat. 19

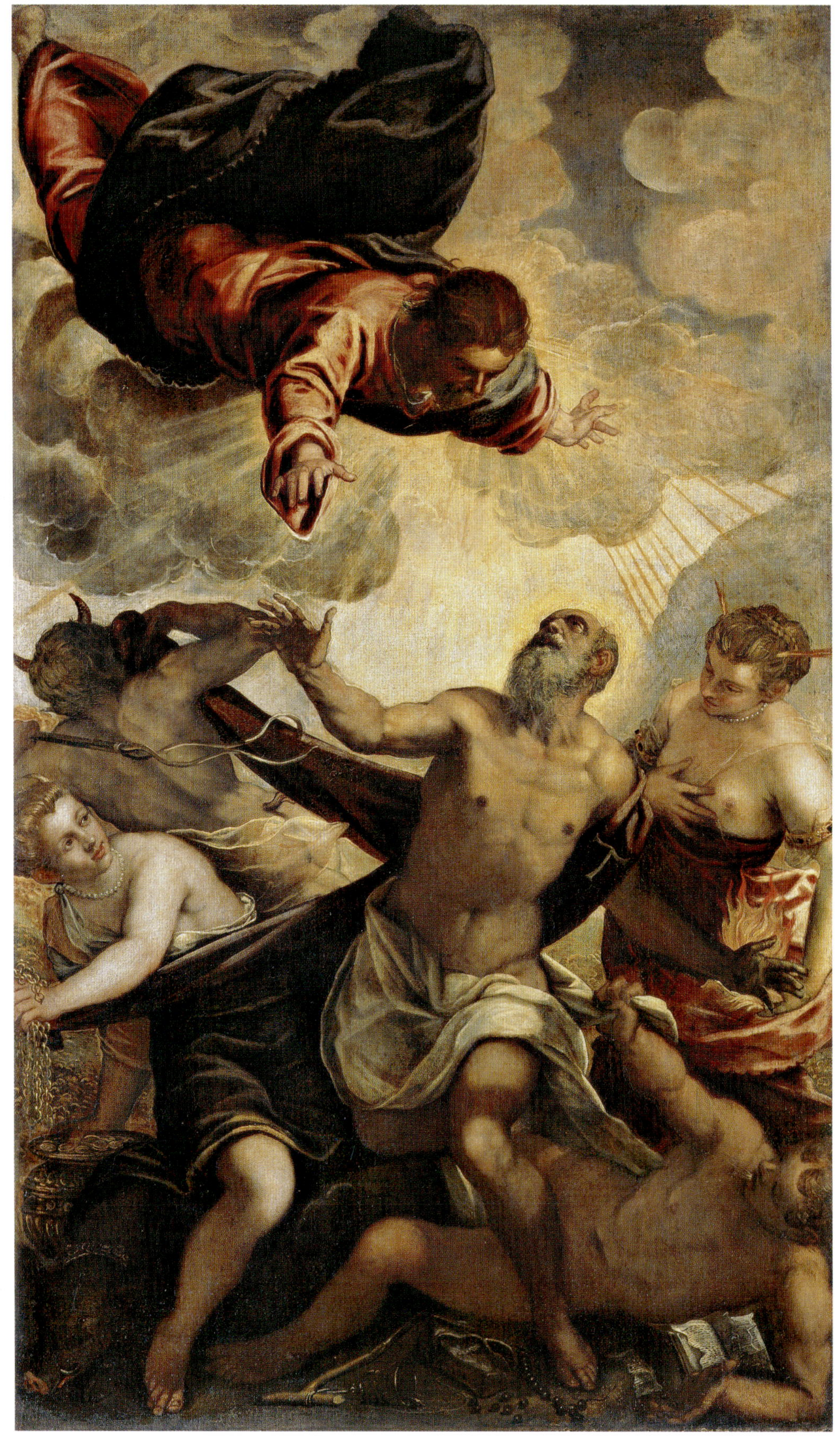

cat. 20

The miraculous vision of the Virgin and Child is seen from a different, higher point of view, so that its spatial relation to the saints is ambiguous. As a result, it seems to move downward and forward, toward the viewer. The disjunction between the heavenly and the earthly planes is emphasized by color: the pearly tonalities of the clouds and the pure blue, green, and yellow of the garments of the Virgin and angels, above, in contrast to the earthy greens, tans, and browns of the terrestrial sphere below. As W. R. Rearick has written of this picture, "Rarely did Paolo evoke the interaction of light and space with such subtlety as in the silvery play of luminescence over the clouds, simultaneously distinct from the warm summer sky in the distance and part of the same reality."[50]

Tintoretto's *Temptation of Saint Anthony*, along with the altar that it adorns, was commissioned by the *cittadino* Antonio Milledonne, who rose to the rank of secretary of the Venetian Senate. The date of 1577 is inscribed on the altar, and it has plausibly been assumed that the altarpiece was commissioned at the same time and executed soon thereafter.[51] Certainly the painting was complete by 1582, when it was engraved by Agostino Carracci.[52] An early biography of Milledone states that the saint is a portrait of the donor, a claim that seems reasonable, given the specificity with which the old man is depicted.[53]

As in Veronese's treatment of the theme for the Duomo at Mantua, Tintoretto shows Saint Anthony tormented by both brutal male demons and seductive female demons, here a pair of each. They tear at his clothes, trample on his book and crutch, and have broken the string of his rosary. Unlike Veronese's picture, however, which evokes no hint of relief for the saint, Anthony is relieved here by the appearance of the Savior amid "a wondrous light," a moment described in *The Golden Legend*, though rarely depicted in art.[54] Christ reassures the besieged saint, commending him for his resistance to temptation: "Anthony, I was here, but I waited to see thee fight; and now thou hast fought the good fight, I shall spread thy glory throughout the whole world!"

Where Veronese's altarpieces are among his greatest creations, this format does not seem to have been as congenial to Tintoretto, and he indeed often delegated the commissions to assistants.[55] The *Temptation of Saint Anthony*, however, is one of Tintoretto's most effective vertical altarpiece compositions. Characteristically for Tintoretto, the figures define the space in the painting. Here they are placed far forward, close to the picture plane. As in Veronese's altarpiece, the use of a different point of view in the upper and lower parts of the picture creates the effect of motion. The male and female demons pulling down and away in different directions from the central figure renders the lower half of the composition unstable. The saint himself twists upward toward the miraculous apparition, which seems to burst forward through the picture plane. It is in the dynamism of this image that we see a fundamental difference between the personalities of Tintoretto and Veronese; as Rearick notes, the vision of the Virgin and Child in Veronese's altarpiece for San Benedetto Po descends with majestic slowness;[56] Tintoretto's Savior, in contrast, swoops down from heaven head first in a burst of golden light, his cloak swirling above and behind him, his arms extended in a gesture that evokes both succor and the physical act of flying.

— RE, FI

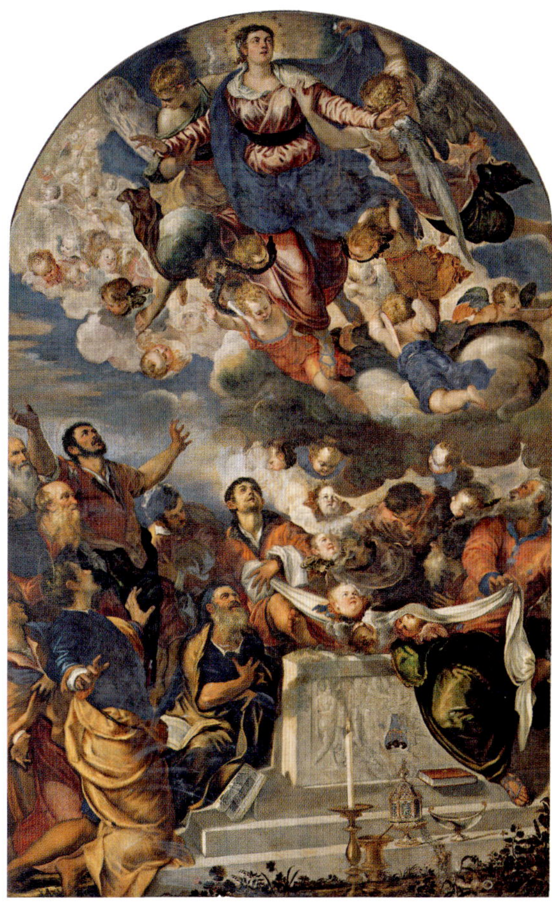

Fig. 53
Tintoretto
Assumption of the Virgin, early–mid-1560s
Oil on canvas
Church of the Gesuiti, Venice

The Supper at Emmaus *and the Biblical Feast*

TITIAN
Supper at Emmaus, 1533–34
Musée du Louvre, Paris
(cat. 21)

TINTORETTO
Supper at Emmaus, about 1542
Szépművészeti Múzeum, Budapest
(cat. 22)

VERONESE
Supper at Emmaus, mid-1570s
Museum Boijmans Van Beuningen, Rotterdam
(cat. 23)

The biblical feast was one of the great themes of the second half of the Cinquecento in Venice, and all three of our protagonists painted monumental examples for important sites in the city. By the 1540s, Titian had largely abandoned large-scale sacred narrative paintings and was channeling his energies toward productions for foreign patrons, but in the mid-1550s he executed a *Last Supper* for the refectory at Santi Giovanni e Paolo. Tintoretto's triumphantly successful *Miracle of the Slave* was just around the corner at the Scuola Grande di San Marco, and Titian may have taken on this hometown commission to demonstrate that he could still compete in the market for big narrative paintings. We can only speculate about the picture's appearance, as it was destroyed by fire in 1571.[57] Veronese was commissioned to replace it; the result was the *Feast in the House of Levi* (1573; fig. 54), the culmination of his great series of banquet scenes—originally a *Last Supper*, but so lavishly depicted and so rich in peripheral characters that it led to a summons from the Inquisition.[58] As for Tintoretto, no theme was more associated with the artist than the Last Supper. Over the course of his career, he painted a number of important treatments of the subject for Venetian churches, among them the one for San Trovaso (datable to about 1563–64; fig. 55). With their humble settings and strong chiaroscuro, Tintoretto's *Last Suppers* could not present a stronger contrast to Veronese's brilliantly lit and sumptuous feasts.[59]

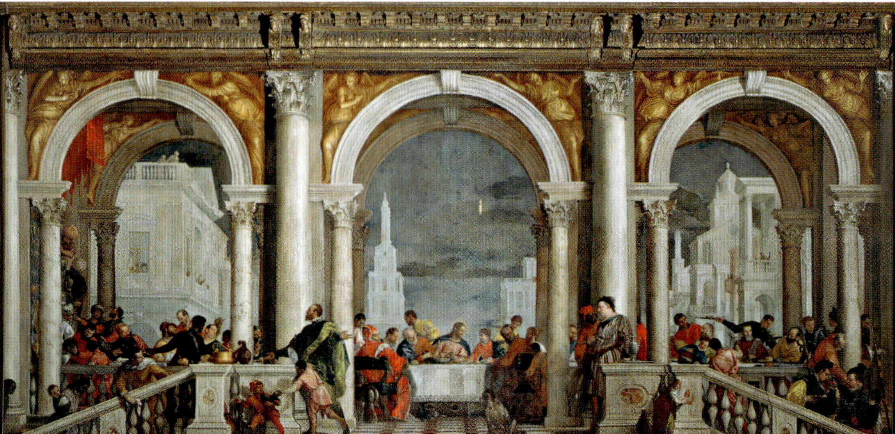

Fig. 54. Veronese, *Feast in the House of Levi*, 1573, oil on canvas, Gallerie dell'Accademia, Venice

Three versions of the *Supper at Emmaus* permit us to survey the rivals' differing approaches to the biblical feast on a smaller scale. Certain elements are common in all three—Christ at the center, with a column behind, a patch of blue sky with clouds—but the divergences reveal the predilections of each painter. As an enactment of the Eucharist soon after the Crucifixion, climaxed by a moment of revelation, the Supper at Emmaus echoes the Last Supper. The story is recounted only in the Gospel of Luke. After the Crucifixion, two of Jesus's disciples (only one of them—Cleopas, who does not appear elsewhere in the New Testament—is named) were walking to Emmaus when the resurrected Jesus joined them, unrecognized. At supper that evening in Emmaus, Christ took the bread, blessed it, broke it, and gave it to them. "And their eyes were opened, and they knew him; and he vanished out of their sight" (Luke 24:30–31).

The Supper at Emmaus first emerged as an independent theme in painting in Venice in the later fifteenth century, often associated with works commissioned for private collections. Before then, it had appeared only in cycles of the life of Christ.[60] Giovanni Bellini executed a painting of the subject in 1490 for Giorgio Cornaro, praised by Vasari.[61] Although the Cornaro painting was lost in a fire in the eighteenth century, its composition is reflected in a number of works by Bellini followers.[62] Vasari's description of "Cristo, Cleofas e Luca" reveals that during this period the second pilgrim was understood to be Luke himself.

Titian supplied versions of the theme for a subsequent generation of collectors. His *Supper at Emmaus* in the Louvre was executed for Count Nicola Maffei, chief minister of Federico II Gonzaga of Mantua, who served as an intermediary between Federico and Titian.[63] Subsequently it entered the Gonzaga collection, passing from there to Charles I

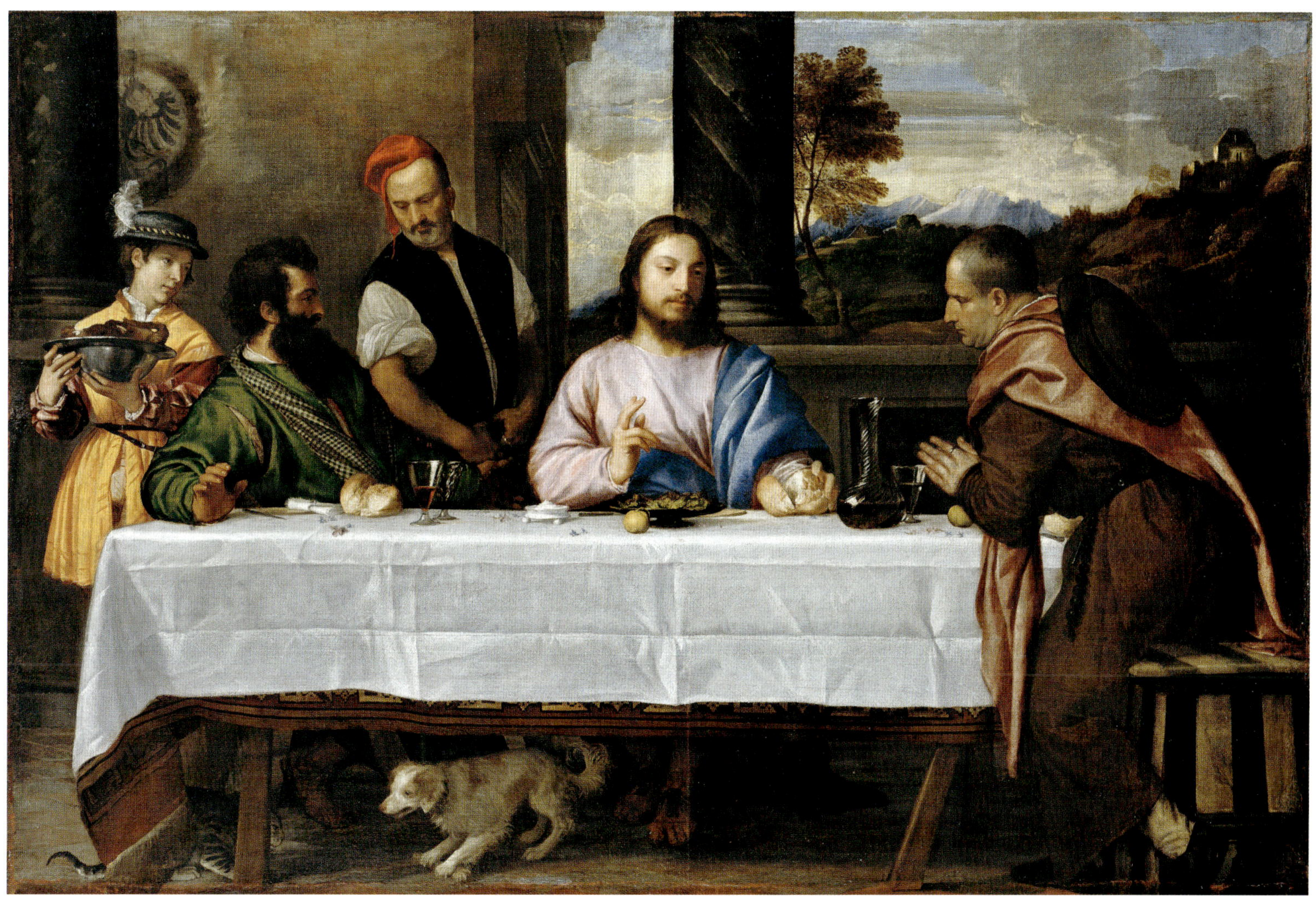

cat. 21

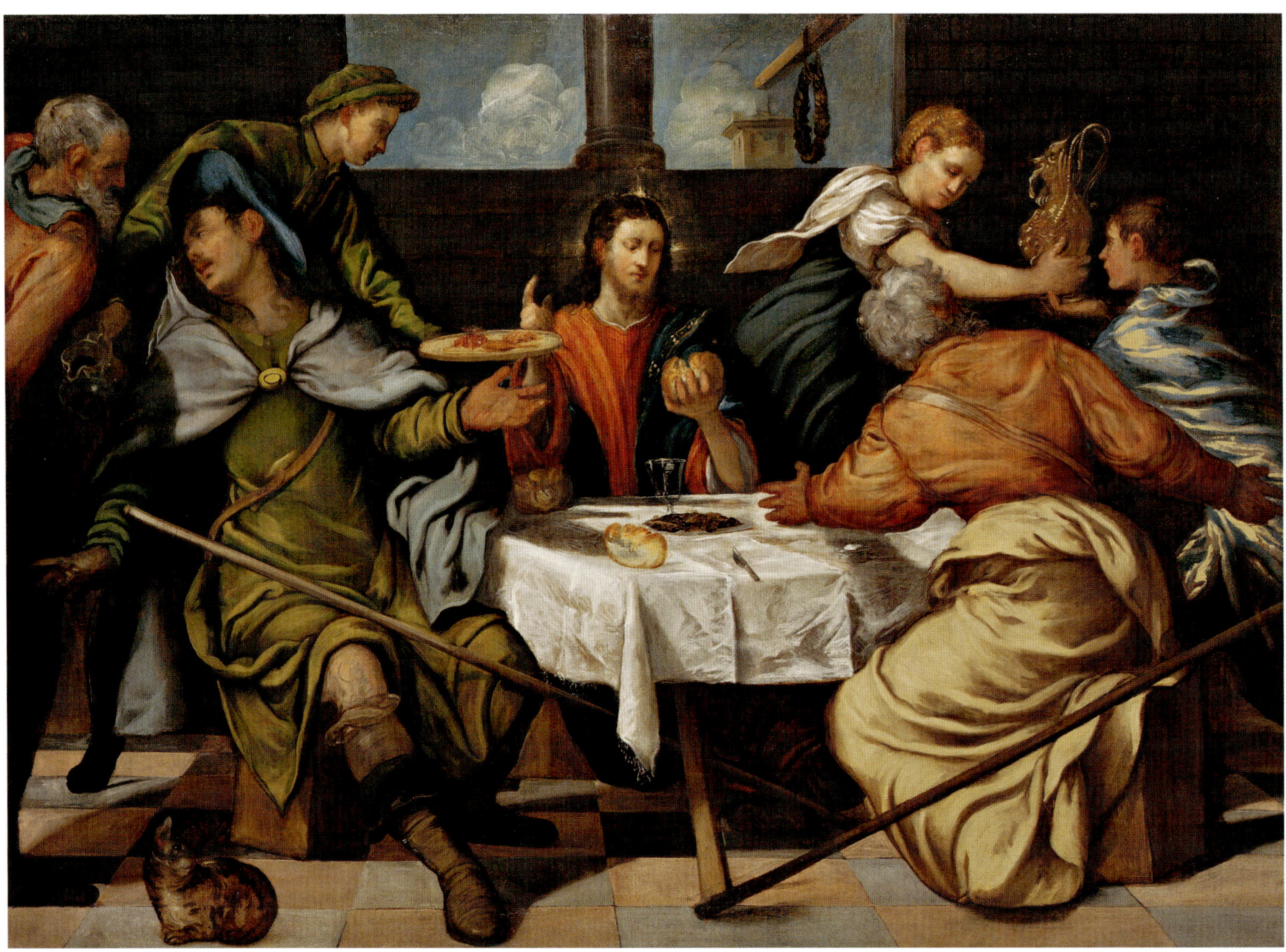

cat. 22

of England and then to Louis XIV of France. The disciple to the right, traditionally identified as Cleopas, is undoubtedly a portrait of Maffei, whose coat of arms appears on the stool from which he rises, barely legible with the naked eye but clearly visible in X-radiographs.[64] The appearance of the patron in the painting is a Venetian tradition that dates back to versions of the theme by Bellini and his studio.[65]

Although the Louvre painting is regarded as Titian's finest version of this composition, it may have been executed after the one that is now in the collection of the Earl of Yarborough (fig. 24), which was painted for the Contarini family of Venice. Subsequently, its owner presented it to La Serenissima, and by 1566 it was on public view in the Palazzo Ducale.[66] As is now visible on the surface of the Louvre picture, as well as in X-radiographs, Titian originally painted two columns in the background in the same position as in the Contarini version, but decided to substitute a single column intersecting with the right side of Christ's head, thereby emphasizing the main figure. Several other differences from the Contarini version heighten the impact of the Louvre composition, suggesting a process of improvement and refinement.[67]

Titian's Louvre *Supper at Emmaus*, like the Contarini version, reflects an awareness of Leonardo's *Last Supper*, evident in the long horizontal table, the facial type of Christ, and the overall sense of High Renaissance balance, reinforced by the strong grid pattern created by the architectural forms. A specific link to Leonardo's painting appears in the pose of Luke, which echoes that of Judas in the Milan *Last Supper*.[68] As in Leonardo's painting, Titian depicts the moment of revelation—in this instance, when the disciples understand that the mysterious pilgrim is Christ himself. Luke draws back in amazement. Cleopas rises from his seat, but his pose and praying hands suggest adoration rather than shock, allowing the figure to be read as both a participant in the action and the donor meditating on the scene (and, in the latter sense, as a model for the viewer).

Titian makes the most of the still-life opportunities the subject offers, devoting special care to the prominent white tablecloth, with its beautiful brocaded pattern and many folds, as well as to the Central Asian carpet visible beneath it.[69] He captures with subtlety such details as the delicate violets, the salt cellar with its pyramidal mound of salt, Cleopas's ring, and light reflecting off the wine carafe and glasses. Symbolic associations have been proposed for all of the items on the table, the most important of which, of course, are the bread and wine of the Eucharist.[70]

Tintoretto's *Supper at Emmaus* dates from the first few years of the 1540s, perhaps around 1541–42, very early in his career.[71] That this is a youthful work is evident in the extent to which Tintoretto borrows from prototypes by Bonifazio de' Pitati, with whom he seems to have maintained some kind of working association during his early years. Tintoretto's primary model here was the *Supper at Emmaus* painted by Bonifazio and his assistants for the Palazzo dei Camerlenghi, from which he borrowed the column directly above Christ's head, the pilgrim staff at the right, and the gesture of the disciple to the left.[72]

Although it was painted only about a decade later than Titian's *Supper at Emmaus* for Nicola Maffei, Tintoretto's picture clearly belongs to a new artistic generation. Some passages in the painting show that the young artist had mastered a traditional Venetian pictorial technique, particularly the dazzling white tablecloth, with its folds and wrinkles. In most of the picture, however, Tintoretto employs what would have seemed an unsettling and rough technique, with long, ribbonlike strokes of the brush defining the drapery folds, and the faces lacking the finish that Venetian audiences were accustomed to in oil paintings. The matte quality of the paint and the prominent impasto contrast with Titian's luminous and sensuous surfaces.

Even more unsettling to contemporary viewers would have been the aggressive dynamism and three-dimensionality of the figures. Tintoretto depicts the moment a few seconds later than that shown in Titian's painting. The two disciples have registered Christ's identity and turn away to others seeking confirmation. The young Tintoretto's study of sculpture is reflected in the emphatic plasticity of the disciple to the left, coupled with an added element of torsion as he swivels away from Christ. The disciple to the right turns in the opposite direction, while the serving woman, who may be oblivious to what is taking place, seems to gyrate as she carries the wine. In contrast to Titian's stable composition, based on a rectangular grid, Tintoretto's is organized around diagonals. The table itself is not horizontal to the picture plane, but appears askew, its corner pushing forward. This compositional structure supports a plunging centrifugal movement outward from the figure of Christ.

Like many of Tintoretto's early works, the Budapest painting can be seen as a deliberate challenge to Titian and the Venetian tradition. But equally

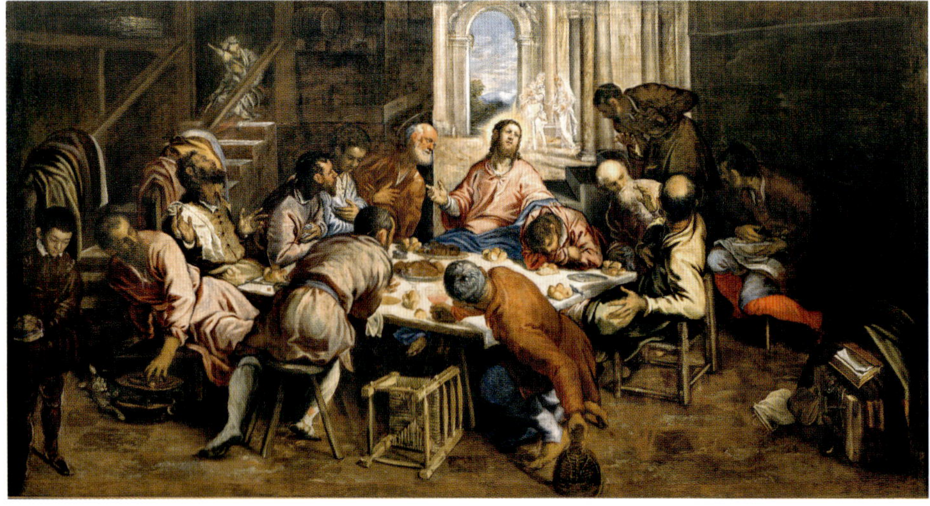

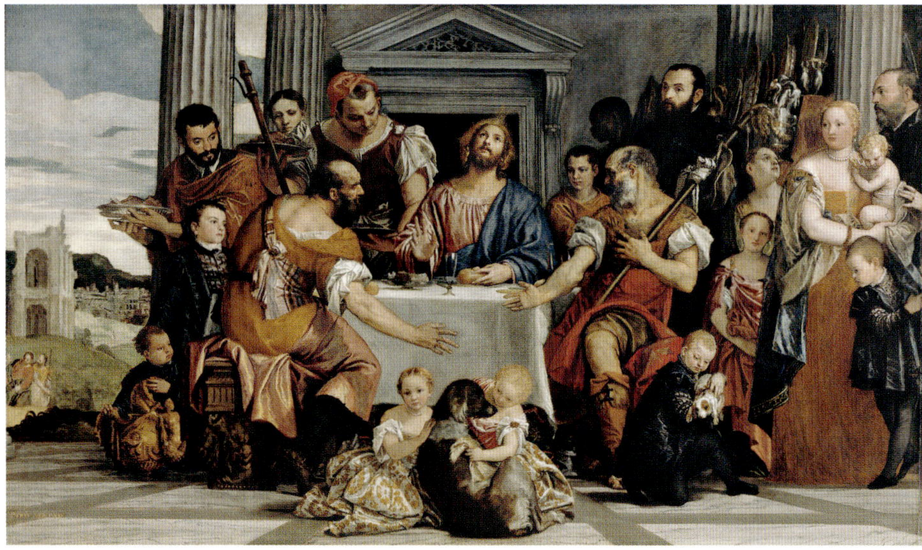

Fig. 55
Tintoretto
Last Supper, about 1563–64
Oil on canvas
Church of San Trovaso, Venice

Fig. 56
Veronese
Supper at Emmaus, about 1559–60
Oil on canvas
Musée du Louvre, Paris

typical, the young artist's ambition here exceeds his ability to achieve the effects he seeks. Over the course of the 1540s, through his continued study of sculpture and of the human body and its mechanics, Tintoretto would master the use of the human form as his primary mode of expression. Here the anatomies are still awkward—the torso of the disciple to the left and the legs of the serving youth are both impossibly long, for example—and the composition lacks the control that characterizes the artist's mature works. Yet the *Supper at Emmaus* contains the embryo of Tintoretto's great depictions of the Last Supper, for example that in San Trovaso (fig. 55). The most important elements of that painting are visible here—the diagonal table, pushing forward into the viewer's space; the centrifugal composition, radiating from Christ at the center; the dynamic physical response of the apostles to the revelation of Christ's identity.[73] As in all of Tintoretto's *Last Suppers*, the overall atmosphere of the scene is homely and quotidian, despite the classicizing elements of the architecture and the luxurious wine ewer. The protagonists are dusty travelers who have stopped at a small-town inn, their modest station embodying the Christian ideal of humility.

Veronese's Rotterdam *Supper at Emmaus* is derived from the artist's magnificent version of the subject now in the Louvre (datable to around 1560; fig. 56).[74] The Paris *Supper at Emmaus* is at once a depiction of the biblical story and a group portrait of an unidentified wealthy Venetian family, who observe the scene as though it were taking place on the veranda of their villa on the *terraferma*.[75] The younger children frolic with the family dogs in the foreground. With its mingling of the sacred and the profane, so typical of Veronese, the Louvre picture foreshadows the artist's series of sumptuous feast paintings and their expansive cast of characters, luxuriant costumes, and elaborate architectural settings.

The little Rotterdam *Supper at Emmaus* takes the theme in a different direction, reminding us that Veronese, like Titian, worked effectively in a range of scales—unlike Tintoretto, who executed very few small religious paintings.[76] While it lacks the magnificence and luxuriant display of the Louvre canvas, the depiction of the biblical scene in the Rotterdam picture improves on the original in certain ways, presenting an intensity lacking in the larger picture. This results not only from the absence of the patrician onlookers, but also from a tighter focus on the participants that encourages the viewer to peer into the scene, following the gaze of both disciples, which is directed intently at Christ's gesture of blessing. (Veronese cannot resist retaining a touch of sentimentality, however, and maintains the little girl playing with the dog in the foreground, both of whom gaze sweetly at the viewer.)[77] As in the Louvre version, Christ looks heavenward, a motif that recalls the depiction of Christ in Raphael's *Transfiguration* (Vatican Museums).[78] In addition, in the Rotterdam painting, the reaction of the disciples is far more dramatic than in the Louvre version, where the gestures of surprise are more conventionally rhetorical. Particularly the disciple to the left, who appears to start up from his seat while his hands tense in shock,

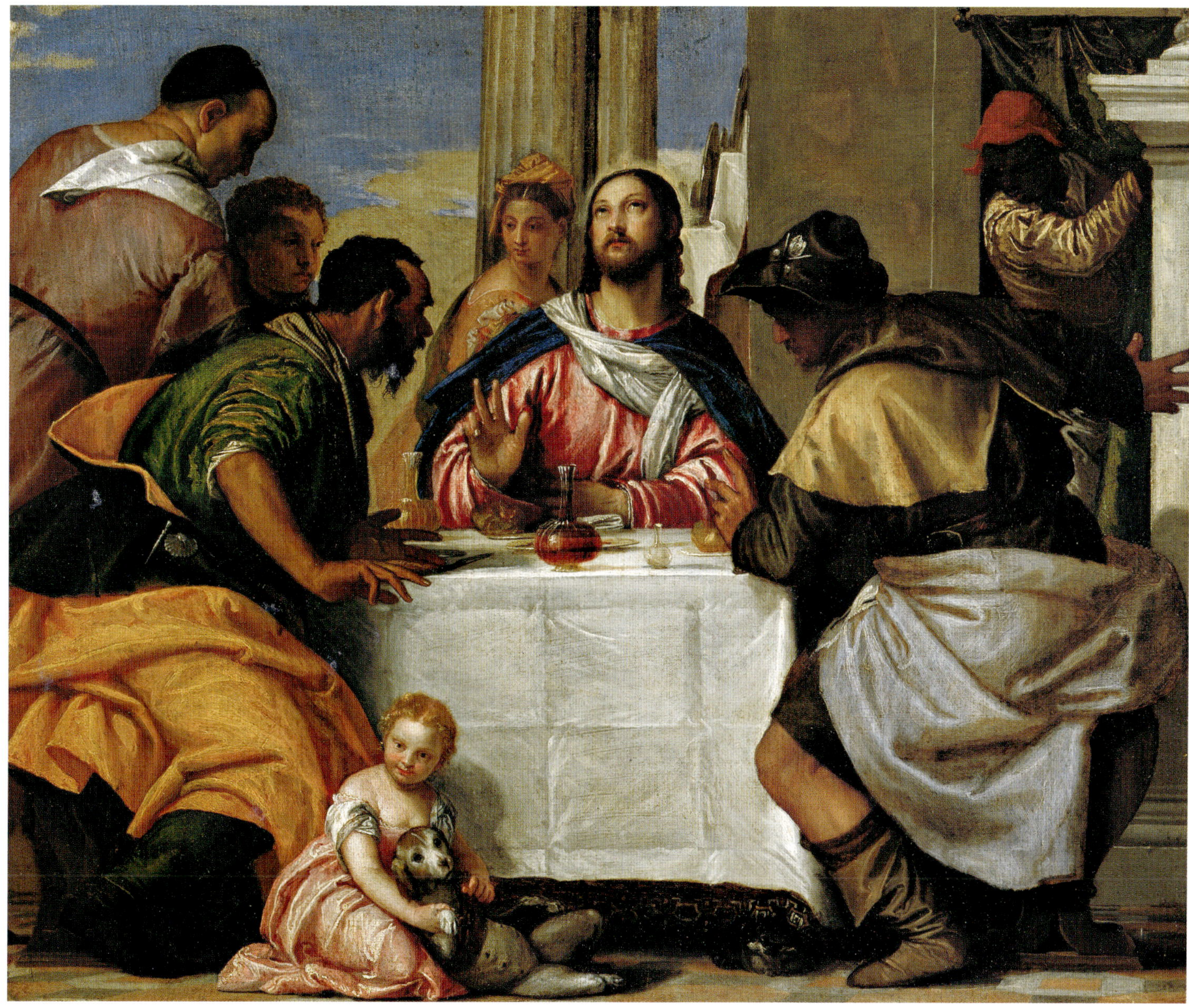

cat. 23

seems to echo Titian's treatments of the theme (of which the Contarini version would have been visible in the Palazzo Ducale by 1566), as well as Tintoretto's great *Last Supper* for San Trovaso.[79]

The dynamic interaction of gesture and gaze in Veronese's Rotterdam *Supper at Emmaus* is contained in a classically harmonious composition. The strong silhouettes of the disciples and the host against a light background draw attention to the figure of Christ, which is further strengthened by the paired columns rising directly behind him. As in Titian's versions, the horizontals and verticals of the architecture provide a stabilizing grid, contrasting markedly with the unstable composition in Tintoretto's *Supper at Emmaus*. Thus the Rotterdam *Supper at Emmaus* offers a synthesis of the approaches of Titian and Tintoretto to the theme, combining the balance of Titian's versions with the energy and depth of feeling of Tintoretto's (more fully realized in the latter's San Trovaso *Last Supper* than his *Supper at Emmaus*). Veronese brings a personal innovation to the theme, however, in his concentrated focus on the gesture of Christ blessing the bread, which highlights the moment of revelation so dramatically.
— RE, FI

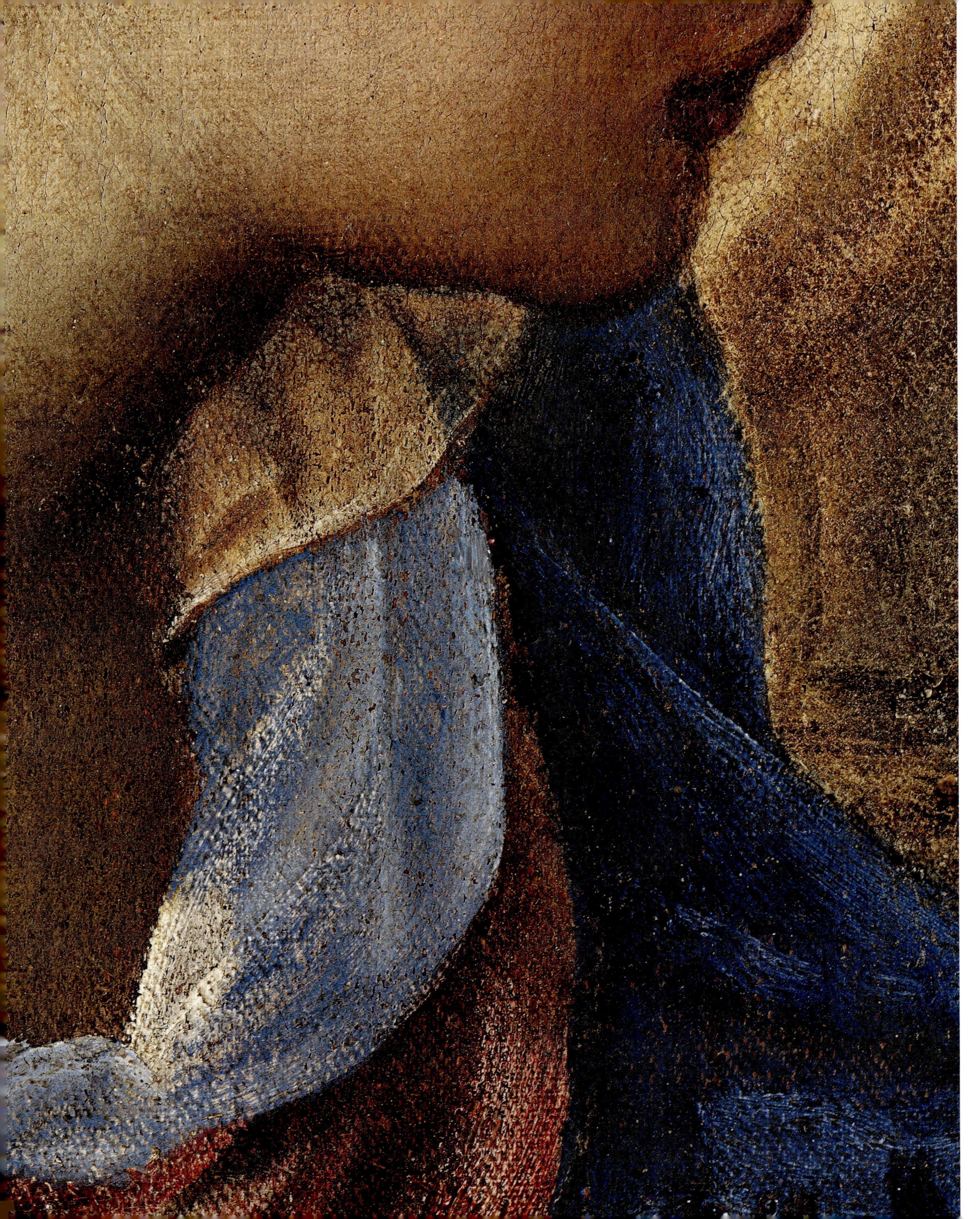

Beneath the Surface: Revelations from Three Works by Veronese, Titian, and Tintoretto

The Museum of Fine Arts is well known for its gold-ground Italian paintings, with a particular strength in Sienese works from the Trecento and Quattrocento.[1] The Venetian Renaissance paintings in the collection, however, are less heralded, though the holdings include some of the major names of the period: Bartolomeo Vivarini, Lotto, Titian, Tintoretto, Veronese, and Bassano. In part, these pictures are all overshadowed by the one truly outstanding Venetian painting in Boston, Titian's *Europa* at the Isabella Stewart Gardner Museum (fig. 106). Moreover, the attributions of two works by Titian and one by Tintoretto were questioned in standard catalogues raisonnés some thirty or forty years ago, causing them to disappear from subsequent literature. Finally, while most of the paintings have been on continuous public display in the permanent-collection galleries, until recently they have received little technical examination or scholarly attention.

The present volume, and the exhibition it accompanies, presents an opportunity to reconsider this collection, digging a little deeper, as it were, for the first time in many years. Among the works in the Museum's collection that have been subject to recent examination and restoration, three paintings—one each by Tintoretto, Titian, and Veronese—have been chosen to serve as case studies. Together, they are the starting point for a reevaluation of a neglected collection; individually, they offer insight into the creative processes of the artists who produced them, with three instances of surprising discoveries below the surface.

Jupiter and a Nude: *Veronese at Small Scale*

VERONESE
Jupiter and a Nude, 1560s
Museum of Fine Arts, Boston
(cat. 24)

Veronese's large-scale works—not only his huge feats for refectories and frescoes but also his sumptuous mythological paintings, suave portraits, and stirring altarpieces—justify his reputation as a master of the grand gesture. By contrast, the small-format *Jupiter and a Nude* provides an opportunity to consider the artist's methods when working at an intimate scale for a domestic setting.

Jupiter and a Nude is one of a set of four identically sized canvases in the Museum's collection. The paintings probably once constituted part of the decoration of a private interior, perhaps a frieze under a cornice.[2] This particular work, the only one of the group with a setting of classical architecture, has traditionally been called "Jupiter and Venus," based on the two primary figures in the center of the painting. Jupiter's identity is confirmed by the prominent eagle, his attribute, perched on the fountain at left; the identity of the beautiful young woman he embraces is not clear, but it is in fact unlikely she is Venus, given that there are no stories in the literary sources about an incestuous love between Jupiter and his daughter. A 1658 inventory calls this painting "the story of Jupiter and Io,"[3] yet this, too, seems doubtful: in the mythology, Jupiter appears to Io in the form of a cloud, which is not the case here. Semele has also been suggested as the female figure, but in that story Jupiter is depicted in a blaze of divine light that kills the heroine.[4] Moreover, neither figure appears particularly godlike; it is only their nudity that sets them apart from the elegantly clothed characters in the background. Absent a more precise identification for this painting, *Jupiter and a Nude* seems a reasonable alternative.

Of Tintoretto, Titian, and Veronese, the last was the most enthusiastic draftsman, and in scale and style, the figures in this painting resemble those found in his many drawings.[5] While the size of the painting might suggest that it was conceived and executed with minimal planning, the variety of techniques used is considerable. The support is a single piece of finely woven twill canvas with a light-toned preparation layer. Examination with infrared reflectography has revealed a large amount of finely executed underdrawing (fig. 58). Most, though not all, of the drawing relates to the placement of the architecture, and much of it is done using a straightedge to work out precisely the proportions of the columns and balustrade, including the spacing of the smallest details (fig. 57). Other details are worked in freehand, however, including the quick lyrical sketch of the statue in the middle of the fountain and the fluid lines describing the placement of the small fruit trees (fig. 59). These underdrawings resemble Veronese's pen-and-ink drawings in their freshness and economy and were probably preceded by a variety of sketches on paper.

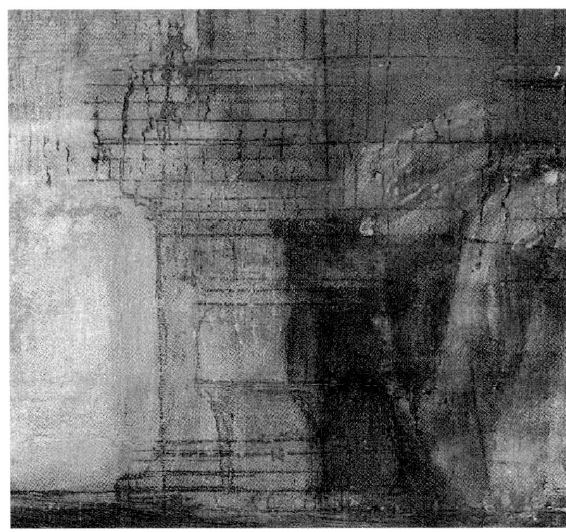

Fig. 57
Infrared reflectogram detail of the bottom of the column at center left of *Jupiter and a Nude*, showing underdrawing using a straightedge

Although drawn by the same hand, a different, broader style of soft brush drawing is visible at the lower right of the canvas: fluidly rendered legs extend upward into the composition from the

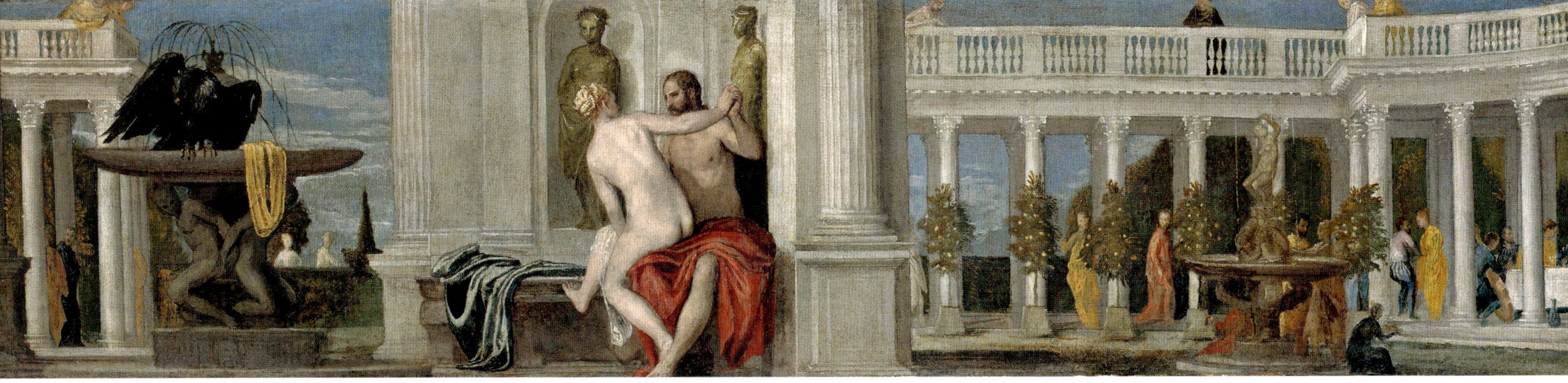

cat. 24

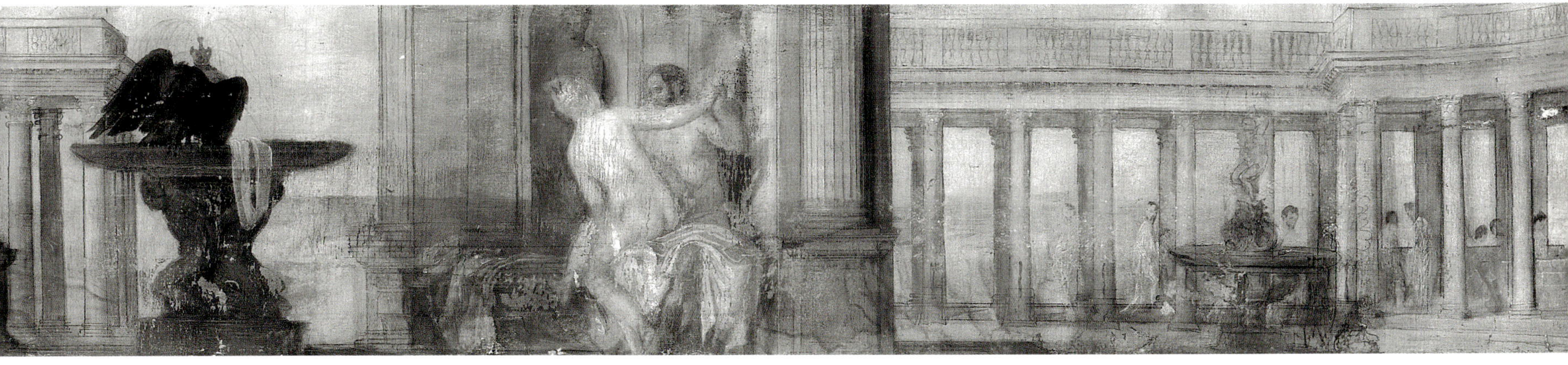

Fig. 58
Infrared reflectogram of *Jupiter and a Nude*, showing the variety of underdrawing styles

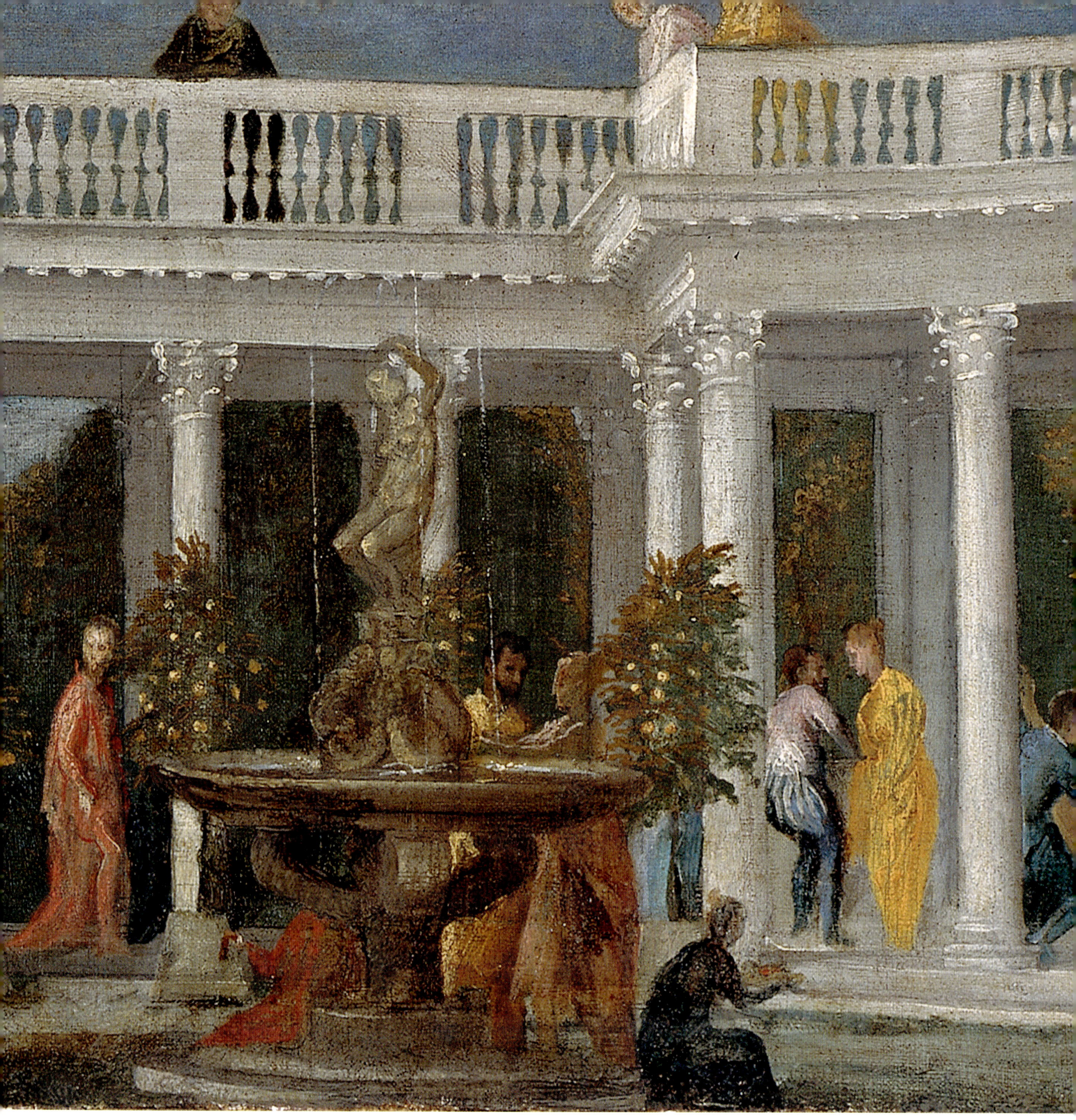

bottom of the support (fig. 60). It became clear during analysis that this drawing related to a different composition; these legs were drawn before the canvas was used for the current painting, and it is quite possible that the rest of this truncated drawing might be found below the surface of one of the other canvases in the group. In scale, it appears similar to figures in other paintings in the set, suggesting that this drawing relates to one of those compositions. As examination of these four paintings continues, we hope that it will shed further light on their production and relationship to each other.

A number of cross sections were taken from *Jupiter and a Nude* in 2001, and visible in all the samples is what appears to be a light pink priming layer, made up of a mixture of lead white and red lake. The prevalent use of red lake pigment in all stages of the painting process, from its appearance in the ground to its use as a final glaze, seems to be a consistent factor in the work of all three artists, and may relate to its low cost and ready availability in Venice at the time.[6] Notable in this painting are the range of colors and high-quality pigments in Veronese's palette, which, combined with pale-colored grounds, gave his works great clarity and light.[7] Even in a small work such as this, Veronese planned and executed the composition with great care, devoting to it the same methods and high-quality materials that he lavished on his largest and most impressive works.

— RM, FI

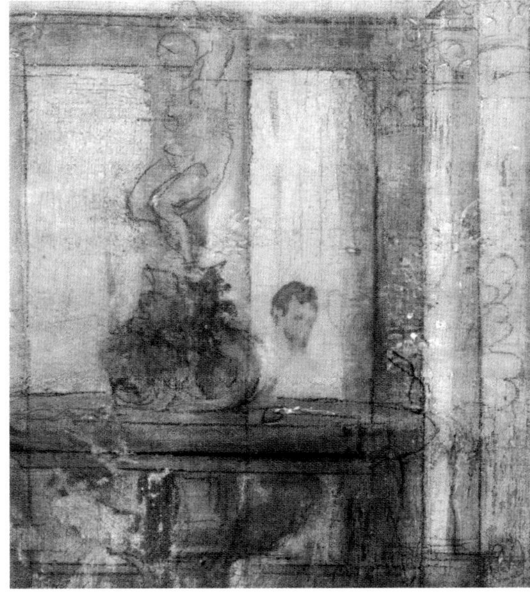

Fig. 59
Infrared reflectogram detail of the fountain, showing the freehand underdrawing below the statue and the trees

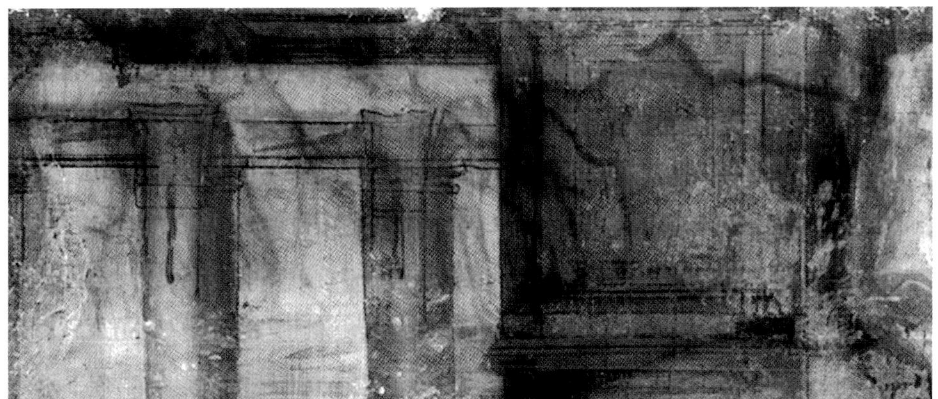

Fig. 60
Infrared reflectogram detail of the inverted painting, showing a fluid brush underdrawing of what appear to be walking or running legs

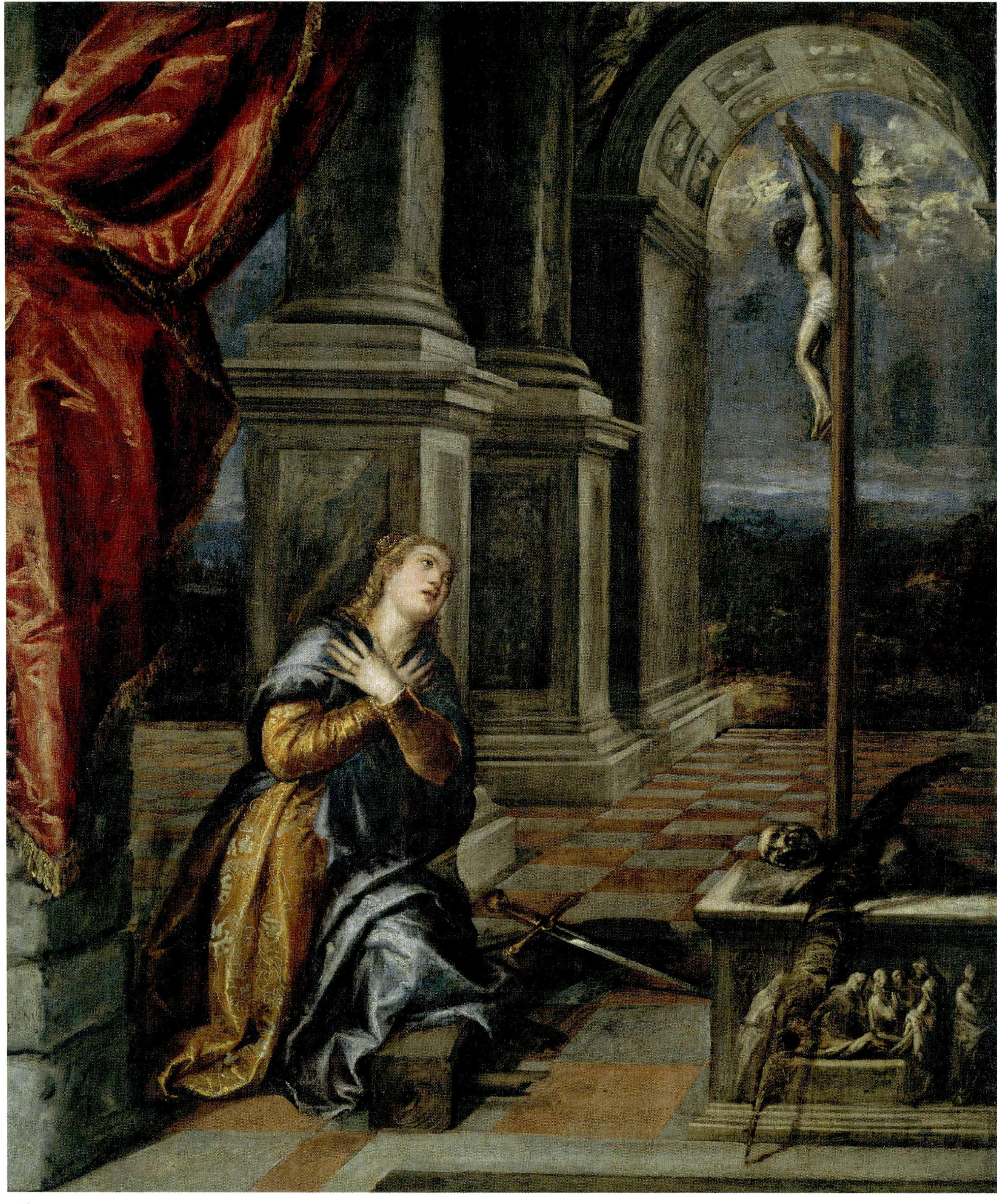

cat. 25

Saint Catherine of Alexandria at Prayer: *The Elderly Titian and the Authorship of Late Paintings*

TITIAN
Saint Catherine of Alexandria at Prayer, about 1567
Museum of Fine Arts, Boston
(cat. 25)

Compared with the mysterious nature of Veronese's *Jupiter and a Nude*, the subject matter of Titian's *Saint Catherine of Alexandria at Prayer*, of about 1567, is immediately recognizable. But while the theme is less puzzling, the painting's overall effect is mixed, which has led to critical neglect over the past three decades. Many passages of the *Saint Catherine* are admirably, even beautifully, rendered, particularly the relief on the sarcophagus and the dramatic, cloudy sky that emphasizes the Crucifixion statuette. These sections seem likely to have been painted by Titian himself, rather than by his workshop assistants. The highlights on the saint's embroidered clothing and the bulky curtain at the upper left evince a level of detail that might seem foreign to Titian's looser style of the 1560s; yet completed paintings sent by Titian to Philip II of Spain, such as *Tarquin and Lucretia* (fig. 107) and the signed *Saint Jerome* in El Escorial, have equivalent careful passages of embroidered fabrics and still-life objects. Other areas, by contrast, including much of the heavy architectural setting and the perspective paving of the floor, are frankly disappointing, rote, or awkward in execution. The unevenness of the paint handling and the banality of this setting have caused some critics to unfairly dismiss the whole picture. The question of Titian's delegation of parts of the painting to assistants must therefore be part of any reassessment of this work.

The presence of a broken wheel, crown, sword, ring, and palm of martyrdom makes clear that the work depicts the legendary Saint Catherine of Alexandria. Often depicted in contemplative pose, the kneeling saint here gazes in rapture at a crucifix, an act of devotion far more typically associated with Saint Jerome (cats. 51–52). The painting bears the artist's signature and can boast impressive documentation, starting with a letter of December 10, 1568, from Titian to Cardinal Alessandro Farnese, which mentions a painting of Saint Catherine ordered by an intermediary, "Cardinal Alessandrino" (Michele di Bonelli), that Titian had sent to Bonelli "many months ago." A 1598 inventory of Bonelli's possessions lists "A kneeling Saint Catherine of the Wheel with crucifix, in Titian's hand." The specificity of the description—which mentions Saint Catherine and her wheel, in a kneeling pose, with a crucifix, in Titian's style and with his signature—confirms that the painting listed in the document is the one at the MFA, especially in the absence of other candidates in Titian's oeuvre. The picture seems to have later hung in El Escorial before passing through prominent English collections (for a more detailed provenance, see the checklist to this volume).

Despite this notable provenance, the painting's unusual composition and its strange array of attributes led to its being first misunderstood and later neglected. In 1954, Erica Tietze-Conrat argued that the emphasis on the Crucifixion and sarcophagus within the picture—not normally associated with Catherine of Alexandria—might be explained because the painting originally depicted Saint Catherine of Siena, a Dominican nun who had numerous visions of the crucified Christ, and eventually received the stigmata.[8] Tietze-Conrat also believed that the deep perspective setting, seen in only one other example in Titian's oeuvre, the *Annunciation* in Treviso, painted around 1520, meant that the Boston picture was begun about that time as a Saint Catherine of Siena. As such, the main figure was transformed nearly fifty years later to make a Saint Catherine of Alexandria, mostly by workshop assistants who added attributes like the "squeezed in" broken wheel.[9] Without the benefit of X-radiography, Tietze-Conrat had proposed a radical but efficient transformation of an earlier painting—which did sometimes occur. Although the painting had been accepted as autograph by most earlier scholars, Tietze-Conrat's dismissal of its quality and pronouncement of extensive intervention by assistants must have influenced Harold E. Wethey's estimation when preparing his 1969 catalogue, in which he declared the picture to be by Titian's workshop.[10] This verdict implied that Titian himself contributed little to the planning and execution, even though the connection with the important patron (and the possibility that this was a specific commis-

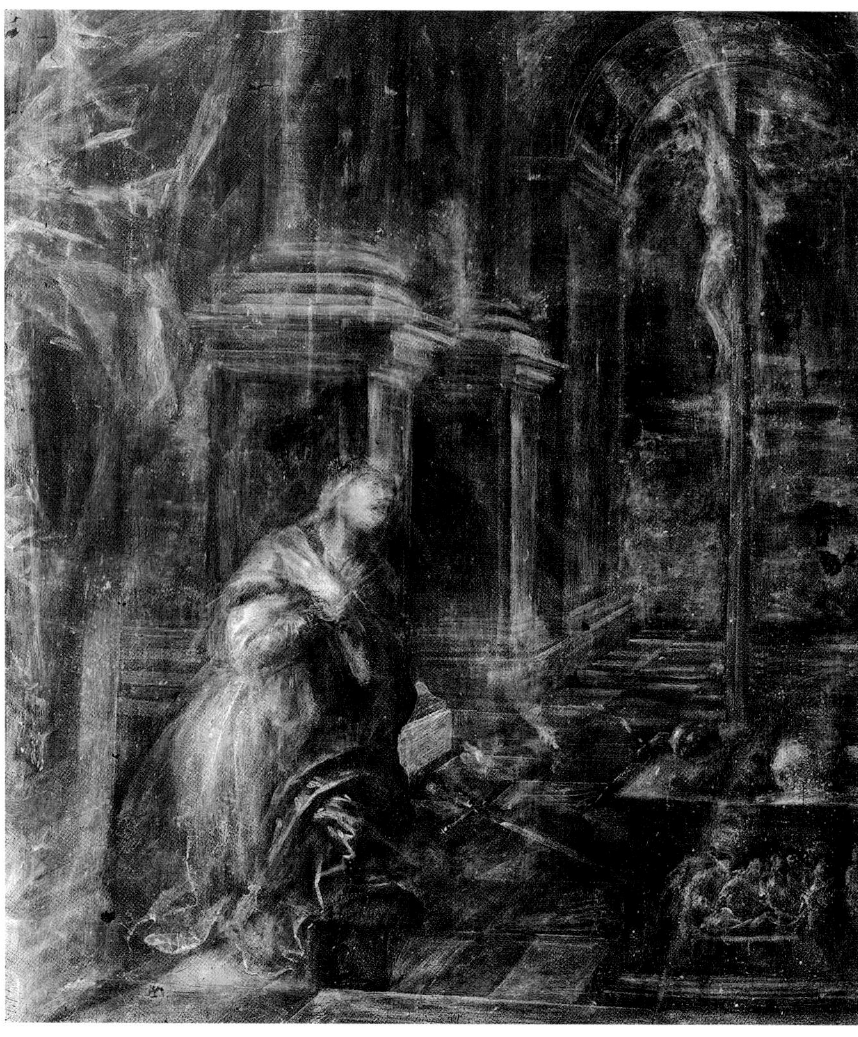

Fig. 61
X-radiograph of *Saint Catherine of Alexandria at Prayer*, showing edits and revisions

sion) was acknowledged in the entry. Although Titian was about seventy-seven years old at the time of this painting, in his last decade of work he produced more than a dozen autograph canvases. The cleaning undertaken for the present exhibition has restored legibility to the composition and its distinctive brushwork, and the case for the painting's substantially autograph status can now be made anew.

Although Wethey's dismissal of the painting led to years of critical neglect, other scholarship of the 1960s proved both the priority of Catherine of Alexandria as subject and the interest of this late work in Titian's oeuvre.[11] The painting's particular emphasis on the vision of the crucified Christ recalls another Catherine, Caterina de' Ricci, a Tuscan nun from Prato who mystically experienced all the stages of Christ's Passion on a weekly basis for more than a decade. Her deep devotions prompted the visits of many ecclesiastical dignitaries to her convent, including Michele di Bonelli, the owner of Titian's picture and a fellow Dominican. From the correspondence with Alessandro Farnese, it appears that Bonelli had requested a Saint Catherine from Titian, and may even have given specific instructions for the depiction also to reflect Caterina de' Ricci. Several authors have suggested that the elderly Titian may have paid special attention to this commission, since he was hoping that Bonelli and Cardinal Farnese might pull strings to help him in a dispute over money owed to his son Pomponio.[12]

In addition to the quality of the picture, now more apparent after the most recent cleaning, the very circumstances of its commission suggest that the *Saint Catherine* for Bonelli was too important to have been simply delegated to the workshop. Although it has been argued that Titian needed to complete this painting quickly (and potentially without payment), and thus recycled compositional ideas from earlier works,[13] preliminary findings from technical examination, particularly by X-radiograph (fig. 61), confirm that the composition in fact went through numerous edits and revisions during the painting process.[14]

The painting's composition was anything but straightforward, with some assumed revisions proving to have been integral concepts and vice versa. For one thing, despite Tietze-Conrat's assertion that the wheel under Catherine's knees was added at a late stage, X-radiography reveals a reserve left in the floor-tile pattern for a curved object, demonstrating that the wheel was always intended to be in the composition. Moreover, Catherine's pose was not changed from the initial composition, and thus she was always intended to be kneeling on an object. On the other hand, the massive column prominently positioned at the front left edge—the only pillar in the composition depicted as rusticated, composed of heavy, unfinished blocks of stone—was not part of the original composition. The X-radiograph shows that this column was first conceived as a marble cylindrical shaft, similar to those that recede behind the saint, and that the change was made relatively late in the process. A significant amount of detail in this lower structure is visible in the X-radiograph, suggesting it was taken to quite a high level of finish before ultimately being discarded. It seems likely that Titian was responsible for this decision, even if he did not execute the change himself; perhaps it is significant that his signature was placed in this area.

Other revisions took place in the floor space just beyond the kneeling saint. The X-radiograph unveils the first position of her sword, initially placed slightly higher and to the right of where it now rests on the wheel. More mysterious are the two forms painted on the floor just behind the sword: they appear to have been barely roughed in with just a few quick strokes of paint before they were eliminated altogether. One form seems circular and may be emitting flames or smoke, suggesting perhaps a small fire. The second, placed just to the right of the first (and more clearly visible in infrared light), resembles a discarded bundle of cloth. At this time, neither form can be definitively identified, nor their relationship to each other clarified. Compared with the changes going on around her, the figure of Saint Catherine herself has remained relatively close to the initial conception. The expression on her face, however, does appear to have evolved: her mouth was originally more open, perhaps suggesting a more painfully ecstatic state than the final, rather subdued and reserved expression seen in the paint surface.

X-radiography also reveals the use of scoring (into both the ground layer and the paint layer) to define architectural details and clarify areas of confusion in the perspective (fig. 62). The initial drawing of the arch, which was lower and flatter in appearance, was roughed in by hand, with scoring then used to raise the arch's height and clarify and correct the perspective of its vaulted ceiling. This redrawing was made with a fine, sharp implement or stylus. The uniform lines were certainly created with the aid of a mechanical device such as a compass—a common practice. While the scoring can be seen with the naked eye, its role in the evolution of the archway is more clearly elucidated by X-radiography, where the marks are visible as either white or black lines. The white lines show the placement of the initial score marks and were probably made into the ground or the very early paint layers. As the painting progressed, the voids left by the scoring became filled with paint, creating small dense areas that are opaque and show up white on X-rays. Conversely, the dark lines, which are not filled with paint and hence are not as opaque under X-ray, most likely reveal later adjustments to the position and perspective of the arch. Similar finely scored lines, also made into the later paint layers with the help of a straightedge, can be seen in the floor behind Saint Catherine. These lines, as in the archway, seem to be

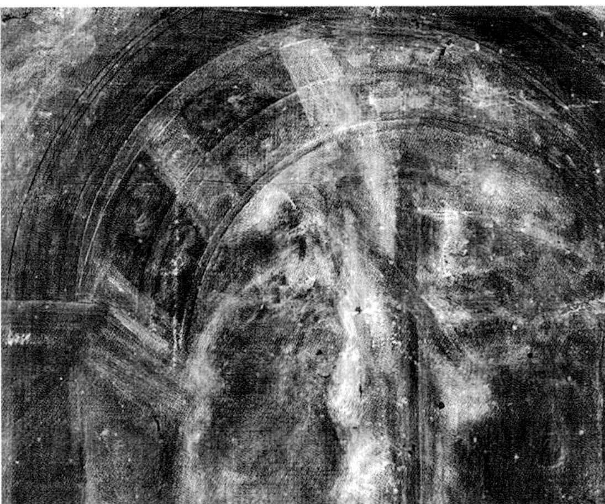

Fig. 62
X-radiograph detail of the archway and the Crucifixion, showing the use of scoring

adjustments and corrections to the rather confused perspective of the tiled floor. The rough, broken appearance of some of these dark lines suggests that the scoring was made into already-dry ground and paint, possibly supporting the suggestion that the painting was worked on over a period of time. The mechanical execution of the architecture is precisely the kind of rote task that an assistant would undertake.

The numerous changes and edits visible in the X-radiograph, combined with the uneven handling of the medium evident in the paint surface, seem to suggest a somewhat confused evolution for this small painting, perhaps exacerbated by the unusual imagery needed to express the specific (and obscure) subject matter, and the urge to complete this picture quickly for its influential recipient. This process of continuous revision and recycling of earlier ideas is a known practice of Titian and his workshop in his later career.[15]

Further technical examination will likely reveal more about the painting, but what we find below the surface reveals a sense of improvised execution, suggesting the master's planning, changes of mind, and apparent delegation of much of the architectural setting to assistants. On the picture's surface, the effects of caressed contours, rich fabrics, palpable atmosphere, and expressive impasto all argue for Titian's own intervention in some areas, even if other parts were carried out by others. The final product, if not uniformly by Titian's hand (and admittedly not possessing the quality of his finest late paintings), contains enough of his supervision and intervention to justify the wording in the 1598 inventory "fatto di mano di Tiziano."

— RM, FI

Tintoretto's Nativity: *More than One Artist, More than One Painting*

TINTORETTO
Nativity, late 1550s, reworked 1570s
Museum of Fine Arts, Boston
(cat. 26)

The *Nativity* is an enigmatic painting, and, in contrast to Titian's *Saint Catherine*, many of its complexities are visible even on the surface. The painting had been treated at least four times before its present restoration, and three of these treatments took place at the MFA. The number of treatments suggests that curators and conservators continued to be unsure about the true nature of the painting's condition and intended appearance.[16] The technical examination of the painting's genesis undertaken for this current restoration has resulted in some unexpected discoveries, which begin to resolve the earlier puzzlement of art historians and conservators.

As with the Veronese and Titian examples, Tintoretto's subject matter is not straightforward. His primary subject is obviously the Adoration of the Christ Child, and while the large figures on the left must be the Virgin and Saint Joseph, the identification of the other pair is problematic. Both lack halos. The woman at right wears the same colors as the Virgin and would seem to be Anne, the mother of Mary, though Anne is not normally present in depictions of the Nativity. An unusual aspect of her appearance is the forceful way she throws out her arms, an oddly energetic gesture in this context. The man at right might be Joachim, Anne's husband. Or, given the Venetian tradition of devotion to Zacharias, the father of John the Baptist, the two figures at right might instead be Zacharias and Elizabeth, the Virgin's cousin.[17] Alternatively, the man at right may simply be a shepherd, which would make sense given his modest clothing and staff. Absent more conclusive evidence, in this essay we will identify the two figures as Anne and a shepherd.

The next problem concerns the artist, or rather artists. Assigned to Domenico Tintoretto in Pallucchini and Rossi's standard catalogue, the picture contains evidence of at least two distinct hands, with that of the primary figures—particularly the Virgin, Anne, and the shepherd—clearly revealing the Michelangelesque body types, confident handling of contours, and bold folds in draperies characteristic of Jacopo Tintoretto.[18] Jacopo's authorship of these figures is confirmed, and a dating for the Boston picture suggested, by comparing the Virgin with her counterpart in the *Adoration of the Shepherds* at the Fitzwilliam Museum in Cambridge, England, which dates from the late 1540s or early 1550s. The Virgin in the present painting is somewhat grander and more loosely rendered, suggesting a later date, and in fact more closely resembles the woman holding the baby (almost certainly the Virgin) in the *Birth of John the Baptist* from the late 1550s in the church of San Zaccaria.[19] These two women share the same physical type and treatment of fabrics in their draperies. The shepherd at the right of the present painting also finds a close analogy with the Zacharias at the right edge of the San Zaccaria altarpiece. Comparisons of the shepherd can also be made with figures in Tintoretto paintings from the 1560s and even 1570s, however, proving that the artist could tighten his handling of faces and other details when he desired. These comparisons suggest that the Virgin was painted in the late 1550s, but open up the possibilities that Jacopo painted, or repainted, at least one of the main figures subsequently.

Some of the confusion about the *Nativity* results from its uneven execution. Portions of the paint surface are beautifully and confidently executed, while others appear more tentative and almost clumsy. Overall, the quality of brushwork is so varied that it is a difficult to date the painting with any confidence: the points of comparison suggested above range over two decades. A completely different hand seems to have executed the passages in the upper corners of the canvas. The left corner shows a courtly cavalcade representing the Journey of the Magi that recalls Domenico's contributions to the Gonzaga Cycle (now at the Alte Pinakothek, Munich) dating from 1578–80.[20] The right corner shows an

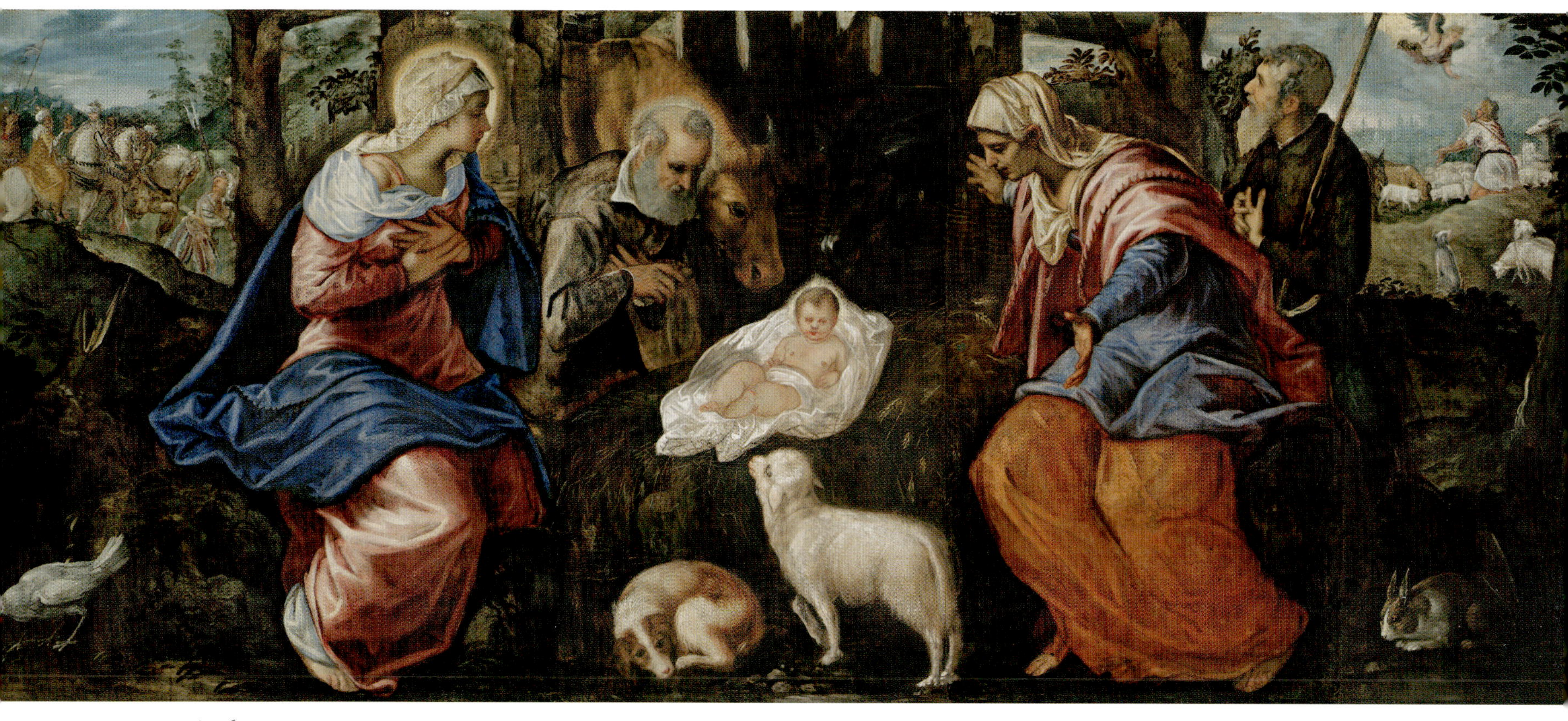

cat. 26

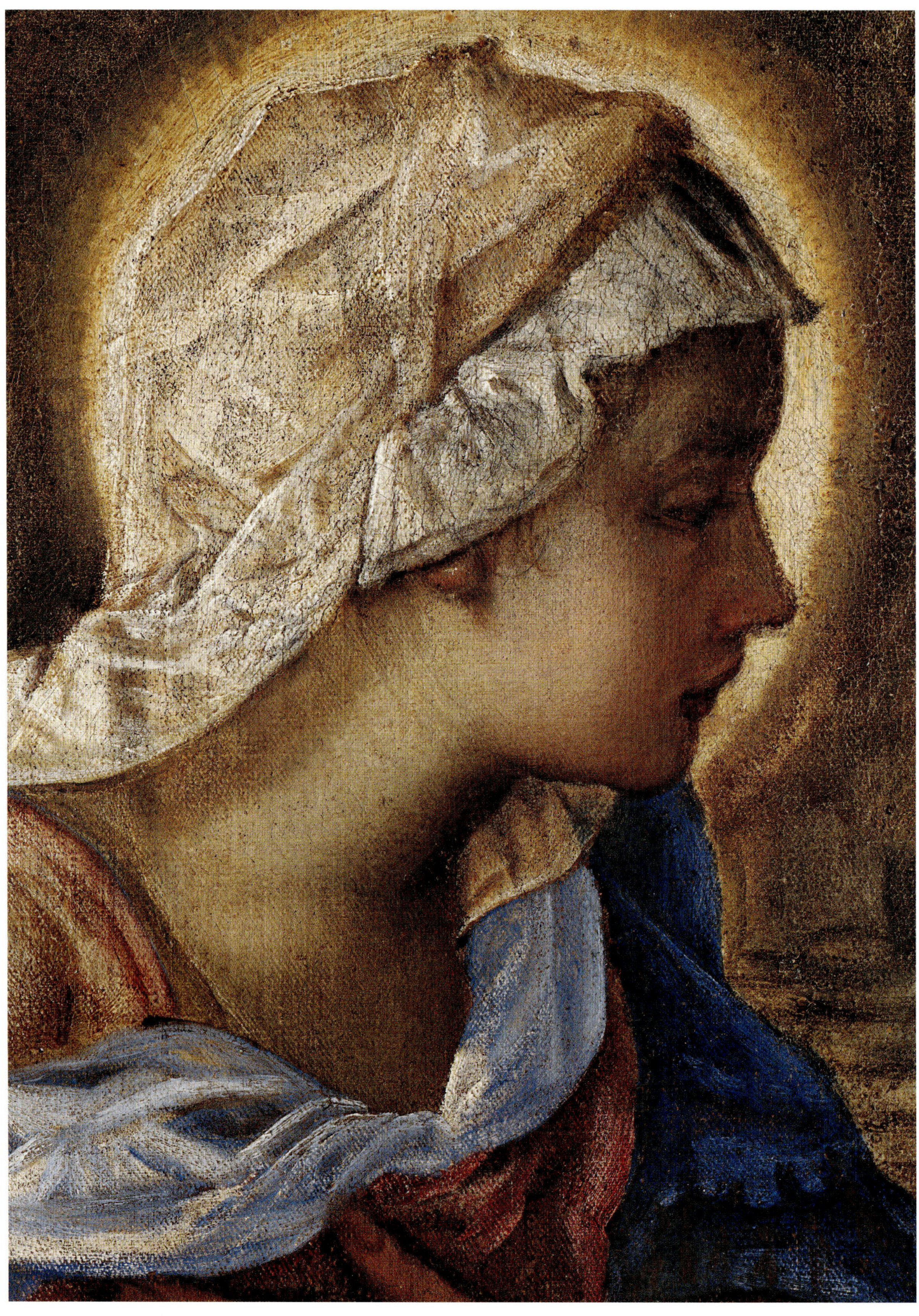

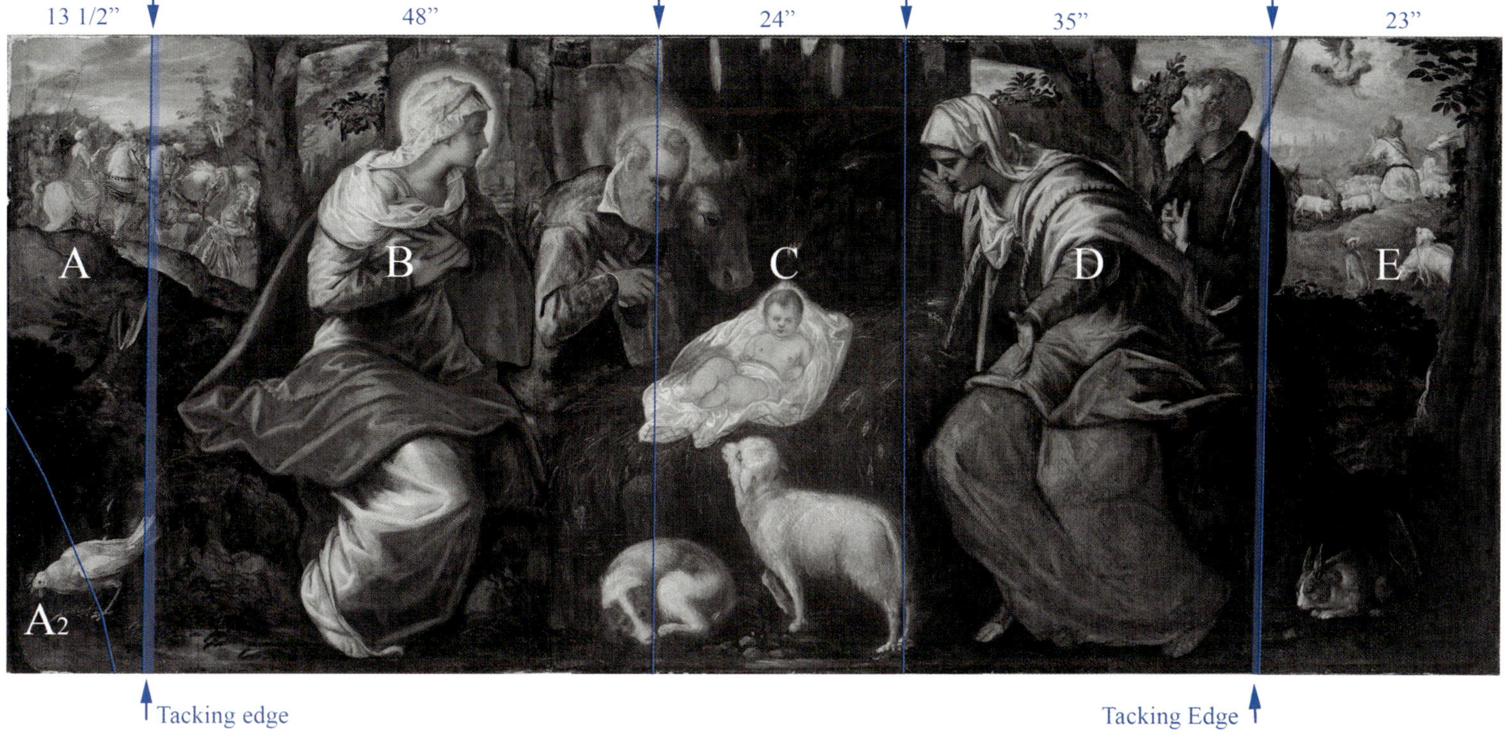

Fig. 63
Diagram of the *Nativity*, showing the position of the canvas joins and older tacking edges

Fig. 64
X-radiograph detail of the join to the right of the standing shepherd, showing damage indicative of a tacking edge

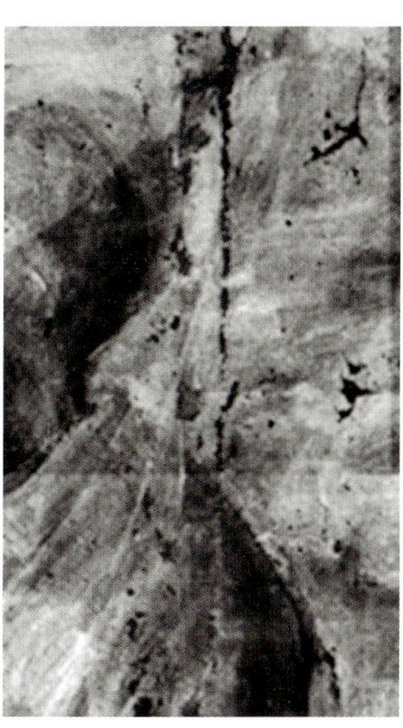

Annunciation to the Shepherds that recalls the imagery of Bassano, with the half-length angel Gabriel, the crouching shepherd, and numerous sheep. These two scenes seem to have been executed by the same hand, while perhaps a third was responsible for the foreground animals. Of these, the rooster at far left and the rabbit at far right are nearly as accomplished as the animals at the base of the tall *Adoration* in El Escorial (fig. 21), documented to 1583 and designed by Jacopo Tintoretto but largely executed by Domenico.[21] There are many other instances in Tintoretto's oeuvre where Jacopo executed the principal figures but delegated other portions to assistants, particularly in paintings as large as this one.

As is often the case in Tintoretto's larger canvases, the support for the *Nativity* is made up of several pieces of cloth sewn together.[22] The long, narrow canvas is composed of five main sections of twill-weave fabric joined with vertical seams. The left-most section of canvas is itself made up of two pieces of canvas sewn together with a diagonal seam at the lower left corner. All the fabric pieces are of a similar weight but of slightly different width (fig. 63).

More surprisingly, close inspection reveals that the outer edges of two internal pieces of canvas, the second and fourth sections from the left (canvas B and canvas D in fig. 63), had once been tacking edges—that is, they had once been attached with metal nails to a wooden stretcher (fig. 64), and thus were once finished supports, or perhaps even finished paintings, before their repurposing for the *Nativity*. The damage to these edges suggests that they had existed as tacking edges for a significant length of time. Paint from the sky and landscape behind the central Nativity grouping had covered these damages, indicating that the alteration to the canvas must be contemporary with those parts of the composition. At first glance, these observations suggest that the composition was enlarged after the inner section had been executed by Jacopo, and that the figures in the background landscape were painted by a different, perhaps later, hand. Alternatively, some of the fabric might have been reused, possibly even cut from another painting, to make up the Nativity grouping's support. But X-radiography, with its ability to look below the paint surface and provide information on the canvas structure, tells of a more complex genesis for the painting.

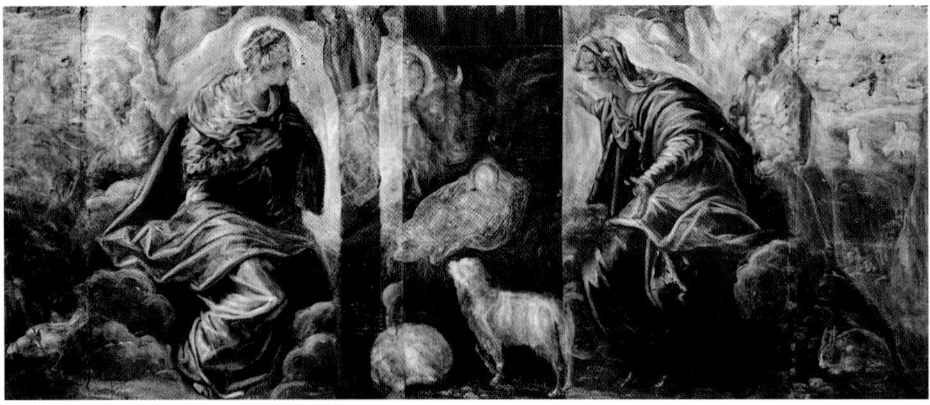

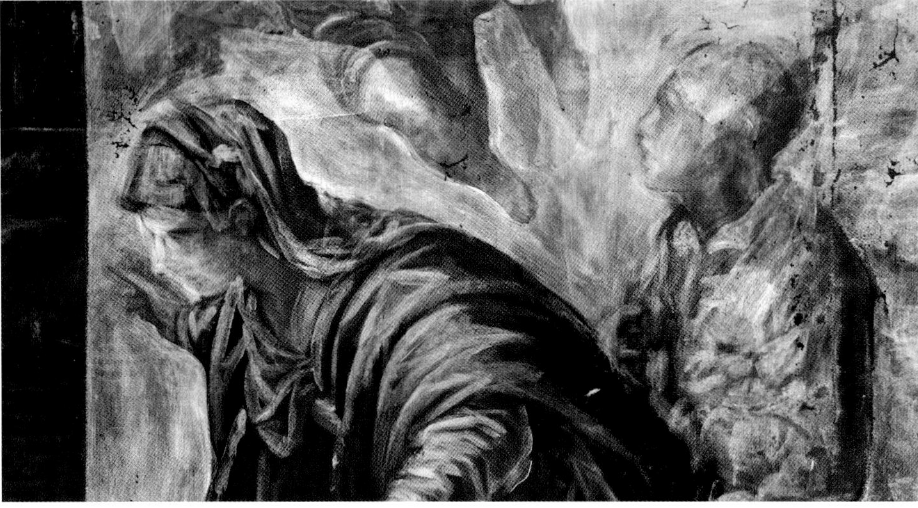

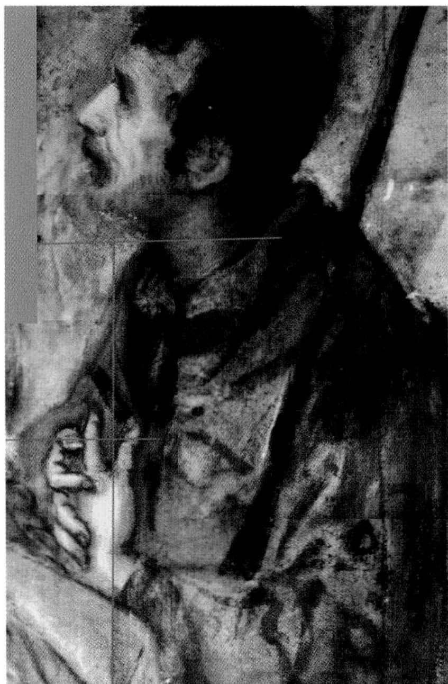

Fig. 65
X-radiograph of the *Nativity*, showing evidence of an earlier composition in two sections of canvas (B and D in fig. 63)

Fig. 66
X-radiograph detail of the heads of Saint Anne and the shepherd, showing the legs and arm of another figure

Fig. 67
Infrared reflectogram detail of the shepherd, showing loose brush underdrawing and use of a transfer grid (emphasized in blue)

A new X-radiograph of the whole painting (fig. 65) quickly made it apparent that the two main sections, the Virgin to the left and Saint Anne and the shepherd to the right—the largest pieces of canvas and the areas that contain the most beautiful and resolved figures in the composition (canvas B and D in fig. 63)—once were part of another painting altogether. Indeed, these two canvases share a similar clarity of form and luminosity, while the piece of canvas in between, showing the Christ Child, Joseph, and several animals (canvas C in fig. 63), looks noticeably darker and duller.

In the background above the heads of Saint Anne and the shepherd, a space filled with foliage and a tree trunk in the finished work, X-radiography revealed the bent legs and left arm of a figure, presumably an angel, hovering just above Saint Anne's back (fig. 66). As is often the case, once a viewer knows to look for the presence of this fugitive angel, it is easily visible to the naked eye. Although the brown paint of the tree trunk covering the angel is somewhat abraded and has become more transparent over time, it is also apparent that minimal effort was made to conceal this figure, suggesting a speed of execution and economy of means frequently ascribed to the working practices of the Tintoretto studio.[23] The bearded shepherd also differs considerably from the figure underneath, which, although still gazing up, is younger and appears to be clean shaven. This underlying figure may be a bishop saint, as the forms around the head seem to evoke the curved front of a bishop's miter (cf. cat. 15). This section is harder to read in the X-radiograph because paint that is opaque under X-rays was used in the sections of sky added later. In particular, a cross section taken from the shepherd's head reveals that later additions of flesh paint (or flesh and hair) represent an efficient adjustment to the figure's hairline, a few daubs of paint both covering the edge of the miter and pushing back the hairline—a neat trick that turns the young saint into a mature shepherd. The underpainted figure's clothing also appears to be different from what we now see on the surface (although this has been further confused by later repainting);[24] the forms revealed in the X-radiograph are suggestive of a garment that could be a bishop's vestment, with its wide collar clasped at the upper chest. The adjacent female figure, the presumed Saint Anne, was also adjusted, although here the alterations were less dramatic and may only have changed slightly the position of the woman's head and aged her features.

An examination of this area made with infrared reflectography (IRR) (fig. 67) clearly shows bold brushstrokes under the drapery of the shepherd that have little to do with what we now see on the surface. Broad dark lines that meet in the area of the figure's chest again indicate the gathered folds of a cloak or vestment, suggestive of an ecclesiastical personage. Most interestingly, the IRR exam also revealed the presence of an underdrawn grid in the area of these two figures. The use of a grid to transfer drawings onto paintings is well documented in the work of Tintoretto and his workshop.[25] What seems particularly significant in the present case is that the use of this transfer method was observed only in relation to Saint Anne, the shepherd, and the Virgin (fig. 68), but nowhere else, which again indicates a different approach to the conception and production of these three figures. Saint Anne's energetic pose has been linked with a figure drawing in the Uffizi, rendered in black chalk and squared for transfer to canvas, which has been attributed variously to the Tintoretto workshop, Palma Giovane, and Domenico Tintoretto. The IRR investigation, however, shows that the squaring on the Uffizi drawing does not match the squaring grid under the surface of the painting, and thus the drawing was not made in preparation for the figure on the Boston canvas.[26]

The upturned gaze of the shepherd, looking away from the Christ Child, seems to present an odd element for a Nativity. It is puzzling that the gazes of the principal figures are not more focused on the infant, but X-radiography provided the solution to this mystery (fig. 69). Plainly visible to the right of the Virgin's face are the knees and calves of a figure who seems to hover above her, but who on closer inspection is hanging on a cross. Turned toward the viewer, the knees were part of a figure of Christ on the cross. Reinforcing this scenario was the discovery of a second male figure, standing to the left of the Virgin, who also gazes up and toward the crucified figure. Unlike the other standing figures, he had been completely painted out, presumably because having a second main figure gazing away from the Christ Child would undermine the coherence of the Nativity scene.

The final discovery in this area of the painting was another foot (possibly two feet) and a portion of a leg; these belong undoubtedly to a second angel floating above the Virgin's head, turned toward the figure on the cross. The angel's leg in the foliage behind the Virgin is visible in the X-radiograph (fig. 69); a cross section taken from the foliage reveals flesh-colored paint underlying sky and landscape. With the discovery of this foot and leg hidden by the topmost layers of paint, it became apparent that these two pieces of canvas (sections B and D in fig. 63) were cannibalized from an earlier painting. The subject of that original composition, perhaps a Crucifixion or a Deposition, remained murky, however. Even the relationship of these two canvas fragments to each other was not clearly established. If the two female figures were not looking up at Christ on the cross, what was the focus of their gazes? Had there originally been more space between them? And might we question their identities? Presumably

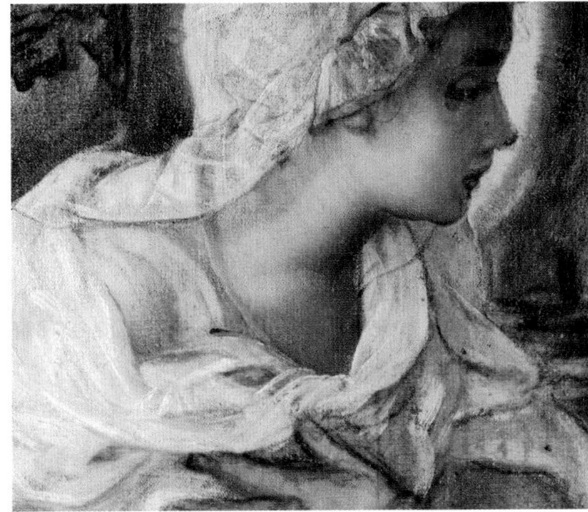

Fig. 68
Infrared reflectogram detail of the head of the Virgin, showing part of the transfer grid

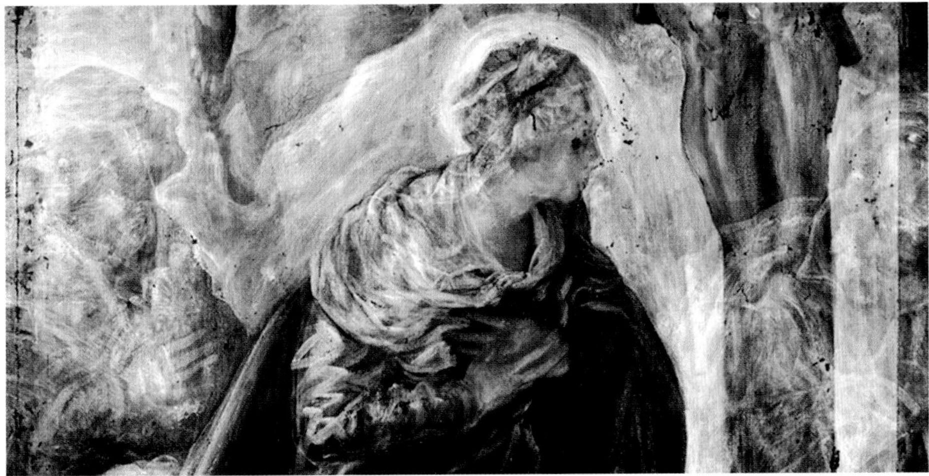

Fig. 69
X-radiograph detail of area around the Virgin, showing additional figures

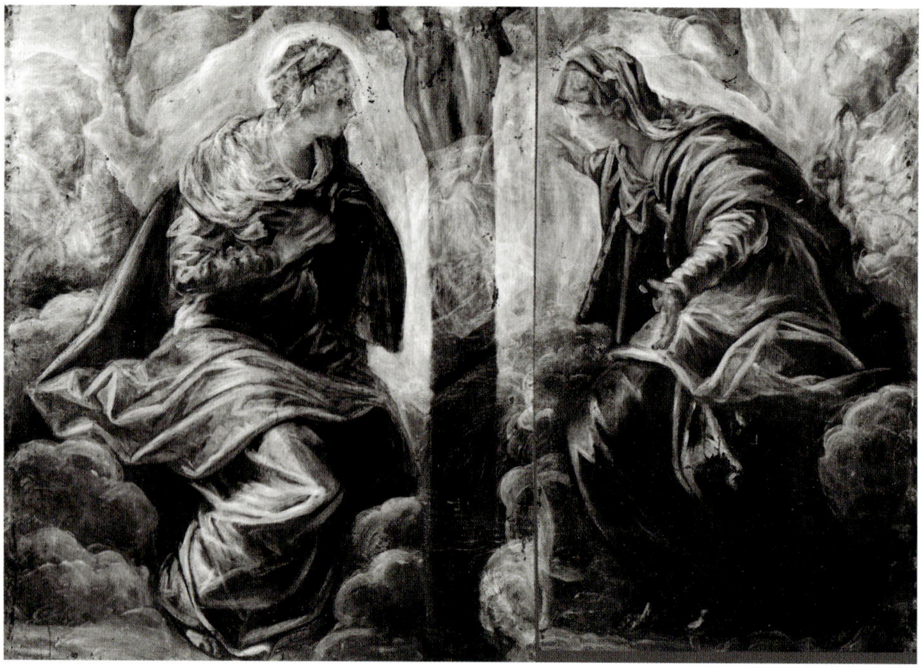

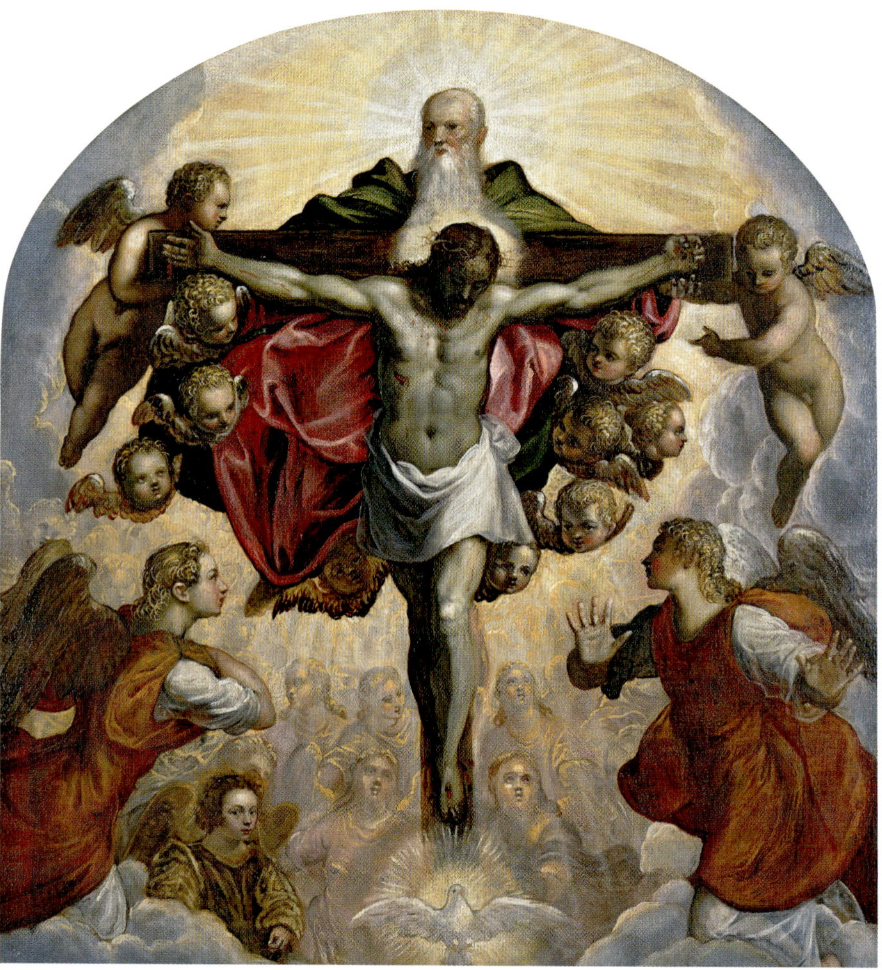

the woman on the left has always been the Virgin Mary (fig. 68); the woman on the right is older but may not always have been so (fig. 66).

At this point, another unexpected detail offered new insights. The X-radiograph shows that the main figures were not standing on the ground but were clearly positioned on large, puffy clouds that billowed up around them and around the base of the cross. Startlingly, when the X-radiographs of the two fragments are positioned next to each other, the broadly painted brushstrokes of the clouds clearly continue almost seamlessly from the edge of one piece of canvas onto the next, with little or no support missing (fig. 70). The original work made from these reunited canvases would have been large and of vertical format (about 200 cm [78 ¾ in.] wide and 300 cm [118 in.] high), proportions appropriate for a midsize altarpiece by Tintoretto or Veronese—taken together with the evident subject matter, this suggests that the work was originally intended for a church.

Finally, with the X-radiograph of the two "original" pieces of canvas placed side by side, a much clearer idea of the original composition emerged. Under the surface of the *Nativity* appears to be the lower section of a vertical, symmetrically composed depiction of a heavenly vision of Christ on the cross amid clouds. Christ is supported on either side by angels, with the figures of the Virgin Mary and a second female saint (Saint Anne or Mary Magdalen?) gazing at him. They stare at his wounds, or perhaps at the nail through his feet, or even at the cross itself. The two female saints are accompanied by two standing male saints (or perhaps the figure on the left is a donor); both look up at Christ. The space is tightly conceived, with the outer figures cropped by the edges of the canvas. It is tempting to speculate that the original subject of the painting, with the two principal women relating so closely to the bottom of the cross, reflects a particular devotion to the cross, the nails, or the wounds of Christ. Such a cult might have been based on a relic housed in the painting's original or intended location, perhaps a setting like the Cappella del Santo Chiodo (Chapel of the Holy Nail) in the Venetian church of San Pantalon.

Some of the same elements in the painting beneath—Christ on the cross, set in the clouds, flanked by symmetrically disposed figures, some with arms folded over their chests, and others with arms flung out—also appear in a small canvas probably executed by Domenico Tintoretto, *The Trinity Adored by a Heavenly Choir*, now in the Columbia Museum of Art in South Carolina (fig. 71). Perhaps the Columbia painting is Domenico's echo of Jacopo's composition beneath the *Nativity*.

It should be stressed that the Crucifixion visible in the X-radiograph is presented as a subject of veneration rather than in a straightforward narrative depiction. Ridolfi describes a similar painting by Tintoretto, already lost at the time that he wrote in 1648: "Above the door of the church of the Carità there once was seen a painting of the Savior on the Cross, a work so noble and delicate that it breathed divinity. At the foot of the Cross there was the usual group of the weeping Marys and on the sides some bishops. But of that painting one may now say with the Angel: *Surrexit non est hic* [He has arisen, he is not here]." The Carità painting may have been very close to the composition visible in the X-radiograph, with the crucified Christ above, the mourning women below, and the bishop saints to the side. Indeed, the passage in Ridolfi contains a tantalizing hint that the Carità picture was somehow "resurrected." Might this be the actual painting that was reused in the MFA composition? Ridolfi does not specify its fate, and it is possible that his reference to the resurrection was intended as an inside joke, indicating that he knew that the picture, after having been damaged or returned, had been reborn in another work.[27]

Having established the origins of the Boston *Nativity*, we must try to determine when and how this drastic alteration happened. The first thing one notices when looking at the X-radiograph is the darker tone of the central piece of canvas (section C in fig. 63), indicating a significant difference in the materials used to prepare it. The second is the way the figures of Joseph and the Christ Child are drawn, or underpainted, with broadly applied lines of lead white paint (fig. 72), much closer in technique to paintings produced in Tintoretto's workshop in the later 1570s. Furthermore, Joseph, who is painted over the legs of the Crucified Christ and across the seams of the two pieces of canvas (B and C in fig. 63), evidently was part of the later campaign of painting. This area was also studied with IRR, and, although difficult to interpret, the strong black lines seem to indicate that the Christ Child was initially drawn facing in the other direction (fig. 72), perhaps looking at the gesturing female figure at the left.

Finally, we come to the outermost sections of canvas (sections A, A2, and E in fig. 63). Presumably added at the same time as the central section, the continuation of the figure of the shepherd at the right seems to be constructed in a similar way to the central canvas (section C). Drawn directly on the dark brown ground, the shepherd's lower body and legs are barely realized, left as a few swift strokes of lead white paint. The lack of finish in this area seems very similar to that of the boy holding a torch in the left-hand side of the *Washing of the Feet* (National Gallery, London), dating to the second half of the 1570s (fig. 73). In both cases, the lower part of the standing figure's body seems to have been left as the briefest of contours, and this might, as has been suggested for the London painting, also indicate something about the lighting in the original location of the Boston *Nativity*.[28]

The surprising genesis of the *Nativity* leads us to question why the picture was so radically altered. Was the first composition left unfinished? Did the

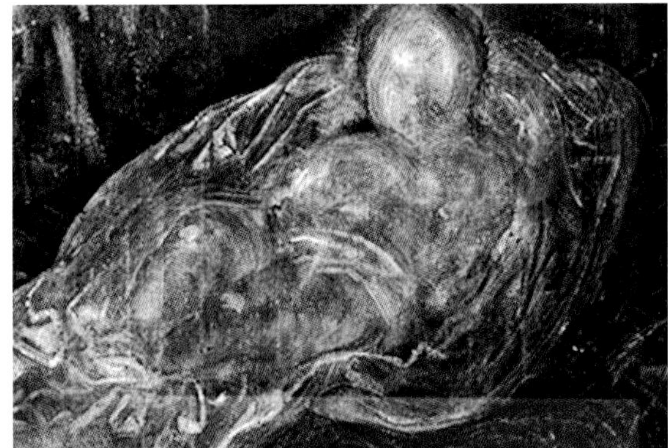

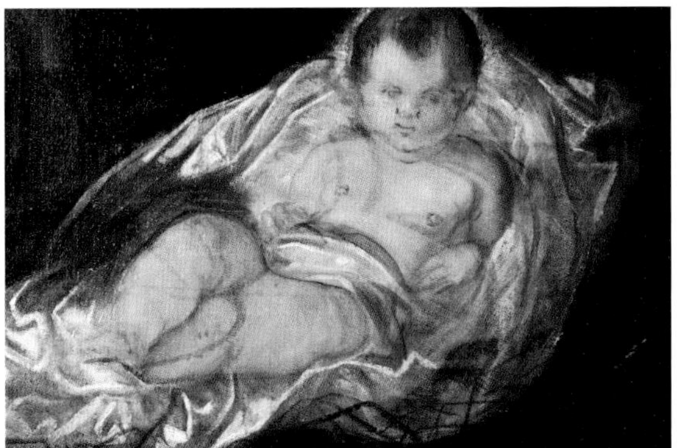

Fig. 70 (*opposite top*)
X-radiograph composite, showing the two pieces of canvas from the earlier composition joined together (sections B and D in fig. 63)

Fig. 71 (*opposite bottom*)
Workshop of Tintoretto, possibly Domenico Tintoretto (Italian, 1560–1635)
The Trinity Adored by a Heavenly Choir, about 1600
Oil on canvas
Columbia Museum of Art, South Carolina

Fig. 72
Detail of the Christ Child in X-radiograph (top) and infrared reflectogram (bottom), showing underpainting

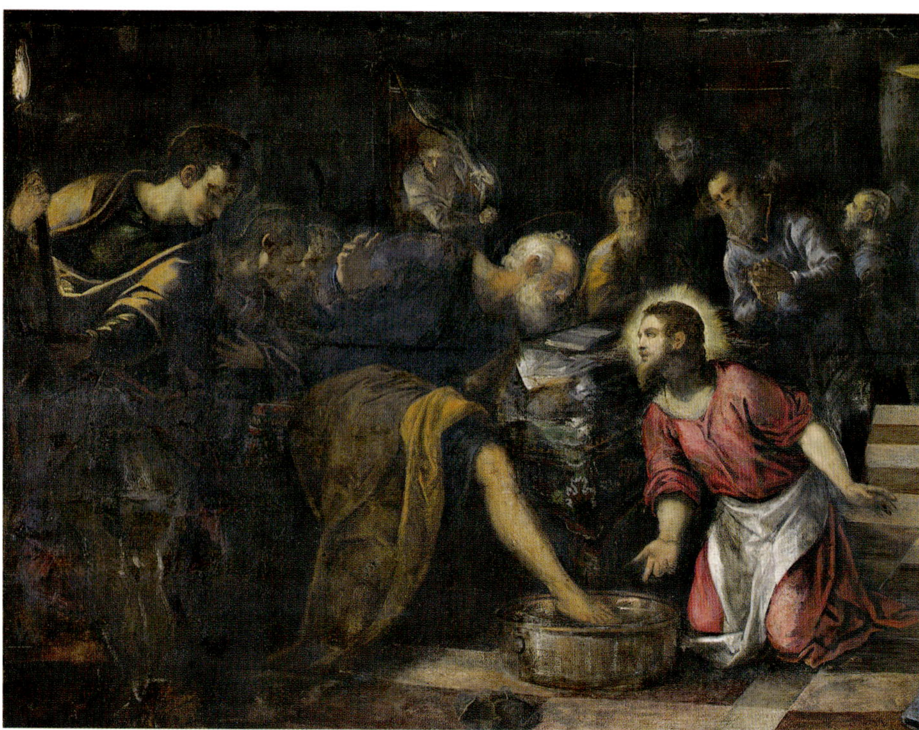

Fig. 73
Tintoretto (detail)
Washing of the Feet, about 1575–80
Oil on canvas
The National Gallery, London

client abandon the commission or refuse to pay for it? Did Tintoretto decide not to finish the painting? Or was the painting finished but damaged? It is also possible that the upper portion of the original composition was reused in a separate painting. This upper section, perhaps including most of the body of Christ on the cross, attendant angels, and even God the Father and the dove of the Holy Spirit, may in fact be hidden beneath another painting. The gigantic scale of many of Tintoretto's paintings makes this proposition difficult to test using X-radiography, but it remains an enticing possibility, given other cases of Tintoretto's reuse of materials.

While for the moment many questions remain unsolved, some preliminary conclusions can be proposed. The original vertical-format painting was completed, or completed in part, in the late 1550s, with at least the Virgin painted by Jacopo Tintoretto himself. In the 1570s, this picture was cut down and other pieces of canvas added, transforming it into a horizontal-format painting with a different subject. Tintoretto repainted the male figure at the far right, turning him into an older shepherd. The figures of Saint Joseph and the Christ Child, which lack inner volume, were painted at the same time by a workshop assistant, thus completing the central group of the *Nativity*. The scenes in the upper corners were most likely added at the same time, perhaps by a third hand; further technical investigation may help clarify this issue.

It is tempting to seek an explanation for the drastic modification to the Nativity in a similarly puzzling document, which lists a work by Tintoretto that has never been connected with an extant picture. On July 31, 1571, the Procurators of San Marco recorded payments to the artist against paintings of philosophers for the Libreria Marciana, as well as other paintings, including a "Nativity of Our Lord to be placed on the high altar of San Marco on Christmas Day." This Tintoretto Nativity is also mentioned in Borghini's *Il riposo* of 1584, but not in any guidebooks or other biographies, which suggests the painting was on the high altar of the church only during the Christmas season. If Tintoretto were to create a work for a seasonal purpose, it might very well look like the present painting, a recycled work adapted in haste for a new role. Its temporary function would also explain why it was discarded before being recorded by later writers. The high altar of San Marco is decorated by a magnificent horizontal altarpiece of medieval enamels, gems, and gold, the so-called Pala d'Oro, similar in format to the MFA's *Nativity*. Although the dimensions of the two altarpieces do not match precisely—the Pala d'Oro is 212 x 334 cm (83½ x 131½ in.), the Nativity about 155 x 358 cm (61 x 141 in.)—they may be close enough for the painting to have served as a temporary altar cover. The composition, with the Christ Child conspicuously at the center, would underscore the Eucharistic function of the altarpiece.[29]

The reuse of materials, such as canvas scraps sewn together for supports and palette scrapings recycled for colored grounds, has been well documented as a normal working practice in the Tintoretto studio. In this context, perhaps the cannibalization of whole passages of an earlier painting should not be surprising, but rather be seen as a logical efficiency for a studio that produced work at an extraordinarily fast pace. Only with the help of technical investigations has it been possible to explore the vicissitudes of this painting, a work far more complicated and fascinating than its reputation would suggest.

— RM, FI

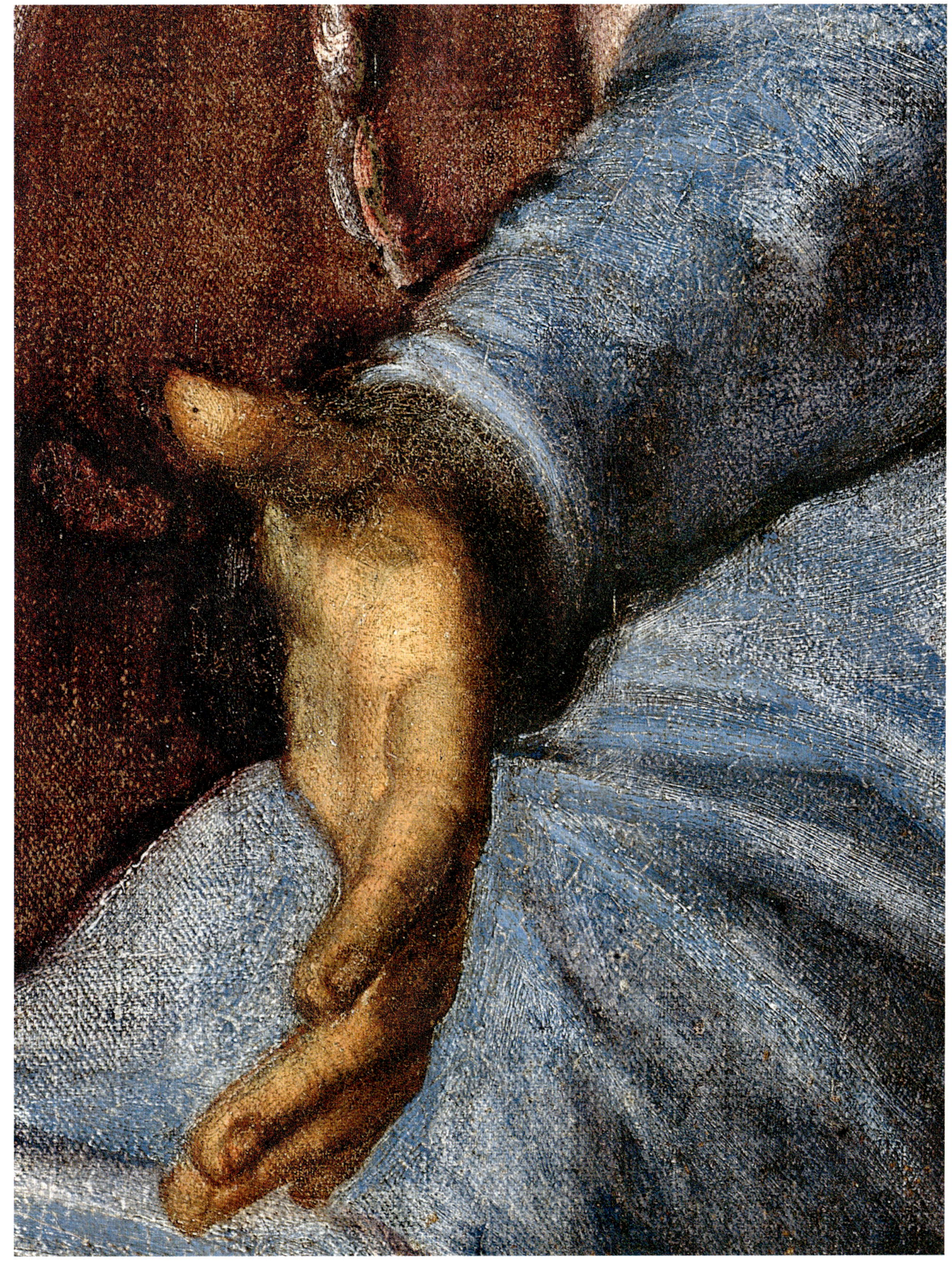

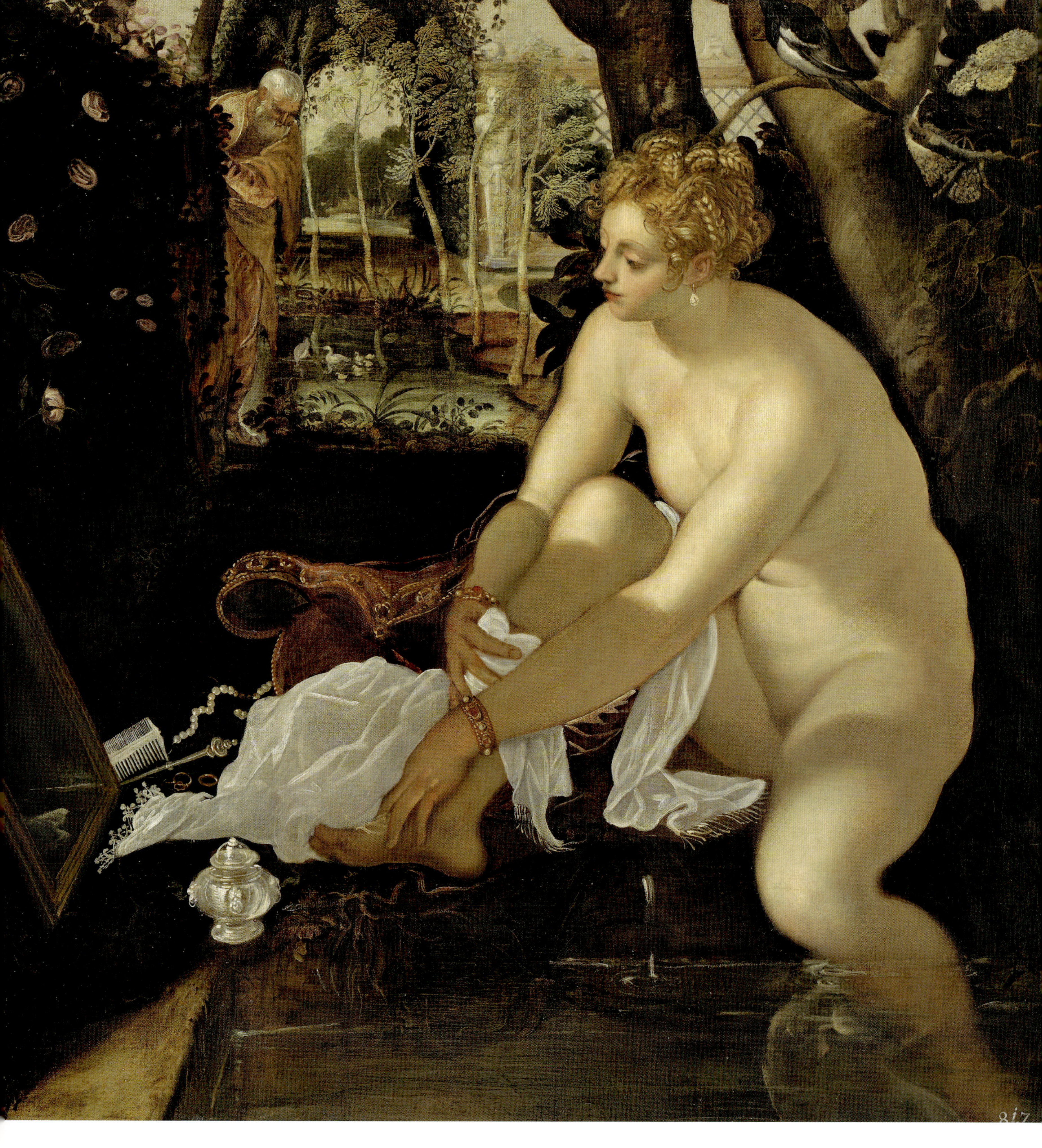
8i7

Tactile Vision: The Female Nude

A major motif in painting since the Renaissance, the female body had been central to any understanding of the art. In Leon Battista Alberti's little book *On Painting* (1435), the first modern treatise on the medium, the Florentine humanist articulated the sensual appeal of that body, especially when vision was simultaneously seduced and obstructed by transparent draperies, gossamer veils that in turn frustrated tactile desire.[1] Hardly an invention of the Renaissance, the sensual allure of female nudity, in particular to a male gaze, had been a central theme in Western culture since antiquity. At least since Paris's fateful judgment of the relative beauty of three goddesses and his reward of the most beautiful of mortal women, the appeal of female beauty to male desire has been a powerful cultural force.

In the Renaissance, then, pictorial occasions for the exploitation of such appeal were to be found most readily in the realm of classical mythology. Among the Olympian deities, Venus embodied the very idea of female beauty; hers was the body that sanctioned nudity in artistic representation (cat. 6). Other goddesses disrobed less willingly; chaste Diana, for example, might be glimpsed at her bath—but only at mortal peril, as poor Actaeon discovered to his doom (fig. 105).[2] And yet the subject of Diana at her bath, accompanied by her court of nymphs, would come to be viewed without repercussion in the lush landscape of Venetian painting in the early sixteenth century (fig. 74).[3] Such bathing scenes acquired a certain generic independence; transcending any specific mythological reference—although never quite surrendering the lingering resonance of such an association—the image type came to be known as a *bagno*. Classical antiquity afforded cultural sanction for the pictorial pleasures of the flesh.

The unveiling of the female nude, usually by a leering satyr, had been represented in ancient art—generally the discovery of a sleeping Ariadne by the raucous train of Bacchus—and had more recently been carved on a fountain illustrating the *Hypnerotomachia Poliphili*, the marvelous archaeological romance published by Aldus Manutius in Venice in 1499 (fig. 75). Indeed, the illustrations of this book were to play an inspirational role in the exploration and invention of classical themes in sixteenth-century imagery.

It is, of course, the motif of the reclining female nude that has come to be associated most traditionally with Venetian painting. Effectively initiating that tradition is the image of a sleeping Venus that was described by an early sixteenth-century observer as having been begun by Giorgione and finished by Titian (fig. 84).[4] Marcantonio Michiel saw the painting in the collection of Girolamo Marcello, and there is good reason to assume that it was commissioned on the occasion of the latter's marriage in 1507, and that its purpose was thus epithalamic. Whereas the relative responsibilities of the two painters continue to challenge connoisseurship, the significance of the model itself is clear. Some three decades later Titian would

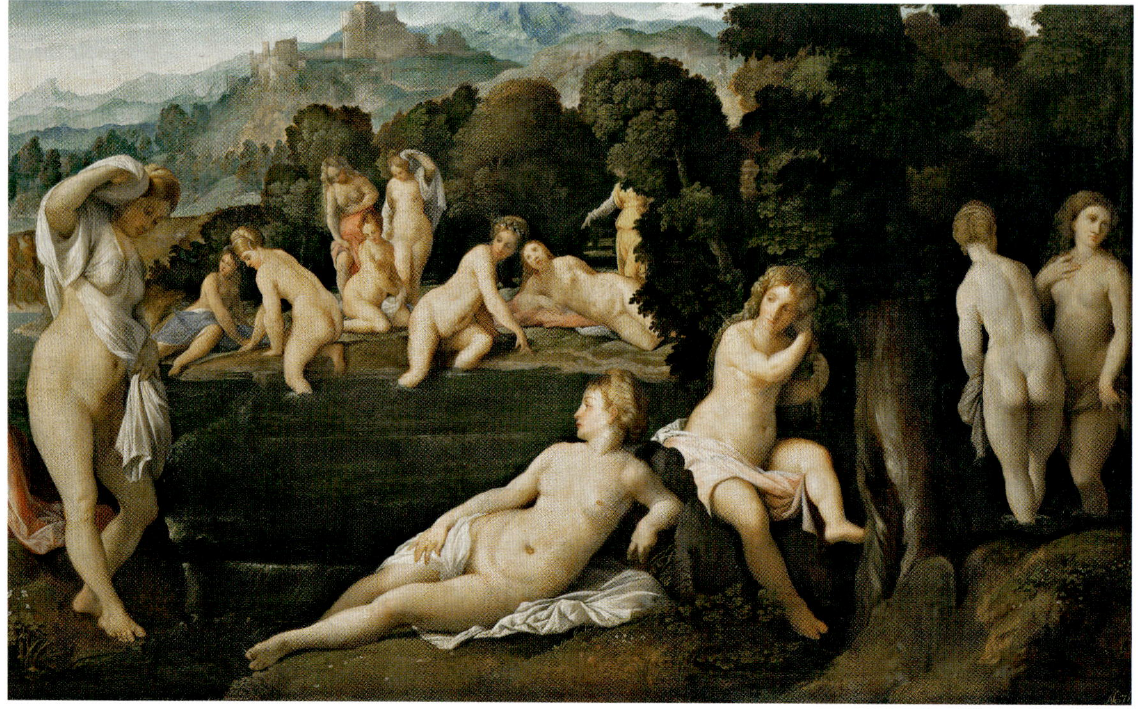

Fig. 74
Palma Vecchio (Italian, about 1479–1528)
Bathing Nymphs, 1525–28
Oil on canvas on wood
Kunsthistorisches Museum, Gemäldegalerie, Vienna

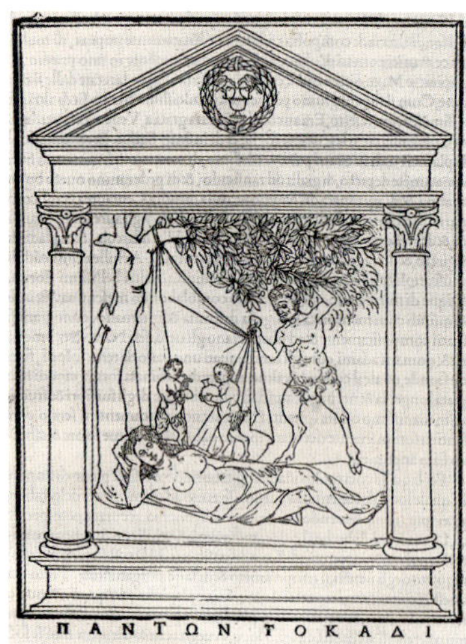

Fig. 75
Unidentified artist
The Fountain of the Sleeping Nymph
Illustrated in Francesco Colonna (?), *Hypnerotomachia Poliphili* (Venice: Aldus Manutius, 1499), fol. e1 recto
Woodcut
Museum of Fine Arts, Boston

bring her indoors, domesticating the goddess, in his *Venus of Urbino* (fig. 76).[5] If the epithalamic function of the Marcello *Sleeping Venus* can be clearly established, Titian's variation on the theme, painted for Guidobaldo II della Rovere, is more equivocal. In the correspondence of 1538, which serves to date the completion of the painting, it is referred to not as Venus but only as "la donna nuda"; Giorgio Vasari, however, had no difficulty in recognizing the goddess of love: "una Venere giovanetta."[6] In the background, the attendants at the *cassone* (marriage chest) are selecting the garments that will clothe the nakedness of divine beauty, making it accessible to natural vision—a theme more iconically rendered half a century earlier in Florence, in Botticelli's *Birth of Venus*. Titian's reclining Venus, however, presents herself directly to the viewer with a confident, not to say challenging, gaze. Although she has been called, with a certain interpretive insouciance, a sixteenth-century "pinup," Titian's nude nonetheless belongs to a visual genre to which it in turn contributes, namely, the epithalamic picture, a painting to celebrate marriage—whether or not this particular image can be associated with a specific marriage.[7]

Whatever its social function or the status of its model, the image of the reclining female nude cannot but carry with it the resonance of classical mythology. The naked lady on the couch, whether intended as the goddess or seen as a posing courtesan, was susceptible to the full range of interpretation: she could represent the lowest level of the hierarchy of love, bestial lust, or the highest, divine love, or an intermediate stage, the licit passion of marital love.

The example of Titian's *poesie*, the mythological narratives painted for King Philip II of Spain, inspired his younger contemporaries to

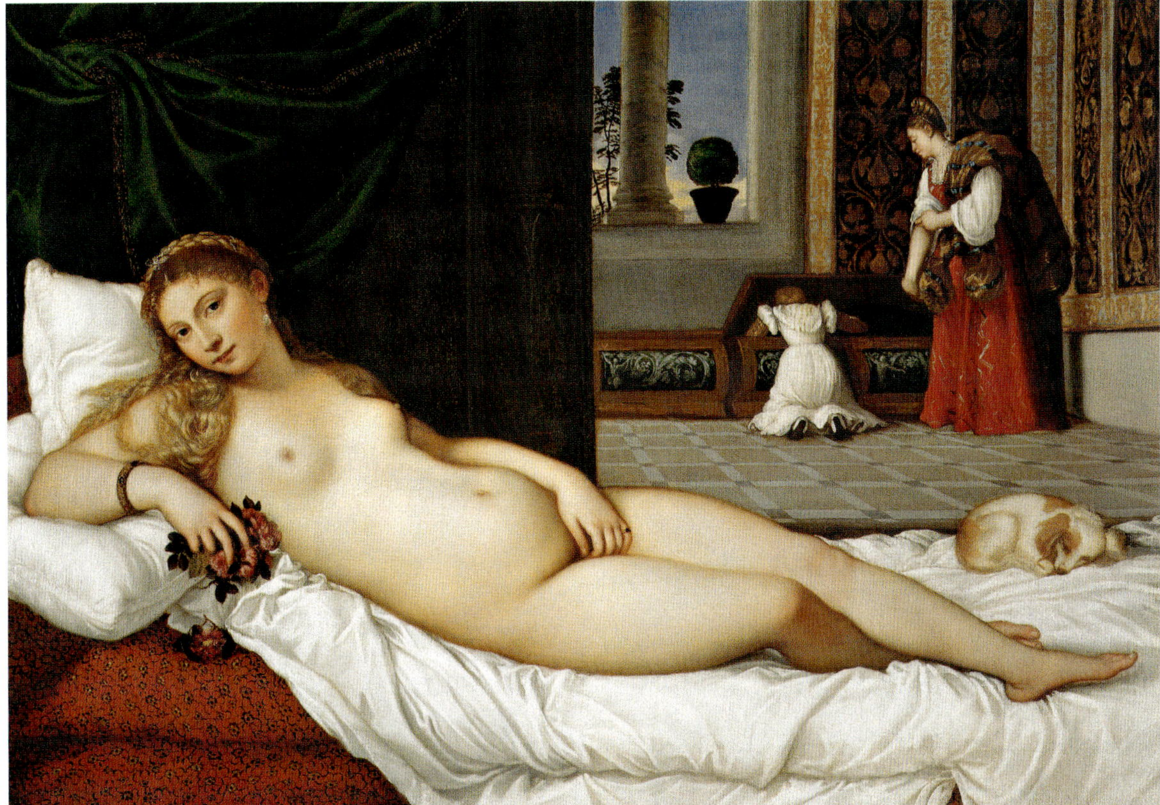

Fig. 76
Titian
Venus of Urbino, about 1538
Oil on canvas
Galleria degli Uffizi, Florence

explore the legends of classical antiquity as occasions for featuring the female nude as more than a passive model of delectation. Danaë ravished by Jupiter or Lucretia threatened by Tarquin were themes actively explored in the studio of Tintoretto (cats. 29, 46). Andromeda chained to a rock, threatened by a monster, and saved by Perseus was another female in distress painted by Titian (fig. 77), in a seascape to which his *Europa* (fig. 106) would subsequently serve as pendant.[8] Veronese took up the challenge of the older master's work to choreograph his own serpentine nude in *Perseus and Andromeda* (cat. 47). Indeed, Titian's art would become the fundamental reference for subsequent pictorial representations of such subjects, the inspiration behind the great masters of mythological narrative of the following century, Rubens and Poussin—and beyond, to Picasso.
— DR

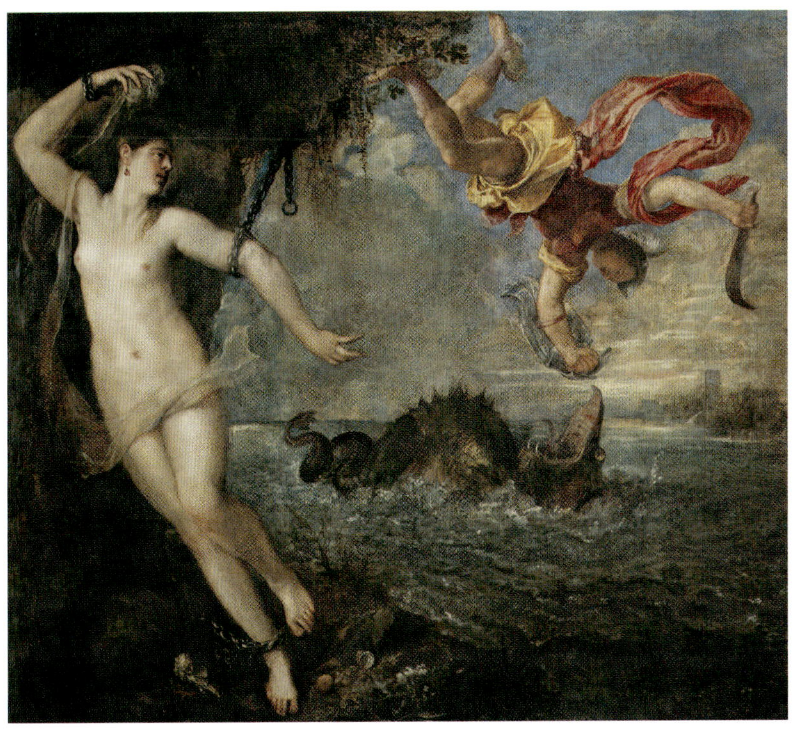

Fig. 77
Titian
Perseus and Andromeda, 1554–56
Oil on canvas
The Wallace Collection, London

Objects of Desire

TITIAN
Danaë, 1544–46
Museo di Capodimonte, Naples
(cat. 27)

TITIAN
Venus with an Organist and a Dog, about 1550
Museo Nacional del Prado, Madrid
(cat. 28)

TINTORETTO
Danaë, late 1570s–early 1580s
Musée des Beaux-Arts, Lyon
(cat. 29)

In painting *Venus Anadyomene* (cat. 6), Titian re-created the achievement of Apelles, the most celebrated painter of Greek antiquity, who had depicted the goddess rising from the sea. Apelles' Venus was "rendered famous by Greek epigrams written in her praise," according to Pliny the Elder, our major source of knowledge of ancient painting. Pliny further reports that when "the lower portion was damaged no one could be found to restore it, and thus the very injury redounded to the glory of the artist."[9] Titian's newborn goddess, wringing the water from her hair, is presented half-length; her legs are hidden in the waves, a possible homage to Apelles—with whom the Venetian master would soon be compared in the patent of nobility conferred in 1533 by the Holy Roman Emperor Charles V. In painting the favorite mistress of Alexander the Great, Apelles fell in love with the nude model, whereupon Alexander, in a gesture of "great magnanimity and still greater self-control," rewarded the artist's desire by making him a present of the beauty herself.[10]

Like his ancient predecessor, Titian was famous for his representation of female beauty, and, also like Apelles, he is said to have become totally absorbed in the human subjects of his art: "When he wanted to draw or paint some figure, and had before him a real woman or man, that object would so affect his sense of sight and his spirit would enter into what he was representing so that he seemed conscious of nothing else."[11] This Neoplatonic commonplace regarding the lover and the object of desire was summarized in the early sixteenth century by none other than Leonardo da Vinci, hardly a committed Platonist: "The lover is moved by the beloved object as the senses are by sensible objects; and they unite and become one and the same thing."[12]

Early in his career Titian acknowledged the direct appeal of female flesh, most explicitly in his *Flora* (cat. 5). Even as she offers her flowers to an admirer off to the side, her body, one breast bared, addresses the viewer of her image more directly. Also offering flowers, in the *Venus of Urbino* the goddess addresses the viewer with both body and gaze. Her pictorial sisters, however, become more fully engaged in the narratives of their respective situations, as, for example, Danaë receiving her shower of gold (cat. 27). Titian's domesticated goddess, reclining on her bed, is returned to mythological narrative as Danaë in his painting for Cardinal Alessandro Farnese. The artist was working on the canvas in 1544, when it was described by the cardinal's representative, Giovanni della Casa, merely as "una nuda"; it was completed during Titian's sojourn to Rome the following year. As X-radiography has revealed, the composition began as a variation on the *Venus of Urbino.* Indeed, whetting the patron's appetite, della Casa explicitly compares the two, declaring that the nude on Titian's easel makes the other one seem as modest as a Theatine nun. Della Casa also writes that the painter is willing to put the face of a famous Roman courtesan, and favorite of the cardinal, on this bedded nude. Evidently, the Ovidian subject—of Danaë locked in the tower and ravished by Jupiter in the form of a shower of gold—was not of immediate concern to the patron. That it was of genuine interest to the painter, however, is confirmed by the way in which he wrought deliberate variations on its narration. A few years later, around 1551, he began another version for Prince Philip of Spain (fig. 78) in which he substituted the attendant Cupid with an old nurse, the girl's guardian, who extends her apron to collect as much of the Olympian passion as possible—a gesture worthy of the comic stage. And yet, for all the comic relief, Titian's *Danaë* retains her heroic stature, including the ominous shadow that falls across her face; ostensibly created by the curtain defining the inner recess of her bed, it adds a tragic note to the otherwise joyous scene—an allusion perhaps to the product of this union, the hero Perseus, who, as foretold, will slay his mother's father. The *Danaë* too may be considered an epithalamic picture, for it celebrates the consummated love of the god for a mortal—as does the last of the *poesie* Titian would deliver to Philip, in 1562, *Europa*, in which the female nude acquires a human fleshiness beyond classical idealization, a carnate realism that seems to reflect the

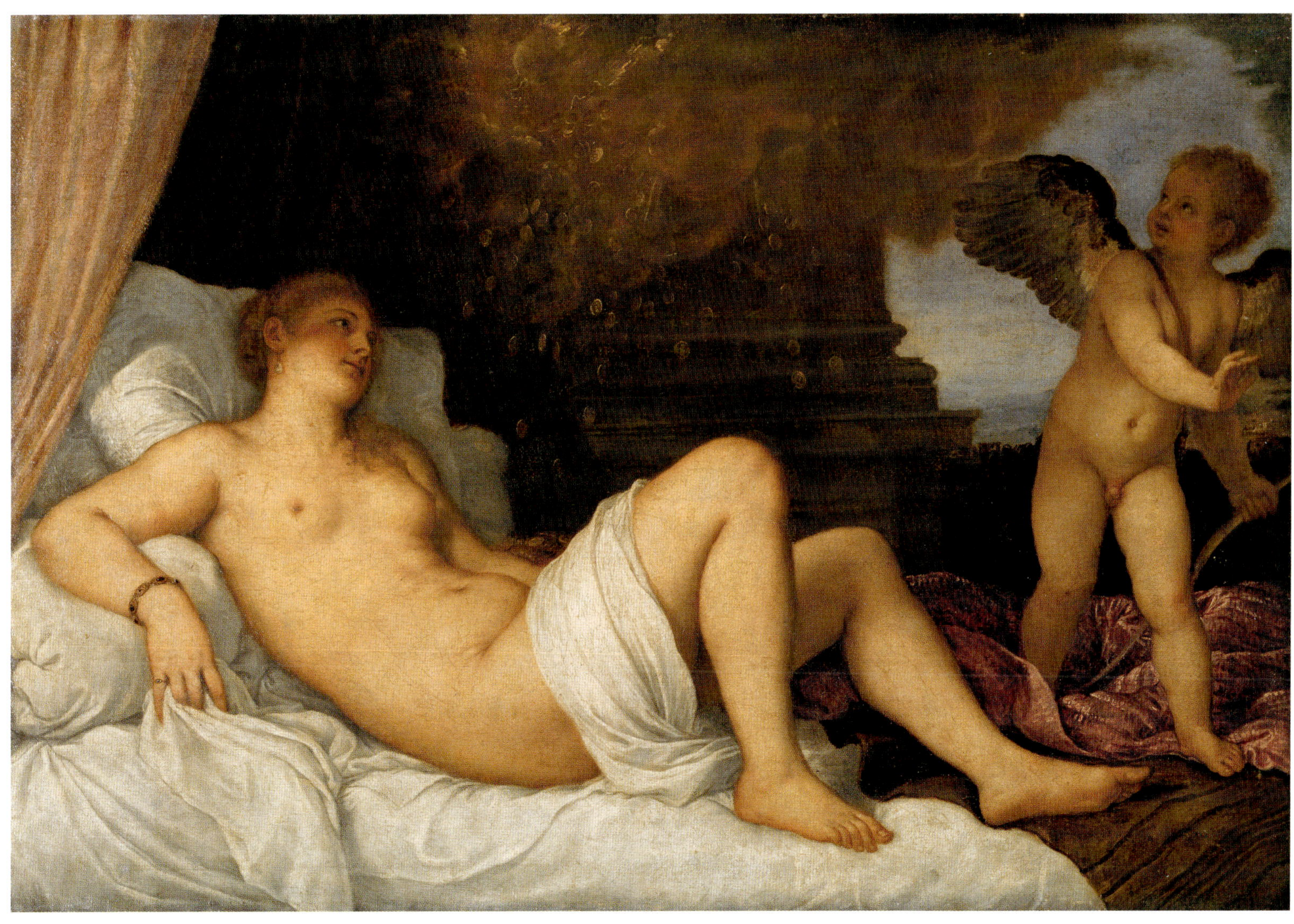

cat. 27

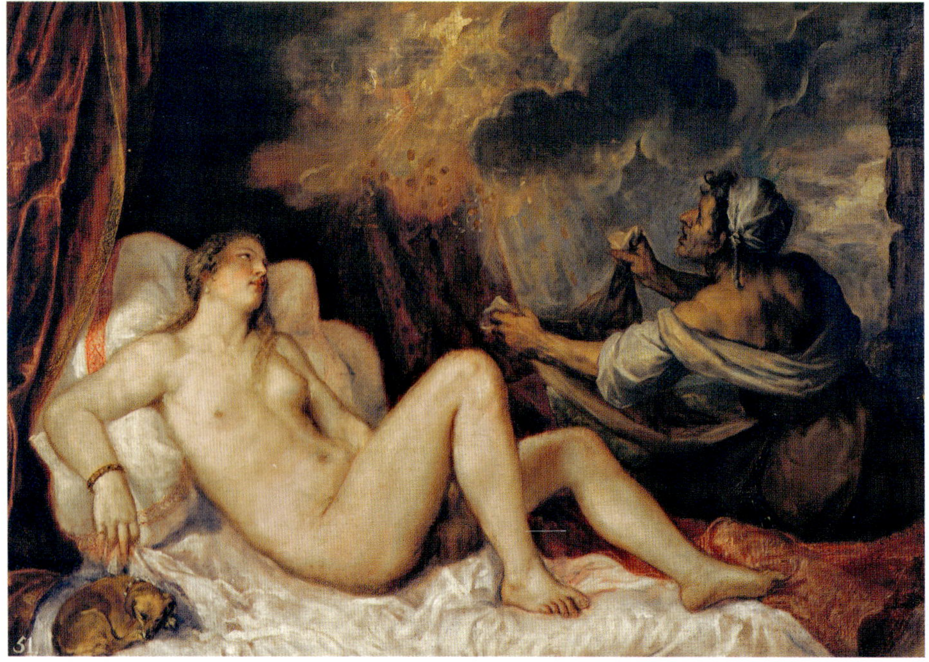

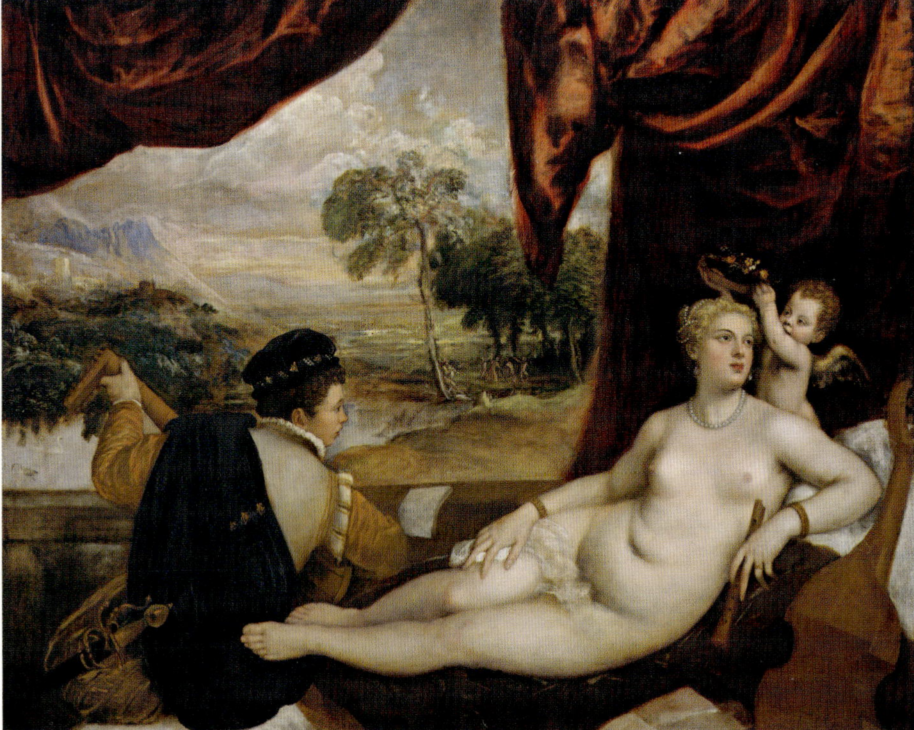

painter's own touch,[13] and which makes her the primary object of the viewer's attention, a carnal object of desire (fig. 106).

As he developed variations on that basic structure, Titian acknowledged the fundamental relationship between object and viewer, making it the very theme of the painting. By adding the figure of a courtier, an attendant musician, he rendered the vision of beauty a narrative action, the admiring male in the picture playing the role of surrogate viewer. The reclining nude may be Venus herself, with Cupid as her attribute to confirm her divinity,[14] or she may be a patron's favorite mistress or bride, playing with her dog, a deliberate mixing of mythological fiction and contemporary reality (cat. 28). The landscape background, too, became a theme for variation. The lover at the keyboard, presumably a portrait of the patron, gazes longingly at the object of desire, probably his mistress—the absence of Cupid deprives this nude of any pretense to Olympian status. Beyond the boudoir scene extends a deer park with strolling lovers; a satyr fountain adds a lascivious note to the setting, its suggestion taken by a buck sniffing his mate in anticipation. This series of variations on the basic theme culminates in the version in which the musician has abandoned the portative organ in favor of the more agile lute (fig. 79).[15] Fundamental to the conception, however, is the position of the musician as ardent courtier, as privileged viewer, drawn to the beauty that is the object of his desire. Significantly, in these later variations Titian adds another instrument, a viola da gamba, propped in the lower right corner of the composition, awaiting its player, who is outside the picture: that is, the viewer, who is thereby invited to participate in this musical celebration of love and beauty.

These images have sometimes been discussed in terms of a Neoplatonic *paragone* of the senses, a comparison of the relative powers of sight, hearing, and touch in the perception of beauty. While these philosophical interpretations may seem rather academic for such overtly sensuous paintings, the range of senses to which they appeal is certainly relevant to our experience of these pictures. On the most obvious level, as paintings, the sense of sight is paramount. Hearing, then, is essential to their subject; as representations of music making they require the projection of the mind's ear. Finally, as pictorial fictions, they invite the viewer to reach out and touch—the nude flesh of the depicted body but, even more immediately, the actual surface of the painting, its fabric of individual brushstrokes and canvas weave. That very tactility, a central aspect of Venetian painting in the later sixteenth century, simultaneously engages vision and touch, each reinforcing and complicating the imagined perception of the other.

It was not only classical mythology, however, that offered pictorial objects of desire. Revealed nudity in the Bible was another source for gazing on bathing females, whether David espying Bathsheba or the elders lusting after Susannah (cat. 31). Here too the viewer of the painting finds himself reflected within its fiction: like the elders, he is a voyeur, but with even more privileged, and aesthetically sanctioned, access to the bathing body. Pictorial desire and sensual desire are conflated.

Amorous desire, however, was hardly limited to such purely carnal eroticism. Within a broad spectrum of Renaissance culture, love was the essential element on a hierarchy of being, from base lust through the licit and necessary passion of the marriage bed to the highest level of divine love, that is, the aspiration of union with the deity and the love of God for humanity. The longing for union with God, as read, for example, in the Psalms, found full pictorial embodiment in the figure of Mary Magdalen, the penitent prostitute who was traditionally favored by an intimacy with the body of Christ.

Titian's renderings of the penitent Magdalen were even more in demand than his pagan nudes (fig. 80);[16] they belong to a particular genre that he created: a religious image, overt in the sensuality of its appeal, that at once sustains delectation and inspires devotion. Although the theme of the repentant prostitute lent itself particularly to such treatment, we recognize in the fervor of the saint a passionate desire for God: her sensual longing is to be read as a metaphor for spiritual yearning. Such existential hierarchies were central to the religious imagination of the Renaissance and expanded the range of experience accessible to painting. Titian's adaptation of the classical Venus *pudica* pose for the shameful Christian sinner adds a further cultural reference to the image, just as the saint's longing for divine love inflects a cultural response to her pagan avatar, Venus herself.

The younger generation of Venetian painters continued the exploration of female flesh that had been pioneered by Titian. Both Veronese and Tintoretto followed the master's lead in exploiting classical subject matter for its access to the nude body, but they brought to the theme different perspectives and attitudes, a certain lightness of touch, and a more self-conscious figural choreography. Even when they carried the weight of allegory, their gods rarely possessed the gravity of Titian's. They seemed more readily to accept mythology as the basis for aesthetic—and sensual—display. For example, although Tintoretto's composition of *Danaë*, which was executed with studio assistance, was clearly inspired by Titian's painting for Philip of Spain, it transforms the old nurse into a younger female companion. For the comic implications of the old woman longing for the passion of youth, Tintoretto substitutes a different pathos through the visual similarity of the nude mistress and her handmaid; in the latter's effort to gather a few coins for herself, there is a social poignancy, which is underscored by that similarity. As in his treatment of the adultery of Venus and Mars (fig. 81), Tintoretto domesticates the ancient myths, transposing them down, as it were, to a level of social reality. The Jovial presence in his *Danaë* has been reduced to hard coinage. Less impressed by the potency of the pagan god, the viewer is left to delight in the female nude, posed for his delectation.

— DR

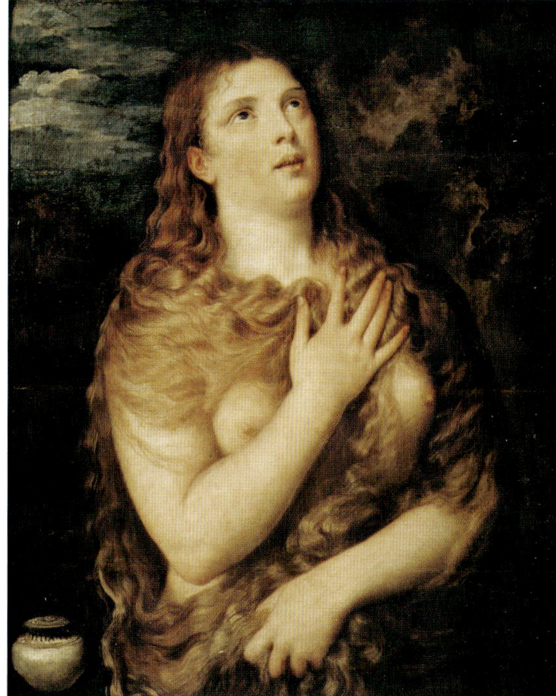

Fig. 78 (*opposite top*)
Titian
Danaë, probably 1551–53
Oil on canvas
Museo Nacional del Prado, Madrid

Fig. 79 (*opposite bottom*)
Titian and workshop
Venus and the Lute Player, about 1565–70
Oil on canvas
The Metropolitan Museum of Art, New York

Fig. 80
Titian
Penitent Magdalen, about 1535
Oil on panel
Galleria Palatina, Palazzo Pitti, Florence

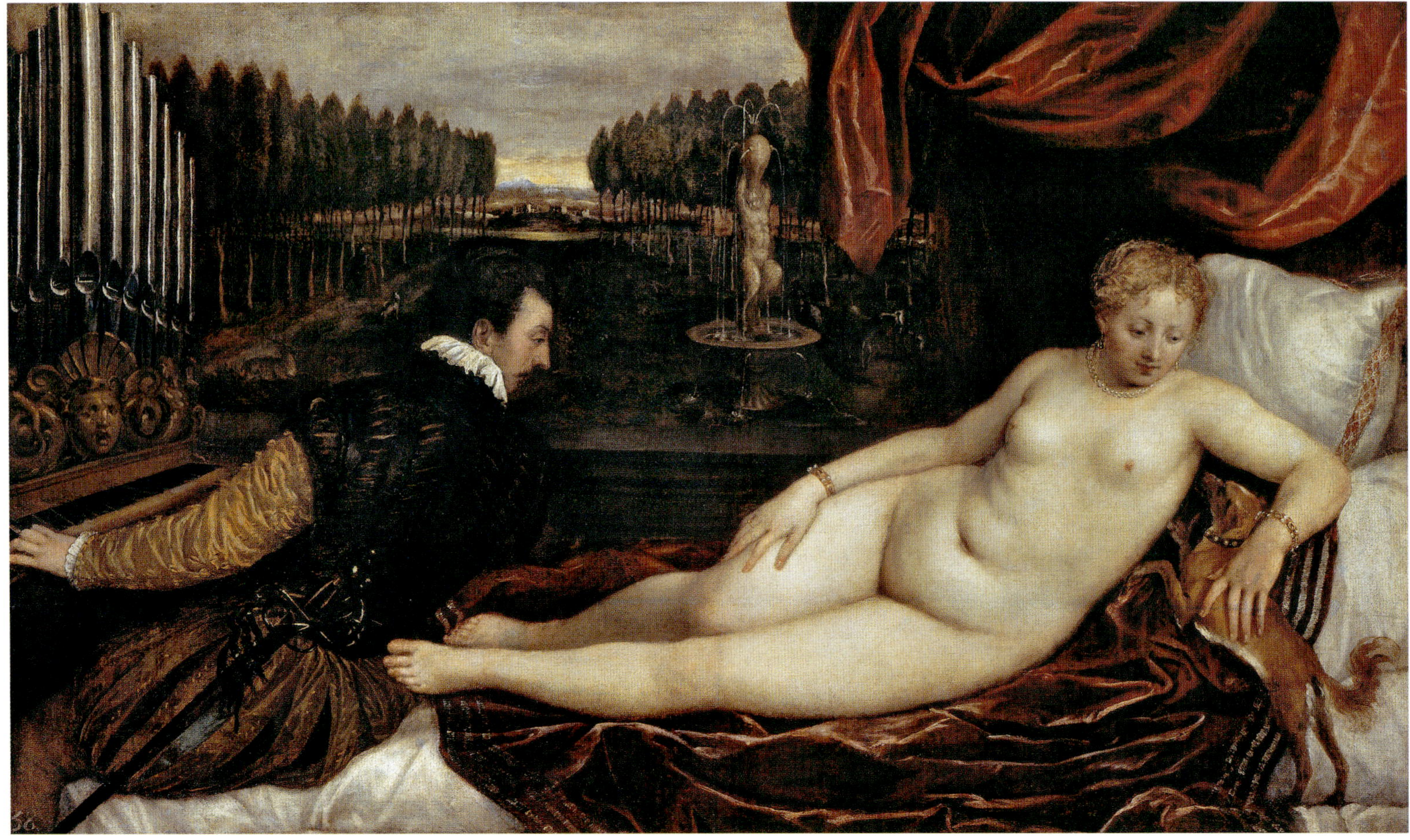

cat. 28

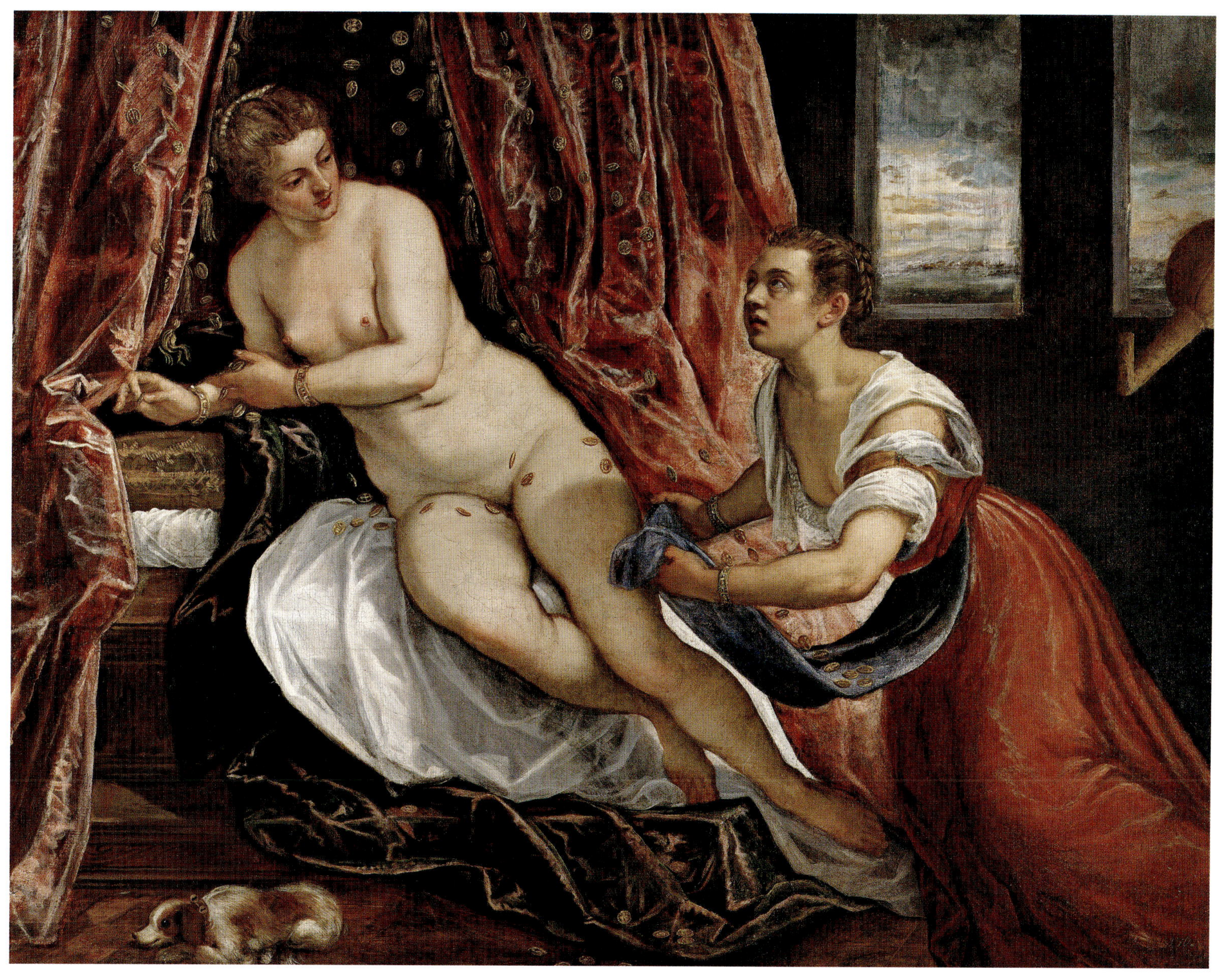

cat. 29

Specular Exchange: The Nude and the Mirror

TITIAN
Venus with a Mirror, about 1555
National Gallery of Art, Washington, DC
(cat. 30)

TINTORETTO
Susannah and the Elders, about 1555–56
Kunsthistorisches Museum, Gemäldegalerie, Vienna
(cat. 31)

VERONESE
Venus with a Mirror (Venus at Her Toilette), mid-1580s
Joslyn Art Museum, Omaha, Nebraska
(cat. 32)

In the Renaissance *paragone* of painting and sculpture, regarding especially which of the two arts offered a more complete imitation of nature, the mirror became a tool on behalf of painting. By including its reflecting surfaces in a composition, the painter could enhance his representation of an object to include a full 360 degrees. Thus did Giorgione triumph over the sculptors by incorporating reflections in armor and water to present a figure in the round, although painted on a flat panel.[17]

The mirror could complicate the visual dimensions of any painting, exposing to view parts of figures otherwise unseen except to others within the notional space of the picture itself. In Tintoretto's bedroom comedy *Venus and Mars Surprised by Vulcan* (fig. 81), for example, the frontal exposure of Venus unveiled is complemented by the mirrored back of her cuckolded husband, a view that might have been available to her martial lover were he not cowering under a table or bed.[18] Even more pointedly does the mirror participate in the visual dynamics of Tintoretto's *Susannah and the Elders*. An integral part of the cosmetic apparatus of the bathing nude, its reflection within the narrative of the picture offers to Susannah the view denied to the leering old men at either end of the rose-covered trellis that marks the boundary of the private space they seek to invade. Despite its dark surface, it even suggests itself as the otherwise unseen light source illuminating her alabaster body.

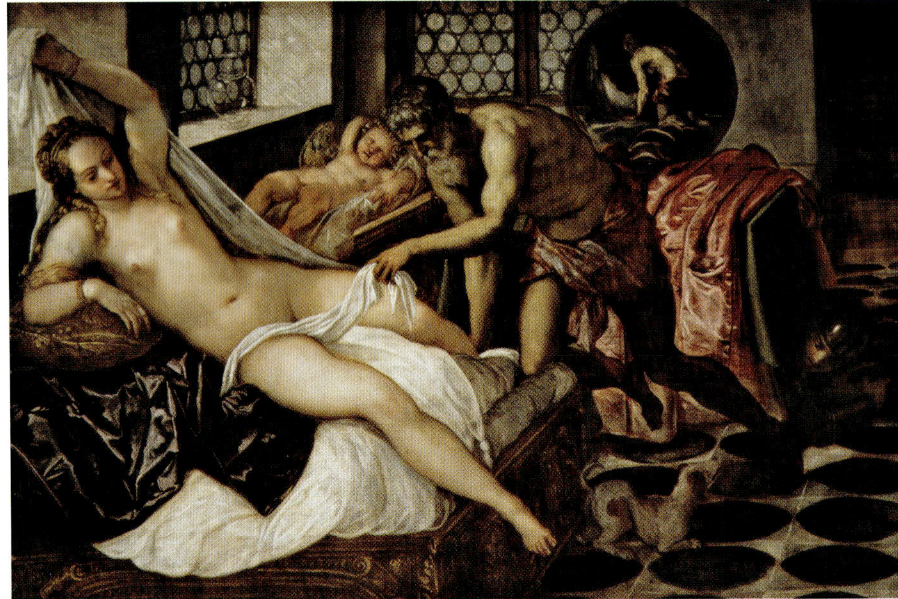

Fig. 81. Tintoretto, *Venus and Mars Surprised by Vulcan*, about 1545, oil on canvas, Bayerische Staatsgemäldesammlungen, Alte Pinakothek, Munich

The association of mirrors and other reflecting surfaces with bathing nude figures was thematically integral to the art of oil painting itself, that is, to an art particularly responsive to the challenge of representing luminosity and surface texture. The earliest such image seems to have been a lost bathing scene by none other than Jan van Eyck, the master who stands at the very origin of this technical tradition in the early fifteenth century.[19] And the juxtaposition of female flesh and reflecting surface would become especially important to the Venetian development of the oil medium in the following century, particularly with the use of a thicker impasto that gave new material substance to the medium.

In making the female figure a specialty of their art, Venetian painters exploited the complementary sensuality of medium and subject. In that context, the mirror became a means of heightening the appeal of surfaces, its cosmetic function commenting on the appeal of beauty as well as its transience. Even the old Giovanni Bellini, the greatest master of the older pictorial tradition, tried to keep up with the tastes of a younger generation; his painting *Woman with a Mirror* is dated 1515, a year before his death (fig. 82).[20] Although in the representation of a beautiful woman the mirror might well be read as a symbol of vanity, frequently the enjoyment of viewing her at her toilette was hardly marred by such moralizing. Instead, the mirror added further visual dimensions to delectation.[21]

It was again Titian who set the example, establishing an epitome of the theme in paintings like *Venus with a Mirror*. The goddess of love and the avatar of female beauty, Venus was the natural model for such scenes of the toilette. Here she admires herself in a mirror held by a cupid, as

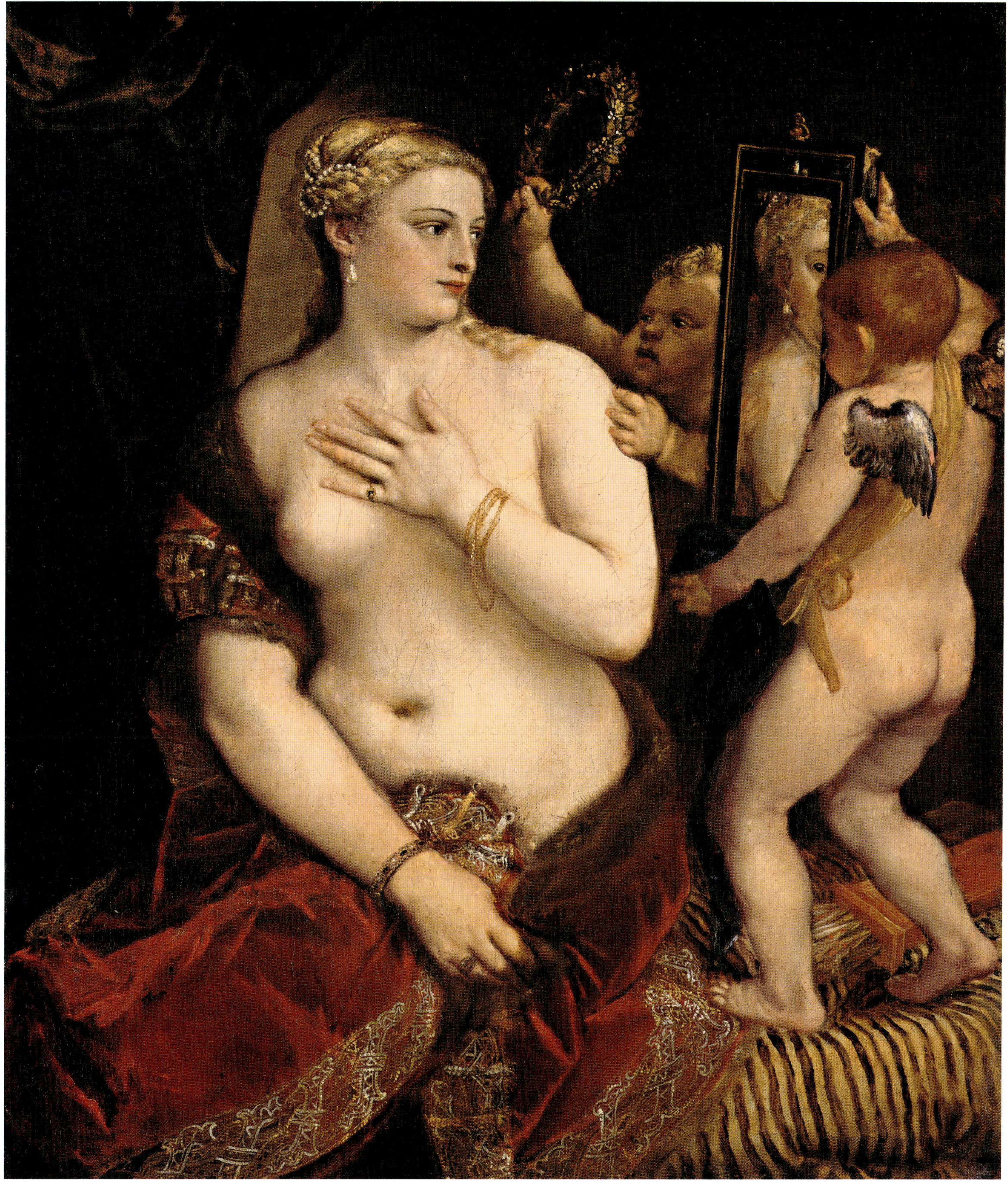

cat. 30

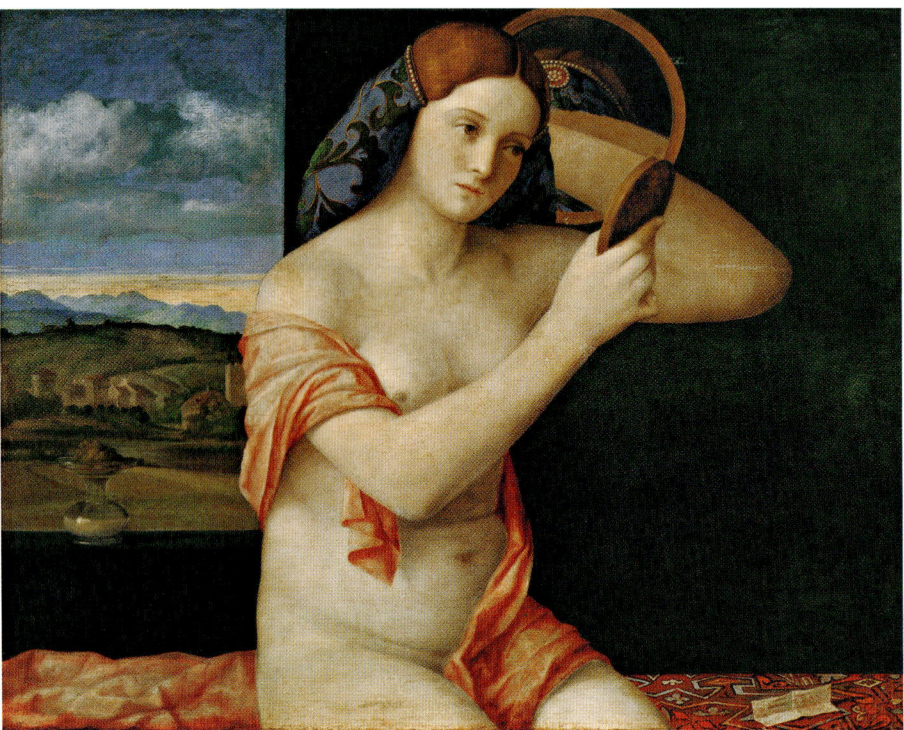

Fig. 82. Giovanni Bellini (Italian, about 1431–1516), *Woman with a Mirror*, 1515, oil on panel, Kunsthistorisches Museum, Gemäldegalerie, Vienna

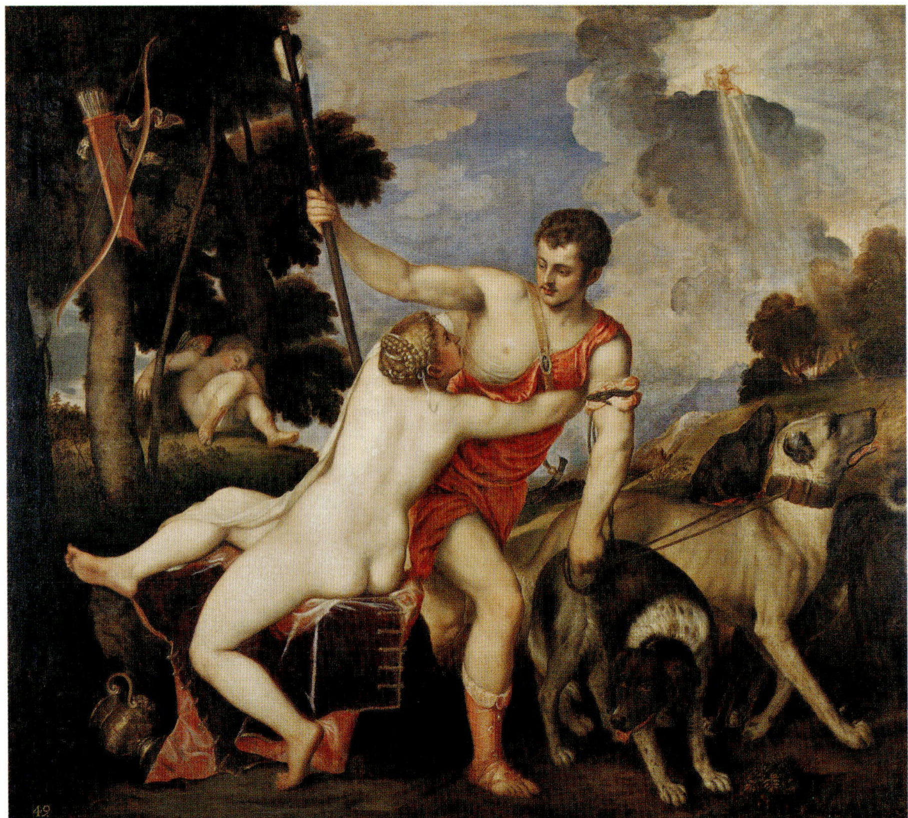

Fig. 83. Titian, *Venus and Adonis*, 1554, oil on canvas, Museo Nacional del Prado, Madrid

another crowns her with a floral wreath. Only a single eye is seen reflected in the mirror, apparently making direct contact with the viewer. The full body of the goddess fills the field, its nudity made symbolically modest by her gesture: one hand over her chest, the other holding her garment over her pudenda. That garment itself, however, plays its role in enhancing tactile invitation; its varied textures—of rich velvet, etched embroidery, and, especially, deep fur lining—set off the broad display of her exposed flesh.

The vision of the female nude from the back, with its invitation to imagine the other side of the body, was one of the most celebrated aspects of the figure of Venus in the composition Titian sent to Philip II in 1554 as a pendant to Philip's *Danaë—Venus and Adonis* (fig. 83), a version of which is in the J. Paul Getty Museum's collection (cat. 33).[22] Titian's depiction of the goddess with her back turned to the viewer was praised as a special demonstration of his art, as sensual a display of female flesh as might be offered by a frontal view of the nude—"in that one recognizes in the hindmost parts here the distension of the flesh caused by sitting."[23] In a letter accompanying the *Venus and Adonis*, the painter explained that since the *Danaë* he had previously sent was shown from the front, he wanted to vary the pose and show the opposite side, and he promised that the Andromeda he would soon send would show yet another view of the nude (fig. 77): "in that way the room in which they are to hang, will be more pleasing to the sight."[24] Titian was vaunting his ability to offer varied views of the female body—without the use of mirrors.

When Paolo Veronese took up the theme of Venus at the mirror, he deliberately varied Titian's model by offering a view of the nude goddess from behind (cat. 32). The apparent modesty of the rear view, however, is compromised by her direct encounter with us via the mirror. What is withheld from vision by the painting is offered, at least potentially, through the mirror. Like so many motifs of erotic invitation, the dorsal view of the female nude enjoyed a tradition going back to classical antiquity, and artists of the High Renaissance such as Raphael and Correggio had fully exploited it. So too had Veronese earlier in his career, in the Olympian dalliance within a villa setting in which Jupiter's nude companion is seen from the rear (cat. 24). Her exact identity is difficult to determine, but her appeal is clear.[25] The privileged lover enjoys the view of her body that the viewer of the picture can only imagine.

— DR

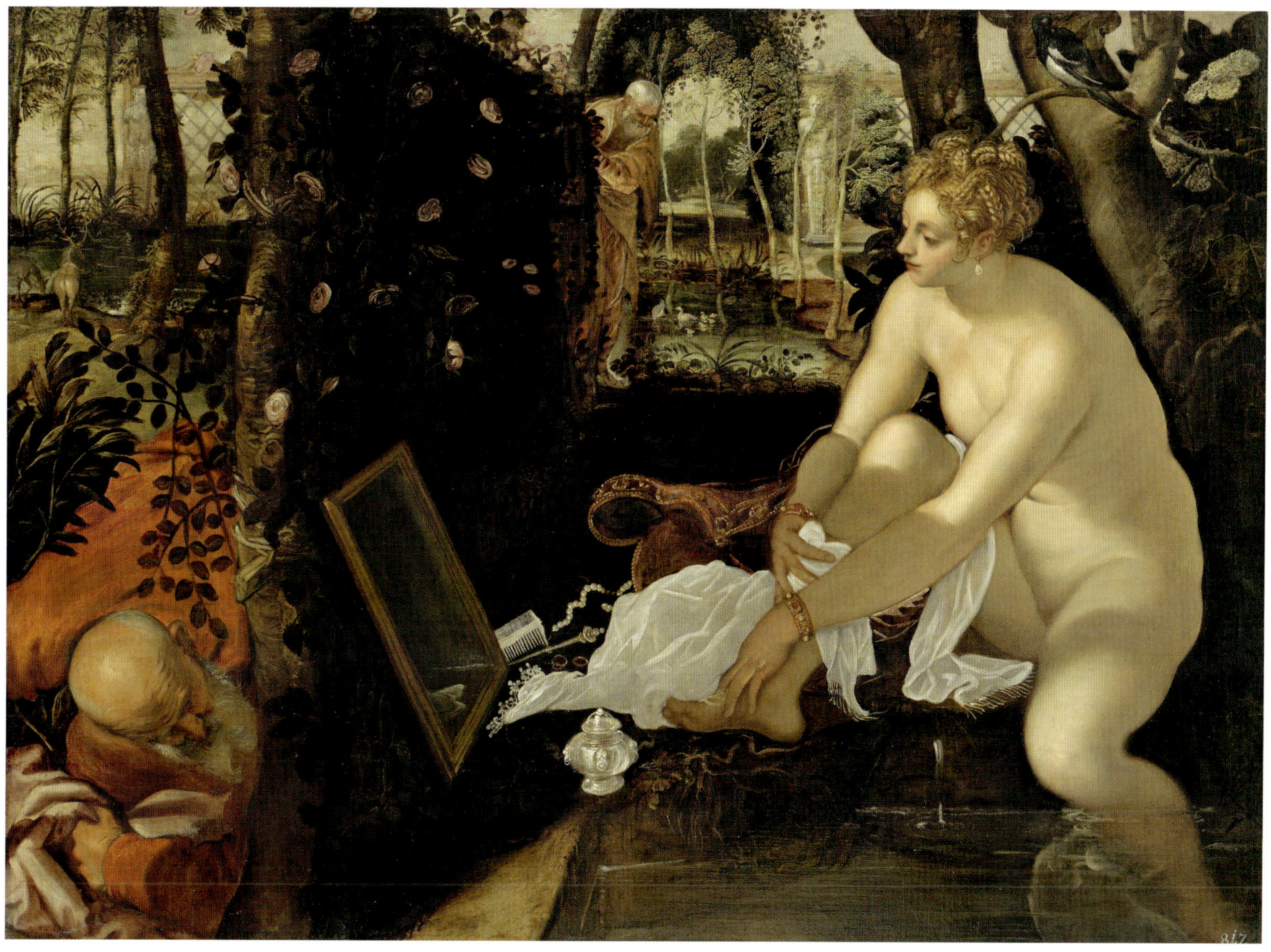

cat. 31

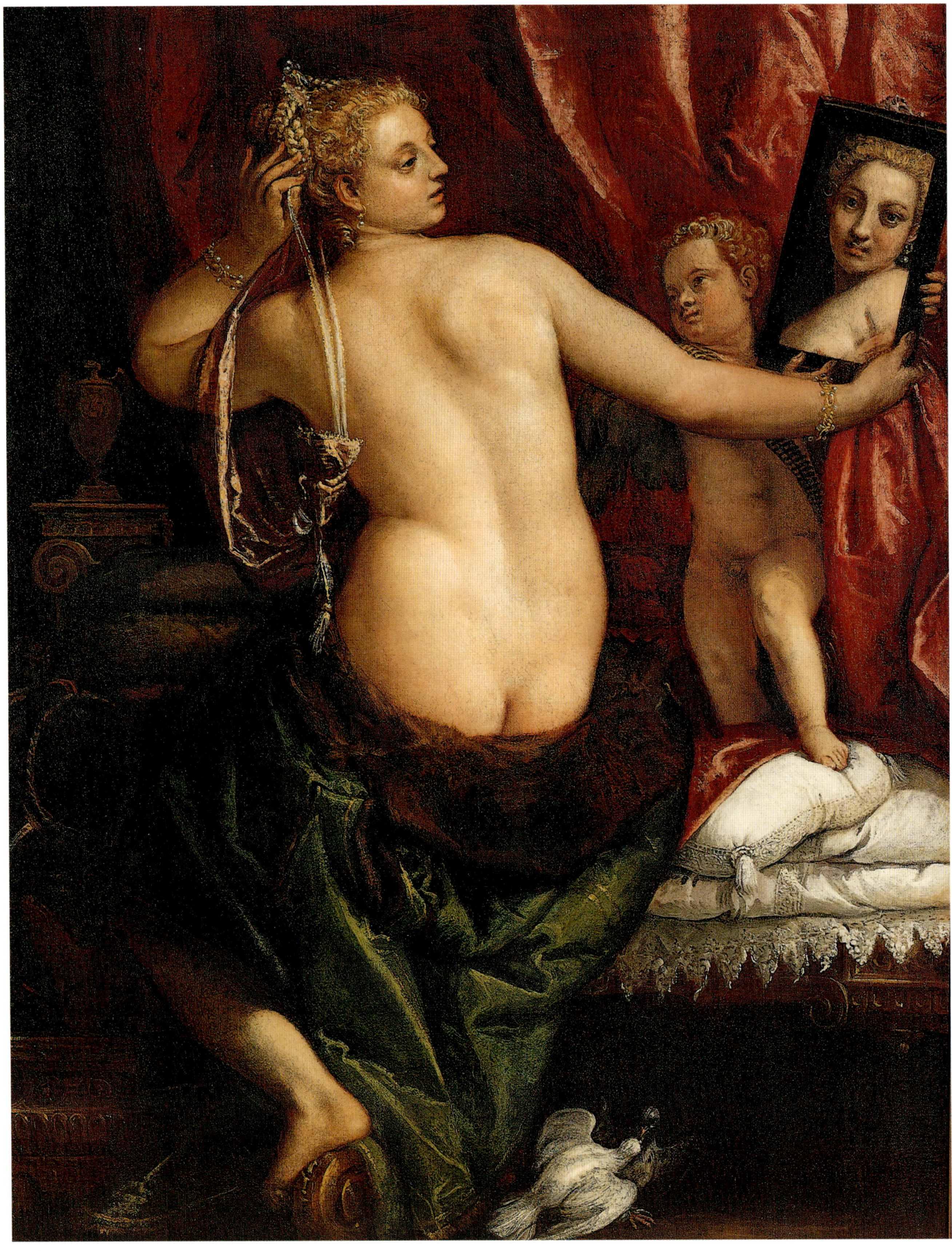

cat. 32

Allegories of Love and Fertility

TITIAN
Venus and Adonis, about 1555–60
The J. Paul Getty Museum, Los Angeles
(cat. 33)

VERONESE
Mars and Venus United by Love, mid-1570s
The Metropolitan Museum of Art, New York
(cat. 34)

However undeniable the basic erotic appeal of the painted female nude, the sensuality of that body nonetheless can carry a socially redeeming value. It was, after all, the essential vessel of procreation and thus of dynastic continuity. As epithalamic image, the female nude was to be found on the inner lids of Quattrocento *cassoni* (bridal chests) and, in the sixteenth century, frequently secured a position over the marital bed; a child conceived under the sign of beauty was all the more likely to be beautiful. This power of "lascivious pictures" in the bedroom not only to arouse sexually but to ensure the conception of beautiful children was acknowledged in antiquity and found renewed articulation in the Renaissance.[26] The self-stimulation of Giorgione's (and Titian's) *Sleeping Venus* (fig. 84) and of her offspring, Titian's *Venus of Urbino*, may be related precisely to the inspiring generative function of such images, in particular to the belief that a woman could conceive only if she achieved orgasm.[27]

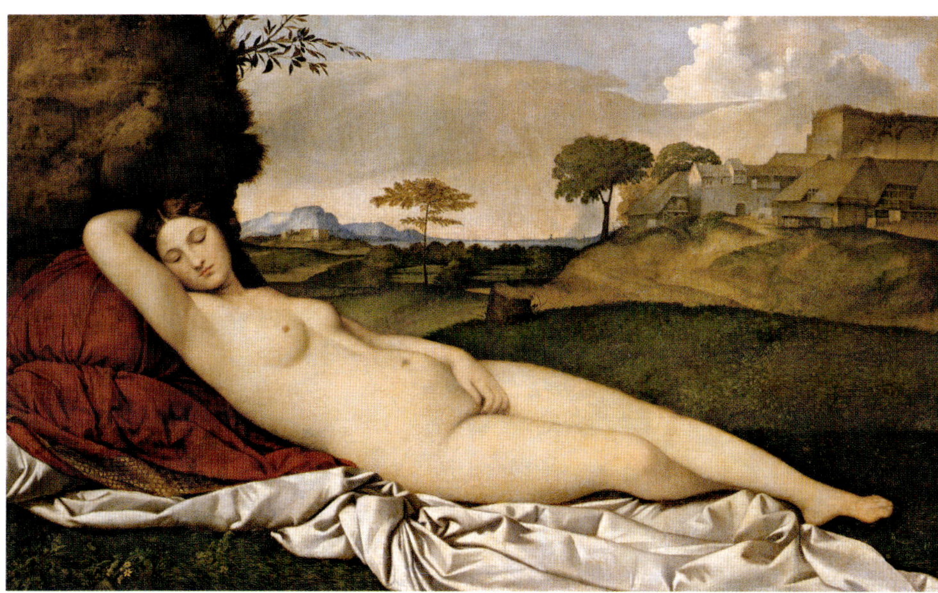

Fig. 84. Giorgione (Italian, about 1477–1510) and Titian, *Sleeping Venus*, 1508–10, oil on canvas, Gemäldegalerie Alte Meister, Staatliche Kunstsammlungen, Dresden

In the ancient pantheon two goddesses were especially relevant to the marital bed: Venus, who despite her celebrated infidelities could nonetheless play the role of *pronuba*, that is, overseer of weddings, and Juno, faithful consort of unfaithful Jupiter, who was a more reliable deity of marriage and childbirth. Juno's maternal fecundity informs one of Tintoretto's most intriguing mythological paintings, the *Origin of the Milky Way* (fig. 85). Presumably executed for Emperor Rudolf II, this complex composition represents Jupiter bringing the infant Hercules, product of his coupling with the mortal Alcmene, to be nursed at the breast of the sleeping Juno and thereby obtain immortality for his progeny. Awakened by the vigorous suckling of the little hero, the goddess pulls away, but her lactating breasts continue to pour forth two streams: one ascends to form the Milky Way; the other falls to earth to create the lily—a scene originally represented in Tintoretto's canvas before it was cut sometime in or before the early eighteenth century.[28]

Rising with a sudden gesture from her Olympian bed, which hovers suspended in the heavens, the goddess reveals her nakedness in a posture of awkward extension. The dynamic counterpoint of the figures animates the heavenly setting of this scene of forced nursing. But the radical foreshortenings of those spatial oppositions are brought under compositional control by the shadowed patterns that impose a larger pictorial order on the design. The picture is executed with an attention to detail—from the feathers of Juno's peacocks to the embroidery of her bedclothes—that belies Tintoretto's reputation as a painter of impetuous haste. This unusual diligence of execution may well be due to the more patient brush of the painter's chief studio assistant, his son Domenico. Such a deliberate demonstration of painterly control may have been intended to appeal to the taste of the imperial court in Prague and to encourage further imperial patronage—especially

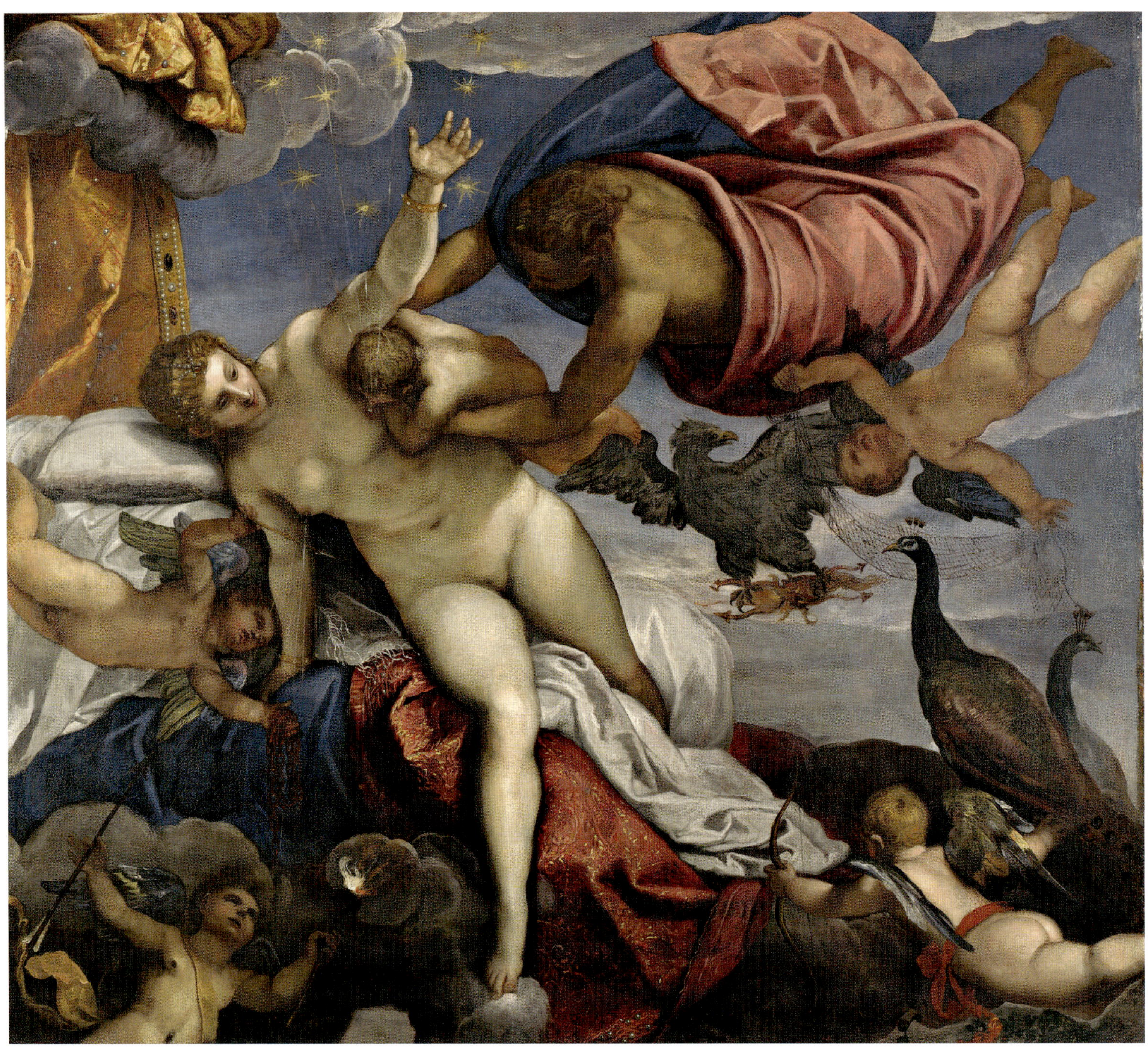

Fig. 85
Tintoretto
Origin of the Milky Way, 1577–79
Oil on canvas
The National Gallery, London

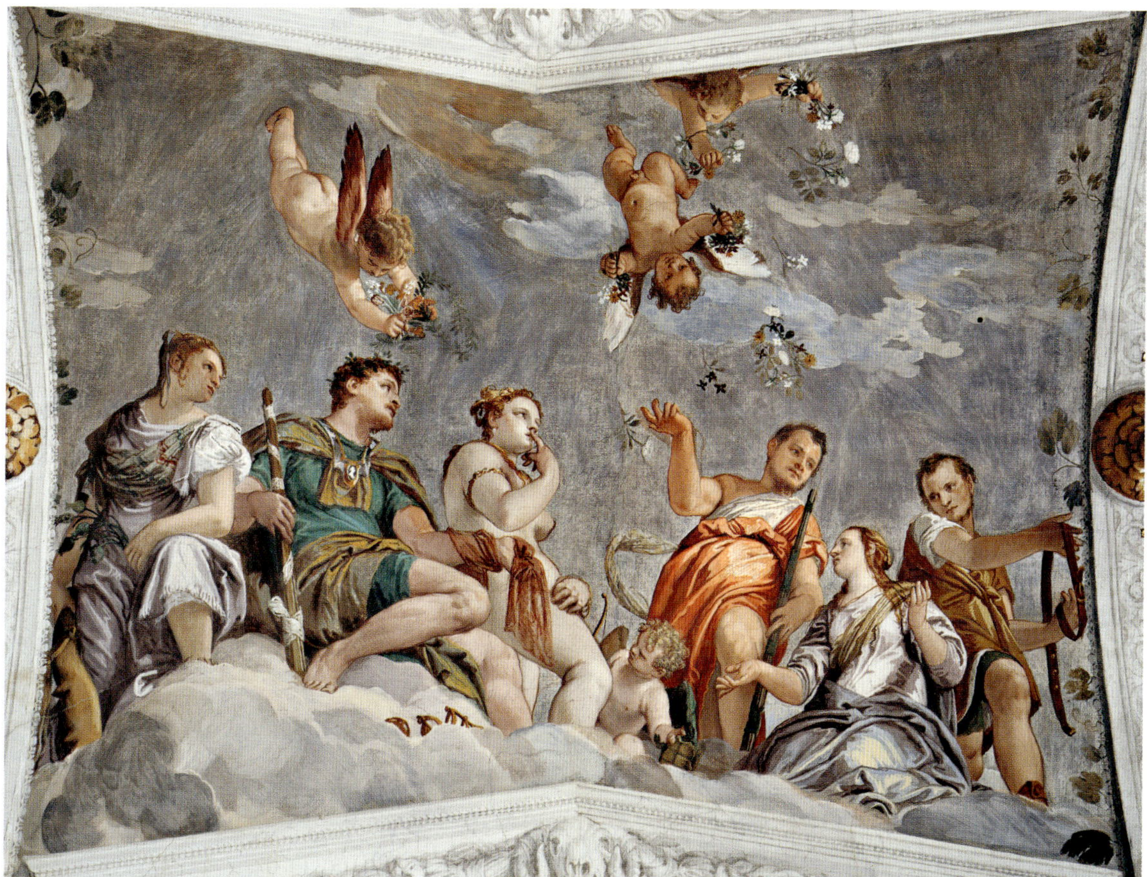

Fig. 86
Veronese
Ceiling of the Room of Married Love, 1560–61
Fresco
Villa Barbaro, Maser

following the death of Titian, who had been the preferred painter of emperors since his elevation to nobility by Charles V.

The invocation of the gods in an epithalamic iconography was a central part of the art of Veronese. From early in his career he enjoyed the patronage of patrician families in the Veneto, and his most monumental exploration of that Olympian realm for the celebration of family values is the fresco decoration of the villa of Daniele and Marcantonio Barbaro, in which the deities are invoked to offer benediction to the prosperity of the clan (fig. 86).[29] The triumph of licit love over base passion is the theme of a set of four canvases (National Gallery, London) clearly designed to decorate a ceiling; temptation is overcome and the series concludes with the celebration of marital union, as the united couple is crowned and rewarded by an allegorical figure of Abundance.[30] Like Tintoretto's *Origin of the Milky Way*, these paintings were in the imperial collection in Prague in the early seventeenth century, but there is no reason to assume they were conceived for Rudolf II; rather, they continue the kind of moralizing elevation of domestic love and resulting reward that inform the program of the Villa Barbaro.

Veronese's most perfect figuration of these values is his painting *Mars and Venus United by Love*. Although listed in the imperial inventories, it is not at all clear for whom the painting was made, whether it was invented for a particular occasion or as an allegorical statement of general appeal.[31] The title on the museum label describes the basic action of the composition: the active agent is Cupid, and his act is one of binding the nude goddess of love with her warrior lover. Venus has disrobed. Her light flesh contrasts with the virile darkness of Mars, her softness with his armor—an opposition, as we have seen, going back to the origins of the bathing scene in Renaissance painting. To the right, another cupid restrains the horse of Mars with the god's own sword. In Titian's *Venus and Adonis*, love is unable to restrain the determined hero, with tragic results; by contrast, Veronese's canvas displays

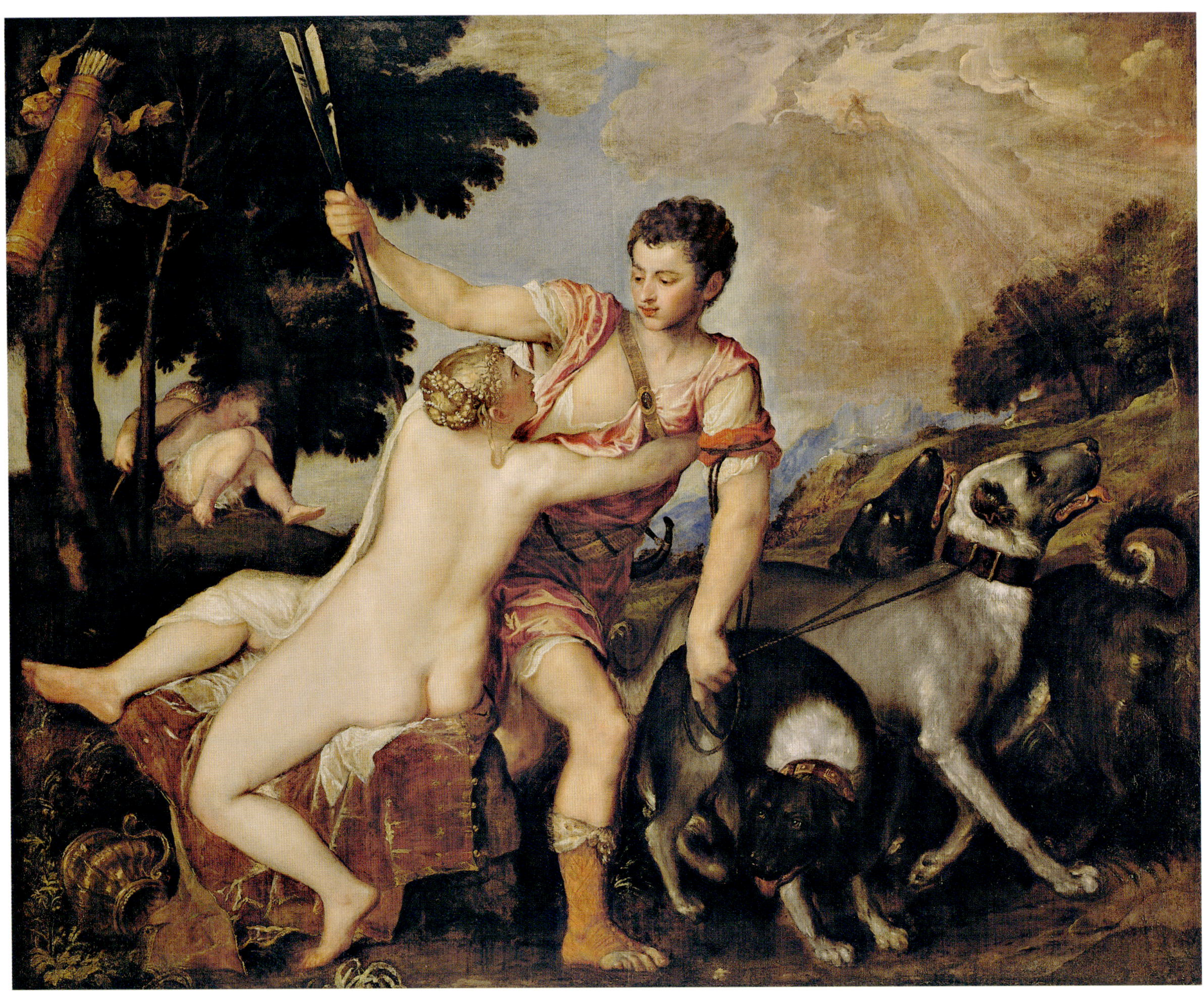

cat. 33

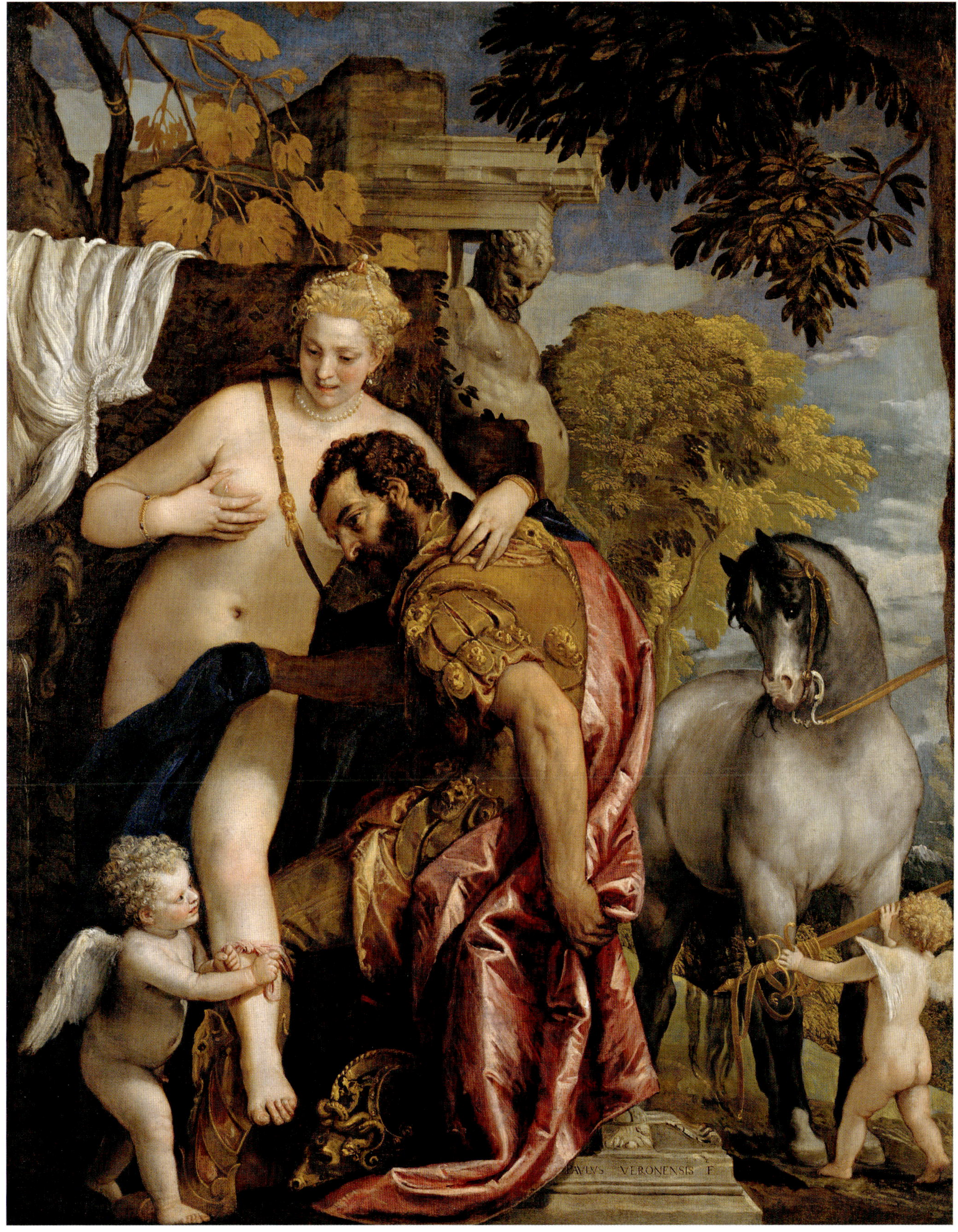

cat. 34

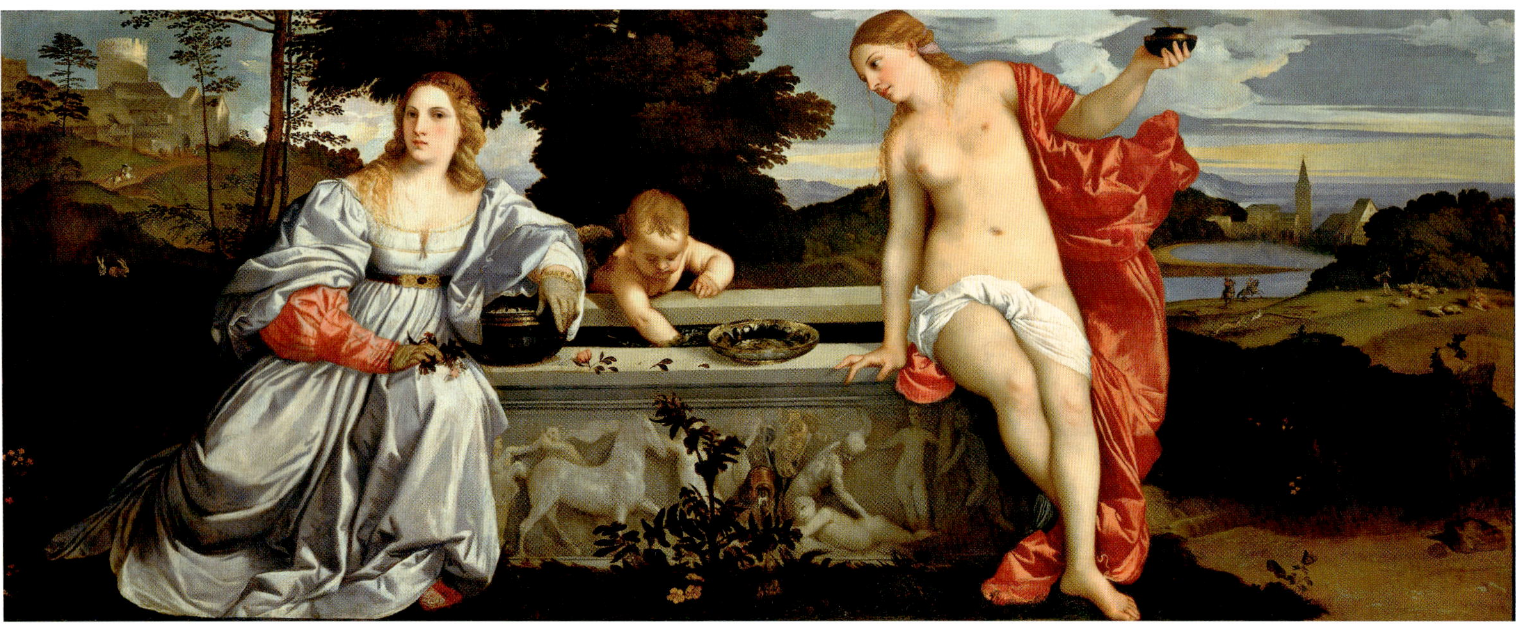

Fig. 87
Titian
Sacred and Profane Love, about 1515–16
Oil on canvas
Galleria Borghese, Rome

love's power and the resulting harmony, as the god of war is successfully restrained. Love conquers all, but this is a noble love. Behind the couple a stone satyr, a favorite creature in Veronese's art, leers down from the architectural ruin he supports; representing the lower level of pure lust, his marmoreal substance renders him impotent. The love of the two deities (whatever her marital infidelity) is a licit passion; her lactating breast signals the fertility of their union.

Even as they followed the example of Titian, working thematic variations on the female nude, Tintoretto and Veronese expanded the symbolic resonance of that basic form. The second part of the sixteenth century witnessed a particularly rich development of inventiveness—the publication of encyclopedias of symbols and allegories and dictionaries of emblems—and it was precisely this younger generation of artists who gave full form to the new imagination, who figured forth this culture of allegory and symbol.[32] Just as the new allegories were inspired by and built on the models of classical antiquity, so the artists themselves developed new possibilities of meaning with traditional forms: the nude goddess arose from her couch to become a more complex player in the construction of meaning.

Having taught a younger generation how the goddess of love was to be painted, Titian continued his pictorial celebration of Venus well into his long career (cat. 28, fig. 79). But she was not always the object of desire. In *Venus Blindfolding Cupid* (fig. 88) of about 1565, also known as the *Education of Cupid*, she appears fully dressed as she covers the eyes of a cupid, while his brother looks on from over her shoulder. These twin cupids represent the pairing of two concepts, Anteros and Eros. One with eyes open, the other blinded, they would come to represent higher and lower—that is, celestial and terrestrial—forms of love. Blind Cupid stands for the passion of the body, while his clear-sighted sibling embodies divine love.[33] Titian had depicted this basic alternative near the beginning of his career in the painting known as *Sacred and Profane Love* (fig. 87), a marriage picture celebrating the licit passion of matrimony and the higher aspirations of divine love. In *Venus Blindfolding Cupid*, Venus is joined by two other female figures; they carry a bow and a quiver of arrows, weapons associated both with love and with the huntress Diana, goddess of chastity. Their presence confirms the moral lesson of Venus's action in restraining libidinous love—implying the function of the canvas as a marriage picture. Titian might indulge here in the tactile appeal of the flesh, but his brush remains in the service of strong social values.

— DR

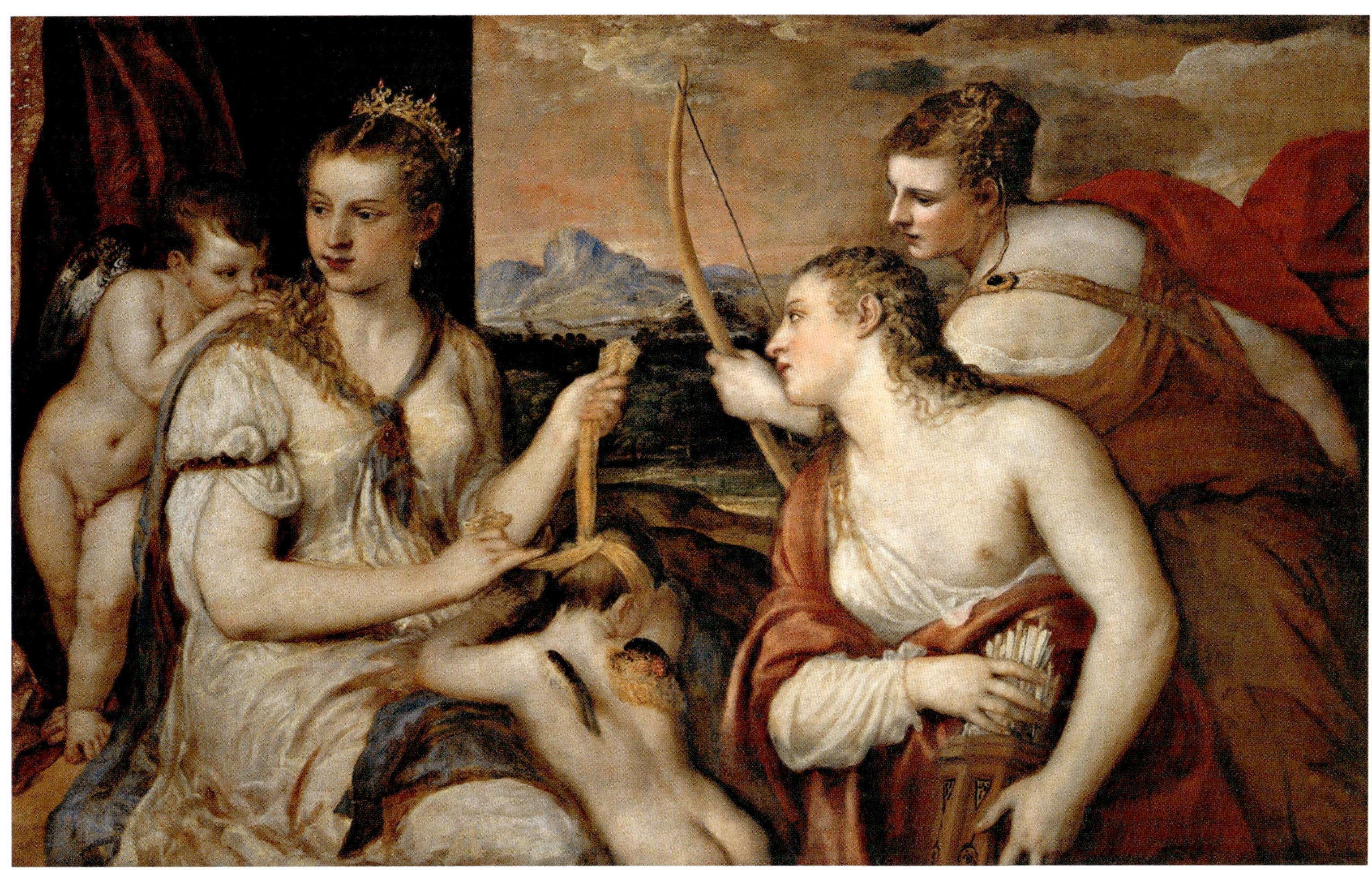

Fig. 88
Titian
Venus Blindfolding Cupid, about 1565
Oil on canvas
Galleria Borghese, Rome

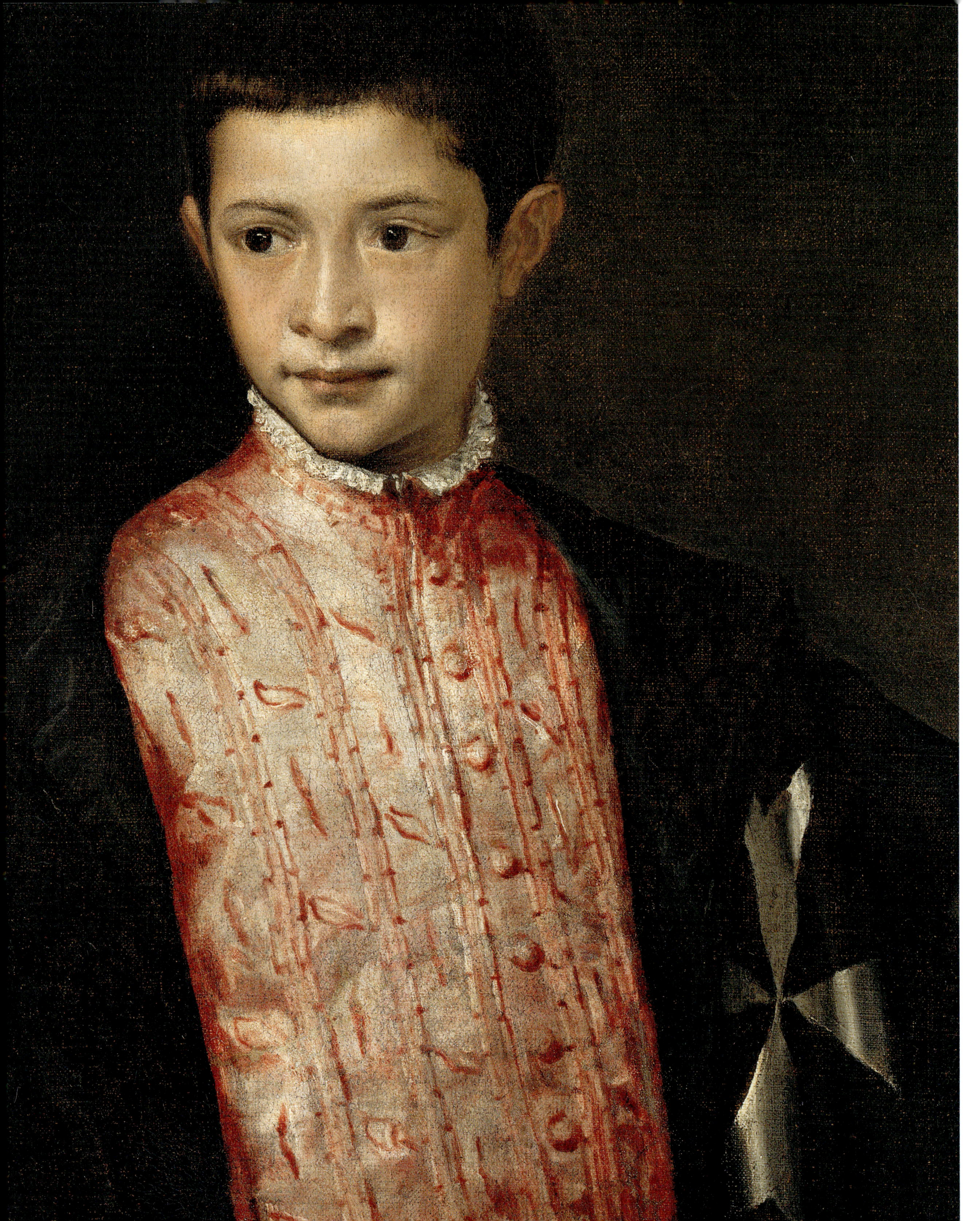

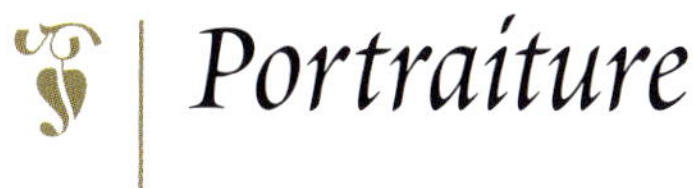

Portraiture

In all the houses of Venice are many portraits and several gentlemen have those of their ancestors to the fourth generation while some of the noblest go even further back. The custom is a most admirable one and was in use among the ancients.

Giorgio Vasari, 1568

Although the Tuscan chauvinist Giorgio Vasari found plenty to fault in Venetian painting, he made a point to praise the city's portraiture.[1] In the sixteenth century, while traditions of donor portraits within religious paintings persisted in Venice (such as the *Madonna di Ca' Pesaro* in Santa Maria Gloriosa dei Frari [fig. 47]), the popularity of independent portraits grew remarkably. Earlier likenesses had followed a limited repertoire of stiff, hieratic portrayals, often showing only the head and shoulders, painted in egg tempera on panel. Gentile Bellini's tempera painting from around 1478 of Doge Giovanni Mocenigo (Museo Correr, Venice) adopts the antique profile pose made popular on ancient Roman coins. By the time Giovanni Bellini assumed his older brother's place as official painter to the Republic in 1479, Roman-inspired formulas were ceding ground to new modes of portrayal.[2] Oil paintings from other parts of Italy and from the Netherlands showed the sitter's face in three-quarter view and greater verisimilitude. Giovanni embraced these innovations, and in the first two decades of the sixteenth century, his younger followers—Giorgione, Lorenzo Lotto, Palma Vecchio, and above all Titian—gradually shifted to painting more often on canvas than panel, simultaneously increasing the size of the painting. Portraits thus gradually lost some of their character as small, precious objects.

Starting around 1500, painters began to depict the sitter's head as life-size and expanded the field to include more of the body, paying particular attention to the hands as vehicles for expression.[3] The profile portrait disappeared as a type, replaced, for the most part, by sitters who looked out at the viewer (see cat. 35), contributing to a sense of connection or even confrontation. A smaller number of portraits depicted the sitter looking away, cultivating an introspective mood. In the case of Titian's *Portrait of a Man in a Red Cap* (fig. 91), the averted gaze invites the viewer to linger over such beautifully painted still-life details as the expansive fur collar and the soft leather gloves. A tangible sensuality also characterizes the flesh and costume of portraits of women, which were relatively rare in comparison to the galleries of male images. Venetian painters like Palma and Titian earned fame in the first three decades of the sixteenth century painting ideal and alluring images of women that reshaped portraiture trends (fig. 89; cat. 5).[4]

Palma and Titian's works displayed the allegorical possibilities of portraiture, contrasting the sitter's lifelike presence with the funereal stoniness of parapets (cat. 35) and other symbolic elements.[5] These images seemed to address the viewer and entreat a response, a poetic

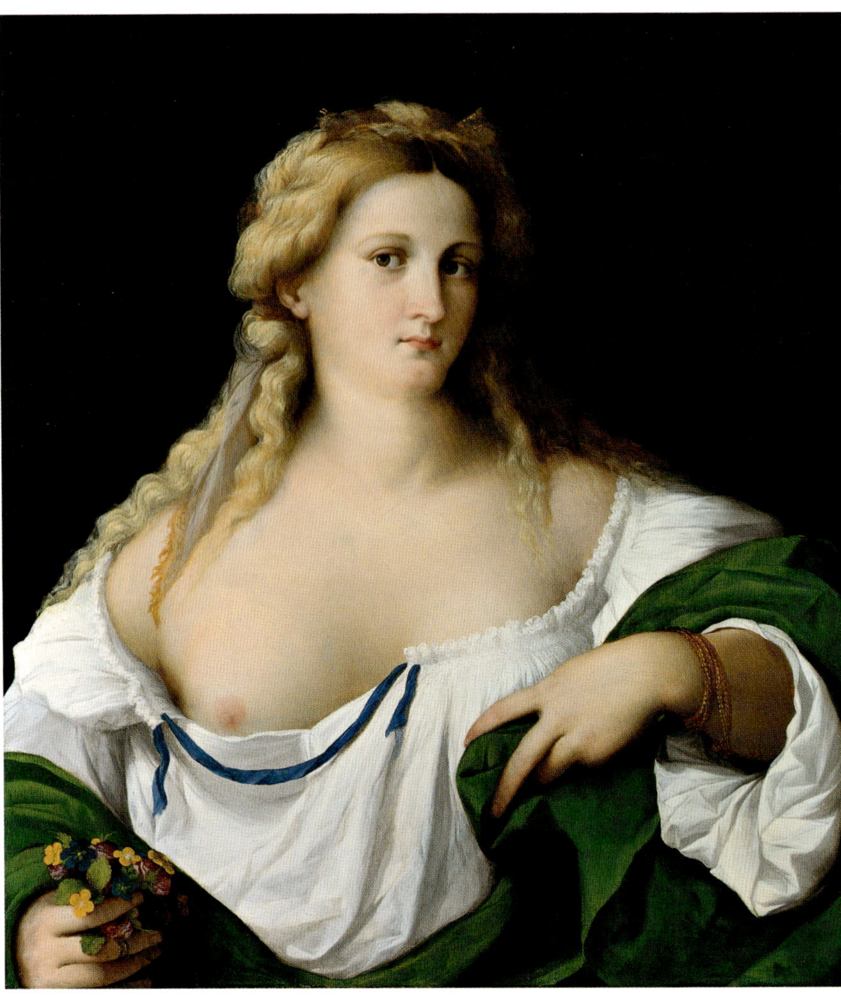

Fig. 89
Palma Vecchio (Italian, about 1479–1528)
A Blonde Woman, about 1520
Oil on wood
The National Gallery, London

yearning, so well known from Petrarch's sonnets. In taking up these goals of portraiture—the illusion of communication, lifelike semblance, and poetic resonance—Titian seized the field from his final teacher, Giorgione. By the time Tintoretto and Veronese emerged to compete with Titian, Venetian portraiture had expanded to include a varied repertoire of poses acted out across ever-larger canvases.

Of the three painters, Titian catered to the most elevated international clientele and may have produced over two hundred portraits, a remarkable number given his abundant output in religious and mythological paintings.[6] As in the case of his encounters with the Hapsburg monarchs Charles V and Philip II, or princes of the church like Pope Paul III (cat. 7), portraiture often provided Titian's entrée to aristocratic clients and helped him secure subsequent commissions in other genres. Tintoretto was even more prolific and seems to have managed a teeming workshop "almost industrial in its size and working methods," resulting in a greater output of portraits than any of his Venetian contemporaries.[7] His patrons included members of the city's highest patrician families.[8] Tintoretto finally received the *senseria*—the sinecure making him in effect Titian's replacement as the official painter of ducal portraits—only on September 17, 1574. This was too late for him to portray the French king Henri III, who had made a state visit to Venice two months earlier. According to Carlo Ridolfi, Tintoretto executed a likeness of the monarch secretly, without commission or explicit permission.[9] By contrast to Titian and Tintoretto's prolific output, only about forty portraits by Veronese survive, yet they are of high quality and feature diverse poses.[10] Although there is no royalty among his sitters, many of the works do record Venice's elite.

All three painters portrayed sitters from across the socioeconomic spectrum, including fellow artists. Veronese painted Titian's portrait (now lost), suggesting a close rapport.[11] Women and children also sat for the artists, though Tintoretto, unlike the other two, never seems to have made the genre a priority: only a few autograph portraits of women (and none of children) by him survive. Portraying women brought its own challenges; for example, the painter could be expected to travel to a female sitter's home, whereas it was socially acceptable and more convenient for a male sitter to pose in the studio. Portrait prices sometimes took into account this inconvenience to the painter. The account book of the Venetian businessman Zuan Paolo da Ponte records an agreement on March 8, 1534, whereby Titian would paint his portrait for 10 ducats and a portrait of his daughter Julia for twice the price.[12] The client agreed to the much higher sum for Julia's portrait, since Titian had to travel to the da Ponte home. Zuan Paolo also records that Titian would be paid an additional 5 ducats to cover the ultramarine pigments required for the blue clothing in his daughter's portrait.

All three painters routinely employed assistants to make their portrait business more efficient. During the face-to-face encounter with the subject, each artist would have sought to work quickly so as to keep the sitter content and alert. Paolo Pino's *Dialogue on Painting* of 1548 made clear that protracted sittings would result in a painter's being "dubbed tedious in his procedure" and he would thus miss out on other commissions.[13] Occasionally the client would not pay the artist for a completed work, and since it was difficult to sell the portrait to someone else, many cases arose of other subjects painted on top of abandoned portraits (cat. 30).

In applying their paints, Titian, Tintoretto, and Veronese exploited the surface textures of the canvas, using it to create illusions of fabric texture or to draw attention to their signature strokes of impasto floating on the surface. In the case of Titian and Tintoretto, open brushwork and sketchy handling even aroused the anxiety or disapproval of some clients. Maria of Hungary cautioned her niece Mary Tudor to view the portrait of Philip II (fig. 97) from a distance, as Titian's portraits were not always decipherable from close-up.[14] Tintoretto's brushwork in portraits ranges from careful, as when he rivals Titian as a painter of fur and leather gloves (cat. 36), to reckless and exciting, such as the reflections on armor (cat. 40). In the latter, the brushwork both conveys the steely surface of the metal plates and celebrates the painter's bold touch.

Admiring these textural effects, poets could praise an image for its lifelike quality while in the same breath professing that it captured the subject's eternal virtues. No poet seized upon this opportunity to win favor or financial support from a sitter quite like Pietro Aretino, who extolled Titian's portrait of Paul III as "animated and true to life" even though he had not seen it.[15] Although Aretino was Titian's great supporter, Tintoretto successfully ingratiated himself with the poet and painted several works for him, including a portrait and a ceiling ensemble for his home (cat. 8).

Veronese, for his part, captured the attention of a later poet, Sir Philip Sidney, who visited Venice in 1574.[16] Writing to a close confidant in Vienna, Sidney declared that he was still undecided whether to give the commission to Tintoretto or Veronese, "who hold by far the highest place in the art."[17] Titian was apparently too old to be considered. In the end, Sidney chose Veronese and sent the portrait on to Vienna. His friend, after initial protests that the painter had depicted Sidney looking too young and slightly sad, warmed to the likeness and declared it the most valuable item in his collection.[18] Though the portrait does not survive, Veronese's pensive-looking *Boy with a Greyhound* (fig. 90) depicts a similar melancholic portrayal.

As Titian, Tintoretto, and Veronese struggled to distinguish themselves, their competition was mediated by one important factor unique to the genre: the presence of the sitter. In some sense a portrait is always a likeness. Yet the artist is often expected to capture qualities that are transcendent or eternal, and as such the genre pulls an artist in opposite directions: being asked to flatter or capture something timeless while being anchored to the time-bound. Several modern writers have analyzed such tensions to great effect.[19] As we consider how our own interpretations, plagued by centuries of distance, are added onto these fictions of the artist's brush, it is useful to note that even sixteenth-century writers recognized that this purportedly truthful genre afforded a wide latitude of fanciful deceit. As Vasari commented, only when portraits are both "like *and* beautiful, then may they be called rare works, and their authors truly excellent craftsmen."[20]
—JG, FI

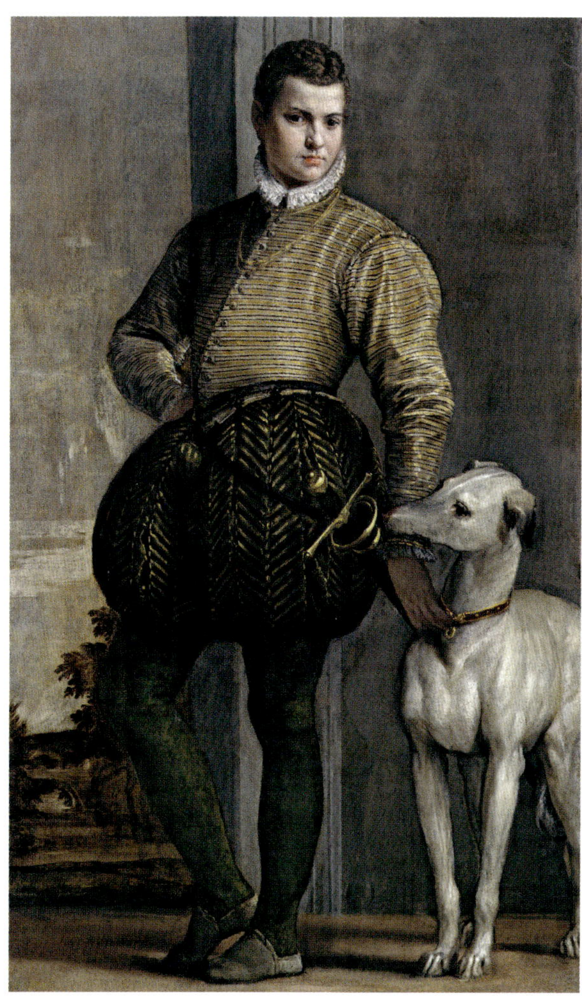

Fig. 90
Veronese
Boy with a Greyhound, mid-1560s
Oil on canvas
The Metropolitan Museum of Art, New York

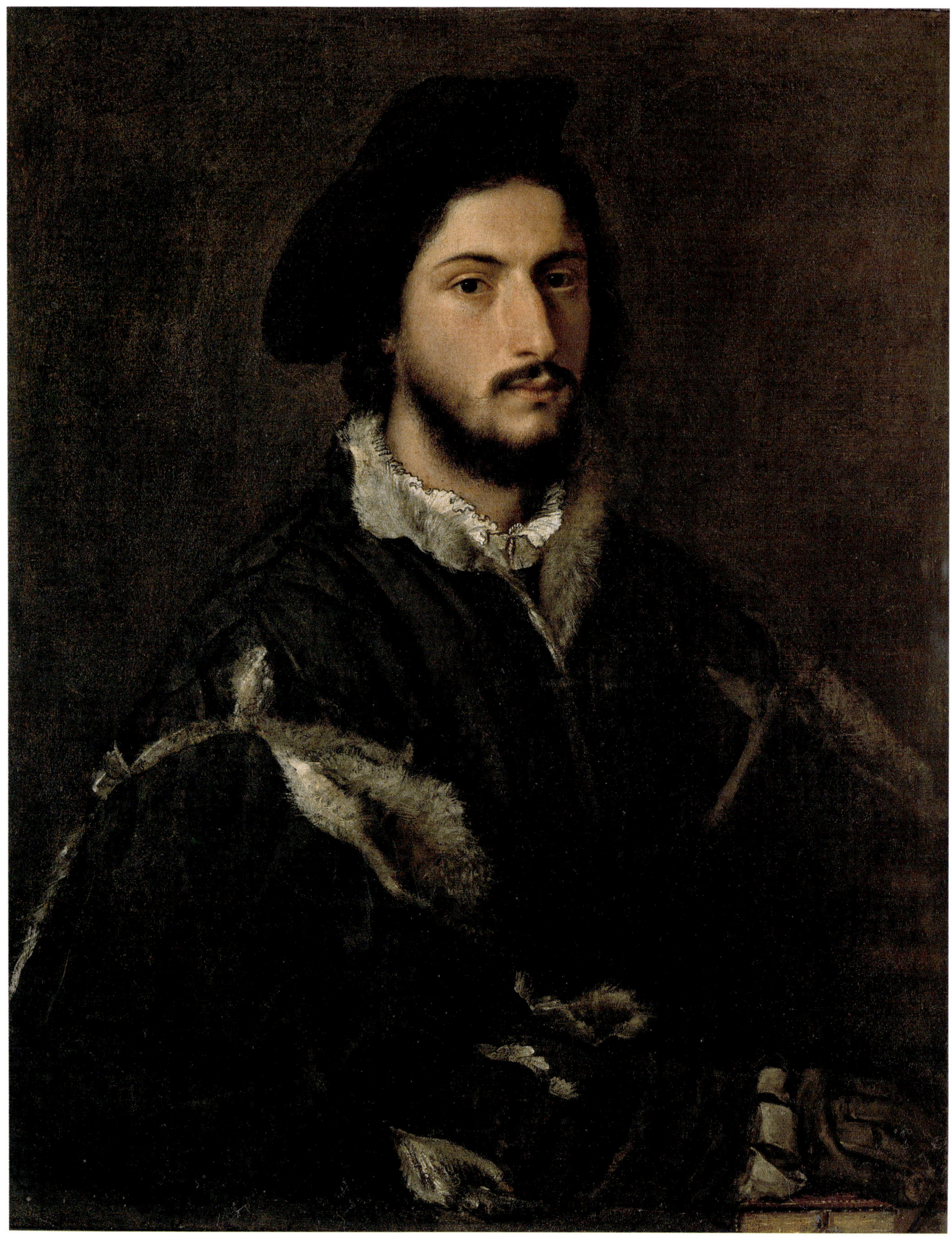

cat. 35

Gentlemen of Fashion

TITIAN
Portrait of a Man (Tommaso Mosti?), about 1520
Galleria Palatina, Florence
(cat. 35)

TINTORETTO
Portrait of a Man Aged Twenty-Six, 1547
Kröller-Müller Museum, Otterlo, the Netherlands
(cat. 36)

VERONESE
Portrait of a Man, about 1551–53
Szépművészeti Múzeum, Budapest
(cat. 37)

In their clothing, the young gentlemen portrayed here appear to follow the etiquette of Baldassare Castiglione, who urged the ideal courtier to don elegant but restrained attire, specifying that "the most agreeable color is black, and if not black, then at least something fairly dark."[21] Castiglione followed these conventions when he posed for his own famous portrait by Raphael (Louvre, Paris), a work that Titian might have seen on a visit to Mantua in 1519.[22] The pyramidal composition of Titian's *Portrait of a Man (Tommaso Mosti?)* closely follows Raphael's example in which the sitter leans confidently on a parapet. Titian's palette is marked by a luxurious sobriety that captures the tactile elements of the picture: the fur lining of the cloak, the supple leather gloves, and the gilt pages of the book. Tintoretto's *Portrait of a Man Aged Twenty-Six* also displays a sensitivity to rich textures. The artist includes a parapet behind the sitter and expands the picture's format to accommodate a standing figure similarly well dressed in lynx-trimmed mantel and displaying a remarkable self-possession.[23] Veronese's *Portrait of a Man* follows in this mode, but a curtain is pulled open to reveal an ivy-clad view of a landscape with antique ruins. In keeping with the tenor of stylishness noted in the preceding portraits, Veronese's sitter rests a gloved hand on his hip in a nonchalant pose that calls to mind Castiglione's idea of *sprezzatura*, or effortlessness.

The names of these sitters do not survive, even if their rich attire makes it clear that they were members of the elite. Only Titian's *Portrait of a Man (Tommaso Mosti?)* offers a tentative identification of the subject. The back of the canvas bears an inscription in what appears to be seventeenth-century script: "DI THOMASO MOSTI IN ETÁ DI ANNI XXV. L'ANNO M.D.XXVI. THITIANO DA CADORO PITTORE" (Tommaso Mosti at the age of twenty-five. The year 1526. Painted by Titian from [Pieve di] Cadore). Most scholars have judged the inscription untrustworthy and prefer to date the work to 1520, based on its style.[24] Given this earlier date, the portrait might still portray Mosti before he took holy orders, but the connection is tenuous enough that the work is sometimes labeled simply *Portrait of a Man*.[25] Tintoretto's sitter remains unidentified, although an inscription declares the date of the painting, June 1547, and the sitter to be twenty-six years old. This handsome work is one of the few dated portraits from Tintoretto's early career, and until recently it was relatively unknown.[26] Veronese's *Portrait of a Man* bears no inscriptions, but the similarity of the ruins in the background to a print of the *Baths of Caracalla* by Hieronymus Cock suggests a date after 1551.[27]

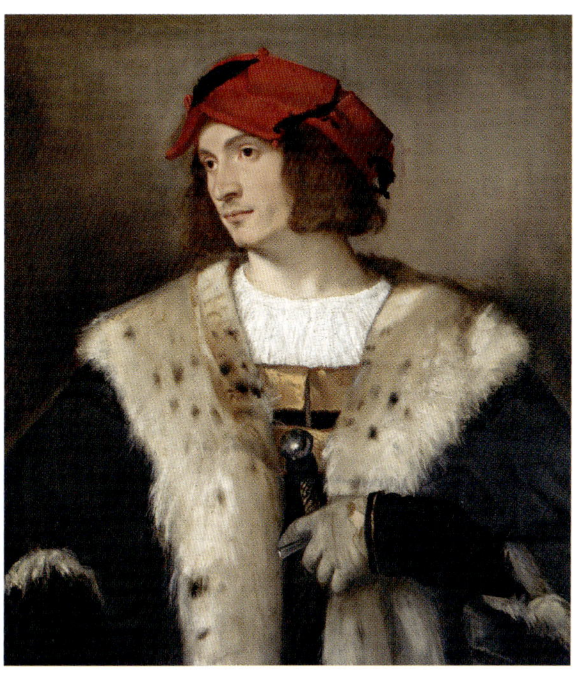

Fig. 91. Titian, *Portrait of a Man in a Red Cap*, 1511–16, oil on canvas, The Frick Collection, New York

Giorgione's sensuous and wistful images set a standard for Titian's early forays into half-length male likenesses, including his *Portrait of a Man in a Red Cap*, from 1511–16 (fig. 91). The yielding sitter in that picture coaxes the viewer's gaze, while Titian's sumptuous brushwork encourages one's eyes to linger on details, such as the light chemise and leather glove. Turning to the *Portrait of a Man*

Fig. 92
Titian
Daniele Barbaro, about 1545
Oil on canvas
Museo Nacional del Prado, Madrid

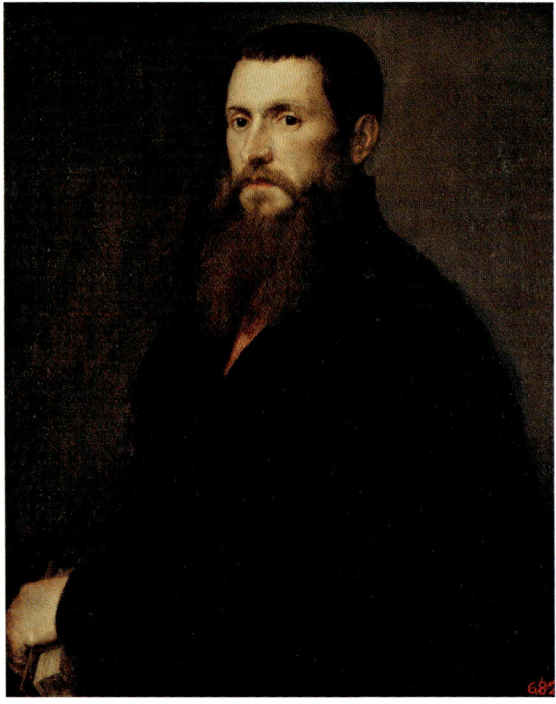

(Tommaso Mosti?) a few years later, Titian continued the intimate half-length portrayal but opted for a more self-assured pose with a book placed under the subject's hand. There is something seductive in the sitter's calm gaze and palpably soft clothing.

In works such as *Portrait of a Man Aged Twenty-Six*, Tintoretto attempts to rival Titian's subdued color harmonies and skillfull evocation of costume, especially in the sitter's gloves. The bright-lit features emulate Titian's canvas, even as the brushwork is more open and unrestrained.[28] As Falomir has noted, Tintoretto's career experienced a "meteoric rise" after 1545, and this assertive portrayal of an upright aristocrat is one of many that document the artist's growing status as portraitist to the elite.[29] The formula of a floating visage on a dark background also characterizes work of the following decades, such as *Giovanni Paolo Cornaro* of 1561 (fig. 25). By the late 1540s, Tintoretto had mastered the skills noted by Cristoforo Sorte in his *Osservationi nella pittura* (1580): "in the portraits and paintings he takes from life, he takes but a moment to insert the contrasts, shadows, half-tones, reliefs and flesh, so well imitated, in their places with such wondrous skill, speed and promptitude that it is a marvel to see him work."[30] Tintoretto's deft handling also meant shorter sitting times for patrons.

No autograph preparatory drawing survives for any of Tintoretto's portraits, and it may not have been important to his working process. Veronese, despite a smaller number of portraits, leaves two drawings of sitters' heads and at least three highly finished drawings of models striking the appropriate pose and wearing the sitter's attire.[31] Veronese's study for *Iseppo da Porto and His Son Adriano* offers a good example—models pose wearing the silk garments of father and son (fig. 99). Such costume studies point to a fundamental difference in the two portraitists that became more pronounced as they aged: Tintoretto prioritized the face and often paid only cursory attention to other parts of the canvas, while Veronese worked more slowly and tended to add more props and sumptuous attire. This difference is evident in Veronese's *Portrait of a Man*, painted when the artist was in his early twenties. The sitter strikes a grandiloquent pose, even if his right hand remains hesitantly placed on the ledge.[32] Veronese stages his fashionably melancholic subject with greater emphasis on connotative props, such as the creeping ivy and overgrown ruins, symbolizing loss and death.[33]

Veronese's interest in objects and staging could also lead him away from Titian's practice, as is evident when both artists were commissioned to portray the same sitter: Daniele Barbaro (figs. 18, 92). Titian's likeness shows the determined features of the young humanist rising out of the dark as the sole conveyor of meaning. In Veronese's image Barbaro's erudition and status are signaled by his seated pose (common to images of scholars or popes), costumes, and books. Daniele also appears in his official vestments as Patriarch-elect of Aquileia, holding his 1556 translation of Vitruvius's *De architectura libri decem*; denotative and connotative elements of his high position and learning conjoin and ultimately contend with the sitter's brightly lit face.

In these portraits, one sees Titian's opulent refinement and relaxed mastery of the pyramidal composition being transformed by his rivals into more upright and forceful portrayals. Tintoretto's depiction exudes self-confidence, while Veronese's likeness approaches a more outwardly theatrical mode, arguably at the expense of the somber tradition pioneered by Titian in the 1520s. Whether restricting the palette to emphasize a sitter's interiority or expanding it to include a sunny landscape with distant ruins, each artist attempts to dignify his sitter with a balance of fashionable presentation and noble sentiment.
—JG

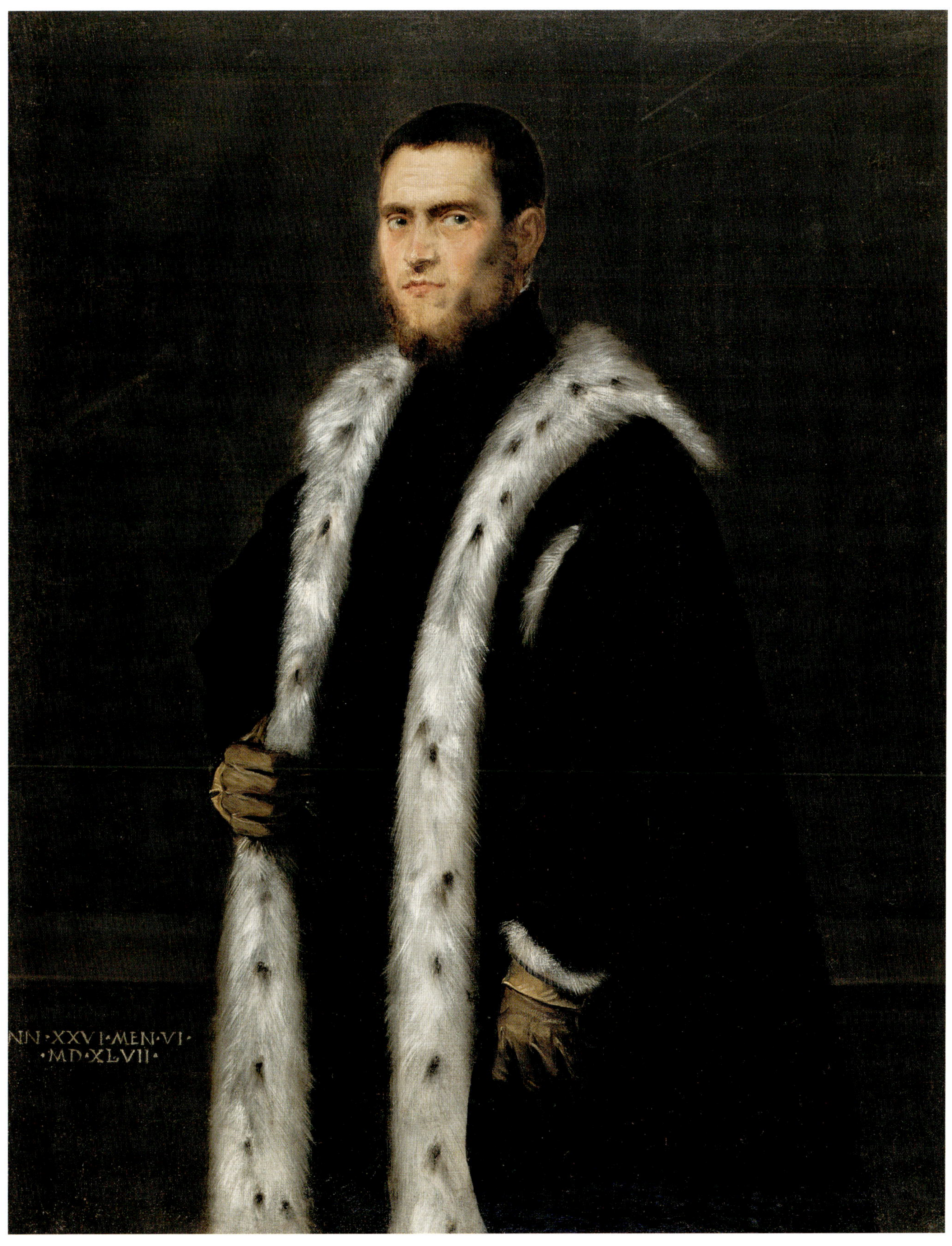

cat. 36

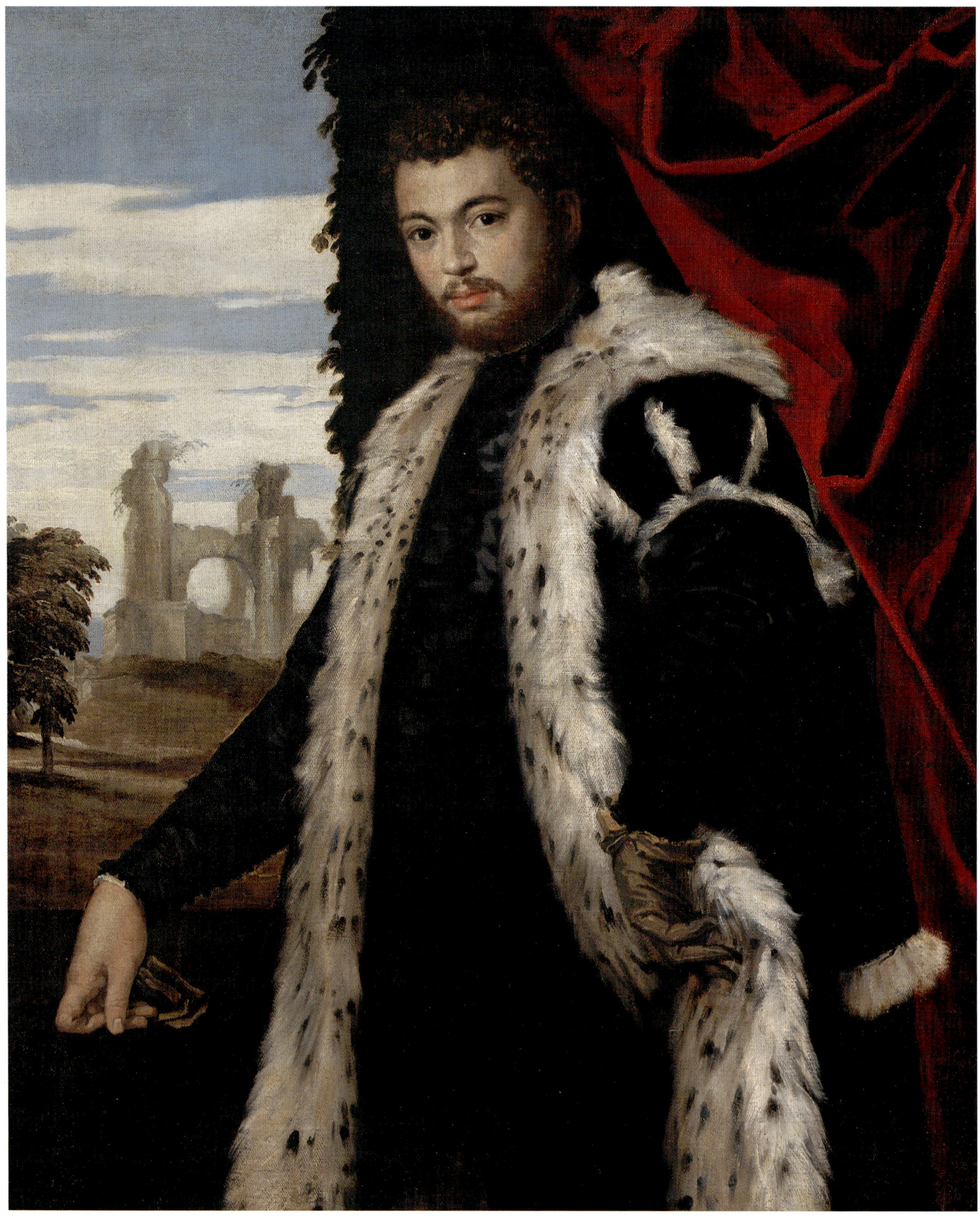

cat. 37

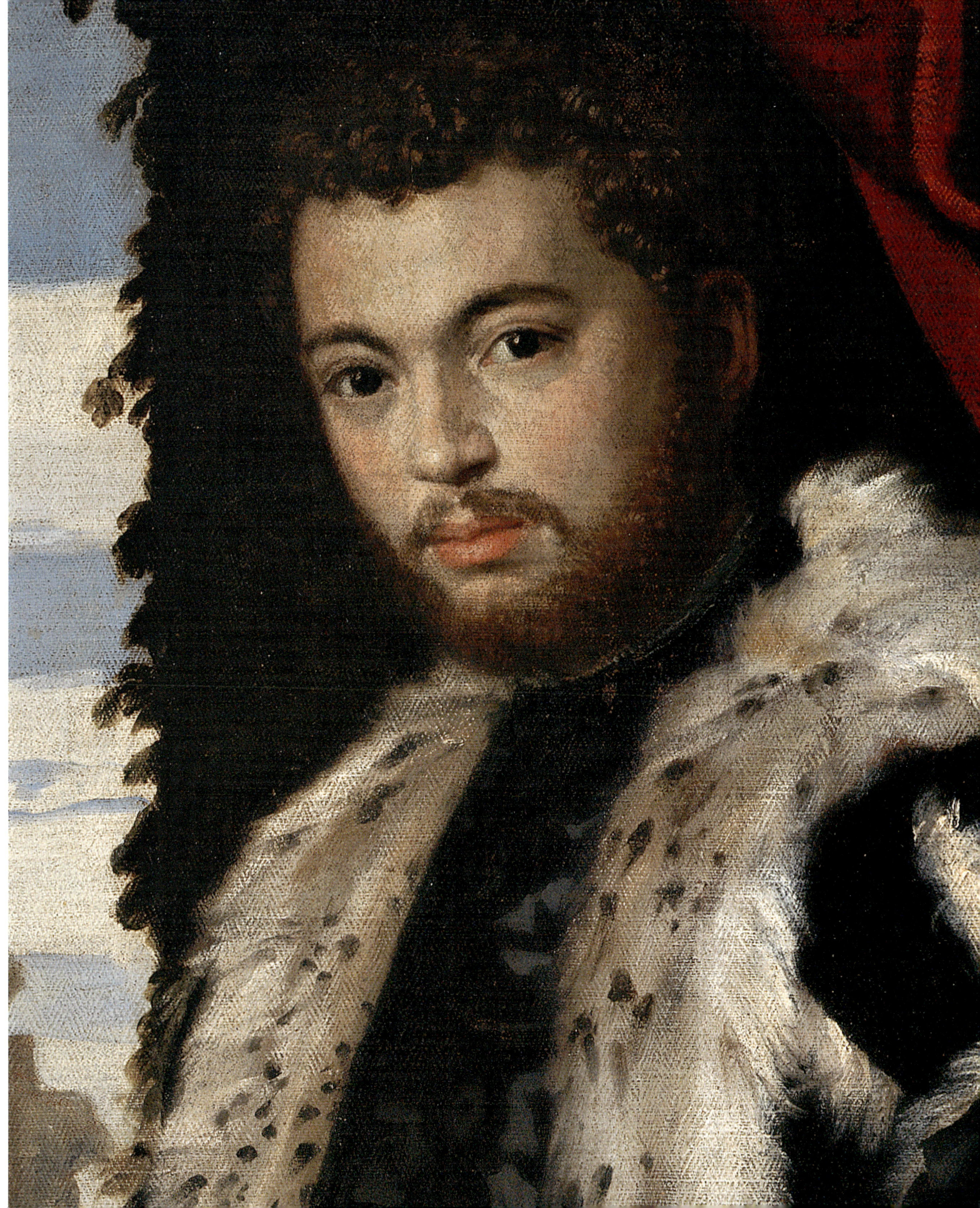

The Titian Formula

TITIAN
Portrait of a Man Holding a Book, about 1540
Museum of Fine Arts, Boston
(cat. 38)

TINTORETTO
Portrait of a Man, about 1548
Private Collection
(cat. 39)

Tintoretto strove to set his religious painting apart from Titian's, repeatedly transforming or overturning the compositions and motifs that the elder artist employed in his work. For example, when Tintoretto painted his *Presentation of the Virgin in the Temple* (fig. 8) for the church of the Madonna dell'Orto, about 1556, he maintained enough of Titian's composition of some two decades earlier (fig. 13) to draw attention to his source, while at the same time introducing changes that make clear his wish to surpass the prototype. Similarly, Tintoretto's *Supper at Emmaus* (cat. 22) seems to explode the harmony and balance in Titian's earlier work of the same subject (cat. 21). Some of Tintoretto's mythological paintings, such as his comical *Venus and Mars Surprised by Vulcan* (fig. 81), should be seen as a pointed parody of Titian's earlier erotic nudes, particularly his *Danaë* (cat. 27). The younger artist wanted his audience—and his rival—to understand his paintings in light of the challenge they posed to Titian's model.

Tintoretto's portraiture, however, does not seem to exhibit the same streak of independence. Indeed, many of Tintoretto's portraits follow Titian's example so closely that they seem to partake of the same formula. The clear resemblance in format, pose, expression, and technique was noted as early as 1584, when Raffaello Borghini claimed that many portraits by the younger painter were "held to be by Titian's hand."[34] Recent studies of Tintoretto's portraiture illuminate how much he depended on Titian's example.[35] Given the antipathy between the two artists, we may presume that Tintoretto's motivation for adhering so closely to Titian's model was not deference or admiration but rather dry acknowledgment of his rival's success. While religious paintings might stray a certain distance from conventional expectations, the latitude for portraits was far narrower, since the patron was both client and subject. Tintoretto seems to have understood that Titian had created a market for a type of portrait that he too could fill. Moreover, the younger artist had learned from Titian how effective portraits could be at advertising a painter's skills—and cultivating new clients.[36] The triumph of Titian's approach may have tempered Tintoretto's impulse to be radical.

Titian's portraiture had of course developed in response to earlier formulas, including those of his teachers, Bellini and Giorgione.[37] Bellini had perfected meticulous portraits painted in oil on panel, which conveyed the physical solidity of the sitter while keeping him behind a parapet: the sitter's eyes did not make contact with the viewer. Giorgione introduced the sitter's hands into the arrangement and endowed the portrait with a sense of interrupted action or particular mood; these portraits created a feeling of atmosphere around the sitter's body, akin to the palpable environment in Venetian religious paintings of the first decade of the Cinquecento.[38] But despite such innovations, portraits by Bellini, Giorgione, and their contemporaries were tightly cropped, focused on the head and upper torso, and allowed little breathing room around the figure.

As Titian's portraiture developed with the use of canvas supports, he freed the sitters, putting them in closer contact with the viewer and expanding the pictorial field. The human figure dominated this larger space, even as Titian's carefully rendered still-life details and textures rivaled Bellini's (fig. 91). By the mid-1520s, Titian had established his portrait formula: a standing figure shown half length or just less than three-quarter length, with at least one hand visible, the torso turned and the sitter often making eye contact with the viewer. The scale is near life-size, the palette relatively somber, and the focus on flattering the subject's features, endowing them with confidence and dignity. Titian produced more than two dozen surviving examples of this formula, including some of female sitters.[39] He had a particular talent for endowing his sitters with the Renaissance ideal of *sprezzatura*, or nonchalance, a quiet confidence abundantly displayed in *Portrait of a Man Holding a Book*.[40]

This portrait was "practically unknown" (in the words of curator W. G. Constable) when the Museum of Fine Arts, Boston, purchased it in 1943.[41] Although dressed conspicuously and possessing a distinctive red beard, the sitter's identity remains a mystery.[42] The

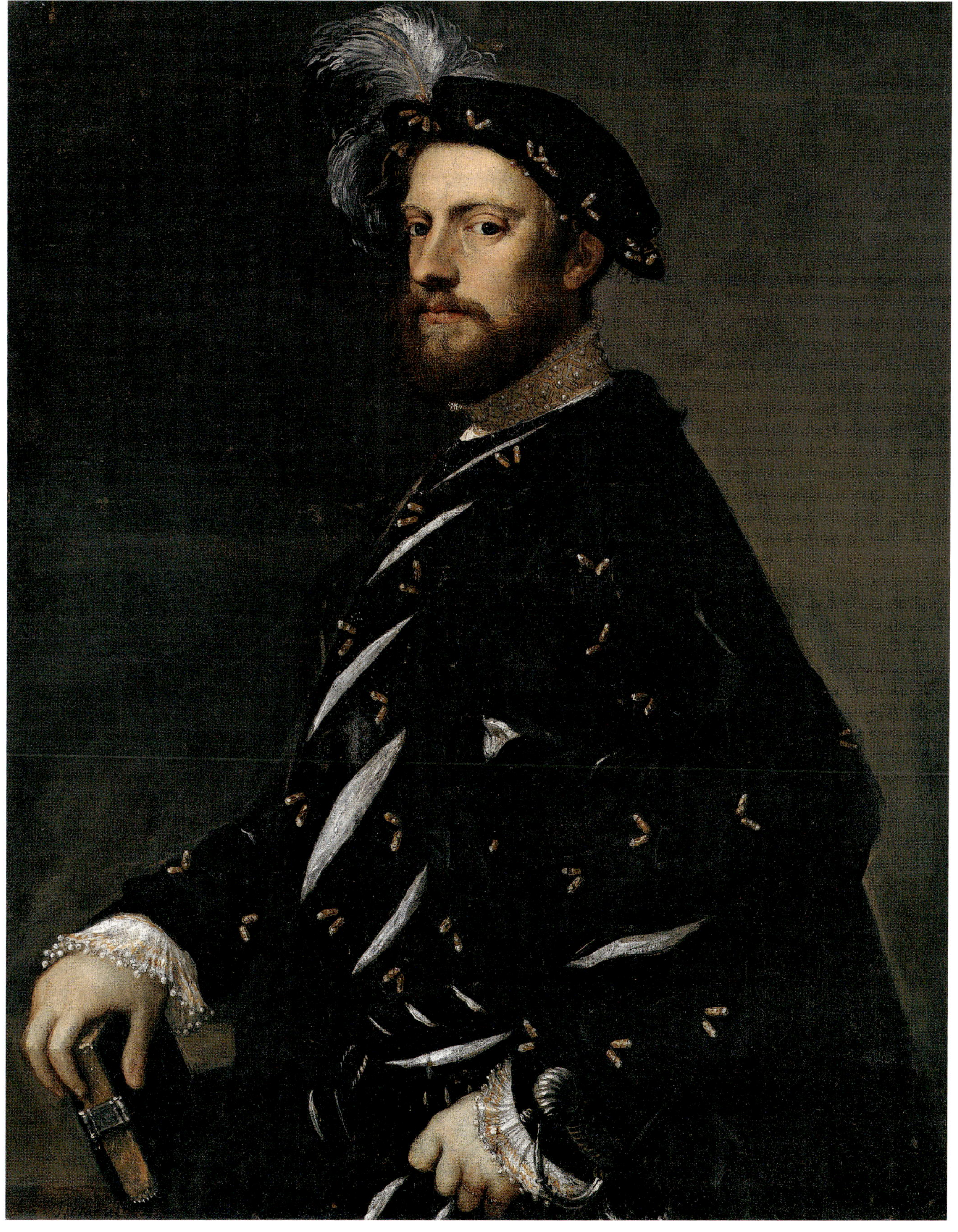

cat. 38

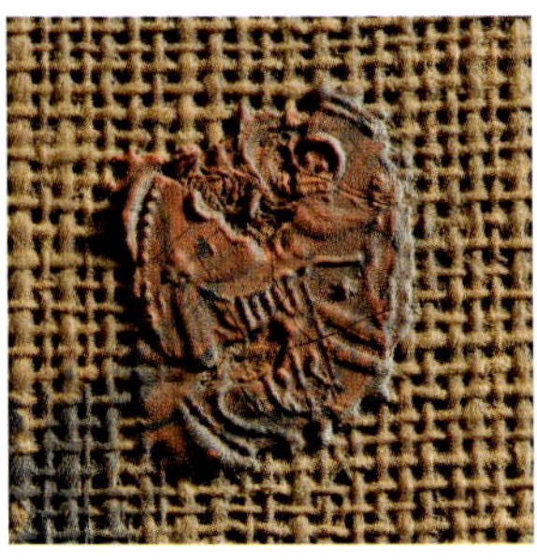

Fig. 93
Unidentified wax seal on the back of Titian's *Portrait of a Man Holding a Book* (cat. 38), Museum of Fine Arts, Boston

picture's provenance has been traced to Sicily in the second half of the nineteenth century, to the Oneto and then Mortillaro families, but a coat of arms on a wax seal on the reverse of the painting remains to be identified (fig. 93). Constable's letter of April 8, 1943, justifying the purchase declared its autograph status "beyond question" and suggested a date of 1530–35. An article announcing the acquisition by the MFA's director, G. H. Edgell, claimed that the picture's style was "even more convincing than the signature" and argued that it was executed "about 1540," based on the clothing and the resemblance to other Titian portraits.[43] Accepted by Bernard Berenson in 1957, the painting's authenticity began to be questioned in the late 1960s, though specific arguments were rarely given. While Harold Wethey placed the portrait within his main catalogue, rather than in the appendix of "doubtful and wrong attributions," he hinted at doubts on the portrait's authenticity: the attribution is listed as "Titian (?)" and the text adds that the "emphasis on costume exceeds the usual restraint in Titian's works." Wethey seems to have ignored the somber palette of that expensive dress, as well as the possibility that the clothing may have been designated by the sitter. In the nearly four decades following Wethey's entry, the MFA portrait has been largely ignored by scholars.[44]

And yet, the sitter forcefully commands both his space and the attention of the viewer in a way that bespeaks the painting's authenticity. His self-assurance; the particulars of his physiognomy and costume; the confident, efficient brushstrokes defining the facial features; the turn of the head and glance of the eyes; the hairs constituting the beard, carefully executed without being precious—all these argue for an attribution to Titian.[45] The treatment of the sitter's costume and possessions reveals an artist highly sensitive to the varieties and textures of cloth, metal, and feathers. The left hand, decorated by two rings, is consistent with those in other Titian portraits. The single discordant note, the puffy and frankly awkward appearance of the right hand holding the book, is explained by its poor condition, one of the more abraded passages in the picture. One detail of brushwork argues in particular for the picture's autograph status: the bold vertical impasto stroke between the proper left eye and the nose, the touch of a confident master. Portraits by workshop assistants and Titian imitators tended to be tentative and bland.

The subject's flashy dress, clearly not Venetian, is worth further analysis, though the sunken colors of the portrait have made distinguishing the components difficult. According to Jane Bridgeman, a specialist on Renaissance dress, the sitter is wearing a shirt and a black padded doublet with prominent slashes, with a fur-lined gown (an antecedent of the academic gown) on top, and breeches and a codpiece below the waist.[46] His doublet and coordinated hat are decorated with aglets, gilded tips that were originally used on the ends of laces that tie up clothing but here are simply for decoration.[47] An ostrich feather embellishes the hat. The unusual cuffs (ruffles with pearls) and the elaborate collar, embroidered with gold and also decorated with pearls, seem very specific and probably reflect an actual outfit owned by the sitter, rather than the painter's creation. By wearing a sword, he can be identified as a nobleman, and he holds a small book with a silver clasp, probably a religious text such as a book of hours. The details of the costume would seem to date the picture to about 1540, and find analogies (particularly in the hat) to the portrait of the weary young man by Moretto da Brescia in the National Gallery, London, dated to about 1540–45.[48] Based on his dress, the sitter may be from Lombardy or the Veneto.[49]

As Rearick noted, Titian's example inspired European portraiture in general and that of Tintoretto in particular.[50] The younger artist, who came of age professionally during Titian's peak production in the 1530s and 1540s, often adopted his elder's formula, as visible in the recently rediscovered *Portrait of a Man*. Tintoretto produced even more examples of this type than Titian: a slightly more than half-length portrait of a standing figure with turned body, facing the viewer. The backgrounds in the two paintings are equally somber, and the strong lighting in each seems to underscore the sitter's presence. Where the sitter's carriage is similar to the Titian portrait, his facial expression seems apprehensive and unusually vulnerable for a Tintoretto. He stands alongside an elaborately carved pilaster or column base with stylized acanthus and other foliage, an uncommon detail in Venetian portraits and perhaps the only clue in the painting that may aid research into its provenance or the sitter's identity.[51] The freedom of this passage is impressive, and Tintoretto is almost audacious in using similar slashing brushstrokes to depict the blue sleeve of the sitter's doublet and the carved stone base. It is hard to imagine Titian or Veronese, both generally more careful in their technique, rendering such different textures the same way. Tintoretto must have painted this picture about 1548, based on the resemblance to a portrait from that year (Staatsgalerie, Stuttgart), noted by Paola Rossi, as well as the similarity to Tintoretto's slightly earlier *Self-Portrait* (cat. 9) and portraits within the *Miracle of the Slave* of 1548 (fig. 5).[52] I should stress that Tintoretto's consistent use of the formula seen in this portrait was not simply for his own convenience but also because it met the expectations of clients accustomed to Titian's portraiture.

— FI

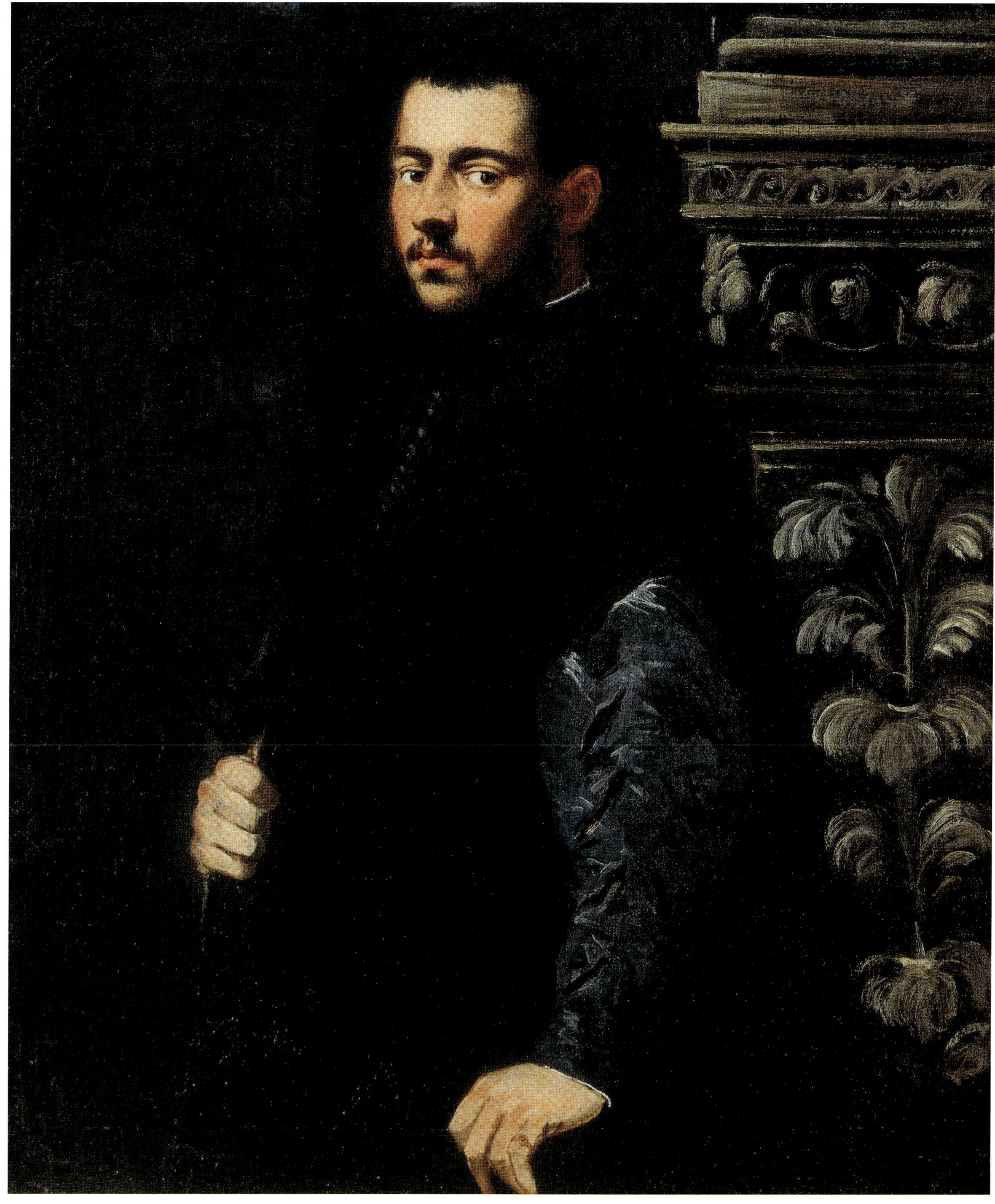

cat. **39**

Portraits of Warriors

TINTORETTO
Sebastiano Venier, about 1571–72
Kunsthistorisches Museum,
Gemäldegalerie, Vienna
(cat. 40)

VERONESE
Agostino Barbarigo, about 1571–72
Cleveland Museum of Art
(cat. 41)

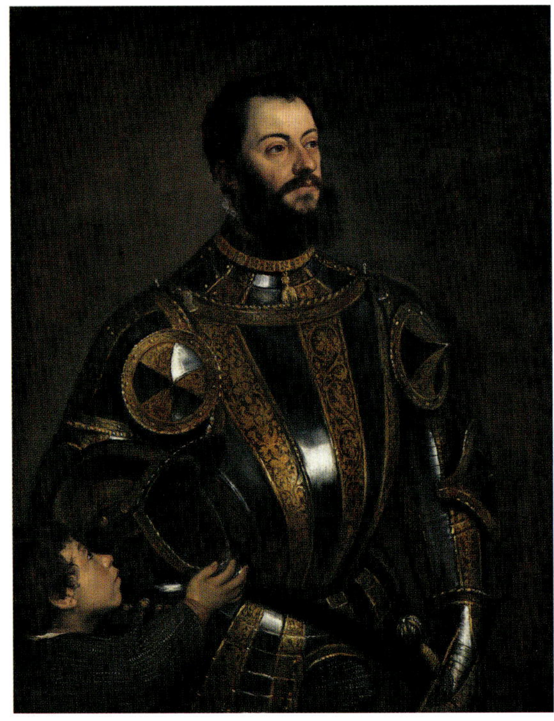

Fig. 94. Titian, *Alfonso d'Avalos*, 1533, oil on canvas, The J. Paul Getty Museum, Los Angeles

The self-assurance and indeed serenity of La Serenissima was based on a powerful navy led by formidable admirals. These warriors sat for Titian, Tintoretto, and Veronese in the hopes that their portraits might secure their fame and inspire the military prowess of their successors, thus keeping alive a lineage of classical portraiture stretching back to the time of Alexander the Great. According to Pliny the Elder's *Natural History*, the famous portraits of Alexander by the painter Apelles were displayed in the Roman forum as exempla of strength and virtue.[53] Ancient biographers noted that Julius Caesar carried a portrait of Alexander on military campaigns to inspire him to victory, an anecdote frequently repeated by Renaissance theorists writing on the merits of portraiture.[54] This essay includes likenesses of three of the most revered Venetian commanders: Admiral Vincenzo Cappello, who led the Venetian navy in numerous Turkish skirmishes; and Admirals Sebastiano Venier and Agostino Barbarigo, who distinguished themselves in the epic Battle of Lepanto in 1571, Venier surviving to rise to an even higher rank, doge of the Venetian Republic. Their portraits made their deeds live on.

Titian's portraiture determined subsequent Venetian and European taste; he was endorsed by his contemporaries as a modern Apelles and celebrated as such in the poetry of Pietro Aretino.[55] Although Titian's portraits of sitters in armor included full-length images, multifigure compositions, and a large equestrian portrait (*Charles V at the Battle of Mühlberg*, in the Museo Nacional del Prado, Madrid), the format he perfected—the three-quarter-length portrait of a sitter in armor, on canvas—was the one most popular in Venice, and one embraced by Tintoretto and Veronese in their own distinctive styles. Titian's pioneering effort in this genre, a nearly three-quarter-length portrait of Charles V in armor, has been lost. The picture seems to have been painted in 1530 in Bologna on the occasion of Charles's coronation as Holy Roman Emperor, and its appearance can be reconstructed from a print by Giovanni Britto and a painting by Rubens.[56] These copies reveal that Titian depicted the emperor without a helmet but otherwise fully armed, bearing a sword in his hand. He turns his body slightly and offers the viewer an expression of composed command. The influence of this lost portrait can be seen in other works by Titian that soon followed in its wake: *Francesco Maria della Rovere, Duke of Urbino* of 1536 (Galleria degli Uffizi, Florence), *Alfonso d'Avalos* of 1533 (fig. 94), and *Vincenzo Cappello*, probably of 1540 (fig. 95). D'Avalos and Titian probably met in 1530 in Bologna at the coronation of Charles V. The Getty *Alfonso d'Avalos* follows the formula of the lost work quite closely, suggesting that the emperor's chief of command in Italy wanted his portrait to pay

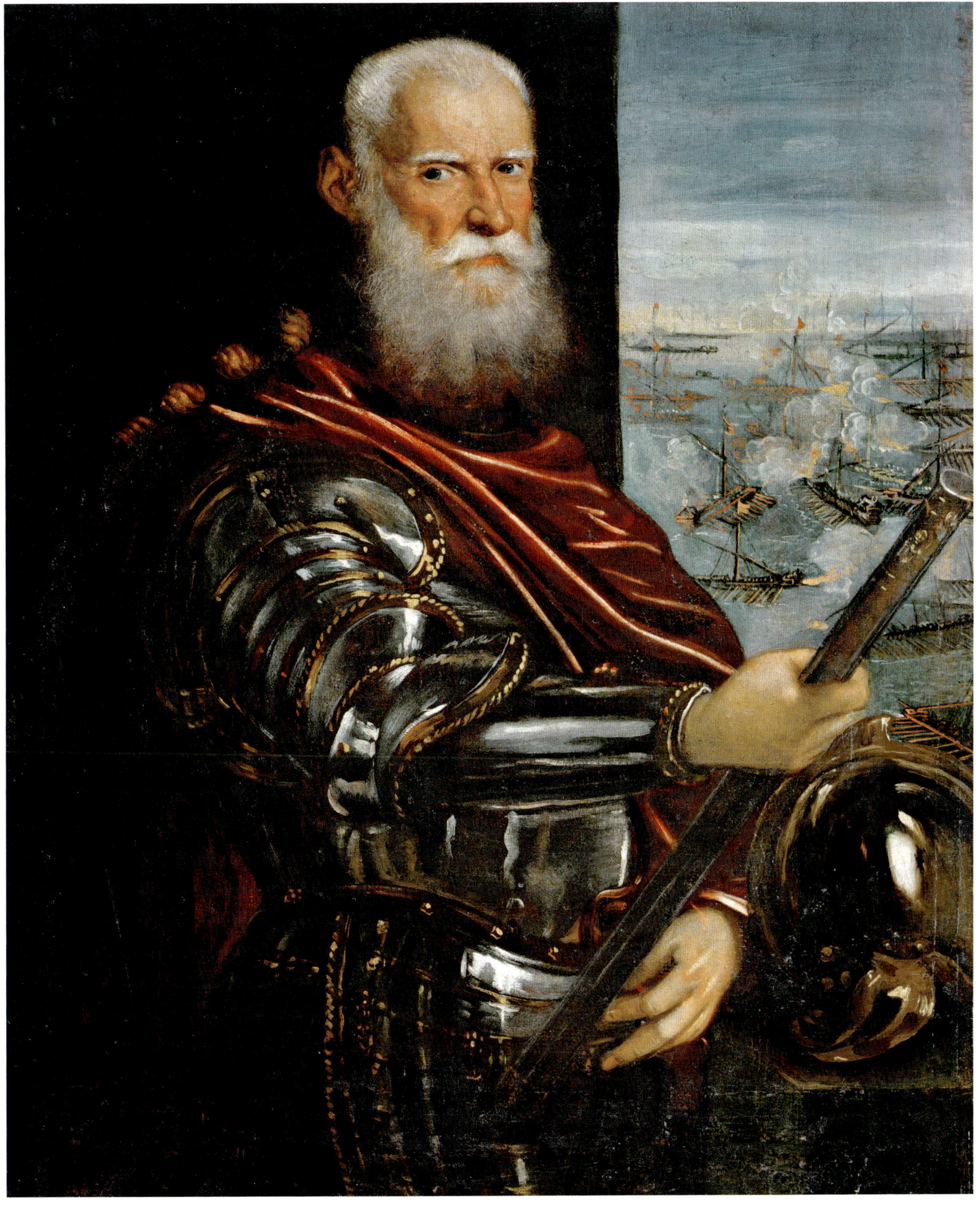

cat. 40

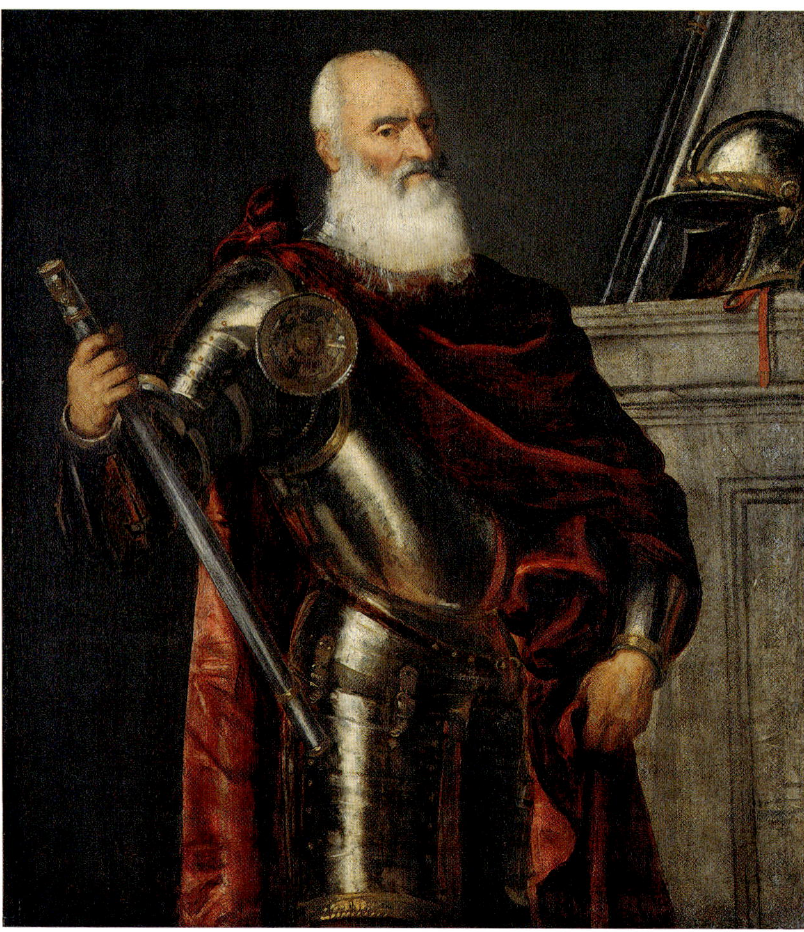

Fig. 95
Titian
Vincenzo Cappello, 1540
Oil on canvas
National Gallery of Art, Washington, DC

homage to the emperor's earlier likeness.[57] The lapse of three years would allow for the appropriate decorum, D'Avalos's image complementing rather than competing with the model. Unlike Charles, who is represented holding a sword aloft, D'Avalos stands firm beside a small page carrying his helmet. The contrast of the formidable general and tiny page lends the image a sense of monumentality and hints at the human interaction that Titian attained with the same sitter about seven years later in a multifigure composition, the *Allocution of Alfonso d'Avalos* (Museo Nacional del Prado, Madrid), where Alfonso addresses his troops.[58]

The confrontational stare in *Vincenzo Cappello* announces a development, that of a newly aggressive sitter who seems as if he could crush his foes through sheer force of will. Cappello (1469–1541) served five times as the Venetian supreme naval commander, the Capitano Generale da Mar, and was knighted by Henry VII of England. Although his naval career ended unhappily at the hands of the Ottoman forces, Cappello returned to Venice and was elected procurator in 1539. The splendid portrait, generally attributed to Titian, derives from Titian's *Francesco Maria della Rovere*, but now a larger figure dominates the pictorial field, and the expression is more bellicose than thoughtful. Cappello brandishes the baton of command, while other attributes of military leadership, stacked on a shelf in the background, allude to his many appointments as Capitano Generale da Mar.[59] The various copies of Titian's *Vincenzo Cappello* attest to its popularity.[60] In fact, its portrait formula inspired Tintoretto and Veronese, as illustrated by *Sebastiano Venier* and *Agostino Barbarigo* respectively.

Pietro Aretino, in a letter of December 25, 1540, to Nicolò Molino, opens a sonnet devoted to a just-completed portrait by Titian of Admiral Vincenzo Cappello.[61] Those who judge the Washington picture to be from Titian's hand have generally accepted this to be the canvas to which Aretino refers.[62] Yet, the earliest inventory of the painting in William Beckford's Scottish collection in 1844 lists it as a Tintoretto, an attribution that continues to persuade some scholars.[63] The current volume therefore offers readers a chance to revisit these lively questions of connoisseurship.[64]

On the question of authorship, many observe a quality of finish suggestive of Titian's hand, and the highlights on the armor and helmet seem typical of Titian.[65] Yet, the linear treatment of the beard, the broad and summary handling of the crimson fabric, and the anatomical conception of the sitter's hands are slightly uncharacteristic of his practice. The treatment of the face is very similar to that in portraits of older men by Tintoretto, such as *Jacopo Soranzo* (fig. 17) and *Giovanni Mocenigo* (Gemäldegalerie, Berlin).[66] The *Portrait of a Widow* (Staatliche Kunstsammlungen, Dresden) stands as a testament to the manner in which some of the softer, more carefully executed works by Tintoretto have historically been assigned to Titian.[67] Raffaello Borghini's praise of Tintoretto in *Il riposo* (1584) remains relevant here: "in coloring he is said to have truly imitated nature, and most particularly Titian, so much so that many portraits done by him are held to be by Titian's hand."[68] The sometimes close stylistic affinity among the artists leaves open the possibility that, similar to the sixteenth-century audiences Borghini mentions, we may have under-

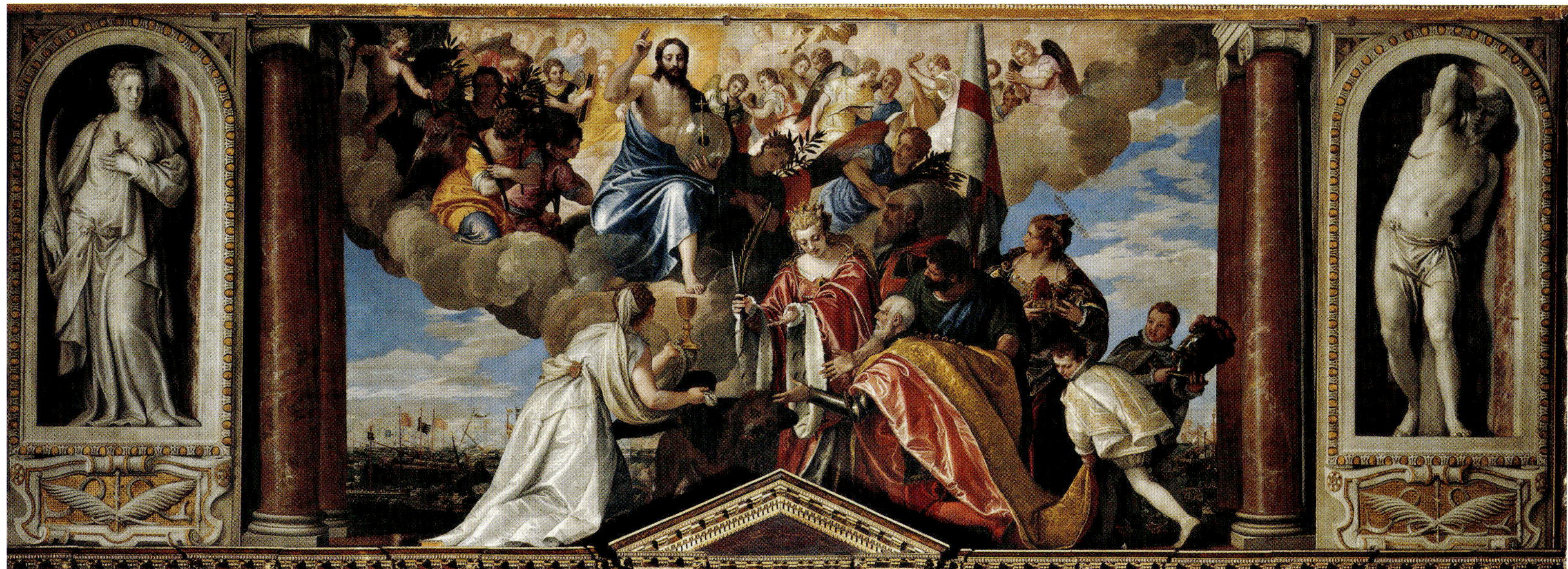

Fig. 96
Veronese
Allegory of the Battle of Lepanto with Sebastiano Venier, after 1574
Oil on canvas
Sala del Collegio, Palazzo Ducale, Venice

estimated Tintoretto's skills of emulation, attributing one of his works to Titian. Whether by Titian or Tintoretto, the *Vincenzo Cappello* represents a memorable portrayal of this powerful admiral.

The *Vincenzo Cappello* set a standard that Tintoretto's *Sebastiano Venier* and Veronese's *Agostino Barbarigo* would uphold in the early 1570s. By the autumn of 1571, the Venetian Republic had spent more than a decade arranging a counteroffensive to the spreading Turkish domination in the Eastern Mediterranean. A Holy League, combining fleets from Venice, Spain, the Papal States, and other Christian powers, confronted an even larger Ottoman armada on October 7 off the western coast of Greece. The crushing defeat of the Ottoman forces was taken as a sign of God's favor, although subsequent Christian naval supremacy in the Eastern Mediterranean was short-lived. For this battle, the leader of the Venetian forces was Sebastiano Venier (1496–1578), whose portrait by Tintoretto celebrates the victory.[69] The elderly but formidable sitter dominates the field to a greater extent than most earlier portraits of warriors; the brushwork constituting the reflections on the armor shows Tintoretto at his most economical and dazzling. Venier's cloak, with its awkward folds, must be by the hand of an assistant, who may also have been responsible for the background scene of raging cannon fire and smoke from the galleys. Heavier fighting, however, was actually sustained by the men under Venice's second in command, Agostino Barbarigo (d. 1571), whose posthumous portrait was painted by Veronese. In the course of the battle, Barbarigo took a crossbow arrow in his left eye and died of the wound two days later.[70] He appears in Veronese's canvas holding an arrow, like Saint Sebastian, but here an attribute of civic martyrdom.[71] In addition, Veronese's *Agostino Barbarigo* has been cut down, trimmed on both sides and the bottom, suggesting that it too perhaps once included a battle scene at the lower right.[72]

The many portraits surrounding the Battle of Lepanto testify to a lucrative competition between Tintoretto and Veronese. Certainly the magnitude of the glorious military victory spurred demand for portraits of all major protagonists and opportunities for the painters to upstage each other. For example, Ridolfi singled out the episode of the wounding of Agostino Barbarigo within Tintoretto's huge narrative painting of the Battle of Lepanto for the Palazzo Ducale (lost), and Veronese executed the large canvas titled *Allegory of the Battle of Lepanto with Sebastiano Venier* (fig. 96).[73] In each case, the painter of the great narrative painting in the seat of government would have known that his rival had executed a superlative portrait of the same individual. Something of their stylistic differences is apparent in these two admiral portraits, both of which seem to have been calibrated to fit the sitter's disposition and painter's predilection. Barbarigo is gener-

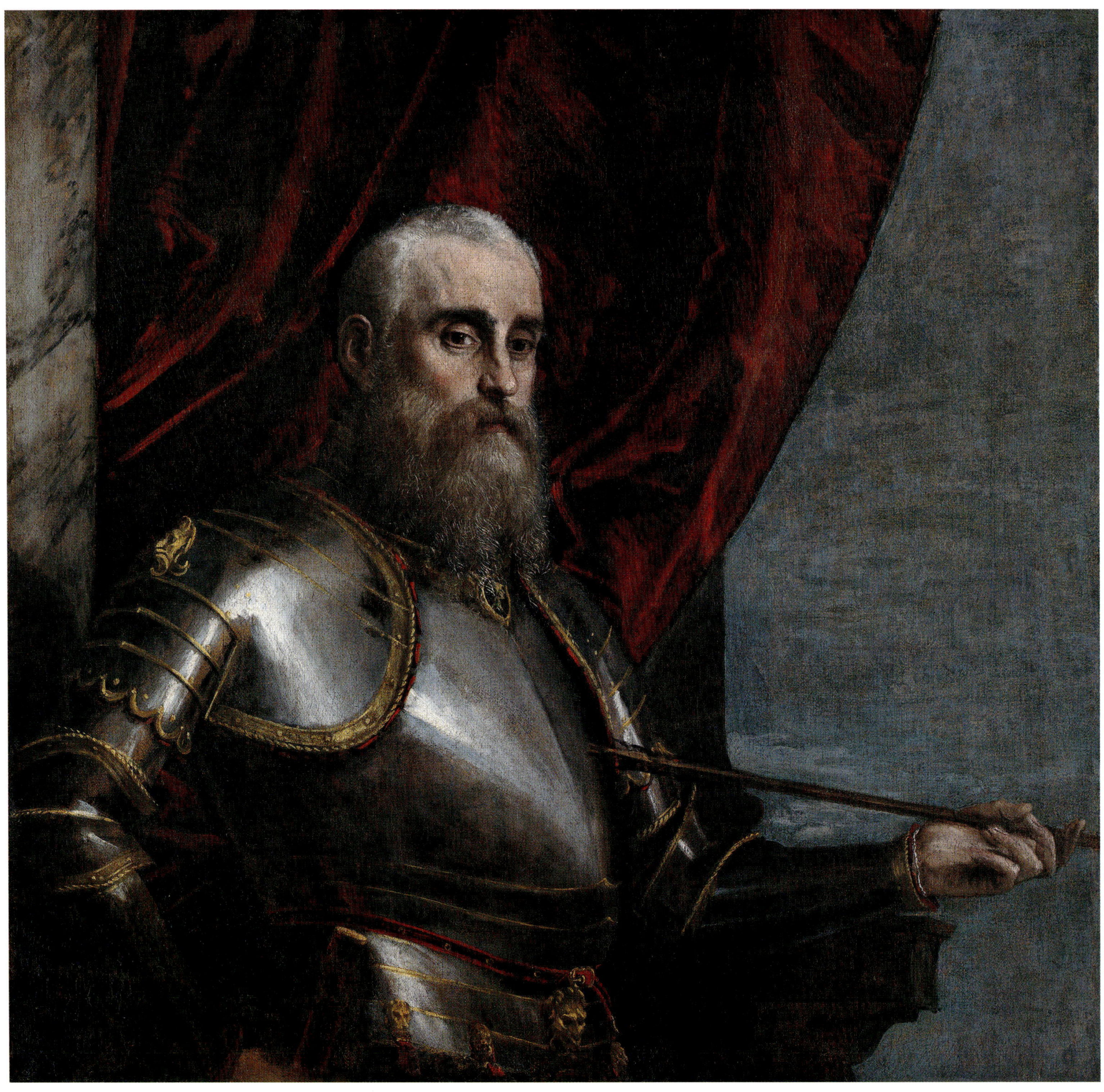

cat. 41

ally praised in the historical sources as a thoughtful moderator between the acerbic Venier and the rest of the Holy League, and Veronese shows a conciliatory leader, albeit rendered in silvery, funereal hues, appropriate for a memorial portrait. Veronese's usual repertoire of props has been edited to the essentials of marble columns, a plinth, and crimson curtain. Long a symbol of fortitude, the gray marble column in this context carries the hint of the tomb; the tone is less valedictory and more elegiac. Tintoretto's *Sebastiano Venier*, by contrast, depicts a vibrant, even cantankerous character whose acute stare and incisive posture communicate authority. His extended battle baton keeps the viewer at a distance. Tintoretto rose to the challenge of representing this imposing figure, deploying his own artistic forces across the parts of the canvas that depict the admiral's mantel and armor; the heavy impastos on the polished steel generate fireworks of their own.[74]

While Tintoretto painted Venier's costume deftly, without recourse to underdrawing, other studies of armor do survive among the drawings of Titian and Veronese.[75] Titian's *Philip II* (fig. 97) of 1551 may be the portrait shipped by the Spanish prince to his aunt Mary of Hungary, with a letter apologizing for the haste with which Titian had painted his armor, adding that "if there were time it would have been done over again."[76] Despite such reservations, the work initiated a long stream of imperial commissions in other genres. One wonders what Titian might have thought of Philip's critique, since the armor in the picture appears reasonably well painted, and Titian's *Alfonso d'Avalos* suggests that the artist had mastered this skill decades earlier. Titian's steely portrayals in three-quarter length proved formative for a subsequent generation of artists. Tintoretto adopts this formula, even as he transforms it with a painterly bravura that seems to match the volatility of Sebastiano Venier. In Veronese's example, the heroics of pain, death, and human valor find a quieter painterly requiem, meant to preserve the fame of the fallen Barbarigo. Each painter in his own way builds on the antique legacy of Apelles and Alexander.

— JG, FI

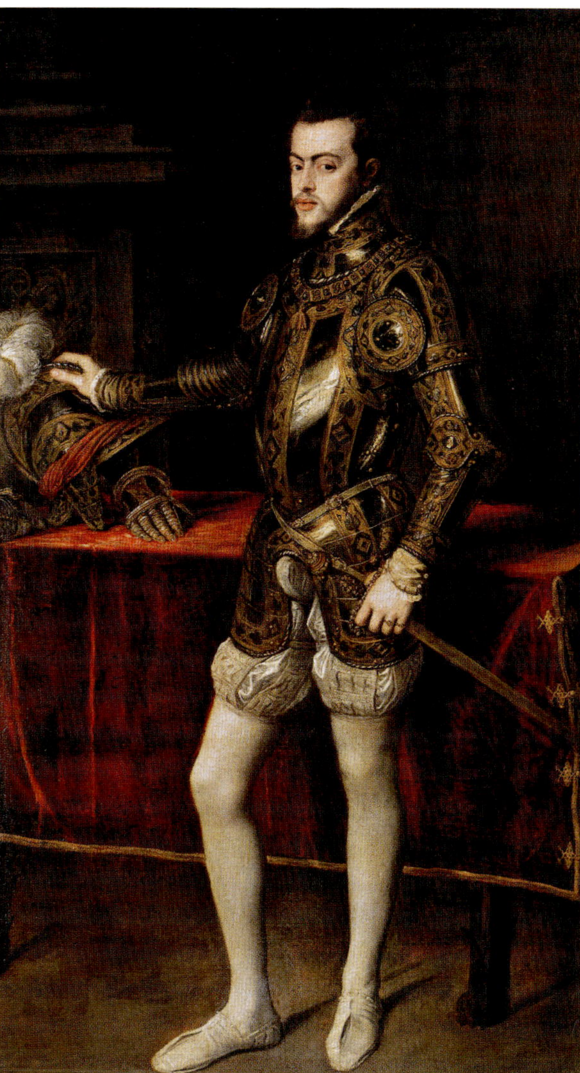

Fig. 97
Titian
Philip II, 1551
Oil on canvas
Museo Nacional del Prado, Madrid

Portraits of Family and Children

TITIAN
Ranuccio Farnese, 1542
National Gallery of Art,
Washington, DC
(cat. 42)

VERONESE
Iseppo da Porto and His Son Adriano, about 1551
Galleria degli Uffizi,
Florence
(cat. 43)

VERONESE
Livia da Porto Thiene and Her Daughter Porzia, about 1551
The Walters Art Museum,
Baltimore
(cat. 44)

In the Renaissance, having one's progeny recorded in portraiture allowed for a certain "shoring up" against the vagaries of fate—only about 60 percent of children survived to adulthood.[77] Likenesses of children were a sign of status and could even be circulated in the hope of furthering the marriage prospects of the sitter.[78] Not surprisingly, portraits of the young frequently show the son or daughter with the comportment and costume of the parent, suggesting a continuity of virtue and elegance across generations. This is true of Veronese's *Iseppo da Porto and His Son Adriano* and *Livia da Porto Thiene and Her Daughter Porzia*, where the finery of the children's attire is coordinated with that of the parents, down to the jewelry and embroidered and fur trims. Although these children are quite young—Adriano is perhaps five years old, and Porzia perhaps four—their gender roles are already distinguished by their outfits.[79]

The costume shown in children's portraits also often signals family ambition and power. Titian's *Ranuccio Farnese* shows the twelve-year-old wearing an oversize cloak bearing the insignia of the Knights of Malta, a reference to his priorship of the Knights' property of San Giovanni dei Forlani in Venice.[80] Yet in the midst of all this parading of status and familial expectation, both Titian and Veronese manage to introduce notes of humor and empathy that naturalize and validate the roles of children. Children are not simply shown, in the words of Leon Battista Alberti, as solemn "pledges and securities of marital love"; they also appear with a lighthearted innocence and spontaneity appropriate to their age.[81] Tintoretto, by contrast, contributed little to the genre, only occasionally depicting children as onlookers in religious narrative paintings.[82]

Childish buoyancy and charm lie at the heart of Titian's *Clarissa Strozzi* of 1542 (fig. 98). The two-year-old daughter of a rich Florentine banking family appears in pearl necklace and bracelet wearing a bejeweled belt (*cintura*) that swings gently from her waist. She has stopped long enough to embrace a timid dog and offer him a biscuit. As Jaffé has noted,

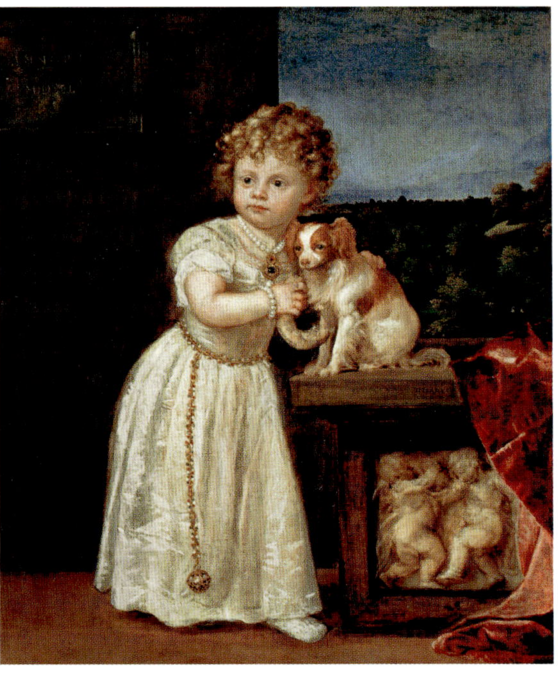

Fig. 98. Titian, *Clarissa Strozzi*, 1542, oil on canvas, Gemäldegalerie, Staatliche Museen zu Berlin

Clarissa's pose follows an ancient prototype of Cupid stringing his bow, which, together with the frolicking putti on the relief at lower right and the pair of distant swans in the background, suggests that love and marriage are intended for the sitter's future.[83] Presumably a parent or attendant accompanied the two-year-old during the sitting, and it may have been painted in her family's residence in exile in San Canciano in Venice.[84] Not all of Titian's attempts to capture and hold a child's attention succeeded as well as the Strozzi portrait: when the young Archduchess Catherine sat for Titian at Innsbruck in 1548, she grew bored, and her portrait was later judged to be too severe.[85]

A hint of youthful impetuosity also marks Titian's *Ranuccio Farnese* in the boy's alert face and searching eyes. The rest of his gesture and costume, however, resembles Titian's formula for depicting fashionable gentlemen holding gloves. According to a letter of 1542 written to Ranuccio's older brother,

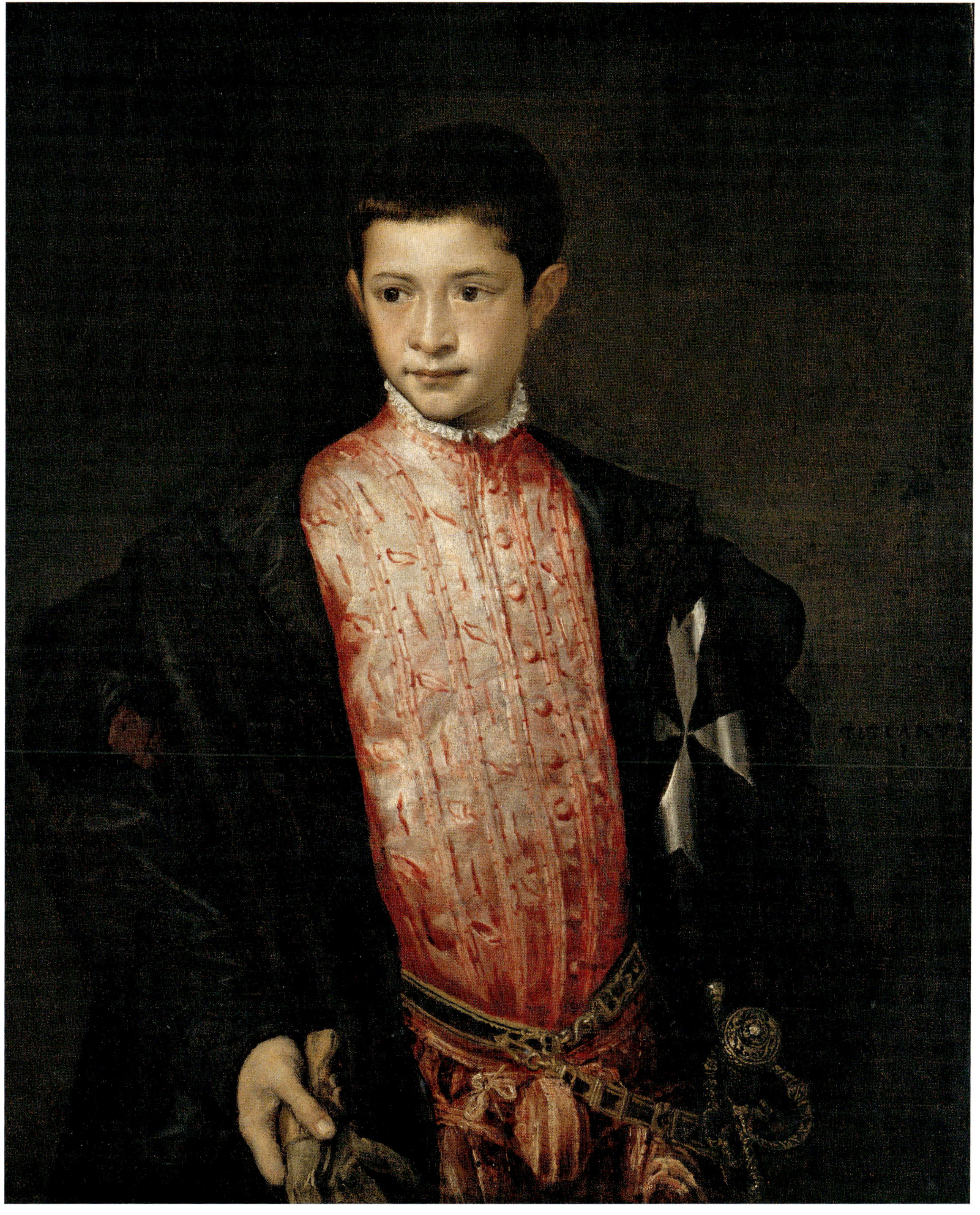

cat. 42

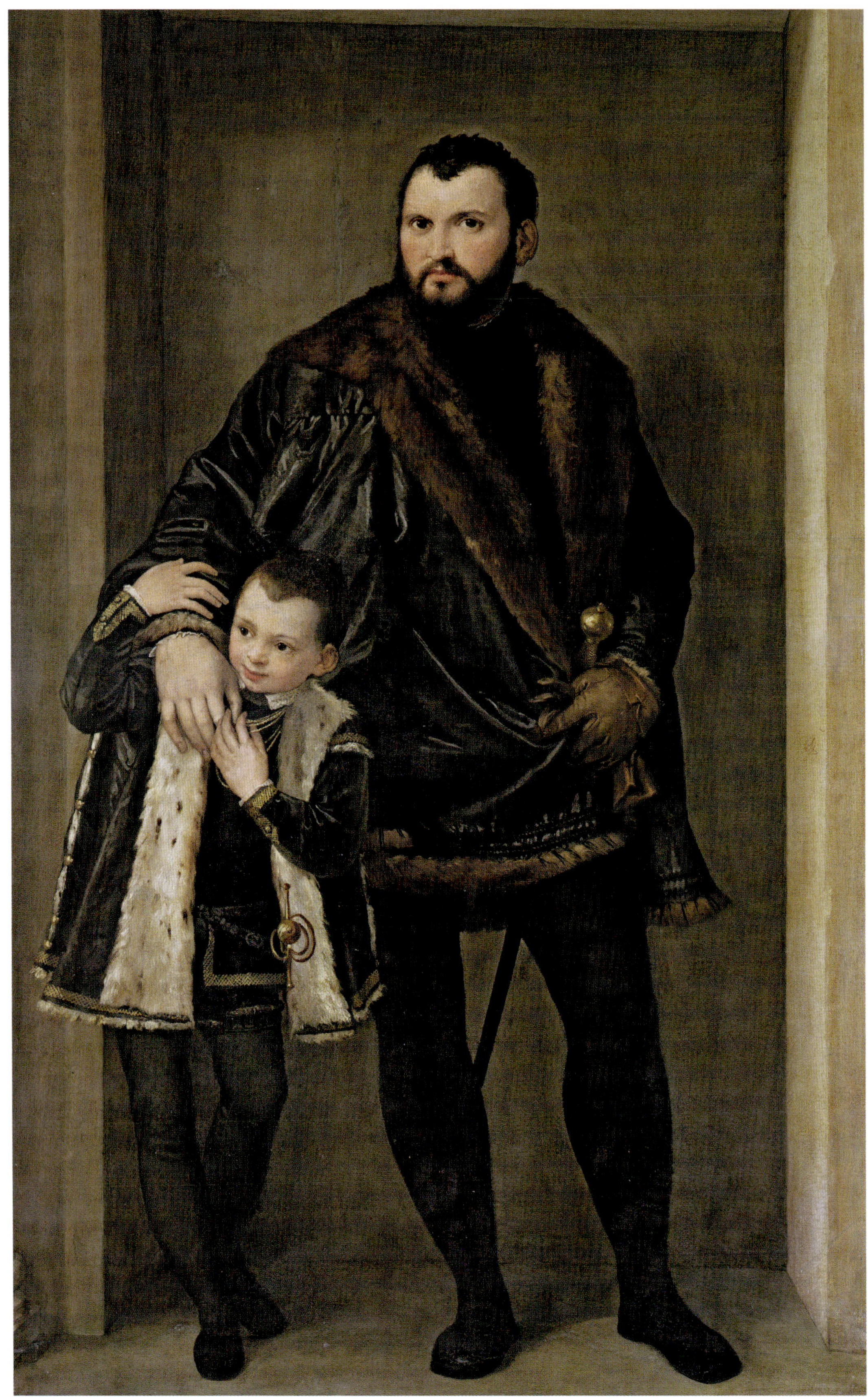

cat. 43

"Titian's excellence is to be admired, particularly since he did it [the portrait] partly in the presence of and partly without Signor Prior [Ranuccio]."[86] Titian depicts Ranuccio with a draped Maltese mantle slipping from his shoulders, a clever use of scale that reminds us of the sitter's tenderness even as it projects a distinguished future. Three years after the portrait was painted, Ranuccio's grandfather Pope Paul III saw to the boy's elevation to the College of Cardinals.[87] Following the warm reception of Ranuccio's portrait, other members of the Farnese commissioned important works from Titian, including portraits like *Pope Paul III* (cat. 7) and mythological subjects such as the *Danaë* (cat. 27).

Like Titian, Veronese captured spontaneous effects and appearances of youthful élan in his family portraits. The brilliant, high-key colors of Veronese's *Livia da Porto Thiene and Her Daughter Porzia* are quite different from the hues of Titian's *Clarissa Strozzi*, even if both works are rare full-length portraits of females. In general, full-length portraits of adults were not yet common in Italian art, and were more frequent on the Venetian *terraferma* than in Venice.[88] Painted about 1551, before the artist had moved definitively to Venice, these early works show his assurance even in a novel format. The Veronese canvas was meant to hang with its pendant, *Iseppo da Porto and His Son Adriano*, probably in the family's palace in Vicenza.[89]

The setting of Veronese's pendants corresponds to the Palladian fabric of Palazzo Iseppo da Porto: the monumental, planar surfaces, the warm, buff-colored stone and plaster, and an engaged half-column that appears at the far left in Iseppo and Adriano's portrait (a similar element was likely eliminated when the female portrait was cut down and the strange floor patterning added at the bottom).[90] The mother's solid, triangular form extends to protect her daughter, who spontaneously twists around from behind her and looks wide-eyed at the viewer. Livia's gaze points us toward the completion of the family's image in the nearby pendant of husband and son. Both Iseppo and Livia came from noble families involved in Vicenza's burgeoning silk trade, so it is appropriate that Veronese gives such painterly attention to their silk clothing.[91] A drawing in the Louvre shows that the artist used models wearing the da Porto's garments during the preparation of their portraits (fig. 99); the man is clearly not Iseppo, and the boy's face is highly idealized. In the final painted version, Iseppo holds his head slightly more erect, and his fingers touch Adriano's. In fact, he seems to have removed one of his gloves for the very purpose of connecting with his son; paternal gallantry contrasts charmingly with filial innocence.[92] Veronese's representation is notable, then, in that few Renaissance portraitists depict such a tender exchange between father and son.

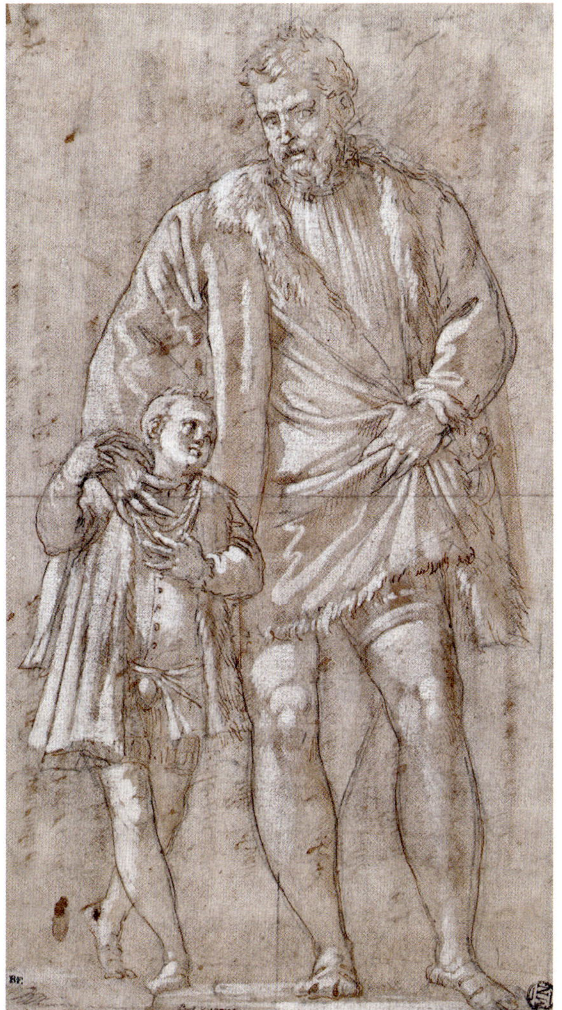

Fig. 99
Veronese
Study for Iseppo da Porto and His Son Adriano, about 1551
Pen and ink and wash over gray chalk on paper
Musée du Louvre, Paris

The Venetian willingness to represent children and families in full-length format and with greater expression corresponds with developments in religious paintings as well. Both Titian and Veronese painted large votive works in which children provide a counterpoint of charming naïveté to the pious narrative of solemn veneration. In Titian's altarpiece the *Madonna di Ca' Pesaro* (fig. 47), at the bottom right corner, little Nicolò seems to disobey instructions to look straight ahead, and instead turns to

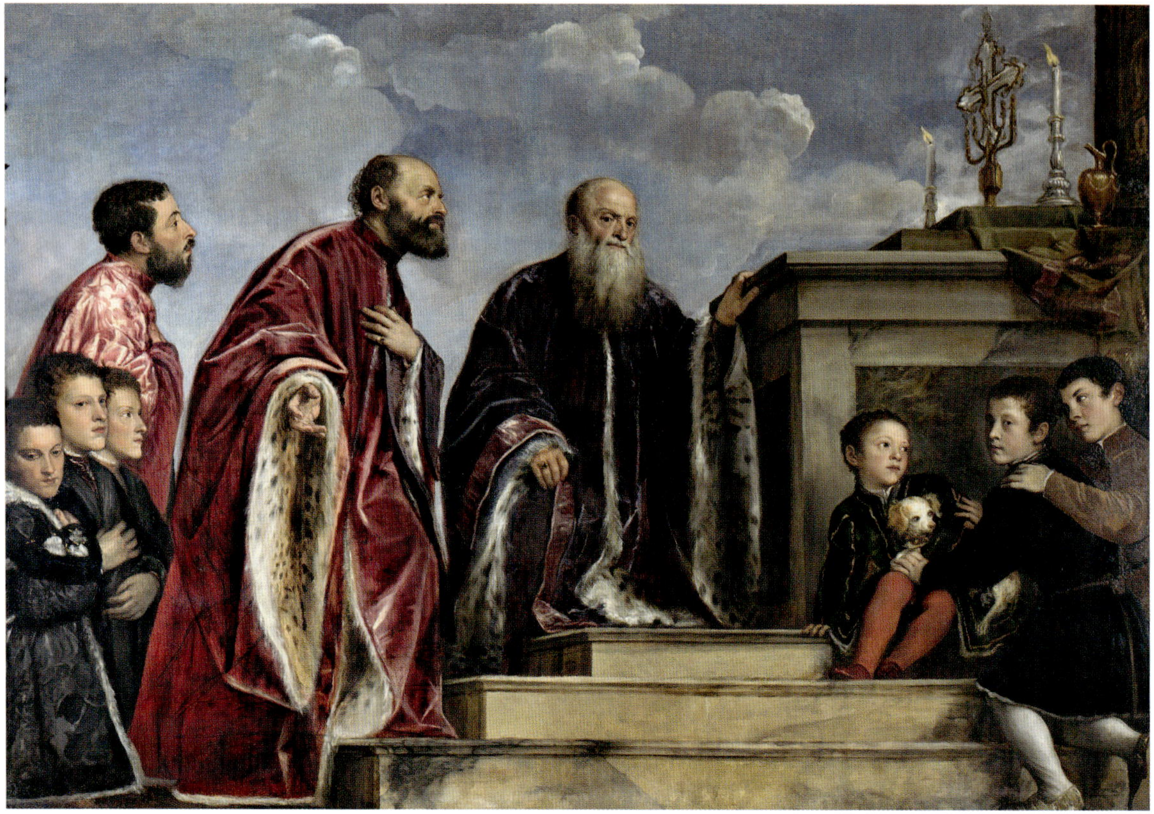

Fig. 100
Titian
The Vendramin Family, Venerating a Relic of the True Cross, about 1540–45, reworked mid-1550s
Oil on canvas
The National Gallery, London

connect with the viewer's gaze, thus bringing us into the world of the picture. When Titian is later commissioned to record the Vendramin family at the foot of a reliquary containing splinters from the True Cross (fig. 100), he casts the seven sons in roles appropriate to their respective ages: the eldest, Lunardo, mimics the posture of his father, who looks to the cross, while the group of the youngest three at lower right pay more attention to the dog and the approaching viewer than to the altar. The boys' postures and wrinkled hose suggest that requirements of decorum and familial duty have not yet subdued their playfulness and curiosity.

In a similar spirit, Veronese's *Supper at Emmaus* (fig. 56) depicts no fewer than ten children, offspring of the patrons who stand at the right, interspersed around Christ's table. The much expanded cast thus both witnesses the miracle and links the events to daily life. In his *Madonna of the Cuccina Family* (about 1571, Staatliche Kunstsammlungen, Dresden), Veronese masters what one might call a "choreography of cuteness" in which the restless energy of the six children activates the tableaux: one climbs a column, another hugs his mother, while a third, in matching costume, grabs at the hind leg of a dog.

Whereas patrons would initiate portrait commissions, and presumably have the final say on which family members are depicted, it seems that Tintoretto had little interest in child portraiture, in contrast to Titian and Veronese, who evidently took great delight in the subject and its potential for charm. No independent portraits of very young children survive from Tintoretto's hand, and very few inhabit his larger oeuvre.[93] While Tintoretto approaches votive portraiture with innovative compositions—witness his *Madonna of the Treasurers* (fig. 12)—youthful tenderness never intrudes upon the adult sphere. Part of the reason is that Tintoretto's multifigure portraits generally depict figures as officeholders in the Venetian government, and not as members of families. But perhaps Tintoretto's temperament was simply less suited than Titian's or Veronese's to the jesting counterpoint and innocence of the genre.

—JG

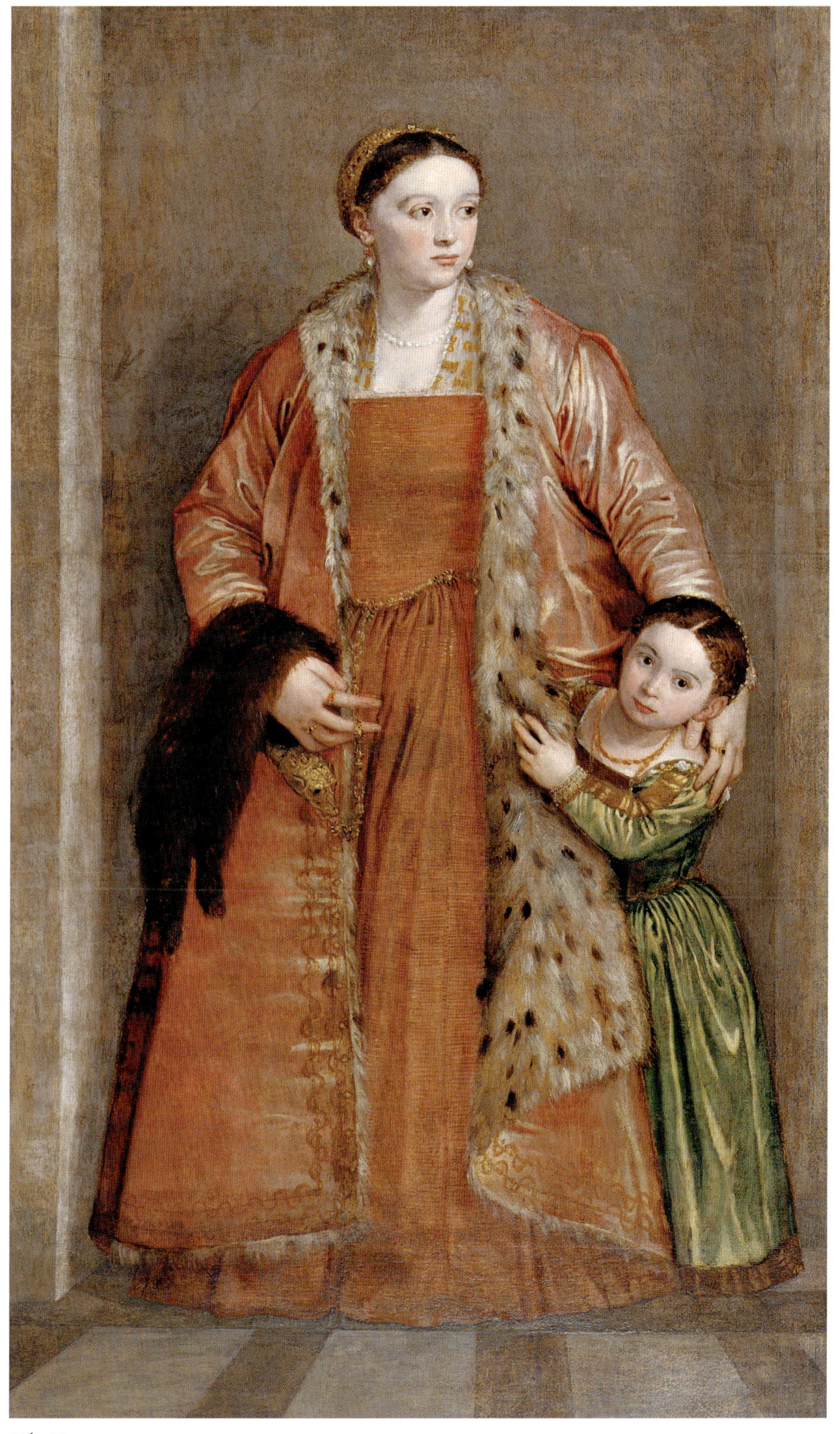

cat. 44

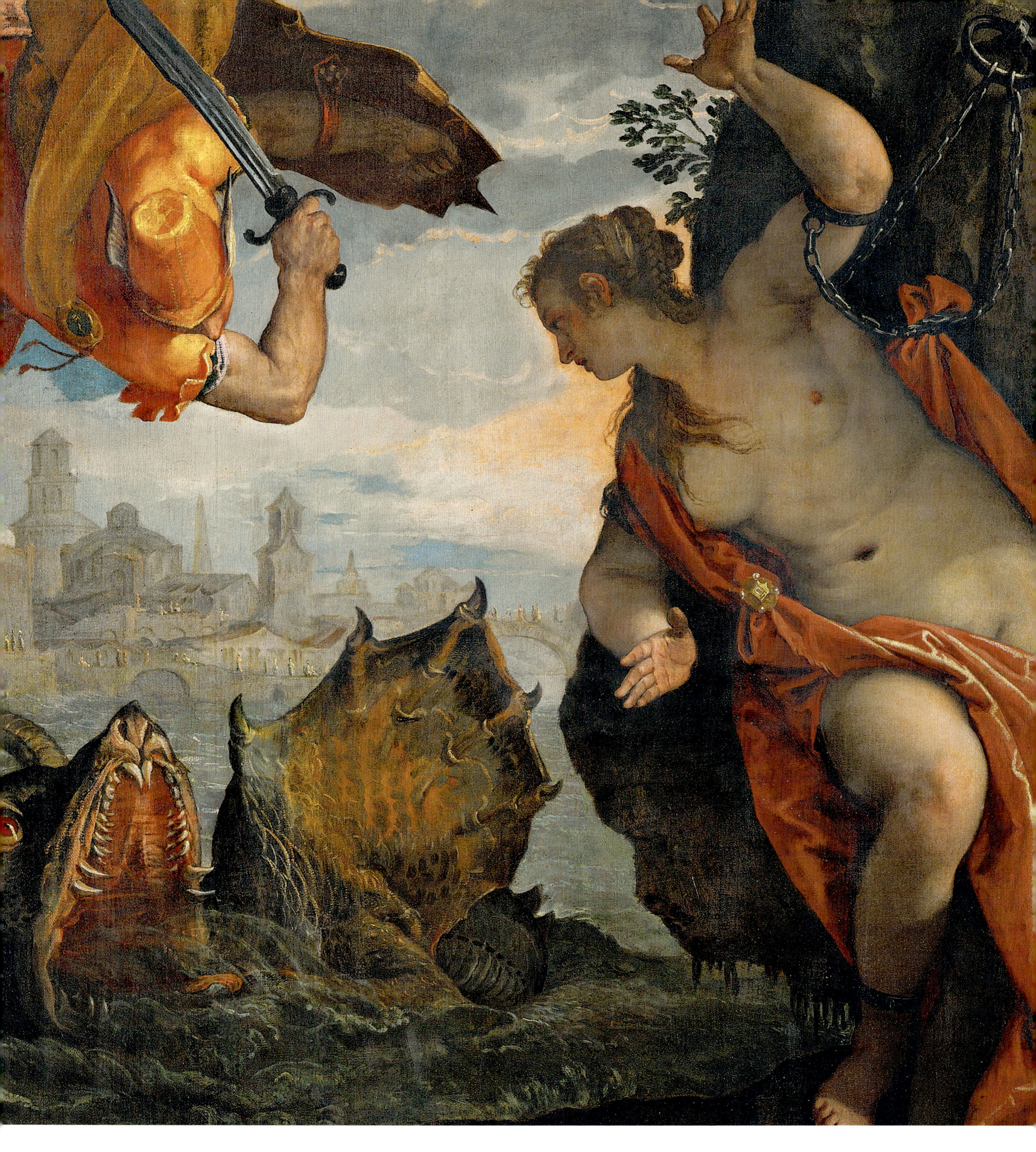

Late Styles

With its thick accumulation of visible brushstrokes, Titian's *Christ Carrying the Cross* (cat. 4) from 1565–70 makes clear the extraordinary evolution of the painter's style, particularly when compared with the pictures from the time of his apprenticeship some sixty years earlier (cat. 3). Titian's late manner was a result of decades spent experimenting with the possibilities of oil paint on canvas. The paintings he created in the 1550s through the 1570s—the last quarter century of his career—are not only manifestly different from those made in his youth, but also from those of his maturity (cat. 21). Titian's late style, or styles, can be seen as a consequence of several factors: his reactions to other artists, physical limitations related to his advancing age, and, above all, his continued painterly development. Titian was referred to as "elderly" (by himself as well as by others) as early as the 1540s. He was already sixty when Tintoretto rose to prominence with the *Miracle of the Slave* in 1548 (fig. 5), and according to the norms of his time and place, there was no question that he had reached old age. Thus, much of the drama of Titian's *ultima maniera* played out while Tintoretto and Veronese were in the first decades of their development as independent painters.

The stylistic traits that characterize "late Titian" begin to emerge in works of the early 1550s. A good example is the *Danaë* painted for Philip II of Spain about 1551–53 (fig. 78), which differs from the version of 1544–45 (cat. 27) in its looser pictorial technique, with individual brushstrokes left visible as dabs of color. Following his visit to Rome in 1545–46, where he encountered first-hand great numbers of works by Michelangelo and other adherents of Central Italian *disegno*, Titian seems to have cast his lot decisively with Venetian *colorito*, a term that refers not simply to color but also to the application of paint, and carries with it the implication of a mode of creation based on direct perception through the senses rather than an apprehension of ideal form.[1] The first distinction between "the *disegno* of Michelangelo and the *colorito* of Titian" as aesthetic ideals appeared in 1548, and Titian seems to have made a strategic decision that the way to secure his reputation as Michelangelo's equal lay in exploiting that distinction, forgoing the values of *disegno* in favor of the visual potential of coloring through oil on canvas.[2] Indeed, when questioned about the increased freedom of his brushwork, Titian commented that he had chosen a "new path" that would bring him fame in the same way that their more refined manners had brought fame to Michelangelo, Raphael, Correggio, and Parmigianino. Otherwise, Titian said, he might be considered their imitator.[3]

Titian's contemporaries recognized the change in his style and its unprecedented visible brushstrokes, which seemed like blotches. A letter by Ludovico Dolce from about 1554 comments on the landscape in Titian's *Venus and Adonis* (fig. 83), calling it a "painterly piece of landscape [*una macchia d'un paese*], of such quality that the reality is not so real."[4] Dolce's wording emphasizes that he found the brushwork distinctive as marks, and not simply as the conveyor of naturalistic space and volume. Vasari, who traveled to Venice in 1566, also used the word *macchie* in describing the technique of Titian's recent works: "The method of work which he employed in these last pictures is no little different from the method of his youth, for the reason that the early works are executed with a certain delicacy and a diligence that are incredible, and they can be seen both from near and from a distance, and these last works are executed with bold strokes, broadly and with blotches of color [*condotte di colpi, tirate via di grosso e con macchie*], insomuch that from near little can be seen, but from a distance they appear perfect."[5] Vasari further warned that this new, loose style was deceptively difficult to master, and that many imitators had failed in their attempts. Paintings in Titian's late style, the biographer asserted, conceal how much effort went into making them.

In the last decades of his career, Titian not only expanded the nature of his brushstrokes but also reduced the scale of his paintings. Indeed, the two developments are related, since the caressing touch of Titian's brushwork—the "old painter's indulgent focus and unhurried pace," in the words of David Rosand—presupposed the hand of the master himself, and this was not easily delegated to others. His laborious manner of applying paint further limited the amount of canvas he could cover. After Tintoretto's public success with the *Miracle of the Slave*, Titian largely abandoned large-scale narrative painting, recognizing that his physical limitations would prevent him from undertaking pictures himself on such a monumental scale.[6] Although Titian had earlier staked a claim as a painter of Venice with large paintings for the Palazzo Ducale and the Venetian *scuole* (fig. 13), by his sixties he had ceded this category to ambitious newcomers. His best later works— those likely to be fully or largely autograph—tend to be moderate in size and focus on fewer principal characters; only a small number include the great crowds of figures that appear in paintings by Tintoretto or Veronese (and that populated many of Titian's own earlier works). Consequently, the few commissions for large-scale paintings that he accepted were assigned primarily to studio assistants.[7]

In a number of paintings from Titian's final years, such as the *Crowning with Thorns* (fig. 22), *Saint Jerome in the Wilderness* (cat. 51), *Boy with Dogs in a Landscape* (cat. 48), and the *Pietà* (fig. 109), the palette is increasingly monochromatic and tenebrous, the forms are increasingly dissolved, and many details are not brought to a conventional finish. These pictures call to mind Palma Giovane's description, reported by the seventeenth-century critic and biographer Marco Boschini, of how the aged Titian worked and reworked his pictures, sometimes turning them to the wall for months without looking at them, then revising them, building them up layer by layer. Like a surgeon, he would remove swelling or excess flesh or "straighten an arm if the bone structure is not quite correct," ignoring his "patient's pain." In the final phases, according to Palma, Titian rubbed the highlights together, to bring them closer to the middle tones, and blended one color with another, painting "more with the finger than with the brush."[8]

These paintings from Titian's last years have come to be seen as a classic example (alongside works by artists such as Michelangelo, Rembrandt, Beethoven, and Goethe) of a "style of old age," in which the artist, at the end of his life, casts off the boundaries of conventional form and achieves a new sublimity of vision. While the style of old age had been a recognized concept in art theory since the sixteenth century, it was twentieth-century German art historians, with eyes accustomed to the techniques of Impressionism and Expressionism, who began to define *Altersstil* as a positive phenomenon, associating it not only with a deepened awareness and spirituality that transcend the artist's physical limitations but also with distinctive aesthetic values arising from the lack of conventional finish.[9] Yet, as Philip Sohm has recently reminded us, the art historian must beware of the tendency to apply this construct indiscriminately—if the "senile sublime" is associated only with the greatest artists, we may find it too readily in the works of an artist we deem great.[10]

Indeed, there has recently been something of a backlash in Titian studies against the special status accorded the group of paintings traditionally held to represent Titian's final style. Charles Hope and others have argued that we should instead take the works sent to Philip II in the late 1560s and 1570s as exemplifying Titian's final style—works, such as *Tarquin and Lucretia* (fig. 107), that include passages of free, expressive brushwork, yet are brought to a higher level of finish. As such, the other group should be considered simply unfinished, the muted color and lack of firm contours seen not as representing a new aesthetic but simply as the result of the old painter's physical decline. This view is buttressed by a letter of 1568 (seconded by later reports), which states that Titian can no longer see what he is painting and that his hand trembles so badly he cannot paint anything.[11] While Charles Hope is right to question received interpretations, he does not allow for the possibility that Titian might intentionally have varied the finish in his paintings, nor does he acknowledge the variety of painting techniques and levels of finish even in the pictures sent to Philip, obvious in very different works, such as *Europa* (fig. 106) and *Perseus and Andromeda* (fig. 77). Moreover, it has long been noted that the *Flaying of Marsyas* (Kromeríz Palace, Archibishopric Olomouc), one of the most characteristic pictures painted in the last years of Titian's life, is in fact signed and therefore presumably completed.[12]

The recent exhibition in Vienna and Venice on Titian's late works seems to have disproved the view that those in the latest style are all unfinished, though some paintings may contain unfinished passages as well as interventions by other hands, perhaps even after Titian's death.[13] While the more colorful and finished paintings may represent Titian's "official" late style, this does not preclude the possibility that the artist was indeed pursuing a different aesthetic in other paintings, especially when he did not have to be particularly concerned about a patron's expectations. This style seems to be particularly associated with subjects that have deep personal resonance for Titian. The *Pietà* was destined to hang above his own tomb; like *Saint Jerome*, it includes a self-portrait of the elderly artist. Both convey a poignant sense of an aging individual confronting death. In other works, such as *Boy with Dogs*, Titian seems to be returning to the elusive poetry of his youth.

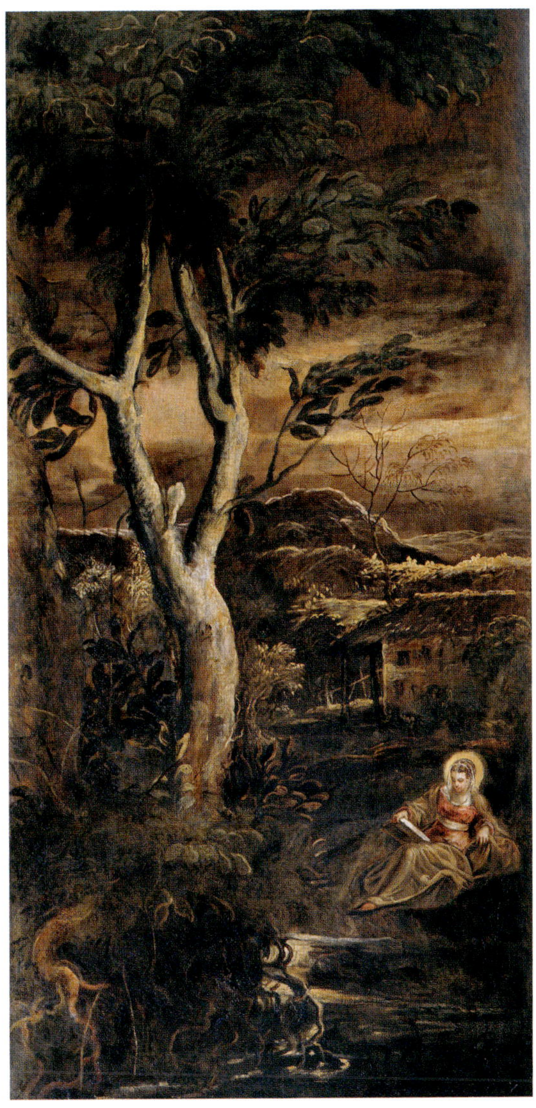

Fig. 101
Tintoretto
Saint Reading (*Saint Mary Magdalen*), about 1582–83
Oil on canvas
Scuola Grande di San Rocco, Venice

In the oeuvre of Tintoretto, the closest analogue to Titian's late style appears in the younger artist's visionary works in the Sala Superiore and Sala Inferiore at the Scuola Grande di San Rocco, such as the *Saint Reading* (*Saint Mary Magdalen*) from the Sala Terrena (fig. 101) of about 1582–83. Here, the phosphorescent light flowing over the dark, mysterious landscape suggests a world charged with currents of divine energy. Other works in this vein include Tintoretto's tragic late *Self-Portrait* (cat. 56), the *Baptism of Christ* (cat. 53), and *Tarquin and Lucretia* (cat. 46). All are characterized by strong chiaroscuro, a limited palette, and a brooding intensity.

While Tintoretto's brushwork was strikingly open and free from the beginning of his career, and continued to be so in the later works, his technique was very different from Titian's *pittura di macchia*. Rather than building up form with dabs of color, Tintoretto drew with paint, using long lines and strong contours. Scientific analysis of the *Saint Reading* revealed that the landscape forms were sketched in white paint on a black ground, apparently while the black layer was still wet, and modeled only with brown and golden glazes.[14] Paradoxically, although, of the great Venetian painters, he was the one most strongly attacked by Vasari, it was Tintoretto who was most firmly committed to the Central Italian principle of *disegno* and, indeed, sought to present himself as achieving the ideal combination of *disegno* and *colorito*. The *Baptism* and *Tarquin* both show his lifelong devotion to the study of sculpture, a central tenet of Central Italian *disegno*, enriched with his studies from live models.

Nevertheless, while Tintoretto's paintings for

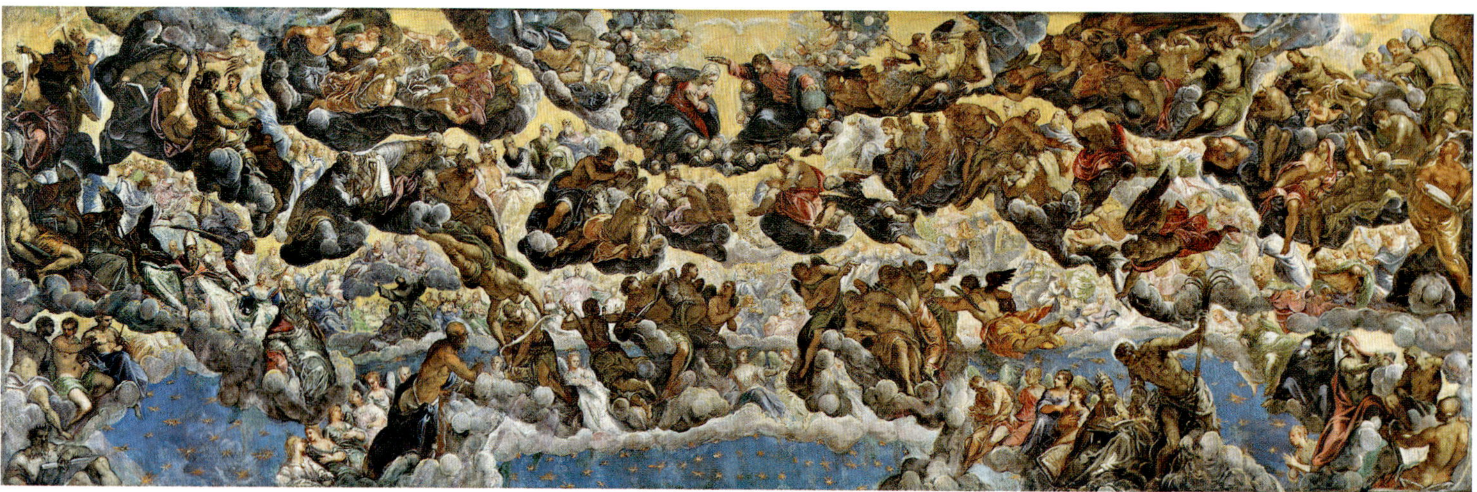

Fig. 102
Tintoretto
Modello for *Paradiso*, 1587–88
Oil on canvas
Museo Thyssen-Bornemisza, Madrid

San Rocco and similar works may represent a particularly compelling aspect of his late career, it is not possible to associate the artist in his last years with a single style. His sketch for the *Paradiso* of 1587–88 (fig. 102), for example, with its pastel tones, conveys a very different feeling from the San Rocco paintings. Hans Tietze suggests a broad distinction between Tintoretto's style at San Rocco, "where he was his own master," and a "Palazzo Ducale style," more conventionally decorative in response to the architectural context and the need to compete with other artists, above all Veronese.[15] Yet Tintoretto's variety is more complex than Tietze's formulation would suggest. The *Baptism of Christ*, the *Temptation of Saint Anthony* (cat. 20), *Tarquin and Lucretia*, and the *Origin of the Milky Way* (fig. 85) were all painted within the span of a few years, yet the two altarpieces differ strikingly from one another in pictorial technique (the *Baptism* much closer to the San Rocco style, the *Temptation* much more finished), as do the two paintings on secular subjects (*Tarquin* almost monochromatic, the *Milky Way* brilliantly colorful). Broadly speaking, it is possible to say that, over the course of his career, Tintoretto's treatment of space becomes more fluid and arbitrary, color more unified, light more diffuse, and brushwork freer—all tendencies that culminate at San Rocco. But the rich variety and unpredictability from commission to commission that characterize Tintoretto's early and middle years continued unabated in his final decades.

Moreover, the difficulty of associating a single style with Tintoretto's later career is compounded by the fact that autograph works by the artist from these years are few and far between. Around 1575, Tintoretto began a major change in his workshop practice. Increasingly, he devoted himself to obtaining commissions, designing compositions, and overseeing their production, while leaving much of the actual painting to his studio assistants. Although he had always had assistants, the *bottega* now became much more of a corporate enterprise. Tintoretto's children Marietta, Domenico, and Marco joined him there, along with a number of other helpers and apprentices, and occasionally other collaborators working on a freelance basis. The degree of the master's involvement, and the resulting level of quality, varied from commission to commission. Even at San Rocco, clearly of great personal importance to Tintoretto, the quality is inconsistent, and in some cases the master seems to have turned the commission entirely over to others.[16]

Although his desire to leave a thriving workshop to his children was undoubtedly the major reason for this change in Tintoretto's artistic practices, also significant were the catastrophic fires in the Palazzo Ducale in 1574 and 1577, which destroyed the important paintings in the halls of the Maggior Consiglio, Senato, and Collegio and resulted in an enormous bounty of commissions for Tintoretto and the other prominent painters of the day, Veronese included. Significantly overextended, Tintoretto delegated much of the execution of his works to his assistants. In the case of one prominent painting, the enormous central section of the ceiling for the Sala del Maggior Consiglio, the middling quality of the studio's production led to complaints, and a public relations campaign led by Tintoretto's associates was necessary to quell the dissatisfaction.[17]

Titian's death in 1576 had also opened up new opportunities for Tintoretto. He made a determined effort to obtain the patronage of Titian's princely clientele, notably the Gonzaga of Mantua and the Hapsburg courts in Madrid and Vienna. Again, success in obtaining commissions from these sources did not necessarily mean that Tintoretto would play a major role in their execution or even their design. His participation in the Gonzaga Cycle (Alte Pinakothek, Munich) seems to have been limited to individual figure drawings and a few rough compositional sketches. In the *Adoration of the Shepherds* (fig. 21), painted for Philip II in 1583, the design, an imaginative reworking of the composition of the same subject at San Rocco, is surely that of Tintoretto himself, but the execution was obviously left to Domenico and other assistants.[18] The years after Titian's death also saw Tintoretto move into an area of subject matter he had left largely unexplored since his youthful *Venus and Mars Surprised by Vulcan* (fig. 81): erotic *poesie*. Pictures such as *Tarquin and Lucretia* and *Danaë* (cat. 29) make clear an intention to serve as Titian's replacement.

Despite the variable quality of his studio productions during his final decades, Tintoretto remained at the summit of Venetian painting until his death in 1594, the last survivor of what was already coming to be recognized as a golden age of Venetian painting. The great *Last Supper* and the *Entombment* (fig. 52) for the Palladian church of San Giorgio Maggiore, probably his final compositions, show his imagination for innovative narrative paintings undiminished, even if Domenico and other assistants wielded the brushes that brought the project to completion.

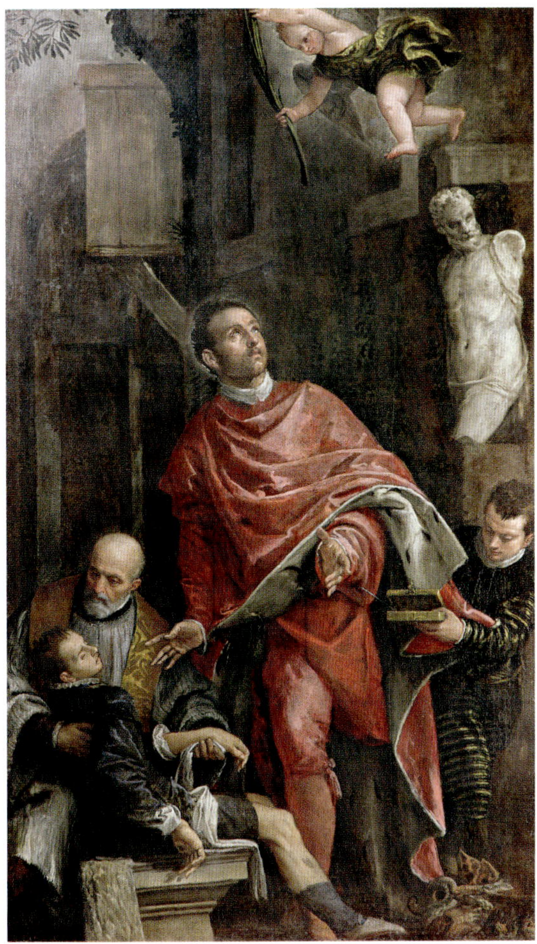

Fig. 103
Veronese
Saint Pantaleon Healing a Child, 1587
Oil on canvas
Church of San Pantalon, Venice

Veronese had barely turned sixty when he was carried away by pneumonia in 1588, after catching cold on a business trip to Treviso. His paintings of the 1580s show him still at the height of his powers, although by the standards of the day he was a man verging on old age. Thus the contemporary complaints about Titian's decrepitude in his last years—and modern questions about the relationship between physical disability and the appearance of his paintings—are less obviously relevant in the case of Veronese.

During these years, new qualities begin to emerge in Veronese's painting that, by virtue of their break with his past work, must be deemed to constitute a late style. The pomp and sunny skies of the earlier works largely disappear; tonalities are increasingly crepuscular. In *Perseus and Andromeda* (cat. 47), the splendor of the mythological paintings of the 1570s—such as *Mars and Venus United by Love* (cat. 34), with its rich, autumnal glow—is replaced with a more somber atmosphere. In Veronese's religious paintings, a new devotional intensity begins to emerge, evident in the *Baptism of Christ* (cat. 54) and *Saint Jerome in the Wilderness* (cat. 52) and especially in the deeply moving *Agony in the Garden* (fig. 112), where the tragic pathos of the subject is accentuated by the extreme chiaroscuro and the intense color glowing in the darkness. The latter painting ushers in the pictorial style of Veronese's final works, which reaches its apogee in *Saint Pantaleon Healing a Child* (fig. 103), completed the year before his death, and marked by strikingly loose, flickering brushwork, thick impasto, and deeply saturated color. While the examples of Titian and Tintoretto undoubtedly had an impact on these developments, Veronese's late style is distinctly his own, particularly his use of rich color to expressive emotional ends.

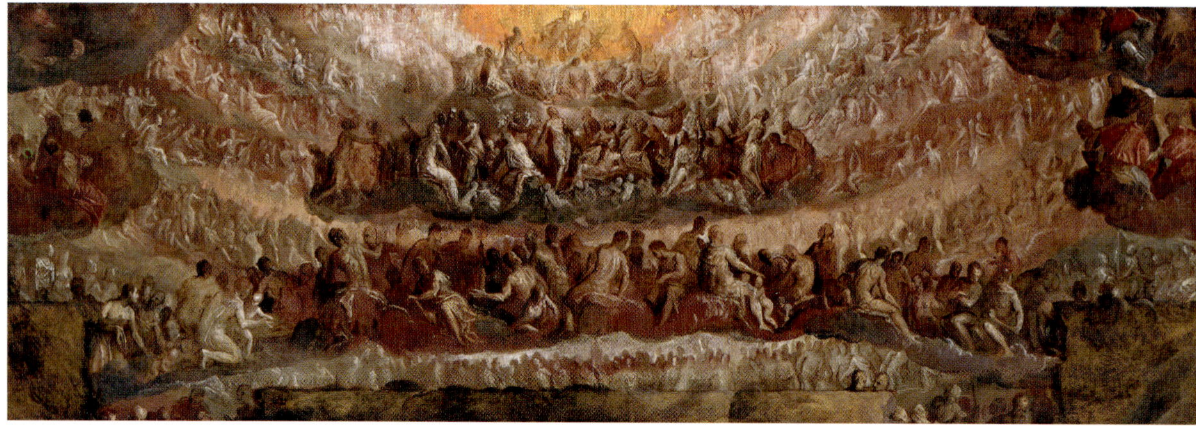

Fig. 104
Veronese
Modello for *Paradiso*, about 1578–82
Oil and tempera (?) on canvas
Palais des Beaux-Arts, Lille

Like Titian and Tintoretto, Veronese maintained an active studio full of relatives, which in his last years included his brother Benedetto; his sons Gabriele and Carletto, still in their teens; and a nephew, Alvise dal Friso, along with a sequence of apprentices.[19] Like Tintoretto, he was busy in the 1580s with commissions for princely patrons around Europe and with major projects for the redecoration of the Palazzo Ducale. Although he too relied on his assistants for these large-scale productions, he was more scrupulous in his quality control than Tintoretto, especially in paintings destined for the most prestigious settings. Where Tintoretto's ceiling for the Sala del Maggior Consiglio excited complaints, Veronese's *Triumph of Venice* on the same ceiling fulfills its function splendidly. Veronese's *Allegory of the Battle of Lepanto with Sebastiano Venier* in the Sala del Collegio (fig. 96) similarly outshines the Tintoretto studio productions from this phase of the palace's decoration. Veronese's skill at monumental public decoration was recognized with the coveted commission, awarded jointly to him and Francesco Bassano, for the *Paradiso*. His *modello* (fig. 104) provides a glimpse of what might have been had death not intervened. Veronese was also more successful than Tintoretto in finding favor with the most important patron of Venetian painting, Philip II. Tintoretto's *Adoration of the Shepherds* (fig. 21) and Veronese's *Annunciation* (fig. 20) were apparently commissioned for the lower part of the high altar at El Escorial as a kind of audition that would permit the king to choose between the two leading painters in Venice after Titian's death. Veronese was the winner; Philip awarded him the commission to complete the altar, which the painter declined, and, in 1586, further offered him the enormous sum of 9000 ducats to move to Spain and join the court. Clearly Philip found in Veronese, not Tintoretto, the heir to Titian that he sought.[20]

By the time of Veronese's death, Tintoretto may have felt like the last man standing, an impression his late *Self-Portrait* seems to convey (cat. 56). Later critics noted that an age ended with the death of these three artists. The seventeenth-century Roman biographer Giovanni Pietro Bellori saw the Venetian school, embodied in Tintoretto, as the last holdout of the Renaissance style: "And although painting endured longer in Venice than elsewhere, neither there nor in Lombardy was that bright tumult of colors more to be heard. It ceased with Tintoretto, the last of the Venetian painters until the present."[21]

At their most personal and distinctive, what the late styles of Titian, Tintoretto, and Veronese have in common is the looseness of their brushwork and the freedom of their approach to color. Each in his own way explored and exploited the potential of *colorito* and, in particular, the possibilities of oil paint on canvas. It might be said that each in his last years became more fully a Venetian painter. From this perspective, their late styles seem to embody the last stage of a great chapter in the history of painting as much as they do the final phases in the individual careers of three painters. Following Bellori and his Venetian contemporaries, we might define the final pictorial achievement of Titian, Tintoretto, and Veronese as the end of the golden age of Venetian painting, the end of the Renaissance, or even the end of the beginning of oil-on-canvas painting.

— RE, FI

Women in Peril

TITIAN
Tarquin and Lucretia, about 1568–71
Musée des Beaux-Arts, Bordeaux
(cat. 45)

TINTORETTO
Tarquin and Lucretia, 1578–80
The Art Institute of Chicago
(cat. 46)

VERONESE
Perseus and Andromeda, late 1570s–early 1580s
Musée des Beaux-Arts, Rennes
(cat. 47)

Titian's paintings of classical myth fall within three distinct phases. The earliest are antiquarian in outlook, culminating in the "Bacchanals" for the Camerino d'Alabastro of 1518–24, which offer vivid reconstructions of ancient ekphrases—verbal descriptions of real or fictive works of art, or literary passages that present veritable word paintings.[22] From the 1530s through the 1550s, Titian cultivated the type of the reclining Venus that originated in the matrimonial context of the *Venus of Urbino* (about 1538; fig. 76) but evolved into allegories of sensual delight (cat. 27).[23] The later mythological paintings for Philip II, which Titian himself termed *poesie*, endowed erotic imagery with the ethos and gravity of tragedy. Although the ravishing figure of a goddess or heroine remains at the core of these compositions, Titian harnesses its seductive power to ensure the viewer's empathy for the fate of the female protagonist. This ranges from commiseration with Venus's futile embrace of Adonis (cat. 33) to trepidation at Actaeon's luckless glimpse of Diana's chaste beauty even as it lures our own gaze (fig. 105). The viewer's sensual enchantment provokes an emotional catharsis, the purgation of pity and fear that Aristotle defined as the principal purpose of tragedy.[24] In two works from around 1560, *Perseus and Andromeda* (1554–56, fig. 77) and *Europa* (1559–62, fig. 106), Titian mesmerizes the viewer with erotic bodies that are exposed, imperiled, and on the verge of being violated or devoured.

Tarquin and Lucretia (fig. 107), which Titian delivered to Philip II a decade later and which is now at the Fitzwilliam Museum, Cambridge, England, pushes this tragic dialectic of beauty and horror further. Titian also executed a variant with a subdued palette and a more uniform level of pictorial detail, now in Bordeaux (cat. 45). Despite its impressive seventeenth-century provenance in the French and English royal collections, some scholars have demoted the Bordeaux canvas to workshop status, though its distinct approach to the theme and reworking of the surface argues that it may be a largely autograph variation, produced during the long gestation of the Cambridge picture.[25] Both versions depict the Etruscan prince Tarquin's assault of Lucretia, the virtuous wife of the Roman general Collatinus. While Collatinus is in the field, Tarquin bursts into Lucretia's chamber and forcibly demands relations at knifepoint, which she valiantly resists. Only when Tarquin finally threatens to kill Lucretia and a male servant, leaving their naked corpses as proof of adultery, does she yield. When her husband returns, Lucretia confesses the defilement and, impervious to forgiveness, thrusts a concealed dagger into her breast. Public uproar at the craven rape and piteous sacrifice drive the Etruscan monarch from Rome and establish the republic. In Renaissance art, images of Lucretia's suicide became popular emblems of uxorial virtue and chastity, in paint-

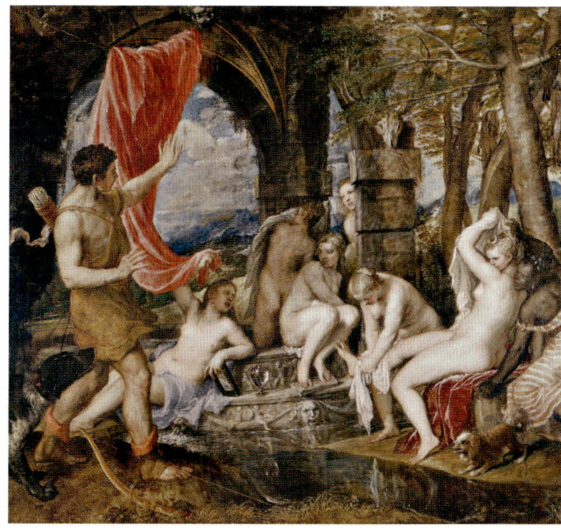
Fig. 105. Titian, *Diana and Actaeon*, 1556–59, oil on canvas, National Gallery of Scotland, Edinburgh

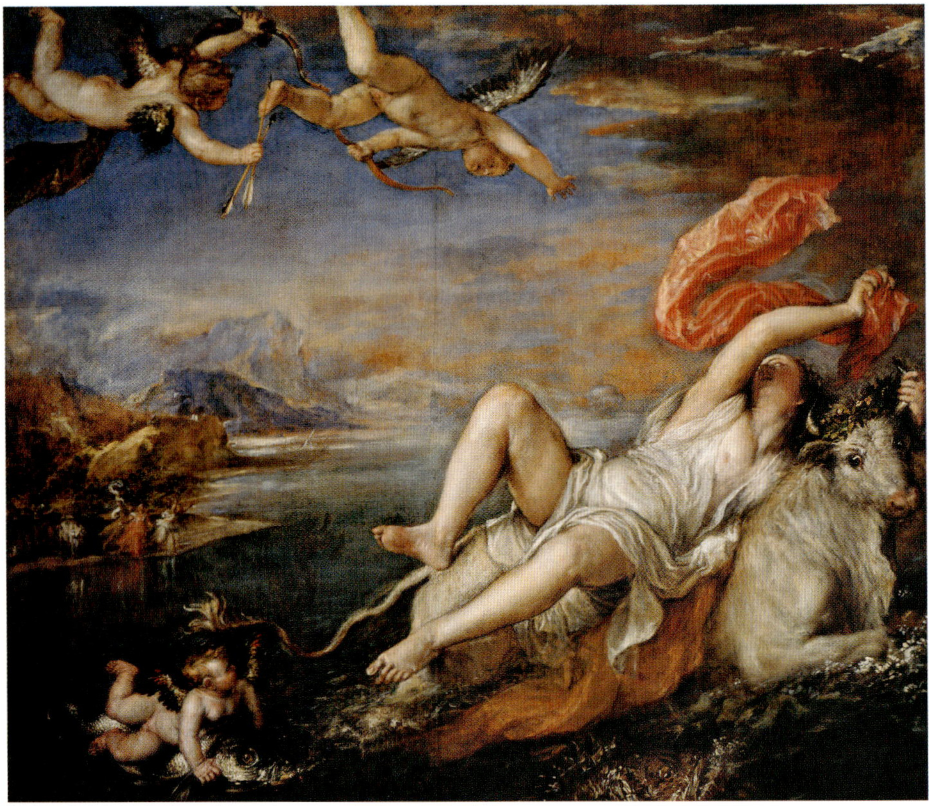

Fig. 106
Titian
Europa, 1559–62
Oil on canvas
Isabella Stewart Gardner Museum, Boston

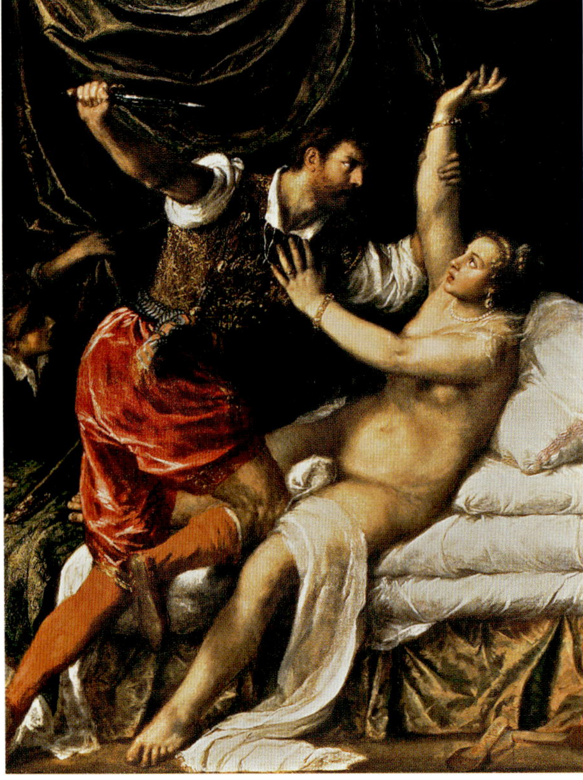

Fig. 107
Titian
Tarquin and Lucretia, 1568–71
Oil on canvas
Fitzwilliam Museum, Cambridge, England

ings acquired in connection with marriages or in prints such as Marcantonio Raimondi's engraving after Raphael.[26] Though Titian had depicted Lucretia's suicide in earlier paintings, he now selects the prior moment, in which Tarquin assaults his victim. The figure peeping from the bed curtains may refer to the servant of Tarquin's sinister bargain, but given the improbability of his proximity during the rape, some have seen him as a surrogate for the viewer as witness.[27] The Bordeaux version omits the witness to focus on the confrontation of rapist and victim.

When beginning work on *Tarquin and Lucretia* in 1568, Titian wrote to Philip, "I am composing another invention of painting of much greater labor and ingenuity than perhaps any I have produced for many years now."[28] At first read, this statement is curious. In contemporary poetics, "invention" referred to the process of devising a subject, and in this regard Titian hardly lacked prototypes: engravings by Heinrich Aldegrever, Giorgio Ghisi (after Giulio Romano), and Leon Davent show a dagger-wielding Tarquin forcing a resisting, nude Lucretia onto her curtained bed.[29] Titian's great innovation was to amplify the brutal mise-en-scène to the full human scale of the Fitzwilliam painting. The only true precedent for this was the artist's own *Saint Peter Martyr* altarpiece of 1530, wherein the executioner straddles the fallen saint reaching out for salvation (see fig. 23). Titian adapts the design, scale, and intensity of this fatal attack in *Tarquin and Lucretia*. Slightly propped up by the mattresses, the victim struggles as her aggressor thrusts his body between her legs, signaling her imminent violation, and pulls his arm back to threaten a blow. The vibrant reds of Tarquin's costume broadcast his carnal passions as much as his furious expression. Thickly applied paint invests surfaces with a tactile immediacy. The texture and gleaming highlights of Lucretia's flesh inevitably seduce the beholder's gaze, forcing the question of whether this renders us complicit in the criminal act. Did the painting's first male viewers see themselves mirrored in the contemporary garments and human scale with which the artist endowed Tarquin? As Rona Goffen has observed, the angle of the dagger parallels the

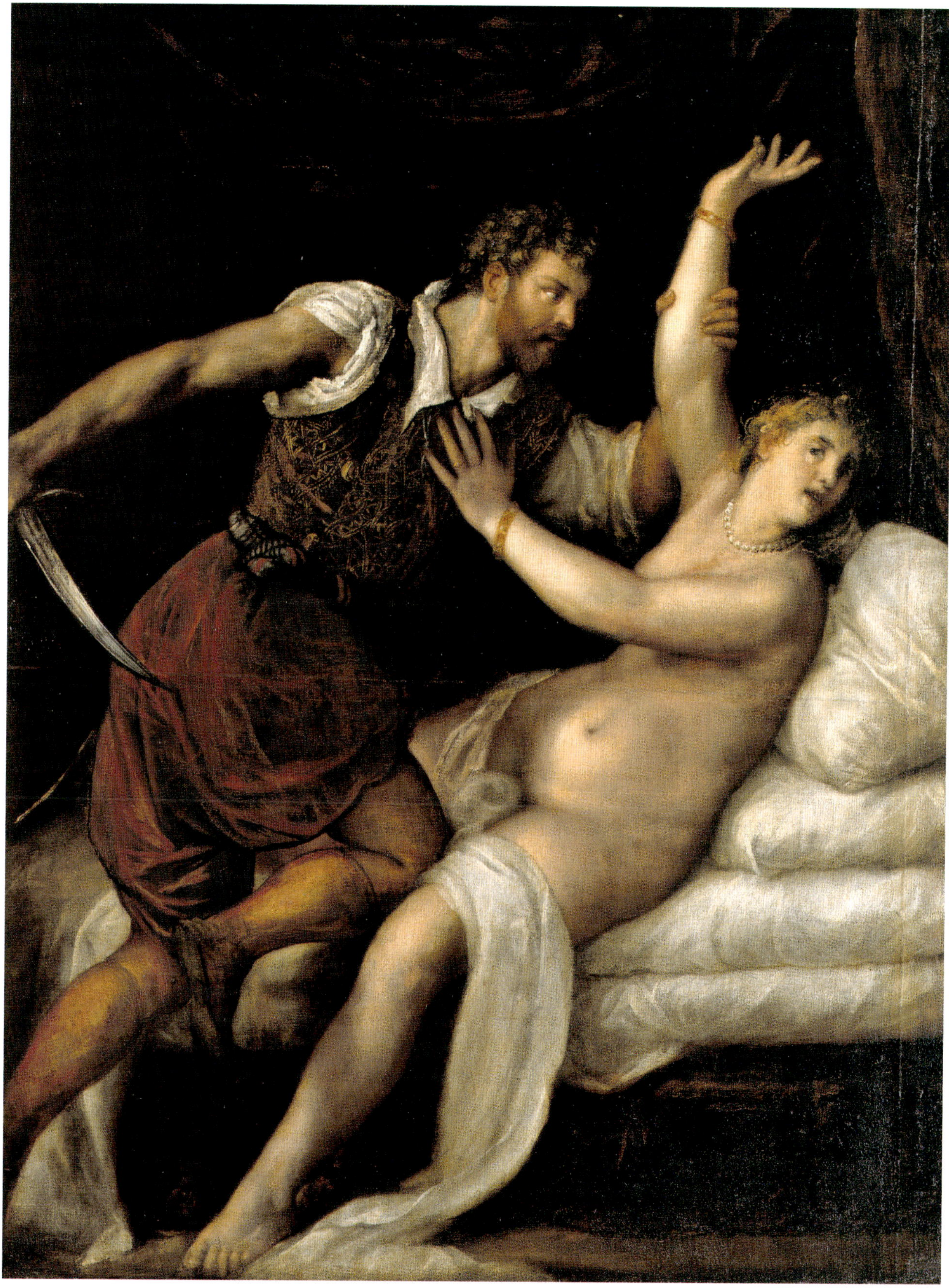

cat. 45

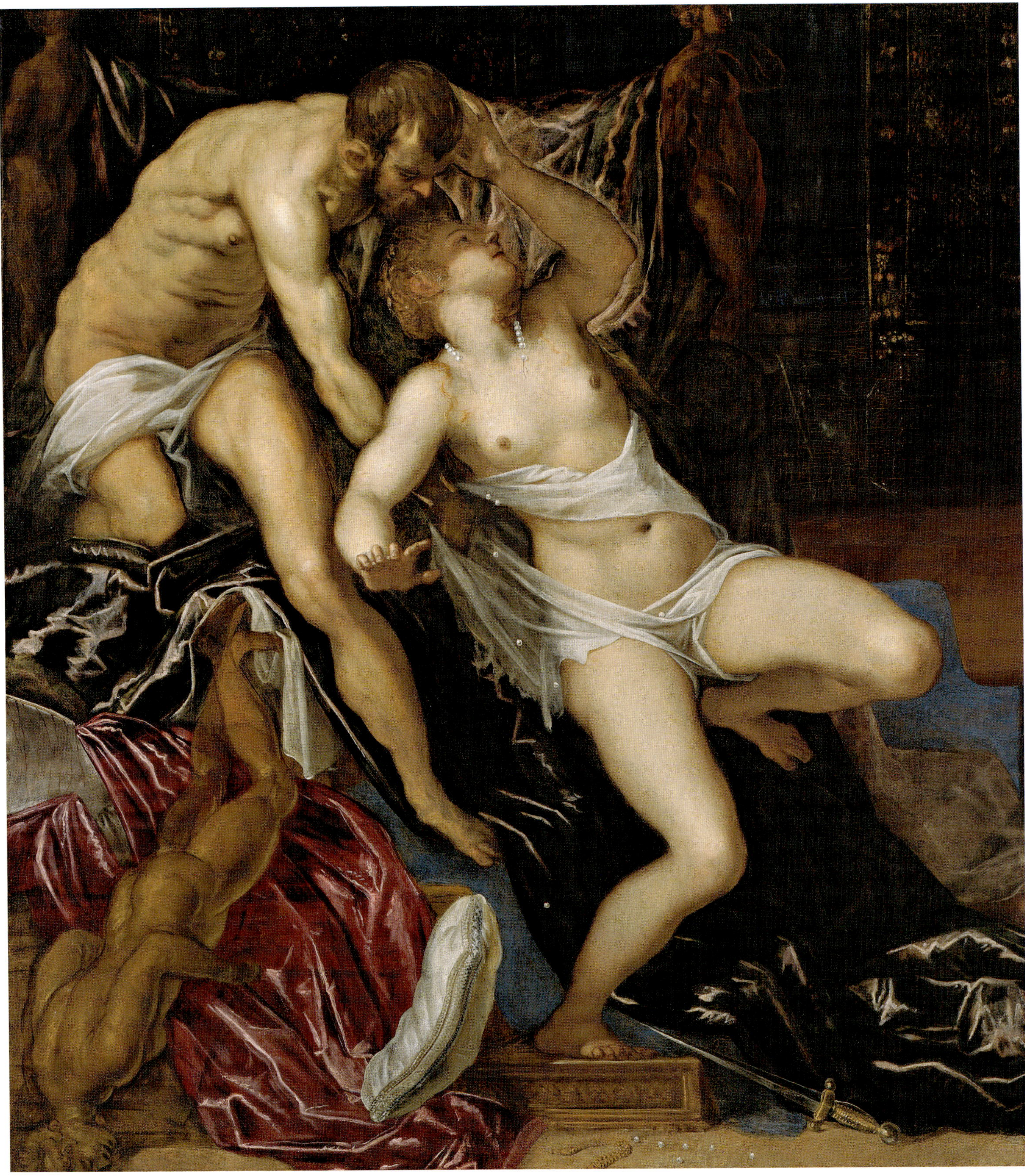

cat. 46

line of sight between Tarquin and Lucretia, underscoring the comparable potential of the gaze for violation. The inevitable attraction of the upstanding viewer (such as Philip II) to the painted flesh transmutes from passion to compassion in an act of catharsis. One shudders at the imminent mutilation, commiserates with Lucretia's tearful plight, and absolves oneself by denouncing Tarquin's depravity.[30]

In the Bordeaux version, Tarquin thrusts the knife underhand toward Lucretia's abdomen. X-ray analysis reveals that Tarquin's arm and weapon were initially raised, as in the Cambridge design, but Titian ultimately elected the lower position. In contrast to the locked gazes of the Cambridge protagonists, the battle of wills has here abated, as Lucretia turns aside and appeals to the viewer directly. In both scenes, the violence is not only staged but indexed through the marks of pigment that trace Titian's bold application of paint in blows and splotches. There is an implicit analogy between the brush that constructs the flesh and the dagger about to plunge into its palpable substance.[31] Indeed, Palma Giovane's famous account of Titian's late technique describes the process of painting in terms of manual assault, "without the slightest pity for the victim": "He scrutinized them [his pictures] as though they were his mortal enemies, in order to discover any faults. . . . With a dab of red, like a drop of blood, he would enliven some surface—in this way bring his animated figures to completion."[32]

Titian's great rival, Tintoretto, offers a similarly unflinching view of Lucretia's rape. Since nothing is known of the commission, proposed dates range widely. Earlier scholars likened the subject to the burlesque *Venus and Mars Surprised by Vulcan* (fig. 81) of about 1545, noting the physiognomic resemblance of Tarquin and Vulcan, and the similar gleam and handling of nude female flesh.[33] Since such correspondences are limited to figure type, more recent opinion has coalesced around the late 1570s, coeval with the *Origin of the Milky Way* (fig. 85) and the *Massacre of the Innocents* in the Scuola Grande di San Rocco. These works share the spatial compression, complex poses, pinwheel figural groupings, and animating chiaroscuro of the Chicago *Tarquin and Lucretia*.[34] The strongest argument for a later date is that Tintoretto seems to respond to Titian's 1571 painting, and even attempts to surpass it in dramatic terms. The close-up view and violence of the composition suggests that Tintoretto had direct knowledge of either the original or, more likely, the Cornelius Cort engraving produced under Titian's supervision before the work was shipped to Spain.[35]

In one sense, Tintoretto clearly supersedes Titian's "ingenious invention," since he illustrates a novel moment, deriving from neither the literary sources nor engravings.[36] Tintoretto shows Tarquin, already disrobed and in bed, brusquely yanking Lucretia upward by her scant remaining garments. She still resists, though not psychologically, since she is already resigned to her fate, but as a physical reflex before the shameful act. Her contorted pose, and the single foot on a pedestal-like base of the bed, may evoke the sculpted statuettes that Tintoretto often studied from multiple viewpoints.[37] Indeed the weight and rigidity of Lucretia undermines the instantaneous force of Tarquin's hoisting, which the toppled bedpost, rumpled linens, and pillow suspended midair all denote, not to mention the scattering pearls from her severed necklace. The latter references her impending loss of virtue, and evocatively metamorphoses her tears into jewels of honor.[38] Yet Tintoretto also encodes the inevitability of rape and injury in the woman's pose, which reverses and slightly tilts upward that of Titian's Europa. The way the drapery clings across Lucretia's thighs and abdomen, and the shadow cast over her face from her upraised arm, also recall Titian's struggling damsel.

When Veronese undertook the theme of Lucretia (Kunsthistorisches Museum, Vienna), he isolated her in solitary remorse just before the suicide. Even though the dagger pierces her flesh, Veronese emphasizes the victim's flawless complexion, her bejeweled coif, and the luxurious fabric that artfully conceals the wound.[39] Only in the dynamic scene of *Perseus and Andromeda* does Veronese approach the interplay of beauty and horror that animates Titian's and Tintoretto's

Lucretia pictures. According to Ovid, Neptune ordered Andromeda chained to a rock as a sacrificial offering to a sea monster in retribution for her mother, Cassiopeia, having boasted that her beauty surpassed that of the Nereids, or sea nymphs. Like Lucretia, Andromeda is an innocent victim, though here fate is kind. Upon the beast's final approach, Perseus, borne aloft on winged sandals and equipped with the gorgon shield, slays the monster and liberates the damsel, ultimately taking her as his bride.[40] Veronese clearly reprises Titian's composition of the same subject for Philip II (fig. 77).[41] Titian presses Andromeda's body, unable to escape the shackles, against the picture plane. Andromeda cranes her neck, the corporeal twist registering a shift in fortune, as her savior dives through the gloom toward the beast. The pallor of her highly modeled torso conveys her petrified terror, which Ovid had compared to a marble statue, but the trembling of her more sketchily rendered extremities heralds her revival.

Veronese's elegance softens the drama, transmuting the terrifying spectacle into a balletic pantomime. The daylight setting and ancillary details such as the distant cityscape and crimson drapery, not to mention the hero's tangerine armor, enrich the picture in decorative terms but dilute the dramatic force of the rescue. While Andromeda's outstretched hands formulaically enact terror, the bent knee and deep bow suggest a curtsey of thanksgiving to her savior. Veronese thereby projects the happy conclusion of the story rather than intensify the suspense at its climax; gallantry takes precedence over terror. Likewise, the turbulent lunge of Titian's Perseus gives way to a nonchalant superhero, gliding onto the scene, whose calibrated limbs achieve a perfect equilibrium. The serpentine twist of Andromeda's pose is much closer to that of Tintoretto's Lucretia, nearly reversing it; perhaps Veronese's Lucretia imitates a similar or even the same sculptural model viewed from a different angle.[42] Yet, for all the similarities, the Mannerist contortion results in a self-conscious gracefulness in Veronese's painting, whereas Tintoretto exploits such devices to animate struggle, revulsion, and turmoil. The congruent poses of the heroines, whether mutually informed or independently conceived, articulate the fundamentally different stylistic and dramatic approaches of each master. Indeed, there is no clear chronological priority between the two paintings.[43]

Veronese's *Andromeda* and Tintoretto's *Lucretia* offer nearly contemporaneous responses to the late masterpieces of Titian, with one of the younger artists perhaps critiquing both Titian and his more immediate rival. Titian's legacy blazed divergent, but equally brilliant, paths for his artistic heirs, whether the dramatic intensity and bravura brushwork of Tintoretto or the sumptuous color harmonies and rarefied elegance of Veronese.

—JU

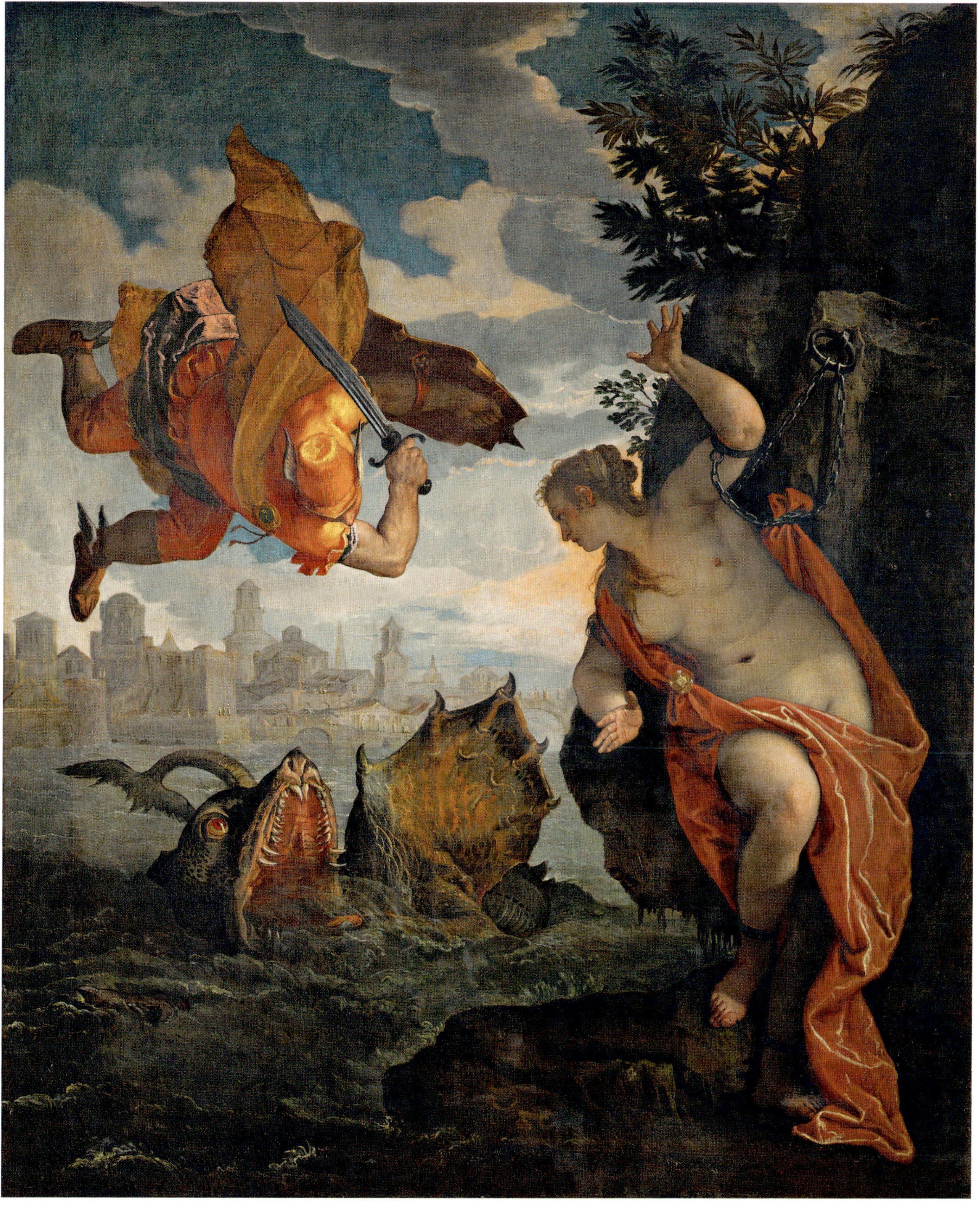

cat. 47

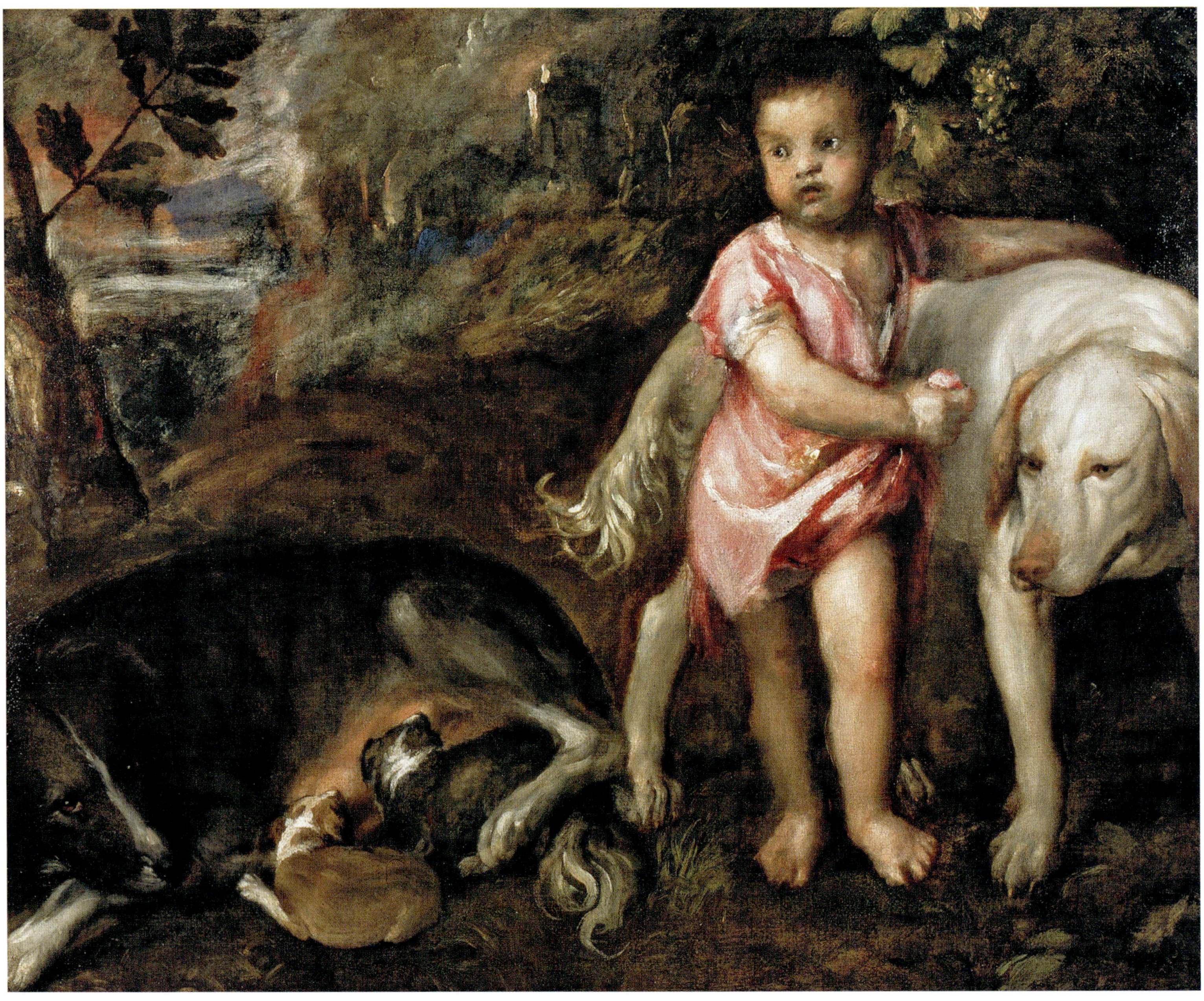

cat. 48

The Dog on Canvas: The Emergence of a New Genre

TITIAN
Boy with Dogs in a Landscape, about 1570–75
Museum Boijmans Van Beuningen, Rotterdam
(cat. 48)

VERONESE
Cupid with Two Dogs, about 1581
Alte Pinakothek, Munich
(cat. 49)

In the diverse bestiary of Renaissance art, by far the most commonly depicted animal is the dog. Faithful hunting companion and friend in daily life, it often sits beside its master in official portraits. In Mantua, for instance, a veritable tradition stretched through the fifteenth and sixteenth centuries: Gianfrancesco Gonzaga had his dogs portrayed in a room of the San Sebastiano palace; Ludovico II hired Mantegna to paint his dog Rubino and his mastiffs in the *camera picta* (Palazzo Ducale, Mantua, 1465–74); Federico II commissioned Giulio Romano to create a funeral monument for his favorite dog in 1526 and soon after had Titian portray him with another of his hounds (*Federico Gonzaga*, about 1527–30, Museo Nacional del Prado, Madrid). Such portraits display not only their subjects' fondness for their animals but also their social standing, given the dog's association with the aristocratic pastime of hunting. In portraits of women, the dog can also symbolize a wife's fidelity (Titian, *Portrait of Eleonora Gonzaga della Rovere*, about 1536–37, Galleria degli Uffizi, Florence).

Still, the image of the dog, as handed down from ancient and medieval traditions, is a complex phenomenon. In ancient times, the animal was considered impure, and in more than one passage of the Bible it stands in for a sinner or the devil himself.[44] Its stature rose during the Middle Ages, probably owing to its gradual acceptance in aristocratic society. Little by little, the dog came to be appreciated for its alertness, intuition, instinct, perseverance, sensitivity, and fidelity.[45] By the Renaissance, its reputation was distinctly more favorable, as attested by Alciati's *Book of Emblems*, in which the dog is shown at rest beneath the legs of the faithful wife, or Ripa's *Iconology*, in which it accompanies Fidelity, Youth, Investigation, and Espionage.[46] Nonetheless, the dog sometimes bears traces of its earlier taint, such that only the specific iconographic context can provide the key to its symbolic meaning.[47]

The mid-sixteenth century saw the first Venetian paintings in which dogs were protagonists rather than ancillary figures. The likely inventor of this conceit was Jacopo Bassano, with *Two Hunting Dogs Tied to a Tree Stump* (1548–50, Musée du Louvre, Paris)[48] and *Two Dogs in a Landscape* (about 1553, Galleria degli Uffizi, Florence).[49] The novelty of these paintings, which portrayed dogs on their own and with frank naturalism, must have fascinated the greatest masters of the period: soon afterward, Tintoretto meticulously reproduced the white-and-brown dog from the Louvre painting in the *Washing of the Feet* (fig. 26), painted about 1548–49 for the church of San Marcuola in Venice.[50] Moreover, the period when he began inserting dogs into his compositions coincides with his great admiration for Bassano.

As Jean Habert has noted,[51] Titian himself might have used the recumbent animal from the Uffizi canvas for the nursing she-dog in *Boy with Dogs in a Landscape*, usually dated to between 1570 and 1576.[52] Titian proved highly imaginative when it came to depicting animals, but he was also quite capable of borrowing from his talented colleague. Indeed, it appears Titian acquired a painting by Bassano of Noah's Ark, a masterful demonstration of the latter's talents as an animal painter.[53]

Bassano's two paintings created a genre, paving the way for Veronese's *Cupid with Two Dogs*.[54] These three works, along with *Boy with Dogs*, form a singular group of canvases in which, for the first time, animals take the lead role. But the meaning of these innovative paintings is not as clear as the simple compositions and humble subject matter would suggest. The lack of contemporary information about them, as well as the rarity and novelty of the subject in the sixteenth century, have yielded contradictory interpretations.

Boy with Dogs in a Landscape is one of Titian's most mysterious works. Its wide brushstrokes and sketchy areas (which some scholars consider unfinished)[55] surely date it from the master's final years, between 1570 and 1576. Little is known of its history before it surfaced on the market in Amsterdam in 1930, most likely from the Serbelloni collection in Milan.[56] The canvas had been trimmed on all four sides, which has inspired various theories about its original dimensions. Some believe the work is a fragment of a larger mythological or allegorical scene,[57] while others argue the dimensions were reduced only slightly.[58] The unusual subject matter—a child picking grapes in a landscape, with a dog and a she-dog nursing two pups nearby—adds another layer of difficulty in understanding the work.

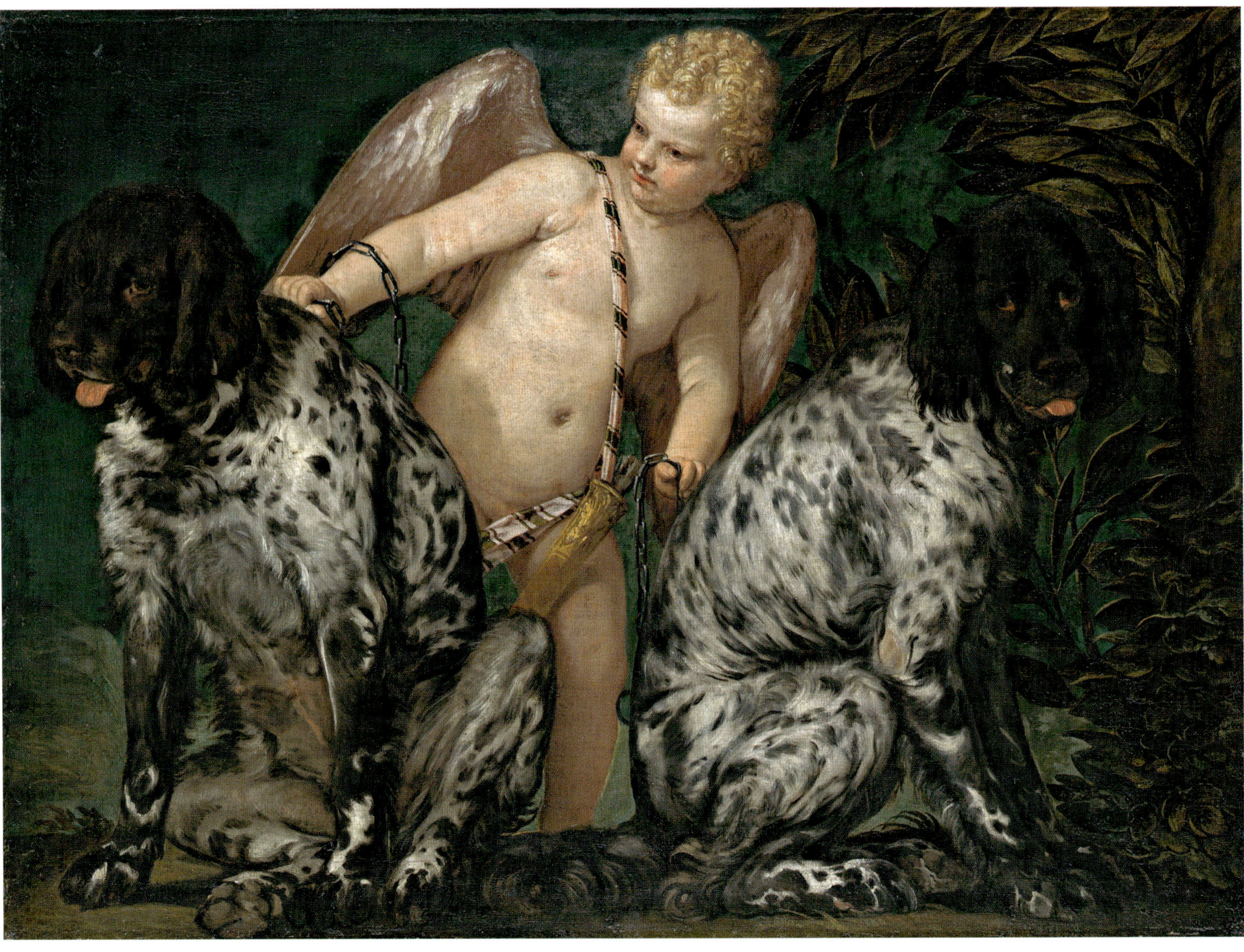

cat. 49

A tradition promoted by the Serbelloni family interprets this painting as illustrating a specific but undocumented event: a young boy saved by his dogs from a fire in the family home.[59] The composition contains no historical elements to support this, however. The tortured landscape, characteristic of Titian's final years, does not necessarily indicate a fire, and the child, similar to the little faun in the *Flaying of Marsyas*,[60] has no specific garments or attributes. Finally, the nursing dog and the act of picking grapes seem more consistent with an allegorical mode.

Tietze has suggested the work might be a fragment of a composition that he relates to an engraving of *Venus and Adonis* by Pietro Testa, which contains a similar group.[61] Wethey disputes this on the grounds that the dogs have no leash, whereas they do in all of Titian's other paintings on the subject. But more to the point, a she-dog nursing her pups would seem out of place in a scene of hunting hounds baying around their master.

Panofsky, who granted the work scant attention, related the motif to Veronese's *Cupid with Two Dogs*, deeming both to represent "Cupid mastering two dogs of different temper."[62] But this rather hasty comparison has been rejected by most subsequent art critics. Indeed, the child has none of Cupid's usual characteristics, while the two dogs do not seem particularly different in character.

Historians have also sought a relation between the Rotterdam canvas and *Portrait of a Soldier with a Cupid and a Dog* in Kassel, in which we find the same standing white dog.[63] While Pallucchini believes the repetition was accidental,[64] Hans Ost has tried to piece together a coherent history despite the paucity of information about the two works.[65] In Ost's view, the gentleman in the Kassel painting is Gabriele Serbelloni, who commissioned Titian to paint his portrait in the 1550s. The unfinished canvas then languished in the master's studio until the 1570s, when Titian completed it by adding the landscape. In that same period, he finished the Rotterdam canvas, a complex allegory of Serbelloni's life replete with his favorite dog and allusions to his time in Rome (the child an imitation of ancient statues of young Bacchus, the nursing dog evoking the Roman she-wolf). In a later text, Ost even posited that the Rotterdam painting was a kind of allegorical lid that fit over the Kassel portrait.[66] Subsequent critics have rejected this hypothesis, finding it hard to believe that the portrait would have sat unfinished in Titian's studio for more than twenty years, and even harder to credit the link between the nursing dog and the she-wolf.[67]

More recently, Mary D. Garrard has interpreted the composition as an allegory of the conflict between nature and culture. The nursing dog would thus be an image of nature, as opposed to the white dog being "civilized" by the child.[68] But here again, the argument seems rather tenuous and ultimately unconvincing.

Absent the discovery of any new documentation, *Boy with Dogs in a Landscape* will remain an enigmatic composition, its allegorical meaning and Bacchic overtones unexplained. Nevertheless, the work attests to the remarkable place that dogs, and animals in general, would henceforth occupy in Venetian painting. It is noteworthy that Titian has rendered the dogs much more precisely than he has the child. The animals here become living creatures on a par with man, able to develop a complex allegorical discourse through their actions and expressions.

Veronese, too, invented a new animal allegory in his *Cupid with Two Dogs*. The artist depicted many animals throughout his career, especially dogs, with great diversity and a consummate talent for naturalism. The Munich canvas, a finished composition,[69] is nonetheless the only one primarily devoted to animals—though, as with the Titian canvas discussed above, there is not enough information available to clarify the artist's intent.

Panofsky saw the painting simply as Cupid training two dogs of different temperaments.[70] For Rolf Kultzen, the dogs incarnate two contradictory aspects of love: the she-dog that Cupid restrains on the left represents passion, while the faithful hound at rest under a laurel bush on the right is a symbol of virtue and constancy.[71] W. R. Rearick, on the other hand, who relates the composition to the one in Rotterdam, sees it as an allegory of the power of love in nature, here uniting two faithful dogs.[72] Attila Scarlini, for her part, has stressed the emblematic character of the work, which she envisions as the pendant to the portrait of a couple or a fiancée. According to her, the allegory celebrates amorous union, without our being able to specify the exact nature of the bond—sensual passion that must be held in check, the solidity of marriage, or the trials of conjugal life.[73]

Kultzen has related the work to the story of Venus and Adonis. And indeed, the image does look like a fragment of a mythical scene, with the young Cupid keeping the dogs from disturbing their master's lovemaking—all the more so in that the animals seem out of breath, their tongues lolling, and that both the young god and the dog on the left appear to be looking toward some event outside the frame. Titian and Veronese depicted this amorous fable several times, in which the main event is subtended by a humorous sidebar enacted by Adonis's dogs. While the Munich canvas might indeed represent metonymically the myth of Venus and Adonis, in its own way it, too, evinces the new role accorded to animals, which are now deemed worthy of evoking human history through their own actions and expressions. At the same time, this metonymy pulls the work away from mythology and toward something more universal. Isolated in the composition, the dogs take on greater symbolic significance. Indeed, the friezelike composition, the movement of Cupid's body toward the right, and the striking similarity between the two animals (drawing a parallel between them) invite us to read the work as a progression from lust—the she-dog held back and exhibiting its teats—toward virtue, as embodied by the dog on the right with its sage gaze.

Singular images from the sixteenth century, these paintings illustrate the extraordinary naturalism of Venetian genius, which discovered through attentive study the expressive and poetic richness of nature. The paintings of dogs foreshadow the culmination of these studies in the emergence of the new genre of animal painting, and prefigure the triumph of that genre in the following century. At the same time, they attest to the complexity of Renaissance imagery, in which myth, allegory, history, and anecdote were allowed to coexist.
— VD

Saint Jerome in the Wilderness

TINTORETTO
Saint Jerome in the Wilderness,
about 1571–72
Kunsthistorisches Museum,
Gemäldegalerie, Vienna
(cat. 50)

TITIAN
Saint Jerome in the Wilderness,
about 1570–75
Museo Thyssen-Bornemisza,
Madrid
(cat. 51)

VERONESE
Saint Jerome in the Wilderness,
about 1580
Gallerie dell'Accademia, Venice
(cat. 52)

Jerome was one of the most frequently represented saints in Venetian Renaissance art, following only the Virgin Mary and John the Baptist. As Peter Humfrey has noted, "The extraordinary popularity of Jerome may be ascribed to the fact that his contrasting guises, alternating between learned cardinal and ascetic penitent, could appeal to quite different constituencies of devotee."[74] Jerome appeared in both painted and sculpted church altarpieces, in paintings for private devotion, and also in pictures acquired primarily by collectors for aesthetic pleasure.[75] This popularity testifies both to the saint's importance in the religious teachings of the day and to his appeal to artists and patrons. Devotional texts urged Christians to contemplate the life of Jerome as an ideal of the "imitation of Christ," following Christ's example to the point of physical suffering.[76] To painters, the theme of the penitent Saint Jerome in the wilderness offered the opportunity to depict a mature male nude as well as an evocative landscape. Moreover, the subject of an elderly, contemplative saint would seem to have provided a potentially resonant and poignant subject matter for an aging painter.

The traditional Venetian image of Jerome the Penitent, as it had evolved by the second half of the Cinquecento, is exemplified by Titian's monumental panel *Saint Jerome*, an altarpiece for the church of Santa Maria Nova (fig. 108), recently dated to between 1557 and 1560.[77] Jerome is shown as a muscular, middle-aged man alone in a remote landscape, beating his breast with a stone and gazing intently at a crucifix. In Titian's painting, the saint's self-mortification is rendered with powerful physicality: his right arm is tensed as he clutches the stone, his left holds fast to a rocky outcropping to steady himself. The trees in the background sway dramatically, recalling Titian's *Saint Peter Martyr* altarpiece of three decades earlier, and their movement underscores the violence and intense emotion

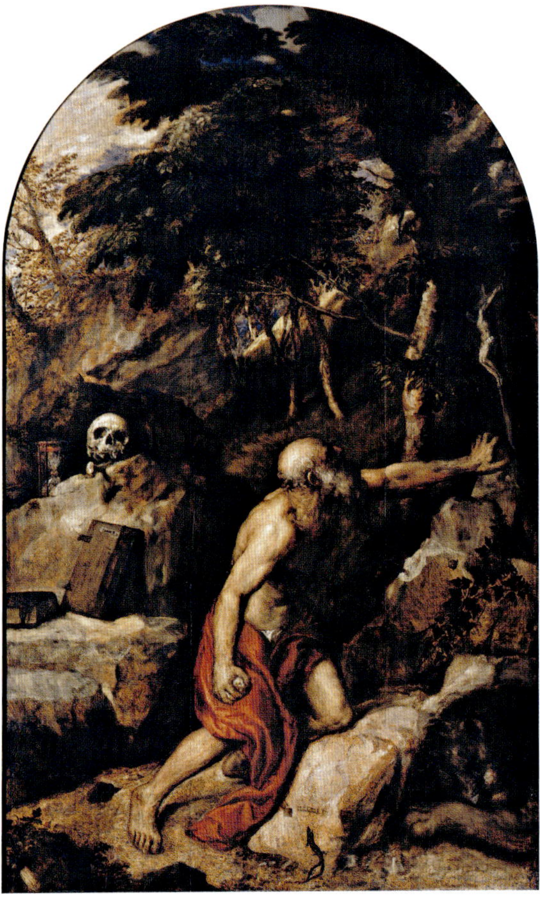

Fig. 108. Titian, *Saint Jerome*, late 1550s, oil on panel, Pinacoteca di Brera, Milan

of Jerome's devotions.[78] Among the saint's usual attributes—including lion, books, and hourglass—the skull is particularly conspicuous, and its effectiveness as a memento mori is heightened since it appears to face the viewer.

By contrast, Tintoretto's *Saint Jerome in the Wilderness* in Vienna portrays the saint as scholar and translator of the scriptures. But this saint is far from the calm elderly man reading or meditating in a landscape seen in the versions by Giovanni Bellini, for example. Tintoretto's Jerome is somewhat

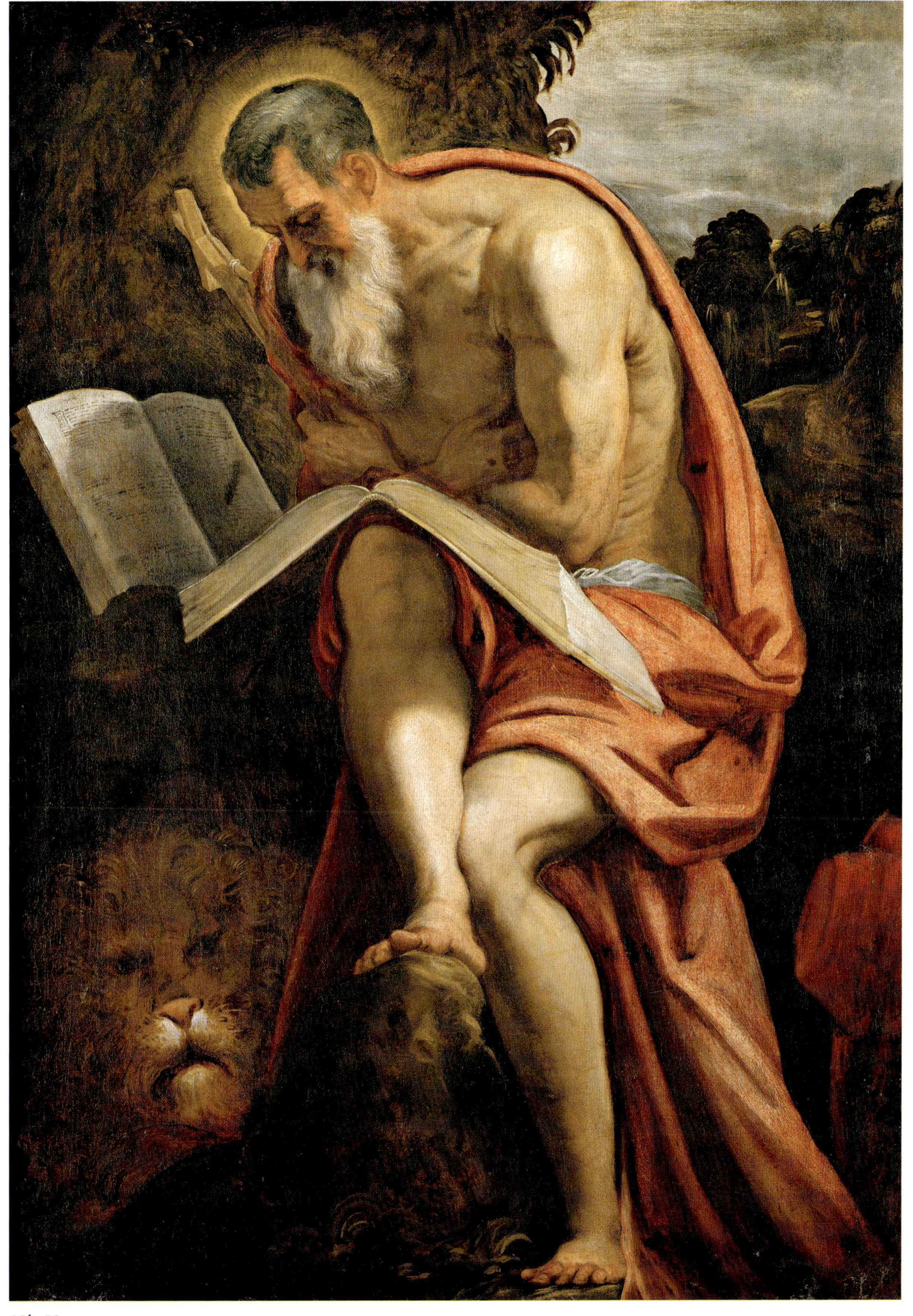

cat. 50

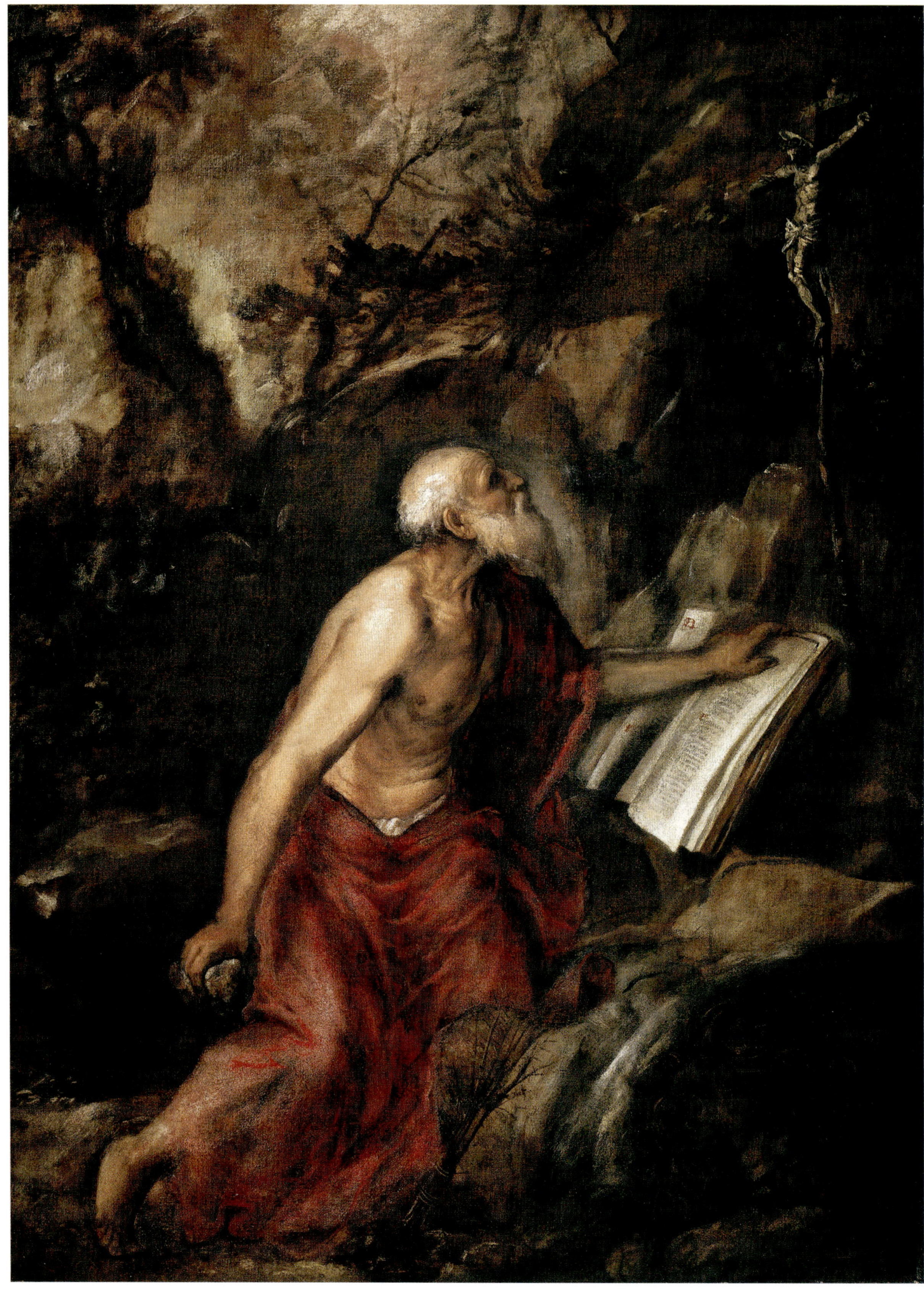

cat. 51

younger than usually shown in Venetian painting, with a full head of dark hair despite his long white beard and a powerfully muscled shoulder and back. As is typical of Tintoretto, the heroic figure conveys no sense of repose, but rather of knotted, potentially explosive energy. Jerome is hunched forward, his limbs tightly folded in toward his chest. The tight focus on the saint's body emphasizes this coiled, constrained quality—if the figure were to stand up, he would burst the boundaries of the frame. The saint's pose reinforces the notion of his deep concentration, suggesting mental activity every bit as brawny as his strapping body. By contrast, the landscape and depiction of Jerome's attributes are perfunctory, albeit necessary to identifying this muscular figure as Jerome.

For this picture, Tintoretto probably relied upon the same figure drawing he employed for one of the *Philosophers* (the so-called *Diogenes*) he painted for the Libreria Marciana in 1571–72. The pose seems to have been conceived for the niche format there, and thus it seems likely that the *Jerome* was executed after the Marciana paintings or around the same time, quite possibly for a private patron.[79] Although any painting of Jerome could have a devotional function, the figure's pronounced Michelangelesque quality suggests that it would have been attractive to a connoisseur who took an interest in the *paragone*, the debate over the relative merits of painting and sculpture, and valued the sculptural quality of Tintoretto's paintings.

While only one autograph Tintoretto painting of Saint Jerome in the wilderness has survived, the subject seems to have been something of a specialty of both Veronese and Titian, each master producing several autograph pictures in addition to further workshop versions.

Titian's *Saint Jerome in the Wilderness*, uniformly assigned to the painter's final years, possesses a composition generally derived from his Santa Maria Nova altarpiece, but the overall effect is very different. This Jerome is no longer heroic; instead, he is an old man with sagging flesh, barely able to hold himself up. Here the emphasis is not on the violence of Jerome's self-castigation but on the contrasting decay of the saint's body and the steadfast intensity of his devotion. Although much of the figure is loosely painted, Titian tightens the focus and finish in certain areas, such as the vein that runs down Jerome's arm from his right shoulder, the strained tendons of his neck, and most effectively his furrowed brow and shadowed eye sockets; all these impart a quality of haunted desperation to Jerome's contemplation of the crucifix. Jerome's attributes, while present, are barely visible, with the exception of the Bible on which he supports himself—a Bible that, in this context, seems to function less as a reference to his translation of the scriptures than as an indication of his hope for eternal life.[80] The wild landscape is conveyed with the loosest brushwork of Titian's late style, creating a vibrating, almost abstract hallucinatory effect, and emphasizes the frailty of the old man's body and the desolation of his setting.

The saint here is the same figure who appears in Titian's *Pietà* (fig. 109), painted for the artist's own

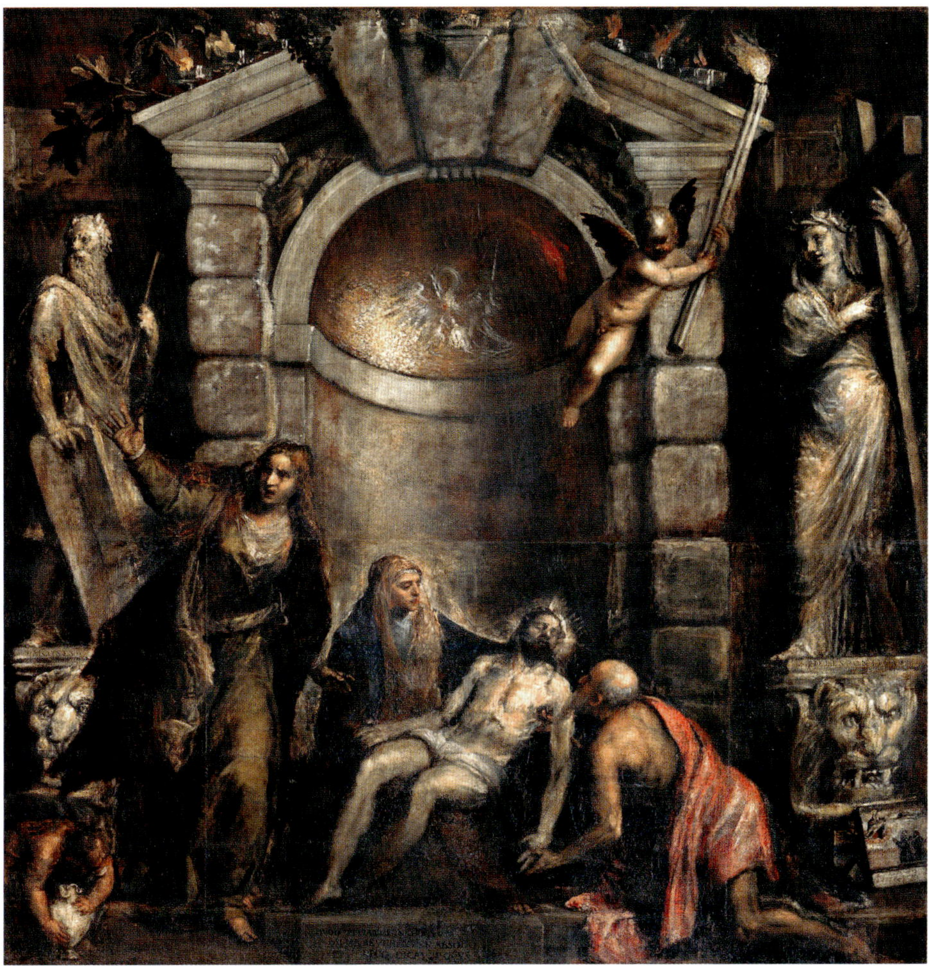

Fig. 109
Titian
Pietà, about 1570–76
Oil on canvas
Gallerie dell'Accademia, Venice

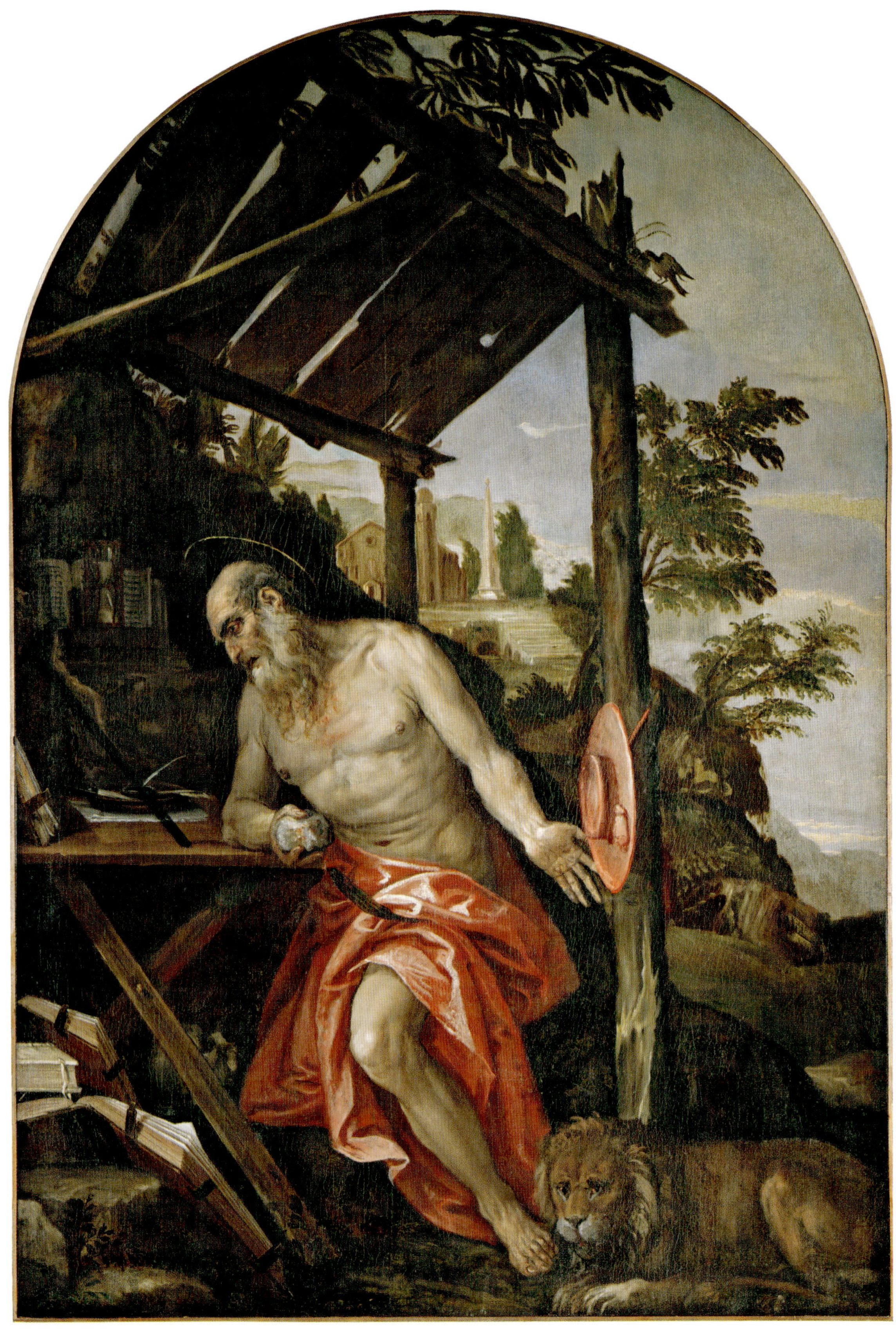

cat. 52

tomb, gazing beseechingly at the Savior. The facial features of the aged Titian have been identified in both figures.[81] At a minimum, both are surely spiritual self-portraits, representing the old artist clinging to his faith in the face of death. Like the *Pietà*, *Saint Jerome* is a highly personal work, a profoundly moving meditation upon bodily decrepitude, suffering, mortality, faith, and the hope of salvation.

As he had done many times in his career, Veronese takes Titian as his point of departure. His *Saint Jerome in the Wilderness* altarpiece for the church of Sant'Andrea della Zirada, Venice (now in the Gallerie dell'Academia), generally dated around 1580 or slightly earlier on stylistic grounds, depicts the penitent. The saint is represented as bald and white-bearded but still powerful—essentially the same physical type seen in Titian's Santa Maria Nova altarpiece. Jerome's body has received particular attention, and was described as the "most beautiful nude this eminent master ever painted" by the eighteenth-century Venetian art chronicler Antonio Zanetti.[82] Here Jerome has paused momentarily in his mortification: his chest is raw and blood is visible on the stone he clutches, an impressive still-life passage. He prays in a rude hut, barely sheltered from the elements, in a dark and inhospitable setting. In the distance, however, the mood is lightened, as the sun strikes a hillside with a church and an obelisk beside it. Blue skies appear beyond.

Veronese's attention to landscape elements seems intended to reinforce the devotional message of the altarpiece, representing eternal salvation (the obelisk is a symbol of eternity), which the devout Christian can achieve by following Jerome's ideal of devotion and mortification of the flesh.[83] Aesthetically, however, the lyricism of the background tends to undermine the penitential mood that characterizes so many Venetian versions of the theme. Where, for example, Titian drains the details of the setting in his painting for Santa Maria Nova to focus on the figure of the saint, Veronese cannot resist adding more elements to his composition and, indeed, imparting a sense of harmony and grace to the picture. The regular grid formed by the horizontals and verticals of Jerome's hut provides compositional balance and support for the figure. The saint's rose-colored robe is disconcertingly sensuous—Veronese creates the highlights with brilliant economy, dragging the loaded brush lightly over the canvas so that only the ridge of the herringbone weave catches it, creating the effect of a plush fabric. The beautifully painted still-life of Jerome's many attributes—books, hourglass, cardinal's hat, writing implements—distracts from rather than enhances the devotional meaning. The balance is righted, however, in the remarkable depiction of the saint's red-rimmed eyes, in which the worshipper would have seen all the penitence and suffering that made Jerome an ideal "imitation of Christ." This effect is emphasized in a final remarkable detail: the eyes of the lion are deeply red as well, as if it were sharing the saint's anguish.

— RE, FI

The Baptism of Christ

TINTORETTO
Baptism of Christ, about 1580
Church of San Silvestro, Venice
(cat. 53)

VERONESE
Baptism of Christ, early 1580s
The J. Paul Getty Museum,
Los Angeles
(cat. 54)

Venetian painters and audiences seem to have had a special attachment to the figure of John the Baptist and the pictorial subject of the Baptism of Christ. Indeed, John the Baptist was the most popular saint represented in altarpieces in Venetian churches in the period 1450–1530, as well as the fourth most popular dedication of altars in 1581.[84] From Giovanni Bellini and Cima da Conegliano through Palma Giovane, most of the leading Venetian painters of the Renaissance executed important depictions of the Baptism of Christ, among which those by Tintoretto and Veronese are particularly noteworthy.

Even divorced from his narrative role, John the Baptist is a prominent presence in Venetian *sacre conversazioni*, in devotional pictures (cat. 1), and in altarpieces. Although John the Baptist was revered throughout Christendom, the unique relationship between the city and its watery setting may have intensified Venetian attention to this saint and the subject of the Baptism. Moreover, many biblical events—from the Flood to the Crossing of the Red Sea to the Baptism of Christ in the river Jordan—involved punishment or salvation with water, and therefore must have had a special resonance for Venetians.[85]

Recounted in all four Gospels, the Baptism of Christ is the first episode in the adulthood of Jesus and marks the start of his public ministry. In Venetian painting, the subject of the Baptism of Christ was codified by Cima in his altarpiece in San Giovanni in Bragora of 1492–94, a composition echoed by Bellini in an altarpiece for Santa Corona, Vicenza, about 1500–1502 (fig. 40)—both pieces for altars dedicated to John the Baptist.[86] In format, both are vertical rectangles with arched tops. Both show Christ standing at the river's edge directly on the central axis, his fixed gaze engaging the viewer and his hands clasped in prayer or arms crossed on his chest. In each, John stands on an outcropping to the right and looks at the head of Christ, occupied in his task of pouring water. Although one might suppose that it would be more dignified for John to stand at the left edge of the composition—to be at Christ's right—the Baptist's placement on the right allows him to employ his right hand for the bowl and to stand partially turned toward the viewer.

John's elevated position also balances the presence of three angels to the left. In both paintings the action takes place before an expansive, hilly landscape resembling the Veneto foothills, with the Dolomites in the distance. The detailed landscapes compete for the viewer's attention with the figures of Christ and John, who take up less than half the height of the field. Although Christ is certainly the focus of the paintings, the Baptist is placed considerably higher in both. Subtle details accentuate this prominence: in Cima's painting, both the head of the Baptist and his hand holding the bowl of water rise above the distant mountains; in Bellini's altarpiece, John's halo in fact projects above the horizon, as Goffen noted. This pictorial emphasis on the Baptist finds confirmation in biblical texts and in Christian theology, where John is accorded special status, simultaneously the last of the prophets and first of the saints, and also the herald of Christ.

Even when depictions of the Baptism were not altarpieces, such as Titian's sole treatment of the theme, a panel for private devotion from about 1513 (Pinacoteca Capitolina, Rome), the head of Christ and the hand of the Baptist often remained on the central axis, underscoring Christ's body and John's action as the most important parts of the composition. Veronese's many depictions, although attuned to subtleties of pose and gesture, also tend to maintain Christ on the central axis, with John on the right. In all of Veronese's pictures, Christ's arms are crossed in front of his chest or held close to his torso.[87]

Not surprisingly, the greatest innovator of this subject in Venetian art was Tintoretto, whose approach to religious narrative painting seems to have involved a fundamental rethinking of how successful compositions were designed and how paintings addressed the viewer.[88] The untraditional com-

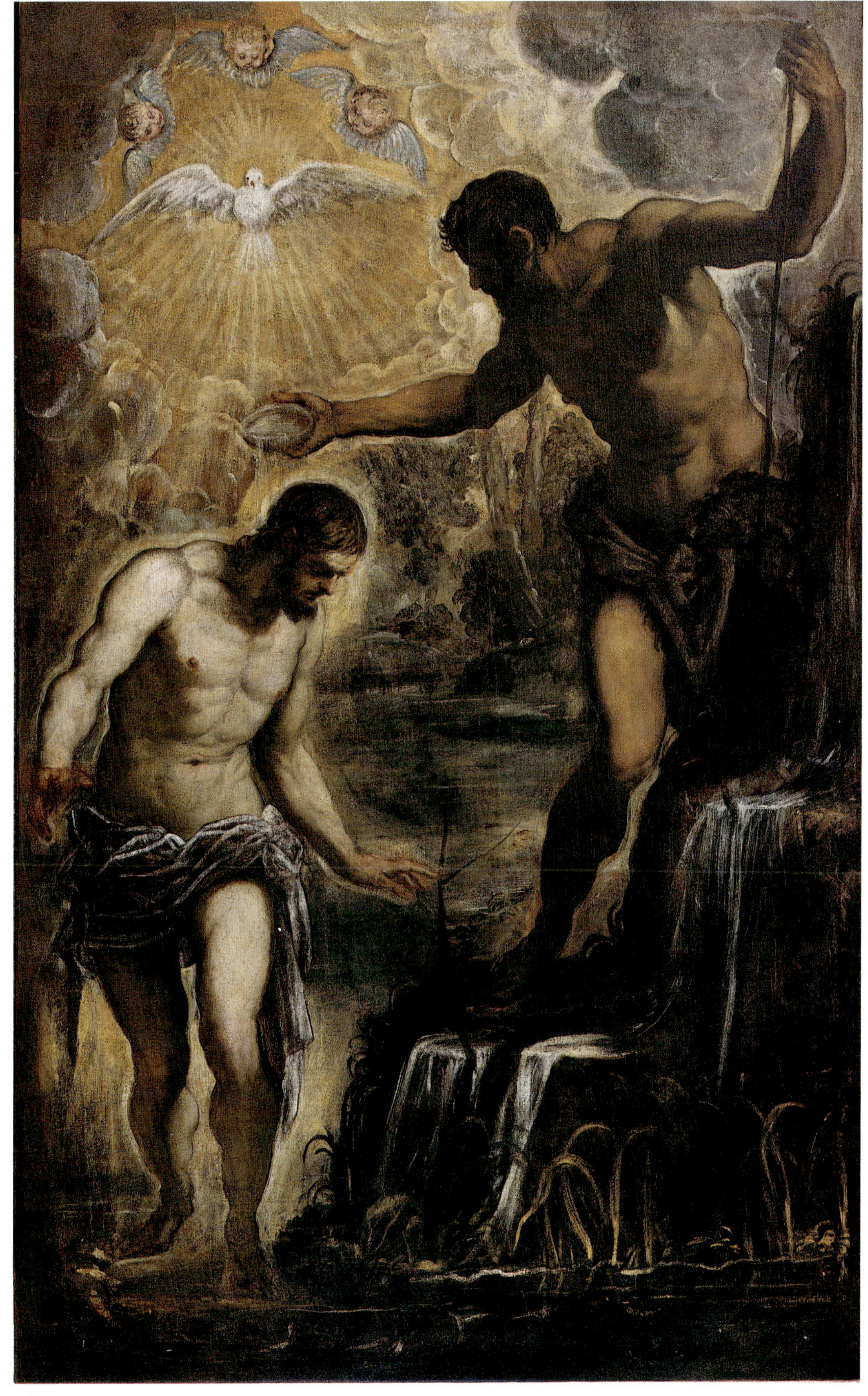

cat. 53

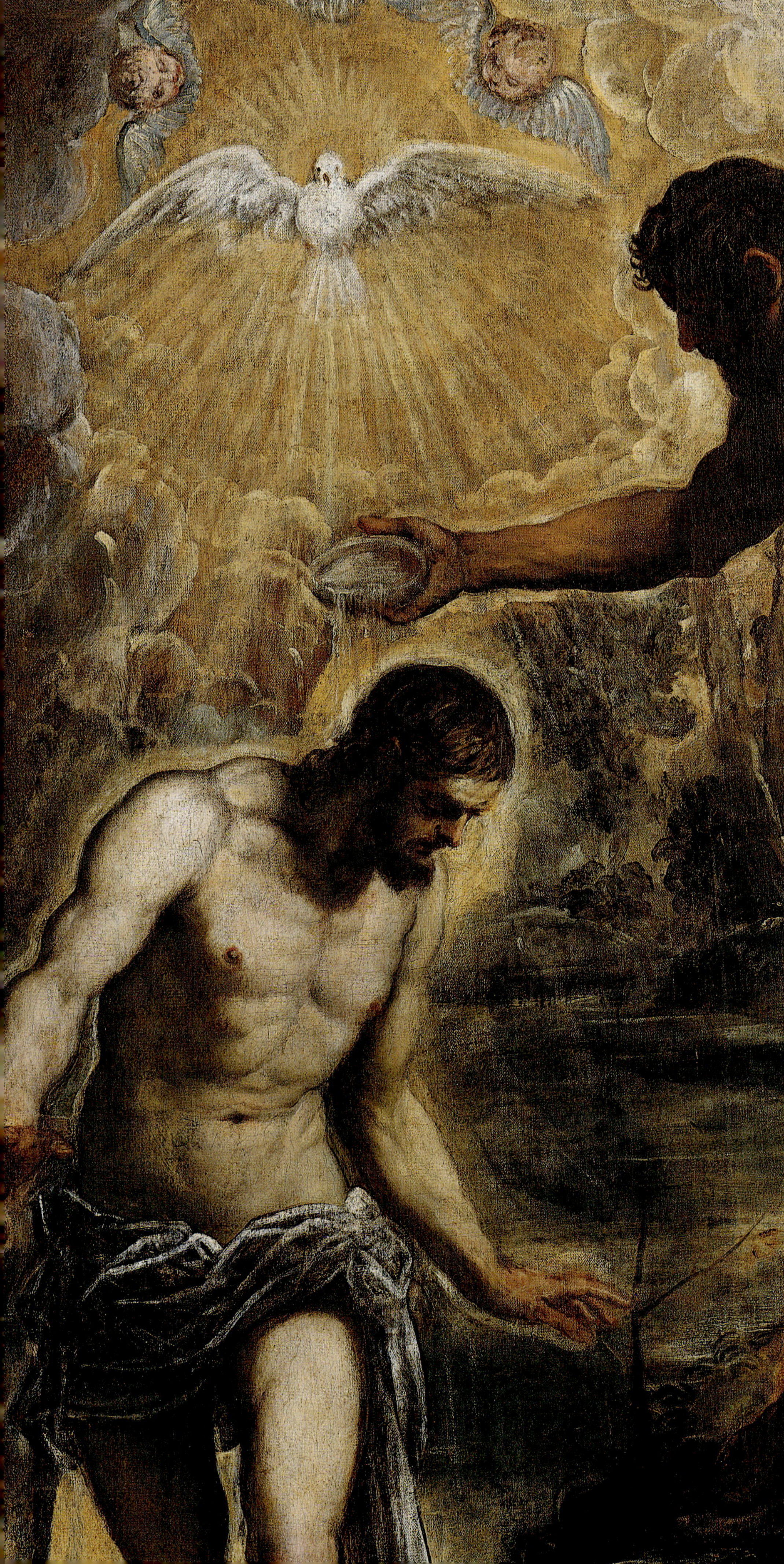

position of Tintoretto's huge *Baptism of Christ* of 1579–81, part of the cycle of the Life of Christ in the Scuola Grande di San Rocco, suggests that the artist was trying to engage the audience and tell the story in a new way.[89] In that painting, Tintoretto broke with Venetian tradition, abandoning the central axis and the emphasis on the foreground, and instead placed Christ kneeling modestly in the left midground, head downcast. Christ and the Baptist, far from the largest figures in the painting, are set well back from the picture plane. Rather than a light-filled setting, the action takes place in an enveloping darkness, emphasizing the drama. Finally, the remarkable variety of brushwork in the canvas appears to be unprecedented.[90] Tintoretto might have employed these divergences from Venetian compositional practice to encourage greater concentration on the viewer's part.

Within this context, a comparison of Veronese and Tintoretto gets to the heart of the temperamental differences between the two painters. Both men's versions of the Baptism of Christ were painted within a few years of each other, and each probably represents the final autograph painting of the subject by the artist—in other words, the culmination of a lifetime's reflection on a central biblical theme. Both paintings have a vertical format, and the two compositions share some common elements, ascribable to Venetian tradition: Christ bows his head humbly below the dove of the Holy Spirit, and John is placed at the right edge. The discrepancies, however, are more revealing, and show each painter's awareness of his own strength: fertile landscape for Veronese, muscular figures for Tintoretto.

Although Tintoretto's altarpiece—painted for the Venetian church of San Silvestro and still housed there—is one of very few outstanding autograph works from the artist's last two decades, when the majority of his paintings included extensive workshop participation, it remained little known until its restoration in 2003–4.[91] The painting is justifiably dated to about 1580 in the literature, contemporaneous with or just after Tintoretto's paintings in the Sala Superiore of the Scuola Grande di San Rocco, which includes the *Baptism* mentioned above. The Apostolic Visitation of 1581, a survey of Venetian churches and their altars, notes that the first altar on the right was dedicated to John the Baptist and owned by the *peateri*, the trade guild of bargemen, seemingly too humble a patron to have received so late in Tintoretto's career a painting as exceptional as this.[92]

Tintoretto's looming, muscular figures of Christ and the Baptist, painted with confident contours and foreshortenings and a secure control of anatomy, immediately bring to mind the figures of Michelangelo, from whom Tintoretto received much inspiration. Although Vasari had attacked Tintoretto for a lack of finish in his paintings and for neglecting to make preparatory drawings, two surviving sheets, one for each of the principal figures, demonstrate how carefully Tintoretto worked out their poses.[93] Indeed, the sheet establishing John's pose originally showed the figure's left arm bent more tightly, with his left hand close to the shoulder. Evidently dissatisfied, Tintoretto redrew the arm extended, thus creating the beautiful sinuous line formed by John's arms, stretching from the upper right corner to above Christ's head. Tintoretto might have been the first to use John's outstretched arms to compose such a graceful pairing, and, indeed, a hallmark of his style is the use of linked figures to structure compositions. The arrangement of the two main individuals in the San Silvestro *Baptism* offers a particularly elegant pas de deux of two massive, sculptural figures.

The positioning and scale of the figures point to two further innovative aspects of this altarpiece. First, spurning tradition, Tintoretto removes the standing Christ from the central axis, placing the figures symmetrically on either side; this underscores John's role as the initiator of the ritual and Christ's as the recipient. Second, the figures are considerably larger in proportion to the picture surface than in previous Venetian treatments of the subject. The standing figures, well over half the height of the canvas, dominate the space; their massive forms appear too big for the pictorial field, a typical effect in Tintoretto. To be sure, the artist has paid attention to the setting. His river Jordan resembles the shore of the Venetian lagoon. He also makes clear that the locale was not chosen for its beauty, at a gentle river bend or inlet common in Venetian tradition, but rather that the action takes place at the source of the river itself, where the water spurts out of the rock at the right edge—thereby emphasizing that the soul's rebirth into Christianity flows from John and the sacrament he has introduced. Despite Tintoretto's efforts in the landscape, the figures are not set in a believable space as in Veronese's versions of the theme. Indeed, Tintoretto uses the two substantial figures to define the space, their energy relating more to the picture plane than to the depth of the rural setting. Tintoretto's figures in general do not stand, in the words of Hans Tietze, "on a firm stage, but on the rolling deck of a ship in rough sea." Without a doubt, the human figure is the cornerstone of Tintoretto's art.[94]

Moreover, Tintoretto carefully uses lighting to accentuate the two principal figures. As in many of his paintings, the use of light and shadow within a restricted palette brings out the full, sculptural solidity of the figures.[95] Subtle paired contrasts of lighting provide a sense of balance: Christ's head and torso in light but John's in shadow, for instance, or Christ's left leg and John's right both illuminated.[96] This attention to light implies a further theological message, exemplifying John 2:6–8: "There was a man named John, sent from God. He came to be a witness to testify regarding the Light, so that every one might believe through him. He was not himself the Light, but came in order to testify regarding the Light." The strong illumination on Christ, as well as the light of the Holy Spirit directly above, underscores the passage from John to Christ, from the old to the new order.

The relative austerity of Tintoretto's treatment—the simplified landscape, the near-monochrome palette, the absence of compositional details such as angel attendants—is typical of many of his later paintings. Yet it is worth considering that this stark picture may have been a response to Veronese, who had already executed a teeming and grandiose *Adoration of the Kings* in 1573 (National Gallery, London) for the same church of San Silvestro. Offered the opportunity to paint in a church containing the magnificent Veronese, Tintoretto seems to have poured himself into the task, which was certainly not the case with his many indifferent paintings from the same years in the Palazzo Ducale, where weak pictures from the Tintoretto *bottega* compare unfavorably with Veronese's productions. Tintoretto may have been trying here to make a statement about the importance of figure over setting, reducing a painting to its essentials. That the elderly, prominent artist produced a masterpiece for humble clients indicates that he cared deeply about this commission. Unlike Titian, who reserved his

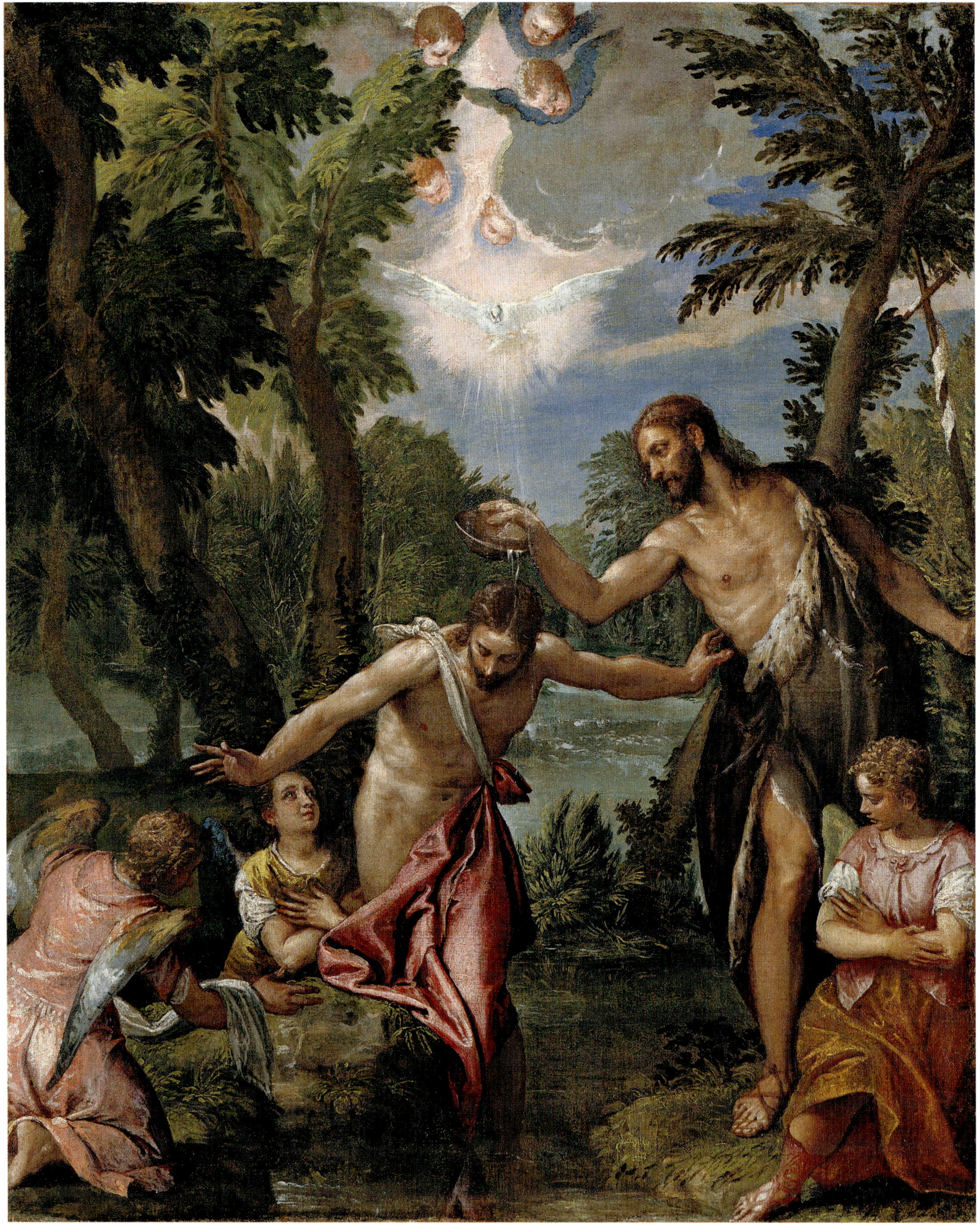

cat. 54

high-quality works in his later career for prestigious (generally royal) patrons, the amount of Tintoretto's own hand depended on his personal interest in the commission, not on the client's status.[97]

Tintoretto appears to acknowledge Veronese in one detail: the elegant rhetorical stance of the striding Christ, complete with a graceful turned body and gesturing arms. This is a pose closer to Veronese's types than Tintoretto's more typically tense and violent poses. Even as he refuted Veronese's predilections for bright and populated compositions with his *Baptism*, Tintoretto seems to have tipped his cap to his rival.

In turn, Veronese's probable final autograph treatment of the subject, now in the J. Paul Getty Museum, seems to be part of this dialogue with Tintoretto. Although presumed by Goldner to have been painted for a private chapel, the canvas at 104.8 x 88.3 cm (41¼ x 34¾ in.) would be quite small for an altarpiece.[98] It may have been intended for private devotion, perhaps for a client named Giovanni Battista, as Humfrey posited.[99] Unlike Tintoretto's painting, the palette is brighter, and the addition of three angels makes for a crowded foreground. Veronese's landscape is lush and specific, celebrating the beauty of God's creation. The various rivulets and grassy banks of the river are clearly delineated, constituting a specific and believable setting. Whereas Tintoretto used his two principal figures to define the painted space, Veronese has inserted the figures of Christ, John, and three kneeling angels into measurable and logical surroundings. Veronese breaks with his earlier paintings of the Baptism by showing Christ with his arms extended; this may be read as a gesture of his acceptance of the ritual and perhaps future sacrifice on the cross. This new pose, as well as the concentrated, even serious mood, may be attributed to Tintoretto's example. Although the painting's quality has been occasionally dismissed by scholars, it stands up to repeated scrutiny.[100] The weak sections—the cherubs at the top, and especially the awkward angel wearing yellow immediately behind Christ—were probably painted by an assistant; otherwise, this is an autograph painting by Veronese, displaying his confident anatomy, verdant landscape, and luminous draperies, all skillfully rendered.

The date of the Getty painting remains uncertain, although the more tremulous brushwork and dappled light mark it as a late work, and it is generally assigned to the first half of the 1580s.[101] The question of its chronology is complicated by the existence of a set of sketches by Veronese for Baptisms (Fogg Art Museum, Cambridge, MA) drawn on the back of a letter in his handwriting, dated February 1587 (1588, modern style).[102] The letter, presumably never sent, and thus the drawings, would date from the very last months of the painter's life, since he died on April 19, 1588. The sketch on the upper left of the Fogg sheet shows a grouping of figures of Christ and the Baptist clearly dependent on Tintoretto's altarpiece. As Goldner has argued, Veronese used the San Silvestro painting as his point of departure for his sketch, eventually evolving a pose with the arms of Christ even further extended, and employed this in the Getty painting.[103] By this line of reasoning, the canvas was executed in the last weeks of the painter's life. Although definitely a picture from the 1580s, the canvas does not share the markedly fragmented forms, tenebrous lighting, and vibrant brushwork of such works as *Saint Pantaleon Healing a Child* (fig. 103), securely dated to 1587.[104] Rather, it seems more likely that Veronese painted the Getty *Baptism* within a few years of Tintoretto's prototype, deciding to employ the unprecedented pose within a more traditional and beautiful landscape. Then, not long before his death, he returned to the theme as he planned further paintings, including an altarpiece for the Church of the Redentore.[105] With the Fogg drawing, Veronese again demonstrated his admiration for Tintoretto's figural invention, conceding his competitor's creativity.

— FI

The Passion of Christ

TITIAN
Entombment, 1559
Museo Nacional del Prado, Madrid
(cat. 55)

The Passion of Christ, the central narrative of the Christian faith, is rich in events and imagery that inspired Venetian painters to some of their most powerful works. These range from the intimate (cat. 3) to the monumentally panoramic (fig. 110). Although the Passion story is often defined as consisting of all episodes from the entry into Jerusalem through Pentecost, the events of Holy Thursday and Good Friday—particularly those around Christ's crucifixion and entombment—are typically the most moving and heartfelt. These scenes underscore the fragility of the human body; as Christ admonishes his most trusted disciples during the Agony in the Garden, "The spirit is willing, but the flesh is weak."

The Passion story is especially associated with the late works of Titian, Tintoretto, and Veronese. It is striking, however, that almost none of the surviving paintings of these subjects dates from the early decades of the artists' careers. With only few exceptions, Christ's final days, death, and burial are simply not part of their youthful production, and begin to be depicted in a major way only when Titian was in his midfifties, Tintoretto in his late thirties, and Veronese in his midforties.[106] The rarity of certain subject matter in the works of the three painters may depend more on the luck of physical survival and the demands of patrons than on the artists' preferences, but the relative absence of these topics in early productions makes their predominance in mature and late work all the more conspicuous.

The few examples of Titian's paintings of Passion scenes from his youth and early maturity show depth of feeling but lack the special intensity characteristic of those from his final decades. Conversely, Veronese's late scenes from the Passion carry an emotional charge not present in pictures of the subject from his earlier maturity. Tintoretto, finally, presents a slightly different case: his greatest and most moving Passion scenes are from the years of his maturity, from the mid-1550s through the late 1560s, when his brilliant conceptions were brought to completion with his own virtuoso brush. Aside

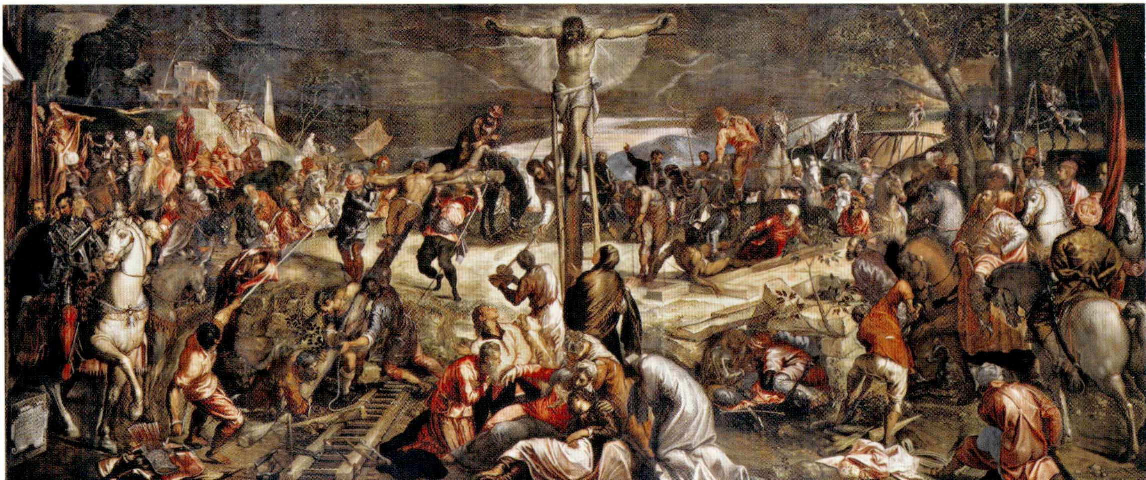

Fig. 110. Tintoretto, *Crucifixion*, 1565, oil on canvas, Scuola Grande di San Rocco, Venice

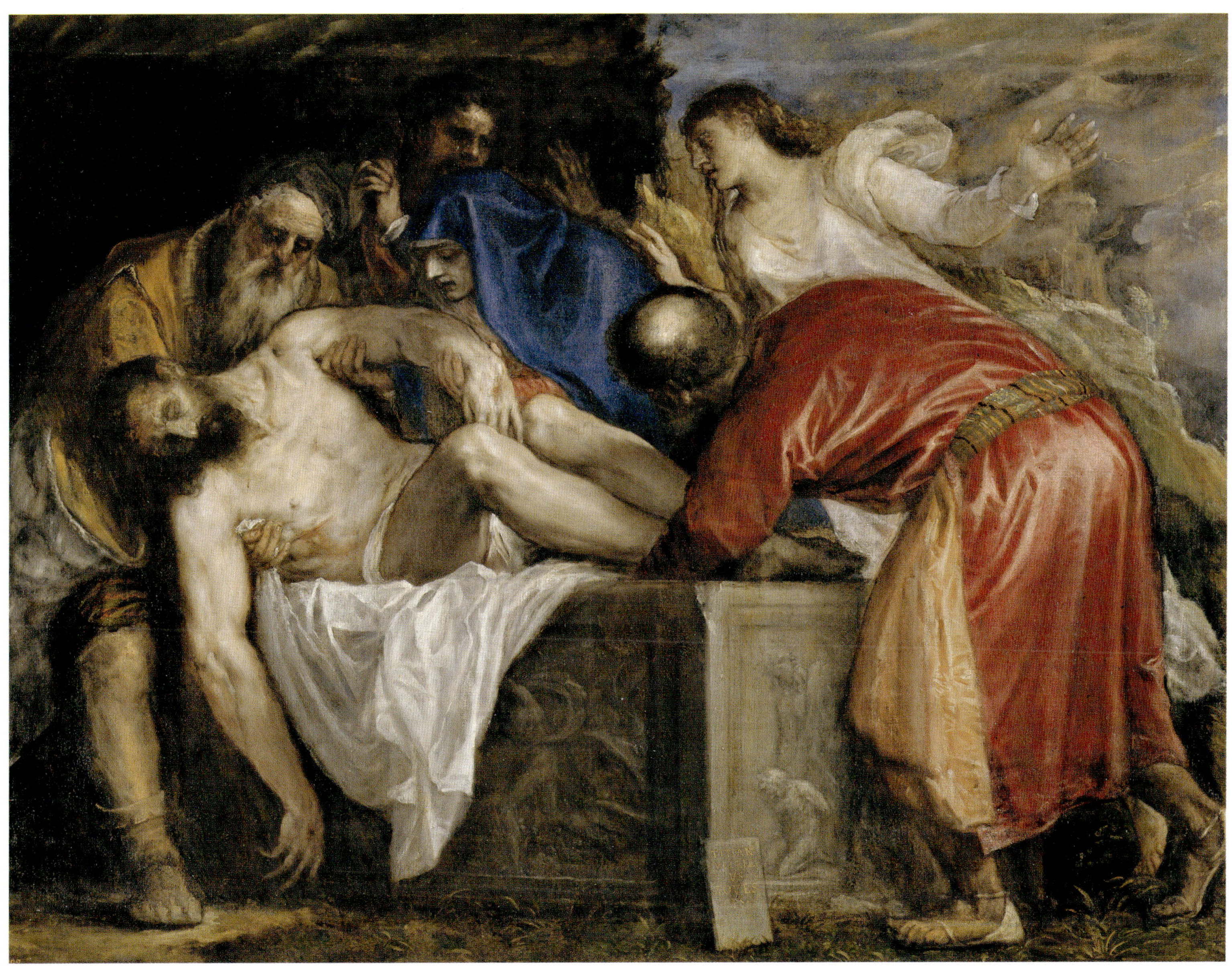

cat. 55

Fig. 111
Titian
Entombment of Christ, about 1520
Oil on canvas
Musée du Louvre, Paris

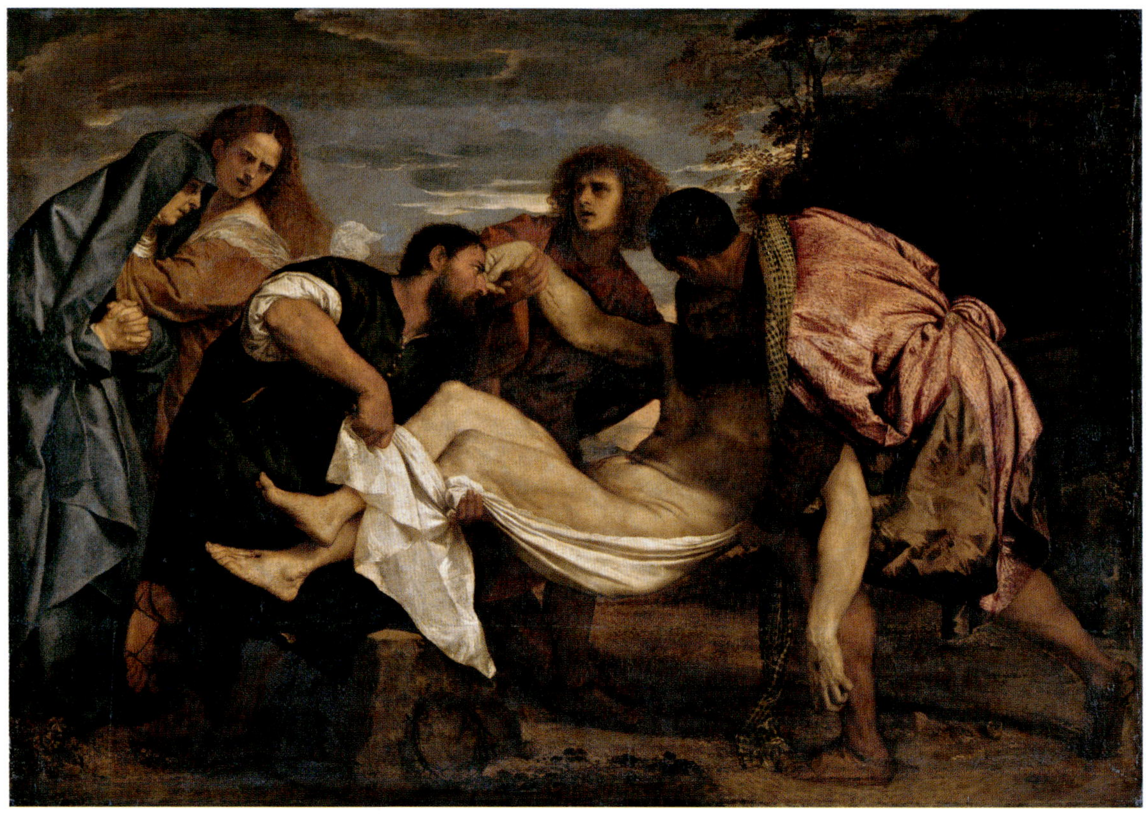

from works in the Scuola Grande di San Rocco (which date from 1578 to 1581), there are few if any primarily autograph Passion paintings by Tintoretto from the last two decades of his life. Titian's *Entombment* and Veronese's *Agony in the Garden* demonstrate the special compatibility of the two artists' late styles with these tragic subjects. (Tintoretto's *Deposition* [cat. 18] can also be considered in this context.)

Titian's *Entombment* was sent to Phillip II in 1559 to replace a painting of the same subject that had been mysteriously lost in transit two years earlier. Titian had previously treated the subject much earlier in his career, in a painting of about 1520 (fig. 111).[107] That picture shows a slightly earlier moment in the narrative: Christ's body is being carried toward the tomb at the right edge of the canvas, rather than lowered into the sarcophagus at the edge of the cave, as in the present painting. Taking inspiration from prototypes by Raphael and a frieze on an antique sarcophagus, Titian adds an aspect of naturalism through his attention to effects of light and atmosphere, achieved through his mastery of oil technique.[108] The distressed facial expressions of John the Evangelist and Mary Magdalen, as well as the palpably heavy and limp body of Christ, convey immense sorrow.

In the painting for Philip II, the emotional pitch of the scene is higher, as exemplified by the anguish expressed in Magdalen's out-flung arms. The figure of Christ is given greater emphasis, propped up frontally toward the viewer and bathed in a more dramatic light, rendering it particularly ashen. The grieving Virgin supports Christ's arm, her face juxtaposed with his hand and its prominent nail wound. Miguel Falomir has identified the textual source for the motif of the Virgin holding Christ's arm (which does not appear in the Gospels) as Pietro Aretino's *I quattro libri de la humanità di Cristo* (1535).[109] If Aretino's devotional text was indeed Titian's point of departure, the figure supporting Christ by his shoulders in the painting would be Nicodemus, while the one holding his feet would be Joseph of Arimathea, since this is how Aretino describes their roles. As Augusto Gentili has noted, the former strongly resembles portraits of Titian himself from this period, and is probably a self-portrait.[110] The relief most clearly visible on the sarcophagus depicts the Sacrifice of Isaac, an Old Testament prefiguration of Christ's sacrifice.

The High Renaissance logic and showy passages of still life—particularly the crisp areas of gathered folds of fabric—that characterized the earlier treatment of the theme are absent in Titian's later *Entombment*. Here the figures fill up the frame, overlapping one another without any clear definition of space. Broken brushstrokes dissolve form and firm contour; in the suggestion of a landscape and dramatic sky at the right edge, they approach abstraction. Much of the painting shows the blended, almost monochromatic tones of Titian's final works, but here such passages set off areas of brilliant local color: the intense blue of the Virgin's mantle, the rich red and orange of Joseph's robe, and the pure white of Christ's shroud, so dazzling that it takes on an affirmative value equal to the other passages of color. The saturation of the color and agitation of the brushwork enhance the picture's dramatic urgency.

Tintoretto's *Deposition* (cat. 18) was probably completed at roughly the same time as Titian's painting, or perhaps several years earlier, although it can be dated only on stylistic grounds.[111] The two pictures have much in common: the grief-stricken gesture of the Magdalen; the emphasis on the weight of the body of Christ; the deep chiaroscuro, with the brightest illumination playing over and drawing attention to these two principal figures; and the manner in which the interlocking bodies fill up almost the entire pictorial space, forming a rectangle out of many individual elements. Although the sequence in which the two pictures were painted is not known, the qualities that they share are more characteristic of Tintoretto than Titian. Thus it may not be too much to suggest that, even at this late date, and despite his professed disdain for his younger rival, Titian found much to admire in Tintoretto's work, and indeed perhaps had the younger painter's version in mind when he executed the canvas for Philip.

Tintoretto, at the end of his life, returned to the subject of the Entombment in the altarpiece for the Cappella dei Morti at the church of San Giorgio Maggiore (fig. 52), probably the last picture to emerge from his *bottega* before his death in 1594. Here the Eucharistic aspect of the picture, already evident in the earlier painting, is particularly plain: the open tomb finds an analogy in the space in front of the picture plane, where the altar would be, and Christ's body is held up by the mourners as though it were a sacrificial offering. John Shearman has noted the iconographic similarity to Pontormo's *Entombment* (church of Santa Felicità, Florence), and how both altarpieces depict a moment different from the more conventional images of the Lamentation, as seen in Titian's pictures. Moreover, both Pontormo's and Tintoretto's altarpiece take into account the position of the viewer: "The moment again freezes at the point where the body is presented sacramentally to the spectator."[112]

Although the focus is on Christ and the figures supporting him in the painting's foreground, Tintoretto uses elements in the distance to make the viewer recall two distinct earlier moments in the narrative: Calvary, where Christ's crucifixion took place, is shown at the top of the pictorial field, while in the middle ground are the Virgin and her two attendants, who only moments earlier had formed a Pietà. Specific gestures reinforce the sense of unfolding action: Christ's arms are stretched out as though he was still on the cross, echoed by the arms of the swooning Virgin.

It is often suggested that the face of Joseph of Arimathea is a self-portrait of Tintoretto, analogous to Titian's self-portrait in the figure of Saint Jerome he painted for his own tomb (fig. 108). Certainly one would like to think that there is something of Tintoretto's hand in this final work. It is more likely, however, that the execution of the painting is entirely by Tintoretto's son Domenico, whose characteristic figure types can be detected in almost all of the protagonists. Nevertheless, it is surely to the elder Tintoretto that we owe the composition and the compelling emotional impact of the altarpiece, which with good reason has long been considered a capstone to his career.

Veronese's *Agony in the Garden* (fig. 112) is first documented in the will, dated 1584, of the ducal sec-

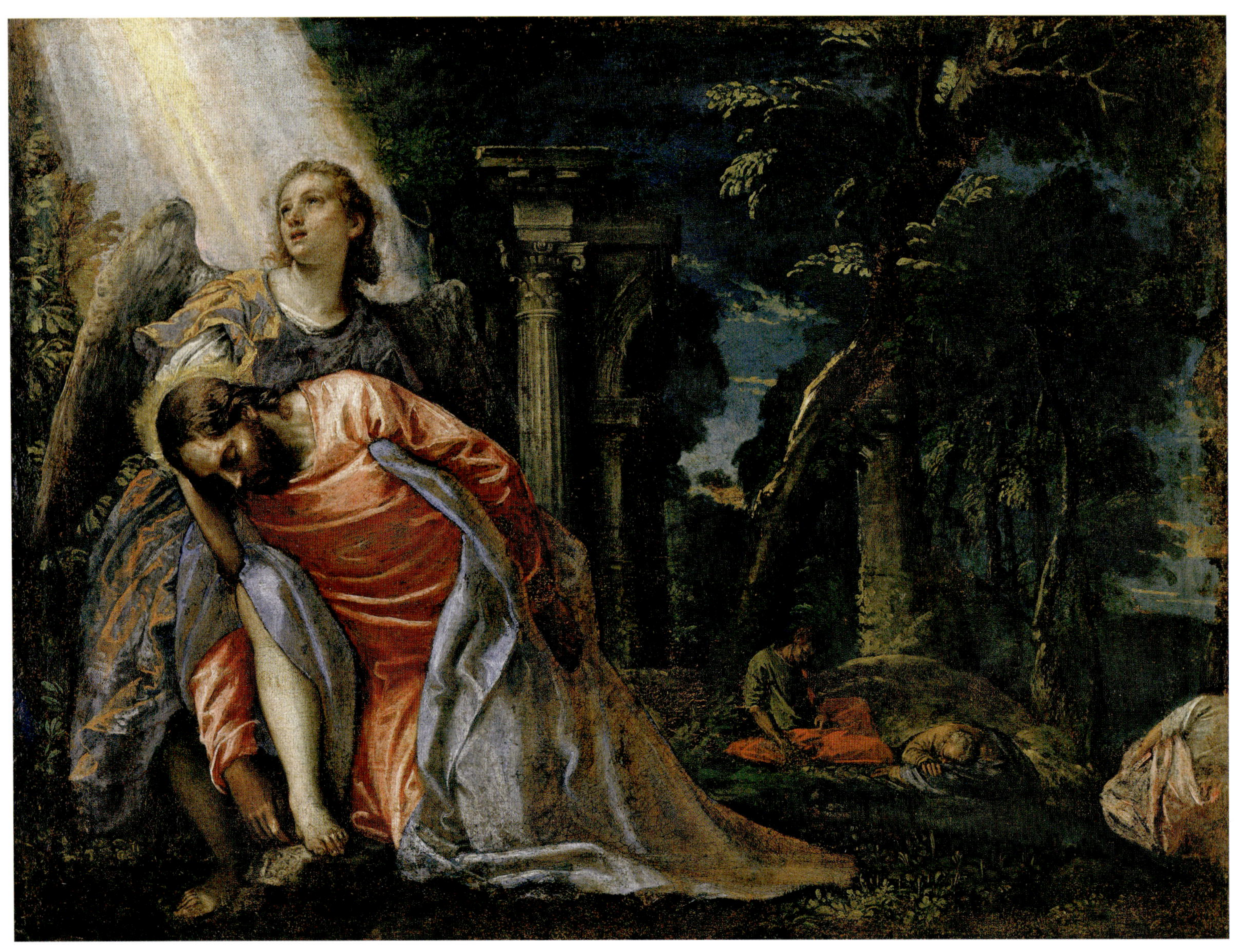

Fig. 112
Veronese
Agony in the Garden, about 1583
Oil on canvas
Pinacoteca di Brera, Milan

retary Simone Lando, who left the sum of 1000 ducats and a group of paintings by Jacopo Bassano and Veronese to beautify the church of the Franciscan convent of Santa Maria Maggiore.[113] Based on its style, current scholars agree that the picture should be dated shortly before Lando's will. A drawing in Berlin shows Veronese working out the pose of the two principal figures.[114] The picture's relatively intimate size and meditative mood would be consistent with devotional purposes, suggesting that it was originally commissioned by Lando for his private collection. Most earlier depictions of the subject, including examples by Titian and Tintoretto, and one possibly by Veronese himself, show Christ in prayer, gazing upward as the angel descends bearing a cup. This traditional iconography illustrates the passages in the Gospels of Mark and Matthew in which Christ reveals his fear of his fate, and prays that the cup might be taken away from him. Veronese, in contrast, depicts Christ slumped, possibly fainting, having understood the sacrifice that is demanded of him. Christ is sustained and comforted by the angel, whose eyes look heavenward in commiseration, both figures bathed in heavenly light. Richard Cocke has pointed out that Veronese's painting can be related to Luke 22:43: "'Father, if thou be willing, remove this cup from me: nevertheless not my will, but thine, be done.' And there appeared an angel unto him from heaven, strengthening him." As Cocke notes, Veronese's *Agony in the Garden* is an early example of a formation that was to become very popular in later decades. A recent study by Lucia Casellato identifies Veronese's picture as the first in which Christ's agony was depicted as a state of complete prostration, and describes it as a critical step in the development of an approach to the theme in which Christ is presented as the object of sympathy, because of his suffering, rather than as a model to be admired and emulated, on account of his humility and resignation.[115]

Veronese's composition is pared down to the essential forms of Christ and the angel; the other apostles, asleep in the garden, are barely visible in the landscape to the right. The emotional power of the picture derives from the mystical light that creates a shimmering play of color over the forms of Christ and the angel. Always a brilliant colorist, Veronese uses color in a new way here, free from any allegiance to naturalism or decorative effect, as a means of expressing the divine. His flickering brushwork dematerializes the forms and imparts a soft, liquid quality to the wondering face of the angel. Although the appearance of the two paintings are very different, Veronese's *Agony in the Garden* shares with Tintoretto's visionary *Saint Reading* from the Scuola Grande di San Rocco (fig. 101), dating from almost exactly the same time, the sense that the artist is painting with light, his brush rendering a divine energy that transfigures the natural world.

— RE, FI

Self-Portrait in Old Age

TINTORETTO
Self-Portrait, about 1588
Musée du Louvre, Paris
(cat. 56)

If Tintoretto's youthful *Self-Portrait* of about 1546–47 (cat. 9) can be read as a declaration of his fiery ambition, his later one of about 1588 seems to embody resignation. The earlier portrait emphasized a young painter apparently on the verge of fame; four decades later, that spark seems almost extinguished. Tintoretto's frontal pose fills the lower half of the pictorial field, and he addresses the viewer (and himself, since it is his own face he confronts) with a solemn stare.[116] Yet even this connection is muted: his eyes are in shadow, their sunken and weary aspect emphasized by the strong light from overhead. Tintoretto typically depicted his sitters soberly, grounding them in a quiet dignity. Here, where the sitter was also the elderly painter, such gravity is taken to an extreme. Tintoretto, an artist with a remarkable ability to convey the textures of fur and rich cloth, has retreated from showy display in the treatment of the fur collar. Instead, the only flashy passages are the hair and bushy, seemingly windblown beard that wreaths his face. The palette has been drained of color, "a chromatic range from impenetrable black to frosty white."[117] This stillness extends to an apparent silence: both the lips and ears are hidden.[118] The hollow eyes dominate.

The present portrait can be dated to around 1588, based on an engraving by the Flemish artist Gijsbert van Veen (about 1562–1628) that includes this image at the center of elaborate allegorical montage, with an inscription noting that it represents the celebrated Venetian painter at age seventy.[119] Although the portrait may have been painted to provide a model for the print, one senses that Tintoretto created this picture primarily for himself, rather than for reproduction and dissemination. The painting's unyielding austerity clashes with the celebratory air of the print, and the artist's expression does not reflect any sign of pride at his remarkable public accomplishments. It is hard to see this as the image of a man who had recently completed the cycle of canvases in the Scuola Grande di San Rocco and many paintings for the Palazzo Ducale, a man whose position in Venice by then was virtually unassailable. But perhaps that was the point. Possibly the rivalry that had long impelled him was now dissipating. As Rearick has noted, "It may not be entirely coincidental that his only real rival, Paolo Veronese, had died still in his prime the previous year. Alone and unchallenged, old Jacopo has no more battles to wage."[120] Even if the painted portrait predated Veronese's death, Titian, his only other serious rival, had long departed the scene, and Tintoretto's own working pace and that of his *bottega* had slackened by the late 1580s.

This sense of isolation receives some confirmation in the early sources, Ridolfi remarking that, despite Tintoretto's great success, the artist was frustrated in his later years, "impeded by excessive work," his spirit "battered by turbulence."[121] Venetian painters, particularly Titian, often claimed poverty, and Tintoretto's large family—eight children are mentioned in a petition to the government of 1574—suggests that he may never have felt financially secure.[122] The portrait appears to reflect this disheartened mood. Documents record that Tintoretto painted other self-portraits, now lost, which would help assess the extent to which his self-portraits mirrored the vicissitudes of his career. In any case, the accepted and possible self-portraits of both Titian and Veronese show nothing as unflinching as this.[123]

— FI

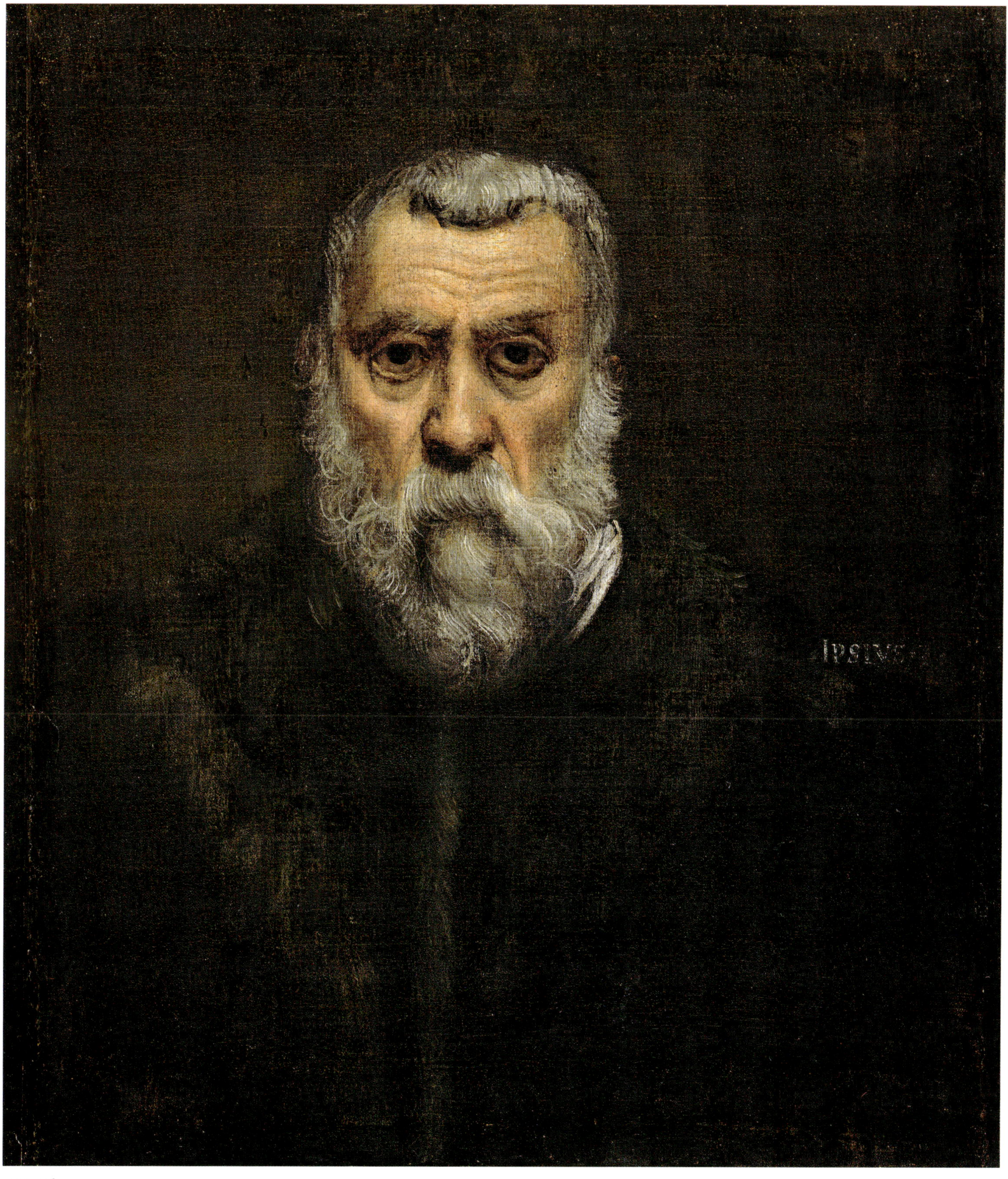

cat. 56

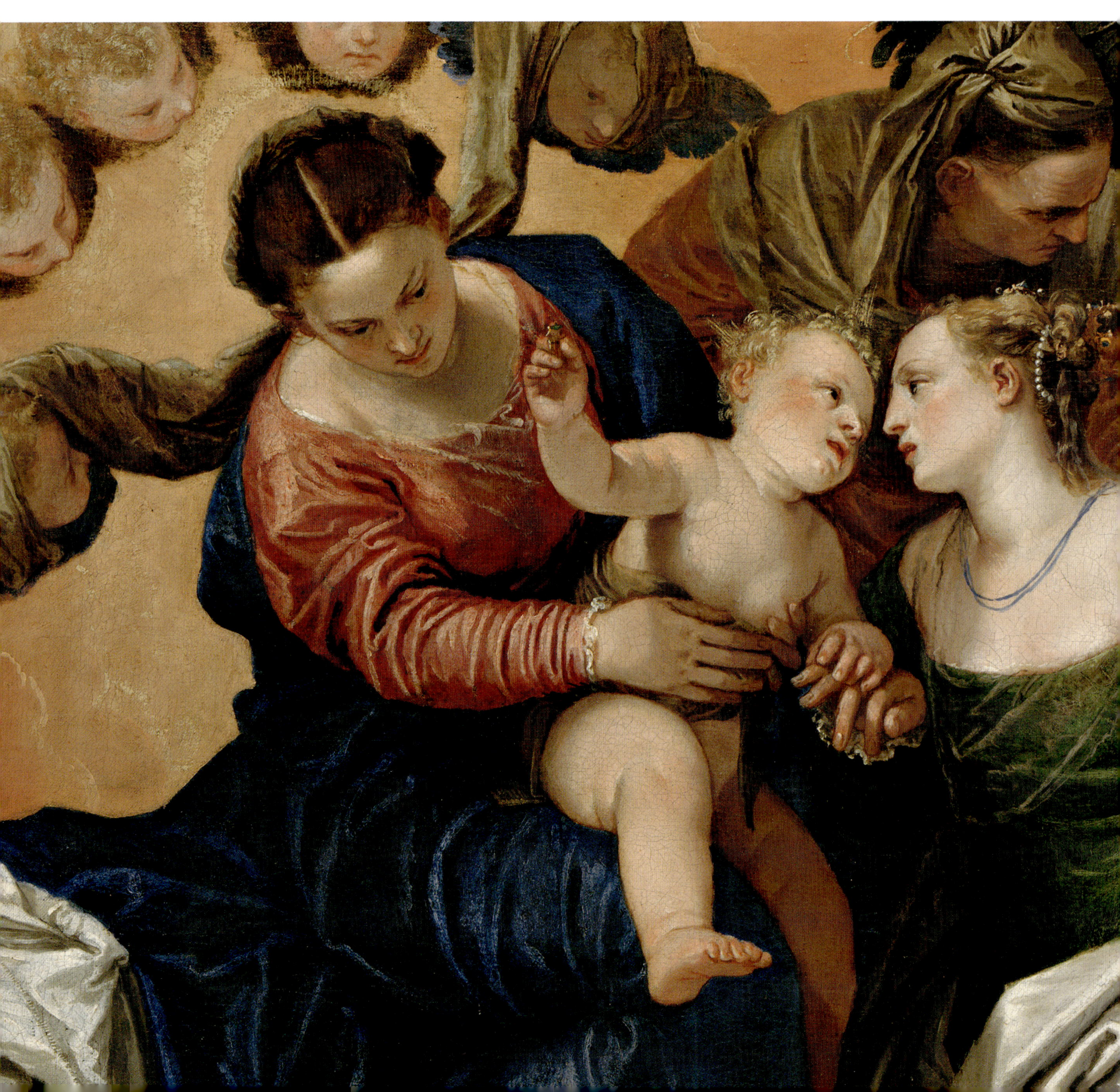

APPENDICES

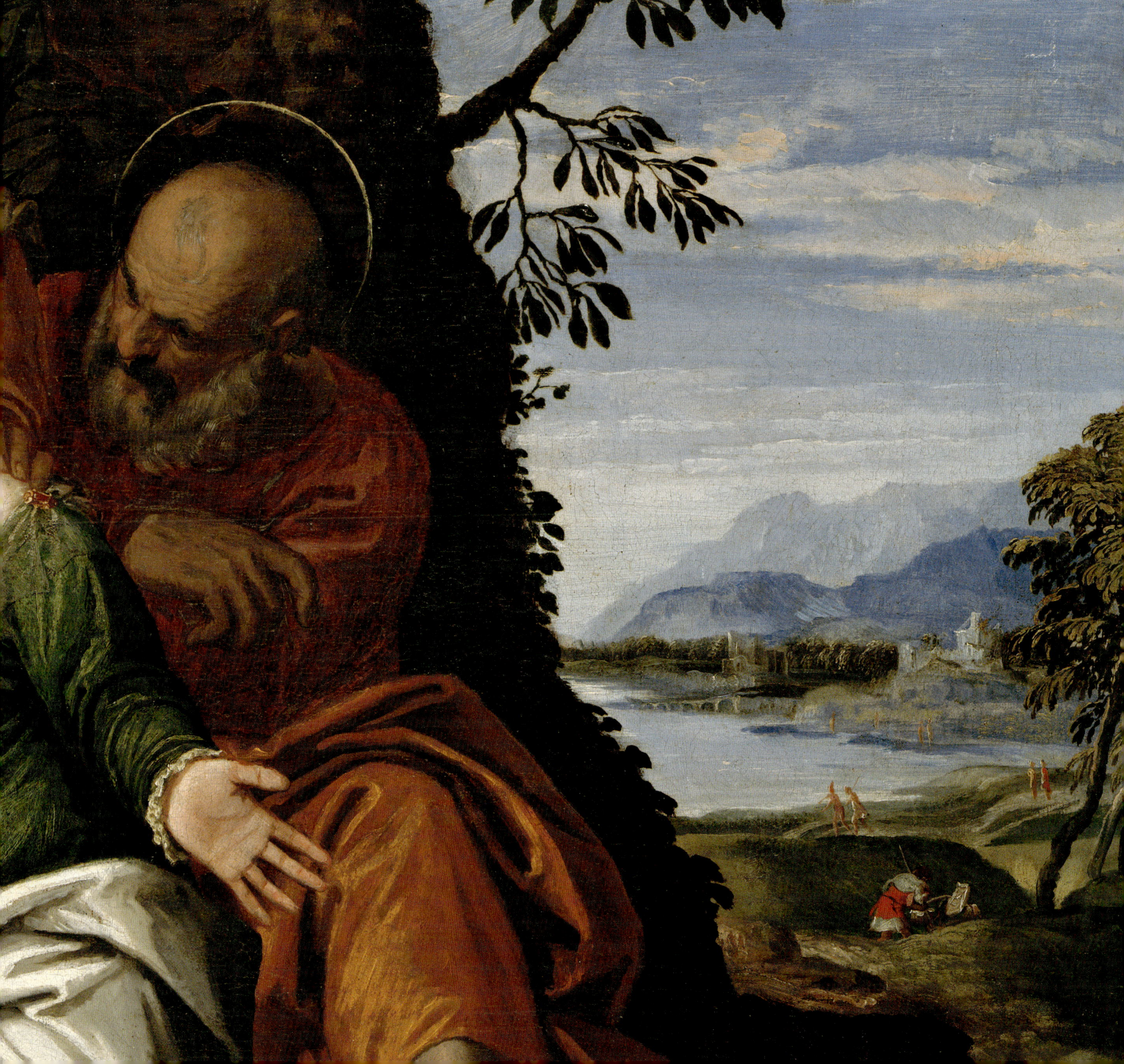

Boston Collects Venetian Paintings

Evidence of Boston's interest in Venetian art goes back nearly two centuries. In 1833, the English telegraph entrepreneur John Watkins Brett displayed his collection, including allegedly authentic works by Titian (an *Entombment*) and Tintoretto (a *Crucifixion*), in one of the earliest exhibitions at the Boston Athenaeum.[1] Boston was also the birthplace of one of the first important American collectors of Italian Renaissance paintings, James Jackson Jarves. Jarves moved to Florence in 1852 and began to acquire a large and important collection of mostly fourteenth- and fifteenth-century "primitives," as well as a few later works, including a notable early Titian painting of the Circumcision. Wishing to convince his fellow Bostonians of the worth of early Italian painting, he wrote several books and in 1859 began actively seeking a Boston institution to buy his collection. But although the trustees of the Boston Athenaeum were initially enthusiastic, putting up $5,000 of the $20,000 total price, they could not attract other donors, and the groundbreaking collection eventually went to Yale University.[2]

Boston collectors in Jarves's wake were less ambitious, but at least some of their acquisitions remained local. The brothers Thomas and Cornelius Felton, sons of the Harvard professor and president Cornelius Conway Felton, acquired paintings in Europe, including some from the dealer Domenico Giobbe in Venice in 1882—paintings that they soon lent to the young Museum of Fine Arts. The collectors may have been poorly advised, or simply in over their heads, as the works they purchased have not stood the test of time. Their big "Titian," the *Mystic Marriage of Saint Catherine* (eventually donated to the MFA in 1942 by Cornelius Felton's widow, Eunice Whitney Felton, in memory of her husband), was later determined to be a copy of a painting by Paris Bordone, and is now kept in the storeroom. Their similarly large "Tintoretto," *Adoration of the Magi*, once prominently hung in the MFA's old premises at Copley Square, was offered for sale to the MFA in 1929, but despite a glowing article in a local paper and the efforts of Cornelius's widow, the Museum declined. The painting was eventually given to Radcliffe College, and transferred to the Fogg Art Museum in 1966. Clearly a derivation of Domenico Tintoretto's large painting of the same subject in the church of San Trovaso, and bearing no sign of Jacopo's hand, this picture is now also held in storage.[3]

According to William Howe Downes, a Boston critic writing in the *Atlantic Monthly* in 1888, local private collections included "genuine paintings by Titian, Tintoretto, Giordano, Il Bassano," but he did not reveal the names of the owners. Downes did mention paintings then on display at the Museum of Fine Arts, including a 1485 Bartolomeo Vivarini altarpiece in "a good state of preservation."[4] This polyptych, combining painting, sculpture, and an unusually intact frame, was eventually donated to the Museum by Quincy Adams Shaw in 1901. Like other ambitious Boston collectors of his era, Shaw sought out large-format paintings—not just the typical "over the sofa picture"—and he also collected in several distinct areas, particularly canvases and pastels by Jean-François Millet, as well as Renaissance relief sculpture, including an outstanding Donatello. The Museum also made some fine purchases of Northern Italian paintings in these early years, including an early Moroni double portrait, *Man and a Boy*, in 1895, purchased through Bernard Berenson.

Perhaps the greatest connoisseur of Italian paintings of his generation, Berenson is also one of the pivotal figures in Boston collecting. Although he was born in Lithuania and lived most of his life near Florence, he was educated at Boston Latin School and Harvard University, and always regarded Boston fondly. His importance to the collecting culture of Boston was grounded in his friendship with Isabella Stewart Gardner, one of the patrons who financed his 1885 *wanderjahre* in Europe. The long correspondence between Berenson and Gardner shows how he shaped her taste in spite of her famously strong will. Gardner loved Venetian painting and architecture enough to build her home, Fenway Court, as a fantasy of a Venetian palazzo, incorporating original architectural fragments, and to fill it with a great collection of art, much of it Italian. Letters such as this 1895 missive to the thirty-year-old Berenson, who was just beginning to serve as her art adviser and purchasing agent, make clear her particular soft spot for Tintoretto: "My foremost desire always is for a Filippino Lippi; and a Velásquez *very* good—and Tintoretto. Only very good need apply!"[5]

Gardner never did acquire a "very good" Tintoretto (though her *Lady in Black* is a fine portrait by his son Domenico). She did, however, obtain what is perhaps the greatest Venetian painting in North America—Berenson acting in this case as both help and hindrance. In the spring of 1896, Gardner was stymied in her attempt to acquire Gainsborough's *Blue Boy*, only to have Berenson offer the possibility of an even greater prize: Titian's *Europa* (fig. 106). Believing that Gardner's money would be tied up in purchasing the Gainsborough, however, he had initially sought another Boston buyer for the Titian. A breathless letter of May 10, 1896, reveals Berenson's patriotic wish to obtain the best for Boston. "The Titian *Europa* is the finest Italian picture ever again to be sold," he justified himself to his patron. "I hated its going elsewhere than to America, and if possible to Boston. Thus in my despair I immediately wrote to Mrs. S. D. Warren urging her to buy it." Happily for Gardner, she was able to pounce on the opportunity before Mrs. Warren did, and by August 25, *Europa* was in her possession.[6] This acquisition marked a shift in her preferences away from English art of the eighteenth century and toward a remarkable zeal for Italian Renaissance painting.

Although Gardner was not nearly as wealthy as some of the Gilded Age collectors to whom she is often compared, she was decisive when it came to purchases, and thus far more nimble than the cautious museum located practically next door to her. On September 11, 1896, Gardner dashed off a note "to say merely that if our stupid and impossible [Boston] Art Museum does not get the Giorgione (the Christ head, you know) please get it for me. I have seen the photographs and like it. They won't move quickly enough to get it I fear." Once it became clear that the MFA would not purchase the painting, Gardner worked with Berenson, obtaining it in 1898. (The picture [cat. 3] is now considered the work of another painter in the circle of Giovanni Bellini rather than by Giorgione.) The occasional squabbles between Gardner and Berenson also illustrate Berenson's continued loyalty to Boston. When Gardner reproached her agent for apparently offering paintings first to other buyers, including the MFA, Berenson replied that she would always have right of first refusal, but that he would remain "guided by the principles which have always actuated me, to use all my influence to get pictures to America, and if possible to Boston."[7]

In subsequent decades, the Museum of Fine Arts continued to receive donations and make judicious purchases, as the limited endowments allowed. In 1930, Curator of Paintings Philip Hendy, who had just completed a catalogue of Gardner's paintings and drawings, recommended that the MFA buy a small late Veronese, *Dead Christ Supported by Angels*, noting its relative bargain price of $16,000: "If the subject were of the frivolous type in demand for apartment decoration the price would be about five times as great. The Museum's best hope of forming a collection with reasonable economy lies with such dignified subjects, too expressive for private, millionaire tastes."[8] With its enforced frugality, the Museum could not compete for magnificent mythological pictures like the Metropolitan Museum of Art's *Mars and Venus United by Love* by Veronese (cat. 34), but tried instead to fill other gaps with works like the somber, late *Dead Christ*. The modesty of available funds may well have helped determine Hendy's return to England in October 1933, only three and a half years after he had joined the MFA.

In the absence of a curator, George Harold Edgell, a trustee and specialist in the painting of Renaissance Siena, took on the role part-time starting in the summer of 1934, and by October was named director of the Museum. The subsequent appointment of an expert in Italian painting, W. G. Constable, as curator in 1937 can be taken as a sign of renewed interest in the Italian collection. It appears that Museum management felt a window was about to close, and wanted to make major acquisitions of paintings while there was still time. In 1938, Edgell traveled to New York to examine Giorgione's Allendale *Nativity*, then owned by the art dealer Joseph Duveen. Although that picture was soon bought instead by the Kress Foundation for the National Gallery of Art, the MFA continued to search for a major Renaissance picture. In a handwritten note of March 25, 1943, Constable described to the director his reaction to a Titian portrait sent up by the New York dealer Knoedler. Declaring that a "truly important picture has just come in," possessing an admirable "swagger," he expressed confidence about raising the purchase price of $70,000, concluding: "I have only lived with it an hour—but I fear [its purchase] may be our fate."[9] A further letter from Constable on April 8 justified the asking price in a very depressed art market: "The present portrait in the late twenties would almost certainly be priced at $250,000 to $300,000." Part of the appeal was its status as a discovery; it was "practically unknown," with a nineteenth-century Sicilian provenance (see fig. 93). Titian's *Portrait of a Man Holding a Book* (cat. 38) was purchased that month, and the director trumpeted the acquisition in the Museum *Bulletin* that autumn, his tone evincing a certain relief: "The Museum has at last obtained a very distinguished portrait by Titian."[10]

Evidently trying to fill another gap, in 1948 the MFA bought a second Titian, a late religious painting, *Saint Catherine of Alexandria at Prayer* (cat. 25), offered by Rosenberg and Steibel. The canvas was signed and had a distinguished provenance going back to the late sixteenth century. After several rounds of negotiation, the price was dropped to $75,000 and the purchase completed.[11] Although both Titians have suffered from scholarly neglect since the publication of Harold Wethey's Titian catalogue raisonné, they have always been on public view.[12] With hindsight it seems clear that the Museum could have done considerably worse with acquisitions of Venetian Renaissance painting at that time, given the rapidly constricting market and the large number of weaker, "school of" pieces available. For example, the National Gallery of Art's superlative holdings of Titian, Tintoretto, and Veronese—largely formed of works purchased by Andrew Mellon and the Samuel Kress Foundation in the 1930s and 1940s—include, in addition to their many masterpieces, a number of pedestrian works by workshop assistants or imitators. Even those buying at the top of the market were not immune to acquisition mistakes. Closer to home, at the time *Saint Catherine* was acquired, Constable was also enthusiastic about buying a Tintoretto portrait from the same dealer, but the proposal died in committee. The picture was then purchased by the Currier Gallery of Art in Manchester, New Hampshire (now the Currier Museum of Art)—though in recent times, the painting, *Pietro Capello, Governor of Fruili*, has been relegated to the storeroom.

While both MFA Titians were purchases, the large Tintoretto *Nativity* (cat. 26) arrived as a donation in 1946. This painting, too, has been largely ignored in the literature, but following its recent conservation treatment, it deserves a place as one of the major Tintoretto paintings in North America.[13] The charming Veronese *Jupiter and a Nude* (cat. 24) came from a group of small mythological paintings probably used to decorate a frieze in a domestic setting. Four of these were donated to the MFA by Mrs. Jackson Holmes between 1959 and 1964.[14] In the past few years, rather than make new acquisitions of Venetian Renaissance paintings, the Museum's goal has been to examine, conserve, and study anew this relatively neglected collection. Of the Venetian paintings at the Museum that have received recent technical examinations, three pictures—Tintoretto's *Nativity*, Titian's *Saint Catherine*, and Veronese's *Jupiter and a Nude*—offer particularly interesting and even surprising case studies into the processes of their creation (see "Beneath the Surface," beginning on page 155). Indeed, *Titian, Tintoretto, Veronese: Rivals in Renaissance Venice* offers a full consideration of the art of these glorious painters, bringing to fruition an exhibition that John Watkins Brett could only have dreamed of in 1833.

– FI

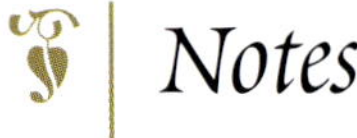

Notes

Note to the reader

The following abbreviations are used throughout the notes for frequently cited sources. For all other sources, the full bibliographic details are given on first mention in each chapter and an abbreviated form is used thereafter.

Echols and Ilchman, "Toward a New Tintoretto Catalogue"
Echols, Robert, and Frederick Ilchman. "Toward a New Tintoretto Catalogue, with a Checklist of Revised Attributions and a New Chronology." In *Jacopo Tintoretto: Actas del congreso internacional/Proceedings of the International Symposium*, Museo Nacional del Prado, Madrid, February 26–27, 2007. Madrid: Museo Nacional del Prado, forthcoming.

Falomir, *Tintoretto*
Falomir, Miguel, ed. *Tintoretto*. Exh. cat. Madrid: Museo Nacional del Prado, 2007.

Humfrey, *Titian: The Complete Paintings*
Humfrey, Peter. *Titian: The Complete Paintings*. Ghent: Ludion, 2007.

Jaffé, *Titian*
Jaffé, David, ed. *Titian*. Exh. cat. London: National Gallery, 2003.

Pallucchini and Rossi, *Opere sacre e profane*
Pallucchini, Rodolfo, and Paola Rossi. *Tintoretto: Le opere sacre e profane*. 2 vols. Venice: Alfieri, 1982.

Penny, *Sixteenth Century Italian Paintings*
Penny, Nicholas. *National Gallery Catalogues: The Sixteenth Century Italian Paintings*. 2 vols. London: National Gallery, 2004–8.

Pignatti and Pedrocco, *Veronese*
Pignatti, Terisio, and Filippo Pedrocco. *Veronese*. 2 vols. Milan: Electa, 1995.

Rearick, *Art of Paolo Veronese*
Rearick, W. R. *The Art of Paolo Veronese, 1528–1588*. Exh. cat. Washington, DC: National Gallery of Art, 1988.

Rosand, *Painting in Sixteenth-Century Venice*
Rosand, David. *Painting in Sixteenth-Century Venice: Titian, Veronese, Tintoretto*. Rev. ed. Cambridge: Cambridge University Press, 1997.

Wethey, *Paintings of Titian*
Wethey, Harold E. *The Paintings of Titian: Complete Edition*. 3 vols. London: Phaidon, 1969–75.

Venetian Painting in an Age of Rivals

1. The epigraph is taken from Carlo Ridolfi, *The Life of Tintoretto and of His Children Domenico and Marietta*, trans. Catherine Enggass and Robert Enggass (University Park, PA: Penn State University Press, 1984), 50.

2. This essay relies on a number of excellent histories of Venetian painting, above all Patricia Fortini Brown, *Art and Life in Renaissance Venice* (New York: Harry N. Abrams, 1997); Peter Humfrey, *Painting in Renaissance Venice* (New Haven, CT: Yale University Press, 1995); Norbert Huse and Wolfgang Wolters, *The Art of Renaissance Venice: Architecture, Sculpture, and Painting, 1460–1590* (Chicago: University of Chicago Press, 1990); and Rosand, *Painting in Sixteenth-Century Venice*, as well as numerous exhibition catalogues, particularly Michel Laclotte, Giovanna Nepi Scirè, et al., *Le siècle de Titien: L'âge d'or de la peinture à Venise*, exh. cat. (Paris: Réunion des musées nationaux, 1993); and David Alan Brown and Sylvia Ferino-Pagden, eds., *Bellini, Giorgione, Titian and the Renaissance of Venetian Painting*, exh. cat. (Washington, DC: National Gallery of Art, 2006). The author would like to thank Martha Clawson, Robert Echols, Shirin Fozi, and Victoria Reed for help and advice. Unless otherwise indicated, the translations are by the author.

3. Many writings by W. R. Rearick employ a lens of rivalry to illuminate sixteenth-century Venetian painting, but a particular debt is owed to the brilliant book by Rona Goffen, *Renaissance Rivals: Michelangelo, Leonardo, Raphael, Titian* (New Haven, CT: Yale University Press, 2002). Although Goffen's focus is on Michelangelo, Leonardo, and Raphael, she includes a perceptive discussion of Titian and an excellent general analysis of rivalry as an interpretive tool for art history. Annibale Carracci was one of the earliest to determine that the rivalry between Tintoretto and Veronese, and the chiaroscuro of the former and the bright coloration of the latter, might help lead the way to a new kind of painting. See Charles Dempsey, *Annibale Carracci and the Beginnings of Baroque Style*, Villa I Tatti, The Harvard University Center for Italian Renaissance Studies (Glückstadt, Germany: Augustin, 1977), esp. 21–32.

4. "Giorgio lasciato a dietro infinite miglia da Titiano." See Mark W. Roskill, *Dolce's "Aretino" and Venetian Art Theory of the Cinquecento* (New York: New York University Press, 1968), 84. For a good summary of the debates regarding Titian's youth and training, see particularly Paul Joannides, *Titian to 1518: The Assumption of Genius* (New Haven, CT: Yale University Press, 2001), as well as the discussions of Titian's early career in this volume.

5. Rearick was a proponent of Tintoretto leaving Titian's *bottega* of his own accord. See, for example, his *Il disegno veneziano del Cinquecento* (Milan: Electa, 2001), 118.

6. On the ceiling of the Libreria Marciana, see Juergen Schulz, *Venetian Painted Ceilings of the Renaissance* (Berkeley: University of California Press, 1968), 93–95, and Antonio Paolucci, "La sala della Libreria e il ciclo pittorico," in *Da Tiziano a El Greco: Per la storia del Manierismo a Venezia* (Milan: Electa, 1981), 287–98. On Tintoretto's difficulties in the 1550s, see Frederick Ilchman, "The Major Pictorial Cycles: 1555–1575," in Falomir, *Tintoretto*, 287–93. It should be remembered that Tintoretto painted a sympathetic portrait of Jacopo Sansovino in 1571 (Galleria degli Uffizi, Florence), cat. 35 in Falomir, *Tintoretto*, suggesting that any dislike of Tintoretto had faded.

7. For a summary of the *disegno-colorito* question, see Rosand, *Painting in Sixteenth-Century Venice*, 10–25, and Humfrey, *Painting in Renaissance Venice*, 212–18, with references to original sources and further bibliography. The historiography of Venetian paint handling is analyzed by Philip Sohm in *Pittoresco: Marco Boschini, His Critics, and Their Critiques of Painterly Brushwork in Seventeenth- and Eighteenth-Century Italy* (Cambridge: Cambridge University Press, 1991).

8. Giovanni Battista Armenini, *I veri precetti della pittura* [1587], ed. M. Gorreri (Turin: Enaudi, 1988). See also the thoughtful analysis of Armenini by Robert Williams, "The Vocation of the Artist as Seen by Giovanni Battista Armenini," *Art History* 18, no. 4 (December 1995): 518–36.

9. Although Titian traveled in Italy and Germany to work for Charles and Philip. he maintained his base in Venice and never went to Spain. See Charles Hope, "Titian as a Court Painter," *Oxford Art Journal* 2 (1979): 7–10.

10. Giorgio Vasari, *Lives of the Painters, Sculptors and Architects*, trans. Gaston de Vere (New York: Alfred A. Knopf, 1996), 1:877, and Vasari, *Le vite de' più eccellenti pittori, scultori ed architettori* [1568], ed. Gaetano Milanesi (Florence: G. C. Sansoni, 1878–85), 5:116. Vasari elsewhere cites cases of rivalry between Pordenone and Titian in the churches of San Giovanni Elemosinario and Santa Maria degli Angeli; Vasari, *Lives* 2:788, and Vasari, *Vite* 7:441.

11. Vasari, *Lives* 1:643, and Vasari, *Vite* 4:95–96.

12. For Tintoretto's lost facade frescoes for a house "al ponte dell'Angelo," see Carlo Ridolfi, *Le maraviglie dell'arte* [Venice, 1648], ed. Detlev von Hadeln (Berlin: Grote'sche Verlagsbuchhandlung, 1914–24), 2:18–19, and Ridolfi, *Life of Tintoretto*, 21. For Tintoretto's self-generated commission for the choir paintings in the Madonna dell'Orto, see Ridolfi, *Le maraviglie dell'arte* 2:19–21 and *Life of Tintoretto*, 21–24. See also Frederick Ilchman, "Tintoretto: Pensare e disegnare in grande," in *Settimo e ottavo incontro in ricordo di Michelangelo Muraro* (Sosanno: Giovani Editori, 2000), 49–75, and "Tintoretto as a Painter of Religious Narrative," in Falomir, *Tintoretto*, 63–94, esp. 85–91, with further bibliography.

13. The phrase in question reads: "sopra qualche mala informatione havuta da quella dell'arte mia, dalli quali son odiato." This document was discovered by Stefania Mason and published by Linda Borean in her compilation "Documentation," in Falomir, *Tintoretto*, 417, 434.

14. For the competition, see the documents compiled by Borean ("Documentation," in Falomir, *Tintoretto*, 426) and the key early sources: Vasari, *Vite* 6:593–94 and *Lives* 2: 513–14; Ridolfi, *Le maraviglie dell'arte* 2:27–28 and *Life of Tintoretto*, 30–31. A good analysis of the competition and Tintoretto's relations with various factions in the Scuola Grande di San Rocco can be found in Maria Elena Massimi, "Jacopo Tintoretto e i confratelli della Scuola Grande di San Rocco: Strategie culturali e committenza artistica," *Venezia Cinquecento* 5 (1995): 5–107 and a helpful alphabetical list of the Scuola's officeholders from 1500 to 1600, 109–69. Ridolfi is wrong both in giving the year as 1560 and in naming Andrea Schiavone as one of the competitors. By the time of the May 31, 1564, announcement of the competition, Schiavone had been dead for six months.

15. Zuccaro's lifelong resentment, which presumably began with the episode of the San Rocco competition and must have been stoked by the 1582 competition for the *Paradiso* in the Sala del Maggior Consiglio, grew until Tintoretto became a villain in Zuccaro's *Lamento della pittura* of 1605. For more on the donation of the ceiling painting, see Massimi,

"Jacopo Tintoretto e i confratelli," 34–35, and Tom Nichols, *Tintoretto: Tradition and Identity* (London: Reaktion Books, 1999), 153–58. That Tintoretto's previous application for membership in 1549 had been ignored would have meant this triumph in 1564 was all the more satisfying.

16. Vasari, *Lives* 2:513.

17. The translation of Marin Sanudo can be found in *Venice: A Documentary History, 1450–1630*, ed. David Chambers and Brian Pullan, with Jennifer Fletcher (Cambridge, MA: Blackwell, 1992), 4.

18. Petrarch is quoted and translated in Rosand, *Painting in Sixteenth-Century Venice*, 1. The quotation from Philippe de Commynes is found in *The Memoirs of Philippe de Commynes*, trans. Isabelle Cazeaux, ed. Samuel Kinser (Columbia: University of South Carolina Press, 1969), 2:490.

19. See the persuasive study of Gentile Bellini's canvas and related narrative paintings by Patricia Fortini Brown, *Venetian Narrative Painting in the Age of Carpaccio* (New Haven, CT: Yale University Press, 1988).

20. On the Fondaco, see Patricia Labalme, Laura Sanguinetti White, and Linda Carroll, *Cità Excelentissima: Selections from the Renaissance Diaries of Marin Sanudo* (Baltimore: Johns Hopkins University Press, 2008), 332–33.

21. William Shakespeare, *The Merchant of Venice*, act 3, scene 3.

22. For more on the physical characteristics of the Venetian lagoon and their influence on Venetian art, see Paul Hills, *Venetian Colour: Marble, Mosaic, Painting and Glass, 1250–1550* (New Haven, CT: Yale University Press, 1999), 1–21, and Brown, *Art and Life in Renaissance Venice*, 1–37.

23. See Borean, "Documentation," in Falomir, *Tintoretto*, 425–26.

24. On Veronese's workshop, see Diana Gisolfi, "Collaboration and Replicas in the Shop of Paolo Veronese and His Heirs," *Artibus et Historiae* 28, no. 55 (2007): 73–86, and Beverly Louise Brown, "Replication and the Art of Veronese," in *Retaining the Original: Multiple Originals, Copies, and Reproductions*, exh. cat. (Washington, DC: National Gallery of Art, 1989), 111–24, with further bibliography.

25. Ottavia's will was first published by Mario Brunetti in 1920; see Rosand, *Painting in Sixteenth-Century Venice*, 6 and 179 n. 22. For new research on Casser, see Fernando Checa Cremades, "El marques de Carpio (1629–1687) y la pintura veneciana del Renaciamento. Negociaciones con Antonio Saurer," *Anales de Historia del Arte* 14 (2004), 193–212, and Miguel Falomir, "Tintoretto and Spain: From El Greco to Velazquez," in Falomir, *Tintoretto*, 159–77, esp. 164–65.

26. This telling example is cited in Rosand, *Painting in Sixteenth-Century Venice*, 4.

27. Ibid., 11–13.

28. David Rosand, *The Invention of Painting in America* (New York: Columbia University Press, 2004), 53.

29. Michelangelo's refusal to acclaim Titian's painting wholeheartedly may also have resulted from the Venetian painter's apparent presumption in basing the pose of this reclining nude on two different prototypes by the Florentine artist, the sculpture *Night* (Medici Chapel, Florence) and the painting *Leda and Swan* (lost, known from copies). For the anecdote of the meeting, see Vasari, *Vite* 7:447, and Vasari, *Lives* 2:791; on the artists' rivalry, see Goffen, *Renaissance Rivals*, 335–38.

30. Pino's original reads, "e se Tiziano e Michelangelo fussero un corpo solo, over al disegno di Michiel Angelo aggiontovi il colore di Tiziano, se gli potrebbe dir lo dio della pittura." Paolo Pino, *Dialogo di pittura* (1548), in *Tratatti d'arte del Cinquecento*, ed. Paola Barocchi (Bari: G. Laterza, 1960), 1:127. See also Rosand, *Painting in Sixteenth-Century Venice*, esp. 15–26.

31. Ridolfi, *Le maraviglie dell'arte* 2:13–14 and *Life of Tintoretto*, 16.

32. Marco Boschini, "Breve instruzione," in *La carta del navegar pitoresco* [1660], ed. Anna Palucchini (Venice: Istituto per la collaborazione culturale, 1966), 752. See also Rosand, *Painting in Sixteenth-Century Venice*, 22, 189 n. 109.

33. Rosand, "Venetian Painting of the Cinquecento," in Giandomenico Romanelli et al., *Venice: Art and Architecture* (Cologne: Könemann, 1977), 451.

34. Louisa C. Matthew, "The Painter's Presence: Signatures in Venetian Renaissance Pictures," *Art Bulletin* 80 (1998): 616–48, esp. 642.

35. Pliny the Elder, *Natural History* (35.81–83), trans. K. Jex-Blake, *The Elder Pliny's Chapters on the History of Art*, ed. E. Sellers (London: Macmillan, 1896), 121–23. See also David Rosand, *Drawing Acts: Studies in Graphic Expression and Representation* (Cambridge: Cambridge University Press, 2002), 4–9.

36. See Creighton Gilbert, "What Did the Renaissance Patron Buy?" *Renaissance Quarterly* 51, no. 2 (Summer 1998): 392–450.

37. Rosand, *Painting in Sixteenth-Century Venice*, 103–6 and doc. 20 on p. 173. It should be recalled that before the Tribunal of the Inquisition, Veronese famously justified his overpopulated *Last Supper* for the convent of Santi Giovanni and Paolo on the grounds of artistic license. When his arguments were rejected, he merely retitled the painting the *Feast in the House of Levi*.

38. Gilbert, "What Did the Renaissance Patron Buy?" 433–34. Given the examples of clients interested simply in a "Bassano," Gilbert aptly concludes, "Art collection in this autonomous way is thus on record from the era of Giorgione." The negotiations between Isabella and Giovanni Bellini are thoroughly analyzed by Goffen in *Renaissance Rivals*, 11–19. The Bembo's letter was published in Giovanni Gaye, *Carteggio inedito d'Artisti dei Secoli XIV.XV.XVI* (Florence: Giuseppe Molini, 1840), 2:71–73.

39. Gilbert, "What Did the Renaissance Patron Buy?" 410 and passim.

40. Robert Echols, "Jacopo Tintoretto and Venetian Painting, 1538–1548" (PhD diss., University of Maryland, 1993), 228–30. Among other quotations, in Tintoretto's painting the man holding the broken mallet cites the astonished apostle with outstretched arms in Titian's *Assunta*, the grouping at the far right recalls Michelangelo's sculptures in the Medici Chapel, Florence, the general composition is drawn from Raphael's *Sacrifice at Lystra* (fig. 46), and the architecture echoes Sansovino's *Loggetta* in Piazza San Marco. Within a wide literature of literary imitation in the Renaissance, two now-classic studies provide models for the concepts of imitation and emulation in the visual arts, whereby citing a source and transforming it allows the later creator to triumph over his prototype: G. W. Pigman III, "Versions of Imitation in the Renaissance," *Renaissance Quarterly* 33 (1980): 1–32, and Thomas M. Green, *The Light in Troy: Imitation and Discovery in Renaissance Poetry* (New Haven, CT: Yale University Press, 1982). Goffen (*Renaissance Rivals*, 3–4, 293, 327) uses this analysis to distinguish among the kinds of allusion employed by sixteenth-century artists.

41. Some scholars endorse the existence of a competition, including Rearick, *Disegno veneziano*, 78–82, and Goffen, *Renaissance Rivals*, 297–300. Patricia Meilman (*Titian and the Altarpiece in Renaissance Venice* [Cambridge: Cambridge University Press, 2000]) concludes that the rivalry with Pordenone started after the *Saint Peter Martyr* altarpiece.

42. For the *Paradiso* competition, see Jean Habert, ed., *Le Paradis de Tintoret: Un concours pour le palais des Doges*, exh. cat. (Paris: Musée du Louvre Editions, 2006). The finished painting was designed by Jacopo but executed by Domenico, with extensive studio assistance. See Echols and Ilchman, "Toward a New Tintoretto Catalogue," cat. 298, and Pallucchini and Rossi, *Opere sacre e profane*, 1:cat. 465.

43. Ridolfi, *Le maraviglie dell'arte* 2:26 and *Life of Tintoretto*, 30.

44. Anton Maria Zanetti, *Della pittura veneziana* (Venice: Giambatista Albrizzi, 1771), 165.

45. Vasari, *Vite* 7:453–54.

46. On the calibration of Titian's paintings to their setting in the Frari, see Rosand, *Painting in Sixteenth-Century Venice*, 35–51. On the brief installation of Titian's *Pietà* in the Frari, see Charles Hope, "A New Document about Titian's Pietà," in *Sight and Insight: Essays on Art and Culture in Honour of E. H. Gombrich at 85*, ed. John Onians (London: Phaidon Press, 1994), 153–68. It can also be argued that Titian's paintings for Santo Spirito in Isola, or particularly for San Salvador, were seen by the painter as opportunities to claim the spaces of these churches as his own. On the patrons of Titian's work in San Salvador, see Lorenzo Finocchi Ghersi, "Artisti e committenti a San Salvador," *Arte Veneta* 51 (1997): 20–39, and Daniela Bohde, "Titian's Three Altar Project for the Church of San Salvador: Strategies of Self-Representation by Members of the Scuola Grande di San Rocco," *Renaissance Studies* 15 (2001): 450–72.

47. On Tintoretto and the choir paintings in the Madonna dell'Orto and their pivotal role in his career, see Ilchman, "Tintoretto as a Painter of Religious Narrative," in Falomir, *Tintoretto*, esp. 85–91, with further bibliography.

48. For Tintoretto's consideration of the intended setting for his paintings, see Jozef Grabski, "The Group of Paintings by Tintoretto in the 'Sala Terena' in the Scuola di San Rocco in Venice and Their Relationship to the Architectural Structure," *Artibus et historiae* 1 (1980): 115–31, and Ilchman, "Tintoretto as a Painter of Religious Narrative," in Falomir, *Tintoretto*, esp. 71–81.

Where the Money Flows: Art Patronage in Sixteenth-Century Venice

1. The epigraph is taken from Francesco Sansovino, *Delle cose notabili che sono in Venetia* (Venice, 1561), 21v, translation by David Chambers and Brian Pullan, with Jennifer Fletcher, eds., *Venice: A Documentary History, 1450–1630* (Cambridge, MA: Blackwell, 1992), 392.

2. For a general overview, see Michel Hochmann, *Peintres et commanditaires à Venise (1540–1628)* (Rome: Ecole française de Rome, 1992); Patricia Fortini Brown, *Art and Life in Renaissance Venice* (New York: Harry N. Abrams, 1997); and Peter Humfrey, ed., *Venice and the Veneto* (Cambridge: Cambridge University Press, 2007), pts. 1 and 2.

3. Charles Hope, *Titian* (London: Chaucer Press, 2003), 135. See also Charles Hope, "Titian and His Patrons," in *Titian: Prince of Painters*, ed. Susanna Biadene and Mary Yakush, exh. cat. (Venice: Marsilio, 1990), 77–84; and Charles Hope, "Titian as a Court Painter," *Oxford Art Journal* 2 (1979): 7–10.

4. Tom Nichols, *Tintoretto: Tradition and Identity* (London: Reaktion Books, 1999), 103, 153–58; Linda Borean, "Documenti," in Falomir, *Tintoretto*, 426; Pallucchini and Rossi, *Opere sacre e profane* 1:cats. 216, 126, 188; Echols and Ilchman, "Toward a New Tintoretto Catalogue," cat. 101.

5. Nichols, *Tintoretto*, 101–10.

6. Carlo Ridolfi, *Le maraviglie dell'arte* [Venice, 1648], ed. Detlev von Hadeln (1914; repr., Rome: Società Multigrafica Editrice Somu, 1965), 1:347–48: "sempre ingenuo ne' suoi trattati; non fece officio giamai per ottenere alcuno impiego; ne' avvili' lo stato suo co' bassi trattamenti; osservo' sempre la promessa e procuro' in ogni sua attione la lode."

7. See Deborah Howard, "The State," in *Venice and the Veneto*, ed. Humfrey, 33–91.

8. Robert Finlay, *Politics in Renaissance Venice* (New Brunswick, NJ: Rutgers University Press, 1980), 40, 26–27.

9. Staale Sinding-Larsen, "Christ in the Council Hall: Studies in the Religious Iconography of the Venetian Republic," *Acta ad archaeologiam et artium historiam pertinentia* 5 (1974): 3–12. For a list of Provveditori for the Palazzo Ducale, 1530–1600, see Tracy E. Cooper, *Palladio's Venice: Architecture and Society in a Renaissance Republic* (New Haven, CT: Yale University Press, 2005), 293–94.

10. Finlay, *Politics in Renaissance Venice*, 165; Sinding-Larsen, "Christ in the Council Hall," 4–5; Philip Cottrell, "Corporate Colors: Bonifacio and Tintoretto at the Palazzo dei Camerlenghi in Venice," *Art Bulletin* 82, no. 4 (Dec. 2000): 659–60.

11. Sinding-Larsen, "Christ in the Council Hall," 1–2; in 1574 the Sala del Collegio, the Anticollegio, the Sala del Pregadi (del Senato), the Antipregadi (Sala delle Quattro Porte), and the ceiling of the Cancelleria were gutted, to be followed in 1577 by the Sala della Libreria (Sala del Scrutinio) and the Sala del Maggior Consiglio. Other painters whose works were destroyed include Gentile and Giovanni Bellini, Carpaccio, Alvise Vivarini, Pordenone, Orazio Vecellio, and Giuseppe Porta Salviati.

12. Giambattista Lorenzi, *Monumenti per servire alla storia del Palazzo Ducale di Venezia: Parte I dal 1253 al 1600* (Venice: M. Visentini, 1868), cat. 337: "quella bataglia da la banda verso de piaza ch e la piu difficile et che homo alcuno, fina questo di non ha voluto tuore tanta impresa." See also Charles Hope, "Titian's Role as Official Painter to the Venetian Republic," in *Tiziano e Venezia: Convegno internazionale di studi, Venezia, 1976* (Vicenza: Neri Pozza, 1980), 301–5; and Wethey, *Paintings of Titian* 3:225–32, cat. L-3.

13. Paul Joannides, *Titian to 1518: The Assumption of Genius* (New Haven, CT: Yale University Press, 2001), 164.

14. Hope, "Titian's Role as Official Painter," 301–5.

15. Lorenzi, *Monumenti*, cats. 354, 366, 373, 462, 591. See also Wolfgang Wolters, *Storia e politica nei dipinti di Palazzo Ducale: Aspetti dell'autocelebrazione della Repubblica di Venezia nel Cinquecento* (Venice: Arsenale Editrice, 1983), 93–135, 239–96; Wethey, *Paintings of Titian* 3:225–33, cats. L-3, L-6.

16. Wolters, *Storia e politica nei dipinti di Palazzo Ducale*, 169.

17. Juergen Schulz, *Venetian Painted Ceilings of the Renaissance* (Berkeley: University of California Press, 1968), 96–101; Giorgio Vasari, *Le vite de' più eccellenti pittori, scultori ed architettori* [1568], ed. Gaetano Milanesi (Florence: G. C. Sansoni, 1878–85), 6:371, 595; Hochmann, *Peintres et commanditaires*, 245–50. Cf. Rearick, *Art of Paolo Veronese*, 50, proposing that the invitation came from Daniele Barbaro and not Ponchino.

18. Rearick, *Art of Paolo Veronese*, 50; Wolters, *Storia e politica nei dipinti di Palazzo Ducale*, 239–40; Pignatti and Pedrocco, *Veronese* 1:cats. 34–36.

19. Rearick, *Art of Paolo Veronese*, 52; Schulz, *Venetian Painted Ceilings*, 93–95; Pignatti and Pedrocco, *Veronese* 1:cats. 66–68. For Tintoretto's portrait with the inscription, see Paola Rossi, *Tintoretto: Ritratti* (Milan: Electa, 1994), 1:cat. 1.

20. Schulz, *Venetian Painted Ceilings*, 95–96; Biadene and Yakush, *Titian: Prince of Painters*, 314; Pallucchini and Rossi, *Opere sacre e profane* 1:cats. 318–23.

21. Wolters, *Storia e politica nei dipinti di Palazzo Ducale*, 169 n. 5; Pignatti and Pedrocco, *Veronese* 2:555, doc. 20; Lorenzi, *Monumenti*, cats. 661, 689; Erika Tietze-Conrat, "Decorative Paintings of the Venetian Renaissance Reconstructed from Drawings," *Art Quarterly* 3 (1940): 15–39.

22. Wolters, *Storia e politica nei dipinti di Palazzo Ducale*, 162–78; Patricia Fortini Brown, *Venetian Narrative Painting in the Age of Carpaccio* (New Haven, CT: Yale University Press, 1988), 272–79; Cooper, *Palladio's Venice*, 165–66.

23. Nichols, *Tintoretto*, 122–23; Sinding-Larsen, "Christ in the Council Hall," 16–21, 24–44, 84–119, 254–60; Wolters, *Storia e politica nei dipinti di Palazzo Ducale*, 93–135, 247–55, 260–65.

24. Sinding-Larsen, "Christ in the Council Hall," 22–24, 45–80, 220–38, and passim; Wolters, *Storia e politica nei dipinti di Palazzo Ducale*, 267–96.

25. Jean Habert, ed., *Le Paradis de Tintoret: Un concours pour le palais des Doges*, exh. cat. (Paris: Musée du Louvre Editions, 2006); Falomir, *Tintoretto*, 370–75.

26. Ridolfi, *Le maraviglie dell'arte* 2:62: "Congratulavansi seco gli stessi Senatori affettuosamente abbracciandolo, poiche con tanta sodisfattione del Senato e della Città tutta haveva condotto à fine quella sì gran fatica."

27. Cottrell, "Corporate Colors," 658–78, esp. 662.

28. Echols in Falomir, *Tintoretto*, 254–56; Philip Cottrell, "Bonifacio Veronese and the Young Tintoretto," *Inferno: St Andrews Journal of Art History* 4 (1997): 17–36; Pallucchini and Rossi, *Opere sacre e profane* 1:cats. 162, 163; Echols and Ilchman, "Toward a New Tintoretto Catalogue," cats. 59, 60.

29. Pallucchini and Rossi, *Opere sacre e profane* 1:cat. 164; Echols and Ilchman, "Toward a New Tintoretto Catalogue," cat. 61 (with extensive studio assistance, notably the face and body of the Virgin).

30. Cottrell, "Corporate Colors," 670–71; Pallucchini and Rossi, *Opere sacre e profane* 1:cat. 302; Echols and Ilchman, "Toward a New Tintoretto Catalogue," cat. 131.

31. Cottrell, "Corporate Colors," 673.

32. Brown, *Venetian Narrative Painting*, 15–30 and passim; Louisa C. Matthew, "Clergy and Confraternities," in *Venice and the Veneto*, ed. Humfrey, 92–150.

33. Peter Humfrey and Richard Mackenney, "The Venetian Trade Guilds as Patrons of Art in the Renaissance," *The Burlington Magazine* 128, no. 998 (May 1986): 317–30; Peter Humfrey, *The Altarpiece in Renaissance Venice* (New Haven, CT: Yale University Press, 1993), 110–21; Patricia Fortini Brown, "Le Scuole," in *Storia di Venezia*, vol. 5, *Il Rinascimento: Società ed economia*, ed. Alberto Tenenti and Ugo Tucci (Rome: Istituto della Enciclopedia Italiana, 1996), 307–54; Thomas Worthen, "Tintoretto's Paintings for the *Banco del Sacramento* in S. Margherita," *Art Bulletin* 78 (1996): 707–32; Paul Hills, "Piety and Patronage in Cinquecento Venice: Tintoretto and the Scuole del Sacramento," *Art History* 6 (1983): 30–42.

34. Brian Pullan, *Rich and Poor in Renaissance Venice* (Cambridge: Cambridge University Press, 1971), 125. See also Patricia Fortini Brown, "Honor and Necessity: The Dynamics of Patronage in the Confraternities of Renaissance Venice," *Studi Veneziani*, n.s., 14 (1987): 179–212; Hochmann, *Peintres et commanditaires*, 319–38.

35. Brown, *Art and Life*, 96–100. At the beginning of the sixteenth century, they included the Scuola Grande di Santa Maria della Carità, Scuola Grande di San Giovanni Evangelista, Scuola Grande di Santa Maria della Misericordia, Scuola Grande di San Marco, and Scuola Grande di San Rocco. The Scuola di San Teodoro was given Grandi status in 1552.

36. For Veronese's *Annunciation*, see Pignatti and Pedrocco, *Veronese* 1:cat. 257. Guido Piovene, in *L'opera completa del Veronese* (Milan: Rizzoli, 1968), lists only two additional paintings by Veronese as scuola commissions: cat. 117 (as school of Veronese), *Adoration of the Shepherds*, for the Chapel of the Setaioli in the Crociferi; and cat. 167, *Madonna del Rosario*, for the Scuola del Rosario in San Pietro Martire in Murano, 1573. Cf. Pignatti and Pedrocco, *Veronese* 1:cats. 99 and 278, respectively.

37. Rosand, *Painting in Sixteenth-Century Venice*, 16, 172–73 (doc. 18): "redur ad effetto tal pittura, et ornamento, come se convien al decoro delalbergo nostro, et come si vede nelli altri alberghi delle schuole grande de questa Illustrissima Città." See also Brown, "Honor and Necessity," 179–212.

38. Wethey, *Paintings of Titian* 1:123–24, cat. 87; Rosand, *Painting in Sixteenth-Century Venice*, 103–16, 172–73, with an appendix of documents, 165–75.

39. See Nicholas Penny's entry on the painting in Jaffé, *Titian*, 144–46, cat. 29; and Penny, *Sixteenth Century Italian Paintings* 2:206–35.

40. Penny, in *Sixteenth Century Italian Paintings*, proposes that it was executed in at least two phases, beginning around 1540–43 and completed around 1550–60.

41. Juergen Schulz, "Titian's Ceiling in the Scuola di San Giovanni Evangelista," *Art Bulletin* 48 (1966): 89–95; Schulz, *Venetian Painted Ceilings*, 84–85, cat. 26.

42. Cited by David Rosand, "Titian's 'Presentation of the Virgin': The Second Door," *The Burlington Magazine* 115 (1973): 603–4: "con quel adornamento necessario che se ricerca a honor della scuola nostra." Cf. Charles Hope, "Documents Concerning

Titian," *The Burlington Magazine* 115, no. 849 (1973): 809–10.

43. Nichols, *Tintoretto*, 137–45; Erasmus Weddigen, "Thomas Philologus Ravennas: Gehehrter, Wohltäter und Mäzen," *Saggi e memorie di storia dell'arte* 9 (1974): 7–76, 149–72; Anne Corneloup, "Le corps de saint Marc et celui de Rangone; ou Le principe d'imitatio selon Tintoret," *Studiolo* 2 (2003): 107–37; Hochmann, *Peintres et commanditaires*, 187–89.

44. Nichols, *Tintoretto*, 103, 149–237, 241–43.

45. See citations in n. 29.

46. Hills, "Piety and Patronage," 33–35; Worthen, "Tintoretto's Paintings for the *Banco del Sacramento*," 711–13, 725–26.

47. Hills, "Piety and Patronage," 36; Pallucchini and Rossi, *Opere sacre e profane* 1:cat. 291; Echols and Ilchman, "Toward a New Tintoretto Catalogue," cat. 124.

48. Hills, "Piety and Patronage," 36–37; Pallucchini and Rossi, *Opere sacre e profane* 1:cats. 303, 304; Echols and Ilchman, "Toward a New Tintoretto Catalogue," cats. 143, 144.

49. See Worthen, "Tintoretto's Paintings for the *Banco del Sacramento*," 710.

50. Humfrey, *Altarpiece in Renaissance Venice*, 87–135; Hochmann, *Peintres et commanditaires*, 293–318.

51. Peter Humfrey, *Titian* (New York: Phaidon, 2007), 126–27; Wethey, *Paintings of Titian* 1:139–40, cat. 114.

52. Daniela Bohde, "Titian's Three Altar Project for the Church of San Salvador: Strategies of Self-Representation by Members of the Scuola Grande di San Rocco," *Renaissance Studies* 15 (2001): 450–72; Blake de Maria, "The Merchants of Venice: A Study in Sixteenth-Century Cittadino Patronage" (PhD diss., Princeton University, 2003), 137–42 (a revised version is to be published by Yale University Press, with the provisional title *Becoming Venetian: Immigrants and the Arts in Early Modern Venice*). For the dynamics of cittadino patronage, see Hochmann, *Peintres et commanditaires*, 187–218.

53. De Maria, "Merchants of Venice," 135–74; Biadene and Yakush, *Titian: Prince of Painters*, 318–20; Wethey, *Paintings of Titian* 1:79–80, 85–86, cats. 21, 31.

54. Wethey, *Paintings of Titian* 1:71–72, cat. 11, *Annunciation*; 163, cat. 146, *Transfiguration*. For the *Crucifixion*, see n. 56.

55. Bohde, "Titian's Three Altar Project," 450–72; de Maria, "Merchants of Venice," 135–74. The ensemble is not cited by Peter Humfrey, "Co-ordinated Altarpieces in Renaissance Venice: The Progress of an Ideal," in *The Altarpiece in the Renaissance*, ed. Peter Humfrey and Martin Kemp (Cambridge: Cambridge University Press, 1990), 190–211.

56. Titian's *Crucifixion* for San Salvador is probably to be identified with a fragment now in the Pinacoteca Nazionale di Bologna: Wethey, *Paintings of Titian* 1:85, cat. 31. See de Maria, "Merchants of Venice," 161–63; and Bohde, "Titian's Three Altar Project," 461 n. 35.

57. De Maria, "Merchants of Venice," 174. Cf. Augusto Gentili, who rejects the notion of a coordinated program in "Titian's Venetian Commissions: Events, Contexts, Images, 1537–1576," in *Late Titian and the Sensuality of Painting*, ed. Sylvia Ferino-Pagden, exh. cat. (Venice: Marsilio, 2008), 43–54, 49–51; and Humfrey, "Co-ordinated Altarpieces," 190–211.

58. Peter Humfrey, "La pala Giustinian a S. Francesco della Vigna: Contesto e committenza," in *Nuovi studi su Paolo Veronese*, ed. Massimo Gemin (Venice: Arsenale Editrice, 1990), 299–307; Peter Humfrey and Stephen Holt, "More on Veronese and His Patrons at San Francesco della Vigna," *Venezia Cinquecento* 5 (1995): 187–214; Nichols, *Tintoretto*, 126–27; Rearick, *Art of Paolo Veronese*, 45.

59. Rearick, *Art of Paolo Veronese*, 50; Augusto Gentili and Michele Di Monte, *Veronese in the Church of San Sebastiano* (Venice: Chorus and Marsilio, 1995), 1–15; Pignatti and Pedrocco, *Veronese* 2:91; Paola Ranieri, "La chiesa di San Sebastiano a Venezia: La rifondazione cinquecentesca e la cappella di Marcantonio Grimani," *Venezia Cinquecento* 12 (2002): 5–139; Pignatti and Pedrocco, *Veronese* 1:cats. 41–49 (sacristy), 56–58 (nave ceiling), 77–84 (nave walls).

60. Rearick, *Art of Paolo Veronese*, 69; Pignatti and Pedrocco, *Veronese* 1:cats. 88–94 (San Sebastiano), 102–104 (San Geminiano).

61. Rearick, *Art of Paolo Veronese*, 69–71; Gentili and Di Monte, *Veronese in the Church of San Sebastiano*, 15–30; Pignatti and Pedrocco, *Veronese* 1:cats. 106–19 (nave frescoes), 157, 171, 172 (presbytery).

62. Pignatti and Pedrocco, *Veronese* 1:252, doc. 16 (January 29, 1559). See Peter Humfrey, "Veronese's High Altar for San Sebastiano: A Patrician Commission for a Counter Reformation Church," in *Venice Reconsidered: The History and Civilization of an Italian City-State, 1297–1797*, ed. John Martin and Dennis Romano (Baltimore: Johns Hopkins University Press, 2000), 365–88.

63. Pignatti and Pedrocco, *Veronese* 1:cat. 157.

64. Rearick, *Art of Paolo Veronese*, 74; Pignatti and Pedrocco, *Veronese* 1:cats. 145–46 (Praglia). For San Benedetto Po, see Penny, *Sixteenth Century Italian Paintings* 2:344–53.

65. Archivio di Stato di Venezia, Archivio San Giorgio Maggiore, processo no. 10, with translation from Chambers and Pullan, *Venice*, 414. See Terisio Pignatti, *Veronese* (Venice: Alfieri, 1976), 1:253–54, doc. 22 (June 6, 1562); and Pignatti and Pedrocco, *Veronese* 1:cat. 149.

66. Pallucchini and Rossi, *Opere sacre e profane* 1:cats. 68–70; Echols and Ilchman, "Toward a New Tintoretto Catalogue," cats. 159–61.

67. Frederick Ilchman, "Tintoretto as a Painter of Religious Narrative," in Falomir, *Tintoretto*, 85–91; Pallucchini and Rossi, *Opere sacre e profane* 1:cats. 236, 237; Echols and Ilchman, "Toward a New Tintoretto Catalogue," cats. 77, 78.

68. Michael Douglas-Scott, "Jacopo Tintoretto's Altarpiece of St. Agnes at the Madonna dell'Orto in Venice and the Memorialisation of Cardinal Contarini," *Journal of the Warburg and Courtauld Institutes* 60 (1997): 130–63; Echols and Ilchman, "Toward a New Tintoretto Catalogue," cat. 198; Pallucchini and Rossi, *Opere sacre e profane* 1:cat. 371.

69. Ridolfi, *Le maraviglie dell'arte* 2:63: "trattenevasi spesse fiate in pie meditationi nella Chiesa dell'horto, & in morali discorsi con que' Padri familgiari suoi." See also Douglas-Scott, "Jacopo Tintoretto's Altarpiece of St. Agnes," 130–63, esp. 140. For Tintoretto's religious beliefs, see Ilchman, "Tintoretto as a Painter of Religious Narrative," 63–94.

70. Francesco Sansovino, *Venetia, città nobillisima et singolare descritta in XIIII libri*, ed. Giustiniano Martinoni (Venice: S. Curti, 1663; repr., Venice: Filippi Editore, 1968), 1:384–85. See Patricia Fortini Brown, *Private Lives in Renaissance Venice: Art, Architecture, and the Family* (New Haven, CT: Yale University Press, 2004), 53–89; and Tracy E. Cooper, "Patricians and Citizens," in *Venice and the Veneto*, ed. Humfrey, 151–206.

71. Luba Freedman, *Titian's Portraits through Aretino's Lens* (University Park, PA: Penn State University Press, 1995), 12.

72. Mark Roskill, *Dolce's "Aretino" and Venetian Art Theory of the Cinquecento* (New York: New York University Press, 1968), 103.

73. Biadene and Yakush, *Titian: Prince of Painters*, 238; Wethey, *Paintings of Titian* 2:82–83, cat. 15.

74. Archivio di Stato di Venezia, Cancelleria Inferiore, Miscellanea Notai Diversi, b. 39, no. 59, March 22, 1557: inventory of Piero Gritti q. Marco de confinio San Salvador, ff. 26–26v. The doge's grandfather Triadano was Piero's great-grandfather; they were first cousins once removed.

75. Wethey, *Paintings of Titian* 2:148, cat. 112; Biadene and Yakush, *Titian: Prince of Painters*, 300–301.

76. Freedman, in *Titian's Portraits*, 12, cites 156 paintings, including 24 portraits, for the period 1554–76.

77. Wethey, *Paintings of Titian* 2:79–80, cat. 21; de Maria, "Merchants of Venice," 89–134.

78. For palace facades, see Nichols, *Tintoretto*, 49–56; Pallucchini and Rossi, *Opere sacre e profane* 1:cats. 21–34; Echols and Ilchman, "Toward a New Tintoretto Catalogue," cats. 13–26; and Diana Gisolfi, "Tintoretto e le facciate affrescate di Venezia," in *Jacopo Tintoretto nel quarto centenario della morte: Atti del convegno internazionale di studi. Venezia, 24–26 Novembre, 1994*, ed. Paola Rossi and Lionello Puppi (Padua: Il Poligrafo, 1996), 111–14. For Aretino's allegories, see Falomir, *Tintoretto*, 196–99; Pallucchini and Rossi, *Opere sacre e profane* 1:25, 143–44, cat. 82; and Echols and Ilchman, "Toward a New Tintoretto Catalogue," cat. 34. For Ca' Pisani, see Stefania Mason Rinaldi, "Intorno al soffito di San Paternian: Gli artisti di Vettor Pisani," 71–75, in *Jacopo Tintoretto nel quarto centenario della morte*, ed. Rossi and Puppi; Pallucchini and Rossi, *Opere sacre e profane* 1:cats. 21–34; and Echols and Ilchman, "Toward a New Tintoretto Catalogue," cats. 13–26. For the Barbo allegories, see Falomir, *Tintoretto*, 204–8; Pallucchini and Rossi, *Opere sacre e profane* 1:328, cats. 209–11; and Echols and Ilchman, "Toward a New Tintoretto Catalogue," cats. 38–41.

79. Falomir, "Tintoretto's Portraiture," in Falomir, *Tintoretto*, 98–104. On patrician patronage in general, see Hochmann, *Peintres et commanditaires*, 219–66.

80. Brown, *Private Lives*, 16–19; Nichols, *Tintoretto*, 127–32; Falomir, *Tintoretto*, 248–50, 266–69; Pallucchini and Rossi, *Opere sacre e profane* 1:79–81; Paola Rossi, *Jacopo Tintoretto*, vol. 1, *I ritratti* (Venice: Alfieri, 1974), 90–95; Giuseppe Maria Pilo, "Il Procuratore di San Marco Jacopo Soranzo Jr. e il ritratto recuperato di Jacopo Tintoretto già in Procuratia 'De Supra,'" in *Storia dell'arte marciana: I mosaici*, ed. Renato Polacco (Venice: Marsilio, 1997), 209–21; Benjamin Paul, "'Erst kein Glück, und dann kam auch noch Pech dazu': Die gescheiterte Karriere des Jacopo Soranzo (1581–1599) im Spiegel seines Grabmals," in *Grab—Kult—Memoria: Studien zur gesellschaftlichen Funktion von Erinnerung*, ed. Carolin Behrmann, Arne Karsten, and Philipp Zitzlsperger (Cologne: Böhlau, 2007), 41–58.

81. Ridolfi, *Le maraviglie dell'arte* 2:70: "Fù honorato con visite di Prelati, Cardinali e Prencipi, che di quando in quando capitavano à Venetia, desiderosi di vedere eternati I volti loro dal sublime suo pennello, ed oltre il Rè di Francia e di Polonia . . . ritrasse ancora molti Duchi e Signori dell'Italia, & altri Prencipe e Baroni oltramontani; ed I particolare I Dolgi tutti di Venetia . . . che vissero nell'età sua, le effigie de' quali si conservano anco nelle case dalle loro famiglie."

82. Falomir, "Tintoretto's Portraiture," 103.

83. Rearick, *Art of Paolo Veronese*, 20–28; Diana Gisolfi Pechukas, "Veronese and His Collaborators at 'La Soranza,'" *Artibus et Historiae* 8 (1987): 67–108; Giampaolo Bordignon Favero, *I Palazzo Soranzo Novello e Spinelli Guidozzi in Castelfranco Veneto* (Castelfranco Veneto:

Banca Popolare di Castelfranco Veneto, 1981); Bernhard Rupprecht, "Sanmichelis Villa Soranza," in *Festschrift Ulrich Middledorf*, ed. Antje Kosegarten and Peter Tigler (Berlin: De Gruyter, 1968), 1:324–32; Pignatti and Pedrocco, *Veronese* 1:cats. 17–22.

84. Rearick, *Art of Paolo Veronese*, 38–39; Pignatti and Pedrocco, *Veronese* 1:cats. 28, 29.

85. Pignatti and Pedrocco, *Veronese* 1:cats. 69–76, 175; Hochmann, *Peintres et commanditaires*, 197–99, 242–51.

86. See de Maria, "Merchants of Venice," 183–285; Brown, *Private Lives*, 19, 96; Hochmann, *Peintres et commanditaires*, 204–6; Pignatti and Pedrocco, *Veronese* 1:cats. 182–85.

87. Roskill, *Dolce's "Aretino,"* 191–93.

88. Hope, "Titian and His Patrons," 80. On Aretino, Dolce, and other literati as intermediaries, see Hochmann, *Peintres et commanditaires*, 95–122.

89. Ridolfi, *Le maraviglie dell'arte* 1:180–82; Freedman, *Titian's Portraits*, 118.

90. Wethey, *Paintings of Titian* 2:16–24, 85–86, and passim.

91. Pietro Aretino, *Lettere sull'arte*, ed. Ettore Camescasa (Milan: Edizioni del Milione, 1957–60), 1:129–31; Biadene and Yakush, *Titian: Prince of Painters*, 244.

92. Cited by Clare Robertson, *"Il Gran Cardinale": Alessandro Farnese, Patron of the Arts* (New Haven, CT: Yale University Press, 1992), 69.

93. Ferino-Pagden, *Late Titian*, 149–51; Robertson, *"Il Gran Cardinale,"* 70.

94. Robertson, *"Il Gran Cardinale,"* 70.

95. Ibid., 70; Wethey, *Paintings of Titian* 2:97–99.

96. Charles Hope, "A Neglected Document about Titian's *Danaë* in Naples," *Arte Veneta* 31 (1977): 188–89; Roberto Zapperi, "Alessandro Farnese, Giovanni Della Casa and Titian's *Danaë* in Naples," *Journal of the Warburg and Courtauld Institutes* 54 (1991): 159–71; Biadene and Yakush, *Titian: Prince of Painters*, 267–69; Wethey, *Paintings of Titian* 3:56–62, 132–36; Robertson, *"Il Gran Cardinale,"* 72.

97. Wethey, *Paintings of Titian* 2:5–6, 1:30 n. 172; Augusto Gentili, "Titian's Venetian Commissions: Events, Contexts, Images, 1537–1576," in *Late Titian*, ed. Ferino-Pagden, 44–45.

98. Andrew John Martin, "La bottega in viaggio. Con Tiziano ad Augusta, Füssen e Innsbruck (1548): Domande e ipotesi," *Studi Tizianeschi* 4 (2006): 99–108, esp. 103; Hope, "Titian and His Patrons," 81–82.

99. Wethey, *Paintings of Titian* 1:21–22, 27–30, 32–33, 2:5–6.

100. Fernando Checa, "Beyond Venice: Titian and the Spanish Court," in *Late Titian*, ed. Ferino-Pagden, 55–61.

101. Ibid., 60. Cf. Humfrey, *Titian*, 168; Hope, *Titian*, 135.

102. Hans von Voltelini, "Urkunden und Regesten aus dem K. u, k. Haus-, Hof- und Staats-Archiv in Wien," *Jahrbuch der Kunsthistorischen Sammlungen des Allerhöchsten Kaiserhauses* 13 (1892): xxvi–clxxiv, docs. 8804, 8806, 8808.

103. Nichols, *Tintoretto*, 133–34, 243; Cornelia Syre, *Tintoretto: The Gonzaga Cycle*, exh. cat. (Ostfildern-Ruit: Hatje Cantz, 2000), 13–22; Pallucchini and Rossi, *Opere sacre e profane* 1:cats. 392–99; Echols and Ilchman, "Toward a New Tintoretto Catalogue," cats. 236–43 (all either Jacopo or studio design, with studio execution).

104. Xavier F. Salomon, *Veronese's Allegories: Virtue, Love, and Exploration in Renaissance Venice*, exh. cat. (New York: Frick Collection, 2006). Salomon argues that the Metropolitan Museum's *Venus and Mars United by Love*, "dating from the first half of the 1570s, seems to have been an ideal candidate for Emperor Maximilian's patronage" (24). Cf. Rearick, in *Art of Paolo Veronese*, 120–24, who sees the *Allegories of Love* as a commission by Rudolf around 1576, and the other allegories as commissions or purchases over the next six years. See Pignatti and Pedrocco, *Veronese* 2:263–66, 268, cats. 247–50.

105. Nichols, *Tintoretto*, 135–37.

106. Rearick, *Art of Paolo Veronese*, 123; Pignatti and Pedrocco, *Veronese* 1:cats. 332–33.

107. Falomir, *Tintoretto*, 362–66; Miguel Falomir, "Tintoretto and Spain: From El Greco to Velázquez," in Falomir, *Tintoretto*, 159–60; Nichols, *Tintoretto*, 134–35; Pignatti and Pedrocco, *Veronese* 1:cat. 341 (with workshop); Pallucchini and Rossi, *Opere sacre e profane* 1:cat. A37; Echols and Ilchman, "Toward a New Tintoretto Catalogue," cat. 271.

108. Ridolfi, as translated in Carlo Ridolfi, *The Life of Tintoretto and of His Children Domenico and Marietta*, trans. Catherine Enggass and Robert Enggass (University Park, PA: Penn State University Press, 1984), 56–57.

109. Ridolfi, *Le maraviglie dell'arte* 1:347: "Le Pitture sparse nelle Galerie più famose dell'Europa . . . non parendo per appunto adorno qualsivoglia Palagio, ove non entri alcuna cosa di questa mano." See also Salomon, *Veronese's Allegories*, 24.

Collecting in Sixteenth- and Seventeenth-Century Venice: Originals, Copies, and "Maniera di"

1. This essay derives from my work on the survey of art-collecting practices in Venice, from their origins to the nineteenth century; it was coordinated by Stefania Mason at the Università di Udine and supported by the Fondazione di Venezia. Algarotti's letter is from Francesco Algarotti, *Opere* (Livorno: Marco Coltellini, 1765), 6:33. The original reads: "nell'acquistare quadri antichi io avrei proceduto sempre, come feci, con cautele grandissime. Non basta che un quadro sia di Tiziano, vuol essere ben conservato, della bella maniera e del fior della bella maniera del pittore. Altrimenti si corre risico di ammirar solamente i nomi."

2. Louisa C. Matthew, "The Painter's Presence: Signatures in Venetian Renaissance Pictures," *Art Bulletin* 80 (1998): 641.

3. Michel Hochmann, *Peintres et commanditaires à Venise (1540–1628)* (Rome: Ecole française de Rome, 1992), 75–91.

4. Marcantonio Michiel, *Notizia d'opere di disegno* [Vienna, 1896], ed. Theodor Frimmel (Florence: Edifir, 2003); Francesco Sansovino, *Venetia città nobilissima et singolare descritta in XIIII libri* (Venice: Jacomo Sansovino, 1581); Vincenzo Scamozzi, *Dell'idea dell'architettura universale* (Venice: for Giorgio Valentino, 1615).

5. On the Vendramin, see Rosella Lauber, "Per un ritratto di Gabriele Vendramin: Nuovi contributi," in *Figure di collezionisti a Venezia tra Cinque e Seicento*, ed. Linda Borean and Stefania Mason (Udine, Italy: Forum, 2002), 25–71.

6. On Simone Lando, see Hochmann, *Peintres et commanditaires*, 199–201. On Cristoforo Barbarigo and his collection, now housed at the State Hermitage Museum, St. Petersburg, see Herbert Siebenhüner, *Der Palazzo Barbarigo della Terrazza in Venedig und sein Tizian Sammlung* (Munich: Deutscher Kunstverlag, 1981), 28, 113; and Charles Hope, "Titian's Family and the Dispersal of His Estate," in *Late Titian and the Sensuality of Painting*, ed. Sylvia Ferino-Pagden, exh. cat. (Venice: Marsilio, 2008), 29–41 (Cristoforo's will is discussed on 37–38).

7. Carlo Ridolfi, *Le maraviglie dell'arte* [Venice, 1648], ed. Detlev von Hadeln, 2 vols. (Berlin: Grote'sche Verlagsbuchhandlung, 1914–24); Marco Boschini, *La carta del navegar pitoresco* [Venice, 1660], ed. Anna Pallucchini (Venice: Istituto per la collaborazione culturale, 1966), 21.

8. Ridolfi (*Le maraviglie dell'arte* 1:347) describes how "i maggiori principi e signori di questo chiaro pittore, havendo eglino con eccessive spese fatto di quelle numerosa raccolta, non parendo adorno qualsivoglia palagio, ove non entri alcuna cosa di questa mano."

9. Ibid., 313.

10. Boschini, *La carta*, 31–33.

11. Ridolfi's original, in *Le maraviglie dell'arte* 2:66, reads: "hor vedete signori, quanto prevaglia nei giudizi l'autorità e l'opinione, e come pochi siano coloro, che bene intendono di pittura."

12. The original reads: "nel colorire dice ha vere imitation la natura, e poi particolarmente Titiano, in tanto che molti ritratti fatti da lui sono stati tenuti di mano di Titiano." Raffaello Borghini, *Il riposo* [Florence, 1584] (Hildesheim: Georg Olms Verlagsbuchhandlung, 1969), 551.

13. Peter Humfrey, "Epilogue: The Demand from Abroad," in *Venice and the Veneto*, ed. Peter Humfrey (Cambridge: Cambridge University Press, 2007), 334, 338, with bibliography. It was not by chance that Veronese had modified his *Annunciation* for El Escorial in a Titianesque manner. On the competition at the Spanish court after the death of Titian, see Miguel Falomir, "Tintoretto and Spain: From El Greco to Velázquez," in Falomir, *Tintoretto*, 159–62; and Philip Cottrell and Rosemarie Mulcahy, "Succeeding Titian: Parrasio Michiel and Venetian Painting at the Court of Philip II," *The Burlington Magazine* 149, no. 1249 (2007): 232–45.

14. See Ridolfi, *Le maraviglie dell'arte* 1:227. Erica Tietze-Conrat ("Titian's Workshop in His Late Years," *Art Bulletin* 28, no. 2 [1946]: 77) hypothesizes that the 50 scudi Girolamo Dente requested to copy the *Martyrdom of Saint Laurence* by Titian at El Escorial could be a standard price for a workshop painting. On Titian's *atelier*, see also Giorgio Tagliaferro, "In the Workshop with Titian, 1548–1576," in *Late Titian*, ed. Ferino-Pagden, 71–77.

15. Wethey, *Paintings of Titian* 1:83 n. 27.

16. Wilhelm Bode, Georg Gronau, and Detlev von Hadeln, *Archivalische Beiträge zur Geschichte der venezianischen Kunst, aus dem Nachlass Gustav Ludwigs* (Berlin: Cassirer, 1911), 156; and Francesca Pitacco, "Fonti per il collezionismo veneziano (1580–1600)" (graduate thesis, Università di Udine, 1999–2000), 143–57.

17. Documentation on sixteenth-century collecting practices is concise, and inventories often lack attributions. See Michel Hochmann, "Quelques réflexions sur les collections des peintures à Venise dans la première moitié du XVI siècle," in *Il collezionismo a Venezia e nel Veneto ai tempi della Serenissima*, conference proceedings, ed. Bernard Aikema, Rosella Lauber, and Max Seidel (Venice: Marsilio, 2005), 117–34.

18. Archivio di Stato di Venezia, Notarile, Atti, notaio Pietro Partenio, b. 10680, cc. 79v–95v, February 20, 1589, inventory of the property of Lorenzo Donà *quondam* Alvise at Santa Maria Formosa.

19. Fabrizio Magani, *Il collezionismo e la committenza artistica della famiglia Widmann dal Seicento all'Ottocento* (Venice: Istituto Veneto di Scienze, Lettere e Arti, 1989), 34.

20. Boschini, *La carta*, 21.

21. Stefania Mason, "'By the hand of Titian,' 'Derives from Titian': Clues from Venetian Collections," in *Late Titian*, ed. Ferino-Pagden, 79–87.

22. Maria Stella Alfonsi, "Cosimo III de Medici e Venezia. I primi anni di regno," in *Figure di collezionisti*, ed. Borean and Mason, 273–77. Among the complaints about the rarity of originals, see that of Paolo del Sera in a letter of 1660 to Leopoldo de' Medici: "in truth, there are no more drawings or paintings, and none to be found on the streets, a sign that if I were ordered to provide something—not necessarily a painting, but a beautiful portrait by Titian or someone else of his stature—even regardless of cost, I would not know where to begin looking"; Gloria Chiarini De Anna, "Nove lettere di Paolo del Sera a Leopoldo de' Medici," *Paragone* 26, no. 307 (1975): 89.

23. The first citation is in Giulio Mancini's *Considerazioni sulla pittura, 1617–1621*, ed. Anna Marucchi and Luigi Salerno (Rome: Accademia Nazionale dei Lincei, 1956), 1:135; the second is in Boschini's *La carta*, 704. Regarding the role of copies from the sixteenth and seventeenth centuries, see Jeffrey M. Muller, "Measures of Authenticity: The Detection of Copies in the Early Literature on Connoisseurship," in *Retaining the Original: Multiple Originals, Copies, and Reproductions*, exh. cat. (Washington, DC: National Gallery of Art, 1989), 141–49; and Maria Loh, "Originals, Reproductions, and a 'Particular Taste' for Pastiche in the Seventeenth-Century Republic of Painting," in *Mapping Markets for Paintings in Europe, 1450–1750*, ed. Neil De Marchi and Hans J. Van Miegroet (Turnhout, Belgium: Brepols, 2006), 237–60.

24. Linda Borean, *La quadreria di Agostino e Giovan Donato Correggio nel collezionismo veneziano del Seicento* (Udine: Forum, 2000), 185, 188.

25. Hochmann, *Peintres et commanditaires*, 90.

26. Linda Borean, "'Desegni e stampa de rame.' La collezione grafica di Gaspar Chechel, mercante tedesco nella Venezia del Seicento," *Aprosiana: Rivista annuale di studi barocchi*, n.s., 10 (2002): 155–78.

27. The document is being published by Stefania Mason, whom I thank for allowing its inclusion here. The actual quotations read as follows: "Madalenna Copia de Titian de man del s[igno]r Geronimo finida" and "Madalena cavada dal Titian de man del s.r Ger finida."

28. Linda Borean, "Il caso Bergonzi," in *Il collezionismo d'arte a Venezia: Il Seicento*, ed. Linda Borean and Stefania Mason (Venice: Marsilio, 2007), 203–21.

29. Isabella Cecchini, *Quadri e mercato di quadri a Venezia nel Seicento: Uno studio sul mercato dell'arte* (Venice: Marsilio, 2000), 236–37, 248–49; Ridolfi, *Le maraviglie dell'arte* 1:194. Ridolfi states that not only did the portrait of a woman come from the Marcello family, but it depicted a member of that family.

30. Mary Frances Neff, "Chancellery Secretaries in Venetian Politics and Society, 1480–1533" (PhD diss., University of California, 1985), 431.

31. Hochmann, *Peintres et commanditaires*, 356–58.

32. Giuseppe Tassini, Cittadini veneziani, Biblioteca del Museo Correr, Venice, ms. P.D. c 4/ 2, p. 240ter.

33. Archivio di Stato di Venezia, Giudici del Proprio, Divisioni, reg. 12, cc. 59v–60v, June 28, 1581. Pietro possessed, therefore, the first version, but current opinion holds that both versions should be dated to around 1532, when the sitter was about to turn sixty. The painting had been first assigned to Pietro's widow, as seen in the inventory compiled three weeks earlier restoring her dowry, which listed "ritrato del Concilior grando Francisci d'età d'anni 60"; Pitacco, "Fonti," 252. The canvas at the Detroit Institute of Arts is generally thought to be of higher quality than the portrait in Washington, DC, which contains workshop intervention and bears the fragmentary inscription "TIS OLX," which may be interpreted as the remnant of the original "AETATIS SUAE LX"; see Wethey, *Paintings of Titian* 2:100–101 nn. 34, 35. Wethey associated the painting in Detroit with the portrait of the chancellor Ridolfi saw at the house of Widmann (in the 1659 inventory of the collection, transcribed in Magani's *Il collezionismo*, 34, is cited a "Ritratto di un cancellier grande di Tiziano"). The 1756 inventory of pictures owned by Costantino Franceschi of the delle Rose branch of the family includes a "Ritratto del nostro antico Cancellier Grande di Tizian" (Donatella Bernardi, "Interni di case veneziane del Settecento," *Studi veneziani*, n.s., 20 [1990]: 241. Alberto Bagnara, in "I De Franceschi collezionisti a Venezia tra XVI e XVIII secolo," *Venezia Arti*, no. 17/18 [2003/2004]: 49–50, published a 1750 inventory of Costantino Franceschi's collection, identical to that of 1756).

34. Siebenhüner, *Der Palazzo*, 32.

35. Mason, "'By the Hand of Titian,'" 81.

36. Boschini, *La carta*, 29.

37. I thank Isabella Cecchini for the annotations to the list. In the preceding inventory of the del Sera collection, compiled in 1674 upon the request of his creditors and without the assistance of an expert, "2 quadreti di bacanali de bona man" are mentioned. The document is published in Borean and Mason, *Il collezionismo d'arte*, 348–54.

38. The replicas (now at Accademia Carrara, Bergamo) were in the possession of Dario Varotari, son and heir to Padovanino (see Boschini, *La carta*, 198) by the middle of the seventeenth century.

39. Boschini, *La carta*, 419.

40. Mitchell F. Merling, "Marco Boschini's *Carta del navegar pitoresco*: Art Theory and *Virtuoso* Culture in Seventeenth-Century Venice" (PhD diss., Brown University, 1992), 97.

41. Maria H. Loh, *Titian Remade* (Los Angeles: Getty Research Institute, 2007), 86–87, 114.

42. The original reads "Signor in Emmaus tre figure soaze nere con fillo d'oro copia del Tician fatta dal Padovanin." Cecilia Corner's inventory of 1699 is transcribed in Borean and Mason, *Il collezionismo d'arte*, 355–61, with further discussion on 246–47.

43. Wethey, *Paintings of Titian* 1:160–61 n. 142. In the manuscript catalogue of paintings sent by Worsley to London in 1797 (soon to be published by this author), the painting does not appear, while an *Ecce Homo* is noted along with a replica of the *Diana and Callisto* made for Philip II and a *Saint Christopher* derived from the fresco in the Palazzo Ducale. For the Louvre's *Supper at Emmaus* (cat. 22, where it is dated about 1533–34), see Guido Rebecchini, "Tiziano e Mantova: *La Cena in Emmaus* per Nicola Maffei," *Venezia Cinquecento* 5, no. 10 (1995): 41–68. Regarding the dispersal of Titian paintings, see Rosella Lauber, "Itinerario di una diaspora: Il giro del mondo alla ricerca dei Tiziano non più a Venezia," *Venezialtrove: Almanacco della presenza veneziana nel mondo* 6 (2007): 77–93.

44. On Tintoretto's critical fortune among Venetian collectors, see Linda Borean, "Jacopo Tintoretto nelle collezioni veneziane tra Sei e Settecento," in *Jacopo Tintoretto: Actas del congreso internacional / Proceedings of the International Symposium*, Museo Nacional del Prado, Madrid, February 26–27, 2007 (Madrid: Museo Nacional del Prado, forthcoming).

45. This information is from a letter from the Venetian ambassador to Madrid, Girolamo Lippomano. See Mary Pittaluga, "L'attività di Tintoretto in Palazzo Ducale," *L'Arte* 25 (1922): 94 n. 6; and Linda Borean, "Documentation," in Falomir, *Tintoretto*, 444, with the complete transcription of the letter.

46. Boschini (*La carta*, 747) recounts: "il Tintoretto dipinse per cinquanta ducati l'uno. Ora, se si dovessero vender, so io che vi sarebbe chi, appresso alle due figure che formano il numero 50, v'aggiungerebbe altri tre zeri, e non in caratteri di penna, ma in caratteri d'oro."

47. Giovanni Prati, *La musa delirante* (Venice, 1677), 208–9. The other artists praised in Prati's sonnets were all from the seventeenth century. Essays in a forthcoming volume edited by Linda Borean, Massimo Favilla, and Ruggero Rugolo discuss Prati and his artistic and literary culture.

48. Archivio di Stato di Venezia, Notarile, Testamenti, Antonio Brinis, b. 157, no. 483, May 30, 1594, will of Jacopo Tintoretto. The document is transcribed in Carlo Ridolfi, *Vite dei Tintoretto da Le Maraviglie dell'arte overo le vite degli illustrissimi pittori veneti e dello stato descritte dal cavalier Carlo Ridolfi (1648)*, introduction by Antonio Manno (Venice: Filippi, 1994), 127–28; and in Borean, "Documentation," 448–49.

49. Francesco Marcolini to Pietro Aretino, September 15, 1551. See Borean, "Documentation," 421, with bibliography.

50. Museum voor Schone Kunsten, Ghent. On the painting, see the entry in Arnout Balis et al., *200 Jaar Verzamelen: Collectieboek Museum voor Schone Kunsten Gent* (Ghent: Ludion, 2000), cat. 71; and Paola Rossi, *Jacopo Tintoretto*, vol. 1, *I ritratti* (Venice: Alfieri, 1974), 107.

51. Ridolfi, *Le maraviglie dell'arte* 2:58.

52. Giovanni Paolo Corner and Pietro Pellegrini will be discussed in my contributions and those by Paola Benussi in *Il collezionismo d'arte a Venezia: Dalle origini al Cinquecento*, ed. Michel Hochmann, Rosella Lauber, and Stefania Mason (Venice: Marsilio, 2008). Pietro Pellegrini's July 16, 1625, inventory was transcribed by Hochmann in *Peintres et commanditaires*, 364–66.

53. The original reads: "ritratto di mano del Tintoretto vecchio, dal ginocchio in su armato in attitudine spiritosissima con architettura di colonne dietro, e da una finestra si vede il mare lontano con una galeazza, della più esquisita maniera di questo autore, essendo anco così belle e terribili le armature, che se non si conoscessi dalla testa, che è mano del Tintoretto, ogn'uno crederebbe che fussi di mano di Tiziano. Il ritratto rappresenta il Veniero che fu poi Capitano Generale de' veneziani nell'Armata Navale del 1571 essendo stato fatto dell'eta' di 40 anni quando era Capitano di Golfo." See Miriam Fileti Mazza, ed., *Archivio del collezionismo mediceo: Il Cardinal Leopoldo*, vol. 1, *Rapporti con il mercato Veneto* (Milan: Ricciardi, 1987), 327–29.

54. This information was graciously provided by Julia Armstrong-Totten (oral communication, September 1, 2004). The coat of arms, however, does not exactly coincide with that of the Giustinian-Lolin, a family that died out in the first half of the nineteenth century, at which point their palace was occupied by Francesco Aglietti (1757–1836), a noted Venetian collector.

55. Archivio di Stato di Venezia, Marco Barbaro-Alessandro Tasca, Arbori de Patritii Veneti, II, c. 183 and 188; and Andrea da Mosto, *I dogi di Venezia* (Florence: Giunti,

2003), 356. Archivio di Stato di Venezia, Giudici del Proprio, Mobili, b. 226, c. 26v.

56. In the 1661 inventory of the Spanish noble Luis Méndez de Haro, a painting of the same subject is listed. See Falomir, "Tintoretto and Spain," 163.

57. Pallucchini and Rossi, *Opere sacre e profane* 1:137, cat. 42.

58. Ridolfi, *Le maraviglie dell'arte* 2:29; Boschini, *La carta*, 146–47; Diane DeGrazia Bohlin, *Prints and Related Drawings by the Carracci Family: A Catalogue Raisonné* (Washington, DC: National Gallery of Art, 1979), 254–57 n. 147a; and Maria Agnese Chiari Moretto Wiel, ed., *Jacopo Tintoretto e i suoi incisori*, exh. cat. (Milan: Electa, 1994), 26 n. 3.2.

59. See Jean Habert, ed., *Le Paradis de Tintoret: Un concours pour le palais des Doges*, exh. cat. (Paris: Musée du Louvre Editions, 2006).

60. Andrea Zannini, *Burocrazia e burocrati a Venezia in età moderna: I cittadini originari (sec. XVI–XVIII)* (Venice: Istituto Veneto di Scienze, Lettere e Arti, 1993), 158. The relationship between the artist and Giovan Francesco Ottobon is noted by Ridolfi in *Le maraviglie dell'arte* 2:69–70.

61. This *modello* is now owned by the Istituti di Ricovero e di Educazione (IRE) in Venice. See Barbara Mazza, "Tracce dei Tintoretto nei fondi archivistici dell'IRE," in *Jacopo Tintoretto nel quarto centenario della morte: Atti del convegno internazionale di studi. Venezia, 24–26 Novembre, 1994*, ed. Paola Rossi and Lionello Puppi (Padua: Il Poligrafo, 1996), 83–88.

62. Del Sera to Leopoldo de' Medici, March 18, 1656, Archivio di Stato di Firenze, Carteggio di Artisti, V.

63. Falomir, *Tintoretto*, 236–40, cat. 12.

64. Marcus B. Burke and Peter Cherry, *Collections of Paintings in Madrid, 1601–1755*, Documents for the History of Collecting, Spanish Inventories, 1 (Los Angeles: Getty Research Institute, 1997), 726–86; Falomir, "Tintoretto and Spain," 159–67.

65. Stefania Mason, "Dallo studiolo al 'camaron' dei quadri. Un itinerario per dipinti, disegni, stampe e qualche curiosità nelle collezioni della Venezia barocca," in *Il collezionismo d'arte*, ed. Borean and Mason, 32–33.

66. Ridolfi, *Le maraviglie dell'arte* 1:354; Hochmann, *Peintres et commanditaires*, 77–78.

67. Gregorio Gattinoni, *Inventario di una casa veneziana del secolo XVII (La casa degli Eccellenti Caliari eredi di Paolo il Veronese)* (Mestre: Officine Grafiche, 1914).

68. Boschini, *La carta*, 735; Beverly L. Brown, "Replication and the Art of Veronese," in *Retaining the Original*, 111–24.

69. The inventory of 1671 reads: "un quadro rappresenta la Nontiata con il Padre Eterno portato da due angioli e tre testine di serafini col spirito santo di Carletto retocata da Paulo Veronese altri si spaza." See Borean, *La quadreria*, 191. The painting was acquired in 1671 for 42 ducats.

70. In 1607, the Patriarch of Aquileia gave to Scipione Borghese *The Preaching of John the Baptist* and *Saint Anthony Preaching to the Fish* (Galleria Borghese, Rome), which may have sparked interest in Veronese within the Barberini circle. See Pignatti and Pedrocco, *Veronese* 2:cats. 210, 382.

71. The original reads: "vi son ben delle cose, che possono essere state disegnate da Paolo, mà non colorite, ò perfettionate da lui; e sono insomma stato assicurato, che tra detti pezzi non ve ne è uno, che meriti di essere stimato per cosa buona di mano di quel maestro." See William L. Barcham and Catherine R. Puglisi, "Paolo Veronese e la Roma dei Barberini," *Saggi e memorie di storia dell'arte* 25 (2001): 86. In addition to publishing this important July 10, 1632, letter by Massani, Barcham and Puglisi discuss the rise of Veronese's popularity among Roman collectors in the first half of the seventeenth century, as well as the general influence of Venetian Renaissance masters on later Italian painters, particularly Pietro da Cortona. The article includes another appendix listing paintings by Veronese in four notable Roman collections of the early Seicento.

72. Klara Garas, "Veronese e il collezionismo del Nord nel XVI–XVII secolo," in *Nuovi studi su Paolo Veronese*, ed. Massimo Gemin (Venice: Arsenale Editrice, 1990): 19–20. See also Xavier F. Salomon, *Veronese's Allegories: Virtue, Love, and Exploration in Renaissance Venice*, exh. cat. (New York: Frick Collection, 2006), 23–24.

73. The original reads: "le opere di questo Maestro non erano qui un tempo fa in molta stima, mà hoggi è salito a segno il credito di esse, che chi hà alcuna cosa di lui, ne tiene assai più conto, che sé fosse di Tiziano istesso, che è stato sempre tenuto il nume de Pittori di questo paese, giudicandosi, che Paolo sia perfetto nel disegno, vago nel colorito…e valente nelle inventioni." See Barcham and Puglisi, "Paolo Veronese," 86. In *Le maraviglie dell'arte* 1:335, Ridolfi underscores that "many were the paintings collected after the Painter's death."

74. Of course, these same collectors would have found it difficult to turn down a painting by Titian; see Ridolfi, *Le maraviglie dell'arte* 1:347. For an exploration of the critical fortune of Veronese, see Richard Cocke, "The Development of Veronese's Critical Reputation," *Arte Veneta* 34 (1980): 96–112.

75. One exception was the collection of Cristoforo Orsetti, a merchant of Greek *malvasia* wine, who seems to have owned the *Venus and Mars* now in the Galleria Sabauda, Turin. See Linda Borean and Stefania Mason, "Cristoforo Orsetti e i suoi quadri di 'perfetta mano,'" in *Figure di collezionisti*, ed. Borean and Mason, 145.

76. In the fiscal declaration to the Ufficio dell'Inquisitorato alle Acque from 1737, on Chiara Pisani's behalf, the value of the painting was fixed at "only" 2,500 ducats. Giuseppe Gullino, *I Pisani dal Banco e Moretta: Storia di due famiglie veneziane in età moderna e delle loro vicende patrimoniali tra 1705 e 1836* (Rome: Istituto Storico Italiano per l'età Moderna e Contemporanea, 1984), 223.

77. Bert W. Meijer, "Per la fortuna di Paolo Veronese sino al 1664," in *Veronese e Verona*, ed. Sergio Marinelli, exh. cat. (Verona: Museo di Castelvecchio, 1988), 122–23. The prohibition on copying this work apparently continued in subsequent centuries; see Penny, *Sixteenth Century Italian Paintings*, 2:354. For a full discussion about the patrons and history of the painting, see 354–87 in the same catalog.

78. Simona Savini Branca, *Il collezionismo veneziano nel Seicento* (Padua: Cedam, 1965), 134–40. Martinioni's 1663 additions to Francesco Sansovino's guidebook, *Venetia, città nobilissima et singolare descritta in XIII libri*, ed. Giustiniano Martinoni (Venice: S. Curti, 1663), contain a list of painters active in Venice, "Quinto catalogo," including one "Bastian Bombello da Udine [who] while he was a student made magnificent copies from Paolo Veronese," 2:21.

79. The February 1704 inventory, drawn up by the owner, mentions "La copia del quadro d'Alessandro di Paulo Veronese che è in Ca Pisani Moreta fatta da Monsù Lefebre." The document is published in Borean and Mason's *Il collezionismo d'arte*, 362–83.

80. Agostino Barbarigo, the Provveditore Generale da Mar, died on October 9, 1571, from an arrow to the eye at the Battle of Lepanto. The 1851 inventory of paintings owned by Marchesa Manfrin Plattis (Library and Archive of the National Gallery, London) lists as no. 31 "P. Veronese. Ritratto d'un generale con freccia in mano." The *Catalogo dei quadri esistenti nella Galleria Manfrin in Venezia*, Venice, 1856, includes as no. 179 a portrait with dimensions close to those of the painting now in Cleveland (102.2 x 104.2 cm [40 ¼ x 41 in.]), assigned to Veronese and believed to depict Onfrè Giustinian, the admiral who communicated the news from Lepanto to Venice. Ridolfi (*Le maraviglie dell'arte* 1:338) records a Veronese portrait of Onfrè Giustinian in the Giustinian house at San Moisé. The Cleveland painting (inv. 1928.16) was published in 1928 as a portrait of the admiral Manfrin, based on the supposed provenance of the painting. See Terisio Pignatti, *Veronese: L'opera completa* (Venice: Arsenale Editrice, 1976), 135, cat. 172; and Pignatti and Pedrocco, *Veronese* 1:284–85, cat. 188. The painting was relined, and without photographic documentation of the back of the canvas during the treatment, it is impossible to verify inscriptions or other marks that might support the Manfrin provenance. I thank Jon Seydl of the Cleveland Museum of Art for this information. A copy of this portrait is housed in the National Gallery of Art, Washington, DC; see Fern R. Shapley, *Catalogue of the Italian Paintings: National Gallery of Art, Washington*, 2 vols. (Washington, DC: National Gallery of Art, 1979), 1:531, cat. 1485.

81. Rearick, *Art of Paolo Veronese*, 108, cat. 54.

82. As was specified in the 1703 will (Borean, "Il caso Bergonzi," 214).

83. Regarding the *Supper* from the Servite monastery, see Laura De Fuccia, "Collezionisti francesi di pittura veneziana nel Seicento" (PhD thesis, Università di Udine–Ecole Pratique des Hautes Etudes, 2007), 1:41–51. In the collections of prints *Opera selectiora* by Valentin Lefèvre, published in 1673 (Ugo Ruggeri, *Valentin Lefèvre [1637–1677]: Dipinti, disegni, incisioni* [Manerba: Merigo Art Books, 2001], 210–26), and *Pitture scelte* by Carla Caterina Patin (Padua: Tipografia del Seminario, 1691), one sees the decline of Tintoretto's fame by comparison to that of Titian and Veronese in French taste. Alvise Molin, who owned a splendid art collection, compiled a list of its contents in 1668, including a *Supper at Emmaus* and a *Risen Christ* by Veronese. See Linda Borean, "Alvise Molin," in *Il collezionismo d'arte*, ed. Borean and Mason, 288–89.

84. Marguerite Allain-Lunay, "A Token of Franco-Venetian Friendship," in *The Feast in the House of Simon: Veronese. History and Restoration of a Masterpiece* (Paris: Alain de Gourcuff, 1997), 65–66.

85. Michel Hochmann, "La Collection de Giacomo Contarini," *Mélanges de l'école française de Rome* 99 (1987): 451–52. The painting reached its present location in 1713 with the donation of the Contarini collection to the Venetian state.

86. The Dresden painting (dimensions 321 x 289 cm [126 1/16 x 113 11/16 in.]) is reproduced in color and discussed by Penny in *Sixteenth Century Italian Paintings* 2:437 and fig. 8. This connection between the Dresden painting and the picture owned by del Sera was advanced by Alfonsi ("Cosimo III," 269). Del Sera's painting would later reach the hands of Francesco Algarotti, who bought it for the Dresden Gallery in 1743. According to Savini Branca (*Il collezionismo veneziano nel Seicento*, 279), del Sera may have purchased the work from the Caliari family. Von Hadeln's notes to Ridolfi (*Le maraviglie dell'arte* 1:357) associated the Dresden painting, which von Hadeln attributed to Carletto, with that mentioned by Ridolfi as owned by Giuseppe Caliari.

87. The original reads: "Historia dell'Europa posta a sedere sopra un toro bianco, con damigelle che la servono, con amorini, et con altre figurette et animali, con paese et alberi bellissimi." See Paola Santin, "Paolo del Sera a Venezia (1640–1672)" (graduate thesis, Università di Udine, 2003/2004), 48.

88. Lucia Procacci and Ugo Procacci, "Carteggio di Marco Boschini con il cardinale Leopoldo de' Medici," *Saggi e memorie di storia dell'arte* 4 (1965): 106–7.

89. Alfonsi, "Cosimo III," 278.

90. Wethey, *Paintings of Titian* 1:112, cat. 70; Pedrocco, *Titian: Complete Paintings*, 202, cat. 149; Humfrey, *Titian: The Complete Paintings*, 219, cat. 161.

91. Alfonsi, "Cosimo III," 274. Some of the aforementioned topics concerning the socio-economic conditions of Venetian painters and the art market, including prices for paintings, are discussed in greater detail in a forthcoming essay by Philip Sohm, "Venice," in *Painting for Profit: The Economic Lives of Painters in Seventeenth-Century Italy*, ed. Richard Spear and Philip Sohm.

Materials and Techniques of Painters in Sixteenth-Century Venice

1. See Paola Lanaro, *At the Centre of the World: Trade and Manufacturing in Venice and the Venetian Mainland, 1400–1800* (Toronto: Centre for Reformation and Renaissance Studies, University of Toronto, 2006).

2. See M. Murano, "Tecniche della pittura murale Veneta," *Pittura murali nel Veneto e tecnica dell'affresco* (Vicenza: Neri Pozza, 1960), 233–34 n. 2.

3. Diana Gisolfi, "Tintoretto e le facciate affrescate di Venezia," in *Jacopo Tintoretto nel quarto centenario della morte: Atti del convegno internazionale di studi. Venezia, 24–26 Novembre, 1994*, ed. Paola Rossi and Lionello Puppi (Padua: Il Poligrafo, 1996), 111–14.

4. See Luca Mola, *The Silk Industry in Venice* (Baltimore: John Hopkins University Press, 2000).

5. Although production stamps have been found on wooden panel and copper supports, little has been documented concerning the manufacture of and market for canvases specifically for artists' use. The illustrated stamp shows a design that is quite similar to weavers' marks on tapestries from the northern regions during this time frame. The stamp/production facility (weaver) has not, as yet, been identified. This stamp is present on Gentileschi's *Way to Cavalry* (about 1604, Kunsthistorisches Museum, Vienna).

6. Andrea Rothe, "Andrea Mantegna's Adoration of the Magi," in *Historical Painting Techniques, Materials, and Studio Practice: Preprints of a Symposium*, University of Leiden, The Netherlands, June 26–29, 1995 (Los Angeles: The J. Paul Getty Trust, 1995), 111–16.

7. The *Wedding Feast at Cana* for the monastery of San Giorgio Maggiore was not stretched onto a wooden frame but mounted directly to the wall with spikes. Hans Dieter Huber, *Paolo Veronese: Kunst als soziales System* (Munich: W. Fink, 2005), 252.

8. Franz Mares, "Beiträge zur Kenntnis der Kunstbestrebungen des Erzherzogs Leopold Wilhelm," in *Jahrbuch der Kunsthistorischen Sammlungen des Allerhöchsten Kaiserhauses* (Vienna: Verlag Holzhuasen, 1887), 5:353.

9. Bruno Heimberg, "'Nostro Apelle Novello': Tintoretto and Italian Easel Painting from the Thirteenth to the Sixteenth Century," in *Tintoretto: The Gonzaga Cycle*, ed. Cornelia Syre, exh. cat. (Ostfildern-Ruit: Hatje Cantz, 2000), 233. The details in fig. 29 are from three paintings in the Kunsthistorisches Museum, Vienna. From left to right, they are Titian, *Ecce Homo* (inv. 73); Veronese and Workshop, *Mystic Marriage of Saint Catherine* (inv. 1529); and Titian, *Danaë* (inv. 90).

10. Robert Wald, "Titian's Vienna *Danaë*: Observations on Execution and Replication in Titian's Studio," in *Late Titian and the Sensuality of Painting*, ed. Sylvia Ferino-Pagden, exh. cat. (Venice: Marsilio, 2008), 124–33. See also Xavier F. Salomon, *Veronese's Allegories: Virtue, Love, and Exploration in Renaissance Venice*, exh. cat. (New York: Frick Collection, 2006), 38.

11. For an example of a painting from the cycle for Philip II (Titian's *Rape of Europa*), see Hilliard Goldfarb, *Titian and Rubens: Power, Politics, and Style*, exh. cat. (Boston: Isabella Stewart Gardner Museum, 1998), 97.

12. Veronika Poll-Frommel, Jan Schmidt, and Cornelia Syre, "The Gonzaga Cycle," in *Tintoretto: The Gonzaga Cycle*, ed. Syre, 28–121.

13. An examination of the ground layers from *Gypsy Madonna*, *Madonna of the Cherries*, and *Madonna and Child with Saints* (all before 1520, Kunsthistorisches Museum, Vienna) reveals monochrome calcium sulphate grounds. Tintoretto's *Susannah and the Elders* as well as *Saint George and the Dragon* (both mid-1550s) are executed on light-colored gesso grounds. See Jill Dunkerton, "Tintoretto's Painting Technique," in Falomir, *Tintoretto*, 146.

14. Armenini writes, "the darker the *imprimatura* the muddier the colors become. But for those who do not want the colors to change in time, the priming should be almost entirely of white lead, with one-sixth of varnish, and a little red that dries at the same rate." He provides alternative recipes as well. See Giovanni Battista Armenini, *On the True Precepts of the Art of Painting*, trans. Edward Olszewski (New York: B. Franklin, 1977), 192. Also see Armenini, *De'veri precetti della pittura* (Ravenna: Libro Secondo, 1587), 122.

15. For a general discussion of the topic, see Arie Wallert and Carlo van Oosterhout, *From Tempera to Oil Paint: Changes in Venetian Painting, 1460–1560* (Amsterdam: Rijksmuseum, 1998).

16. Jill Dunkerton and Marika Spring, "The Development of Painting on Coloured Surfaces in Sixteenth-Century Italy," in *Painting Techniques, History, Materials and Studio Practice: Contributions to the Dublin Congress, 7–11 September 1998* (London: International Institute for Conservation of Historic and Artistic Works, 1998), 120–30.

17. For the examination of grounds and *imprimatura* of selected mid- to late-career works by Titian, see Martina Griesser and Natalia Gustavson, "Observations on Technique and Materials in Titian's Late Work," in *Late Titian*, ed. Ferino-Pagden, 102–11.

18. Jill Dunkerton, "Developments in Colour and Texture in Venetian Painting of the Early 16th Century," in *New Interpretations of Venetian Renaissance Painting*, ed. Francis Ames-Lewis (London: University of London, Birkbeck College, 1994), 71.

19. Joyce Plesters, "Tintoretto's Paintings in the National Gallery," *National Gallery Technical Bulletin* 4 (1980): 32–47. See also Syre, *Tintoretto: The Gonzaga Cycle*, 123.

20. Nicholas Penny, "Paolo Veronese: The Adoration of the Kings," in Penny, *Sixteenth Century Italian Paintings* 2:396.

21. Syre, *Tintoretto: The Gonzaga Cycle*, 124.

22. For the description of the problems associated with the transport of Titian's *Venus and Adonis*, see Wethey, *Paintings of Titian* 3:189. More recent investigations have brought into question which version of *Venus and Adonis* is the canvas that was actually damaged during this initial transport from Italy to England; see also W. R. Rearick, "Titian's Later Mythologies," *Artibus et Historiae* 17, no. 33 (1996): 23–67. The characteristics and subsequent repair (perhaps original) of a series of horizontal losses to the painting *Girl in a Fur Wrap* (Kunsthistorisches Museum, Vienna) suggest that this painting was damaged in transit and repaired (repainted with modifications) by the artist himself. The repairs to the losses were made with original paint from an overlying composition, which considerably modified the underlying composition. See Ferino-Pagden, *Late Titian*, 15.

23. Robert Wald, "Titian's Portrait of Johann Friedrich von Sachsen in the Kunsthistorisches Museum," in *Tiziano: Téchnicas y restauraciones*, exh. cat. (Madrid: Museo Nacional del Prado, 1999), 87–97.

24. Giorgio Vasari, *Vasari on Technique*, ed. G. Baldwin Brown (New York: Dover, 1960), 236–37.

25. Elke Oberthaler and Elizabeth Walmsely, "Technical Studies of Painting Methods," in *Bellini, Giorgione, Titian and the Renaissance of Venetian Painting*, ed. David Alan Brown and Sylvia Ferino-Pagden, exh. cat. (Washington, DC: National Gallery of Art, 2006), 286–300. See also Paolo Spezzani, "Le Indagini non Invasive," in *Il colore ritrovato: Bellini a Venezia*, ed. Rona Goffen and Giovanna Nepi Sciré, exh. cat. (Milan: Electa, 2000), 181–83; and discussion of Giorgione's *Adoration of the Kings* in David Bomford, ed., *Underdrawings in Renaissance Paintings: Art in the Making* (London: National Gallery, 2003), 136–43.

26. Oberthaler and Walmsely, "Technical Studies," 286–300. See also Cavigli Bagarotto et al., "La Tecnica Pittorica di Giovanni Bellini," in *Il colore ritrovato*, ed. Goffen and Sciré, 184–202.

27. Giorgio Vasari, *Das Leben des Tizian*, ed. Alessandro Nova and Christina Irlenbusch, trans. Victoria Lorini (Berlin: Verlag Klaus Wagenbach, 2005), 45.

28. Carmen Bambach, *Drawing and Painting in the Italian Renaissance Workshop: Theory and Practice, 1300–1600* (Cambridge: Cambridge University Press, 1999), 406 n. 70.

29. A woodcut from Cesere Vecellio, 1591, depicts an enlarging/diminishing grid together with a pricking instrument; see Bambach, *Drawing and Painting*, 13.

30. Sylvia Ferino-Pagden and Robert Wald's catalogue entry on *Saint Jerome* in Falomir, *Tintoretto*, 330–32.

31. Bruce Cole, "Titian and the Idea of Originality in the Renaissance," in *The Craft of Art: Originality and Industry in the Italian Renaissance and Baroque Workshop*, ed. Andrew Ladis and Carolyn Wood (Athens, GA: University of Georgia Press, 1995), 86–112. See also Miguel Falomir, "Tiziano: Replicas," in *Tiziano*, ed. Miguel Falomir, exh. cat. (Madrid: Museo Nacional del Prado, 2003), 77–92.

32. Wenke Deiters, "Tizians Sacre Conversazioni im Kunsthistorischen Museum, im Chiswick House und im Musee du Louvre," in *Der Späte Tizian und die Sinnlichkeit der Malerei*, ed. Sylvia Ferino-Pagden, exh. cat. (Vienna: Kunsthistorisches Museum, 2007), 141–47.

33. Robert Wald, "Titian's Vienna *Danaë*: Observations on Execution and Replication in Titian's Studio," in *Late Titian*, ed. Ferino-Pagden, 124–33.

34. Julius von Schlosser, "Aus der Bilderwerkstatt der Renaissance," *Jahrbuch der Kunsthistorischen Sammlungen des Allerhöchsten Kaiserhauses* 31 (1913–14): 10–135.

35. Roland Krischel, *Tintoretto und die Skulptur der Renaissance in Venedig* (Weimar: VDG, 1994); Julius von Schlosser, "Aus der Bilderwerkstatt der Renaissance," *Jahrbuch der Kunsthistorischen Sammlungen des Allerhöchsten Kaiserhauses* 31 (1913–14): 118. See also Lucy Whitaker, "Tintoretto's Drawings after Sculpture and His Workshop Practice," in *The Sculpted Object, 1400–1700*, ed. Stuart Currie and Peta Motture (Aldershot, UK: Scholar Press, 1997), 177–91.

36. An excellent example of the fusion of sculpture and painting integrated into a single visual program is the Grimani chapel, church of San Sebastiano, Venice. See Thomas Martin, "Vittoria e la Committenza," in *La Bellissima Maniera: Alessandro Vittoria e la scultura veneta del Cinquecento*, by Andrea Bacchi, Lia Camerlengo, and Manfred Leithe-Jasper (Trento: Castello del Buonconsiglio, 1999), 63.

37. Beverly Brown, "Titian's Marble Muse: Ravenna, Padua and 'The Miracle of the Speaking Babe,'" in *Studi Tizianeschi* (Milan: Silvana Editoriale, 2005), 23.

38. Marilyn Perry, "On Titian's Borrowings from Ancient Art: A Cautionary Case," in *Tiziano e Venezia: Convegno internazionale di studi, 1976* (Vicenza: Neri Pozza, 1980), 187–91. See also Robert Wald, "Parmigianino's Cupid Carving His Bow: History, Examination, Restoration," in *Parmigianino e il Manierismo Europo: Atti del convegno internazionale di studi, Parma, 13–15 June, 2002*, ed. Lucia Fornari Schianchi (Milan: Silvana Editoriale, 2002), 165–81.

39. Carl Brandon Strehlke and Cecilia Frosinini, *The Panel Paintings of Masolino and Masaccio: The Role of Technique* (Milan: 5 Continents Editions, 2002), 202, 123 (with reference to Raymond White's binding media analysis from 1995, National Gallery, London). See also Paula Nuttall, *From Flanders to Florence: The Impact of Netherlandish Painting, 1400–1500* (New Haven, CT: Yale University Press, 2004), 163.

40. Ernst Berger and Théodore Turquet de Mayerne, *Quellen für Maltechnik während der Renaissance und deren Folgezeit* (Munich: G. D. W. Callwey, 1901), 339.

41. For more comprehensive information regarding historical pigment characteristics, see Nicholas Eastaugh et al., *The Pigment Compendium: Optical Microscopy of Historical Pigments* (Oxford: Elsevier Butterworth Heinemann, 2004); see also Robert Feller et al., eds., *Artist's Pigments*, vols. 1–3 (Oxford: Oxford University Press, 1986–97), vol. 4 (Washington, DC: National Gallery of Art; London: Archetype Publications, 2007).

42. R. Krischel, "Zur Geschichte des Venezianischen Pigmenthandels," *Wallraf-Richartz-Jahrbuch*, 2002, 100. See also Louisa C. Matthew, "Vendecolori a Venezia: The Reconstruction of a Profession," *The Burlington Magazine*, Nov. 2002, 680–86.

43. Goffen and Scirè, *Il colore ritrovato*, 33–35.

44. For a comprehensive discussion of the development of Venetian painting technique, see Marcia Hall, "Venice and the Development of Tonal Painting," in *Color and Meaning: Practice and Theory in Renaissance Painting* (Cambridge: Cambridge University Press, 1992), 199–235. See also Carolin Bohlmann, *Tintorettos Maltechnick: Zur Dialektik von Theorie und Praxis* (Munich: Scaneg, 1998).

45. Marco Boschini, *La carta del navegar pitoresco* [Venice, 1660], ed. Anna Pallucchini (Venice: Istituto per la collaborazione culturale, 1966), 7:711ff. See also Sylvia Pagden-Ferino, "Late Titian and the Sensuality of Painting," in *Late Titian*, ed. Ferino-Pagden, 21–22.

46. Bernard Aikema, "Late Titian and the Others: Between Venice and Europe," in *Late Titian*, ed. Ferino-Pagden, 89–99.

47. Falomir, *Tintoretto*, 100–101.

48. Hubertus Von Sonnenburg, "Beobachtungen zur Arbeitsweise Tintorettos," in *Maltechnik Restauro* (Munich: Callwey Verlag, 1974), 3:133–43.

49. Huber, *Paolo Veronese*, 254–57. For insight into the differences between Central Italian and Venetian theories of painting, see John Gage, *Colour and Culture: Practice and Meaning from Antiquity to Abstraction* (London: Thames and Hudson, 1995), 117–38; see also Wolf-Dietrich Löhr and Stefan Weppelmann, *Fantasie und Handwerk: Cennino Cennini und die Tradition der Toskanischen Malerei von Giotto bis Lorenzo Monaco* (Munich: Hirmer Verlag, 2008).

Prologue: The Transformation of Venetian Painting around 1500

1. Among the many excellent studies of Venetian painting in this period, see in particular David Alan Brown and Sylvia Ferino-Pagden, eds., *Bellini, Giorgione, Titian and the Renaissance of Venetian Painting*, exh. cat. (Washington, DC: National Gallery of Art, 2006); Peter Humfrey, *Painting in Renaissance Venice* (New Haven, CT: Yale University Press, 1995); and Rosand, *Painting in Sixteenth-Century Venice*. See also two surveys of paintings published by the National Gallery, London, which are particularly informative about the working methods of Renaissance artists: Jill Dunkerton, Susan Foister, Dillian Gordon, and Nicholas Penny, *Giotto to Dürer: Early Renaissance Painting in the National Gallery* (London: National Gallery, 1991), and Jill Dunkerton, Susan Foister, and Nicholas Penny, *Dürer to Veronese: Sixteenth-Century Painting in the National Gallery* (London: National Gallery, 1999).

2. See Jaynie Anderson (*Giorgione: The Painter of "Poetic Brevity"* [Paris: Flammarion, 1997], 362) for the letters, amid a rich appendix of documents and sources.

3. Leonardo's stay in Venice and his influence and that of his circle on Venetian art is thoroughly discussed in *Leonardo and Venezia*, ed. Giovanna Nepi Scirè and Pietro C. Mariani (Milan: Bompiani, 1992). In that volume, see in particular the essay by David Alan Brown ("Il Cenacolo di Leonardo: La prima eco a Venezia," 85–96), which surveys the kinds of drawings—especially those related to the *Last Supper*—that would have promoted softer contours, feminized beauty, and increasingly emotional facial expressions and gestures in Venetian art, if not immediately, then by the end of the decade.

4. Giorgio Vasari, *Le vite de' più eccellenti pittori, scultori ed architettori* [1568], ed. Gaetano Milanesi (Florence: G. C. Sansoni, 1878–85), 4:92–93 (see 91–100 for the biography of Giorgione). Written a decade earlier, in 1557, Dolce's *Dialogo della pittura*, also known as the *"Aretino"* (see Mark W. Roskill, *Dolce's Aretino and Venetian Art Theory of the Cinquecento* [New York: New York University Press], 1968, 85), stresses the generational break between Bellini and Titian in the opening comparison of the dialogue, which contrasts two altarpieces in Santi Giovanni e Paolo, the *Saint Catherine of Siena* altarpiece of the 1470s and Titian's *Saint Peter Martyr* altarpiece of 1530. Recent important (and varying) accounts of Giorgione's work include Alessandro Ballarin, "Une nouvelle perspective sur Giorgione: Les portraits des années 1500–1503," and catalogue entries, in *Le siècle de Titien: L'âge d'or de la peinture à Venise*, by Michel Laclotte, Giovanna Nepi Scirè, et al., exh. cat. (Paris: Réunion des musées nationaux, 1993), 281–347; Anderson, *Giorgione*; Sylvia Ferino-Pagden and Giovanna Nepi Scirè, eds., *Giorgione: Myth and Enigma*, exh. cat. (Vienna: Kunsthistorisches Museum, 2004).

5. For example, Gentile Bellini's *Procession in Piazza San Marco* of 1496 for the Scuola Grande di San Giovanni Evangelista (fig. 49), where the narrative is almost overburdened by topographic detail and local color, seems much more than a generation earlier than Titian's fresco the *Miracle of the Speaking Babe* of 1511 in the Scuoletta di Sant'Antonio, Padua, with its clear focus on the primary characters and their actions. Even if these pictures were painted in different media, they were paintings of similar subjects for comparable settings. The standard study of the narrative *istorie* of the late Quattrocento and early Cinquecento is Patricia Fortini Brown, *Venetian Narrative Painting in the Age of Carpaccio* (New Haven, CT: Yale University Press, 1988). On p. 4, Brown defines an "eyewitness style" and argues that the attention to detail and stability reproduced in these paintings was not so much a reflection of Venetian reality but the construction of an "image of life as it should have been." For a recent discussion, see Peter Humfrey, "La pittura narrativa dai Bellini ai Carpaccio," in *Da Bellini a Veronese: Temi di arte Veneta*, ed. Gennaro Toscano and Francesco Valcanover (Venice: Istituto veneto di scienze, lettere ed arti, 2004), 177–95. For Titian's fresco in Padua, see Wethey, *Paintings of Titian* 1:cat. 93; Paul Joannides, *Titian to 1518: The Assumption of Genius* (New Haven, CT: Yale University Press, 2001), 107–21; Humfrey, *Titian: The Complete Paintings*, cat. 15A.

6. This shift can be seen, for example, in Giovanni Bellini's *sacra conversazione* altarpieces in the Frari (1488) and San Zaccaria (1505), paintings recently discussed in *Il colore ritrovato: Bellini a Venezia*, ed. Rona Goffen and Giovanna Nepi Scirè, exh. cat. (Milan: Electa, 2000), cats. 32, 34.

7. On architecture, see the discussions of Mauro Codussi and of architecture during the War of the League of Cambrai in Deborah Howard, *The Architectural History of Venice*, rev. ed. (New Haven, CT: Yale University Press, 2002), 132–59.

8. For a summary of Venice's wars in the late fifteenth and early sixteenth centuries, including the War of the League of Cambrai, see Frederic C. Lane, *Venice: A Maritime Republic* (Baltimore: Johns Hopkins University Press, 1973), 225–49.

9. Sanudo's *Diarii*, which were compiled between January 1496 and September 1533, offer a fundamental window onto Venetian political and social history. The first quotation is taken from *Cità Excelentissima: Selections from the Renaissance Diaries of Marin Sanudo*, ed. Patricia H. Labalme and Laura Sanguineti White, trans. Linda L. Carroll (Baltimore: Johns Hopkins University Press, 2008), 174. The second, Sanudo's entry for May 17, 1509, is translated by David Chambers in *Venice: A Documentary History, 1450–1630*, ed. David Chambers and Brian Pullan, with Jennifer Fletcher (Cambridge, MA: Blackwell, 1992), 75.

10. Deborah Howard, "Giorgione's *Tempesta* and Titian's *Assunta* in the context of the Cambrai Wars," *Art History* 8, no. 3 (Sept. 1985): 271–89; Paul H. D. Kaplan, "The Storm of War: The Paduan Key to Giorgione's *Tempesta*," *Art History* 9, no. 4 (Dec. 1986): 405–27. Other paintings read in light of this crisis include the *Concert Champêtre* (Musée du Louvre, Paris), attributed to Titian, and the *Storm at Sea* (Galleria dell'Accademia, Venice) by Palma Vecchio and Paris Bordone. See Jonathan Unglaub, "The *Concert Champêtre*: The Crises of History and the Limits of Pastoral," *Arion* 5, no. 1 (1997): 46–96; and Philip Sohm, "Palma Vecchio's *Sea Storm*: A Political Allegory," *Revue d'Art Canadienne / Canadian Art Revue* 6, no. 2 (1979–80): 85–96.

11. The documents can be found in Brown, *Venetian Narrative Painting*, 272–73, docs. 1a, 1b.

12. Although the painted cycle in the Sala del Maggior Consiglio was destroyed by fire in 1577, echoes of its appearance can be seen in surviving decoration of Venetian *scuole* in the Galleria dell'Accademia, Venice.

13. For Tintoretto's role in the development of extremely large-format paintings in Venetian art, and the breakthrough paintings in the

Madonna dell'Orto, see Frederick Ilchman, "Tintoretto: Pensare e designare in grande," in *Settimo e ottavo incontro in ricordo di Michelangelo Muraro*, ed. Giuseppina Menin Muraro and Daniela Puppulin (Sosanno: Biblioteca Comunale di Sossano, 2000), 49–75.

14. Rosand, *Painting in Sixteenth-Century Venice*, 11–13. On early oil painting in the broader Italian context, see the section "Oil Painting in Italy" in Dunkerton, Foister, Gordon, and Penny, *Giotto to Dürer*, 197–204.

15. Letter of February 7, 1506, from Dürer to Wilibald Pirkheimer, "Er ist sehr alt und ist noch der pest im gemoll." Hans Rupprich, ed., *Dürer: Schriftlicher Nachlass* (Berlin: Deutscher Verein für Kunstwissenschaft, 1956), 1:44.

16. Rosand, *Painting in Sixteenth-Century Venice*, 13. The same author offers a sensitive analysis of the Venetian development of oil-on-canvas painting in "The Stroke of the Brush," in David Rosand, *The Meaning of the Mark: Leonardo and Titian* (Lawrence, KS: Spencer Museum of Art, 1988), 49–89. See also the chapter "Original Developments," in Dunkerton, Foister, and Penny, *Dürer to Veronese*, 265–91.

17. The question of Sebastiano's San Giovanni Crisostomo altarpiece is complicated because, although on canvas, there is some thought that it may originally have been on panel. Also, the date for the altarpiece is usually given as about 1510, based on documents cited by Michael Hirst (*Sebastiano del Piombo* [Oxford: Oxford University Press, 1981], 25), as well as the *terminus ante quem* of August 1511 when Sebastiano left for Rome. Mauro Lucco has argued that the altarpiece was in fact painted before the San Bartolomeo organ shutters and thus was begun in 1507 or early 1508; if so, according to Lucco, "it acquires an almost revolutionary significance, even though it was not immediately imitated." See Mauro Lucco, "Some Observations on the Dating of Sebastiano del Piombo's S. Giovanni Crisostomo Altarpiece," in *New Interpretations of Venetian Renaissance Painting*, ed. Francis Ames-Lewis (London: University of London, Birkbeck College, 1994), 43–49 (quotation on 47). A final complication is that the paint surfaces of both Bellini's and Sebastiano's paintings have suffered greatly. The most recent study of the San Giovanni Crisostomo altarpiece, by Mauro Lucco, appeared in the catalogue of the 2008 Rome exhibition, *Sebastiano del Piombo, 1485–1547* (Milan: Motta, 2008), cat. 7.

18. Humfrey (*Painting in Renaissance Venice*, 117–20) offers a good summary of the *Tempesta* and how it encapsulates much of what is innovative about Giorgione. See also Anderson, *Giorgione*, 301–2; Salvatore Settis, *Giorgione's Tempesta: Interpreting the Hidden Subject* (Chicago: University of Chicago Press, 1990); and Giovanna Nepi Scirè in *Giorgione: Myth and Enigma*, ed. Ferino-Pagden and Nepi Scirè, cat. 7.

19. For summaries of some of the changes visible through X-radiography and infrared reflectography in the *Tempesta*, see Anderson, *Giorgione*, 96–97; and Nepi Scirè in *Giorgione: Myth and Enigma*, cat. 7, with further bibliography. The technical studies were compiled by Sandra Moschini Marconi in *Giorgione a Venezia*, ed. Adriana Augusti Ruggeri et al. (Milan: Electa, 1978), 99–109.

20. Pliny the Elder, *Natural History* (35.96), trans. H. Rackham (Cambridge, MA: Harvard University Press, 1952), 9:332–33.

21. Settis, in *Giorgione's Tempesta*, surveys and points out the flaws in the many earlier interpretations, but his own definitive reading for the picture—Adam and Eve and the serpent—is unconvincing.

22. Rosand, *Painting in Sixteenth-Century Venice*, 7.

23. In many instances, even when documents about a painting's origins have been lost, we can surmise from the format (altarpiece) or subject matter (portrait) that these works came into being because a patron approached a painter with a commission.

24. Charles Hope, "Titian as a Court Painter," *Oxford Art Journal* 2 (1979): 7–10.

25. Rona Goffen, *Renaissance Rivals: Michelangelo, Leonardo, Raphael, Titian* (New Haven, CT: Yale University Press, 2004), 11–19; see pp. 11–12 for a translation of the letter of June 25, 1501, from the agent Michele Vianello to Isabella.

26. A translation of part of Bembo's letter of January 1, 1506, can be found in ibid., 16.

27. Ibid., 17.

28. Humfrey, *Painting in Renaissance Venice*, 279.

29. The picture has not been on public display since 1974. It was treated at the Metropolitan Museum of Art, New York, in 2003. The author is grateful for the opportunity to consult the treatment report and to discuss the painting with Charlotte Hale. A recent, relatively dismissive account of its quality is found in Keith Christiansen, "Giovanni Bellini and the Practice of Devotional Painting," in *Giovanni Bellini and the Art of Devotion*, ed. Rhonda Kasl, exh. cat. (Indianapolis: Indianapolis Museum of Art, 2004), 18–23, 47–57.

30. See Joannides, *Titian to 1518*, 158–59, including a thorough analysis of the painting.

31. Sixten Ringbom surveys how the "window" format derived from Byzantine half-length icons where "a parapet was introduced as if to justify the truncation of the represented figure." For this format and its particular psychological effectiveness, see Sixten Ringbom, *Icon to Narrative: The Rise of the Dramatic Close-Up in Fifteenth-Century Devotional Painting* (Åbo: Åbo Akademi, 1965), esp. 39–52.

32. Most of the underdrawing visible through infrared reflectography, described in the treatment report and in discussion with Charlotte Hale (see n. 29), shows rather schematic and hard contours, as if the forms were traced, particularly in the drapery of both the Virgin and Saint Peter. Other changes apparently include the cloth of honor added over the sky to emphasize the Virgin and Child, who may have seemed a little lost in the crowd. X-radiography has also disclosed that Saint Catherine's head was originally smaller and more to scale with the other saints, and that she previously wore a more regal, jeweled costume. The treatment report speculates that these changes might have been imposed by the client, or indeed a new patron.

33. Additionally, the Virgin in the Metropolitan Museum of New York painting is not as massive nor as imposing as that in Bellini's 1510 *Virgin and Child* (Pinacoteca di Brera, Milan), and would seem to predate it. On the comparatives used to date Bellini's panel and arguments for dating those pictures, see Goffen and Nepi Scirè, *Il colore ritrovato*, esp. cats. 11, 12, 19; see also Federico Zeri's catalogue entry on the picture in *Italian Paintings: A Catalogue of the Collection of the Metropolitan Museum of Art, Venetian School* (New York: Metropolitan Museum of Art, 1973), 6–7; Peter Humfrey in *The Dictionary of Art*, ed. Jane Turner, 34 vols. (New York: Grove's Dictionaries, 1996), 3:659. Keith Christiansen noted that the Saint Lucy in the Metropolitan's panel is similar to one of the female figures in Bellini's *Feast of the Gods* (National Gallery of Art, Washington, DC) dated 1514, though the rest of the Metropolitan painting does not seem to have been painted as late as that. In terms of relative quality and similar use of figures from other compositions, the Metropolitan picture resembles a *Sacra Conversazione* in the Pierpont Morgan Library, New York, which also has a female saint looking straight ahead. For this painting, see Anchise Tempestini, *Giovanni Bellini* (New York: Abbeville, 1999), cat. 87.

34. Louisa C. Matthew, "The Painter's Presence: Signatures in Venetian Renaissance Pictures," *Art Bulletin* 80, no. 4 (Dec. 1998): 627. See also Rona Goffen, "Signatures: Inscribing Identity in Italian Renaissance Art," *Viator* 32 (2001): 303–70.

35. Caroline Campbell and David Jaffé's catalogue entry in Jaffé, *Titian*, cat. 9.

36. See Matthew 27:32: "And as they came out, they found a man of Cyrene, Simon by name: him they compelled to bear his cross." The episode also occurs in Mark 15:21 and Luke 23:26.

37. Ringbom, *Icon to Narrative*, esp. 11–72.

38. Ibid., 147–55, figs. 118–27. The Scuola Grande di San Rocco painting was confusingly attributed by Vasari both to Giorgione and to Titian. For a summary of the attribution dispute, with arguments in favor of Giorgione, see Anderson, *Giorgione*, 303. For the alternative attribution to Titian, see Humfrey, *Titian: The Complete Paintings*, cat. 11. The miraculous image was replicated in prints; see David Rosand and Michelangelo Muraro, *Titian and the Venetian Woodcut* (Washington, DC: International Exhibitions Foundation, 1976), 108–111.

39. Bernard Berenson, *Venetian Painters of the Renaissance, with an Index to Their Works*, 3rd ed. (New York: G. P. Putnam's Sons, 1894), 108. Berenson's list of the painter's production was conventional for the time, although he accepted only one painting in Vienna.

40. *The Letters of Bernard Berenson and Isabella Stewart Gardner, 1887–1924*, ed. Rollin Van N. Hadley (Boston: Northeastern University Press, 1987), 66–67; on the negotiations for this picture, see 65–90, 98, 105–14.

41. Recently, David Alan Brown has, in oral communications with a number of scholars, suggested Vincenzo Catena, based on similarities to known paintings by the artist, including a comparable head of Christ in three-quarter profile in Catena's *Christ Giving the Keys to Saint Peter* (Isabella Stewart Gardner Museum, Boston); Brown also sees the distinctive treatment of the wood grain of the cross as present in the cupboards of Catena's *Saint Jerome in His Study* (National Gallery, London), of about 1510. The proposal has merit: the hard edge and literally rendered details of *Christ Carrying the Cross* are seen throughout Catena's oeuvre, and the painter was part of the milieu in which the Gardner picture was certainly created. See Alan Chong's mention of this suggestion in *Eye of the Beholder: Masterpieces from the Isabella Stewart Gardner Museum*, ed. Alan Chong, Richard Lingner, and Carl Zahn (Boston: Isabella Stewart Gardner Museum, 2003), 99.

42. Carlo Ridolfi, *Le maraviglie dell'arte* [Venice, 1648], ed. Detlev von Hadeln (Berlin: Grote'sche Verlagsbuchhandlung, 1914–24), 1:200.

43. See Paul Joannides's discussion (*Titian to 1518*, 267) of Titian's half-length subjects of the 1510s, and how this type ceased by about 1520: "Even the subject of *Christ Carrying the Cross*, represented in close-up in canvas of about 1570 in the Prado, is a return to the arrangement pioneered in Venice by Bellini and Giorgione." In a forthcoming study, "Retrospection and Materiality," Jodi Cranston investigates Titian's return to the half length late in his career; see her forthcoming book *The Muddied Mirror: Figuration and Materiality in Titian's Later Paintings* (University Park, PA: Penn State University Press).

Titian to 1545

1. The date of Titian's birth is complicated by the varying ages of the painter given in sources and documents by his contemporaries, and also by the painter's own contradictory statements, which tended to exaggerate his age as a ploy for sympathy. The most reliable datum seems to be the statement in Dolce's *Dialogo della pittura* (also known as the "*Aretino*") of 1557 that Titian was "not yet twenty" when he executed frescoes along with Giorgione at the Fondaco dei Tedeschi, the dating of which is documented by a payment in December 1508. Dolce's account can be found in Mark W. Roskill, *Dolce's "Aretino" and Venetian Art Theory of the Cinquecento* (New York: New York University Press, 1968), 186–87.

2. Ibid.; Giorgio Vasari, *Lives of the Painters, Sculptors and Architects*, trans. Gaston de Vere (New York: Alfred A. Knopf, 1996), 2:783.

3. Titian, quoted in Charles Hope, *Titian* (London: Chaucer, 2003), 41–42.

4. Quoted in J. A. Crowe and G. B. Cavalcaselle, *Titian: His Life and Times* (London: J. Murray, 1877), 2:82. Hope (*Titian*, 98–101) notes that Titian's easygoing reputation would stand in sharp contrast to the temperamental Michelangelo.

5. On Titian's altarpieces in the church of Santa Maria Gloriosa dei Frari and their context, see Rosand, *Painting in Sixteenth-Century Venice*, 38–51. For the *Saint Peter Martyr* altarpiece, see Patricia Meilman, *Titian and the Altarpiece in Renaissance Venice* (New York: Cambridge University Press, 2000).

6. For a recent discussion of these issues and key references, see Sylvia Ferino-Pagden, "Pictures of Women—Pictures of Love," and cat. 42, *"Flora,"* in *Bellini, Giorgione, Titian and the Renaissance of Venetian Painting*, ed. David Alan Brown and Sylvia Ferino-Pagden, exh. cat. (Washington, DC: National Gallery of Art, 2006), 190–99, 224–27.

7. Paul Joannides, *Titian to 1518: The Assumption of Genius* (New Haven, CT: Yale University Press, 2001), 264. While Flora's chemise has been identified as a common contemporary undergarment, it was also used in the theater of the day to identify the player as a nymph. See Emma H. Mellencamp, "A Note on the Costume of Titian's *Flora*," *Art Bulletin* 51, no. 2 (June 1969): 174–77.

8. Peter Humfrey, *The Age of Titian: Venetian Renaissance Art from Scottish Collections*, exh. cat. (Edinburgh: National Galleries of Scotland, 2004), cat. 19. Pliny the Elder, *Natural History* (35.91–92), trans. H. Rackham (Cambridge: Harvard University Press, 1968), 9:329.

9. Humfrey, *Age of Titian*, 94. However, as Humfrey acknowledges, the possibility of a Venetian commission cannot be excluded. Cyprus was a Venetian possession, and Venice, which rises from the sea as Venus did, had adopted the goddess. On Venus and Venice, see David Rosand, *Myths of Venice: The Figuration of a State* (Chapel Hill: University of North Carolina Press, 2001), esp. 117–19.

10. Rona Goffen, *Renaissance Rivals: Michelangelo, Leonardo, Raphael, Titian* (New Haven, CT: Yale University Press, 2002), 301–6. For Pordenone's career and works in general, see Caterina Furlan, *Il Pordenone* (Milan: Electa, 1988); and Charles E. Cohen, *The Art of Giovanni Antonio da Pordenone: Between Dialect and Language* (New York: Cambridge University Press, 1996).

11. On Pordenone at the Scuola Grande della Carità, see Rosand, *Painting in Sixteenth-Century Venice*, 104, 173, docs. 19, 20.

12. Letter from Giovanni della Casa to Alessandro Farnese, September 20, 1545 (which speaks of painting "tutti fino alle gatte"), cited in Lorne Campbell, *Renaissance Portraits: European Portrait-Painting in the 14th, 15th and 16th Centuries* (New Haven, CT: Yale University Press, 1990), 266 n. 99.

13. Wethey, *Paintings of Titian* 2:cat. 72.

14. "...ms. tucian pictor homo della speriencia che a caduano è noto...." Juergen Schulz, "Titian's Ceiling in the Scuola di San Giovanni Evangelista," *Art Bulletin* 48 (1966): 89–95. The April 16, 1544, document is transcribed on p. 93.

New Rivals

1. The two early sources that mention this very brief apprenticeship are Carlo Ridolfi and Marco Boschini. See Carlo Ridolfi, *The Life of Tintoretto and of His Children Domenico and Marietta*, trans. Catherine Enggass and Robert Enggass (University Park, PA: Penn State University Press, 1984), 15, and Carlo Ridolfi, *Le maraviglie dell'arte* [Venice, 1648], ed. Detlev von Hadeln (Berlin: Grote'sche Verlagsbuchhandlung, 1914–24), 2:13; and Marco Boschini, *La carta del navegar pitoresco* [Venice, 1660], ed. Anna Pallucchini (Venice: Istituto per la collaborazione culturale, 1966), 6, 226–27.

2. Calmo's original letter is reprinted in Anna Laura Lepschy, *Davanti a Tintoretto: Una storia del gusto attraverso i secoli* (Venice: Marsilio, 1998), 15. Tom Nichols has surveyed Tintoretto's relationship with the wider literary culture in "Tintoretto, Prestezza and the Poligrafi: A Study in the Literary and Visual Culture of Cinquecento Venice," *Renaissance Studies* 10, no. 1 (1996): 72–100.

3. In his Life of Titian, Vasari recounts that Bordone left Titian's studio after a few years because Titian was not particularly eager to teach his pupils ("non essere molto vago d'insegnare a' suoi giovani"). Giorgio Vasari, *Le vite de' più eccellenti pittori, scultori ed architettori* [1568], ed. Gaetano Milanesi (Florence: G. C. Sansoni, 1878–85), 7:461. Ridolfi's description of Titian locking his paintings away from his assistants is at p. 137 in Carlo Ridolfi, *The Life of Titian*, ed. Julia Conaway Bondanella, Peter Bondanella, Bruce Cole, and Jody Robin Shiffman (University Park, PA: Penn State University Press, 1996). W. R. Rearick promoted the view that Tintoretto may have left the shop because Titian was an ungenerous teacher, for example in *Il disegno veneziano del Cinquecento* (Milan: Electa, 2001), 118.

4. Ridolfi, *Le maraviglie dell'arte* 2:13–15; *Life of Tintoretto*, 16–17.

5. Echols in Falomir, *Tintoretto*, 32–33, 182. Ridolfi seems to have known Domenico, who painted his portrait. It is thus likely that his biography of Tintoretto reflects the version of the painter's history accepted by his family and students. See also Philip Cottrell, "Painters in Practise: Tintoretto, Bassano and the Studio of Bonifacio de' Pitati," in *Jacopo Tintoretto: Actas del congreso internacional / Proceedings of the International Symposium*, Museo Nacional del Prado, Madrid, February 26–27, 2007 (Madrid: Museo Nacional del Prado, forthcoming).

6. On Tintoretto's early paintings, see Echols in Falomir, *Tintoretto*, 31–36, 181–85, and cats. 1–3.

7. On Aretino and painting in Venice, see Mina Gregori, "Tiziano e l'Aretino," in *Tiziano e il manierismo europeo*, ed. Rodolfo Pallucchini (Florence: L. S. Olschki, 1978), 271–306. On Aretino and Vasari, and Vasari's stay in Venice generally, see Juergen Schulz, "Vasari at Venice," *The Burlington Magazine* 103 (1961): 500–511. On Francesco Salviati in Venice, see Iris B. Cheney, "Francesco Salviati's North Italian Journey, *Art Bulletin* 45 (1963): 337–49. There is ample visual evidence in Tintoretto's paintings of the early 1540s that he knew the paintings that Francesco Salviati had executed in Venice, including his ceiling paintings for the patrician Grimani brothers, important members of Aretino's circle. See Echols in Falomir, *Tintoretto*, 33–34 and cat. 1. Documentary evidence of Tintoretto's access to humanist circles is provided by a letter of introduction written in 1541 by the Venetian patrician Girolamo Querini to the Paduan humanist Marco Mantova Benevides; see Linda Borean, "Documentation," in Falomir, *Tintoretto*, 419. On Girolamo Querini and his relationship to Aretino, see Vincenzo Mancini, *Lambert Sustris a Padova* (Commune di Selvazzano Dentro: Biblioteca Pubblica Comunale, 1993), 21; and Christopher Cairns, *Pietro Aretino and the Republic of Venice: Researches on Aretino and His Circle in Venice, 1527–1556* (Florence: L. S. Olschki, 1985), 24.

8. Robert Echols, "'Jacopo nel corso, presso al palio': Dal soffitto per l'Aretino al *Miracolo dello Schiavo*," in *Jacopo Tintoretto nel quarto centenario della morte: Atti del convegno internazionale di studi. Venezia, 24–26 Novembre, 1994*, ed. Paola Rossi and Lionello Puppi (Padua: Il Poligrafo, 1996), 77–81; Echols in Falomir, *Tintoretto*, cat. 5.

9. Robert Echols, "Titian's Venetian Soffitti: Sources and Transformations," in *Titian 500*, ed. Joseph Manca, Studies in the History of Art 45 (Washington, DC: National Gallery of Art, 1993) 29–49; the connection between Titian's *David and Goliath* and Tintoretto's *Deucalion and Pyrrha* is discussed on pp. 33–35. A date of 1542 for Tintoretto's ceiling paintings was established by Stefania Mason ("Intorno al soffitto di San Paternian: Gli artisti di Vettor Pisani," in *Jacopo Tintoretto nel quarto centenario della morte*, ed. Rossi and Puppi, 71–75). Titian's Santo Spirito in Isola painting had until recently been dated by most scholars to 1542–44; however, Paul Joannides (on stylistic grounds) and Charles Hope (based on circumstantial evidence), followed by Peter Humfrey, have adopted a later date, in the vicinity of 1550. See Paul Joannides, "On Some Borrowings and Non-borrowings from Central Italian and Antique Art in the Works of Titian c. 1510–1550," *Paragone*, no. 487 (1990), 21–45, esp. 33–34 (dating it to c. 1550); Charles Hope, "Titian's Life and Times," in *Titian*, exh. cat. (London: National Gallery Company, 2003), 21 (1550–51); and Humfrey, *Titian: The Complete Paintings*, cat. 176 (1548–49).

10. Ridolfi, *Le maraviglie dell'arte* 2:13–14; *Life of Tintoretto*, 25–26. Boschini, *La carta del navegar pitoresco*, 516.

11. See the essay by Miguel Falomir, "Tintoretto y Tiziano" to be published in *Jacopo Tintoretto: Actas del congreso internacional*, Museo Nacional del Prado.

12. Borean, "Documentation," in Falomir, *Tintoretto*, 422–23, for November 5, 1552; May 14, 1556.

13. Ibid., 421. Ridolfi, *Le maraviglie dell'arte* 2:51: "in concorrenza di Titiano."

14. Borean, "Documentation," in Falomir, *Tintoretto*, 422–23.

15. See Anna Laura Lepschy, *Tintoretto Observed: A Documentary Survey of Critical Reactions from the 16th to the 20th Century* (Ravenna: Longo Editore, 1983), 17; Lepschy, *Davanti a Tintoretto*, 14; and Mark W. Roskill, *Dolce's "Aretino" and Venetian Art Theory of the Cinquecento* (New York: New York University Press, 1968), 31–32.

16. For Titian's attempt to block Tintoretto at the Scuola Grande di San Rocco, see the section "Aggressive Tactics" in the essay "Venetian Painting in an Age of Rivals" by Frederick Ilchman in this volume.

17. Borghini and Ridolfi named Antonio Badile IV as Veronese's master, and "Paulus

eius discipulus seu Garsonus 14" is recorded as a member of Badile's household in 1541. Vasari named Giovanni Caroto as Paolo's teacher. Diana Gisolfi Pechukas ("Two Oil Sketches and the Youth of Veronese," *Art Bulletin* 64 [1982], 388–413) has proposed that Paolo trained with Caroto after an initial apprenticeship with Badile.

18. Ridolfi, *Le maraviglie dell'arte* 1:299.

19. On Veronese's early career, see Rearick, *Art of Paolo Veronese*, 20–49, and Penny, *Sixteenth Century Italian Paintings* 2:331–43.

20. Pignatti and Pedrocco, *Veronese* 1:cats. 34–36; see also Jean Habert, "La peinture vénitienne de 1540 à 1560 dans les collections du Louvre," in *Da Bellini a Veronese: Temi di arte Veneta*, ed. Gennaro Toscano and Francesco Valcanover (Venice: Istituto veneto di scienze, lettere ed arti, 2004), 559–87, esp. 570.

21. Pignatti and Pedrocco, *Veronese* 1:cats. 41–49 (sacristy ceiling), 56–58 (nave ceiling), 77–84 (frescoes), 88–94 (organ shutters and decorations), 106–119 (further frescoes), 157 (high altarpiece), 171, 173 (laterali of main chapel). For a recent summary of San Sebastiano, see the periodical *Studies in Venetian Art and Conservation* (New York and Venice: Save Venice Inc., 2008).

22. On the ceiling of the Libreria Marciana, see Juergen Schulz, *Venetian Painted Ceilings of the Renaissance* (Berkeley: University of California Press, 1968), 93–95, and Antonio Paolucci, "La sala della Libreria e il ciclo pittorico," in *Da Tiziano a El Greco: Per la storia del Manierismo a Venezia* (Milan: Electa, 1981), 287–98.

23. This taste was exemplified by the two ceilings that Aretino's friend Francesco Salviati had painted for the grand Grimani palace in 1541, which had a major impact on younger painters such as Giuseppe Porta Salviati, Andrea Schiavone, Veronese, and Tintoretto himself. On the development of Venetian ceiling paintings, see Schulz, *Venetian Painted Ceilings*. On the place of Tintoretto's ceiling for Aretino in this tradition, see Robert Echols, in Falomir, *Tintoretto*, cat. 4. On the patronage and dating of Tintoretto's earlier ceiling paintings, see Stefania Mason, "Intorno al soffitto di San Paternian: Gli artisti di Vettor Pisani," in *Jacopo Tintoretto nel quarto centenario della morte,* ed. Rossi and Puppi, 71–75.

24. On Tintoretto's aggressive business practices, see especially Paul Hills, "Tintoretto's Marketing," in *Venedig und Oberdeutschland in der Renaissance*, ed. Bernd Roeck, Klaus Bergholt, and Andrew John Martin (Venice: Sigmaringen: J. Thorbecke, 1993), 107–20; and Tom Nichols, "Price, 'Prestezza,' and Production in Jacopo Tintoretto's Business Strategy," *Venezia Cinquecento* 12 (1996): 207–33.

25. Pietro Aretino, *Lettere sull'arte*, ed. Ettore Camesasca (Milan: Edizioni del Milioni, 1957–60), 2:52, translated in Lepschy, *Tintoretto Observed*, 16. The original reads: "Et belle et pronte et vive in vive, in pronte, et in belle attitudini da ogni huomo ch'è di perito giudicio sono tentute le due historie, una in la favola di Apollo e di Marsia, e l'altra in la novella di Argo e di Mercurio, da voi così giovane quasi dipinte in meno spatio di tempo che non si mise in pensare al cio che dovevate dipingerere nel palco della camera, che con tanta sodisfazione mia e d'ognuno voi m'havete dipinte."A telling slip in Ridolfi is indicative of the competition between Titian and Tintoretto, as well as Titian's deep friendship with Aretino. Ridolfi misidentifies the painter of the ceiling paintings for Aretino as Titian, rather than Tintoretto. Ridolfi, *Le maraviglie dell'arte* 1:175. This passage is translated—and the error noted—in Ridolfi, *The Life of Titian*, ed. Bondanella, Bondanella, Cole, and Shiffman, 89.

26. Vernacular versions of Ovid available in the sixteenth century embellished the tale in ways reflected in Tintoretto's painting: the contestants play on contemporary instruments, a *lira da braccio* and a *ciamarella* (or shawm), an early reed instrument; Marsyas is depicted as a human youth, not a satyr. In this regard, the painting is also similar to the woodcut illustrating the fable in a vernacular version of the *Metamorphoses* published in Agostini in 1522: see Bodo Guthmüller, "Tintoretto e Ovidio, il problema dei testi mediatori," in *Jacopo Tintoretto nel quarto centenario della morte*, ed. Rossi and Puppi, 258–59.

27. Schulz, *Venetian Painted Ceilings*, cat. 46; Philipp P. Fehl, "Tintoretto's Homage to Titian and Pietro Aretino," in *Decorum and Wit: The Poetry of Venetian Painting* (Vienna: IRSA, 1992), 167–80. Fehl, noting that the tale of Apollo and Marsyas was frequently conflated with the story of the musical contest between Apollo and Pan, argues that the picture is an allegory in which Aretino is represented as an "Anti-Midas . . . a true hero of poetry, a lover of harmony seeking the heights of Parnassus." Fehl identifies the white-bearded figure to the right as Midas, looking with annoyance at Aretino, who, with hand to breast, expresses his allegiance to Minerva and Apollo. If the figure in green at the right is indeed Aretino, as claimed by Fehl and others, this inclusion of an image of Aretino by Tintoretto would follow by just a year or two Titian's portrayal of Aretino as Pontius Pilate in the large *Ecce Homo* of 1543 (Kunsthistorisches Museum, Vienna), an identification that goes back to Ridolfi, *Le maraviglie dell'arte* 1:172. On the identification, see Wethey, *Paintings of Titian* 1:cat. 21.

28. Lora Anne Palladino ("Pietro Aretino, Orator and Art Theorist" [PhD diss., Yale University, 1981], 326–36) suggests that the antithesis between stringed and wind instruments, seen in the Renaissance as symbolizing two modes of poetry, the high and the low, refers to Aretino's mastery of both types of literature, the one celebrating the ideal, the other imitating the human. For the woodcut, see David Rosand and Michelangelo Muraro, *Titian and the Venetian Woodcut*, exh. cat. (Washington, DC: International Exhibitions Foundation, 1976), cat. 41.

29. Aretino to Cosimo, in Aretino, *Lettere sull'arte* 2:108: "se più fussero stati gli scudi che gliene ho conti, invero i drappi sariano lucidi, morbidi, e rigidi, come il da senno raso, velluto, e broccato." In contrast, subsequent writers and scholars have lauded the figure's presence and the remarkable bravura highlights on cloth.

30. Aretino to Titian, in Aretino, *Lettere sull'arte* 2:106.

31. Aretino, *Lettere sull'arte* 2:204–5, translated in Lepschy, *Tintoretto Observed*, 17. The original reads: "E beato il nome vostro se riduceste la prestezza del fatto in la paziena del fare." Aretino's condemnation of hastiness is hypocritical, given his pride in his own speed of writing, which he likened to a divine faculty. See Una Roman D'Elia, "Tintoretto, Aretino, and the Speed of Creation," *Word & Image* 20, no. 3 (2004): 206–18.

32. Aretino, *Lettere sull'arte* 2:14 and 2:73. On Aretino's construction of his image through portraiture, see Joanna Woods-Marsden, "Toward a History of Art Patronage in the Renaissance: The Case of Pietro Aretino," *Journal of Medieval and Renaissance Studies* 24 (1994): 275–99.

33. Falomir in *Tiziano*, ed. Miguel Falomir, exh. cat. (Madrid: Museo Nacional del Prado, 2003), cat. 53.

34. Ridolfi, *Life of Tintoretto*, 18; Ridolfi, *Le maraviglie dell'arte* 2:16. The original verse reads: "Tinctorettus noctis sic lucet in umbris / Exorto faciet quid radiante Die?"

35. See Miguel Falomir in Falomir, *Tintoretto*, cat. 7.

36. The self-portrait, first proposed by Francesco Arcangeli in 1955, is discussed by Echols in Falomir, *Tintoretto*, cat. 2.

37. Most recent scholars have concurred on this dating for the Philadelphia self-portrait: see Terisio Pignatti in *The Golden Century of Venetian Painting*, exh. cat. (Los Angeles: Los Angeles County Museum of Art, 1979), cat. 31; and Falomir in Falomir, *Tintoretto*, cat. 7. The exception is W. R. Rearick, who preferred the date of 1542 in "Reflections on Tintoretto as a Portraitist," *Artibus et Historiae* 31 (1995): 52. Rearick offered the intriguing suggestion that the related—and until recently more admired—portrait in the Victoria and Albert Museum, London (Paola Rossi, *Tintoretto: Ritratti* [Milan: Electa, 1994], cat. 61) could be the "portrait of our father, on panel" mentioned in Domenico's will to be bequeathed to his sister Ottavia. Rearick further argued that the V&A portrait was painted "perhaps by Domenico himself, after the Philadelphia original, and that it passed to Ottavia as a family relic, rather than an original work of art." The attribution to Domenico is doubtful, however, since he is a much better portraitist than the painter who produced this work, with its unconvincing facial structure and eyes out of plane. One would expect Domenico's portrait of his own father to be much better, even if copying another painting, and Domenico to have specified that it was by his hand in the will. Despite its poor quality, the V&A portrait was still accepted as being by Jacopo in the 1994 Venice and Vienna exhibitions (Paola Rossi, *Jacopo Tintoretto: Ritratti* ext. cat. [Milan: Electa, 1994], cat. 3), and by Tom Nichols, *Tintoretto: Tradition and Identity* (London: Reaktion Books, 1999), fig. 3. Katherine T. Brown (*The Painter's Reflection: Self-Portraiture in Renaissance Venice, 1458–1625* [Florence: L. S. Olschki, 2000], cats. 51–52, 164–65), inexplicably deems both the Philadelphia and the V&A paintings to be copies of a lost original; while the V&A painting is almost certainly a copy of the Philadelphia painting or another original, the Philadelphia painting is without doubt an autograph Tintoretto.

38. Alternatively, it is possible that Tintoretto's *Self-Portrait* dates from slightly before Titian's *Aretino*, and that Titian saw Tintoretto's painting and took inspiration from it.

39. Veronese's picture was once identified as "Christ and the Woman Taken in Adultery," but the actions of the other women in the crowd do not fit that story. The kneeling woman's unfastened necklace later led to an identification of the painting as "Mary Magdalen Laying aside Her Jewels," but there is neither a textual source nor another depiction of the Magdalen performing this action, and the woman lacks the Magdalen's usual jar of ointment; see Nicholas Penny and Marika Spring, "Veronese's Paintings in the National Gallery: Techniques and Materials, Part 1," *National Gallery Technical Bulletin* 16, no. 1 (1995): 6, 25 nn. 7–8; and more recently, Penny, *Sixteenth Century Italian Paintings* 2:334–36, for the tentative but convincing suggestion that the composition instead represents the "woman with an issue of blood," who was healed by touching the hem of Christ's robe.

40. For a full discussion of the painting's technical properties, see Penny and Spring, "Veronese's Paintings," 4–29.

41. The connection of Tintoretto's composition to Raphael's cartoon, proposed by John Shearman, has been confirmed in subsequent literature; see Robert Echols, "The Decisive Years: 1547–1555," in Falomir, *Tintoretto*, 221–25, cat. 9, which reproduces Raphael's cartoon as fig. 116.

42. Six additional chapters were interspersed in the Septuagint (Greek) version of the book of Esther. When Jerome was translating and assembling the Latin Vulgate, he noted that these chapters did not originate in the Hebrew text, and so he inserted them at the end.

43. A youth was later painted atop this sketch, presumably by a studio assistant, but that youth was so poorly executed that it was scraped away and repainted at some unknown moment, before twentieth-century restoration campaigns removed it entirely. For details of the conservation history, see Lucy Whitaker and Martin Clayton, *The Art of Italy in the Royal Collection: Renaissance and Baroque*, exh. cat. (London: Royal Collection Publications, 2007), 224–26.

44. For further discussion along these lines, see Robert Echols, "Beginnings: Until 1546" and "The Decisive Years: 1547–1555," in Falomir, *Tintoretto*, 181–245.

45. Although he shared Tintoretto's interest in Raphael and Central Italian art, the young Veronese seems to have looked not to Venice-based mannerists such as Andrea Schiavone and Giuseppe Porta Salviati but to Parmigianino and Giulio Romano.

46. Matthew 9:20–22, Mark 5:25–34, Luke 8:43–48; see Penny, *Sixteenth Century Italian Paintings* 2:337.

47. Since the restoration of the London painting in 1988, there has been little support for Pignatti's prior dating of it to 1555–56. Despite its somewhat unresolved arrangement of space, *Christ Healing a Woman with an Issue of Blood* is a more mature work than the oil sketch for *Raising of the Daughter of Jairus* (preparatory for the Avanzi Chapel in San Bernardino, Verona, almost certainly dated to 1546) and the ambitious but awkward 1546–48 *Virgin and Child with Saints* altarpiece from the Bevilacqua-Lazise Chapel at San Fermo (see Pignatti and Pedrocco, *Veronese* 1:cats. 1, 6, 8). *Christ Healing a Woman with an Issue of Blood*, like the *Mystic Marriage of Saint Catherine of Alexandria* (cat. 13), to which it is often compared, would thus seem to follow, in around 1548 and 1549, respectively, as Penny has also recently argued (*Sixteenth Century Italian Paintings* 2:337–38). For the *Mystic Marriage* and further comments on dating, see n. 55.

48. For a brief summary of the development, see Peter Humfrey, "Sacred Images," in *Bellini, Giorgione, Titian and the Renaissance of Venetian Painting*, ed. David Alan Brown and Sylvia Ferino-Pagden, exh. cat. (Washington, DC: National Gallery of Art, 2006), 55–63; and Philip Rylands, *Palma Vecchio* (Cambridge: Cambridge University Press, 1992), 67–70.

49. *Madonna of the Rabbit* can be compared to Titian's important early *Virgin and Child with Saint Catherine, Saint Dominic, and a Donor* (cat. 2) of about 1513–14. For the most recent discussion of that work, see Brown and Ferino-Pagden, *Bellini, Giorgione, Titian*, 90, cat. 10.

50. For an exploration of the iconography (emphasizing some of the sacred and symbolic aspects of the picture), as well as a discussion of the alternately suggested provenance, see Michel Laclotte, Olivier Le Bihan, Patrick Ramade, and Michel Hochmann, *Splendeur de Venise, 1500–1600*, exh. cat. (Paris: Somogy, 2005), cat. 93. See also the provenance listed in the checklist to this volume, under cat. 12. Paul Joannides, in "Titian in London and Madrid," *Paragone* 55, no. 657 (2004): 7–8, questions not only the provenance but also the dating of the *Madonna of the Rabbit*, rejecting the otherwise universally held view of a date of about 1530 in favor of a date of about 1520, contemporary with the *Worship of Venus*.

51. For the *Aldobrandini Madonna* (Wethey, *Paintings of Titian* 1:cat. 59; Filippo Pedrocco, *Titian* [New York: Rizzoli, 2001], cat. 86), see, most recently, Jaffé, *Titian*, 120–21, no. 19.

52. In contrast, an older artist like Lorenzo Lotto seems to have painted pictures of this type only when he was working in Venice; there are few, if any, examples between his early *Mystic Marriage of Saint Catherine* (Alte Pinakothek, Munich), dating to the period around 1505–6 when he moved back and forth between Venice and Treviso, and his *Madonna and Child with Saints Catherine and James (or Thomas)* (Kunsthistorisches Museum, Vienna), another of the genre's masterpieces, executed around 1530 after his return to Venice.

53. Furthermore, the standard typology for this subject remained essentially unchanged through the first half of the century, such that Veronese's example is no more similar to Titian's than are those painted in the 1530s by Paris Bordon and Bonifazio de' Pitati. One notable exception to the general trend of naturalistic, pastoral pictures of this type is Tintoretto's very early *Holy Family with Saints* of 1540, which instead is an exercise in the rhetorical figures of Central Italian mannerism; see Pallucchini and Rossi, *Opere sacre e profane* 1:cat. 11; Echols, "Beginnings: Until 1546," in Falomir, *Tintoretto*, cat. 1; and Echols and Ilchman, "Toward a New Tintoretto Catalogue," cat. 4.

54. Compare, for example, figures in *Christ Healing a Woman with an Issue of Blood (?)* (cat. 11), as well as the Virgin in the *Holy Family with Saint John* (Rijksmuseum, Amsterdam). Lotto's early *Mystic Marriage of Saint Catherine*, now in the Alte Pinakothek, Munich (a variant copy of which is in the Museum of Fine Arts, Boston), has a remarkably similar figure of the Virgin and might have served as Veronese's model. These figures presage the foreshortening that would later be important in his work as a decorative painter.

55. Like so many of Veronese's early works, the Barker Welfare Foundation *Mystic Marriage* has been dated over a broad span of years, from 1546 (among his first works) to sometime in the 1560s. Apart from the much-disputed chronologies of Pignatti and Pedrocco and Cocke, Rearick and others generally agreed that the Barker painting was from the very late 1540s, at least until the discovery of the similar canvas now in Tokyo; see Diana Gisolfi, "A New Early Veronese in Tokyo," *The Burlington Magazine* 137 (1995): 742–46. The Tokyo picture, alternately attributed to Veronese and Battista Zelotti, has a coat of arms that places it with relative security in 1547; because Rearick felt that it had to derive from the Barker painting, he later rearranged his chronology to place the Barker painting and the similar *Christ Healing a Woman with an Issue of Blood (?)* in 1546 (W. R. Rearick, "Paolo Veronese's Earliest Works," *Artibus et Historiae* 18 [1997]: 147–59). Yet, the similarities between the Barker and the Tokyo paintings are relatively generic and hardly necessitate that one rely on the other; moreover, if the Barker and London canvases date to 1546, it is difficult to see a logical development of Veronese's work. Instead, I propose a sequence as follows: *Resurrection of the Daughter of Jairus*, 1546; the Bevilacqua-Lazise altarpiece, about 1547; *Portrait of a Woman and Her Son (Isabella Guerrieri Gonzaga Canossa?)* (Musée du Louvre, Paris) and the *Lamentation* (Museo Civico di Castelvecchio, Verona), about 1547–48; *Holy Family with Saint John* (Rijksmuseum, Amsterdam) and *Christ Healing a Woman with an Issue of Blood (?)* (National Gallery, London), about 1548; the *Mystic Marriage* (Barker Welfare Foundation/Yale University Art Gallery, New Haven, CT), about 1549; and the Giustiniani altarpiece (see fig. 48), in 1550–51. This arrangement is similar to that set out by Diana Gisolfi. It excludes the Museo Nacional del Prado *Christ Preach-ing in the Temple*, which Cocke continues to date to 1548 on the basis of its fragmentary inscription, but which is otherwise placed in the 1560s by nearly all scholars.

56. The altarpiece takes as its subject a seldom-depicted story from the life of Saint Augustine included in *The Golden Legend*: Saint Augustine appeared to a group of cripples on a pilgrimage to Rome and directed them into a church near Pavia, after which they were healed. For further discussion of the subject, with a similar argument that Tintoretto's deliberately innovative altarpiece was meant to serve as a kind of calling card for the artist among mainland patrons, see the entry by Frederick Ilchman in Falomir, *Tintoretto*, 245–47, cat. 14; see also Filippi's entry in *Pinacoteca civica di Vicenza: Catalogo scientifico delle collezioni*, ed. Maria Elisa Avagnina et al. (Milan: Silvana, 2003), 2:348–51, cat. 180.

57. See Robert Echols, "Tintoretto the Painter," in Falomir, *Tintoretto*, 25–62. The blending of painting and drawing also suggests a comparison with a sheet like the *Study of Limbs* in the British Museum (inv. no. 1946-713-107), which Hans Tietze and Erika Tietze-Conrat (*The Drawings of the Venetian Painters in the 15th and 16th Centuries* [New York: J. J. Augustin, 1944], cat. 1577) believed to be one of the early drawings that Tintoretto made from casts including one after Michelangelo's *Dawn* from the Medici Chapel. Frederick Ilchman has also suggested that the head of the man at lower right may, similarly, be based on the cast of Michelangelo's *Giuliano de' Medici*, albeit drawn from an extreme angle. On Tintoretto, his drawings, and his *michelangelismo*, see especially Frederick Ilchman and Edward Saywell, "Michelangelo and Tintoretto: *Disegno* and Drawing," in Falomir, *Tintoretto*, 385–415.

58. Although Titian's *Madonna di Ca' Pesaro* is the primary and most obvious source for the composition, several altarpieces by Veronese's master, Antonio Badile, had also adopted the off-center Virgin and diagonal spatial composition of that painting and might have served as intermediate influences; these include Badile's *Madonna di Piazzi dei Signori* (Museo Civico di Castelvecchio, Verona; reproduced in *Paolo Veronese Restauri*, ed. Giovanna Nepi Scirè, exh. cat. [Venice: Soprintendenza ai beni artistici e storici di Venezia, 1988], 44, fig. 5).

59. On the viewpoint(s) for the *Madonna di Ca' Pesaro* in the Church of Santa Maria Gloriosa dei Frari, see Rosand, *Painting in Sixteenth-Century Venice*, 45–51. Regarding changes to the architectural background of the *Pala Giustiniani*, as well as the relationship of those changes to the addition of the columns in Titian's *Madonna di Ca' Pesaro*, see Diana Gisolfi Pechukas, "L' 'Anno Veronesiano' and Some Questions about Early Veronese and His Circle," *Arte Veneta* 43 (1989–90): 33–37.

60. Diane DeGrazia Bohlin, *Prints and Related Drawings by the Carracci Family: A Catalogue Raisonné* (Washington, DC: National Gallery of Art, 1979), cats. 102–7, 133.

Sacred Themes

1. Francesco Sansovino, *Venetia, città nobillisima et singolare descritta in XIII libri*, ed. Giustiniano Martinoni (Venice: S. Curti, 1663), 3.

2. Edward Muir, *Civic Ritual in Renaissance Venice* (Princeton, NJ: Princeton University Press, 1981), 16.

3. For a persuasive argument linking Venetian public piety, history writing, and modes of visual representation in narrative painting, see Patricia Fortini Brown, "Painting and History in Renaissance Venice," *Art History* 7 (1984): 263–94; and Patricia Fortini Brown, *Venetian Narrative Painting in the Age of Carpaccio* (New Haven, CT: Yale University Press, 1988).

4. The essential work on the altarpiece in Venice is Peter Humfrey, *The Altarpiece in Renaissance Venice* (New Haven, CT: Yale University Press, 1993). Among many useful discussions, he analyzes the validity of the term *sacra conversazione* on pp. 12–18.

5. On the question of multiple intended viewpoints for the *Madonna di Ca' Pesaro*, see Rosand, *Painting in Sixteenth-Century Venice*, 45–51. After the Basilica di San Marco and Venice's cathedral (San Pietro di Castello), the two most important churches in Renaissance Venice were the Franciscan church of Santa Maria Gloriosa dei Frari and the Dominican church of Santi Giovanni e Paolo. It is a mark of Titian's status that he had painted the high altar of the former, the *Assunta*, and the most notable altarpiece in the latter, the *Saint Peter Martyr* altarpiece.

6. Patricia Fortini Brown's *Venetian Narrative Painting*, 258–98, includes a catalogue of "Early Venetian Cycles of Narrative Paintings" (up to 1534), which contains records of lost cycles, as well as those not for scuole but for government structures, such as the Palazzo Ducale. For the artistic decorations of the Venetian scuole, see Terisio Pignatti, ed., *Le scuole di Venezia* (Milan: Electa, 1981).

7. The seminal work on this subject is Paul Hills, "Piety and Patronage in Cinquecento Venice: Tintoretto and the Scuole del Sacramento," *Art History* 6 (1983): 30–43. An important recent clarification of some issues has been provided by Thomas Worthen, "Tintoretto's Paintings for the *Banco del Sacramento* in S. Margherita," *Art Bulletin* 78 (1996): 707–32.

8. The two Tintoretto *Last Suppers* not commissioned by Venetian *scuole del Sacramento* were the one for the Benedictine church of San Giorgio Maggiore (Pallucchini and Rossi, *Opere sacre e profane* 1:cat. 467; Echols and Ilchman, "Toward a New Tintoretto Catalogue," cat. 309), and the one for the Lucca Duomo (Pallucchini and Rossi, *Opere sacre e profane* 1:A52; Echols and Ilchman, "Toward a New Tintoretto Catalogue," 310).

9. Although those figures in Tintoretto's painting seem energetic for an iconic altarpiece, there are precedents of jostling saints in the altarpieces of Pordenone, a painter who greatly influenced Tintoretto, such as *Saint Sebastian, Saint Catherine, Saint Roch* (church of San Giovanni Elemosinario, Venice). On Pordenone's altarpiece for San Giovanni Elemosinario, see Caterina Furlan, *Il Pordenone* (Milan: Electa, 1988), cat. 91. On the importance of Pordenone as an example for Tintoretto—for his *michelangelismo* and as a model of challenging the hegemony of Titian—see Robert Echols, "Tintoretto the Painter," in Falomir, *Tintoretto*, 32. Likewise, Veronese's proud *Saint Menna* has many antecedents in Venetian *sacre conversazione*.

10. For a sensitive analysis of Venetian visual culture and artistic materials, see Paul Hills, *Venetian Colour: Marble, Mosaic, Painting and Glass, 1250–1550* (New Haven, CT: Yale University Press, 1999). For the rich settings depicted in Bellini's altarpieces and their analogies to Venetian church interiors, see Rosand, *Painting in Sixteenth-Century Venice*, 29–30.

11. The anecdotes of Pino and Vasari about Giorgione's painting are discussed by Rona Goffen, with her translations, in *Renaissance Rivals: Michelangelo, Leonardo, Raphael, Titian* (New Haven, CT: Yale University Press, 2002), 60–64. Leonardo da Vinci's commentary on the *paragone* is well known and was part of contemporary discourse, even if not published until 1651. His claims for the superiority of painting over sculpture can be found in *Leonardo on Painting*, ed. Martin Kemp (New Haven, CT: Yale University Press, 1989), 38–46; his notebooks also discuss mirrors as an aid to painters (202–3).

12. Moreover, Rona Goffen (*Renaissance Rivals*, 62–63) has reasonably argued that the existence of Giorgione's painting receives credence from paintings that seem to be inspired by it, such as Giovanni Gerolamo Savoldo's *Self-Portrait* (Musée du Louvre, Paris), which shows the artist wearing armor and reflected in two mirrors. Savoldo's painting was executed about 1525, well before either text.

13. For a discussion of the mirror within Bellini's *Woman with a Mirror* and further bibliography on mirrors, see Hills, *Venetian Colour*, 130–31.

14. On Tintoretto's *Venus and Mars Surprised by Vulcan*, now convincingly dated to the mid-1540s, see Pallucchini and Rossi, *Opere sacre e profane* 1:cat. 155; Echols in Falomir, *Tintoretto*, cat. 5; and Echols and Ilchman, "Toward a New Tintoretto Catalogue," 36. Two important essays on this picture can be found in *Jacopo Tintoretto nel quarto centenario della morte: Atti del convegno internazionale di studi. Venezia, 24–26 Novembre, 1994*, ed. Paola Rossi and Lionello Puppi (Padua: Il Poligrafo, 1996): Beverly Louise Brown, "Mars's Hot Minion or Tintoretto's Fractured Fable," 199–205, 347–48; and Erasmus Weddigen, "Nuovi percorsi di avvicinamento a Jacopo Tintoretto. Venere, Vulcano e Marte: L'inquisizione dell'informatica," 155–61, 335–38. Weddigen's essay uses computer-aided design technology to support a clever argument with mirrors playing a central role in disclosing the activities of the adulterous couple to Vulcan. By this theory, Apollo reveals the commotion in the bedroom to Vulcan at his forge, seen through the open door at the painting's upper right corner, by means of rays of sunlight that penetrate the window and the glass vase and reflect through two different mirrors, one visible behind the table and another in the foreground outside of the picture (scarcely visible in the first mirror).

15. A perceptive and sympathetic analysis of the decoration of the Palazzo dei Camerlenghi, with an appendix listing extant paintings from the cycle, can be found in Philip Cottrell, "Corporate Colors: Bonifacio and Tintoretto at the Palazzo dei Camerlenghi in Venice," *Art Bulletin* 82, no. 4 (Dec. 2000): 658–78. The characterization of Bonifazio's modus operandi quoted above is on p. 661, where Cottrell also argues that Bonifazio's employment of many "semi-independent" young painters permitted his *bottega* to dominate a single government commission, normally discouraged in favor of equitable distribution of opportunities to different workshops. On the Venetian disapproval of monuments to single artists, see Rosand, *Painting in Sixteenth-Century Venice*, 4.

16. Cottrell, "Corporate Colors," 667–68.

17. Tintoretto's *Madonna of the Treasurers* (Gallerie dell'Accademia, Venice) was painted about 1567. See Pallucchini and Rossi, *Opere sacre e profane* 1:cat. 302; Echols and Ilchman, "Toward a New Tintoretto Catalogue," cat. 131.

18. Cottrell ("Corporate Colors," 668–69) speculates on how the painting would have pleased or displeased the clients.

19. Dolce's original reads: "mostrò di haver bene avuto poca consideratione [lack of judgment] alhora, ch'ei dipinse la Santa Margherita a cavallo del Serpente." For the Italian text, translation, and commentary, see Mark W. Roskill, *Dolce's "Aretino" and Venetian Art Theory of the Cinquecento* (New York: New York University Press, 1968), 126–27, 286. Although Roskill questioned whether Tintoretto's picture was the one in question (in Dolce's dialogue, the female figure is misidentified as Saint Margaret), this has not been doubted by subsequent scholars.

20. Tom Nichols, *Tintoretto: Tradition and Identity* (London: Reaktion Books, 1999), 67.

21. On the dating of the new organ, see Rodolfo Gallo, "Per la datazione delle opere del Veronese," *Emporium* 89 (March 1939): 145–52. When the organ was not in use, the two outer shutters, depicting Saints Geminanus and Severus, were closed. When the instrument was played, the shutters were opened, with Saint Menna on the right and Saint John the Baptist on the left of the organ pipes. The two paintings on the outer shutters have been unified as a single canvas. The three pictures are now in the Galleria Estense, Modena. See Rearick, *Art of Paolo Veronese*, cats. 29–31; and Pignatti and Pedrocco, *Veronese* 1:cats. 102–4.

22. The many documented Venetian examples include Titian's choosing the subjects to send to Philip II as well as Pordenone convincing the members of the Scuola della Carità through arguments of iconography and format to accept his choice of subject matter rather than that first proposed by the patrons. For the latter episode and a transcription of the document, see Rosand, *Painting in Sixteenth-Century Venice*, 104, 173.

23. Flaminio Corner, *Notizie storiche delle Chiese e monastery di Venezia e Torcello* (Padua: Giovanni Manfrè, 1758), 203; Alvise Zorzi, *Venezia scomparsa* (Milan: Mondadori, 2001), 223–27.

24. Rearick, *Art of Paolo Veronese*, 53. John Garton discusses Rearick's proposal that Menna is a sort of self-portrait in *Grace and Grandeur: The Portraiture of Paolo Veronese* (London: Brepols Publishers, 2008), 94–97.

25. Within the many Michelangelesque figures in Tintoretto's oeuvre, certain paintings from the 1550s seem to be deliberate invocations of Michelangelo's work: for example, the 1550–52 facade frescoes at the Palazzo Gussoni and the enormous choir paintings for the Madonna dell'Orto, the *Last Judgment* and the *Making of the Golden Calf*, about 1559–60. On the Palazzo Gussoni frescoes, see Echols and Ilchman, "Toward a New Tintoretto Catalogue," cat. 54; and Diana Gisolfi, "Tintoretto e le facciate affrescate di Venezia," in *Jacopo Tintoretto nel quarto centenario della morte*, ed. Rossi and Puppi, 111–14. The date of 1550–52 was established by Roland Krischel, *Tintoretto und die Skulptur der Renaissance in Venedig* (Weimar: Verlag und Datenbank für Geisteswissenschaften, 1994), 40; and Michel Hochmann, "Tintoret au Palais Gussoni," in *Jacopo Tintoretto nel quarto centenario della morte*, ed. Rossi and Puppi, 101–7. On the Madonna dell'Orto paintings, see Pallucchini and Rossi, *Opere sacre e profane* 1:cats. 236, 237; and Echols and Ilchman, "Toward a New Tintoretto Catalogue," cats. 78, 79. On Tintoretto's artistic engagement with Michelangelo, see also Frederick Ilchman and Edward Saywell, "Michelangelo and Tintoretto: *Disegno* and Drawing," in Falomir, *Tintoretto*, 385–93.

26. The textual sources for this iconography include the life of Anthony composed by Saint Athanasius, the fourth-century Patriarch of Alexandria, and integrated into the *Vitae patrum*, a compilation of the Egyptian church fathers. See H. Ellershaw, trans., *Life of Antony: Select Writings of Athanasius*, Library of Nicene and post Nicene Fathers II.4 (New York, 1924; repr., 1957), 195–221, esp. 197, 198–99. For a useful analysis and further bibliography, see Charles D. Cuttler, "Some Grünewald Sources," *Art Quarterly* 19, no. 2 (1956): 101–24, esp. 102, 119 n. 6. Another enormously influential text about Anthony was Jacobus de Voragine, *The Golden Legend of Jacobus de Voragine*, trans. Granger Ryan and Helmut Ripperger (New York: Longmans, Green, 1941), 99–103. *The Golden Legend*, however, does not describe a separate temptation by a demon in the form of a beautiful woman.

27. Cuttler concludes that the subject is uncommon in later Italian Renaissance art: "It was far from popular in Italian painting after the decline of the Sienese school, and the few examples which can be cited are to be found chiefly in the comparatively minor arts of woodcut and engraving." He also notes how Spanish art tended to follow the iconographic example of Siena. See Cuttler, "Some Grünewald Sources," 107, 120 n. 22. The examples cited of Italian and Spanish art suggest that the two moments of Saint Anthony attacked by demons and his temptation by the devil in the form of a beautiful woman were usually treated as distinct episodes. In addition, see the examples compiled by George Kaftal, *Iconography of the Saints in Tuscan Painting* (Florence: Sansoni, 1952), 61–76; Kaftal, *Iconography of the Saints in the Painting of North East Italy* (Florence: Sansoni, 1978), 52–72; Kaftal, *Iconography of the Saints in the Painting of North West Italy* (Florence: Le Lettere, 1985), 68–86. The Saint Anthony panels by the Master of the Osservanza offer clear examples of episodes of erotic temptation and physical punishment depicted in separate panels (both at Yale University Art Gallery, New Haven, CT); Keith Christiansen's comprehensive study of these panels cites as their main textual source the fourteenth-century *Vite dei santi padri* of Domenico Cavalca, a rewriting in Italian of the *Vitae patrum*. See Christiansen, "Saint Anthony Abbot Series," in *Painting in Renaissance Siena, 1420–1500*, by Keith Christiansen, Laurence B. Kanter, and Carl Brandon Strehlke (New York: Metropolitan Museum of Art, 1988), 104–23, esp. 113–17, cats. 10d, 10e.

28. An elaborate drawing by Veronese of the subject, showing a quite different composition (Musée du Louvre, inv. 4842), has been considered, variously, as a modello for the altarpiece (David Rosand, "An Early Chiaroscuro Drawing by Paolo Veronese," *The Burlington Magazine* 108, no. 761 [1966]: 421–22), a later variant (Richard Cocke, *Veronese's Drawings* [Ithaca, NY: Cornell University Press, 1984], 106–7, cat. 36), or an independent presentation drawing from roughly the same time as the altarpiece (Rearick, *Art of Paolo Veronese*, 48–49, cat. 17; W. R. Rearick, *Il disegno veneziano del Cinquecento* [Milan: Electa, 2001], 128–29).

29. Richard Cocke, in "An Early Drawing by P. Veronese," *The Burlington Magazine* 113 (1971): 726–34, relates the figure of the male demon to that of Hercules in Caraglio's engraving *Hercules and Cacus*, after a design by Rosso Fiorentino (see Walter L. Strauss, ed., *The Illustrated Bartsch* [New York: Abaris Books, 1978–2000], 28:cat. 49), which looks back to a modello by Michelangelo. Cocke relates the saint and the female temptress to Saint Jerome and the Virgin in Parmigianino's *Virgin and Child with Saints John the Baptist and Jerome* (National Gallery, London). Rearick, in *Art of Paolo Veronese*, 47, cat. 16, cites an overall similarity to Correggio's mythologies then at the Palazzo del Te, "metamorphoized into a sinister nightmare." Patrick Ramade, in *Splendeur de Venise, 1500–1600*, by Michel Laclotte, Olivier Le Bihan, Patrick Ramade, and Michel Hochmann, exh. cat. (Paris: Somogy, 2005), suggests works by Rosso Fiorentino and Giulio Romano as models. Remigio Marini, in *L'opera completa del Veronese* (Milan: Rizzoli, 1968), cat. 16, identifies Andrea Schiavone's *Samson Killing a Philistine* (Galleria Palatina, Palazzo Pitti, Florence) as a likely source for the pose of the male demon. That figure is derived from one in Raimondi's engraving of the *Massacre of the Innocents* after Baccio Bandelli (Strauss, *The Illustrated Bartsch*, 26:cat. 21), or possibly Baccio's original figure study (Gabinetto Disegni e Stampe degli Uffizi, Florence, 6911F). The same figure provided the source for Tintoretto's *Lician Peasants Changed into Frogs*, one of the ceiling panels for the Palazzo Pisani a San Paternian of 1542 (Galleria Estense, Modena; see Pallucchini and Rossi, *Opere sacre e profane* 1:cat. 22; and Echols and Ilchman, "Toward a New Tintoretto Catalogue," cat. 14), as well as his painting *Cain Killing Abel* (see Pallucchini and Rossi, *Opere sacre e profane* 1:cat. 152; and Echols and Ilchman "Toward a New Tintoretto Catalogue," cat. 58). It is possible that Tintoretto, Schiavone, and Veronese were familiar with the print or some version of the original figure study by Bandinelli.

30. See Pignatti and Pedrocco, *Veronese* 2:553, doc. 5. The commissions for the other three Mantua altarpieces also went to painters of the Verona school: Domenico Brusasorci, Paolo Farinati, and Battista del Moro.

31. Although some scholars have proposed that the painting has been cut down slightly, a recent review of the work's recorded dimensions indicates that they have remained constant, according to Ramade, *Splendeur de Venise*, cat. 104.

32. Pallucchini and Rossi, *Opere sacre e profane* 1:cat. 227. On Daniele da Volterra as a source of Tintoretto, see Simon H. Levie, "Daniele da Volterra e Tintoretto," *Arte Veneta* 7 (1954): 168–70. Other possible models include the traditional image of the dead Christ supported by angels, of which there are versions from Venice and Central Italy (e.g., fig. 4). Rossi also suggested Pordenone's *Crucifixion* in the Duomo at Cremona as a source for the image of the fainting Virgin; see Pallucchini and Rossi, *Opere sacre e profane* 1:180.

33. For the organ shutters, see Pallucchini and Rossi, *Opere sacre e profane* 1:cats. 159–61; and Echols and Ilchman, "Toward a New Tintoretto Catalogue," cats. 68–70. For the *Pool of Betheseda*, see Pallucchini and Rossi, *Opere sacre e profane*, 1:226; and Echols and Ilchman, "Toward a New Tintoretto Catalogue," cat. 75.

34. Marco Boschini, *Le minere della pittura* (Venice: F. Nicolini, 1664), 346; Anton Maria Zanetti, *Descrizione di tutte le pubbliche pitture della città di venezia* (Venice: Pietro Bassaglia, 1733), 333; Zanetti, *Della pittura veneziana* (Venice: Giambatista Albrizzi, 1771), 159.

35. For the demolished church and monastery of the Umiltà, see Zorzi, *Venezia scomparsa*, 244–45.

36. Pignatti and Pedrocco, *Veronese* 1:130–33, cats. 95–97.

37. When Boschini described the church a century later, there was a tabernacle on the high altar, with paintings by Bassano and Veronese towering up on four separate levels; for the various citations, see Zorzi, *Venezia scomparsa*, 244. These paintings seem to be lost, and so the date of the tabernacle is unknown. Over the course of the second half of the sixteenth century, in many churches the tabernacle holding the Host was moved with increasing frequency from side altars to the high altar, in accordance with the church's growing emphasis on the doctrine of transubstantiation (on this point, see Paul Hills, "Piety and Patronage in Cinquecento Venice: Tintoretto and the Scuole del Sacramento," *Art History* 6 [1983]: 30–43, esp. 35–39). We are indebted to Thomas Worthen (personal communication, April 2008) for this intriguing proposal concerning the *Deposition*'s possible origins, which we hope will be the subject of further exploration.

38. For example, Titian's *Transfiguration* for the high altar at San Salvador, painted to cover a medieval *pala*, functioned as an altarpiece.

39. This point was also suggested to us by Worthen.

40. On the Eucharistic imagery in the San Francesco della Vigna and San Giorgio Maggiore altarpieces, see the entries on the two paintings in Falomir, *Tintoretto*, cats. 33 and 49.

41. See Giovanna Nepi Sciré, *Guida alla Quadreria* (Venice: Marsilio, 1995), 74–76, cat. 38. The conservation treatment, sponsored by Save Venice Inc., undertaken for the present exhibition has clarified its beauty and importance.

42. Carlo Ridolfi, *The Life of Tintoretto and of His Children Domenico and Marietta*, trans. Catherine Enggass and Robert Enggass (University Park, PA: Penn State University Press, 1984), 43; the original is in Carlo Ridolfi, *Le maraviglie dell'arte ovvero le vite degli illustri pittori veneti e dello stato* (Venice, 1648), 2:38.

43. Ridolfi, *Life of Tintoretto*, 44; the original is in Ridolfi, *Le maraviglie dell'arte* 2:39–40.

44. We suggest that a sense of rivalry with Veronese is a more likely explanation for the unusually high degree of finish in the *Temptation of Saint Anthony*, rather than the experience of painting mythological works, such as the *Origin of the Milky Way*, for foreign patrons, as argued by Tom Nichols (*Tintoretto*, 137): "Despite the moralizing content, however, the luxuriant handling of the painting reflects the impact of secular work for Prague, an overlap which indicates the spread of courtly tastes through the ranks of the city's patricians and citizens."

45. The other two altarpieces that Veronese executed for the church are the *Consecration of Saint Nicholas* (National Gallery, London) and *Saint Jerome in the Wilderness with the Madonna in Glory* (destroyed; the composition is known from a copy still in the church). The altarpieces were removed from the church in the Napoleonic era; see the provenance narrative in the checklist for this catalogue. See also Beverley Louise Brown, "Veronese and the Church Triumphant: The Altarpieces for San Benedetto Po," *Artibus et Historiae* 25 (1997): 51–64; and Penny, *Sixteenth Century Italian Paintings* 2:346–51.

46. W. R. Rearick offers a compelling summary of the sheer volume of Veronese's production in the early 1560s; see "Fame, Fortune, Family: Maser, Venice, Verona, 1561–1570," in *Art of Paolo Veronese*, 72–75.

47. Penny, *Sixteenth Century Italian Paintings* 2:349.

48. The encounter between Saints Anthony and Paul the Hermit is mentioned only in the life of Paul the Hermit in *The Golden Legend*. By this account, Saint Anthony, learning in a dream that he had been preceded by another hermit, "better than himself," set off to find Paul, who had spent most of his life in solitude. After initially resisting a meeting, Paul opened the door of his cell to Anthony, and the two men fell into a warm embrace. At mealtime, a raven descended, bringing a loaf of bread divided into two, and Paul revealed that God had provided him daily with food in this manner; on that day, the ration was doubled. See Jacobus de Voragine, *The Golden Legend of Jacobus de Voragine*, trans. Granger Ryan and Helmut Ripperger (1941; repr., New York: Arno Press, 1969), 88–90. The embrace between the two saints and the descent of the raven were common subjects in medieval and Renaissance art; see the examples listed under the iconography of Saint Anthony Abbot in Kaftal, *Iconography of the Saints in Tuscan Painting*, 70.

49. Brown, "Veronese and the Church Triumphant," 57–58.

50. Rearick, *Art of Paolo Veronese*, 88.

51. Pallucchini and Rossi, *Opere sacre e profane* 1:208, cat. 370; Echols and Ilchman, "Toward a New Tintoretto Catalogue," cat. 197.

52. Maria Agnese Chiari Moretto Wiel, ed. *Jacopo Tintoretto e i suoi incisori*, exh. cat. (Milan: Electa, 1994), 19, cat. 1. Diane DeGrazia Bohlin, *Prints and Related Drawings by the Carracci Family: A Catalogue Raisonné* (Washington, DC: National Gallery of Art, 1979), cat. 101.

53. See Pallucchini and Rossi, *Opere sacre e profane* 1:208, cat. 370.

54. De Voragine, *The Golden Legend*, 100. See also note 26 for the sources for this text, which include, besides *The Golden Legend*, the earlier texts that constituted the *Vitae partum*; for example, Ellershaw, *Life of Antony*, 195–221, esp. 197, 198–99.

55. Ilchman, "Tintoretto as a Painter of Religious Narrative," 63–94, esp. 77.

56. Rearick, *Art of Paolo Veronese*, 86.

57. Brian D'Arganville, "Titian's *Cenacolo* for the Refectory of SS. Giovanni e Paolo Reconsidered," in *Tiziano e Venezia: Convegno internazionale di studi, 1976* (Vicenza: Neri Pozza, 1980), 161–67. The lost *Last Supper* at Santi Giovanni e Paolo may be reflected in the *Last Supper* that Titian sent to Philip II in 1564 (Real Monasterio de El Escorial). See Wethey, *Paintings of Titian* 1:96–98, cat. 46; Humfrey, *Titian: The Complete Paintings*, 321, cat. 253. Charles Hope, in *Titian* (London: Chaucer Press, 2003), 164–65, suggests that the Escorial *Last Supper* was originally begun for Santi Giovanni e Paolo in 1557 and that Titian supplied another, later version to the church. Echoes of Titian's *Supper at Emmaus* compositions are apparent in the Escorial *Last Supper*, as noted by Jean Habert in *Le siècle de Titien: L'âge d'or de la peinture à Venise*, by Michel Laclotte, Giovanna Nepi Scirè, et al., exh. cat. (Paris: Réunion des musées nationaux, 1993), 518, cat. 161. The Santi Giovanni e Paolo picture may similarly have reflected the *Supper at Emmaus* composition.

58. Pignatti and Pedrocco, *Veronese* 1:288–89, cat. 194, On the *Last Supper* as the original subject, see Paul Kaplan, "Veronese and the Inquisition: The Geopolitical Conflict," in *Suspended License: Censorship and the Visual Arts*, ed. Elizabeth Childs (Seattle: University of Washington Press, 1997), 85–124. For a recent discussion, see Maria Elena Massimi, "La cosiddetta *Cena in casa di Levi* di Paolo Veronese: Descrizione preliminare all'identificazione del soggetto come *Cena in casa del fariseo*," *Venezia Cinquecento* 14 (2004): 123–68.

59. Robert Echols and Frederick Ilchman, "*The Last Supper*," in Falomir, *Tintoretto*, 304–9, cat. 32; Pallucchini and Rossi, *Opere sacre e profane* 1:cat. 259; Echols and Ilchman, "Toward a New Tintoretto Catalogue," cat. 95. For a perceptive analysis of Tintoretto's *Last Suppers*, see Rosand, *Painting in Sixteenth-Century Venice*, 153–59. For questions of authorship and chronology, see Echols and Ilchman in Falomir, *Tintoretto*, 304–9; and for a more complete discussion, see the section devoted to this subject in Echols and Ilchman, "Toward a New Tintoretto Catalogue."

60. For the general background of the Supper at Emmaus as a theme in European art, see Gertrud Schiller, *Ikonographie der christlichen Kunst*, vol. 3, *Die Auferstehung und Ehrhöhung Christi* (Gütersloh: Gütersloh Verlagshaus G. Mohn, 1971), 99–103. For a recent discussion of the emergence of the Supper at Emmaus as an independent theme in Venice, see Francesco Saracino, "Vincitore e Pellegrino: I pittori veneziani e l'immaginazione del Risorto," in *La Cena di Tiziano: Immagini del Risorto tra Louvre e Ambrosiana*, ed. Giovanni Morale, exh. cat. (Milan: Pinacoteca Ambrosiana, 2006), 33–89, esp. 59–61.

61. On the lost Bellini, see Rona Goffen, "*Cena in Emmaus*," in *Il colore ritrovato: Bellini a Venezia*, ed. Rona Goffen and Giovanna Nepi Scirè, exh. cat. (Milan: Electa, 2000), 166–67, cat. 38. Vasari writes: "ed in casa Messer Giorgio Cornaro è un quadro similmente bellissimo, dentro Cristo, Cleofas, e Luca." See Giorgio Vasari, *Le vite de' più eccellenti pittori, scultori ed architettori* [1568], ed. Gaetano Milanesi (Florence: G. C. Sansoni, 1878–85), 3:164.

62. Of the examples by Bellini and his followers, the most prominent is the one dated 1513 in the Contarini chapel in the church of San Salvador, Venice; it is attributed to Bellini and his assistants or possibly Carpaccio, commissioned by Girolamo Priuli, who is both identified by an inscription and depicted in the painting. See Goffen, "*Cena in Emmaus*," 166–67; and Saracino, "Vincitore e Pellegrino," fig. 21. Other examples include versions attributed to Benedetto Diana and Marco Marziale, both in the Gemäldegalerie, Berlin (Saracino, "Vincitore e Pellegrino," figs. 19, 21). Another version by Marco Marziale is in the Gallerie dell'Accademia, Venice; see Sandra Moschini Marconi, *Gallerie dell'Accademia di Venezia: Opere d'arte dei secoli XIV e XV* (Rome: Istituto Poligrafico dello Stato, 1955), 143, cat. 153. Goffen ("*Cena in Emmaus*," 166) also cites examples in the Galleria degli Uffizi, Florence, possibly by a follower of Vicenzo Catena, and the Accademia Carrara, Bergamo. Versions by artists outside Venice include a design for a tapestry from the school of Raphael (Musei Vaticani); a woodcut in Dürer's Small Passion series; and paintings by Romanino (Pinacoteca Tosio-Martinengo, Brescia), Pontormo (Galleria degli Uffizi, Florence), and Moretto (Pinacoteca Tosio-Martinengo, Brescia); see Guido Rebecchini, "Tiziano e Mantova: *La Cena in Emmaus* per Nicola Maffei," *Venezia Cinquecento* 5, no. 10 (1995): 41–68, figs. 3–5, 7–9.

63. Rebecchini, "Tiziano e Mantova," 42–48.

64. Ibid., 52. Rebecchini further reaffirms earlier suggestions that Luke is a portrait of Duke Federico Gonzaga. This is less convincing. Luke here has a sharper nose than Federico, according to Titian's well-known portrait of him in the Museo Nacional del Prado (Wethey, *Paintings of Titian* 2:107–8, cat. 49) or his presumed likeness in the *Virgin and Child with Saint Catherine of Alexandria and a Rabbit* (cat. 12). Moreover, the same figure appears in the Earl of Yarborough's version (fig. 24), discussed below, which has no Mantuan connection.

65. As noted earlier, the patron Girolamo Priuli is depicted in the *Supper at Emmaus* now at San Salvador (Goffen, "*Cena in Emmaus*," 166–67). The patron Tommaso Raimondi is depicted as the host in Marco Marziale's *Supper at Emmaus* in Berlin (Saracino, "Vincitore e Pellegrino," 59).

66. The respective patronage and the chronological relationship of Titian's two versions of the *Supper of Emmaus* have been much debated over the decades. Recent scholars have generally considered the Contarini/Yarborough/Brocklesby Park version the earlier of the two, dating from 1525–30, while regarding it as somewhat weaker and probably created with studio assistance. For a thorough review of the literature on the subject, see Jean Habert, "Tiziano Vecellio: *La Cena in Emmaus*," in *La Cena di Tiziano*, ed. Morale, 146–49, as well as Habert's catalogue entry on the Maffei/Musée du Louvre picture in *Le siècle de Titien*, by Laclotte, Nepi Scirè, et al., 515–17, cat. 161 (the latter was published prior to Rebecchini's identification of the Maffei provenance). However, Humfrey (*Titian: The Complete Paintings*, 139, 156, cats. 90, 106) dates the Brocklesby Park version after the Louvre picture, around 1534–36. Humfrey argues that the fact that the Louvre picture originally included features that appear in the Brocklesby Park version does not necessarily mean that the Louvre picture must be later; he points out that Titian occasionally uses discarded ideas in later variants. It is possible that the two pictures were executed virtually contemporaneously in Titian's studio, with the Contarini commission having been begun first and the Maffei version adapted from it before the earlier version had left the shop.

67. By extending the wall in the background farther into the center of the picture in the Paris painting, Titian reduced the emphasis on the subsidiary figure of the host, who is silhouetted against the sky in the Contarini version. He also moved the figure of Cleopas to the viewer's side of the table, thus reducing the hieratic quality of the scene.

68. Wethey (*Paintings of Titian* 1:161) notes that "nearly all writers have observed" Titian's quotation from Leonardo's *Last Supper*. An early example of such observations that has not appeared previously in the Titian literature is Johann Boloz Antoniewicz's "O wieczerzy Lionarda da Vinci (Das Abendmahl Lionardos)," *Bulletin international de l'Académie des Sciences de Cracovie*, no. 6 (June 1904): 53–66, reprinted and translated by Leo Steinberg in *Leonardo's Incessant Last Supper* (New York: Zone Books, 2001), appendix B, 203.

69. A seventeenth-century engraving of the picture by Antoine Masson, which emphasized the lozenge pattern of the cloth, was known simply as "la Nappe." See Habert, "Tiziano Vecellio," 146; and Habert in *Le siècle de Titien*, by Laclotte, Nepi Scirè, et al., 517. Similar carpets are so frequently depicted in Venetian Cinquecento painting that in Italy they are known as "Lotto carpets."

70. Rebecchini ("Tiziano e Mantova," 49) suggests that the plate of lettuce, a bitter herb, before Christ represents penitence, while the quince is a symbol of resurrection, and the common violets are symbols of humility. The dog and cat beneath the table are interpreted as representing faith (the dog was a common symbol of fidelity) standing firm against doubts and heresy; the cat traditionally had negative, even diabolical associations. (One might note that here its tail is particularly serpentine.) These suggestions are amplified by Saracino ("Vincitore e pellegrino," 72–75), who adds that the mound of salt in the salt cellar should be understood as symbolizing brotherhood and peace.

71. Scholars are in accord about the early date of this painting; see, for example, Pallucchini and Rossi, *Opere sacre e profane* 1:cat. 41 (1542–43); Vilmos Tátrai, "*The Supper at Emmaus*," in *Treasures of Venice: Paintings from the Museum of Fine Arts, Budapest*, ed. George Keyes, Istvan Bárkóczi, and Jane Satkowski, exh. cat. (New York: Harry N. Abrams, 1995), 150–51, cat. 9 (around 1543); and Echols and Ilchman, "Toward a New Tintoretto Catalogue," cat. 27 (early 1540s).

72. On Bonifazio's Palazzo dei Camerlenghi *Supper at Emmaus*, see Cottrell, "Corporate Colors," 658–78; and Simonetta Simonetti, "Profilo di Bonifacio de' Pitati," *Saggi e memorie di storia dell'arte* 15 (1986): 83–133, cat. 35, fig. 42. In the Budapest painting, Tintoretto also quotes from other works by Bonifazio, including versions of the *Last Supper*. For example, the pose of the disciple to the right in Tintoretto's painting is based upon that of an apostle in a similar position in Bonifazio's *Last Supper* at the church of Santa Maria Mater Domini, Venice (Simonetti, "Profilo di Bonifacio de' Pitati," cat. 27, fig. 31). The specific quotations from Bonifazio's paintings were first discussed by Robert Echols in "Jacopo Tintoretto and Venetian Painting in the 1540s" (PhD diss., University of Maryland, 1993), 113–16. The general relationship to Bonifazio and the Camerlenghi painting in particular had been noted by Rodolfo Pallucchini (*La giovinezza del Tintoretto* [Milan: D. Guarnati, 1950], 81–82) and subsequent scholars.

73. See Echols and Ilchman, *"The Last Supper,"* in Falomir, *Tintoretto*, 304–9, cat. 32; and Rosand, *Painting in Sixteenth-Century Venice*, 153–59.

74. Most recent scholars date the Louvre painting around 1559–60. See Pignatti and Pedrocco, *Veronese* 1:135, cat. 100; Terisio Pignatti and Filippo Pedrocco, *Veronese: Catalogo completo dei dipinti* (Florence: Cantini, 1991), 93, cat. 49; Terisio Pignatti, *Veronese* (Venice: Alfieri, 1976), 1:116, cat. 91 (around 1559); and Jean Habert, "La peinture vénitienne de 1540 à 1560 dans les collections du Louvre," in *Da Bellini a Veronese: Temi di arte Veneta*, ed. Gennaro Toscano and Francesco Valcanover (Venice: Istituto veneto di scienze, lettere ed arti, 2004), 571 (1560). The exceptions are Rearick, *Art of Paolo Veronese*, 33 (around 1555); and Richard Cocke, *Paolo Veronese: Piety and Display in an Age of Religious Reform* (Aldershot, UK: Ashgate, 2001), 144 ("Soon after the artist's arrival in Venice"). The picture was acquired by Louis XIII from Cardinal Richelieu and is said to have been the favorite Venetian painting of the Bourbons; see Habert, "La peinture vénitienne," 571.

75. Habert, in "La peinture vénitienne," 571, suggests the possibility that the painting depicts members of the Barbaro family.

76. An exception among Tintoretto's works is the *Raising of Lazarus* (private collection); see Falomir, *Tintoretto*, cat. 39.

77. Given that Veronese's paintings often contain many details and subsidiary figures whose roles seem essentially decorative, there is no need to read the inclusion of the child embracing the dog as a representation of "the love of Christ," as suggested by Erik Beenker in *The Collection: Museum Boijmans Van Beuningen, Rotterdam, the Netherlands* (Rotterdam: Museum Boijmans Van Beuningen, 2005), 58.

78. In a version of the *Supper of Emmaus* from Titian's studio (National Gallery of Ireland, Dublin), Christ's gaze is also directed upward, although less strongly than in Veronese's paintings. See Wethey, *Paintings of Titian* 1:179, cat. X-38 (Wethey doubts that Titian participated even in the design of the picture); Francesco Valcanover, *L'opera completa di Tiziano* (Milan: Rizzoli, 1969), 113 (Titian with studio assistance, around 1542); Rodolfo Pallucchini, *Tiziano* (Florence: G. C. Sansoni, 1969), 1:97 (Titian with studio assistance, not before 1542–43). See also Saracino, "Vincitore e Pellegrino," 67. The Raphaelesque quality of the motif of Christ looking heavenward is pointed out by Habert in "La peinture vénitienne," 571.

79. The Rotterdam painting shows some studio participation in its execution but is accepted by all recent scholars as a primarily autograph work of Veronese's design. See Rodolfo Pallucchini, *Veronese* (Milan: Mondadori, 1984), 179, cat. 140; Pignatti and Pedrocco, *Veronese: Catalogo completo dei dipinti*, 200, cat. 119; and Pignatti and Pedrocco, *Veronese* 1:295–96, cat. 200. All of the preceding scholars date the painting to around 1574, following Cocke, *Veronese's Drawings*, 176–77, cat. 74. Cocke relates the Rotterdam painting to a drawing (Staatliche Museen, Berlin-Dahlem, KdZ 26358) that includes a sketch for a *Supper at Emmaus*. Another sketch on the sheet shows a Lamentation that Cocke relates to an altarpiece Veronese executed for a church in Ostuni, Puglia, in 1574. Dating the Rotterdam painting to around 1574 on this basis may be overly precise. The sketch in the Berlin drawing is only generally similar to the Rotterdam picture; at most, it suggests that Veronese was thinking about the Supper at Emmaus theme at roughly the same time that he was designing the altarpiece for Ostuni. The Rotterdam picture does show the gray or metallic tonalities and compact poses that characterize some of Veronese's paintings of the mid-1570s, however, such as his *Adoration of the Kings* (National Gallery, London), dated 1573. The painting is probably the one seen by Ridolfi in the Muselli collection in Verona; before arriving in Rotterdam, it passed through a number of distinguished collections, including those of the Duc d'Orléans and the Duke of Sutherland at Stafford House. Pignatti and Pedrocco (*Veronese: Catalogo completo dei dipinti*, 328, cat. 16A) properly consider a version roughly twice as large as the Rotterdam composition (Gemäldegalerie, Dresden) a later studio production by Veronese's heirs. The Dresden painting is included in Pignatti's *Veronese* 1:116–17, cat. 92, 2:fig. 187. With the addition of space around the figures, the impact of the composition is diminished. Early in his career, Veronese executed a presentation drawing of the *Supper at Emmaus* (Chatsworth), as well as a preliminary sketch; see Rearick, *Art of Paolo Veronese*, 32–33, cats. 4, 5; Cocke, *Veronese's Drawings*, 104, cat. 35; and Rearick, *Disegno veneziano*, 127–28. The composition shows few similarities to the Louvre or Rotterdam paintings.

Beneath the Surface: Revelations from Three Works by Veronese, Titian, and Tintoretto

1. The authors of this essay would particularly like to acknowledge the extensive and generous assistance of Meta Chavannes, Andrew W. Mellon Fellow, and Sandra Kelberlau, Cunningham Assistant Conservator, for the technical investigations. Other colleagues who have helped us analyze these puzzling paintings include Jean Woodward, Robert Echols, and Robert Wald. The finest Sienese works in the MFA, including examples by Duccio, Ugolino, "Barna da Siena," Simone Martini, Giovanni di Paolo, the Master of the Osservanza, and Sano di Pietro, as well as early Renaissance works of other schools, are discussed in the excellent catalogue by Laurence Kanter, *Italian Paintings in the Museum of Fine Arts, Boston*, vol. 1, *13th–15th Century* (Boston: Museum of Fine Arts, 1994). The introduction offers a rich view of Boston collecting and an ideal starting point for further research.

2. Pignatti and Pedrocco date the set of paintings to the second half of the 1560s; see Pignatti and Pedrocco, *Veronese* 1:260, cats. 158–61. The four Boston canvases have also been linked in the literature with three small canvases, slightly taller (28 vs. 25 cm [11 1/16 vs. 9 11/16 in.]) but similar in scale, depicting Painting, Diana, and Minerva; see ibid., cats. 162–64.

3. Piero Boccardo, in *L'età di Rubens: Dimore, committenti e collezionisti genovesi* (Milan: Skira, 2004), 372, cat. 94.

4. Robert Echols, oral communication, June 2008, noting that Jupiter originally seduced Semele in human guise.

5. See Richard Cocke, *Veronese's Drawings* (Ithaca, NY: Cornell University Press, 1984); and Rearick, *Art of Paolo Veronese*.

6. See Louisa C. Matthew, "'Vendecolori a Venezia': The Reconstruction of a Profession," *The Burlington Magazine* 144 (2002): 680–86.

7. Veronese's grounds and layering of colors have been studied in great detail recently; see particularly the relevant catalogue entries in Penny, *Sixteenth Century Italian Paintings*, vol. 2; and Dorothy Mahon, Silvia A. Centeno, Mark T. Wypski, Xavier F. Salomon, and Andrea Bayer, "A Technical Study of Three Allegorical Paintings by Paolo Veronese," in the forthcoming issue of *The Metropolitan Museum of Art Technical Journal*.

8. Erika Tietze-Conrat, "Titian's *Saint Catherine*," *Gazette des beaux-arts* 43 (1954): 257–61.

9. For the Treviso *Annuciation*, see Wethey, *Paintings of Titian* 1:69–70, cat. 8; Filippo Pedrocco, *Titian* (New York: Rizzoli International, 2001), 132, cat. 65; and Peter Humfrey, *Titian* (New York: Phaidon, 2007), 107, cat. 61.

10. Wethey, *Paintings of Titian* 1:129–30, cat. 96.

11. X-radiographs taken in 1963 had made clear that the figure was not originally a nun, and that the sword and ring had always been there. Two articles appearing in 1969 refuted Tietze-Conrat's analysis: Joy Kenseth, "Titian's St. Catherine of Alexandria," *Bulletin: Museum of Fine Arts, Boston* 67 (1969): 174–88; and Henry T. Blodget, "Titian's 'St. Catherine' in Boston," *The Burlington Magazine* 111 (1969): 544–48. All three writers—Tietze-Conrat, Kenseth, and Blodget—plumb the iconographic questions of the painting but question its quality and beauty.

12. Kenseth, "Titian's St. Catherine," 181; J. A. Crowe and G. B. Cavalcaselle, *Titian: His Life and Times* (London: J. Murray, 1877), 2:374–78.

13. Blodget, "Titian's 'St. Catherine,'" 547.

14. Some of the changes have already been noted in the 1969 publications by Kenseth and Blodget (see n. 11), who had access to earlier X-radiographs of *Saint Catherine*.

15. See Miguel Falomir, "Titian's Replicas and Variants," in Jaffé, *Titian*, 60–68, as well as the technical essays in the recent catalogue *Der Späte Tizian und die Sinnlichkeit der Malerei*, ed. Sylvia Ferino-Pagden, exh. cat. (Vienna: Kunsthistorisches Museum, 2007).

16. Correspondence and notes in the MFA Department of Art of Europe curatorial files indicate at least five earlier conservation treatments for the Tintoretto *Nativity*. The picture, perhaps acquired during an 1874 visit to Italy, was hung in Quincy Adams Shaw's Jamaica Plain dining room relatively soon after its purchase, and sometime before it was first lent to the MFA in 1894–95. The picture was later lent again from 1917 to 1923, when a further treatment appears to have taken place. Another cleaning is listed in March 1932 and yet another between December 1946 and March 1947, at which point it was relined and the "old canvas found to be in excellent condition." A further removal of yellowed varnish occurred in July 1949.

17. For a painting by Tintoretto connected to the cult of Zacharias, see Frederick Ilchman and Victoria S. Reed, "*The Birth of Saint John the Baptist* by Tintoretto in the Church of San Zaccaria: Conservation and Iconography," in *Arte nelle Venezie: Scritti di amici per Sandro Sponza*, ed. Chiara Ceschi, Pierluigi Fantelli, and Francesca Flores d'Arcais (Saonara, Italy: Il Prato, 2007), 107–14.

18. The *Nativity* was accepted by Fredericksen and Zeri, but Pallucchini and Rossi dismissed this and earlier opinions; see Burton B. Fredericksen and Federico Zeri, *Census of Pre-Nineteenth-Century Italian Paintings in North American Public Collections* (Cambridge, MA: Harvard University Press, 1972), 199; and Pallucchini and Rossi, *Opere sacre e profane* 1:241, cat. A13. In linking the painting with Domenico, Pallucchini and Rossi cited the depiction of the animals and the landscape, particularly the "reminiscenza dei modi del Bassano," ignoring the possibility that these peripheral details need not be by the same hand that planned the composition and executed the large figures. They further compare the Boston painting to a picture in Grenoble, France, *Mary Magdalen Presenting Matteo Soranzo to the Holy Family* (1:244–45, cat. A42), yet neither the facial types nor the limp draperies (much closer to Domenico) in the Grenoble painting are seen in the *Nativity*. Finally, Pallucchini and Rossi do not aid their case by illustrating the MFA's two large narra-

tive paintings (both of which they consider to be by Domenico) on the same page (2:631, figs. 640, 641). The principal sections of these two paintings simply cannot be by the same hand. The *Adoration of the Magi* (26.142) contains slender figures with large shoulders and small heads, each with a high center of gravity and a silvery palette; all these features are typical of Domenico. Conversely, the *Nativity* (46.1430) shows massive and bulky figures, strong contours and foreshortening, and stronger contrast of colors, all characteristic of Jacopo. See Echols and Ilchman, "Toward a New Tintoretto Catalogue," cat. 280.

19. Pallucchini and Rossi, *Opere sacre e profane* 1:153, cat. 121, 1:185–86, cat. 248; Echols and Ilchman, "Toward a New Tintoretto Catalogue," cats. 43 and 73. See also Ilchman and Reed, "*The Birth of Saint John the Baptist*."

20. Frederick Ilchman, under "*The Virgin and Child with Saints Mark and Luke*," in Falomir, *Tintoretto*, 323 n. 6.

21. Pallucchini and Rossi, *Opere sacre e profane* 1:244, cat. A37; Echols and Ilchman, "Toward a New Tintoretto Catalogue," cat. 271.

22. See Jill Dunkerton, "Tintoretto's Painting Technique," in Falomir, *Tintoretto*, 139–58; Joyce Plesters, "Tintoretto's Paintings in the National Gallery: Part I," *National Gallery Technical Bulletin*, 3 (1979): 3–24; and Joyce Plesters and Lorenzo Lazzarini, "Preliminary Observations on the Technique and Materials of Tintoretto," in *Conservation and Restoration of Pictorial Art*, ed. Norman Brommelle and Perry Smith (London: Butterworths, 1976), 7–26.

23. See Dunkerton, "Tintoretto's Painting Technique"; and Plesters and Lazzarini, "Preliminary Observations."

24. The cross section shows that the upper layer of paint on the shepherd's jacket is composed of a much more finely ground pigment than was found in the rest of the painting. However, the pigment is azurite, indicating that the repainting may be pre-nineteenth century.

25. See Dunkerton, "Tintoretto's Painting Technique"; and Plesters, "Tintoretto's Paintings in the National Gallery."

26. The drawing in the Galleria degli Uffizi is no. 13025F. Hans Tietze and Erika Tietze-Conrat (*The Drawings of the Venetian Painters in the 15th and 16th Centuries* [New York: J. J. Augustin, 1944], 300, cat. 1810) propose that it was perhaps used for a Magdalen in a Lamentation, and then reused in the MFA painting; they further argue that the artist was a Tintoretto pupil influenced by Palma Giovane. Anna Forlani attributed the sheet to Palma Giovane, and said that it was a study for a Virgin Annunciate: see Anna Forlani, "In margine a una mostra di disegni del Tintoretto," *Arte Veneta* 11 (1957): 88–89, fig. 90. The attribution to Palma was rejected by Paola Rossi (Pallucchini and Rossi, *Opere sacre e profane* 2:241, cat. A13), as well as by Stefania Mason (oral communication), both of whom preferred an attribution to Domenico Tintoretto. The drawing is clearly not by Jacopo, who was the author of the corresponding figure in the painting, and the position of the knees is not the same. Given that the squaring in the painting visible in infrared reflectography does not correspond with that on the drawing, the most likely scenario is that Domenico asked a model (perhaps a studio assistant, since the face is that of a young man) to hold a pose similar to that in the painting.

27. This suggestion was made by Robert Echols. Carlo Ridolfi, *The Life of Tintoretto and of His Children Domenico and Marietta*, trans. Catherine Enggass and Robert Enggass (University Park, PA: Penn State University Press, 1984), 45. The original reads: "Sopra la porta della Chiesa della Carità vedevasi un quadro col Salvatore levato di Croce così gentile e delicate, che spirava divinità; e à piedi l'ordinario drapello delle Marie piangenti, & alcuni Vescovi ne'lati; ma di quello si può dire con l'Angelo: *Surrexit non est hic*." Ridolfi, *Le maraviglie dell'arte* 2:40. It should be noted that there is no cusping along the bottom edge of the existing canvas, leaving the possibility that the earlier painting may have extended below the two female figures.

28. See Dunkerton, "Tintoretto's Painting Technique," 154–55.

29. The document, first published by Detlev von Hadeln in 1911, can be found in Pallucchini and Rossi, *Opere sacre e profane* 1:127 (which also lists the San Marco *Nativity* among the lost works, p. 263), and in Borean, "Documentation," in Falomir, *Tintoretto*, 430. Paul Hills discusses the lost painting in "The Renaissance Altarpiece: A Valid Category?" in Peter Humfrey and Martin Kemp, *The Altarpiece in the Renaissance* (Cambridge: Cambridge University Press, 1990), 48. In the mid-seventeenth century, Ridolfi described two large Tintoretto paintings of the *Nativity* with life-size figures, in private collections in Paris and Antwerp, and one of these may be connected to the MFA painting. See Carlo Ridolfi, *Le maraviglie dell'arte* [Venice, 1648], ed. Detlev von Hadeln (Berlin: Grote'sche Verlagsbuchhandlung, 1914–24), 2:51; Ridolfi, *Life of Tintoretto*, 57. Benjamin Paul discusses another lost Tintoretto *Nativity*, perhaps a small picture, painted just about the same year for the church of San Benedetto, in "Jacopo Tintoretto and the Church of San Benedetto in Venice," *Mitteilungen des Kunsthistorischen Institutes in Florenz* 49.2005 (2006), 377–412, esp. 377, 382, 400 n. 32.

Tactile Vision: The Female Nude

1. Leon Battista Alberti, *De Pictura*, ed. Cecil Grayson (Rome: Laterza, 1975), 45.

2. Among his *poesie* for Philip II, Titian painted Actaeon's accidental glimpse of the naked Diana (National Gallery of Scotland, Edinburgh, on loan from the Duke of Sutherland); see Wethey, *Paintings of Titian* 3:cat. 9; Filippo Pedrocco, *Titian* (New York: Rizzoli, 2001), cat. 205; and Humfrey, *Titian: The Complete Paintings*, cat. 221. In a later canvas he depicted the wrath of the goddess and the destruction of the hunter by his own hounds (National Gallery, London): see Wethey, *Paintings of Titian* 3:cat. 8; Pedrocco, *Titian*, cat. 213; and Humfrey, *Titian: The Complete Paintings*, cat. 286.

3. Philip Rylands, *Palma Vecchio* (Cambridge: Cambridge University Press, 1992), cat. 85.

4. Jaynie Anderson, *Giorgione: The Painter of "Poetic Brevity"* (Paris: Flammarion, 1997), 217–30, 307–8; Terisio Pignatti and Filippo Pedrocco, *Giorgione* (New York: Rizzoli, 1999), cat. 27. That the painting is in fact entirely by Titian has been argued, most recently, by Paul Joannides in *Titian to 1518: The Assumption of Genius* (New Haven, CT: Yale University Press, 2001), 179–85. Joannides has also denied the identity of the nude as Venus.

5. Wethey, *Paintings of Titian* 3:cat. 54; Pedrocco, *Titian*, cat. 106; Humfrey, *Titian: The Complete Paintings*, cat. 115.

6. Giorgio Vasari, *Le vite de' più eccellenti pittori, scultori, ed architettori* [1568], ed. Gaetano Milanesi (Florence: G. C. Sansoni, 1878–85), 7:443.

7. See David Rosand, "'So-And-So Reclining on Her Couch,'" in *Titian 500*, ed. Joseph Manca, Studies in the History of Art 45 (Washington, DC: National Gallery of Art, 1993), 101–19. The labeling of this nude and others as "mere pin-ups" is owed to Charles Hope, "Problems of Interpretation in Titian's Erotic Paintings," in *Tiziano e Venezia: Convegno internazionale di studi, Venezia, 1976* (Vicenza: Neri Pozza, 1980), 111–24, esp. 119. A fuller discussion of the picture and its interpretive challenge will be found in the contributions to the volume edited by Rona Goffen, *Titian's "Venus of Urbino"* (Cambridge: Cambridge University Press, 1997).

8. Wethey, *Paintings of Titian* 3:cat. 30; Pedrocco, *Titian*, cat. 211; Humfrey, *Titian: The Complete Paintings*, cat. 212.

9. Pliny the Elder, *Natural History* (35.91), trans. K. Jex-Blake, *The Elder Pliny's Chapters on the History of Art*, ed. E. Sellers (London: Macmillan, 1896), 127–29.

10. Pliny the Elder, *Natural History* (35.89), trans. Jex-Blake, *The Elder Pliny's Chapters*, 125.

11. Antonio Persio, *Trattato dell'ingegno dell'huomo* (Venice, 1576), 98. This important passage was first cited by Charles Hope in *Titian* (London: Jupiter Books, 1980), 170.

12. Jean Paul Richter, ed., *The Literary Works of Leonardo da Vinci*, 2nd ed. (London: Oxford University Press, 1939), 2:249, no. 1202.

13. Wethey, *Paintings of Titian* 3:cat. 32; Pedrocco, *Titian*, cat. 212; Humfrey, *Titian: The Complete Paintings*, cat. 229. On the carnal quality of the brushwork in the *Europa*, see David Rosand, "Titian and the Eloquence of the Brush," *Artibus et Historiae* 2, no. 3 (1981): 85–96.

14. Wethey, *Paintings of Titian* 3:cat. 47; Pedrocco, *Titian*, cat. 173; Humfrey, *Titian: The Complete Paintings*, cat. 193.

15. Wethey, *Paintings of Titian* 3:cat. 45; Pedrocco, *Titian*, cat. 215; Humfrey, *Titian: The Complete Paintings*, cat. 238. See also the entry by Keith Christiansen in *Late Titian and the Sensuality of Painting*, ed. Sylvia Ferino-Pagden (Venice: Marsilio, 2008), cat. 2.4.

16. Wethey, *Paintings of Titian* 1:cat. 96; Humfrey, *Titian: The Complete Paintings*, cat. 111.

17. The story of Giorgione confounding the sculptors appears first in Paolo Pino, *Dialogo di pittura* [1548], reprinted in *Trattati d'arte del Cinquecento, fra Manierismo e Controriforma*, ed. Paola Barocchi (Bari: G. Laterza, 1960), 1:131; it was then repeated, with some variation, by Vasari in *Le vite de' più eccellenti* 4:98.

18. Pallucchini and Rossi, *Opere sacre e profane* 1:cat. 155; Echols and Ilchman, "Toward a New Tintoretto Catalogue," cat. 36; Echols in Falomir, *Tintoretto*, cat. 5.

19. For Van Eyck's lost painting, see Julius S. Held, "Artis Pictoriae Amator: An Antwerp Art Patron and His Collection," in *Rubens and His Circle* (Princeton, NJ: Princeton University Press, 1982), 45–51.

20. See David Alan Brown and Sylvia Ferino-Pagden, *Bellini, Giorgione, Titian and the Renaissance of Venetian Painting*, exh. cat. (Washington, DC: National Gallery of Art, 2006), cat. 41.

21. For further discussion of this theme, see Rona Goffen, *Titian's Women* (New Haven, CT: Yale University Press, 1997), 65–86; see also Sylvia Ferino-Pagden, "Pictures of Women—Pictures of Love," in *Bellini, Giorgione, Titian*, ed. Brown and Ferino-Pagden, 189–235.

22. Wethey, *Paintings of Titian* 3:cat. 40; Pedrocco, *Titian*, cat. 180; Humfrey, *Titian: The Complete Paintings*, cat. 191.

23. Ludovico Dolce's letter in praise of Titian's *Venus and Adonis* is reprinted, with translation, in Mark W. Roskill, *Dolce's "Aretino" and Venetian Art Theory of the Cinquecento* (New York: New York University Press, 1968), 212–17.

24. Celso Fabbro, ed., *Tiziano: Le lettere* (Pieve di Cadore: Magnifica Comunità di Cadore, 1977), 171, no. 135.

25. A seventeenth-century inventory describes the couple as Jupiter and Io, but that fable requires the god to ravish the mortal in the form of a great cloud. The modern identification of the nude as Venus makes no more sense mythologically.

26. See Rosand, "'So-And-So Reclining on Her Couch,'" 101–19, with further bibliography on the subject.

27. This dimension of such imagery was first explored by Rona Goffen in "Renaissance Dreams," *Renaissance Quarterly* 40 (1987): 683–706, and *Titian's Women*, 146–59 ("Epithalamium and the Goddess").

28. For the literary sources of this myth and the full painted copy of the original composition, see the entry by Miguel Falomir in Falomir, *Tintoretto*, cat. 40; and, for the fullest discussion of the picture and its subject, Penny, *Sixteenth Century Italian Paintings* 2:154–63. See also Pallucchini and Rossi, *Opere sacre e profane* 1:cat. 390; Echols and Ilchman, "Toward a New Tintoretto Catalogue," cat. 213.

29. Pignatti and Pedrocco, *Veronese* 1:174–228, cat. 123. For the identity of the mythological figures on the vault of the so-called Stanza dell'Amore Coniugale, see Charles Hope, "Veronese and the Venetian Tradition of Allegory," *Proceedings of the British Academy* 71 (1985): esp. 419–20.

30. Although never fully satisfactory, the titles first assigned to the four Allegories of Love in the eighteenth century have by now become traditional; they are surveyed along with more recent interpretive efforts by Penny, *Sixteenth Century Italian Paintings* 2:410–29, esp. 421–24. To that survey should now be added the readings suggested by Augusto Gentili, based on an opposition of honorable and dishonorable love (*amore onesto* and *amore disonesto*); see "Miti e allegorie d'amore," in *Veronese: La pittura profana* (*Arte e Dossier*), ed. Augusto Gentili et al. (Florence: Giunti Editore, 2005), 4–15.

31. On the imperial inventories and the question of patronage, see Xavier F. Salomon, *Veronese's Allegories: Virtue, Love, and Exploration in Renaissance Venice*, exh. cat. (New York: Frick Collection, 2006).

32. Still an invaluable guide to this development is Jean Seznec's *The Survival of the Pagan Gods: The Mythological Tradition and Its Place in Renaissance Humanism and Art* (New York: Pantheon Books, 1953); see also Don Cameron Allen, *Mysteriously Meant: The Rediscovery of Pagan Symbolism and Allegorical Interpretation in the Renaissance* (Baltimore: Johns Hopkins University Press, 1970).

33. The fullest discussion of this picture remains that of Erwin Panofsky, "Blind Cupid," in *Studies in Iconology: Humanistic Themes in the Art of the Renaissance* (1939; repr., New York and Evanston: Harper Torchbooks, 1962), 95–106, and again in *Studies in Titian, Mostly Iconographic* (New York: New York University Press, 1969), 129–37. For the painting itself, see, most recently, Miguel Falomir, ed., *Tiziano*, exh. cat. (Madrid: Museo Nacional del Prado, 2003), cat. 49, and the entry by Stefan Albl in *Late Titian*, ed. Ferino-Pagden, cat. 2.3.

Portraiture

1. The epigraph to this essay is taken from Giorgio Vasari, *Le vite de' più eccellenti pittori, scultori ed architettori* [1568], ed. Gaetano Milanesi (Florence: G. C. Sansoni, 1878–85), 3:168–69, translated by Lorne Campbell in *Renaissance Portraits: European Portrait-Painting in the 14th, 15th and 16th Centuries* (New Haven, CT: Yale University Press, 1990), 193–94.

2. When Gentile was sent to work for Sultan Mehmet II in Constantinople in 1479, the Maggior Consiglio assigned Giovanni to continue the decoration of the meeting, and he would be rewarded with the next vacant *senseria* as a salary. For the document of August 29, 1479, see Patricia Fortini Brown, *Venetian Narrative Painting in the Age of Carpaccio* (New Haven, CT: Yale University Press, 1988), 278.

3. An insightful summary of the development of male portraiture in the early Cinquecento is found in David Alan Brown's "Portraits of Men," in *Bellini, Giorgione, Titian and the Renaissance of Venetian Painting*, ed. David Alan Brown and Sylvia Ferino-Pagden, exh. cat. (Washington, DC: National Gallery of Art, 2006), 237–45. Good recent summaries of Titian's portraiture have been written by Jennifer Fletcher, "Titian as a Painter of Portraits," in Jaffé, *Titian*, 31–42, and "'La vraie ressemblance': Les portraits de Titien," in *Titien: Le pouvoir en face*, ed. Giovanna Rocchi (Paris: Skira, 2006), 35–50. W. R. Rearick contributed two useful reconsiderations of the development of Venetian portraiture in the sixteenth century (focusing on the role of Tintoretto) in a catalogue entry in *Italian Paintings, XIV–XVIIIth Centuries, from the Collection of the Baltimore Museum of Art*, ed. Gertrude Rosenthal (Baltimore: Baltimore Museum of Art, 1981), 129–47, and a review of the 1994 Venice Tintoretto portraits exhibition, "Reflections on Tintoretto as a Portraitist," *Artibus et Historiae* 31 (1995): 51–68.

4. Sylvia Ferino-Pagden surveys these two overlapping categories in her essay and catalogue entries "Pictures of Women—Pictures of Love," in *Bellini, Giorgione, Titian*, ed. Brown and Ferino-Pagden, 189–235.

5. On the subject of parapets and funereal symbolism, see David Rosand, "The Portrait, the Courtier, and Death," in *Castiglione: The Ideal and the Real in Renaissance Culture*, ed. Robert W. Hanning and David Rosand (New Haven, CT: Yale University Press, 1983), 91–129.

6. This count remains highly speculative, given the unpredictable rate of survival. Luba Freedman proposes 204 portraits by Titian if no-longer surviving works and recorded commissions are included; see Luba Freedman, *Titian's Portraits through Aretino's Lens* (University Park, PA: Penn State University Press, 1995), 12.

7. Miguel Falomir, "Tintoretto's Portraiture," in Falomir, *Tintoretto*, 110.

8. Tintoretto's independent portrait of Vincenzo Morosini (National Gallery, London, NG 4004) seems to have served both as the model for subsequent (workshop) portraits of the sitter and as a starting point for further (nonportrait) commissions from the client, including an altarpiece in San Giorgio Maggiore. See Tracy E. Cooper, *Palladio's Venice: Architecture and Society in a Renaissance Republic* (New Haven, CT: Yale University Press, 2005), 126; and Penny, *Sixteenth Century Italian Paintings* 2:176–85.

9. Carlo Ridolfi, *Le maraviglie dell'arte* [Venice, 1648], ed. Detlev von Hadeln (Berlin: Grote'sche Verlagsbuchhandlung, 1914–24), 2:69. According to Raffaello Borghini (*Il riposo* [Florence, 1584], 558), Tintoretto received 100 crowns from the king, who made a gift of the portrait to Doge Mocenigo. The portrait is now lost. See the analysis of this incident by Falomir ("Tintoretto's Portraiture," 103), who notes that Ridolfi wanted to make an analogy to Titian's meeting Charles V in 1533, and how Tintoretto in fact seems to have profited from this opening by selling paintings to a member of the French royal entourage.

10. See the catalogue raisonné in John Garton's *Grace and Grandeur: The Portraiture of Paolo Veronese* (London: Brepols Publishers, 2008), 183–242. This count includes only independent portraits and therefore does not include the portraits in Villa Maser, donor portraits, or the family members in the Cuccina votive painting, Gemäldegalerie, Dresden.

11. Veronese's portrait of Titian was recorded in the inventory of Alessandro Vittoria's estate in 1608; see Victoria J. Avery, "Documenti sulla vita e opere di Alessandro Vittoria (c. 1525–1608)," *Studi trentini di scienze storiche* 78, no. 1 (1999): supplemento, 233. Another portrait of Titian is recorded in the 1682 inventory of Veronese's heirs: Gregorio Gattinoni, *Inventario di una casa veneziana del secolo XVII (La casa degli Eccellenti Caliari eredi di Paolo il Veronese)* (Mestre: Officine Grafiche, 1914), nos. 26, 61. Neither work survives. Of Veronese's rapport with Titian, we have only the evidence that Titian (together with Sansovino) awarded Veronese a gold chain for the completion of his roundels for the Marciana Library ceiling competition; his entries were judged the best among works completed by such Mannerist-inspired painters as Andrea Schiavone, Del Moro, Zelotti, Battista Franco, and the Tuscan Giuseppe Porta Salviati. The competition is recorded in Ridolfi, *Le maraviglie dell'arte* 2:305–7.

12. The document is Zuan Paolo da Ponte's account book, "Memorial C": March 8, 1534: "S. Tucian de Cadore picttor die dar adi 8 marzo per contadi a lui a bon conto di duj retrati me die far uno quello de Julia mia fia el qual die venir a farlo qui a casa et son rimasto daccordo in ducati 20 di L6 S4 per ducato et li debbo pagar lo azuro oltramarin che anderà nelli pani l'altro retrato e el mio che lo die far a casa sua delo qual li debbo dar ducati 10 da L6 S4 che son in tutto ducati 30." The price of the ultramarine pigment is specified on October 3, 1534: "disse have speso per azuro per el retratto de Julia mia fia ducati 5." The full documentation is transcribed in *Tiziano ritrovato: Il ritratto di messer Zuan Paulo da Ponte* (Venice: Antichità Pietro Scarpa, 1998). See also Michelangelo Muraro, "Il memoriale di Zuan Paolo da Ponte," *Nuovo archivio Veneto* (1949): 77–88. Both portraits are mentioned by Vasari (*Le vite de' più eccellenti* 7:454–55), and Titian's portrait of Zuan Paolo is now in a private collection in Venice.

13. Paolo Pino, *Dialogo di pittura* [1548], reprinted in *Trattati d'arte del Cinquecento, fra Manierismo e Controriforma*, ed. Paolo Barocchi (Bari: G. Laterza, 1960), 1:137. The original Italian reads, "acquista un nome di troppo tedioso."

14. Cited in Fletcher, "Titian as a Painter of Portraits," 31.

15. Freedman, *Titian's Portraits*, 98.

16. On Sidney's now-lost portrait, see Garton, *Grace and Grandeur*, 148; and Michelangelo Muraro, "Un celebre ritratto: Sir Philip Sidney a Venezia nel 1574 scegli Veronese per farsi ritrarre," in *Nuovi studi su Paolo Veronese*, ed. Massimo Gemin (Venice: Arsenale Editrice, 1990), 391–96.

17. John Buxton, *Sir Philip Sidney and the English Renaissance* (London: Macmillan, 1954), 69–70.

18. Ibid.

19. See, for instance, Berger's 1994 study of the portrait as an index of "what sitter and painter 'have in mind,' an expression of their designs on the observer"; Harry Berger, "Fictions of the Pose: Facing the Gaze in Early Modern Portraiture," *Representations* 46

(Spring 1994): 89. The burgeoning literature on Renaissance portraiture is too copious to list here, but *The Image of the Individual: Portraits in the Renaissance*, ed. Nicholas Mann and Luke Syson (London: British Museum, 1998), is one milestone in approaching portraits as conditional statements that rely on the viewer to complete their meaning.

20. Vasari, *Le vite de' più eccellenti* 4:462–63.

21. Baldassare Castiglione, *The Book of the Courtier*, trans. George Bull (New York: Penguin, 1978), 135.

22. Charles Hope, *Titian* (London: Jupiter Books, 1980), 62–64.

23. Falomir (*Tintoretto*, 218) has identified the material of the lining as lynx. On the inclusion of lynx in other sixteenth-century portraits, see Penny, *Sixteenth Century Italian Paintings* 1:178.

24. By 1526 Tommaso Mosti held an ecclesiastical office, and he likely would have wanted to celebrate by wearing the appropriate vestments. For a review of scholars who have questioned the inscription, see Enrico Maria Dal Pozzolo's catalogue entry in *Renaissance Venice and the North: Crosscurrents in the Time of Bellini, Dürer, and Titian*, ed. Bernard Aikema and Beverly Louise Brown, exh. cat. (New York: Rizzoli, 1999), 378; and Serena Padovani's catalogue entry in *Titian: Prince of Painters*, ed. Susanna Biadene and Mary Yakush, exh. cat. (Venice: Marsilio, 1990), 187.

25. Dal Pozzolo, in *Renaissance Venice*, 378.

26. Though Paola Rossi noted in 1974 that this portrait is one of the youthful period's highest achievements, "uno dei più alti raggiungimenti del periodo giovanile," it had been overlooked in several exhibitions until the 2007 Museo Nacional del Prado show. See Paola Rossi, *Jacopo Tintoretto*, vol. 1, *I ritratti* (Venice: Alfieri, 1974), 28; and Falomir, *Tintoretto*, 218, cat. 8.

27. For an illustration of the print from Cock's *Praecipua aliquot romanae antiqutiatis ruinarium monumenta* (1551), see Garton, *Grace and Grandeur*, 144.

28. For Tintoretto's place in the field of Venetian portraiture, with special attention to his early career, see Rearick, "Reflections on Tintoretto as a Portraitist," 51–68.

29. Falomir, *Tintoretto*, 218.

30. Translated in ibid., 104.

31. Garton, *Grace and Grandeur*, 54, 161, 169, 187, 197, 207.

32. One wonders if Tintoretto's 1548 *Portrait of a Gentleman Aged Twenty-Eight* (Staatsgalerie, Stuttgart) was known to Veronese, since a similar pose, curtain pulled aside, and leafy landscape appear in that picture. For the Stuttgart portrait, see Falomir, *Tintoretto*, 226–27, cat. 10.

33. As Shearman has noted, many classical sources, including the *Greek Anthology*, speak of ivy covering tombs, including Propertius's vivid elegy in which his dead Cynthia begs him to restrain "the ivy from my tomb, that with aggressive cluster and twining leaves binds my frail bones." See John Shearman, *Only Connect . . . : Art and the Spectator in the Italian Renaissance* (Princeton, NJ: Princeton University Press, 1992), 15–16.

34. Raffaello Borghini, *Il riposo* (Florence, 1584), translated in Falomir, *Tintoretto*, 112.

35. For example, see Rearick, "Reflections on Tintoretto as a Portraitist," 3; and Falomir, "Tintoretto's Portraiture," 96–98.

36. Falomir, "Tintoretto's Portraiture," 95–96.

37. For a recent account, see Brown, "Portraits of Men," 238–45, and the catalogue entries that follow.

38. For example, this effect is present in Sebastiano's altarpiece for San Giovanni Crisostomo and Giorgione's Castelfranco altarpiece. Bellini's late religious paintings, such as the San Zaccaria altarpiece (1505) and particularly that for San Giovanni Crisostomo (1513), set the figures within a heavy atmosphere. Only in Bellini's later portraits, such as his latest surviving portrait, the *Portrait of a Young Man* in the Royal Collection (about 1505), does some sense of golden light and palpable atmosphere appear. On this portrait, see Lucy Whitaker in Lucy Whitaker and Martin Clayton, *The Art of Italy in the Royal Collection: Renaissance and Baroque*, exh. cat. (London: Royal Collection Publications, 2007), cat. 56.

39. The portraits of female sitters include that of Isabella d'Este (Wethey, *Paintings of Titian* 2:cat. 27; Humfrey, *Titian: The Complete Paintings*, cat. 107) and *La Bella* (Wethey, *Paintings of Titian* 2:cat. 14; Humfrey, *Titian: The Complete Paintings*, cat. 112).

40. This ideal of *sprezzatura* was codified in Baldassare Castiglione's *Il Cortegiano* (1528), bk. 1, chap. 27. See the discussion of Castiglione and Titian's portraiture in David Alan Brown, "Man with a Glove," in *Bellini, Giorgione, Titian*, ed. Brown and Ferino-Pagden, cat. 56.

41. See the discussion of its purchase in the appendix "Boston Collects Venetian Paintings" and the provenance narrative in the checklist to this catalogue.

42. The identification of the sitter as Gian Paolo Baglione (d. 1520), based on a later, probably eighteenth-century, inscription on the back of the canvas, was rightly rejected by Edgell as chronologically impossible. Edgell did entertain but ultimately rejected Constable's suggestion that the Boston canvas was one of the lost Titian portraits of Guidobaldo II della Rovere, Duke of Urbino, the patron of the *Venus of Urbino*; a comparison with Bronzino's 1532 portrait of that sitter (Galleria Palatina, Florence) suggests that Edgell was right to dismiss this identification. See G. H. Edgell, "A Recently Acquired Portrait by Titian," *Bulletin of the Museum of Fine Arts* 41 (October 1943): 40–42.

43. Edgell, "A Recently Acquired Portrait."

44. Wethey, *Paintings of Titian* 2:cat. 47. About the same time as Wethey's catalogue, the portrait was published by Fredericksen and Zeri as "studio" (Burton B. Fredericksen and Federico Zeri, *Census of Pre-Nineteenth-Century Italian Paintings in North American Public Collections* [Cambridge, MA: Harvard University Press, 1972], 201) and considered one step below securely autograph in the catalogue by Francesco Valcanover, *L'opera completa di Tiziano* (Milan: Rizzoli, 1969), cat. 250.

45. Paul Joannides has noted that the expression and costume resemble strongly Titian's *Charles V with a Dog* of 1533; thus the scholar proposed dating the Boston painting to that period and speculated that the sitter was employed by the emperor ("Tiziano e il ritratto di corte," *Studi Tizianeschi* 4 [2006]: 184–85, a review of the exhibition "Tiziano e il ritratto di corte da Raffaello ai Carracci" at the Museo di Capodimonte, Naples, March 25–June 4, 2006). Joannides had earlier affirmed the authenticity of the portrait during a visit to the MFA in 2005. In his own review of the Naples exhibition, however, Peter Humfrey maintained that he was "not convince[d]" ("Titian and Portraiture," *The Burlington Magazine* 148, no. 1239 [June 2006]: 442 n. 4). Finally, Miguel Falomir, in a message of November 14, 2005, agreed with Joannides and stated that this is "an original by Titian from the very early 1530s."

46. Jane Bridgeman, communication with the author, June 2008.

47. On aglets, see Penny (*Sixteenth Century Italian Paintings* 1:174), who notes such ornaments decorating the sleeve of the far left young boy in Titian's *Vendramin Family, Venerating a Relic of the True Cross* (fig. 100).

48. For Moretto's *Portrait of Conte Fortunato Martinengo Cesaresco* (National Gallery, London, NG299), see Penny, *Sixteenth Century Italian Paintings* 1:172–81, and Nicola Spinosa, ed., *Tiziano e il ritratto di corte da Raffaello ai Carracci*, exh. cat. (Naples: Museo di Capodimonte, 2006), cat. C50.

49. This conclusion reinforces some earlier determinations, such as that of Richard McLanathan, in "Dipinti veneziani acquistati negli ultimi anni dal Museo di Belli Arti di Boston," *Arte Veneta* 4 (1950): 162, who dated this portrait on the basis of its costume to between 1540–45, and more specifically to 1544–45 based on the similarity to the *Daniele Barbaro* in the Museo Nacional del Prado.

50. "By 1540 portraiture in most of Europe had evolved into a kind of International Style, one in which Titian had played a significant formulative role" (Rearick, "Reflections on Tintoretto as Portraitist," 52). Rearick's review argues for Tintoretto's strong dependence on Titian's example, and he later cited the present portrait within a group Tintoretto executed between about 1540 and 1547, described as a "list of tributes rendered to Titian by Tintoretto the portrait painter" (W. R. Rearick, "I ritratti giovanili di Tintoretto," in *La Pinacoteca di Palazzo Thiene: Collezione della Banca Popolare di Vicenza*, ed. Fernando Rigon [Milan: Skira, 2001], 47). Rearick's claims for Titian's influence on Tintoretto's portraiture are seconded and expanded in Falomir, "Tintoretto's Portraiture," 95–98.

51. Titian's *Portrait of a Young Man*, from about 1515–20 (Halifax Collection; see Wethey, *Paintings of Titian* 2:cat. 115), and a contemporary *Allegory of Youth and Age* by Giovanni Cariani (State Hermitage Museum, St. Petersburg) share the same *all'antica* carved pilaster. See Amanda Bradley in Jaffé, *Titian*, cat. 6, fig. 44. The carvings in the Tintoretto portrait bear some resemblance to those near the Sala dei Giganti in the Palazzo Ducale and the choir in San Giobbe. See Wolfgang Wolters, *Architektur und Ornament: Venezianischer Bauschmuck der Renaissance* (Munich: Verlag C. H. Beck, 2000), figs. 79, 95.

52. On the Stuttgart portrait, see Rossi, *Jacopo Tintoretto* 1:28; Paola Rossi, *Jacopo Tintoretto: Ritratti*, exh. cat. (Milan: Electa, 1994), cat. 6; and Falomir, in Falomir, *Tintoretto*, cat. 10.

53. The Roman emperor Augustus displayed two images of Alexander in the most frequented parts of his forum. Pliny the Elder, *Natural History* (35.94), trans. H. Rackham (Cambridge, MA: Harvard University Press, 1962), 9:331.

54. Suetonius, *Divus Iulius*, 7; a similar account appears in Valerius Maximus's *Facta et dicta memorabilia*, ed. John Briscoe (Stuttgart: B. G. Teubner, 1998), 2:bk. 3, no. 5.1. The dialogue of Ludovico Dolce (Venice, 1557) and the treatises of Giovan Paolo Lomazzo (Milan, 1584) and Romano Alberti (Rome, 1585) retell this account: see Paola Barocchi, ed., *Trattati d'arte del Cinquecento, fra Manierismo e Controriforma* (Bari: G. Laterza, 1960), 1:162 (Dolce); Paola Barocchi, ed., *Scritti d'arte del Cinquecento* (Turin: Einaudi, 1977), 1:374–75 (Lomazzo); Barocchi, *Trattati d'arte del Cinquecento* 3:216–17 (Alberti).

55. For a discussion of Titian's reputation as a new Apelles and Pietro Aretino's sonnet that claimed the superiority of Titian's *Francesco Maria della Rovere* over Apelles' Alexander the Great, see Hilliard Goldfarb, "Titian: *Colore* and *Ingegno* in the Service of Power," in *Titian and Rubens: Power, Politics, and Style*, exh. cat. (Boston: Isabella Stewart Gardner Museum, 1998), 3–19, esp. 3–12; and Freedman, *Titian's Portraits*, 69–90.

56. Britto's print (Adam von Bartsch, *Italian Chiaroscuro Woodcuts [Bartsch Vol. XII]* [University Park, PA: Penn State University Press, 1971], 140, plate 1), which probably simplified and cropped the original, is published in Scott Schaefer, *Titian and the Commander: A Renaissance Artist and His Patron*, brochure (Los Angeles: Getty Publications, 2005). A copy by Rubens probably also records the lost portrait of Charles; see Humfrey, *Titian: The Complete Paintings*, 144, cat. 95.

57. On *Alfonso d'Avalos*, see the well-rounded study by Habert in *Le siècle de Titien*, by Laclotte, Nepi Scirè, et al., 574–76, cat. 166; and Schaefer, *Titian and the Commander*.

58. Wethey, *Paintings of Titian* 2:cat. 10; Humfrey, *Titian: The Complete Paintings*, cat. 127.

59. See Peter Humfrey, *The Age of Titian: Venetian Renaissance Art from Scottish Collections*, exh. cat. (Edinburgh: National Galleries of Scotland, 2004), cat. 35.

60. Two of the copies are illustrated in Humfrey, *Age of Titian*, figs. 115, 116, where he attributes the painting in the Chrysler Museum, Norfolk, to Tintoretto and writes that the portrait in the Koelliker Collection was produced by Titian's workshop. In his entry (cat. 35), Humfrey argues that the Chrysler Museum version appears closer to Tintoretto's style, and therefore "helps to confirm the attribution of the present portrait [in Washington] to Titian." Unfortunately, the captions to the two photographs were reversed, and the conclusions on authorship are debatable. Robert Echols and Frederick Ilchman examined the Chrysler portrait in August 2007 and decided that the handling was closer to Titian and his workshop than Tintoretto. Overall, the fine and even soft rendering of details seems unlike Tintoretto's manner. Certain points in the Chrysler picture appear to be derived from Titian's practice, such as the red cloak seen behind the baton, which is very similar in handling to the upholstery on the chair in Titian's *Pope Paul III* (cat. 7). While the Koelliker portrait has been recently assigned to Tintoretto (Rocchi, *Titien: Le pouvoir en face*, 136–37, cat. 28), apparently reviving Gustav Friedrich Waagen's attribution in 1857, it seems highly unlikely that the mature Tintoretto would produce a straightforward copy of a painting by his rival Titian. There is no surviving example of a Tintoretto copy after a Titian portrait. It seems more logical that the copies would be produced by the same workshop (albeit by different hands within the *bottega*) that created the Washington original.

61. Pietro Aretino, *Lettere sull'arte*, ed. Ettore Camesasca (Milan: Edizioni del Milioni, 1957–60), 1:177–78, no. 109.

62. Those who support the attribution to Titian include: Wilhelm Suida and F. R. Shapley, *Paintings and Sculpture from the Kress Collection: Acquired by the Samuel H. Kress Foundation 1951–1956* (Wasington, DC: National Gallery of Art, 1956), 182–85; F. R. Shapley, *Paintings from the Samuel H. Kress Collection: Italian Schools, XV–XVI Century* (London: Phaidon, 1968), 181–82, Wethey, *Paintings of Titian* 2:83–84; and Humfrey, *Age of Titian*, 2004, 124.

63. Those in favor of Tintoretto's authorship include: Bernard Berenson, *The Venetian Painters of the Renaissance with an Index to Their Works* (New York: G. P. Putnam's Sons, 1894), 136; Bernard Berenson, *The North Italian Painters of the Reniassance* (New York: G. P. Putnam's Sons, 1906), 136; Henry Thode, *Tintoretto* (Bielefeld, Germany: Velhagen and Klasing, 1901), 80; Rodolfo Pallucchini, *Tiziano* (Florence: Sansoni, 1969), 90; W. R. Rearick, in *Venezia da stato a mito*, ed. Alessandro Bettagno, exh. cat. (Venice: Fondazione Giorgio Cini, 1997), 335–36; and Stefania Mason, "Tiziano nelle collezioni scozzesi: Note in margine alla mostra di Edimburgo," *Studi tizianeschi* 3 (2005): 84–88. The Cappello portrait is omitted from two recent Titian monographs: Francesco Valcanover, *Tiziano: I suoi pennelli sempre partorirono espressioni di vita* (Florence: Il Fiorino, 1999); and Filippo Pedrocco, *Titian* (New York: Rizzoli, 2001).

64. Aretino's letter confirms that a portrait by Titian was made around 1540, and that Cappello died in 1541, when Tintoretto was too young and unproven to have painted such an important sitter. Yet, an attribution to Tintoretto can also draw upon documentary support. Rearick introduced archival evidence, a codicil to the 1601 will of Vincenzo's nephew, which lists a family portrait of "Ser Vincenzo che è de J. Tintoretto." For Rearick, the portrait is thus posthumous and can be dated to 1572–75, part of a campaign by his family to rehabilitate his reputation as commander. See Rearick, in *Venezia da stato*, ed. Bettagno, 335.

65. Similar reflections on armor include the aforementioned *Francesco Maria della Rovere* and the J. Paul Getty Museum and Museo Nacional del Prado portraits of Alfonso d'Avalos.

66. When one studies the beard of Tintoretto's *Jacopo Soranzo* (Castello Sforzesco, Milan) or the hand of his *Jacopo Sansovino* (Galleria degli Uffizi, Florence), similarities to the present work are observable. For color illustrations of these works, see Falomir, *Tintoretto*, 249, 319, cats. 15, 35. The Berlin portrait of Morosini is reproduced in Rossi, *Jacopo Tintoretto: Ritratti*, 160–61, cat. 39.

67. Illustrated in Falomir, *Tintoretto*, 253, cat. 16.

68. Borghini, *Il riposo*, translated in Falomir, *Tintoretto*, 112. The original reads: "nel colorire dice ha vere imitation la natura, e poi particolarmente Titiano, in tanto che molti ritratti fatti da lui sono stati tenuti di mano di Titiano"; see Raffaello Borghini, *Il riposo* [Florence, 1584] (Hildesheim: Georg Olms Verlagsbuchhandlung, 1969), 551.

69. On Venier's role, see Pompeo Molmenti, *Sebastiano Veniero e la battaglia di Lepanto* (Florence, 1899).

70. György Gombosi was the first to recognize the sitter as Barbarigo on the basis of comparison with other works, including the Venier votive in Palazzo Ducale; see György Gombosi, "Veronese," *Magyar Muveszet* 4 (1928): 724, 728. For the circumstances of Barbarigo's death, see Girolamo Diedo, *Lettera all'Ill.mo Sig. Marcantonio Barbaro* (Venice, 1588); cited in "Le virtù della repubblica e le gesta dei capitani dipinti votivi, ritratti, pietà," in *Venezia e la difesa del Levante: Da Lepanto a Candia, 1570–1670*, by Stefania Mason Rinaldi (Venice: Arsenale, 1986), 28.

71. Either his features were copied from an earlier portrait or he sat for Veronese before his departure, depending on whether one sees the small painting of the same sitter in Budapest as a *ricordo* (record) of the Cleveland picture or as a preliminary study done from life. The painting is reproduced in color and discussed in Garton, *Grace and Grandeur*, 111, 203.

72. That Veronese's *Agostino Barbarigo* may once have been larger, perhaps even full-length, as Rearick has proposed, is suggested by its odd cropping; the larger dimensions of a copy in Washington, DC; a full-length copy (from the hand of a minor artist) now preserved in the castle of Archduke Ferdinand II of Austria at Ambras; and other full-length portraits by Veronese. See Rearick, *Art of Paolo Veronese*, 108.

73. Ridolfi, *Le maraviglie dell'arte* 2:36; Carlo Ridolfi, *The Life of Tintoretto and of His Children Domenico and Marietta*, trans. Catherine Enggass and Robert Enggass (University Park, PA: Penn State University Press, 1984), 40. For Veronese's votive painting, see Pignatti and Pedrocco, *Veronese* 2:373–74, cat. 261.

74. Tintoretto considered the armor successful enough that he used it again in the Museo Nacional del Prado *Portrait of a Venetian Admiral*, the contours copied exactly; the portrait is illustrated in Falomir, *Tintoretto*, 106, fig. 51.

75. For Titian, see the *Study for Francesco Maria della Rovere* in the Gabinetto Disegni e Stampe degli Uffizi, Florence (no. 29767), reproduced in Goldfarb, *Titian and Rubens*, pl. 5, and in the same collection the *Helmet* (no. 566 Orn.), reproduced in Habert in *Le siècle de Titien*, by Laclotte, Nepi Scirè, et al., 578–79, cat. 230, pl. 230. For Veronese, see the armor study in the Kupferstichkabinett Berlin (kdz 5120), reproduced in Rearick, *Art of Paolo Veronese*, 132, cat. 67.

76. Letter from Augsburg on May 16, 1551, cited in Wethey, *Paintings of Titian* 2:127, cat. 78.

77. See Patricia Fortini Brown, "Children and Education," in *At Home in Renaissance Italy*, ed. Marta Ajmar-Wollheim and Flora Dennis (London: Victoria and Albert Museum, 2006), 143.

78. Lorne Campbell, *Renaissance Portraits*, 178–79, 196–97, 214; Cristina Cortese, "Immagini e ritratti infantili dal XVI al XX secolo," in *La scoperta dell'infanzia: Cura, educazione e rappresentazione; Venezia, 1750–1930* (Venice: Marsilio, 1999), 235–47.

79. For a good survey of children's gender roles and education, see Brown, "Children and Education," 137–43.

80. Caroline Campbell, *Titian* (London: National Gallery, 2003), 136–37, cat. 25.

81. Leon Battista Alberti, *The Family in Renaissance Florence: A Translation of "I libri della famiglia" by Leon Battista Alberti*, trans. R. Neu Watkins (New York: Columbia University Press, 1969), 112–13, cited in Brown, "Children and Education," 136.

82. Robert Echols and Frederick Ilchman (in Falomir, *Tintoretto*, 308) noted that the serving boy at the far left of the San Trovaso *Last Supper* is "perhaps the most tender and distinctive depiction of a child in all of Tintoretto's oeuvre, and unmistakably taken from life." They speculate that this figure could be the painter's daughter Marietta, who as a child was dressed as a boy and accompanied her father, according to Ridolfi.

83. Jaffé, *Titian*, 134, cat. 24.

84. Fletcher, "Titian as a Painter of Portraits," 36.

85. Hope, *Titian*, 116.

86. Caroline Campbell, *Titian*, 136.

87. Ibid.

88. Penny summarizes that Vasari evidently thought full-length independent portraits were a novelty in Italy and claims that Moretto's *Portrait of a Man* (National Gallery, London, NG1025), dated 1526, is the "earliest surviving example in Italy of a life-size, full-length, independent portrait on either canvas or panel." He also notes that the formula of a sitter resting an elbow on a column plinth was later taken up some thirty years later by Veronese. See Penny, *Sixteenth Century Italian Paintings* 1:156.

89. The dating is based on style, as well as the apparent ages of the children, given that Iseppo and Livia married in 1545. See Garton, *Grace and Grandeur*, 26–33. The MFA's exhibition reunites the two paintings for only the second time in at least a hundred years, and possibly longer. The previous occasion was the exhibition at the Victoria and Albert Museum in 2006, "At Home in Renaissance Italy," where the present paintings were cats.
4 and 5.

90. The door frame and part of a column at Livia's right, devices that once gave architectural unity to the portraits, have been all but eliminated. A close examination of the Baltimore canvas for the 1988 exhibition "The Art of Paolo Veronese, 1528–1588" revealed that the work was cut down at least three inches along each side and six along the bottom, where a crude floor pattern was added with subsequent changes to the door frame at right. See Rearick, *Art of Paolo Veronese*, 40.

91. Garton, *Grace and Grandeur*, 27.

92. Ibid., 31.

93. The few youthful sitters in Tintoretto's canvases appear to be in their late teens and already assume the reserve and comportment of young gentlemen. An example of this kind is the *Portrait of a Young Man* in the Metropolitan Museum of Art, New York, illustrated in the exhibition catalogue Rossi, *Jacopo Tintoretto: Ritratti*, 19. In the sphere of votive portraits, only the *Venetian Family Presented to the Madonna of San Lorenzo* (National Gallery of Scotland, Edinburgh) ventures into children's portrayals, and this studio work must date from the 1570s. See Pallucchini and Rossi, *Opere sacre e profane* 1:196, cat. 313, for a dating from 1570–75 and attribution substantially to Tintoretto himself. Echols and Ilchman ("Toward a New Tintoretto Catalogue," cat. S11) consider this a workshop production, with no intervention by Jacopo. The large and dismembered group portrait of the extended family of Jacopo Soranzo (Castello Sforzesco, Milan) is a strangely stiff and formal affair revealing extensive workshop intervention, with only the central figure by Jacopo. See Falomir, *Tintoretto*, 248–50, cat. 15. For the Cuccina family and their patronage, see Blake de Maria, "The Merchants of Venice: A Study in Sixteenth-Century Cittadino Patronage" (PhD diss., Princeton University, 2003), esp. 243–85.

Late Styles

1. Several publications by Rosand stress the important semantic distinction between *colore* and *colorito*, where the latter must be understood as "the *act* of coloring, the manipulation of pigment, the operations of the brush"; see David Rosand, "Titian and the Eloquence of the Brush," *Artibus et Historiae* 2, no. 3 (1981): 86.

2. Paolo Pino, *Dialogo di pittura* [1548], reprinted in *Trattati d'arte del Cinquecento, fra Manierismo e Controriforma*, ed. Paola Barocchi, vol. 1 (Bari: G. Laterza, 1960), 127.

3. The point that the increasing freedom of Titian's brushwork was not simply a stylistic development but represented a strategic choice has been emphasized by Miguel Falomir in *Tiziano*, ed. Falomir, exh. cat. (Madrid: Museo Nacional del Prado, 2003), 392, and Sylvia Ferino-Pagden in *Late Titian and the Sensuality of Painting*, exh. cat. (Venice: Marsilio, 2008), 17. For Titian's comment, see, for example, David Rosand, "La mano di Tiziano," in *Tiziano: Téchnicas y restauraciones*, exh. cat. (Madrid: Museo Nacional del Prado, 1999), 127–28.

4. Ludovico Dolce's letter to Alessandro Contarini is transcribed and translated in Mark W. Roskill's *Dolce's "Aretino" and Venetian Art Theory of the Cinquecento* (New York: New York University Press, 1968), 212–17.

5. Giorgio Vasari, *Lives of the Painters, Sculptors and Architects*, trans. Gaston de Vere (New York: Alfred A. Knopf, 1996), 2:794; except that de Vere translates "condotte di colpi, tirate via di grosso e con macchie" as "with bold strokes, and dashed off with a broad and even coarse sweep of the brush," which loses the sense of *"con macchie,"* literally "with blotches" or "with patches of paint." For the original, see Giorgio Vasari, *Le vite de' più eccellenti pittori, scultori ed architettori* [1568], ed. Gaetano Milanesi (Florence: G. C. Sansoni, 1878–85), 7:452.

6. This conclusion has been advanced by Miguel Falomir in "Tintoretto y Tiziano" (lecture, Congreso Jacopo Tintoretto, Museo Nacional del Prado, Madrid, February 26, 2007) and "Titian vs. Tintoretto" (lecture, Museum of Fine Arts, Boston, May 25, 2007). The former will be published in the volume of Tintoretto conference papers from the Prado: *Jacopo Tintoretto: Actas del congreso internacional / Proceedings of the International Symposium*, Museo Nacional del Prado, Madrid, February 26–27, 2007 (Madrid: Museo Nacional del Prado, forthcoming). It should be emphasized that some of Titian's autograph late altarpieces are very large.

7. Examples of paintings primarily by Titian's studio include the *Last Supper* (El Escorial monastery) and the *Votive Picture of Doge Antonio Grimani* (Palazzo Ducale, Venice), and probably the allegories for the ceiling of the council chamber in the Palazzo Communale in Brescia, for which the patrons subsequently refused to pay in full, suspecting that Titian had not painted them himself; see Wethey, *Paintings of Titian* 3:87–89, 225 (cat. L-1), 251–55. The shop's inner circle included Titian's son Orazio, Orazio's cousin Marco, and several others; see Giorgio Tagliaferro, "In the Workshop of Titian," in *Late Titian*, ed. Ferino-Pagden, 71–77.

8. From Palma Giovane's recollections as recorded by Marco Boschini in 1674; see *Venice: A Documentary History, 1450–1630*, ed. David Chambers and Brian Pullan, with Jennifer Fletcher (Cambridge, MA: Blackwell, 1992), 440–41. Recent technical examination of many of Titian's paintings dating from the mid-1550s to the end of his career has confirmed the accuracy of Palma's description. Among many examples, see "Titian's Late Style as Seen in the Nymph and Shepherd," in Ferino-Pagden, *Late Titian*, 113–23; and Jill Dunkerton, Susan Foister, and Nicholas Penny, *Dürer to Veronese: Sixteenth-Century Paintings in the National Gallery* (London: National Gallery, 1999), 282–86.

9. For a recent discussion of the historiography of the "old-age style" in art, see Philip Sohm, *The Artist Grows Old: The Aging of Art and Artists in Italy, 1500–1800* (New Haven, CT: Yale University Press, 2007), 7–12. The late works of Beethoven have received particular scrutiny, beginning with Theodor Adorno's 1937 essay "Late Style in Beethoven." Adorno sees that these late works possess a "ravaged character [that] does not always bespeak deathly resolve and demonic humor, but is often ultimately mysterious in a way that can be sensed in pieces that have a serene, almost idyllic tone." Adorno saw commonalities in the late works of "significant artists" that were the opposite of ripened fruit; instead, these artist creations can be "furrowed, even ravaged. Devoid of sweetness, bitter and spiny, they do not surrender themselves to mere delectation." See Theodor W. Adorno, *Essays on Music*, ed. Richard Leppert (Berkeley: University of California Press, 2002), 564–68.

10. Sohm, *The Artist Grows Old*, 9. The term "senile sublime," not used by Sohm, is from the literary critic Barbara Herrnstein Smith.

11. Charles Hope first advanced this argument in his *Titian* (London: Jupiter Books, 1980), 161–66, and he most recently made the case in "Titian's Life and Times," in *Tiziano*, ed. Falomir, 306–7. For a summary of recent debate on this issue, see Ferino-Pagden, *Late Titian*, 15–27. Sohm (*The Artist Grows Old*, 91–103) argues that Titian, aware that the public expected to see him painting in an "elderly" way, deliberately exaggerated his old age, manipulating his patrons artistically and financially.

12. Sohm, *The Artist Grows Old*, 93–96. See also Falomir in *Tiziano*, ed. Falomir, cat. 63; and Ferino-Pagden in *Late Titian*, cat. 2.10.

13. "Der späte Tizian und die Sinnlichkeit der Malerei" (Kunsthistorisches Museum, Vienna, October 18, 2007–January 6, 2008) and "L'ultimo Tiziano e la sensualità della pittura" (Gallerie dell'Accademia, Venice, January 16, 2008–April 20, 2008).

14. Joyce Plesters and Lorenzo Lazzarini, "I materiali e la tecnica dei Tintoretto della Scuola di San Rocco," in *Jacopo Tintoretto nel quarto centenario della morte: Atti del convegno internazionale di studi. Venezia, 24–26 Novembre, 1994*, ed. Paola Rossi and Lionello Puppi (Padua: Il Poligrafo, 1996), 275–80. Plesters and Lazzarini note that Tintoretto's minimalist technique in this painting finds a counterpart only in certain late paintings of Rembrandt.

15. Hans Tietze, *Tintoretto* (New York: Phaidon, 1948), 53.

16. On the Tintoretto studio, see generally Pallucchini and Rossi, *Opere sacre e profane* 1:81–82; and the excellent discussion in Hans Tietze and Erika Tietze-Conrat, *The Drawings of the Venetian Painters in the 15th and 16th Centuries* (repr., New York: Hacker Art Books, 1979), 256–97. On issues of attribution relating to the studio, see Echols and Ilchman, "Toward a New Tintoretto Catalogue."

17. The painting is the *Triumph of Doge Nicolò da Ponte*; see Pallucchini and Rossi, *Opere sacre e profane* 1:cat. 401; and Echols and Ilchman, "Toward a New Tintoretto Catalogue," cat. 244. The attempt to sway public opinion is mentioned in Carlo Ridolfi, *Le maraviglie dell'arte ovvero le vite degli illustri pittori veneti e dello stato* (Venice, 1648), 2:47–48; English translation in Carlo Ridolfi, *The Life of Tintoretto and of His Children Domenico and Marietta*, trans. Catherine Enggass and Robert Enggass (University Park, PA: Penn State University Press, 1984), 53.

18. Pallucchini and Rossi, *Opere sacre e profane* 1:cats. A13, 392–99; Echols and Ilchman, "Toward a New Tintoretto Catalogue," cats. 236–43, 280; Falomir, *Tintoretto*, cat. 49.

19. For Veronese's studio, see Hans Tietze and Erika Tietze-Conrat, *The Drawings of the Venetian Painters in the 15th and 16th Centuries* (New York: J. J. Augustin, 1944), 165–66, 191, 352–54; David Rosand, *Veronese and His Studio in North American Collections*, exh. cat. (Birmingham, AL: Birmingham Museum of Art, 1972); Beverly Louise Brown, "Replication and the Art of Veronese," in *Retaining the Original: Multiple Originals, Copies, and Reproductions*, exh. cat. (Washington, DC: National Gallery of Art, 1989), 111–24; Luciana Larcher Crosato, "La Bottega di Paolo Veronese," in *Nuovi studi su Paolo Veronese*, ed. Massimo Gemin (Venice: Arsenale Editrice, 1990), 256–65; and Diana Gisolfi, "Collaboration and Replicas in the Shop of Paolo Veronese and His Heirs," *Artibus et Historiae* 28, no. 55 (2007): 73–86.

20. See Falomir, "Tintoretto and Spain: From El Greco to Velázquez," in Falomir, *Tintoretto*, 159–60.

21. G. P. Bellori, *Le vite de' pittori*, ed. Evelina Borea (Turin: Einaudi, 1976), 32. The translation is from Anna Laura Lepschy, *Tintoretto Observed: A Documentary Survey of Critical Reactions from the 16th to the 20th Century* (Ravenna: Longo Editore, 1983), 58.

22. On the Camerino paintings, see most recently, with bibliography, Jaffé, *Titian*, 101–11; and Falomir, in *Tiziano*, ed. Falomir, cats. 11, 12.

23. On the interpretations of Titian's Venus images, see Rona Goffen, *Titian's Women* (New Haven, CT: Yale University Press, 1997),

107–69; and the various essays assembled in Rona Goffen, ed., *Titian's Venus of Urbino* (New York: Cambridge University Press, 1997).

24. On the foregoing, see especially Thomas Puttfarken, *Titian and Tragic Painting* (New Haven, CT: Yale University Press, 2006), 150–81; Philipp P. Fehl, "The Camerino for Philip II," in *Decorum and Wit: The Poetry of Venetian Painting* (Vienna: IRSA, 1992), 115–29; and David Rosand, "Ut pictor poeta: Meaning in Titian's poesie," *New Literary History* 3 (1972): 527–46.

25. For varying opinions on the status of the Bordeaux picture in relation to the Fitzwilliam, see J. W. Goodison and G. H. Robertson, *Fitzwilliam Museum Cambridge: Catalogue of Paintings*, vol. 2, *Italian Schools* (Cambridge: Syndics of the Fitzwilliam Museum, 1967), 172–75, cat. 914; Wethey, *Paintings of Titian* 3:181, cat. 35; Filippo Pedrocco, *Titian* (New York: Rizzoli, 2001), 297, cats. 259, 260; and the entries of Jean Habert and Sylvia Ferino-Pagden in *Late Titian*, ed. Ferino-Pagden, 496–97, cats. 2.8, 2.9.

26. The standard sources for the Lucretia story are Livy, *Ab urbe condita* 1:58, Ovid, *Fasti* 2:752–852, and Boccaccio, *De Claris Mulieribus*, ch. 46; see Wethey, *Paintings of Titian* 3:180, no. 34. On earlier Lucretia imagery, and Titian's paintings of the suicide, see Goffen, *Titian's Women*, 192–204; and Ferino-Pagden, *Late Titian*, 216. On Marcantonio's *Lucretia*, see David Rosand, "Raphael, Marcantonio, and the Icon of Pathos," *Source* 3 (1984): 34–52.

27. On the witness, see Goffen, *Titian's Women*, 208; and Philipp P. Fehl, "Mourning for Lucretia," in *Decorum and Wit*, 199.

28. Letter of October 26, 1568, in J. A Crowe and G. B. Cavalcaselle, *The Life and Times of Titian*, 2nd ed. (London: J. Murray, 1881), 2:537–38.

29. On the importance of these prints for Titian's design, see Fehl, "Mourning for Lucretia," 202–9; Goffen, *Titian's Women*, 204–6; Ferino-Pagden, *Late Titian*, 496; and Jane Martineau in *The Genius of Venice, 1500–1600*, ed. Jane Martineau and Charles Hope, exh. cat. (London: Royal Academy of Arts, 1983), 229–30, cat. 130.

30. Goffen, *Titian's Women*, 209–12.

31. Jodi Cranston, "Theorising Materiality: Titian's *Flaying of Marsyas*," in *Titian: Materiality, Likeness, Istoria*, ed. Joanna Woods-Marsden (Turnhout, Belgium: Brepols, 2007), 13–14.

32. Reported in Marco Boschini, *La carta del navegar pitoresco* (Venice, 1660), translated in David Rosand, "Titian and the Critical Tradition," in *Titian: His World and His Legacy*, ed. David Rosand (New York: Columbia University Press, 1982), 24.

33. For the Munich picture, see Echols and Ilchman, "Toward a New Tintoretto Catalogue," cat. 36; Robert Echols in Falomir, *Tintoretto*, cat. 5; and Pallucchini and Rossi, *Opere sacre e profane* 1:cat. 155. For a summary of the early dating of the *Lucretia*, see Christopher Lloyd, *Italian Paintings before 1600 in the Art Institute of Chicago: A Catalogue of the Collection* (Princeton, NJ: Princeton University Press, 1993), 244. For the consequent case that Tintoretto is a source for Titian's Fitzwilliam *Lucretia*, see Fehl, "Mourning for Lucretia," 208–9.

34. For prevailing later dating of the Chicago picture and stylistic comparisons, see Pallucchini and Rossi, *Opere sacre e profane* 1:cat. 450 (1585–90); Lloyd, *Italian Paintings*, 244 (1580–90); Falomir, *Tintoretto*, 354, cat. 42 (1578–80); and Echols and Ilchman, "Toward a New Tintoretto Catalogue," cat. 219 (1578–80).

35. On the Cort engraving, see Wethey, *Paintings of Titian* 3:181, pl. 229.

36. Falomir in Falomir, *Tintoretto*, 354, cat. 42.

37. On this aspect of Tintoretto's draftsmanship, see Frederick Ilchman and Edward Saywell, "Michelangelo and Tintoretto: *Disegno* and Drawing," in Falomir, *Tintoretto*, 385–405.

38. E. de Jongh, "Pearls of Virtue and Pearls of Vice," *Simiolus* 8 (1975–76): 88; Falomir, *Tintoretto*, 354, cat. 42.

39. On Veronese's *Lucretia*, see Pignatti and Pedrocco, *Veronese* 2:cat. 353; and Giandomenico Romanelli and Claudio Strinati, *Veronese: Gods, Heroes, and Allegories*, exh. cat. (Milan: Skira, 2004), cat. 39.

40. Ovid, *Metamorphoses* 4:663–764.

41. On Titian's *Andromeda*, see Wethey, *Paintings of Titian* 3:cat. 30; Pedrocco, *Titian*, cat. 211; Puttfarken, *Titian and Tragic Painting*, 166–70; Cecil Gould, "The *Perseus and Andromeda* and Titian's Poesie," *The Burlington Magazine* 105 (1963): 112–17.

42. This is Frederick Ilchman's suggestion.

43. The Rennes Veronese is generally dated to the mid- to late 1570s or early 1580s, based on similarities with the London *Allegories of Love*, such as the rhythmic design and accomplished foreshortening from a low viewpoint. Given Andromeda's monumentality and torsion, W. R. Rearick placed the work later into the 1580s, just ahead of *Venus with a Mirror* (cat. 32). On the late 1576–78 date, see Pignatti and Pedrocco, *Veronese* 2:cat. 256; and Mylène Allano, *La collection des peintures italiennes du musée des Beaux-Arts de Rennes* (Paris: Somogy, 2004), 114–16, no. 43. For a somewhat later date of 1584, see Rearick, *Art of Paolo Veronese*, cat. 86.

44. Louis Réau, *Iconographie de l'art chrétien* (Paris: Presses universitaires de France, 1955), 1:77, 101, 128.

45. Karl Joseph Höltgen, "Clever Dogs and Nimble Spaniels: On the Iconography of Logic, Invention, and Imagination," *Explorations in Renaissance Culture* 24 (1998): 29–30.

46. In Cesare Ripa's *Iconology* (New York: Garland, 1979), the dog is also presented in negative allegories, but never alone; rather, it faces off against another dog in "Civil War" and against a cat in "Opposition."

47. On this subject, see the Venetian example discussed by Beatrice Peria in "Tintoretto e l'*Ultima Cena*," *Venezia Cinquecento* 7, no. 13 (1997): 104 nn. 65–73.

48. The most complete studies of the work (Musée du Louvre, R.F.1994-23) are: Alessandro Ballarin, "L'orto del Bassano (a proposito di alcuni quadri e disegni inediti singolari)," *Arte Veneta* 18 (1964): 55–61, and "Jacopo Bassano: *Ritratto di Levriero*" (1994), in *Jacopo Bassano*, vol. 1, *Scritti 1964–1995* (Citadella, Italy: Bertoncello, 1995), pt. 2, 378–408; and Jean Habert in Musée du Louvre, *Nouvelles acquisitions du département des Peintures, 1991–1995* (Paris: Editions de la Réunion des musées nationaux, 1996), 212–20. Bassano's account book mentions this work, thereby dating it between 1548 and 1550; see Michelangelo Muraro, *Il libro secondo di Francesco e Jacopo dal Ponte* (Bassano, Italy: G. B. Verci, 1992), 43, 70, 71.

49. The date of this second work (Galleria degli Uffizi, inv. 1890 n. 965) has been contested, but most critics now agree on about 1553. Ballarin ("L'orto del Bassano," 67) first suggested a date of about 1555, followed by Magagnato and Avagnina; see Licisco Magagnato in *Genius of Venice*, ed. Martineau and Hope, 148; and Maria Elisa Avagnina in *Jacopo Bassano, c. 1510–1592*, ed. Beverley Louise Brown and Paola Marini, exh. cat. (Fort Worth, TX: Kimbell Art Museum, 1993), cat. 26. In 1973, Ballarin shifted the date to about 1554; see Ballarin, "Introduzione ad un catalogo dei disegni di Jacopo Bassano III," in *Jacopo Bassano* 1:208–9. For Rearick, the painting should be dated about 1553; see Vittore Branca and Carlo Ossola, eds., *Cultura e società nel Rinascimento tra riforme e manierismi* (Florence: L. S. Olschki, 1984), 304 n. 20. Reexamining *Lazarus and the Rich Man* at the Cleveland Museum of Art, Ballarin also suggested a date of 1553; see Ballarin, "Jacopo Bassano: *Ritratto di Levriero*," 394–97. A later date, late 1550s– early 1560s, is proposed in the Uffizi's catalogues; see, for instance, Gloria Chiarini, *Tiziano nelle Gallerie fiorentine* (Florence: Centro Di, 1978), 174. In addition to the portrait of a greyhound published by Ballarin ("Jacopo Bassano: *Ritratto di Levriero*," 397–405), there might have been other paintings of dogs by Bassano; see Linda Borean, "Collezione Nani di Cannaregio," in *Il collezionismo d'arte a Venezia: Il Seicento*, ed. Linda Borean and Stefania Mason (Venice: Marsilio, 2007), 292.

50. Opinions are divided as to who—Bassano or Tintoretto—truly invented the motif of the dog at rest. The answer obviously depends on the date of the *Two Dogs* and the *Washing of the Feet*. The publication of Bassano's second account book allows us to situate definitively the creation of the Musée du Louvre canvas between 1548 and 1550. The San Marcuola *Washing of the Feet*, on the other hand, has generally been dated about 1547 because that date figures on its pendant, *The Last Supper* (Prado), suggesting that Tintoretto's work came first. Ballarin ("L'orto del Bassano," 72 n. 2) was the first to note the similarity between the two animals and to see it as an indication of Tintoretto's influence on Bassano. Rearick (Branca and Ossola, *Cultura e società*, 303, 304 n. 21; W. R. Rearick, "The Life and Works of Jacopo dal Ponte, Called Bassano, c. 1510–1592," in *Jacopo Bassano, c. 1510–1592*, ed. Brown and Marini, 85 n. 125) sees it the other way around, noting that Tintoretto's dog was ill adapted to the flat surface of the floor and that no other canvas of his from that period features such a precise depiction of an animal. Bernard Aikema takes the same position in *Jacopo Bassano and His Public: Moralizing Pictures in an Age of Reform, ca. 1535–1600* (Princeton, NJ: Princeton University Press, 1996), 183 n. 159. In 1994, Ballarin (*Jacopo Bassano* 1:392–93) reaffirmed his position by claiming that Tintoretto's dog was "a good point of departure" for a "study from nature [by Bassano] and an opportunity to show his young colleague that he could best him on his own terrain." Rossi also seems to favor this hypothesis; see Paola Rossi, "I Bassano e i Tintoretto: Due generazioni a confronto," *Venezia Arti* 11 (1997): 51–52. But the later dating of the *Washing of the Feet*—in other words, not 1547 but the more recently adopted date of 1548–49—has lent more credence to Rearick's position, which is also supported by Jean Habert (Musée du Louvre, *Nouvelles acquisitions*, 218–19) and Robert Echols ("*Jacopo nel corso, presso al palio*: Dal soffitto per l'Aretino al *Miracolo dello schiavo*," in *Jacopo Tintoretto nel quarto centenario della morte*, ed. Rossi and Puppi, 80 nn. 34, 35, and Falomir, *Tintoretto*, 39, 229–40).

51. Habert in Musée du Louvre, *Nouvelles acquisitions*, 219; Jean Habert and Catherine Loisel Legrand, *Bassano et ses fils dans les musées français*, exh. cat. (Paris: Réunion des musées nationaux, 1998), 69.

52. Rearick has noted a case of reverse influence between Titian and Bassano: according to him, the dog in Bassano's *Adoration of the Magi* (Marquis of Exeter Collection, Burghley House, Stamford) is taken from the one in Titian's earlier *Venus of Urbino*. The pose of the sleeping dog, however, is too conventional to be considered an obvious borrowing. See W. R. Rearick, "The Burghley House 'Adoration' of Jacopo Bassano," *Arte Veneta* 12 (1957): 198.

53. This information, noted by Michelangelo Muraro, was first published by Carlo Ridolfi. See Muraro, *Il libro secondo di Francesco e Jacopo dal Ponte*, 43 n. 113; and Carlo Ridolfi, "Vita di Iacopo da Ponte da Bassano. Pittore," in *Le maraviglie dell'arte* 1:379.

54. The dating of the work oscillates between 1575 and 1583.

55. Charles Hope in *Genius of Venice*, ed. Martineau and Hope, 228.

56. This information is given in the first publications of the work, but does not seem to be supported by any documentation; nor has any contemporary information been found about the work. Wethey (*Paintings of Titian* 3:129) was the first to conjecture that the painting was commissioned by Gabriele Serbelloni (1509–1580).

57. Hans Tietze, *Titian* (London: Phaidon, 1950), 393; Francesco Valcanover, *L'opera completa di Tiziano* (Milan: Rizzoli, 1969), 135 n. 500; Erwin Panofsky, *Problems in Titian, Mostly Iconographic: The Wrightsman Lectures Delivered under the Auspices of the New York University, Institute of Fine Arts* (New York: New York University Press, 1969), 171 n. 85; Wethey, *Paintings of Titian* 3:90–91, 129–130; Aikema, *Jacopo Bassano and His Public*, 183 n. 152; Augusto Gentili, "Ancora sul non finito di Tiziano, materia e linguaggio," in *Tiziano: Téchnicas y restauraciones*, 171–79.

58. Hans Ost, *Tizians Kasseler Kavalier: Ein Beitrag zum höfischen Porträt unter Karl V* (Cologne: Copy-Star, 1982), 49–66; Charles Hope in *Genius of Venice*, ed. Martineau and Hope, 228; *Van Titiaan tot Tiepolo: Italiaanse schilderkenst in Nederlands bezit*, exh. cat. (Rotterdam: Nilsson & Lamm, 1989), 39; Susanna Biadene and Mary Yakush, eds. *Titian: Prince of Painters*, exh. cat. (Venice: Marsilio, 1990), 358; Ferino-Pagden, *Late Titian*, 227.

59. The anecdote changes depending on the critic: a prince saved by dogs (D. Hannema, *Chefs d'oeuvre de la collection D. G. van Beuningen*, exh. cat. [Paris: Musée du Petit Palais, 1952], no. 32; Francesco Valcanover in *Le siècle de Titien: L'âge d'or de la peinture á Venise*, by Michel Laclotte, Giovanna Nepi Scirè, et al., exh. cat. [Paris: Réunion des musées nationaux, 1993]) or dogs saved by the prince (Biadene and Yakush, *Titian*; Pedrocco, *Titian*).

60. Tietze, *Titien*, 393; Ost, *Tizians Kasseler Kavalier*, 49; Valcanover in *Le siècle de Titien*, by Laclotte, Nepi Scirè, et al., 678.

61. Tietze, *Titien*, 393.

62. Panofsky, *Problems in Titian*, 171 n. 85.

63. However, some slight differences have been noted in the rendering of the tail.

64. Rodolfo Pallucchini, *Tiziano*, 2 vols. (Florence: GC Sansoni Editore, 1969), 1:195–96.

65. Ost, *Tizians Kasseler Kavalier*, 49–66.

66. Hans Ost, *Tizian-Studien* (Cologne: Böhlau, 1992), 62–65.

67. Charles Hope in *Genius of Venice*, ed. Martineau and Hope, 228; Biadene and Yakush, *Titian*, 358; Valcanover in *Le siècle de Titien*, by Laclotte, Nepi Scirè, et al., 678; Valeska von Rosen, *Mimesis und selbstbezüglichkeit in Werken Tizians* (Emsdetten, Germany: Edition Imorde, 2001), 370–71.

68. Mary D. Garrard, "'Art More Powerful than Nature'? Titian's Motto Reconsidered," in *The Cambridge Companion to Titian*, ed. Patricia Meilman (New York: Cambridge University Press, 2004), 251–52.

69. Unlike Titian's *Boy with Two Dogs*, the Munich canvas has not been trimmed. See Cornelia Syre, *Alte Pinakothek: Italienische Malerei* (Munich: Hatje Cantz, 2007), 278.

70. Panofsky, *Problems in Titian*, 171 n. 85.

71. Rolf Kultzen and Peter Eikemeier, *Venezianische Gemälde des 15. und 16. Jahrhunderts* (Munich: Bayerische Staatsgemäldesammlungen, 1971), 219–21.

72. Rearick, *Art of Paolo Veronese*, 135–36.

73. Attilia Scarlini in *Veronese e Verona*, ed. Sergio Marinelli, exh. cat. (Verona: Museo di Castelvecchio, 1988), 250–51. The emblematic character was also noted by Wethey (*Paintings of Titian* 3:129) and Ferino-Pagden (*L'ultimo Tiziano*, 228).

74. Peter Humfrey, *The Altarpiece in Renaissance Venice* (New Haven, CT: Yale University Press, 1993), 65. Humfrey offers useful tabulations of "Dedications of Altars in Venetian Churches, 1581" (table 2, p. 64), where Jerome is the third most popular saint listed, after the Virgin Mary and Saint John the Baptist, and "Saints most commonly represented in altarpieces for Venetian churches, 1450–1530," (p. 65), where Jerome is the second most popular saint after the Baptist. In each case, Jerome appears more often than any Evangelist, even Mark. Jerome had close personal associations with the shores of the Adriatic; he was born in Dalmatia; he visited sites on what was to become the Venetian *terraferma*, such as Aquileia and Altino, and engaged in correspondence with many local ecclesiastics. See S. Tramontin, A. Niero, G. Musolino, and C. Candiani, *Culto dei santi a Venezia* (Venice: Edizioni Studium Cattolico Veneziano, 1965), 144.

75. Prominent examples include paintings by Giovanni Bellini, Cima da Conegliano, Lorenzo Lotto, and Paris Bordone. For illustrations, and on the general development of the theme, see Adolfo Venturi, *L'arte a san Girolamo* (Milan: Fratelli Treves, 1924); Herbert Friedmann, *A Bestiary for Saint Jerome: Animal Symbolism in European Religious Art* (Washington, DC: Smithsonian Institution Press, 1980); Eugene F. Rice, Jr., *Saint Jerome in the Renaissance* (Baltimore: Johns Hopkins University Press, 1985); and Daniel Russo, *Saint Jérôme en Italie: Etude d'iconographie et de spiritualité XIIIe–VXe siècle* (Paris: Découverte, 1987).

76. In *The Golden Legend*, Jerome is described as "dipped in blood through his contemplation of the Passion of Our Lord"; see *The Golden Legend of Jacobus de Voragine*, trans. Granger Ryan and Helmut Ripperger (1941; repr., New York: Arno Press, 1969), 588–89. The image of the penitent Jerome is based on the description of the saint's four-year sojourn in the Syrian desert, written by Jerome himself in a letter quoted in *The Golden Legend* and other devotional texts. Jerome describes how, tormented by carnal fantasies, he beat his breast until he retained peace of spirit. The mortification of the flesh that Jerome described principally in terms of purifying himself of sexual desires was interpreted in later texts as a means of participating in Christ's suffering. Thus he is shown beating his breast as he contemplates a crucifix.

77. The discovery and forthcoming publication of the documents establishing the dates will appear in the journal *Venezia Cinquecento*. This was announced by Valentina Sapienza in her catalogue entry on the Museo Thyssen-Bornemisza *Saint Jerome* in Sylvia Ferino-Pagden, ed., *Der späte Tizian und die Sinnlichkeit der Malerei*, exh. cat. (Vienna: Kunshistorisches Museum, 2007), 347, cat. 3.20.

78. The depiction of the wilderness in which Jerome exiled himself changed along with the approach to landscape in Venetian painting. The snakes, scorpions, plants, and animals with particular symbolic associations that appear in earlier representations tended to disappear by the early Cinquecento, as the quality of Jerome's exile began to be conveyed increasingly by the mood of the landscape itself—variously bleak and harsh, austere but almost idyllic, or wild and mysterious. On this development in the paintings of Cima da Conegliano, see Robert Echols, "Cima da Conegliano and the Theme of Saint Jerome in the Wilderness," *Venezia Cinquecento* 4, no. 8 (1994): 47–69. Augusto Gentili ("Titian's Prudent Dissent: Painting Religion in the Disciplinary Years," in *Der späte Tizian*, ed. Ferino-Pagden, 503–4) relates the shift to a more dramatic landscape over the course of the Cinquecento to the increasing spiritual tension of the times; Gentili describes meditation on the meaning of religious experience as having become, by mid-Cinquecento, "a frightening storm of emotions, an extreme confrontation with himself and with a hostile nature."

79. The drawing is in the Museo della Fondazione Horne, Florence; see Falomir, *Tintoretto*, fig. 172. See also Pallucchini and Rossi, *Opere sacre e profane* 1:cat. 320; Echols and Ilchman, "Toward a New Tintoretto Catalogue," cat. 151. As noted by Sylvia Ferino-Pagden and Robert Wald in their catalogue entry on Tintoretto's *Saint Jerome* in Falomir, *Tintoretto*, 330, infrared examination of the painting reveals grid lines on the same scale as those in the drawing. Thanks to a tracing on acetate provided by Robert Wald, Frederick Ilchman has been able to determine that the figure of Jerome varies somewhat from the *Philosopher* in the Biblioteca Nazionale Marciana, Venice; the latter is much more massive overall, some 20 percent larger in the legs and approximately 40 percent in the chest and shoulders. This confirms that the figure of Jerome was painted freehand from the drawing, without the use of a tracing from the Marciana figure.

80. Ferino-Pagden, *Der späte Tizian*, cat. 3.20; Susanna Biadene and Mary Yakush, eds., *Titian: Prince of Painters*, exh. cat. (Venice: Marsilio, 1990), cat. 68; Wethey, *Paintings of Titian* 1:135–36, cat. 107. The Bible also appears in a similar position in the El Escorial version.

81. Most recently by Gentili in Ferino-Pagden, *Der späte Tizian*, 503–4. Wethey (*Paintings of Titian* 1:135–36) pointed out the similarity of the Museo Thyssen-Bornemisza *Jerome* to Titian's late self-portraits. For Saint Jerome in the *Pietà* as a self-portrait, see most recently Giovanna Nepi Scirè in *Der späte Tizian*, ed. Ferino-Pagden, 528.

82. Anton Maria Zanetti, *Della pittura veneziana* [1771] (Venice: Filippi, 1972), 190.

83. Bernard Aikema, "L'immagine devozionale nell'opera di Paolo Veronese," in *Nuovi studi su Paolo Veronese*, ed. Gemin, 198–99. Aikema links the imagery to passages in Lorenzo Scupoli's devotional manual *Combattimento spirituale*, published in 1589 and dedicated to the abbess of Sant'Andrea della Zirada, arguing that, although published after the painting, the text illuminates the devotional practices at the convent at the time Veronese received the commission.

84. With thirty-three appearances, the Baptist was represented more than twice as often in Venetian altarpieces as Saint Mark, Venice's patron saint. A 1581 survey of dedications of Venetian altars shows that John the Baptist was the fourth most popular dedicatee, with thirty-one altars, after the Virgin Mary, the Holy Sacrament, and the Holy Cross. These compilations appear in Humfrey, *Altarpiece in Renaissance Venice*, 65, 64, amid a useful broader discussion of altar dedications and subjects.

85. There are numerous major works spanning the history of Venetian art that emphasize a prominent or even miraculous role for the sea, including the *Last Judgment* mosaic (12th–13th century) at Torcello and Tintoretto's giant canvas of the same subject in the Madonna dell'Orto (about 1560). Some works suggesting divine protection from

water—not to mention the city's improbable physical setting—have been linked with the survival of Venice from the threat of the League of Cambrai, such as the *Sea Storm* painted by Palma Vecchio for the Scuola Grande di San Marco (Philip Sohm, "Palma Vecchio's *Sea Storm*: A Political Allegory," *Revue d'Art Canadienne / Canadian Art Revue* 6, no. 2 [1979–80]: 85–96) or Titian's large woodcut *Submersion of Pharaoh's Army in the Red Sea*, which furthermore casts the Venetians as a Chosen People. On Titian's print, see David Rosand and Michelangelo Muraro, *Titian and the Venetian Woodcut*, exh. cat. (Washington, DC: International Exhibitions Foundation, 1976), cat. 4.

86. For Cima's pioneering altarpiece—one of the "very earliest altar paintings to survive in situ about the high altar of a Venetian church" and its original setting—see Peter Humfrey, "Cima da Conegliano, Sebastiano Mariani, and Alvise Vivarini at the East End of S. Giovanni in Bragora in Venice," *Art Bulletin* 62, no. 3 (Sept. 1980): 350–63, and *Altarpiece in Renaissance Venice*, 225–29, cat. 43. For Bellini's painting, see Rona Goffen, *Giovanni Bellini* (New Haven, CT: Yale University Press, 1989), 163–71; Humfrey, *Altarpiece in Renaissance Venice*, 248, cat. 55; and Anchise Tempestini, *Giovanni Bellini* (New York: Abbeville, 1999), 160–61.

87. For example, the horizontal-format *Baptism of Christ* in the North Carolina Museum of Art, Raleigh, probably dating from the 1550s; see Rearick, *Art of Paolo Veronese*, cat. 39; Pignatti and Pedrocco, *Veronese* 1:cat. 14; and David Steel, "The Baptism of Christ," in *A Gift to America: Masterpieces of European Painting from the Samuel H. Kress Collection*, by Chiyo Ishikawa et al. (New York: Harry N. Abrams, 1994), cat. 4. For Veronese's treatments of the theme in general, see George R. Goldner, "A *Baptism of Christ* by Veronese in the Getty Museum," *The J. Paul Getty Museum Journal* 9 (1981): 111–26. Twelve of the thirteen depictions of the Baptism by Veronese and his workshop illustrated by Goldner maintain Christ on or fairly close to the central axis. See also Giuseppe M. Pilo, "Paolo Veronese e il Tema del Battesimo di Gesù Cristo," in *Nuovi studi su Paolo Veronese*, ed. Gemin, 400–411.

88. Frederick Ilchman, "Tintoretto as a Painter of Religious Narrative," in Falomir, *Tintoretto*, 63–94.

89. On Tintoretto's *Baptism of Christ* in the Scuola Grande di San Rocco, see Pallucchini and Rossi, *Opere sacre e profane* 1:cat. 348; and Echols and Ilchman, "Toward a New Tintoretto Catalogue," cat. 226. For an analysis of this painting within an investigation of Tintoretto's unconventional compositions, see Ilchman, "Tintoretto as a Painter of Religious Narrative," 77–79.

90. The variety of brushwork and finish in this painting may have expressed a theological point; see Ilchman, "Tintoretto as a Painter of Religious Narrative," 78–79.

91. A summary of the treatment can be found in Frederick Ilchman, "Two Altarpieces of John the Baptist by Jacopo Tintoretto," *Studies in Venetian Art and Conservation*, 2004, 24–29.

92. Silvio Tramontin, "La visita apostolica del 1581 a Venezia," *Studi Veneziani* 9 (1967): 503; Peter Humfrey and Richard MacKenney, "The Venetian Trade Guilds as Patrons of Art in the Renaissance," *The Burlington Magazine* 128, no. 998 (May 1986): 317–30, esp. 329.

93. On Vasari's criticism of Tintoretto's approach to *disegno* and his drawings, see Ilchman and Saywell, "Michelangelo and Tintoretto," 390. The two sheets—one for the figure of Christ and one for the Baptist—are in the Gabinetto Disegni e Stampe degli Uffizi, Florence (nos. 12961 F and 12943 F). See Paola Rossi, *I disegni di Jacopo Tintoretto* (Florence: La Nuova Italia, 1975), 28, 24.

94. For the role of the human figure in Tintoretto's art, see Robert Echols, "Tintoretto the Painter," in Falomir, *Tintoretto*, 25–62, esp. 28–29; Tietze's quotation is on p. 29.

95. The vibrating contours of Christ's figures are also bathed in light, and may be a late Renaissance version of the *mandorla* (Italian for "almond"), the almond-shaped frame surrounding Christ in medieval and early Renaissance depictions of the Ascension.

96. On these paired contrasts of lighting in the San Silvestro *Baptism* and other Tintoretto paintings, see Ilchman, "Tintoretto as a Painter of Religious Narrative," 69.

97. That Tintoretto devoted so much attention and his own brushwork to an apparently minor client offers a marked contrast with the business practices of Titian, who was motivated primarily by the prestige of the patron (and the fee to be paid). See Miguel Falomir, "The Final Years: 1575–1594," in Falomir, *Tintoretto*, 342–43, and "Titian's Replicas," in *Tiziano*, ed. Falomir, 326–32.

98. Goldner, "A *Baptism of Christ*," 111. This article also notes and illustrates the modern additions on all four sides of the canvas, removed during the conservation treatment by Mark Leonard in 1987–88. See Penny, *Sixteenth Century Italian Paintings* 2:147, for a discussion of the size of Tintoretto's *Saint George and the Dragon* (National Gallery, London) in relation to other small altarpieces. At 158.3 cm (62 ⅜ in.) tall, the Tintoretto is more than 50 cm (19 ⅝ in.) taller than the Getty Veronese.

99. Peter Humfrey in *The Age of Titian: Venetian Renaissance Art from Scottish Collections*, ed. Peter Humfrey, exh. cat. (Edinburgh: National Galleries of Scotland, 2004), cat. 70. Humfrey's entry, as well as Victoria Reed's summary in the checklist to this volume, has clarified the complicated provenance of the Getty picture, in marked contrast to the Tintoretto that still belongs to its original church.

100. Richard Cocke assigned it "entirely to the workshop," insisting that this judgment would meet "a measure of agreement amongst Veronese scholars." See Cocke's review of three 1988 Veronese exhibitions in *The Burlington Magazine* 131, no. 1030 (Jan. 1989): 61–64, with the verdict on the *Baptism* on p. 62. Rosand also expressed an uncertainty with the quality of this painting in a review of Pignatti's 1976 catalogue raisonné. *Art Bulletin* 63, no. 1 (March 1981): 163–64, with the specific opinion on p. 164.

101. Rearick (*Art of Paolo Veronese*, cat. 105) proposed the perhaps overly precise date of 1582, while Humfrey (*Age of Titian*, cat. 80) offered "c. 1580–5."

102. The Fogg Art Museum drawing (no. 1924.101), has been reproduced and discussed in Agnes Mongan and Paul Sachs, *Drawings in the Fogg Museum of Art* (Cambridge, MA: Harvard University Press, 1940), 1:cat. 205, 2:figs. 112–13; Richard Cocke, *Veronese's Drawings* (Ithaca, NY: Cornell University Press, 1984), cat. 125; and Rearick, *Art of Paolo Veronese*, cat. 105. The date on the letter is variously read as February 2 (Mongan and Sachs), or February 4 (Cocke and Rearick).

103. Goldner, "A Baptism of Christ," 121–25.

104. For Veronese's *Miracle of Saint Pantaleon* (church of San Pantalon, Venice), see Rearick, *Art of Paolo Veronese*, cat. 103; Adriana Augusti in *Le siècle de Titien*, by Laclotte, Nepi Scirè, et al., cat. 271; and Pignatti and Pedrocco, *Veronese* 2:cat. 403. The features mentioned above that are seen in some of Veronese's last paintings seem to have been inspired by the late works of Titian and Bassano.

105. See Rearick, *Art of Paolo Veronese*, 200, fig. 60.

106. Among Titian's surviving paintings of Passion images, his only generally accepted early treatments are *Christ Carrying the Cross* of about 1510 (Scuola Grande di San Rocco) and the *Noli me tangere* of about 1513 (National Gallery, London; some scholars prefer a date of 1510–11). Titian paints several important treatments around 1520, but only starting in the 1540s are there large numbers of paintings with Passion subjects. Tintoretto paints his first depiction of the *Last Supper* for San Marcuola in 1547 and two versions of the *Washing of the Feet* (Museo Nacional del Prado and Shipley Art Gallery, Gateshead) in subsequent years, but the great production of Passion imagery begins only in the mid-1560s. In the case of Veronese, with the exception of the *Lamentation* of about 1546–48 (Museo del Castelvecchio, Verona), an *Entombment* attributed to him (private collection), and the great Musée du Louvre *Supper at Emmaus* of about 1560, the important surviving paintings on Passion themes date from the 1570s and later.

107. Wethey, *Paintings of Titian* 1:cat. 36; Pedrocco, *Titian*, 2001, cat. 66; Humfrey, *Titian: The Complete Paintings*, cat. 64.

108. Titian's sources for the composition have been identified as Raphael's *Entombment* of 1507 (Galleria Borghese, Rome), as noted by Georg Gronau in 1911, and the sarcophagus depicting the *Death of Meleager* (Pinacoteca Capitolina, Rome), a connection made by Ludwig Curtius in 1938; see Jean Habert's catalogue entry on the Musée du Louvre *Entombment* in *Le siècle de Titien*, by Laclotte, Nepi Scirè, et al., cat. 159.

109. Falomir, *Tiziano*, 399–401, cat. 47.

110. Augusto Gentili, "Tiziano e la religione," in *Titian 500*, ed. Joseph Manca, Studies in the History of Art 45 (Washington, DC: National Gallery of Art, 1993), 147–65. Pedrocco (*Titian*, cat. 207) also accepts the figure as a self-portrait, although he identifies it as Joseph of Arimathea.

111. Pallucchini and Rossi (*Opere sacre e profane* 1:cat. 227) assign Tintoretto's *Deposition* from the church of the Umiltà a date of 1559–60; Echols and Ilchman ("Toward a New Tintoretto Catalogue," cat. 66) argue instead for a date of the mid-1550s.

112. John Shearman, *Only Connect . . . : Art and the Spectator in the Italian Renaissance* (Princeton, NJ: Princeton University Press, 1992), 92. Shearman reasonably argues that Tintoretto was probably not "innocent of the Central Italian tradition," though there is no specific evidence that his knowledge of Florentine art was gained on a trip to Florence. Recent scholars agree that Tintoretto seems not to have traveled further than Mantua; see Echols, "Beginnings: Until 1546," in Falomir, *Tintoretto*, 185.

113. Rearick, *Art of Paolo Veronese*, 178, cat. 91.

114. Kupferstichkabinett, Staatliche Museen Preussicher Kulturbesitz, Berlin (no. KdZ 18 457). Cocke, *Veronese's Drawings*, cat. 109; Rearick, *Art of Paolo Veronese*, cat. 90.

115. Cocke, *Veronese: Piety and Display*, 130; Cocke identifies the broken arch in the background with the "empty promise of paganism." Lucia Casellato, "Agonia e apologia: L'orazione nell'orto nella cultura figurativa veneziana del Cinquecento," *Venezia Cinquecento* 13 (2003): 5–98.

116. Falomir ("Self-Portrait," in Falomir, *Tintoretto*, cat. 48) argued that Tintoretto may have modeled the Musée du Louvre *Self-por-*

trait on Albrecht Dürer's *Self-portrait* of 1500 (Alte Pinakothek, Munich), given the formal similarities and the German origin of the picture's first recorded owner, Hans Jacob König.

117. W. R. Rearick, "Reflections on Tintoretto as a Portraitist," *Artibus et Historiae* 31 (1995), 51–68.

118. Roland Krischel, *Tintoretto* (Cologne: Könemann, 2000), 129.

119. The inscription reads, "IAC. TINTORETVS. VENET. PICT. CELEBERR. ANNVM AGENS SEPTVAG." The print is discussed in Maria Agnese Chiari Moretto Wiel, ed., *Jacopo Tintoretto e i suoi incisori*, exh. cat. (Milan: Electa, 1994), cat. 6; it is reproduced in Paola Rossi, *Jacopo Tintoretto: Ritratti*, exh. cat. (Milan: Electa, 1994), 164; and Falomir, *Tintoretto*, 379.

120. Rearick, "Reflections on Tintoretto," 65. Veronese died on April 19, 1588, and Rearick dates the Musée du Louvre portrait to 1589.

121. Ridolfi, *Life of Tintoretto*, trans. Enggass and Enggass, 78; Ridolfi, *Le maraviglie dell'arte* 2:70–71.

122. Tintoretto's petition to the Council of Ten to obtain a *senseria*, a sinecure at the Fondaco dei Tedeschi, mentions "my and my eight children's poverty" and was filed on September 17, 1574. The tone of Tintoretto's will of May 30, 1594, also underscores the financial necessity of keeping the family business in operation, rather than specifying large cash sums to be given to his heirs. See Linda Borean, "Documentation," in Falomir, *Tintoretto*, 431, 448–49. Titian's greed is well documented in the scholarly literature. For a reading of his "public reputation [as] a tightwad" in his later years, see Sohm, *The Artist Grows Old*, 87–88.

123. The Berlin and Prado self-portraits of Titian are discussed in many sources, including Jaffé, *Titian*, cats. 28, 33; Rearick, "The Venetian Self-Portrait," in *Le metamorfosi del ritratto*, ed. Renzo Zorzi (Florence: L. S. Olschki, 2002), 167–68; and Katherine T. Brown, *The Painter's Reflection: Self-Portraiture in Renaissance Venice, 1458–1625* (Florence: L. S. Olschki, 2000), cats. 33, 34. John Garton (*Grace and Grandeur*, cat. 2) makes a good case for the small canvas painting in the State Hermitage Museum, St. Petersburg, as an early self-portrait by Veronese. While there is no surviving mature independent self-portrait by Veronese, many scholars grudgingly accept Boschini's identification of the figure in white playing the viola da gamba in the foreground of the *Wedding Feast at Cana* as Paolo.

Boston Collects Venetian Paintings

1. For much of the information in this essay, I am indebted to Eric M. Zafran, "On the Collecting of Early Italian Paintings in Boston," in *Italian Paintings in the Museum of Fine Arts, Boston*, vol. 1, *13th–15th Century*, ed. Laurence Kanter (Boston: Museum of Fine Arts, 1994), 11–49. See also Mabel Munson Swan, *The Athenaeum Gallery, 1827–1873* (Boston: Boston Athenaeum, 1940); and Pamela Hoyle, *A Climate for Art: The History of the Boston Athenaeum Gallery, 1827–1873* (Boston: Boston Athenaeum, 1980), esp. 9–22. Although the three major Boston museums—the Museum of Fine Arts, the Isabella Steward Gardner Museum, and the Fogg Art Museum—all possess very strong and similar collections of fourteenth- and fifteenth-century Italian painting, only the MFA and the Gardner have significant holdings of Venetian Renaissance pictures.

2. The Titian *Circumcision* is no. 1871.95 at the Yale University Art Gallery; although Wethey denied that this panel was by Titian (*Paintings of Titian* 1:171, cat. X-8), it has been accepted by most subsequent scholars, including Filippo Pedrocco, *Titian* (New York: Rizzoli, 2001), 71, cat. 4; Paul Joannides, *Titian to 1518: The Assumption of Genius* (New Haven, CT: Yale University Press, 2001), 87–88; and Humfrey, *Titian: The Complete Paintings*, 5.

3. The painting is no. 42.388. Letters from 1929 in the curatorial files of the Art of Europe department disclose that the MFA originally did not wish to acquire the painting, and indeed helped the owner contact seventeen other American museums that might want to purchase the work. Apparently none did, and the picture came to Boston. The article supporting the attribution of the Felton *Adoration of the Magi*, "'School Painting' May Soon Be Judged Priceless Tintoretto," was published in the *Boston Evening Transcript*, Magazine, Jan. 29, 1929, 1, 8. The painting is shown hanging on the walls of the MFA's first building at Copley Square in a 1902 photograph, reproduced in Zafran, "On the Collecting of Early Italian Paintings," 17.

4. Zafran, "On the Collecting of Early Italian Paintings," 15–17. The altarpiece, no. 01.4, was signed and dated by Bartolomeo Vivarini, and came originally from the church of Sant' Andrea, on the island of Rab (Arbe) off the Dalmatian coast. It was first recorded at the MFA in 1876, when Shaw lent it to the Museum.

5. Isabella Stewart Gardner to Bernard Berenson, Dec. 2, 1895, in *The Letters of Bernard Berenson and Isabella Stewart Gardner, 1887–1924*, ed. Rollin Hadley (Boston: Northeastern University Press, 1987), 43. For a good introduction to Gardner's home and collections, see Alan Chong, Richard Lingner, and Carl Zahn, eds., *Eye of the Beholder: Masterpieces from the Isabella Stewart Gardner Museum* (Boston: Isabella Stewart Gardner Museum, 2003).

6. Hadley, *Letters of Berenson and Gardner*, 55–64. In this case, "happily for Gardner" no doubt also meant "unhappily for the MFA," as Mrs. Warren, a huge supporter, might very well have chosen the Museum as *Europa*'s eventual home.

7. Bernard Berenson to Isabella Stewart Gardner, Oct. 9, 1903, in *Letters of Berenson and Gardner*, ed. Hadley, 323.

8. The painting, no. 30.773, was purchased from Durlacher Bros. of London. Hendy's recommendation is in the curatorial file, Art of Europe department. Although this understated painting is of sufficient quality, it has been occasionally regarded as less than fully autograph; see, for example, Terisio Pignatti and Filippo Pedrocco, *Veronese: Catalogo completo dei dipinti* (Florence: Cantini, 1991), 321, cat. 6A; or Pignatti and Pedrocco, *Veronese* (Milan: Electa, 1995), 2:505, cat. A7. On Hendy's tenure at the MFA, see Walter Muir Whitehill, *Museum of Fine Arts, Boston: A Centennial History* (Cambridge, MA: Harvard University Press, 1970), 1:428–30.

9. This and the following letter are in the archives of the Museum of Fine Arts, Boston.

10. G. H. Edgell, "A Recently Acquired Portrait by Titian," *Bulletin of the Museum of Fine Arts* 61, no. 245 (Oct. 1943): 40–42.

11. Letter of April 8, 1943, from W. G. Constable to George Harold Edgell, in Collections Committee minutes, Museum of Fine Arts, Boston. An article in the 1950 issue of *Arte Veneta* formed part of a public relations effort on behalf of these new acquisitions. Written by Richard McLanathan, assistant curator of decorative arts at the MFA, the article celebrated several recent acquisitions of Venetian paintings, leading with the Titian *Portrait of a Man*. See Richard McLanathan, "Dipinti veneziani acquistati negli ultimi anni dal Museo di Belle Arti di Boston," *Arte Veneta* 4 (1950): 162–63. *Saint Catherine*, on the other hand, was not discussed, perhaps because the curators felt it had already received enough attention (the picture had been featured in "The Year's Best: 1948," *ArtNews* 47, no. 9 [Jan. 1949]: 40–41) or because it was slated for a separate essay. In either case, the article and its MFA authorship suggest that Constable and his colleagues were orchestrating a plan to build up a key area of the collection and then promote the new acquisitions. Apparently not everything by Titian made the cut: Constable's letter also mentioned that the MFA had recently passed on acquiring the painter's *Man with a Hawk*, which later went to the Joslyn Art Museum in Omaha, Nebraska.

12. Wethey, in *Paintings of Titian* 2:106, cat. 47, assigned the *Portrait of a Man with a Book* (43.83) the vague category "Titian (?)," and in *Paintings of Titian* 1:129–30, cat. 96, listed the *Saint Catherine* (48.499) under "Workshop of Titian."

13. This painting (46.1430) has minimal provenance (by family tradition, it was acquired by the senior Shaw in Italy in the 1860s or 1870s, perhaps during an 1874 trip to Italy). Although it was assigned to Domenico Tintoretto by Pallucchini and Rossi (*Opere sacre e profane* 1:241, cat. A13), the main figures are identifiably by Jacopo's hand.

14. The other three Veronese canvases are *Actaeon Watching Diana and Her Nymphs Bathing* (59.260), *Jupiter with Gods and Goddesses on Olympus* (64.2078), and *Atalanta Receiving the Boar's Head from Meleager* (64.2079).

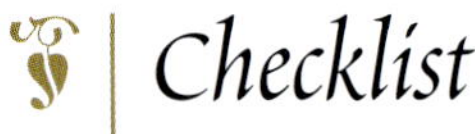

Checklist

Note to the Reader
This checklist includes provenance information and a selection of references for each painting displayed in the 2009 exhibition at the Museum of Fine Arts, Boston. The references, listed in abbreviated form and in chronological order by date of publication, represent the most significant citations to each painting; the full bibliographic details for each source can be found in the Selected Bibliography. The provenance entries were compiled by Victoria S. Reed, the Monica S. Sadler Assistant Curator for Provenance at the MFA. The entries are given chronologically and are based on information provided by the lending institutions and found in published works. Owners are separated by semicolons, with a period denoting a break in the provenance. Whenever possible, names and life dates have been standardized and follow those given in the Grove *Dictionary of Art*. Thus certain names or dates may differ slightly from the accounts published by the lending institutions. Further clarification or discussion is provided in the notes that follow.

The fact that many of the paintings can be traced back to inventories of the sixteenth or seventeenth centuries is a testament to the value placed on Venetian Renaissance painting from an early date. As the taste for easel paintings grew and the practice of collecting spread, the works of Titian, Tintoretto, and Veronese were among the most sought-after throughout Europe. Many names appear repeatedly in the provenance entries—Queen Christina of Sweden, the Ducs d'Orléans, the Gonzaga family, King Charles I—demonstrating not only that some of the earliest and most prominent collections in Europe included the works assembled here, but also that this exhibition does not mark the first time that many of these pictures have been seen together.

For readers seeking further information on specific paintings, the standard exhibition catalogues and catalogues raisonnés on the individual painters (e.g., Wethey, *The Paintings of Titian* or Humfrey, *Titian: The Complete Paintings*; Pallucchini and Rossi, *Tintoretto: Le opere sacre e profane*; and Pignatti and Pedrocco, *Veronese*) are all listed in the selected bibliography.

A painting's title can influence the opinions of the reader; for example, one might suppose that a *Portrait of a Gentleman* depicts a more prestigious sitter than a comparable *Portrait of a Man*. Since titles are sometimes arbitrary, certain ones have been standardized here, with the permission of the lending institutions, in the absence of specific information to the contrary. The dates listed for the paintings are generally those determined by the authors of the relevant text, typically based on current scholarship. Similarly, the life dates used for the three protagonists are those accepted by most scholars: Titian (about 1488–1576), Tintoretto (about 1518–1594), and Veronese (1528–1588). The dimensions of the paintings are unframed, with height preceding width, and the medium and support are oil on canvas unless otherwise specified.

1.
GIOVANNI BELLINI AND WORKSHOP
Virgin and Child with Saints, about 1505–8
Oil and tempera on wood
Signed on *cartellino*, "Ioannes Bellinus"; inscribed on scroll held by John the Baptist, "ECCE AGNVS. DEI"
97.2 x 153.7 cm (38¼ x 60½ in.)
The Metropolitan Museum of Art, New York
The Jules Bache Collection, 1949, 49.7.1
Image © The Metropolitan Museum of Art

PROVENANCE
Possibly Philip Stephens (b. 1723–d. 1809), 1st Bt., London; May 17, 1810, possibly posthumous Stephens sale, Christie's, London, lot 76, bought in; June 23, 1821, possibly posthumous Stephens sale, Christie's, London, lot 90, to Noseda. Wynn Ellis (b. 1790–d. 1875), London; June 17, 1876, Ellis estate sale, Christie's, London, lot 55, to Waters, possibly for William Graham (b. 1817–d. 1885), Oakdene, near Guildford, Surrey; April 2–10, 1886, Graham estate sale, Christie's, London, lot 486, to Colnaghi. By 1893, Robert H. and Evelyn Benson, London; 1927, sold by the Bensons to Duveen, London and New York; sold by Duveen to Jules S. Bache (b. 1861–d. 1944), New York; 1949, bequest of Bache to the Metropolitan Museum of Art.

SELECTED REFERENCES
Berenson, *Italian Pictures* 1:32; Pallucchini, *Giovanni Bellini*, 106, 156; Heinemann, *Giovanni Bellini* 1:cat. 131; Bottari, *Tutta la pittura* 2:36; Zeri and Gardner, *Catalogue of the Collection*, 6–7; Christiansen, "Giovanni Bellini," 18–22; Christiansen in Toscano and Valcanover, *Da Bellini a Veronese*, 131–32.

2.
TITIAN
Virgin and Child with Saint Catherine, Saint Dominic, and a Donor, about 1513–14
137 x 184 cm (53^15/16 x 72^7/16 in.)
Fondazione Magnani Rocca, Mamiano di Traversetolo
Inv. n.3
Photo: Scala / Art Resource, NY

PROVENANCE
By 1701, Balbi family, Palazzo Balbi, Genoa; by descent within the family, through Maria Balbi Doria, Genoa, to Andrea D'Oria, Milan, and his brother; 1962, sold by the D'Oria brothers to Luigi Magnani (b. 1906–d. 1984), Mamiano; 1977, passed to the Fondazione Magnani Rocca.

SELECTED REFERENCES
Crowe and Cavalcaselle, *Life and Times of Titian* 2:417; Berenson, *Italian Pictures* 1:186; Valcanover, *L'opera completa di Tiziano*, cat. 46; Wethey, *Paintings of Titian* 1:cat. 61; Hope, *Titian* (1980), 34; Biadene and Yakush, *Titian: Prince of Painters*, cat. 9; Laclotte, Nepi Scirè, et al., *Le siècle de Titien*, cat. 47; Pedrocco, *Titian*, cat. 32; Joannides, *Titian to 1518*, 157–59; Jaffé, *Titian*, cat. 9; Brown and Ferino-Pagden, *Bellini, Giorgione, Titian*, cat. 10; Kennedy, *Titian*, 15, 17–18; Humfrey, *Titian: The Complete Paintings*, cat. 36.

3.
CIRCLE OF GIOVANNI BELLINI
Christ Carrying the Cross, about 1505–10
Oil on panel
49.5 x 38.5 cm (20^13/16 x 16⅝ in.)
Isabella Stewart Gardner Museum, Boston
P26n17
Photo: © Isabella Stewart Gardner Museum, Boston

PROVENANCE
Probably Camillo Zileri dal Verme (b. 1830–d. 1896), Palazzo Loschi, Vicenza; 1898, sold by the heirs of Zileri dal Verme, through Bernard Berenson, to Isabella Stewart Gardner (b. 1840–d. 1924), Boston.

SELECTED REFERENCES
Berenson, *Italian Pictures* 1:83 (Giorgione); Wethey, *Paintings of Titian* 1:cat. x-5 (Giorgionesque); Fredericksen and Zeri, *Census*, 22 (Bellini); Joannides, *Titian to 1518*, 241.

4.
TITIAN
Christ Carrying the Cross, 1565–70
Signed on cross, "TITIANVS AEQ CAES. F."
67 x 77 cm (26⅜ x 30⅜ in.)
Museo Nacional del Prado, Madrid
438
Photo: Scala / Art Resource, NY

PROVENANCE
By 1666, Charles II (b. 1661–d. 1700), king of Spain, Alcázar, Madrid; by inheritance within the Spanish royal family; 1843, transferred to the Museo Nacional del Prado.

SELECTED REFERENCES
Crowe and Cavalcaselle, *Life and Times of Titian* 2:405–6; Suida, *Le Titien*, 144, 180; Berenson, *Italian Pictures* 1:188; Wethey, *Paintings of Titian* 1:36, cat. 24, fig. 127; Valcanover, *L'opera completa di Tiziano*, cat. 492; Biadene and Yakush, *Titian: Prince of Painters*, cat. 71; Pedrocco, *Titian*, cat. 256; Falomir, *Tiziano*, cat. 51; Humfrey, *Titian: The Complete Paintings*, cat. 262.

5.
TITIAN
Flora, about 1516–18
79.7 x 63.5 cm (31⅜ x 25 in.)
Galleria degli Uffizi, Florence
Inv. 1890 n. 1462
Photo: Scala / Ministero per i Beni e le Attività culturali / Art Resource, NY

PROVENANCE
By about 1637/40, Alfonso López (b. about 1582–d. 1649), Amsterdam; 1641, sold by Lopez in Paris. By 1728, Charles VI (b. 1685–d. 1740), Holy Roman Emperor, Vienna; by descent within the Hapsburg dynasty to Francis II (b. 1768–d. 1835), Holy Roman Emperor, Vienna; December 18, 1793, exchanged by Francis II with his brother Ferdinand III (b. 1769–d. 1824), Grand Duke of Tuscany, Florence, and placed at the Galleria degli Uffizi; June 13, 1940, removed from the Uffizi to the Villa Medici, Poggio a Caiano; October 31, 1940, taken to the Hermitage of Camaldoli, Poppi; October 17, 1945, returned to the Galleria degli Uffizi.

SELECTED REFERENCES
Crowe and Cavalcaselle, *Life and Times of Titian* 1:270–73; Suida, *Le Titien*, 31, 158; Berenson, *Italian Pictures* 1:186; Valcanover, *L'opera completa di Tiziano*, cat. 60; Wethey, *Paintings of Titian* 3:cat. 17; Hope, *Titian* (1980), 62, 81; Laclotte, Nepi Scirè, et al., *Le siècle de Titien*, cat. 49; Pedrocco, *Titian*, cat. 40; Joannides, *Titian to 1518*, 264–66; Jaffé, *Titian*, cat. 11; Spinosa, *Tiziano e il ritratto di corte*, cat. 4; Brown and Ferino-Pagden, *Bellini, Giorgione, Titian*, cat. 42; Kennedy, *Titian*, 18, 20; Humfrey, *Titian: The Complete Paintings*, cat. 53.

6.
TITIAN
Venus Rising from the Sea (Venus Anadyomene), about 1520
75.8 x 57.6 cm (29⅞ x 22¾ in.)
National Gallery of Scotland, Edinburgh
NG 2751
Photo: Scala / Art Resource, NY

PROVENANCE
By about 1662, Christina, queen of Sweden (b. 1626–d. 1689), Stockholm and Rome; 1689, by inheritance to Cardinal Decio Azzolino (b. 1623–d. 1689), Rome; 1689, by inheritance to his nephew Marchese Pompeo Azzolino (d. 1696), Rome; 1692, sold by Pompeo Azzolino to Livio Odescalchi (b. 1652–d. 1713), Duke of Bracciano, Rome; 1713, by inheritance to his nephew Baldassare Erba Odescalchi (d. 1746), Rome; 1721, sold by Odescalchi to Pierre Crozat (b. 1665–d. 1740), Paris, for Philippe II (b. 1674–d. 1723), Duc d'Orléans, Paris; by descent within the House of Orléans to Louis-Philippe-Joseph (b. 1747–d. 1793), Duc d'Orléans, Paris; 1792, sold from the Orléans collection to Edouard Walkiers (b. 1764?–d. 1844), Brussels; 1792, sold by Walkiers to François-Louis-Joseph de Laborde-Méréville (b. 1761–d. 1802), Paris and London; 1798, consigned by Laborde-Méréville to Jeremiah Harman (b. 1764–d. 1844), London; 1798, sold

by Harman to Michael Bryan (b. 1757–d. 1821), London, for a consortium of Francis Egerton (b. 1736–d. 1803), 3rd Duke of Bridgewater, Frederick Howard (b. 1748–d. 1825), 5th Earl of Carlisle, and George Granville Leveson-Gower (b. 1758–d. 1833), Earl Gower and 1st Duke of Sutherland, London; December 26, 1798, Orléans collection sale, Bryan's Gallery, London, lot 49, but reserved for Francis Egerton; until 2003, by inheritance within the family to Francis Ronald Egerton, 7th Duke of Sutherland; 2003, acquired from the Duke of Sutherland by the National Gallery of Scotland.

SELECTED REFERENCES

Crowe and Cavalcaselle, *Life and Times of Titian* 1:275–77; Suida, *Le Titien*, 43, 72, 160; Berenson, *Italian Pictures* 1:185; Valcanover, *L'opera completa di Tiziano*, cat. 98; Wethey, *Paintings of Titian* 3:cat. 39; Goffen, *Titian's Women*, 126–33; Pedrocco, *Titian*, cat. 55; Humfrey, *Age of Titian*, cat. 19; Humfrey, *Titian: The Complete Paintings*, cat. 60.

7.

TITIAN

Pope Paul III, 1543
113.7 x 88.8 cm (44¾ x 34^{15}⁄$_{16}$ in.)
Museo di Capodimonte, Naples
Inv. Q130
Photo: Erich Lessing / Art Resource, NY

PROVENANCE

1543, Pope Paul III (Alessandro Farnese, b. 1468–d. 1549), Rome (original commission); by descent to his grandson Cardinal Alessandro Farnese (b. 1520–d. 1589), Palazzo Farnese, Rome; by inheritance within the Farnese family; 1649, moved to the Palazzo del Giardino, Parma; 1734, moved by Charles VII (b. 1716–d. 1788), king of Naples, to Naples; 1798, moved from Naples to Palermo; 1815, returned to Naples and placed in the Palazzo Capodi-monte (later Museo di Capodimonte).

SELECTED REFERENCES

Vasari, *Vite* 7:442–43; Fishel, *Tizian*, xxi; Suida, *Le Titien*, 104–5; Berenson, *Italian Pictures* 1:189; Valcanover, *L'opera completa di Tiziano*, cat. 236; Wethey, *Paintings of Titian* 2:28–29, 122, cat. 72; Hope, *Titian* (1980), 86; Laclotte, Nepi Scirè, et al., *Le siècle de Titien*, cat. 172; Freedman, *Titian's Portraits*, 91–105; Pedrocco, *Titian*, cat. 127; Jaffé, *Titian*, cat. 26; Falomir, *Tiziano*, cat. 23; Spinosa, *Tiziano e il ritratto di corte*, cat. 17; Ferino-Pagden, *Der späte Tizian*, cat. 1.4; Kennedy, *Titian*, 67; Humfrey, *Titian: The Complete Paintings*, cat. 136.

8.

TINTORETTO

Contest between Apollo and Marsyas, 1544–45
137 x 236 cm (53^{15}⁄$_{16}$ x 92^{15}⁄$_{16}$ in.)
Wadsworth Atheneum Museum of Art, Hartford, Connecticut
The Ella Gallup Sumner and Mary Catlin Sumner Collection Fund, 1950.438
Photo: Wadsworth Atheneum Museum of Art, Hartford, CT

PROVENANCE

1545, Pietro Aretino (b. 1492–d. 1556), Ca' Bollani, Venice (original commission). By 1618, Sir Dudley Carlton (b. 1573–d. 1632), The Hague, London, and Oxfordshire. Duke of Abercorn. By 1892, William Bromley-Davenport (b. 1862–d. 1949), Capesthorn, Cheshire; July 28, 1926, Bromley-Davenport sale, Christie's, London, lot 149, to Gordon. Thomas Agnew and Sons, London. Stephen Lewis Courtauld (b. 1883–d. 1967), London. By 1949, Thomas Agnew and Sons, London; 1950, sold by Agnew to the Wadsworth Atheneum.

PROVENANCE NOTES

William Bromley-Davenport was the son of noted collector Walter Davenport Bromley; however, Waagen makes no mention of this painting in the Davenport Bromley collection (Gustav Friedrich Waagen, *Treasures of Art in Great Britain* [London, 1854], 3:371–80, and *Galleries and Cabinets of Art in Great Britain* [London, 1857], 166–68).

SELECTED REFERENCES

Tietze, *Tintoretto*, 353; Pallucchini, *La giovinezza*, 93–94, 157 n. 56; Berenson, *Italian Pictures* 1:173; Schultz, *Venetian Painted Ceilings*, 25, 117, cat. 46; De Vecchi, *L'opera completa del Tintoretto*, cat. 28A; Fredricksen and Zeri, *Census*, 200; Pallucchini and Rossi, *Opere sacre e profane* 1:cat. 82; Martineau and Hope, *Genius of Venice*, cat. 100; Nichols, *Tintoretto*, 38; Zafran, *Renaissance to Rococo*, cat. 4; Falomir, *Tintoretto*, cat. 4; Echols and Ilchman, "Toward a New Tintoretto Catalogue," cat. 34.

9.

TINTORETTO

Self-Portrait, about 1546–47
45.1 x 38.1 cm (17¾ x 15 in.)
Philadelphia Museum of Art
Gift of Marion R. Ascoli and the Marion R. and Max Ascoli Fund in honor of Lessing Rosenwald, 1983, 1983-190-1
Photo by Graydon Wood

PROVENANCE

Possibly Alessandro Vittoria (b. 1525–d. 1608), Venice. Manfrin collection, Venice. By 1896, Charles Eliot Norton (b. 1827–d. 1908), Boston; 1908 until at least 1939, the Misses Norton, Boston. 1948, Wildenstein and Co., New York. By 1957, Max Ascoli, New York; to his wife, Marion R. Ascoli; 1983, gift of Marion R. Ascoli to Philadelphia Museum of Art.

SELECTED REFERENCES

Ridolfi, *Le maraviglie* 1:i, 119–24, 2:54; Tietze, *Tintoretto*, 352; Pallucchini, *La giovinezza*, 107–8; Berenson, *Italian Pictures* 1:176; De Vecchi, *L'opera completa del Tintoretto*, cat. 62b; Rossi, *Jacopo Tintoretto* (1974) 1:24, 117–18; Pignatti, *Golden Century*, 96, 165, cat. 31; Laclotte, Nepi Scirè, et al., *Le siècle de Titien*, cat. 191; Rossi, *Jacopo Tintoretto: Ritratti* (1994), cat. 4; Rearick, "Reflections on Tintoretto as a Portraitist," 52; Brown, *Painter's Reflection*, 164–65; Falomir, *Tintoretto*, cat. 7.

10.

TINTORETTO

Esther before Ahasuerus, about 1547–48
207.7 x 275.5 cm (81¾ x 108^{7}⁄$_{16}$ in.)
The Royal Collection, London
RCIN 407247
Photo: © 2008 Her Majesty Queen Elizabeth II

PROVENANCE

By 1627, Vincenzo II Gonzaga (b. 1594–d. 1627), 7th Duke of Mantua; by inheritance to Carlo I Gonzaga (b. 1580–d. 1637), 8th Duke of Mantua and Duke of Nevers; 1628/31, sold by Gonzaga, through Daniel Nys and Nicholas Lanier, to Charles I (b. 1600–d. 1649), king of England and Scotland, St. James's Palace, London; 1649, collected by the House of Commons for sale; June 18, 1650, sold by the Trustees of the Commonwealth to Smith. Emanuel de Critz (b. 1608–d. 1665); 1660, recovered from de Critz by the House of Commons for Charles II (b. 1630–d. 1685), king of England and Scotland; by descent within the royal family.

SELECTED REFERENCES

Waagen, *Treasures of Art* 2:478; Tietze, *Tintoretto*, 351; Pallucchini, *La giovinezza*, 106–7; Berenson, *Italian Pictures* 1:173; De Vecchi, *L'opera completa del Tintoretto*, cat. 63a; Pallucchini and Rossi, *Opere sacre e profane* 1:33, cat. 129; Falomir, *Tintoretto*, cat. 9; Whitaker and Clayton, *Art of Italy*, cat. 75; Echols and Ilchman, "Toward a New Tintoretto Catalogue," cat. 45.

11.

VERONESE

Christ Healing a Woman with an Issue of Blood (?), about 1548
117.5 x 163.5 cm (46¼ x 64⅜ in.)
The National Gallery, London
Wynn Ellis Bequest, 1876, NG931
Photo: © The National Gallery 2008

PROVENANCE

Possibly Josiah Burchett (b. 1666?–d. 1746), London; April 6–9, 1747, possibly posthumous Burchett sale, Cock, London, lot 233. By 1761, Sir Gregory Page (b. 1689–d. 1775), Bt., London; 1775, by inheritance within the family to Sir Gregory Osborne Page Turner (b.1785–d.1843), 4th Bt., London. By 1823, William Smith (b. 1756–d. 1835); May 16, 1829, Smith sale, Christie's, London, lot 69, to Wynn Ellis (b. 1790–d. 1875), London; 1876, bequest of Ellis to the National Gallery.

SELECTED REFERENCES

Marini, *L'opera completa*, cat. 24; Pallucchini, *Veronese*, 9, 15, cat. 9; Pignatti, *Veronese* 1:cat. 47; Rearick, *Paolo Veronese: Disegni e dipinti*, cat. 50; Pignatti and Pedrocco, *Veronese: Catalogo completo dei dipinti*, cat. 34; Pignatti and Pedrocco, *Veronese* 1:cat. 55; Penny, *Sixteenth Century Italian Paintings* 2:334–43.

12.

TITIAN

Virgin and Child with Saint Catherine of Alexandria and a Rabbit, about 1530
Signed on Saint Catherine's wheel, "Ticianus . F."
71 x 87 cm (27^{15}⁄$_{16}$ x 34¼ in.)
Musée du Louvre, Paris
Inv. 743
Photo: Réunion des Musées Nationaux / Art Resource, NY

PROVENANCE

Possibly Francesco d'Este (b. 1610–d. 1658), 8th Duke of Modena and Reggio. 1665, Duc de Richelieu (b. 1629–d. 1715), Paris; 1665, sold by Richelieu to Louis XIV (b. 1638–d. 1715), king of France, Paris and Versailles; by inheritance within the French royal family; 1792 or 1793, transferred to the Musée du Louvre.

PROVENANCE NOTES

Traditionally, this is considered to be the painting commissioned from Titian by Federico II Gonzaga in 1530, which is supposed to have passed in the 1620s to Cardinal Richelieu and then by inheritance to the Duc de Richelieu. Nevertheless, a painting in Francesco d'Este's posthumous inventory of 1663, described as "quadro ove la Vergine tiene con una mano un coniglio et una donna che ha nelle braccia il Bambino, di mano di Titiano," more accurately describes the Louvre picture than does the "quadro dipintovi la Madonna con il bambino in braccio et S. Catterina con cornice di violino, opera di Titiano" in the Gonzaga inventory.

SELECTED REFERENCES

Crowe and Cavalcaselle, *Life and Times of Titian* 1:336–41; Suida, *Tiziano*, 154; Berenson, *Italian Pictures* 1:189; Wethey, *Paintings of Titian*

1:cat. 60; Valcanover, *L'opera completa di Tiziano*, cat. 142; Hope, *Titian* (1980), 74–75; Biadene and Yakush, *Titian: Prince of Painters*, cat. 23; Laclotte, Nepi Scirè, et al., *Le siècle de Titien*, cat. 160; Pedrocco, *Titian*, cat. 85; Jaffé, *Titian*, cat. 18; Habert and Pomarède, *Tiziano e la Pittura del Cinquecento*, 36–37; Laclotte et al., *Splendeur de Venise*, cat. 93; Kennedy, *Titian*, 41; Humfrey, *Titian: The Complete Paintings*, cat. 88.

13.
VERONESE
Mystic Marriage of Saint Catherine of Alexandria, about 1549
57.68 x 91.44 cm (22¾ x 36 in.)
Yale University Art Gallery, New Haven, Connecticut
Lent by The Barker Welfare Foundation, in memory of Catherine Barker and Charles V Hickox, B.A. 1911
Photo: Yale University Art Gallery

PROVENANCE
By 1767, Joseph Wenzel (b. 1696–d. 1772), Prince of Liechtenstein, Vienna; until at least 1873, by inheritance within the princely family of Liechtenstein. 1926, Van Diemen Galleries, New York; sold by Van Diemen to Catherine Barker Spaulding Hickox (b. 1896–d. 1970); 1970, bequeathed by Catherine Hickox to the Barker Welfare Foundation.

SELECTED REFERENCES
Berenson, *Italian Pictures* 1:134; Marini, *L'opera completa*, cat. 56; Pignatti, *Veronese* 1:cat. 113; Pallucchini, *Veronese*, 38, cat. 48; Rearick, *Art of Paolo Veronese*, cat. 6; Pignatti and Pedrocco, *Veronese: Catalogo completo dei dipinti*, cat. 12; Pignatti and Pedrocco, *Veronese* 1:cat. 11; Cocke, *Veronese: Piety and Display*, 138–39, 142.

14.
TINTORETTO
Saint Augustine Healing the Lame, about 1549–50
255 x 175 cm (100⅜ x 68⅞ in.)
Musei Civici, Pinacoteca di Palazzo Chiericati, Vicenza
Inv. A 74
Photo: Scala / Art Resource, NY

PROVENANCE
About 1549/50, Porto Godi family, chapel of Saint Augustine, church of San Michele, Vicenza (original commission); 1810/12, removed from the church in preparation for its demolition and kept by the Porto Godi family, Vicenza; 1826, given by Paolina Porto Godi Pigafetta Bissari to the Museo Civico.

SELECTED REFERENCES
Tietze, *Tintoretto*, 378; Pallucchini, *La giovinezza*, 126–27; Berenson, *Italian Pictures* 1:182; De Vecchi, *L'opera completa del Tintoretto*, cat. 74; Pallucchini and Rossi, *Opere sacre e profane* 1:cat. 136; Falomir, *Tintoretto*, cat. 14; Echols and Ilchman, "Toward a New Tintoretto Catalogue," cat. 51.

15.
TINTORETTO
Saint George, Saint Louis, and the Princess, 1552
226 x 146 cm (89 x 57½ in.)
Gallerie dell'Accademia, Venice
No. 899
Photo: Cameraphoto Arte, Venice / Art Resource, NY

PROVENANCE
1552, first room of the Magistrato del Sale, Palazzo dei Camerlenghi, Venice (original commission); 1777, removed and transferred to the *antichiesetta* of the Palazzo Ducale, Venice; 1937, transferred to the Gallerie dell'Accademia.

SELECTED REFERENCES
Ridolfi, *Le maraviglie* 2:58; Boschini, *Le minere*, 271; Tietze, *Tintoretto*, 361; Pallucchini, *La giovinezza*, 135–36; Berenson, *Italian Pictures* 1:179; De Vecchi, *L'opera completa del Tintoretto*, cat. 98; Pallucchini and Rossi, *Opere sacre e profane* 1:cat. 162; Valcanover and Pignatti, *Tintoretto*, 88; Nichols, *Tintoretto*, 67; Cottrell, "Corporate Colors," 668–70; Falomir, *Tintoretto*, cat. 17; Echols and Ilchman, "Toward a New Tintoretto Catalogue," cat. 59.

16.
VERONESE
Saint Menna, about 1560
247 x 122 cm (96¾ x 47½ in.)
Galleria Estense, Modena
Inv. 4133
Photo: Cameraphoto Arte, Venice / Art Resource, NY

PROVENANCE
About 1560, executed as the inner shutter for the organ in the church of San Geminiano, Venice (original commission); by 1733, shutter paintings removed and placed above the organ; 1807, removed from the church in preparation for its demolition and placed at the Gallerie dell'Accademia, Venice; 1811, exchanged by the Accademia with the Galleria Estense, Modena.

SELECTED REFERENCES
Ridolfi, *Le maraviglie* 1:326; Boschini, *Le minere*, 101; Berenson, *Italian Pictures* 1:134; Marini, *L'opera completa*, cat. 66C; Pignatti, *Veronese* 1:cat. 122; Pallucchini, *Veronese*, 50–51, cat. 66c; Marinelli, *Veronese e Verona*, 208–10; Rearick, *Art of Paolo Veronese*, cat. 31; Pignatti and Pedrocco, *Veronese: Catologo completo dei dipinti*, cat. 51C; Pignatti and Pedrocco, *Veronese* 1:cat. 104; Cocke, *Veronese: Piety and Display*, 91, cat. 8; Romanelli and Strinati, *Gods, Heroes, and Allegories*, cat. 8.

17.
VERONESE
Temptation of Saint Anthony, 1552–53
198 x 151 cm (77 15/16 x 59 7/16 in.)
Musée des Beaux-Arts, Caen
Inv. 6
Photo: Cameraphoto Arte, Venice / Art Resource, NY

PROVENANCE
1552, one of four altarpieces commissioned for the Duomo of Mantua (original commission); 1797, removed from the church; 1798, seized by French troops and taken to Paris; 1801, transferred to Caen and placed in the Musée des Beaux-Arts.

SELECTED REFERENCES
Vasari, *Vite* 6:367, 488–89; Borghini, *Il riposo*, 561; Berenson, *Italian Pictures* 1:130; Marini, *L'opera completa*, cat. 16; Pignatti, *Veronese* 1:cat. 22; Martineau and Hope, *Genius of Venice*, cat. 134; Rearick, *Art of Paolo Veronese*, cat. 16; Pignatti and Pedrocco, *Veronese: Catalogo completo dei dipinti*, cat. 25; Pignatti and Pedrocco, *Veronese* 1:cat. 33; Cocke, *Veronese: Piety and Display*, 3–5, cat. 2; Laclotte et al., *Splendeur de Venise*, cat. 104; Romanelli and Strinati, *Gods, Heroes, and Allegories*, cat. 7.

18.
TINTORETTO
Deposition of Christ, mid-1550s
227 x 294 cm (89.4 x 115.7 in.)
Gallerie dell'Accademia, Venice
No. 217
Photograph taken before cleaning and restoration
Photo: Scala / Art Resource, NY

PROVENANCE
Mid-1550s, church of Santa Maria dell'Umiltà, Venice (original commission); by 1821, removed from the church in preparation for its demolition and transferred to the Gallerie dell'Accademia.

SELECTED REFERENCES
Boschini, *Le minere*, 346; Tietze, *Tintoretto*, 42, 361; Pallucchini, *La giovinezza*, 152; Berenson, *Italian Pictures* 1:178; De Vecchi, *L'opera completa del Tintoretto*, cat. 130; Zorzi, *Venezia scomparsa*, 244–45; Pallucchini and Rossi, *Opere sacre e profane* 1:cat. 227; Echols and Ilchman, "Toward a New Tintoretto Catalogue," cat. 66.

19.
VERONESE
Virgin and Child with Angels Appearing to Saint Anthony Abbot and Saint Paul the Hermit, 1562
284.5 x 168.9 cm (112 x 66½ in.)
The Chrysler Museum of Art, Norfolk, Virginia
Gift of Walter P. Chrysler, Jr., in memory of Della Viola Forker Chrysler, 71.527
Photograph taken before cleaning and restoration
Photo: The Chrysler Museum of Art, Norfolk, VA

PROVENANCE
1562, chapel of Saint Anthony, church of San Benedetto Po, Mantua (original commission; second chapel on the right, when facing the high altar); about 1792, removed from the church to the abbey at San Benedetto Po; 1797, removed from the abbey by occupying French troops and sold to Jean Frédéric Guillaume de Sahuguet d'Amarzit (b. 1750–d. 1817), comte d'Espagnac, in partnership with Giovanni Giorgio Müller; about 1800, taken by Müller and Espagnac to France; April 4, 1820, Espagnac sale, Bonnefons de Lavialle, Paris, lot 59, to Vignot. 1950, private collection, France. 1954, Jean Neger, Paris; 1954, sold by Neger to Walter P. Chrysler, Jr. (b. 1909–d. 1988), Norfolk; 1971, gift of Chrysler to the Chrysler Museum of Art.

SELECTED REFERENCES
Vasari, *Vite* 6:490–91; Borghini, *Il riposo*, 561; Berenson, *Italian Pictures* 1:134; Marini, *L'opera completa*, cat. 77b; Rosand, *Veronese and His Studio*, 20; Pignatti, *Veronese* 1:cat. 124; Pignatti, *Golden Century*, 116, 167–68, cat. 40; Martineau and Hope, *Genius of Venice*, cat. 135; Pallucchini, *Veronese*, 73–74, cat. 73; Rearick, *Art of Paolo Veronese*, cat. 41; Pignatti and Pedrocco, *Veronese: Catalogo completo dei dipinti*, cat. 70; Pignatti and Pedrocco, *Veronese* 1:cat. 143; Cocke, *Veronese: Piety and Display*, 91–92, cat. 10; Huber, *Paolo Veronese*, 149–50.

20.
TINTORETTO
Temptation of Saint Anthony, about 1577
282 x 165 cm (111 x 64 15/16 in.)
Church of San Trovaso, Venice
Milledonne family chapel, left of high altar
Photo: © Cameraphoto Arte, Venezia

SELECTED REFERENCES
Borghini, *Il riposo*, 554; Ridolfi, *Le maraviglie* 2:39–40; Boschini, *Le minere*, 364; Tietze, *Tintoretto*, 374; Berenson, *Italian Pictures* 1:181; De Vecchi, *L'opera completa del Tintoretto*, cat. 224; Pallucchini and Rossi, *Opere sacre e profane* 1:cat. 370; Echols and Ilchman, "Toward a New Tintoretto Catalogue," cat. 197.

21.
TITIAN
Supper at Emmaus, 1533–34
Signed on leg of table at left, "ticiAn."
169 x 244 cm (66 9/16 x 96 1/16 in.)
Musée du Louvre, Paris
Inv. 746
Photo: R. G. Ojeda / Réunion des Musées Nationaux / Art Resource, NY

PROVENANCE
1533/34, Nicola Maffei (b. about 1486–d. 1536), Mantua (original commission); by inheritance to his daughter-in-law, Olimpia Martinengo Maffei; about 1593, sold from the Maffei collection to Vincenzo I Gonzaga (b. 1562–d. 1612), 4th Duke of Mantua; by inheritance to Carlo I Gonzaga (b. 1580–d. 1637), 8th Duke of Mantua and Duke of Nevers; 1628–31, sold by Gonzaga, through Daniel Nys and Nicholas Lanier, to Charles I (b. 1600–d. 1649), king of England and Scotland, Whitehall Palace, London; 1649, collected by the House of Commons for sale; October 23, 1651, sold by the Trustees of the Commonwealth to Robert Houghton, London. By 1656, Everard Jabach (b. 1618–d. 1695), Paris; 1662, sold by Jabach to Louis XIV (b. 1638–d. 1715), king of France, Paris and Versailles; by inheritance within the French royal family; 1792, transferred to the Musée du Louvre.

PROVENANCE NOTES

Although Titian's *Supper at Emmaus* does not appear in the 1627 Gonzaga inventory, it is presumed to have been sold, along with the rest of the collection, to Charles I between 1628 and 1631. It appears in the king's 1639 inventory and in the 1649/50 inventory drawn up after the king's execution.

SELECTED REFERENCES

Crowe and Cavalcaselle, *Life and Times of Titian* 2:152–55; Suida, *Tiziano*, 67; Berenson, *Italian Pictures* 1:189; Valcanover, *L'opera completa di Tiziano*, cat. 201; Wethey, *Paintings of Titian* 1:cat. 143; Laclotte, Nepi Scirè, et al., *Le siècle de Titien*, cat. 161; Rebecchini, "Tiziano e Mantova," 42–48; Pedrocco, *Titian*, cat. 97; Joannides, *Titian to 1518*, 161; Morale, *La Cena di Tiziano*, 146–49; Kennedy, *Titian*, 41–42; Humfrey, *Titian: The Complete Paintings*, cat. 90.

22.

TINTORETTO

Supper at Emmaus, about 1542

156 x 212 cm (61⅜ x 86⅞ in.)

Szépművészeti Múzeum, Budapest

Inv. no. 111

Photo: Szépművészeti Múzeum, Budapest

PROVENANCE

Probably Manuel José Antonio Hilario Negrete de la Torre (b. 1736–d. 1818), Paris. Edmund de Bourke (b. 1761–d. 1821), Paris; 1821, sold by Bourke's widow to Nicholas II Esterházy (b. 1765–d. 1833), Budapest and Vienna; 1870, purchased with the Esterházy collection by the Szépművészeti Múzeum.

PROVENANCE NOTES

According to the 1821 catalogue of the Bourke bequest, the painting comes from the collection of a certain "Duc de Campo Alagne," probably Manuel José Antonio Hilario Negrete de la Torre, Marqués and later Duque de Campo Alanje, who was ambassador to London between about 1878 and 1807/8 and ambassador to France from 1811.

Edmund de Bourke was the Danish ambassador to Naples, Madrid, and London, and invested in paintings on the Spanish art market between 1801 and 1811. When he sold this in 1821, it was attributed to Andrea Schiavone.

SELECTED REFERENCES

Pallucchini, *La giovinezza*, 81–82, 155, and n. 35; Berenson, *Italian Pictures* 1:171; De Vecchi, *L'opera completa del Tintoretto*, cat. 18; Pallucchini and Rossi, *Opere sacre e profane* 1:cat. 42; Keyes, Bárkóczi, and Satkowski, *Treasures of Venice*, cat. 9; Echols and Ilchman, "Toward a New Tintoretto Catalogue," cat. 27.

23.

VERONESE

Supper at Emmaus, mid-1570s

66 x 79 cm (25¹⁵⁄₁₆ x 30¹⁵⁄₁₆ in.)

Museum Boijmans Van Beuningen, Rotterdam

Inv. No. 2571

Photograph taken before cleaning and restoration

Photo: Museum Boijmans Van Beuningen, Rotterdam

PROVENANCE

Probably Giacomo Muselli (b. 1550–d. 1641), Verona; by inheritance within the family; 1685/86, sold by the Muselli family to Louis Alvarez (d. after 1692); acquired at Alvarez's death by Pierre Crozat (b. 1665–d. 1740), Paris, for Philippe II (b. 1674–d. 1723), Duc d'Orléans, Paris; by descent within the House of Orléans to Louis-Philippe-Joseph (b. 1747–d. 1793), Duc d'Orléans, Paris; 1792, sold from the Orléans collection to Edouard Walkiers (b. 1764?–d. 1844), Brussels; 1792, sold by Walkiers to François-Louis-Joseph de Laborde-Méréville (b. 1761–d. 1802), Paris and London; 1798, consigned by Laborde-Méréville to Jeremiah Harman (b. 1764–d. 1844), London; 1798, sold by Harman to Michael Bryan (b. 1757–d. 1821), London, for a consortium of Francis Egerton (b. 1736–d. 1803), 3rd Duke of Bridgewater, Frederick Howard (b. 1748–d. 1825), 5th Earl of Carlisle, and George Granville Leveson-Gower (b. 1758–d. 1833), Earl Gower and 1st Duke of Sutherland, London; December 26, 1798, Orléans collection sale, Bryan's Gallery, London, lot 67, but reserved for George Granville Leveson-Gower; until 1913, by descent within the family; July 11, 1913, Duke of Sutherland sale, Christie's, London, lot 95, to Agnew. 1931, Stefan von Auspitz (b. 1869–d. 1945), Vienna; 1932, sold to Daniël George van Beuningen (b. 1877–d. 1955), Rotterdam; 1958, purchased by the city of Rotterdam for the Museum Boijmans (later Boijmans Van Beuningen).

PROVENANCE NOTES

Stefan von Auspitz was a banker at the Bankhaus Auspitz, Lieben, and Co., Vienna. After the company declared bankruptcy in 1931 the Austrian government seized the bank and the property of its directors. Auspitz's collection of art was sold to Daniël George van Beuningen, who kept some objects for himself and sold the remainder through the Bachstitz Gallery.

SELECTED REFERENCES

Ridolfi, *Le maraviglie* 1:320; Waagen, *Treasures of Art* 2:60, 198; Berenson, *Italian Pictures* 1:139; Marini, *L'opera completa*, cat. 136; Pignatti, *Veronese* 1:cat. 171; Pallucchini, *Veronese*, cat. 140; Pignatti and Pedroco, *Veronese: Catalogo completo dei dipinti*, cat. 119; Pignatti and Pedroco, *Veronese* 1:cat. 200.

24.

VERONESE

Jupiter and a Nude, 1560s

27.1 x 101 cm (10⅝ x 39¾ in.)

Museum of Fine Arts, Boston

Gift of Mrs. Edward J. Holmes, 60.125

Photo: © Museum of Fine Arts, Boston

PROVENANCE

Until 1657, Giovanni Batta Raggi (b. 1613–d. 1657), Genoa; 1658, by inheritance to his brother, Cardinal Lorenzo Raggi (b. 1615–d. 1687), Rome; until at least 1780, probably by descent within the family, to Giulio Raggi, Genoa; 1818, possibly still at the Raggi palace, Genoa. By 1939, Edward Jackson Holmes (b. 1873–d. 1950), Boston; by inheritance to his widow, Mary Stacy (Mrs. Edward Jackson) Holmes (b. 1875), Boston; 1960, gift of Mrs. Edward Jackson Holmes to the Museum of Fine Arts, Boston.

SELECTED REFERENCES

Berenson, *Italian Pictures* 1:130; Marini, *L'opera completa*, cat. 64d; Pignatti, *Veronese* 1:cat. 150; Fredericksen and Zeri, *Census*, 38, 565; Pignatti and Pedrocco, *Veronese: Catalogo completo*, cat. 87d; Pignatti and Pedrocco, *Veronese* 1:cat. 161; Romanelli and Strinati, *Gods, Heroes, and Allegories*, cat. 14.

25.

TITIAN

Saint Catherine of Alexandria at Prayer, about 1567

Signed at lower left, "[TI]TIANVS F."

119.1 x 100 cm (46⅞ x 39⅜ in.)

Museum of Fine Arts, Boston

1948 Fund and Otis Norcross Fund, 48.499

Photograph taken before cleaning and restoration

Photo: © Museum of Fine Arts, Boston

PROVENANCE

1567 until 1598, Cardinal Alessandrino Farnese (Michele di Bonelli) (b. 1541–d. 1598), Rome. 1653, Manuel de Acevedo y Zúñiga (b. about 1590–d. 1653), 6th Count of Monterrey, Madrid; 1653, transferred to Gaspar de Haro y Guzmán (b. 1629–d. 1687), 7th Marqués de Carpio, Madrid; 1691, possibly transferred from the Haro y Guzmán collection to Charles II (b. 1661–d. 1700), king of Spain, and kept at the Real Monasterio del Escorial, Madrid. William Waldegrave (b. 1753–d. 1825), 1st Baron Radstock, Longford Castle, Wiltshire, England; May 12–13, 1826, Radstock sale, Christie's, London, lot 39, to Charles Dixon; by descent at Dixon's death to his nephew George Wilder, Stansted Park, Hampshire, England; May 19, 1911, Wilder sale, Christie's, London, lot 37, to Arthur. By 1912, F. Nicholson, London. 1913, Agnew and Sons, London; 1913, sold by Agnew to Leopold Koppel (b. 1854–d. 1933), Berlin; around 1927, by descent to his son, Albert Koppel, Toronto; 1948, sold by Albert Koppel to Rosenberg and Stiebel, New York, for the Museum of Fine Arts, Boston.

SELECTED REFERENCES

Fischel, *Tizian*, 246, 323; Berenson, *Italian Pictures* 1:184; Valcanover, *L'opera completa di Tiziano*, cat. 478; Panofsky, *Problems in Titian*, 69–70; Wethey, *Paintings of Titian* 1:cat. 96; Wethey, *Paintings of Titian* 3:262 (addenda to volume 1); Hope, *Titian* (1980), 154, 160, 166; Hope, *Titian* (2004), 171–72, 177, 184.

26.

TINTORETTO

Nativity, late 1550s, reworked 1570s

155.6 x 358.1 cm (61¼ x 141 in.)

Museum of Fine Arts, Boston

Gift of Quincy A. Shaw, 46.1430

Photograph taken before cleaning and restoration

Photo: © Museum of Fine Arts, Boston

PROVENANCE

Until about 1860s or 1870s, said to be in a church in a town north of Florence; about 1860s or 1870s (possibly in 1874), sold by the church to Quincy Adams Shaw (b. 1825–d. 1908), Boston; by descent to his son, Quincy Adams Shaw, Jr., Boston; 1946, gift of Quincy Adams Shaw, Jr., to the Museum of Fine Arts, Boston.

SELECTED REFERENCES

Tietze and Tietze-Conrat, *Drawings of the Venetian Painters*, 300; Fredericksen and Zeri, *Census*, 199, 565; Pallucchini and Rossi, *Opere sacre e profane* 1:cat. A13; Ilchman in Falomir, *Tintoretto*, 322–23; Echols and Ilchman, "Toward a New Tintoretto Catalogue," cat. 280.

27.

TITIAN

Danaë, 1544–46

120 x 172 cm (47¼ x 67¹¹⁄₁₆ in.)

Museo di Capodimonte, Naples

Inv. Q134

Photo: Scala / Ministero per i Beni e le Attività culturali / Art Resource, NY

PROVENANCE

1544/46, Cardinal Alessandro Farnese (b. 1520–d. 1589), Palazzo Farnese, Rome (original commission); by inheritance within the Farnese family, Rome; by 1680, kept at the Palazzo Giardino, Parma; 1734, moved by Charles VII (b. 1716–d. 1788), king of Naples, and from 1759 on, kept at the Palazzo Capodimonte (later Museo di Capodimonte), Naples, and the royal palace at Portici; 1798, moved from Portici to Palermo; 1815, returned to Naples and kept at the Palazzo Capodimonte; 1943, removed from the Museo di Capodimonte to the abbey at Monte Cassino; 1943, seized by Nazi officers of the Hermann Goering Division and taken to Berlin; 1944, sent to Carinhall for presentation to Hermann Goering, but refused by him and placed in his bunker at Kurfürst; 1945, taken to the Reichschancellery, Berlin, and moved to Alt Aussee; July 15, 1945, recovered by Allied troops and taken to the Munich Central Collecting Point (no. 4360); August 13, 1947, restituted to Italy and returned to the Museo di Capodimonte.

SELECTED REFERENCES

Vasari, *Vite* 7:447; Ridolfi, *Le maraviglie* 1:178; Crowe and Cavalcaselle, *Life and Times of Titian* 2:119–21; Suida, *Le Titien*, 117, 175; Valcanover, *L'opera completa di Tiziano*, cat. 264; Panofsky, *Problems in Titian*, 23, 144–47; Wethey, *Paintings of Titian* 3:cat. 5; Hope, *Titian* (1980), 89–90; Rosand, *Titian*, 122; Biadene and Yakush, *Titian: Prince of Painters*, cat. 40; Laclotte, Nepi Scirè, et al., *Le siècle de Titien*, cat. 177; Goffen, *Titian's Women*, 215–18; Pedrocco, *Titian*, cat. 137; Jaffé, *Titian*, cat. 23; Falomir, *Tiziano*, cat. 27; Spinosa, *Tiziano e il ritratto di corte*, cat. 19; Kennedy, *Titian*, 62, 64–65, 67; Humfrey, *Titian: The Complete Paintings*, cat. 144.

28.
TITIAN
Venus with an Organist and a Dog, about 1550
138 x 222.4 cm (54⁵⁄₁₆ x 87⁹⁄₁₆ in.)
Museo Nacional del Prado, Madrid
420
Photo: Scala / Art Resource, NY

PROVENANCE

About 1550, Francesco Assonica, Venice (original commission). By 1639, Charles I (b. 1600–d. 1649), king of England and Scotland, Whitehall Palace, London; 1649, collected by the House of Commons for sale; November 8, 1649, sold by the Trustees of the Commonwealth to Colonel John Hutchinson (b. 1615–d. 1664), London; 1651, sold by Hutchinson to David Teniers (b. 1610–d. 1690), on behalf of Alonso Pérez de Vivero (b. 1603–d. 1661), 3rd Count of Fuensaldaña, for Philip IV (b. 1605–d. 1665), king of Spain, Madrid; by inheritance within the Spanish royal family; 1814, seized by French troops and taken to Paris; 1816, returned to Spain; 1827, transferred to the Museo Nacional del Prado.

SELECTED REFERENCES

Ridolfi, *Le maraviglie* 1:194; Crowe and Cavalcaselle, *Life and Times of Titian* 2:158 n.*; Suida, *Tiziano*, 175; Berenson, *Italian Pictures* 1:187; Valcanover, *L'opera completa di Tiziano*, cat. 341; Wethey, *Paintings of Titian* 3:cat. 50; Biadene and Yakush, *Titian: Prince of Painters*, cat. 48; Goffen, *Titian's Women*, 160–64; Falomir, *Tiziano*, cat. 41; Pedrocco, *Titian*, cat. 189; Humfrey, *Titian: The Complete Paintings*, cat. 192.

29.
TINTORETTO
Danaë, late 1570s–early 1580s
142 x 182 cm (55⅞ x 71⅝ in.)
Musée des Beaux-Arts, Lyon
Inv. A 91
Photo: Erich Lessing / Art Resource, NY

PROVENANCE

1624, acquired in France by Balthazar Gerbier (b. 1592–d. 1663) for George Villiers (b. 1592–d. 1628), 1st Duke of Buckingham, York House, London; by inheritance to George Villiers (b. 1628–d. 1687), 2nd Duke of Buckingham; 1648, sent to Amsterdam and then Antwerp; 1650, sold by Buckingham's financial advisers to Leopold Wilhelm (b. 1614–d. 1662), Archduke of Austria, for his brother, Ferdinand III (b. 1608–d. 1657), Holy Roman Emperor, Hradčany Castle, Prague, and Vienna; by descent within the Hapsburg dynasty to Francis II (b. 1768–d. 1835), Holy Roman Emperor, Vienna; 1792, exchanged by Francis II with his brother Ferdinand III (b. 1769–d. 1824), Grand Duke of Tuscany, Florence; 1796, returned to the imperial collection, Vienna; 1809, seized by French troops and taken to Paris; 1811, deposited at the Musée des Beaux-Arts, Lyon.

SELECTED REFERENCES

Tietze, *Tintoretto*, 43, 353; Berenson, *Italian Pictures* 1:174; De Vecchi, *L'opera completa del Tintoretto*, cat. 242; Pallucchini and Rossi, *Opere sacre e profane* 1:cat. 378; Laclotte, Nepi Scirè, et al., *Le siècle de Titien*, cat. 195; Laclotte et al., *Splendeur de Venise*, cat. 82; Falomir, *Tintoretto*, cat. 46; Echols and Ilchman, "Toward a New Tintoretto Catalogue," cat. 217 (as Jacopo responsible for the figure of Danaë, with the remainder by an assistant).

30.
TITIAN
Venus with a Mirror, about 1555
124.5 x 105.5 cm (49 x 41⁹⁄₁₆ in.)
National Gallery of Art, Washington, DC
Andrew W. Mellon Collection, 1937.1.34
Image courtesy of the Board of Trustees, National Gallery of Art, Washington, DC

PROVENANCE

By inheritance from the artist to his son, Pomponio Vecellio, Venice; 1581, sold by Vecellio to Cristoforo Barbarigo, Venice; until about 1850, by inheritance within the Barbarigo family; 1850, sold by the Barbarigo family to Czar Nicholas I of Russia (d. 1855), St. Petersburg; transferred to the State Hermitage Museum, St. Petersburg; 1931, deaccessioned by the Hermitage and sold through Matthiesen Gallery, Berlin, Colnaghi, London, and Knoedler, New York, to Andrew W. Mellon (b. 1855–d. 1937), Pittsburgh and Washington, DC; June 5, 1931, deeded by Mellon to the A. W. Mellon Educational and Charitable Trust, Pittsburgh; 1937, gift of the Mellon Trust to the National Gallery of Art.

SELECTED REFERENCES

Ridolfi, *Le maraviglie* 1:200; Boschini, *La carta*, 665; Crowe and Cavalcaselle, *Life and Times of Titian* 2:334–36; Valcanover, *L'opera completa di Tiziano*, cat. 384; Wethey, *Paintings of Titian* 3:cat. 51; Rosand, *Titian*, 33–34; Pignatti, *Golden Century*, 76, 162, cat. 21; Hope, *Titian* (1980), 149, 158–60; Rearick, *Art of Paolo Veronese*, 172–73; Biadene and Yakush, *Titian: Prince of Painters*, cat. 51; Goffen, *Titian's Women*, 133–39; Pedrocco, *Titian*, cat. 218; Kennedy, *Titian*, 79, 91; Ferino-Pagden, *Der Späte Tizian*, 484–88, 492–93, cat. 2.5; Humfrey, *Titian: The Complete Paintings*, cat. 194.

31.
TINTORETTO
Susannah and the Elders, about 1555–56
146.5 x 193.6 cm (57¹¹⁄₁₆ x 76¼ in.)
Kunsthistorisches Museum, Gemäldegalerie, Vienna
GG Inv. Nr. 1530
Photo: Kunsthistorisches Museum, Wien oder KHM, Wien

PROVENANCE

By 1648, Nicolas Regnier (b. 1591–d. 1667), Venice. 1677, Giovanni Battista Rovetta (b. about 1620–d. 1691), Venice. By 1712, Charles VI (b. 1685–d. 1740), Holy Roman Emperor, Vienna; by inheritance within the Hapsburg dynasty; 1919, transferred to the Kunsthistorisches Museum.

PROVENANCE NOTES

Probably the painting recorded by Ridolfi in 1648 in the collection of the painter Nicolas Regnier (Niccolo Renieri); unlike other paintings owned by Regnier, however, this did not make its way to the imperial collection in Vienna through James Hamilton, as it does not appear in the 1649 Hamilton inventory. It is not known precisely how or when it arrived in Vienna.

SELECTED REFERENCES

Ridolfi, *Le maraviglie* 2:56; Tietze, *Tintoretto*, 379; Berenson, *Italian Pictures* 1:182; De Vecchi, *L'opera completa del Tintoretto*, cat. 123; Pallucchini and Rossi, *Opere sacre e profane* 1:cat. 200; Nichols, *Tintoretto*, 90–93; Falomir, *Tintoretto*, cat. 31; Echols and Ilchman, "Toward a New Tintoretto Catalogue," cat. 64.

32.
VERONESE
Venus with a Mirror (*Venus at Her Toilette*), mid-1580s
161.3 x 120.7 cm (65 x 49 in.)
Joslyn Art Museum, Omaha, Nebraska
Joslyn Endowment Fund Purchase, 1942.4
Photo: Joslyn Art Museum, Omaha, Nebraska

PROVENANCE

By 1648, owned jointly by the Bevilacqua and Muselli families, Verona; mid-seventeenth century, ownership passed in full to the Bevilacqua family, Palazzo Bevilacqua, Modena; 1805, sold by Bevilacqua to Richard Pryor, London; February 6, 1810, Pryor sale, Christie's, London, lot 3, bought in. Thomas Lawrence (b. 1769–d. 1830), London; May 15, 1830, posthumous Lawrence sale, Christie's, London, lot 114, to Wood. By 1929, Alexander von Frey (b. 1882–d. 1951), Paris. By 1938, Jacob Hirsch, New York; 1942, sold by Hirsch to the Joslyn Art Museum.

SELECTED REFERENCES

Borghini, *Il riposo*, 563; Ridolfi, *Le maraviglie* 1:320, 335; Marini, *L'opera completa*, cat. 218c; Fredericksen and Zeri, *Census*, 39; Pignatti, *Veronese* 1:cat. 275; Pignatti, *Golden Century*, 128, 169, cat. 46; Pallucchini, *Veronese*, cat. 213; Rearick, *Art of Paolo Veronese*, cat. 87; Pignatti and Pedrocco, *Veronese: Catalogo completo dei dipinti*, cat. 231; Pignatti and Pedrocco, *Veronese* 2:cat. 357.

33.
TITIAN
Venus and Adonis, about 1555–60
160 x 196.5 cm (63 x 77⅜ in.)
The J. Paul Getty Museum, Los Angeles
92.PA.42
Photo: The J. Paul Getty Museum, Los Angeles, California

PROVENANCE

Giovanni Vincenzo Imperiale (b. 1582–d. 1648), Genoa; 1648, by inheritance to his heirs; 1665, sold by the heirs of Imperiale to Francesco Maria Balbi, Genoa; 1665, sold by Balbi to Christina, Queen of Sweden (b. 1626–d. 1689), Stockholm and Rome; 1689, by inheritance to Cardinal Decio Azzolino (b. 1623–d. 1689), Rome; 1689, by inheritance to his nephew, Marchese Pompeo Azzolino (d. 1696), Rome; 1692, sold by Pompeo Azzolino to Livio Odescalchi (b. 1652–d. 1713), Duke of Bracciano, Rome; 1713, by inheritance to his nephew Baldassare Erba Odescalchi (d. 1746), Rome; 1721, sold by Odescalchi to Pierre Crozat (b. 1665–d. 1740), Paris, for Philippe II (b. 1674–d. 1723), Duc d'Orléans, Paris; by descent within the House of Orléans to Louis-Philippe-Joseph (b. 1747–d. 1793), Duc d'Orléans, Paris; 1792, sold by Walkiers to François-Louis-Joseph de Laborde-Méréville (b. 1761–d. 1802), Paris and London; 1798, consigned by Laborde-Méréville to Jeremiah Harman (b. 1764–d. 1844), London; 1798, sold by Harman to Michael Bryan (b. 1757–d. 1821), London, for a consortium of Francis Egerton (b. 1736–d. 1803), 3rd Duke of Bridgewater, Frederick Howard (b. 1748–d. 1825), 5th Earl of Carlisle, and George Granville Leveson-Gower (b. 1758–d. 1833), Earl Gower and 1st Duke of Sutherland, London; December 26, 1798, Orléans collection sale, London, lot 224, to Fitzhugh; 1844, sold by Fitzhugh to Welbore Ellis Agar (b. 1778–d. 1868), 2nd Earl of Normanton, Somerly, England; by inheritance within the family to Shaun James Christian Welbore Ellis Agar, 6th Earl of Normanton, Somerly; December 13, 1991, Normanton sale, Christie's, London, lot 85, to Hazlitt, Gooden, and Fox, London, and Herman Shickman Gallery, New York; 1992, sold by Hazlitt, Gooden, and Fox and Shickman Gallery to the J. Paul Getty Museum.

SELECTED REFERENCES

Waagen, *Treasures of Art* 3:219; Wethey, *Paintings of Titian* 3:60, cat. 42; Laclotte, Nepi Scirè, et al., *Le siècle de Titien*, 617; Goffen, *Titian's Women*, 248, 250; Penny, *Sixteenth Century Italian Paintings*, 2:280–81.

34.
VERONESE
Mars and Venus United by Love, mid-1570s
Signed on stone fragment at bottom, "PAVLVS VERONENSIS F"
205.7 x 161 cm (81 x 63⅜ in.)
The Metropolitan Museum of Art, New York
John Stewart Kennedy Fund, 1910, 10.189
Image © The Metropolitan Museum of Art

PROVENANCE

Rudolph II (b. 1552–d. 1612), Holy Roman Emperor, Prague; by inheritance to Ferdinand III (b. 1608–d. 1657), Holy Roman Emperor, Prague; 1648, seized by Swedish troops and given to the collection of Christina, queen of Sweden (b. 1626–d. 1689), Stockholm and Rome; 1689, by inheritance to Cardinal Decio Azzolino (b. 1623–d. 1689), Rome; 1689, by inheritance to his nephew, Marchese Pompeo Azzolino (d. 1696), Rome; 1692, sold by Pompeo Azzolino to Livio Odescalchi (b. 1652–d. 1713), Duke of Bracciano, Rome; 1713, by inheritance to his nephew, Baldassare Erba Odescalchi (d. 1746), Rome; 1721, sold by Odescalchi to Pierre Crozat (b. 1665–d. 1740), Paris, for Philippe II (b. 1674–d. 1723), Duc d'Orléans, Paris; by descent within the House of Orléans to Louis-Philippe-Joseph (b. 1747–d. 1793), Duc d'Orléans, Paris; 1792, sold from the Orléans collection to Edouard Walkiers (b. 1764?–d. 1844), Brussels; 1792, sold by Walkiers to François-Louis-Joseph de

Laborde-Méréville (b. 1761–d. 1802), Paris and London; 1798, consigned by Laborde-Méréville to Jeremiah Harman (b. 1764–d. 1844), London; 1798, sold by Harman to Michael Bryan (b. 1757–d. 1821), London, for a consortium of Francis Egerton (b. 1736–d. 1803), 3rd Duke of Bridgewater, Frederick Howard (b. 1748–d. 1825), 5th Earl of Carlisle, and George Granville Leveson-Gower (b. 1758–d. 1833), Earl Gower and 1st Duke of Sutherland, London; December 26, 1798, Orléans collection sale, Bryan's Gallery, London, lot 273, to Hastings Elwyn, Booten; May 23, 1806, Elwyn sale, Phillips, London, lot 23, sold to an unknown buyer. 1866, Campbell, London; 1866, sold by Campbell to Ivor Bertie Guest (b. 1835–d. 1914), 1st Baron Wimborne of Canford Magna, Dorset; May 23, 1903, Wimborne sale, Christie's, London, lot 75. With Lepper. 1909, Asher Wertheimer, London, 1910, sold by Wertheimer, through Blakeslee Galleries, to the Metropolitan Museum of Art.

SELECTED REFERENCES

Borghini, *Il riposo*, 563; Ridolfi, *Le maraviglie* 1:334; Fredericksen and Zeri, *Census*, 39; Pignatti, *Veronese* 1:cat. 248; Pallucchini, *Veronese*, 114, 126, cat. 174; Rearick, *Art of Paolo Veronese*, cat. 68; Pignatti and Pedrocco, *Veronese: Catalogo completo dei dipinti*, cat. 165; Pignatti and Pedrocco, *Veronese* 2:cat. 265; Salomon, *Veronese's Allegories*, cat. 3.

35.

TITIAN

Portrait of a Man (Tommaso Mosti?), about 1520
85 x 69 cm (33⁷⁄₁₆ x 27³⁄₁₆ in.)
Galleria Palatina, Florence
Inv. 1912: n. 495
Photo: Scala / Art Resource, NY

PROVENANCE

By about 1663–67, Leopoldo de' Medici (b. 1617–d. 1675), Florence; by descent within the Medici family and kept at the Palazzo Pitti, Florence; June 12, 1940, removed from the Palazzo Pitti to the Villa Medici, Poggio a Caiano; October 31, 1940, taken to the Hermitage of Camaldoli, Poppi; July 6, 1945, returned to the Palazzo Pitti, Florence.

SELECTED REFERENCES

Crowe and Cavalcaselle, *Life and Times of Titian* 1:303; Suida, *Le Titien*, 33, 161; Berenson, *Italian Pictures* 1:185; Valcanover, *L'opera completa di Tiziano*, cat. 95; Wethey, *Paintings of Titian* 2:cat. 67; Hope, *Titian* (1980), 62, 64; Martineau and Hope, *Genius of Venice*, cat. 118; Biadene and Yakush, *Titian: Prince of Painters*, cat. 16; Aikema and Brown, *Renaissance Venice*, cat. 88; Humfrey, *Titian: The Complete Paintings*, cat. 70.

36.

TINTORETTO

Portrait of a Man Aged Twenty-Six, 1547
Inscribed at left,
"ANN.XXVI.MEN.VI.MD.XLVII."
130 x 97 cm (51⅛ x 38⅛ in.)
Kröller-Müller Museum, Otterlo, the Netherlands
KM 108.448
Photo: Kröller-Müller Museum, Otterlo, the Netherlands

PROVENANCE

Balbi collection, Venice. Possibly Giustinian-Lolin collection, Venice. 1900, Reinhold von Liphart (b. 1864–d. 1940?), Rathshof, near Dorpat; October 11, 1921, Liphart sale, Mak van Waay, Amsterdam, lot 1, to Helene Kröller-Müller (b. 1869–d. 1939), Otterlo; transferred to the Kröller-Müller Museum.

SELECTED REFERENCES

Pallucchini, *La giovinezza*, 118; Berenson, *Italian Pictures* 1:176; De Vecchi, *L'opera completa*, cat. 60; Rossi, *Jacopo Tintoretto* (1974) 1:118; Rossi, *Jacopo Tintoretto: Ritratti* (1994), 16; Falomir, *Tintoretto*, cat. 8.

37.

VERONESE

Portrait of a Man, about 1551–53
120 x 102 cm (47¼ x 40⅛ in.)
Szépművészeti Múzeum, Budapest
Inv. no. 4228
Photo: Szépművészeti Múzeum, Budapest

PROVENANCE

Count János Pálffy (b. 1829–d. 1908), Pozsony, Bratislava; 1912, bequest of Pálffy to the Szépművészeti Múzeum.

SELECTED REFERENCES

Berenson, *Italian Pictures* 1:130; Marini, *L'opera completa*, cat. 114; Pignatti, *Veronese* 1:cat. 107; Pallucchini, *Veronese*, 71, cat. 51; Rearick, *Paolo Veronese: Disegni e dipinti*, cat. 54; Pignatti and Pedrocco, *Veronese: Catalogo completo*, cat. 60; Pignatti and Pedrocco, *Veronese* 1:cat. 129; Keyes, Bárkóczi, and Satkowski, *Treasures of Venice*, cat. 48; Garton, *Grace and Grandeur*, 145–46, cat. 7.

38.

TITIAN

Portrait of a Man Holding a Book, about 1540
Signed at lower left, "Ticianus"
97.8 x 77.2 cm (38½ x 30⅜ in.)
Museum of Fine Arts, Boston
Charles Potter Kling Fund, 43.83
Photo: © Museum of Fine Arts, Boston

PROVENANCE

Until 1650, possibly the Oneto family, Genoa; 1650, possibly brought by Don Giovan Stefano Oneto and Don Agostino Oneto from Genoa to Palermo, Sicily; by descent within the Oneto family to Don Giuseppe Oneto e Lanza (d. 1852), Duke of Sperlinga, Palermo, and Naples; 1864, sold by the heirs of Oneto e Lanza to the Count of Francavilla, Palermo; by descent to his son, Luigi Maria Majorca Mortillaro, Count of Francavilla, Palermo; about 1901/7, sold by Majorca Mortillaro to Agnew and Sons, London. Trotti et Companie, Paris. Purchased in Paris by Cottier and Company, New York; April 29, 1907, sold by Cottier to Frederick B. Pratt, Brooklyn; April 3, 1943, sold by Pratt to Knoedler and Co., New York, and Pinakos, Inc., New York; 1943, sold by Knoedler and Pinakos to the Museum of Fine Arts, Boston.

PROVENANCE NOTES

On the reverse of the canvas is an inscription: "Ritratto di Giovan Paolo Baglione Signore di Perugia, che mori in Roma nell'anno 1520. Fatto da Tiziano. Nell'angolo sotto, sotto il libro si legge *Titianus*." Moreover, there are three wax seals on the reverse, of which two are illegible and one bears a coat of arms that is still unidentified. It is not identical to the arms of either the Oneto or Mortillaro families. Because the lining of the canvas dates to about the eighteenth or nineteenth century, the inscription and marks on the reverse of the canvas cannot be earlier than the eighteenth century.

SELECTED REFERENCES

Suida, *Tiziano*, 88, 164; Berenson, *Italian Pictures* 1:184; Valcanover, *L'opera completa di Tiziano*, cat. 250; Wethey, *Paintings of Titian* 2:cat. 47; Fredericksen and Zeri, *Census*, 201; Spinosa, *Tiziano e il ritratto di corte*, cat. 13.

39.

TINTORETTO

Portrait of a Man, about 1548
109.2 x 88.9 cm (43 x 35 in.)
Private Collection

PROVENANCE

By 1927, Jacob von Danzas (b. 1876–d. 1943), Berlin. Hans Duensing, Boizenburg, Germany; probably by descent to his daughter, Alice von Guggenberg (b. 1911–d. 2001), Lucerne; June 26, 1964, probably Guggenberg ("property of a lady") sale, Christie's, London, lot 47, to David. 2002, Derek Johns, London; sold by Derek Johns to a private collection.

SELECTED REFERENCES

Rossi, *Jacopo Tintoretto* (1974) 1:98; Rossi, *Tintoretto: Ritratti* (1994), cat. 16.

40.

TINTORETTO

Sebastiano Venier, about 1571–72
104.5 x 83.5 cm (41⅛ x 32⅞ in.)
Kunsthistorisches Museum, Gemäldegalerie, Vienna
GG Inv. Nr. 32
Photo: Erich Lessing / Art Resource, NY

PROVENANCE

1636, Bartolomeo della Nave, Venice; 1638, sold from the della Nave collection to Basil Fielding (b. about 1608–d. 1675) for his brother-in-law, James Hamilton (b. 1606–d. 1649), 3rd Marquess of Hamilton; about 1649/1650, acquired by Leopold Wilhelm (b. 1614–d. 1662), archduke of Austria, Brussels and Vienna; by inheritance within the Hapsburg dynasty; 1919, transferred to the Kunsthistorisches Museum.

SELECTED REFERENCES

Berenson, *Italian Pictures* 1:182; De Vecchi, *L'opera completa del Tintoretto*, cat. F63; Rossi, *Jacopo Tintoretto* (1974) 1:65, 130; Martineau and Hope, *Genius of Venice*, cat. 108; Rossi, *Jacopo Tintoretto: Ritratti* (1994), cat. 33; Rearick, "Reflections on Tintoretto as a Portraitist," 62; Falomir, *Tintoretto*, 106, 109.

41.

VERONESE

Agostino Barbarigo, about 1571–72
102.2 x 104.2 cm (40¼ x 41 in.)
Cleveland Museum of Art
Gift of Mrs. L. E. Holden, Mr. and Mrs. Guerdon S. Holden and the L. E. Holden Fund, 1928.16
Photo: © The Cleveland Museum of Art

PROVENANCE

Probably by 1648 until at least 1856, Manfrin collection, Venice. 1927, Galerie H. O. Miethke, Vienna; 1927, sold by Miethke to Italico Brass (b. 1870–d. 1943), Venice; 1928, sold by Italico Brass, through Harold W. Parsons, to the Cleveland Museum of Art.

SELECTED REFERENCES

Berenson, *Italian Pictures* 1:130; Marini, *L'opera completa*, cat. 139a; Fredericksen and Zeri, *Census*, 39; Pignatti, *Veronese* 1:cat. 172; Pignatti, *Golden Century*, 124, 168–69, cat. 44; Pallucchini, *Veronese*, 155; Rearick, *Art of Paolo Veronese*, cat. 54; Pignatti and Pedrocco, *Veronese: Catalogo completo dei dipinti*, cat. 108; Pignatti and Pedrocco, *Veronese* 1:cat. 188; Romanelli and Strinati, *Gods, Heroes, and Allegories*, cat. 22; Garton, *Grace and Grandeur*, 99–101, cat. 18.

42.

TITIAN

Ranuccio Farnese, 1542
Signed at right, "TITIANVS .F."
89.7 x 73.6 cm (35⁵⁄₁₆ x 29 in.)
National Gallery of Art, Washington, DC
Samuel H. Kress Collection, 1952.2.11
Image courtesy of the Board of Trustees, National Gallery of Art, Washington, DC

PROVENANCE

By 1620, Farnese family, Parma and Naples; by 1880, acquired in Naples by George Donaldson, London; May 1880, sold by Donaldson to Sir John Charles Robinson (b. 1824–d. 1913), London; by 1885, sold by Robinson to Sir Francis Cook (b. 1817–d. 1901), 1st Bt., Doughty House, Richmond, Surrey; by inheritance within the family to Sir Francis Ferdinand Maurice Cook (b. 1907–d. 1978), 4th Bt., Doughty House and Cothay Manor, Somerset; June or July 1947, sold by Cook to Gualtiero Volterra, London, for Alessandro Contini Bonacossi, Florence; July 1948, sold by Contini Bonacossi to the Samuel H. Kress Foundation, New York; 1952, gift of the Kress Foundation to the National Gallery of Art.

SELECTED REFERENCES

Crowe and Cavalcaselle, *Life and Times of Titian* 2:75–77; Suida, *Le Titien*, 92, 169; Berenson, *Italian Pictures* 1:192; Valcanover, *L'opera completa di Tiziano*, cat. 224; Wethey, *Paintings of Titian* 2:cat. 31; Rosand, *Titian*, 114; Martineau and Hope, *Genius of Venice*, cat. 121; Biadene and Yakush, *Titian: Prince of Painters*, cat. 33; Pedrocco, *Titian*, cat. 122; Jaffé, *Titian*, cat. 25; Kennedy, *Titian*, 62–63; Humfrey, *Titian: The Complete Paintings*, cat. 134.

43.
VERONESE
Iseppo da Porto and His Son Adriano, about 1551
207 x 137 cm (81½ x 53⅞ in.)
Galleria degli Uffizi, Florence
Donazione Contini Bonacossi, Inv. Contini Bonacossi, 16
Photo: Galleria degli Uffizi, Florence, Italy / The Bridgeman Art Library

PROVENANCE
About 1551/52, Giuseppe (Iseppo) da Porto, Vicenza (original commission). Alessandro Contini Bonacossi (b. 1878–d. 1955), Florence; 1969, bequest of Contini Bonacossi to the Italian state.

SELECTED REFERENCES
Berenson, *Italian Pictures* 1:131; Marini, *L'opera completa*, cat. 33; Pignatti, *Veronese* 1:cat. 20; Pallucchini, *Veronese*, 24, cat. 17; Rearick, *Art of Paolo Veronese*, 38–40; Pignatti and Pedrocco, *Veronese: Catalogo completo dei dipinti*, cat. 22; Pignatti and Pedrocco, *Veronese* 1:cat. 28; Ajmar-Wollheim and Dennis, *At Home*, 137–39, cat. 4; Garton, *Grace and Grandeur*, 26–33, 187–88, cat. 5.

44.
VERONESE
Livia da Porto Thiene and Her Daughter Porzia, about 1551
208.4 x 121 cm (82 1/16 x 47⅝ in.)
The Walters Art Museum, Baltimore
Acquired by Henry Walters, 1921, 37.541
Photo: © The Walters Art Museum, Baltimore

PROVENANCE
About 1551/52, Giuseppe (Iseppo) da Porto, Vicenza (original commission). Private collection, Vicenza. 1921, Paolo Paolini, Rome; sold by Paolini to Henry Walters (b. 1848–d. 1931), Baltimore; 1931, bequest of Henry Walters to the Walters Art Museum.

SELECTED REFERENCES
Berenson, *Italian Pictures* 1:129; Marini, *L'opera completa*, cat. 34; Pignatti, *Veronese* 1:cat. 21; Pallucchini, *Veronese*, 24, cat. 18; Rearick, *Art of Paolo Veronese*, cat. 11; Pignatti and Pedrocco, *Veronese: Catalogo completo dei dipinti*, cat. 23; Pignatti and Pedrocco, *Veronese* 1:cat. 29; Ajmar-Wollheim and Dennis, *At Home*, 137–39, cat. 5; Garton, *Grace and Grandeur*, 26–33, cat. 6.

45.
TITIAN
Tarquin and Lucretia, about 1568–71
193 x 143 cm (75.27 x 55.77 in.)
Musée des Beaux-Arts, Bordeaux
Inv. n. E 42
Photo: Cameraphoto Arte, Venice / Art Resource, NY

PROVENANCE
By 1622, Thomas Howard (b. 1685–d. 1646), 2nd Earl of Arundel; by 1639, given by Howard to Charles I (b. 1600–d. 1649), king of Scotland and England, Whitehall Palace; 1649, collected by the House of Commons for sale; October 25, 1649, Commonwealth sale to Colonel William Webb. By 1653, Jules Mazarin (b. 1602–d. 1661), Paris; after 1665, assigned by Mazarin's heirs to Louis XIV (b. 1638–d. 1715), king of France, Paris; by inheritance within the French royal family; 1805, transferred to the Musée des Beaux-Arts, Bordeaux.

SELECTED REFERENCES
Ridolfi, *Le maraviglie* 1:xxviii, 196; Crowe and Cavalcaselle, *Life and Times of Titian* 2:392–93, 538; Valcanover, *L'opera completa di Tiziano*, cat. 497; Wethey, *Paintings of Titian* 3:cat. 35; Pedrocco, *Titian*, cat. 259; Laclotte et al., *Splendeur de Venise*, cat. 95; Ferino-Pagden, *Late Titian*, cat. 2.6.

46.
TINTORETTO
Tarquin and Lucretia, 1578–80
175 x 151.5 cm (68⅞ x 59⅝ in.)
The Art Institute of Chicago
Art Institute Purchase Fund, 1949.203
Photography © The Art Institute of Chicago

PROVENANCE
Private collection, France. 1937, Robert Lebel (b. 1901–d. 1986), Paris. 1939, Richard Goetz, Paris and New York. 1949, E. and A. Silberman Galleries, New York; 1949, sold by Silberman to the Art Institute of Chicago.

PROVENANCE NOTES
A Tintoretto *Tarquin and Lucretia* was recorded in the Tronsarelli collection. Based on the fact that several drawings from the Tronsarelli collection were subsequently with Thomas Lawrence, the *Tarquin and Lucretia* by Tintoretto that later appears in the Lawrence collection may be assumed to come from Tronsarelli as well. Unfortunately, however, the Chicago painting cannot be identified with the Lawrence picture, which measured 39 x 33 cm (15⅜ x 13 in.).

SELECTED REFERENCES
Tietze, *Tintoretto*, 357; Pallucchini, *La giovinezza*, 151; Berenson, *Italian Pictures* 1:171; De Vecchi, *L'opera completa del Tintoretto*, cat. 131a; Fredericksen and Zeri, *Census*, 199; Pallucchini and Rossi, *Opere sacre e profane* 1:cat. 450; Falomir, *Tintoretto*, cat. 42; Echols and Ilchman, "Toward a New Tintoretto Catalogue," cat. 219.

47.
VERONESE
Perseus and Andromeda, late 1570s–early 1580s
260 x 211 cm (102⅜ x 83 1/16 in.)
Musée des Beaux-Arts, Rennes
Inv. 801.1.1
Photo: Erich Lessing / Art Resource, NY

PROVENANCE
By 1662, Nicolas Fouquet (b. about 1615–d. 1680), Paris; 1662, collection seized and impounded; by 1665, purchased by Louis XIV (b. 1638–d. 1715), king of France, Versailles; by inheritance within the French royal family; 1801, deposited at the Musée des Beaux-Arts, Rennes.

SELECTED REFERENCES
Berenson, *Italian Pictures* 1:135; Marini, *L'opera completa*, cat. 282; Pignatti, *Veronese* 1:cat. A262; Rearick, *Art of Paolo Veronese*, cat. 86; Pignatti and Pedrocco, *Veronese: Catalogo completo dei dipinti*, cat. 152; Laclotte, Nepi Scirè, et al., *Le siècle de Titien*, cat. 198; Pignatti and Pedrocco, *Veronese* 2:cat. 256; Laclotte et al., *Splendeur de Venise*, cat. 109.

48.
TITIAN
Boy with Dogs in a Landscape, about 1570–75
99.5 x 117 cm (39 3/16 x 46 1/16 in.)
Museum Boijmans Van Beuningen, Rotterdam
Inv. No. 2569
Photo: Museum Boijmans Van Beuningen, Rotterdam

PROVENANCE
Serbelloni collection, Milan. By 1651 until 1665, Francesco del Cairo (b. 1607–d. 1665), Milan. 1930, Goudstikker, Amsterdam; 1930, sold by Goudstikker to Daniël George van Beuningen (b. 1877–d. 1955), Rotterdam; 1958, purchased by the city of Rotterdam for the Museum Boijmans (later Boijmans Van Beuningen).

SELECTED REFERENCES
Suida, *Tiziano*, 107, 113; Berenson, *Italian Pictures* 1:192; Ballarin, "L'orto del Bassano," 55–56; Panofsky, *Problems in Titian*, 171, n. 85; Valcanover, *L'opera completa di Tiziano*, cat. 500; Wethey, *Paintings of Titian* 3:90–91, cat. 2; Ost, *Tizians Kasseler Kavalier*, 49–55; Martineau and Hope, *Genius of Venice*, cat. 128; Biadene and Yakush, *Titian: Prince of Painters*, cat. 72; Laclotte, Nepi Scirè, et al., *Le siècle de Titien*, cat. 263; Ferino-Pagden, *Late Titian*, cat. 2.8; Humfrey, *Titian: The Complete Paintings*, cat. 288.

49.
VERONESE
Cupid with Two Dogs, about 1581
100 x 134 cm (39⅜ x 52¾ in.)
Alte Pinakothek, Munich
Inv.-Nr. 29
Photo: Bildarchiv Preussischer Kulturbesitz / Art Resource, NY

PROVENANCE
By 1692, Maximilian II Emanuel (b. 1662–d. 1726), Elector of Bavaria, Schleissheim Castle, Oberschleissheim; by inheritance within the Wittelsbach dynasty; 1836, transferred to the Alte Pinakothek.

SELECTED REFERENCES
Berenson, *Italian Pictures* 1:134; Marini, *L'opera completa*, cat. 217; Pignatti, *Veronese* 1:cat. 276; Pallucchini, *Veronese*, cat. 212; Rearick, *Art of Paolo Veronese*, cat. 69; Pignatti and Pedrocco, *Veronese: Catalogo completo dei dipinti*, cat. 232; Pignatti and Pedrocco, *Veronese* 2:cat. 358; Romanelli and Strinati, *Gods, Heroes, and Allegories*, cat. 37.

50.
TINTORETTO
Saint Jerome in the Wilderness, about 1571–72
143.5 x 103 cm (56½ x 40 9/16 in.)
Kunsthistorisches Museum, Gemäldegalerie, Vienna
GG Inv.Nr. 46
Photo: Erich Lessing / Art Resource, NY

PROVENANCE
By 1648, Priuli family, Venice. 1677, Giovanni Battista Rovetta (b. about 1620–d. 1691), Venice. By 1783, Joseph II (b. 1741–d. 1790), Holy Roman Emperor, Vienna; by inheritance within Hapsburg dynasty; 1919, transferred to the Kunsthistorisches Museum.

PROVENANCE NOTES
Probably owned by Michiel Priuli (d. 1638), who built up the Priuli collection, this was thought to be first recorded at the Palazzo Priuli by Ridolfi in 1648. Like Tintoretto's *Susannah*, this painting was with Rovetta in 1677 and does not appear in the 1649 Hamilton inventory.

SELECTED REFERENCES
Ridolfi, *Le maraviglie* 2:55 n. 2; Tietze, *Tintoretto*, 379–80; Berenson, *Italian Pictures* 1:182; De Vecchi, *L'opera completa del Tintoretto*, cat. 211; Pallucchini and Rossi, *Opere sacre e profane* 1:cat. 325; Nichols, *Tintoretto*, 107; Falomir, *Tintoretto*, cat. 38; Echols and Ilchman, "Toward a New Tintoretto Catalogue," cat. 155.

51.
TITIAN
Saint Jerome in the Wilderness, about 1570–75
135 x 96 cm (53⅛ x 37 13/16 in.)
Museo Thyssen-Bornemisza, Madrid
Inv. 1933.4
Photo: Scala / Art Resource, NY

PROVENANCE
S. E. W. Browne, London. 1920, possibly Mordasewicz collection, Paris. 1931, Julius Böhler, Munich; probably passed directly from Böhler to F. Steinmeyer, New York. 1934, acquired by Heinrich Thyssen (b. 1875–d. 1947), Lugano; 1993, acquired by the Museo Thyssen-Bornemisza.

PROVENANCE NOTES
This painting has been identified with the Titian *Saint Jerome* that was in the collection of Francesco Maria Balbi in 1780 and that was sold by the Balbi family in 1806 to Andrew Wilson, who imported it to London. Nevertheless, in the 1807 auction catalogue of Wilson's pictures, the dimensions of the *Saint Jerome* were given as 7 cm high x 7.6 cm wide (2¾ x 3 in.), which do not accord with the Thyssen picture. The Balbi *Saint Jerome* later appeared in the sale of the Duke of Lucca (1841) and was described as being done "in [Titian's] first manner," which would not accurately describe the present composition.

SELECTED REFERENCES
Suida, *Tiziano*, 123–24, 170; Berenson, *Italian Pictures* 1:187; Valcanover, *L'opera completa di Tiziano*, cat. 411; Wethey, *Paintings of Titian* 1:cat. 107; Hope, *Titian* (1980), 155; Biadene and Yakush, *Titian: Prince of Painters*, cat. 68; Pedrocco, *Titian*, 237, cat. 255; Falomir, *Tiziano*, cat. 59; Ferino-Pagden, *Late Titian*, cat. 3.18; Humfrey, *Titian: The Complete Paintings*, cat. 285.

52.
VERONESE
Saint Jerome in the Wilderness, about 1580
251 x 167 cm (98 13/16 x 65 3/4 in.)
Gallerie dell'Accademia, Venice
Photo: Erich Lessing / Art Resource, NY

PROVENANCE

About 1580, church of Sant'Andrea della Zirada, Venice (original commission, small altar to the right of the high altar); 1971, removed from the church and placed on deposit at the Gallerie dell'Accademia.

SELECTED REFERENCES

Ridolfi, *Le maraviglie* 1:325; Marini, *L'opera completa*, cat. 284; Pignatti, *Veronese* 1:cat. 188; Pallucchini, *Veronese*, cat. 151; Pignatti and Pedrocco, *Veronese: Catalogo completo dei dipinti*, cat. 171; Laclotte, Nepi Scirè, et al., *Le siècle de Titien*, cat. 200; Pignatti and Pedrocco, *Veronese* 2:cat. 271.

53.
TINTORETTO
Baptism of Christ, about 1580
283 x 162 cm (111 7/16 x 63 3/4 in.)
Church of San Silvestro, Venice
Photo: Francesco Turio Bohm

SELECTED REFERENCES

Borghini, *Il riposo*, 554; Ridolfi, *Le maraviglie* 2:41; Boschini, *Le minere*, 254; Tietze, *Tintoretto*, 373; Berenson, *Italian Pictures* 1:181; De Vecchi, *L'opera completa del Tintoretto*, cat. 244; Pallucchini and Rossi, *Opere sacre e profane* 1:cat. 408; Echols and Ilchman, "Toward a New Tintoretto Catalogue," cat. 253.

54.
VERONESE
Baptism of Christ, early 1580s
104.8 x 88.3 cm (41 1/4 x 34 3/4 in.)
The J. Paul Getty Museum, Los Angeles
79.PA.19
Photo: The J. Paul Getty Museum, Los Angeles, California

PROVENANCE

Possibly Giacomo Muselli (b. 1550–d. 1641), Verona; by inheritance within the family; 1685/86, possibly sold by the Muselli family to Louis Alvarez (d. after 1692) for Jean-Baptiste Colbert (b. 1651–d. 1690), Marquis de Seignelay. 1829, George Hibbert (b. 1757–d. 1837), London; June 13, 1829, Hibbert sale, Christie's, London, lot 39, to Samuel Woodin, probably on behalf of Thomas Bruce (b. 1766–d. 1841), 7th Earl of Elgin, for his cousin Charles Stirling (b. 1771–d. 1830), Cawder, Scotland; by descent within the family to William Joseph Stirling, Keir, Scotland; July 3, 1963, Stirling sale, Sotheby's, London, lot 48, to Julius H. Weitzner and Hallsborough Gallery, London; 1970s, sold by Weitzner and Hallsborough to Virginia Duffield, Geneva; 1979, sold by Duffield, through P. & D. Colnaghi and Co., New York, to the J. Paul Getty Museum.

PROVENANCE NOTES

The Getty painting cannot be identical with the Veronese *Baptism* that was in the collection of Richard Sullivan, London, as has sometimes been suggested. Two early nineteenth-century sales of Sullivan's collection include a Veronese "Baptism of Our Savior"—described in the 1808 catalogue as "a concert of angels above . . . from the Orléans collection." Because many of the paintings owned by the Marquis de Seignelay made their way to the Orléans collection, the Getty painting is presumed to have come from the Orléans collection as well.

Sullivan's *Baptism* was bought in at both early sales, however, and it reappears in an 1859 auction of his collection. By this date, the Getty *Baptism* was securely in the Stirling collection, as described by Waagen.

SELECTED REFERENCES

Pignatti, *Veronese* 1:cat. 220; Cocke, *Veronese's Drawings*, 198, 245; Pallucchini, *Veronese*, 104, cat. 171; Rearick, *Art of Paolo Veronese*, cat. 79; Pignatti and Pedrocco, *Veronese: Catalogo completo*, cat. 160; Pignatti and Pedrocco, *Veronese* 2:cat. 287; Humfrey, *Age of Titian*, cat. 70.

55.
TITIAN
Entombment, 1559
Signed on tablet, "TITIAN^S VECELL^iVS AEQVES CAES."
137 x 175 cm (53 15/16 x 68 7/8 in.)
Museo Nacional del Prado, Madrid
440
Photo: Photographic Archive, Museo Nacional del Prado, Madrid

PROVENANCE

1559, Philip II (b. 1527–d. 1598), king of Spain, Madrid (original commission); by inheritance within the Spanish royal family at the Real Monasterio del Escorial, Madrid; 1837, transferred to the Museo Nacional del Prado.

SELECTED REFERENCES

Crowe and Cavalcaselle, *Life and Times of Titian* 2:289–92; Berenson, *Italian Pictures* 1:188; Valcanover, *L'opera completa di Tiziano*, cat. 403; Wethey, *Paintings of Titian* 1:cat. 37; Hope, *Titian* (1980), 37, 128, 131, 133; Martineau and Hope, *Genius of Venice*, cat. 127; Laclotte, Nepi Scirè, et al., *Le siècle de Titien*, cat. 253; Pedrocco, *Titian*, cat. 207; Jaffé, *Titian*, cat. 31; Falomir, *Tiziano*, cat. 47; Hope, *Titian* (2003), 40, 146, 148; Humfrey, *Titian: The Complete Paintings*, cat. 222.

56.
TINTORETTO
Self-Portrait, about 1588
Inscribed at right, remaining portion reads, "IPSIVS."
63 x 52 cm (24.8 x 20.5 in.)
Musée du Louvre, Paris
Inv. 572
Photo: Jean-Gilles Berizzi / Réunion des Musées Nationaux / Art Resource, NY

PROVENANCE

Hans Jakob König (b. before 1536–d. 1600), Venice; about 1603, König collection dispersed. Henrietta Anne (b. 1644–d. 1670), princess of England and duchess of Orléans, Palais Royal; by inheritance within the house of Orléans to Louis-Philippe (b. 1725–d. 1785), Duc d'Orléans, Palais Royal and Saint-Cloud; 1785, sold from the Orléans collection to Marie-Antoinette (b. 1755–d. 1793), queen of France; 1792, transferred to the Musée du Louvre.

SELECTED REFERENCES

Tietze, *Tintoretto*, 358; De Vecchi, *L'opera completa del Tintoretto*, cat. 272; Rossi, *Jacopo Tintoretto* (1974) 1:74, 119; Brown, *The Painter's Reflection*, 89–90, cat. 27; Habert and Pomarède, *Tiziano e la Pittura del Cinquecento*, 56–58; Falomir, *Tintoretto*, cat. 48.

Figure Illustrations

Fig. 1
Jacopo Sansovino (about 1486–1570)
Interior of the Reading Room
Libreria Marciana, Venice
Photo: Biblioteca Marciana, Venice, Italy / The Bridgeman Art Library

Fig. 2
Veronese
Allegory of Music, 1556–57
Oil on canvas
230 cm (90 9/16 in.) diameter
Libreria Marciana, Venice
Photo: Biblioteca Marciana, Venice, Italy / The Bridgeman Art Library

Fig. 3
Tintoretto
Saint Roch in Glory, 1564
Oil on canvas
240 x 360 cm (94 1/2 x 141 3/4 in.)
Sala dell'Albergo, Scuola Grande di San Rocco, Venice
Photo: Cameraphoto Arte, Venice / Art Resource, NY

Fig. 4
Rosso Fiorentino (Giovanni Battista di Jacopo) (Italian, 1494–1540)
Dead Christ with Angels, about 1524–27
Oil on panel
133.4 x 104.1 cm (52 1/2 x 41 in.)
Museum of Fine Arts, Boston
Charles Potter Kling Fund, 58.257
Photo: © Museum of Fine Arts, Boston

Fig. 5
Tintoretto
Miracle of the Slave, 1548
Oil on canvas
416 x 544 cm (163 4/5 x 214 3/16 in.)
Gallerie dell'Accademia, Venice
Inv. n. 45
Photo: Scala / Ministero per i Beni e le Attività culturali / Art Resource, NY

Fig. 6
Domenico Tintoretto and Workshop, following designs by Jacopo Tintoretto
Paradiso, 1588–92
Oil on canvas
700 x 2200 cm (275 9/16 x 866 1/8 in.)
Sala del Maggior Consiglio, Palazzo Ducale, Venice
Photo: Cameraphoto Arte, Venice / Art Resource, NY

Fig. 7
Church of Santa Maria Gloriosa dei Frari, Venice, with the high altar and Titian's *Assumption of the Virgin (Assunta)* seen through the arch of the choir
Photo: Erich Lessing / Art Resource, NY

Fig. 8
Tintoretto
Presentation of the Virgin in the Temple, about 1556
Oil on canvas
429 x 480 cm (168 7/8 x 189 in.)
Church of the Madonna dell'Orto, Venice
Photo: Madonna dell'Orto, Venice, Italy / Cameraphoto Arte, Venezia / The Bridgeman Art Library

Fig. 9
View of the Sala Superiore, with paintings by Tintoretto, 1576–81
Scuola Grande di San Rocco, Venice
Photo: Scala / Art Resource, NY

Fig. 10
Titian
Drawing for Battle of Spoleto, about 1538
Charcoal and black chalk on paper
38.2 x 44.4 cm (15 1/16 x 17 1/2 in.)
Musée de Louvre, Paris
Inv. 21788
Photo: Michele Bellot / Réunion des Musées Nationaux / Art Resource, NY

Fig. 11
Federico Zuccaro (Italian, about 1540–1609), study after Veronese
Frederick Barbarossa Kisses the Hand of the Schismatic Pope Victor IV, 1563–65
Black and red chalk on paper
33.6 x 22.8 cm (13 1/4 x 9 in.)
The Pierpont Morgan Library, New York
Gift of Mr. Janos Scholz, 1983.68
Photo: Joseph Zehavi, © The Pierpont Morgan Library, New York, 2008

Fig. 12
Tintoretto
Madonna of the Treasurers, about 1567
Oil on canvas
221 x 521 cm (87 x 205 1/8 in.)
Gallerie dell'Accademia, Venice
Inv. n. 909
Photo: © Cameraphoto Arte, Venezia

Fig. 13
Titian
Presentation of the Virgin in the Temple, 1534–38
Oil on canvas
335 x 775 cm (131 7/8 x 305 1/8 in.)
Gallerie dell'Accademia, Venice
Inv. n. 313
Photo: Cameraphoto Arte, Venice / Art Resource, NY

Fig. 14
High altar of the church of San Cassiano, Venice, with Tintoretto's *Resurrection of Christ with Saints Cassian and Cecilia*, 1565 (center); *Crucifixion*, 1568 (left); and *Descent into Limbo*, 1568 (right)
Photo: © Cameraphoto Arte, Venezia

Fig. 15
Nave of the church of San Sebastiano, Venice, with paintings by Veronese
Photo: Scala / Art Resource, NY

Fig. 16
Titian
Doge Francesco Venier, 1554–56
Oil on canvas
113 x 99 cm (44 1/2 x 39 in.)
Museo Thyssen-Bornemisza, Madrid
Inv. 405
Photo: © Cameraphoto Arte, Venezia

Fig. 17
Tintoretto
Jacopo Soranzo, about 1550
Oil on canvas
75 x 60 cm (29 1/2 x 23 5/8 in.)
Civica Pinacoteca del Castello Sforzesco, Milan
Inv. n. 64
Photo: Castello Sforzesco, Milan, Italy / The Bridgeman Art Library

Fig. 18
Veronese
Daniele Barbaro, about 1567
Oil on canvas
121 x 106 cm (47 5/8 x 41 3/4 in.)
Rijksmuseum, Amsterdam
SK-A-4011
Photo: Rijksmuseum, Amsterdam, The Netherlands / The Bridgeman Art Library

Fig. 19
Titian
Cardinal Alessandro Farnese, 1545–46
Oil on canvas
99 x 79 cm (39 x 31 1/8 in.)
Museo Nazionale di Capodimonte, Naples
Inv. 133
Photo: Scala / Ministero per i Beni e le Attività culturali / Art Resource, NY

Fig. 20
Veronese
Annunciation, 1583
Oil on canvas
440 x 190 cm (173 1/4 x 74 13/16 in.)
Patrimonio Nacional, Real Monasterio de San Lorenzo de El Escorial
Photo: Oronoz

Fig. 21
Jacopo and Domenico Tintoretto
Adoration of the Shepherds, 1583
Oil on canvas
432 x 186 cm (170 1/16 x 73 1/4 in.)
Patrimonio Nacional, Real Monasterio de San Lorenzo de El Escorial
Inv. no. 10014600
Photo: Scala / Art Resource, NY

Fig. 22
Titian
Crowning with Thorns, about 1570–76
Oil on canvas
280 x 181 cm (110 1/4 x 71 1/4 in.)
Bayerische Staatsgemäldesammlungen, Alte Pinakothek, Munich
Inv. 2272
Photo: Scala / Art Resource, NY

Fig. 23
Martino Rota (Croatian, about 1520–1583), after Titian's lost original of 1530
Saint Peter Martyr, about 1560
Etching and engraving
40 x 27.7 cm (15 3/4 x 10 7/8 in.)
The Metropolitan Museum of Art, New York
Bequest of Joseph Pulitzer, 1917, 17.50.16-155
Image © The Metropolitan Museum of Art

Fig. 24
Titian
Supper at Emmaus, about 1530–34, possibly earlier
Oil on panel
169 x 211 cm (66 9/16 x 83 1/16 in.)
Brocklesby Park, Lincolnshire, Earl of Yarborough, on loan to Walker Art Gallery, Liverpool
Photo: © National Museums Liverpool, Walker Art Gallery

Fig. 25
Tintoretto
Giovanni Paolo Cornaro, 1561
Oil on canvas
102 x 81.2 cm (40 3/16 x 31 15/16 in.)
Museum voor Schone Kunsten, Ghent
Photo: Royal Museum of Fine Arts Ghent—© Lukas – Art in Flanders, vzw

Fig. 26
Tintoretto
Washing of the Feet, 1548–49
Oil on canvas
210 x 533 cm (82 11/16 x 209 13/16 in.)
Museo Nacional del Prado, Madrid
2824
Photo: Photographic Archive, Museo Nacional del Prado, Madrid

Fig. 27
Veronese
Allegory of Virtue and Vice (The Choice of Hercules), about 1565
Oil on canvas
219.1 x 169.6 cm (86 1/4 x 66 3/4 in.)
The Frick Collection, New York
Henry Clay Frick Bequest, 1912.1.129
Photo: © The Frick Collection, New York

Fig. 28
Weaver's stamp on reverse of canvas. Orazio Gentileschi, *Road to Calvary*, about 1603
Kunsthistorisches Museum, Vienna
Photo: Photo Studio, Kunsthistorisches Museum, Vienna

Fig. 29
Examples of canvas weaves from the Kunsthistorisches Museum, Vienna.
Left: twill weave (Titian, *Ecce Homo*)
Center: herringbone weave (Veronese and Workshop, *Mystic Marriage of Saint Catherine*)
Right: tabby weave (Titian, *Danaë*)
Photos: Photo Studio, Kunsthistorisches Museum, Vienna

Fig. 30
Canvas support construction with detail from reverse side of canvas (inserted) showing seams.
Titian, *Danaë*, about 1560–65
Kunsthistorisches Museum, Vienna
Photo: Photo Studio, Kunsthistorisches Museum, Vienna

Fig. 31
Detail showing warm medium-brown tone of *imprimatura*.
Jacopo Tintoretto, *Susannah and the Elders*, about 1555–56 (cat. 31)
Kunsthistorisches Museum, Vienna
Photo: Photo Studio, Kunsthistorisches Museum, Vienna

Fig. 32
Detail showing underdrawing in black paint within unfinished passage.
Jacopo Tintoretto, *Doge Alvise Mocenigo Presented to the Redeemer*, about 1571–74
Metropolitan Museum of Art, New York
Photo: Courtesy of Robert Wald

Fig. 33
Top: Titian, *Venus Blindfolding Cupid*, about 1565, Galleria Borghese, Rome.
Middle: X-radiograph revealing the artist's changes to the composition during execution.
Bottom: Unknown (18th-century?) artist's copy of Titian's earlier composition for the Borghese canvas, possibly copied from a version (now reduced in size) in the National Gallery of Art, Washington, DC.
Photos: Courtesy of Robert Wald

Fig. 34
Detail illustrating Tintoretto's construction of form through line.
Jacopo Tintoretto, *Baptism of Christ*, 1579–81
Scuola Grande di San Rocco, Venice
Photo: Courtesy of Robert Wald

Fig. 35
Top: Detail of color separation (*cangianti*) in Tiepolo's figure of Europa, 1751–53, Würzburg Residenz.
Bottom: Detail of color separation in Veronese's *Christ and the Samaritan*, about 1580, Kunsthistorisches Museum, Vienna.
Photos: Photo Studio, Kunsthistorisches Museum, Vienna

Fig. 36
Giovanni Bellini (Italian, about 1431–1516)
Virgin and Child Enthroned with Saints, 1505
Oil on canvas, transferred from panel
402 x 273 cm (158 1/4 x 107 1/2 in.)
Church of San Zaccaria, Venice
Photo: Cameraphoto Arte, Venice / Art Resource, NY

Fig. 37
Sebastiano del Piombo (Italian, about 1485–1547)
Saint Louis of Toulouse, about 1509
Oil on canvas
293 x 137 cm (115 3/8 x 53 15/16 in.)
Church of San Bartolomeo di Rialto, Venice (on deposit at Gallerie dell'Accademia)
Photo: Cameraphoto Arte, Venice / Art Resource, NY

Fig. 38
Sebastiano del Piombo (Italian, about 1485–1547)
San Giovanni Crisostomo Altarpiece, about 1510
Oil on canvas
200 x 156 cm (78 3/4 x 61 7/16 in.)
Church of San Giovanni Crisostomo, Venice
Photo: Scala / Art Resource, NY

Fig. 39
Giorgione (Italian, about 1477–1510)
The Tempest, about 1506
Oil on canvas
82 x 73 cm (32 5/16 x 28 3/4 in.)
Gallerie dell'Accademia, Venice
Inv. n. 881
Photo: Cameraphoto Arte, Venice / Art Resource, NY

Fig. 40
Giovanni Bellini (Italian, about 1431–1516)
Baptism of Christ, 1500–1502
Oil on canvas
400 x 263 cm (157 1/2 x 103 9/16 in.)
Church of Santa Corona, Vicenza
Photo: Scala / Art Resource, NY

Fig. 41
Pordenone (Italian, about 1483–about 1539)
Saint Martin with the Beggar and Saint Christopher, 1528–29
Oil on panels
238 x 268 cm (93 11/16 x 105 1/2 in.)
Church of San Rocco, Venice, Italy
Photo: Cameraphoto Arte, Venice / Art Resource, NY

Fig. 42
Veronese
Jupiter Expelling the Vices, about 1554–55
Oil on canvas
560 x 330 cm (220 1/2 x 129 15/16 in.)
Musée du Louvre, Paris
Inv. 147
Photo: Réunion des Musées Nationaux / Art Resource, NY

Fig. 43
Veronese
Coronation of Esther, about 1555–56
Oil on canvas
450 x 370 cm (177 3/16 x 145 11/16 in.)
Church of San Sebastiano, Venice
Photo: Scala / Art Resource, NY

Fig. 44
Titian
Pietro Aretino, 1545
Oil on canvas
96.7 x 77.6 cm (38 1/16 x 30 9/16 in.)
Galleria Palatina, Florence
Inv. 1912: no. 54
Photo: Scala / Art Resource, NY

Fig. 45
Titian
Self-Portrait, about 1562
Oil on canvas
96 x 75 cm (37 13/16 x 29 1/2 in.)
Gemäldegalerie, Staatliche Museen zu Berlin
Inv. 163
Photo: Jörg P. Anders / Bildarchiv Preussischer Kulturbesitz / Art Resource, NY

Fig. 46
Raphael (Raffaello Sanzio) (1483–1520)
Sacrifice at Lystra, 1515–16
Bodycolor on paper mounted on canvas (tapestry cartoon)
305 x 506 cm (120 1/16 x 199 3/16 in.)
Victoria and Albert Museum, London
Photo: V&A Images / Victoria and Albert Museum

Fig. 47
Titian
Madonna di Ca' Pesaro, 1519–26
Oil on canvas
478 x 266 cm (188 3/16 x 104 3/4 in.)
Church of Santa Maria Gloriosa dei Frari, Venice
Photo: Cameraphoto Arte, Venice / Art Resource, NY

Fig. 48
Veronese
Holy Family with Saint John the Baptist, Saint Anthony Abbot, and Saint Catherine, about 1551
Oil on canvas
313 x 190 cm (123 1/4 x 74 13/16 in.)
Church of San Francesco della Vigna, Venice
Photo: San Francesco della Vigna, Venice, Italy / The Bridgeman Art Library

Fig. 49
Gentile Bellini (Italian, about 1429–1507)
Procession in Piazza San Marco, 1496
Oil on canvas
367 x 745 cm (144 1/2 x 293 5/16 in.)
Gallerie dell'Accademia, Venice
Inv. n. 382
Photo: Scala / Ministero per i Beni e le Attività culturali / Art Resource, NY

Fig. 50
Titian
Assumption of the Virgin (Assunta), 1516–18
Oil on panel
690 x 360 cm (271 5/8 x 141 3/4 in.)
Church of Santa Maria Gloriosa dei Frari, Venice
Photo: Scala / Art Resource, NY

Fig. 51
Vittore Carpaccio (Italian, about 1465–about 1525)
Healing of a Possessed Man at Rialto, about 1496
Oil on canvas
365 x 389 cm (143 11/16 x 153 1/8 in.)
Gallerie dell'Accademia, Venice
Inv. n. 391
Photo: Scala / Ministero per i Beni e le Attività culturali / Art Resource, NY

Fig. 52
Tintoretto and workshop
Entombment, 1592–94
Oil on canvas
288 x 166 cm (113 3/8 x 65 3/8 in.)
Church of San Giorgio Maggiore, Venice
Photo: © Cameraphoto Arte, Venezia

Fig. 53
Tintoretto
Assumption of the Virgin, early–mid-1560s
Oil on canvas
440 x 260 cm (173 1/4 x 102 3/8 in.)
Church of the Gesuiti, Venice
Photo: Gesuiti, Venice, Italy / Cameraphoto Arte, Venezia / The Bridgeman Art Library

Fig. 54
Veronese
Feast in the House of Levi, 1573
Oil on canvas
555 x 1280 cm (218 1/2 x 503 15/16 in.)
Gallerie dell'Accademia, Venice
Inv. n. 374
Photo: Scala / Art Resource, NY

Fig. 55
Tintoretto
Last Supper, about 1563–64
Oil on canvas
221 x 413 cm (87 x 162 5/8 in.)
Church of San Trovaso, Venice
Photo: Cameraphoto Arte, Venice / Art Resource, NY

Fig. 56
Veronese
Supper at Emmaus, about 1559–60
Oil on canvas

241 x 415 cm (94⅞ x 163⅜ in.)
Musée du Louvre, Paris
Inv. 146
Photo: Gérard Blot / Réunion des Musées Nationaux / Art Resource, NY

Fig. 57
Infrared reflectogram detail of the bottom of the column at center left of *Jupiter and a Nude*, showing underdrawing using a straightedge
Photo: © Museum of Fine Arts, Boston (Department of Conservation and Collections Management)

Fig. 58
Infrared reflectogram of *Jupiter and a Nude*, showing the variety of underdrawing styles
Photo: © Museum of Fine Arts, Boston (Department of Conservation and Collections Management)

Fig. 59
Infrared reflectogram detail of the fountain, showing the freehand underdrawing below the statue and the trees
Photo: © Museum of Fine Arts, Boston (Department of Conservation and Collections Management)

Fig.60
Infrared reflectogram detail of the inverted painting, showing a fluid brush underdrawing of what appear to be walking or running legs
Photo: © Museum of Fine Arts, Boston (Department of Conservation and Collections Management)

Fig. 61
X-radiograph of *Saint Catherine of Alexandria at Prayer*, showing edits and revisions
Photo: © Museum of Fine Arts, Boston (Department of Conservation and Collections Management)

Fig. 62
X-radiograph detail of the archway and the Crucifixion, showing the use of scoring
Photo: © Museum of Fine Arts, Boston (Department of Conservation and Collections Management)

Fig. 63
Diagram of the *Nativity*, showing the position of the canvas joins and older tacking edges
Photo: © Museum of Fine Arts, Boston (Department of Conservation and Collections Management)

Fig. 64
X-radiograph detail of the join to the right of the standing shepherd, showing damage indicative of a tacking edge
Photo: © Museum of Fine Arts, Boston (Department of Conservation and Collections Management)

Fig. 65
X-radiograph of the *Nativity*, showing evidence of an earlier composition in two sections of canvas (B and D in fig. 63)
Photo: © Museum of Fine Arts, Boston (Department of Conservation and Collections Management)

Fig. 66
X-radiograph detail of the heads of Saint Anne and the shepherd, showing the legs and arm of another figure
Photo: © Museum of Fine Arts, Boston (Department of Conservation and Collections Management)

Fig. 67
Infrared reflectogram detail of the shepherd, showing loose brush underdrawing and use of a transfer grid (emphasized in blue)
Photo: © Museum of Fine Arts, Boston (Department of Conservation and Collections Management)

Fig. 68
Infrared reflectogram detail of the head of the Virgin, showing part of the transfer grid
Photo: © Museum of Fine Arts, Boston (Department of Conservation and Collections Management)

Fig. 69
X-radiograph detail of area around the Virgin, showing additional figures
Photo: © Museum of Fine Arts, Boston (Department of Conservation and Collections Management)

Fig. 70
X-radiograph composite, showing the two pieces of canvas from the earlier composition joined together (sections B and D in fig. 63)
Photo: © Museum of Fine Arts, Boston (Department of Conservation and Collections Management)

Fig. 71
Workshop of Tintoretto, possibly Domenico Tintoretto (Italian, 1560–1635)
The Trinity Adored by a Heavenly Choir, about 1600
Oil on canvas
116.8 x 108.3 cm (46 x 42⅝ in.)
Columbia Museum of Art, South Carolina
Gift of the Samuel H. Kress Foundation
CMA 1954.36
Photo: Columbia Museum of Art

Fig. 72
Detail of the Christ Child in X-radiograph (top) and infrared reflectogram (bottom), showing underpainting
Photo: © Museum of Fine Arts, Boston (Department of Conservation and Collections Management)

Fig. 73
Tintoretto (detail)
Washing of the Feet, about 1575–80
Oil on canvas
200.6 x 408.3 cm (78¾ x 160¾ in.)
The National Gallery, London
Bought, 1882, NG 1130
Photo: © The National Gallery 2008

Fig. 74
Palma Vecchio (Italian, about 1479–1528)
Bathing Nymphs, 1525–28
Oil on canvas on wood
77.5 x 124 cm (30½ x 48 13⁄16 in.)
Kunsthistorisches Museum, Gemäldegalerie, Vienna
GG Inv. Nr. 6803
Photo: Erich Lessing / Art Resource, NY

Fig. 75
Unidentified artist
The Fountain of the Sleeping Nymph
Illustrated in Francesco Colonna (?), *Hypnerotomachia Poliphili* (Venice: Aldus Manutius, 1499), fol. e1 recto
Woodcut
Museum of Fine Arts, Boston
George Nixon Black Fund, 35.654
Photo: © Museum of Fine Arts, Boston

Fig. 76
Titian
Venus of Urbino, about 1538
Oil on canvas
119 x 165 cm (46⅞ x 64 15⁄16 in.)
Galleria degli Uffizi, Florence
Inv. 1437
Photo: Scala / Ministero per i Beni e le Attività culturali / Art Resource, NY

Fig. 77
Titian
Perseus and Andromeda, 1554–56
Oil on canvas
175 x 189.5 cm (68⅞ x 74⅝ in.)
The Wallace Collection, London
Inv. P011
Photo: © By kind permission of the Trustees of the Wallace Collection, London

Fig. 78
Titian
Danaë, probably 1551–53
Oil on canvas
129.8 x 181.2 cm (51⅛ x 71 5⁄16 in.)
Museo Nacional del Prado, Madrid
425
Photo: Scala / Art Resource, NY

Fig. 79
Titian and workshop
Venus and the Lute Player, about 1565–70
Oil on canvas
165 x 209.5 cm (64 15⁄16 x 82½ in.)
The Metropolitan Museum of Art, New York
Munsey Fund, 1936, 36.29
Image © The Metropolitan Museum of Art

Fig. 80
Titian
Penitent Magdalen, about 1535
Oil on panel
84 x 69.2 cm (33 1⁄16 x 27¼ in.)
Galleria Palatina, Palazzo Pitti, Florence
Inv. n. 67
Photo: Scala / Art Resource, NY

Fig. 81
Tintoretto
Venus and Mars Surprised by Vulcan, about 1545
Oil on canvas
135 x 198 cm (53⅛ x 77 15⁄16 in.)
Bayerische Staatsgemäldesammlungen, Alte Pinakothek, Munich
Inv. 9257
Photo: Kavaler / Art Resource, NY

Fig. 82
Giovanni Bellini (Italian, about 1431–1516)
Woman with a Mirror, 1515
Oil on panel
62 x 79 (24 7⁄16 x 31⅛ in.)
Kunsthistorisches Museum, Gemäldegalerie, Vienna
GG Inv. No. 97
Photo: Erich Lessing / Art Resource, NY

Fig. 83
Titian
Venus and Adonis, 1554
Oil on canvas
186 x 207 cm (73¼ x 81½ in.)
Museo Nacional del Prado, Madrid
422
Photo: Scala / Art Resource, NY

Fig. 84
Giorgione (Italian, about 1477–1510) and Titian
Sleeping Venus, 1508–10
Oil on canvas
108.5 x 175 cm (42 11⁄16 x 68⅞ in.)
Gemäldegalerie Alte Meister, Staatliche Kunstsammlungen, Dresden
Gal. Nr. 185
Photo: Hans-Peter Klut / Bildarchiv Preussischer Kulturbesitz / Art Resource, NY

Fig. 85
Tintoretto
Origin of the Milky Way, 1577–79
Oil on canvas
149.4 x 168 cm (58 13⁄16 x 66⅛ in.)
The National Gallery, London
Bought, 1890, NG 1313
Photo: © The National Gallery 2008

Fig. 86
Veronese
Ceiling of the Room of Married Love, 1560–61
Fresco
Villa Barbaro, Maser
Photo: Scala / Art Resource, NY

Fig. 87
Titian
Sacred and Profane Love, about 1515–16
Oil on canvas
118 x 279 cm (46 7⁄16 x 109 13⁄16 in.)
Galleria Borghese, Rome
Inv. 147
Photo: Scala / Ministero per i Beni e le Attività culturali / Art Resource, NY

Fig. 88
Titian
Venus Blindfolding Cupid, about 1565
Oil on canvas
118 x 185 cm (46 7⁄16 x 72 13⁄16 in.)
Galleria Borghese, Rome
Photo: Scala / Ministero per i Beni e le Attività culturali / Art Resource, NY

Fig. 89
Palma Vecchio (Italian, about 1479–1528)
A Blonde Woman, about 1520
Oil on wood
77.5 x 64.12 cm (30½ x 25¼ in.)
The National Gallery, London
Mond Bequest, 1924, NG 3939
Photo: © The National Gallery 2008

Fig. 90
Veronese
Boy with a Greyhound, mid-1560s
Oil on canvas
173.7 x 102 cm (68⅜ x 40 3/16 in.)
The Metropolitan Museum of Art, New York
H. O. Havemeyer Collection, Bequest of Mrs. H. O. Havemeyer, 1929, 29.100.105
Image © The Metropolitan Museum of Art

Fig. 91
Titian
Portrait of a Man in a Red Cap, 1511–16
Oil on canvas
82.2 cm x 71.1 cm (32⅜ x 28 in.)
The Frick Collection, New York
Henry Clay Frick Bequest, 1915.1.116
Photo: © The Frick Collection, New York

Fig. 92
Titian
Daniele Barbaro, about 1545
Oil on canvas
81 x 69 cm (31⅞ x 27 3/16 in.)
Museo Nacional del Prado, Madrid
414
Photo: © Cameraphoto Arte, Venezia

Fig. 93
Unidentified wax seal on the back of Titian's *Portrait of a Man Holding a Book* (cat. 38), Museum of Fine Arts, Boston
Photo: © Museum of Fine Arts, Boston

Fig. 94
Titian
Alfonso d'Avalos, 1533
Oil on canvas
110 x 80 cm (43 5/16 x 31½ in.)
The J. Paul Getty Museum, Los Angeles
2003.486
Photo: The J. Paul Getty Museum, Los Angeles, California

Fig. 95
Titian
Vincenzo Cappello, 1540
Oil on canvas
141 x 118.1 cm (55½ x 46½ in.)
National Gallery of Art, Washington, DC
Samuel H. Kress Collection, 1957.14.3
Image courtesy of the Board of Trustees, National Gallery of Art, Washington, DC

Fig. 96
Veronese
Allegory of the Battle of Lepanto with Sebastiano Venier, after 1574
Oil on canvas
285 x 565 cm (112 3/16 x 222 7/16 in.)
Sala del Collegio, Palazzo Ducale, Venice
Photo: Scala / Art Resource, NY

Fig. 97
Titian
Philip II, 1551
Oil on canvas
193 x 111 cm (76 x 43 11/16 in.)
Museo Nacional del Prado, Madrid
411
Photo: Scala / Art Resource, NY

Fig. 98
Titian
Clarissa Strozzi, 1542
Oil on canvas
115 x 98 cm (45¼ x 38 9/16 in.)
Gemäldegalerie, Staatliche Museen zu Berlin
Inv. 160A
Photo: Jörg P. Anders / Bildarchiv Preussischer Kulturbesitz / Art Resource, NY

Fig. 99
Veronese
Study for Iseppo da Porto and His Son Adriano, about 1551
Pen and ink and wash over gray chalk on paper
34.2 x 18.8 cm (13 7/16 x 7⅜ in.)
Musée du Louvre, Paris
Inv. 4678, Recto
Photo: Bellot / Réunion des Musées Nationaux / Art Resource, NY

Fig. 100
Titian
The Vendramin Family, Venerating a Relic of the True Cross, about 1540–45, reworked mid-1550s
Oil on canvas
206.1 x 288.5 cm (81⅛ x 113 9/16 in.)
The National Gallery, London
Bought with a special grant and contributions from Samuel Courtauld, Sir Joseph Duveen, The Art Fund and the Phillips Fund, 1929, NG 4452
Photo: © The National Gallery 2008

Fig. 101
Tintoretto
Saint Reading (*Saint Mary Magdalen*), about 1582–83
Oil on canvas
425 x 209 cm (167 5/16 x 82 5/16 in.)
Scuola Grande di San Rocco, Venice
Photo: Cameraphoto Arte, Venice / Art Resource, NY

Fig. 102
Tintoretto
Modello for *Paradiso*, 1587–88
Oil on canvas
164 x 492 cm (64 9/16 x 193 11/16 in.)
Museo Thyssen-Bornemisza, Madrid
Inv. 1980.43
Photo: Erich Lessing / Art Resource, NY

Fig. 103
Veronese
Saint Pantaleon Healing a Child, 1587
Oil on canvas
277 x 160 (109 1/16 x 63 in.)
Church of San Pantalon, Venice
Photo: San Pantalon, Venice, Italy / The Bridgeman Art Library

Fig. 104
Veronese
Modello for *Paradiso*, about 1578–82
Oil and tempera (?) on canvas
87 x 234 cm (34¼ x 92⅛ in.)
Palais des Beaux-Arts, Lille
Inv. P 20
Photo: Hervé Lewandowski / Réunion des Musées Nationaux / Art Resource, NY

Fig. 105
Titian
Diana and Actaeon, 1556–59
Oil on canvas
184.5 x 202.2 cm (72⅝ x 79⅝ in.)
National Gallery of Scotland, Edinburgh
Lent by the Duke of Sutherland 1945, NGL 058.46
Photo: Scala / Art Resource, NY

Fig. 106
Titian
Europa, 1559–62
Oil on canvas
178 x 205 cm (70 1/16 x 80 11/16 in.)
Isabella Stewart Gardner Museum, Boston
P26e1
Photo: © Isabella Stewart Gardner Museum, Boston

Fig. 107
Titian
Tarquin and Lucretia, 1568–71
Oil on canvas
188.9 x 145.1 cm (74⅜ x 57⅛ in.)
Fitzwilliam Museum, Cambridge, England
914
Photo: Fitzwilliam Museum, University of Cambridge, UK / The Bridgeman Art Library

Fig. 108
Titian
Saint Jerome, late 1550s
Oil on panel
235 x 125 cm (92½ x 49 3/16 in.)
Pinacoteca di Brera, Milan
Inv. 182
Photo: Scala / Ministero per i Beni e le Attività culturali / Art Resource, NY

Fig. 109
Titian
Pietà, about 1570–76
Oil on canvas
378 x 347 cm (148 13/16 x 136⅝ in.)
Gallerie dell'Accademia, Venice
Inv. n. 400
Photo: Scala / Art Resource, NY

Fig. 110
Tintoretto
Crucifixion, 1565
Oil on canvas
536 x 1224 cm (211 x 481⅞ in.)
Scuola Grande di San Rocco, Venice
Photo: Cameraphoto Arte, Venice / Art Resource, NY

Fig. 111
Titian
Entombment of Christ, about 1520
Oil on canvas
148 x 213 cm (58¼ x 83⅞ in.)
Musée du Louvre, Paris
Inv. 749
Photo: R. G. Ojeda / Réunion des Musées Nationaux / Art Resource, NY

Fig. 112
Veronese
Agony in the Garden, about 1583
Oil on canvas
108 x 180 cm (42½ x 70⅞ in.)
Pinacoteca di Brera, Milan
Inv. 241
Photo: Mauro Magliani, 1998 / Alinari / Art Resource, NY

Chronology

Titles in bold indicate paintings that are catalogue plates in this book.

Date	Historical Events	TITIAN	TINTORETTO	VERONESE
1488		Tiziano Vecellio (Titian) is born in Pieve di Cadore, perhaps in this year.		
1508	The League of Cambrai is formed. Michelangelo begins to paint the Sistine Chapel ceiling (1508–12).	Paints frescoes on the facade of Fondaco dei Tedeschi.		
1509	Forces of the League of Cambrai rout the Venetian army at Agnadello.			
1510	Giorgione dies. Plague strikes Venice.	Contracted to paint frescoes in the Scuola del Santo, Padua.		
1513	Pope Julius II is succeeded by Leo X. Machiavelli writes *Il principe.*	Petitions the Council of Ten to paint the *Battle of Spoleto* (destroyed in 1577) for the Sala del Maggior Consiglio in the Palazzo Ducale.		
1514	Fire destroys large portion of Rialto area in Venice.	***Virgin and Child with Saint Catherine, Saint Dominic, and a Donor*** (about 1513–14)		
1516	Giovanni Bellini dies.	Makes first visit to the court of Alfonso d'Este in Ferrara.		
1518		*Assumption of the Virgin* (*Assunta*) in Santa Maria Gloriosa dei Frari unveiled. ***Flora*** (about 1516–18)	Jacopo Robusti (Tintoretto) is born in Venice, probably in this year.	
1520	Raphael dies. Michelangelo begins work on the Medici Chapel at San Lorenzo, Florence.	***Venus Rising from the Sea*** **(*Venus Anadyomene*)** (about 1520); ***Portrait of a Man*** **(*Tommaso Mosti?*)** (about 1520)		
1523	Clement VII is elected pope. Andrea Gritti is elected doge.			
1526	Carpaccio dies, probably in this year.	Completes the *Madonna di Ca' Pesaro* in Santa Maria Gloriosa dei Frari.		
1527	Imperial troops sack Rome; many artists abandon the city, some settling in Venice.			
1528	Michelangelo travels to Venice.			Paolo Caliari (Veronese) is born in Verona.
1529		Travels to Mantua and Ferrara and first meets Charles V in Parma.		
1530	Charles V is crowned as Holy Roman Emperor and king of Italy by Pope Clement VII in Bologna.	Completes the *Saint Peter Martyr* altarpiece (lost in 1867 fire) for the church of Santi Giovanni e Paolo. ***Virgin and Child with Saint Catherine of Alexandria and a Rabbit*** (about 1530)		

Date	Historical Events	TITIAN	TINTORETTO	VERONESE
1533		Made Count Palatine and Knight of the Golden Spur by Charles V. ***Supper at Emmaus*** (1533–34)		
1538	Venetians, allies of Pope Paul III, are defeated by the Turks at Prevesa.	In competition with Titian, Pordenone is engaged to decorate the Sala dello Scrutinio in the Palazzo Ducale. Titian finishes the *Battle of Spoleto* for the Sala del Maggior Consiglio, Palazzo Ducale. Completes the *Venus of Urbino* (about 1538) and *Presentation of the Virgin in the Temple.*	Probably completes his first known painting this year, *Virgin and Child with Saints Joseph and Jerome and Procurator Giralmo Marcello* (1537–38, location unknown). "Jacopo depentor" is recorded as renting a house and studio in San Geremia.	
1540		***Portrait of a Man Holding a Book*** (about 1540)	Completes first signed and dated painting, *Holy Family with Saints.*	
1541	Vasari visits Venice.			Documented as a fourteen-year-old apprentice of painter Antonio Badile in Verona.
1542		***Ranuccio Farnese***	***Supper at Emmaus*** (about 1542)	
1543		***Pope Paul III***		
1545	Council of Trent opens (concludes in 1563).	Paints the portrait of Pietro Aretino. Travels to Rome.	Pietro Aretino writes to thank Tintoretto for the ceiling painting ***Contest between Apollo and Marsyas.***	
1546		Meets Michelangelo in Rome and delivers ***Danaë*** to Cardinal Alessandro Farnese, in this year or the previous one.	***Self-Portrait*** (about 1546–47)	Probably completes his first independent painting, the *Raising of the Daughter of Jairus* (now lost) for the church of San Bernardino in Verona.
1547			***Portrait of a Man Aged Twenty-Six***	
1548	Paolo Pino publishes *Dialogo di pittura* in Venice.	Leaves for Augsburg. In Milan, meets the future Philip II of Spain, who will serve as his principal patron for the remainder of his career.	Paints *Miracle of the Slave* for the Scuola Grande di San Marco, to great acclaim. ***Esther before Ahasuerus*** (about 1547–48); ***Portrait of a Man*** (about 1548)	***Christ Healing a Woman with an Issue of Blood (?)*** (about 1548)
1549			Completes an altarpiece for the church of San Marziale.	***Mystic Marriage of Saint Catherine of Alexandria*** (about 1549)
1550	First edition of Vasari's *Lives* is published. Julius III succeeds Paul III as pope.	On invitation of Philip II, returns to Augsburg. ***Venus with an Organist and a Dog*** (about 1550)	***Saint Augustine Healing the Lame*** (about 1549–50)	
1551		By August, returns to Venice.		Completes his first commission for a Venetian church at San Francesco della Vigna. ***Iseppo da Porto and His Son Adriano*** and ***Livia da Porto Thiene and Her Daughter Porzia*** (about 1551)
1552			***Saint George, Saint Louis, and the Princess***	***Temptation of Saint Anthony*** (1552–53)

Date	Historical Events	TITIAN	TINTORETTO	VERONESE
1553	Doge Marcantonio Trevisan is succeeded by Francesco Venier.	Offers to paint a large picture for the Scuola Grande di San Rocco.	Is paid 100 ducats for a painting in the Sala del Maggior Consiglio in the Palazzo Ducale.	With Ponchino and Zelotti, decorates the ceiling of the Sala of the Council of Ten in the Palazzo Ducale (1553–56). ***Portrait of a Man*** (about 1551–53)
1555		Probably completes *Portrait of Doge Francesco Venier.* ***Venus with a Mirror*** (about 1555); ***Venus and Adonis*** (about 1555–56)	***Susannah and the Elders*** (about 1555–56)	Delivers ceiling paintings for the sacristy of the church of San Sebastiano; signs contract for the nave ceiling paintings.
1556	Charles V abdicates (dies in 1558). Pietro Aretino dies.			Receives payments for paintings in the nave of the church of San Sebastiano.
1557	Ludovico Dolce's *Dialogo della pittura intitolato l'Aretino* praises Titian and seems to slight Tintoretto, apparently disparaging his ***Saint George, Saint Louis, and the Princess.***			Titian and Jacopo Sansovino award Veronese a gold chain for the best contribution to the ceiling decoration of the Libreria Marciana, a prestigious commission from which Tintoretto is excluded.
1559		Advises Philip II that a new ***Entombment*** was sent to replace the original lost in Trent in 1557; also sends *Diana and Actaeon* and *Venus and Adonis*; at work on *Europa* (1559–62).	Completes *Christ at the Pool of Bethesda* for the church of San Rocco; probably at work on the *Last Judgment* and *Making the Golden Calf* for the church of Madonna dell'Orto.	Designs a stone frame for the new high altar of the church of San Sebastiano.
1560				Begins fresco decoration at Villa Barbaro at Maser (finishes in 1561). ***Saint Menna*** (about 1560)
1562				***Virgin and Child with Angels Appearing to Saint Anthony Abbot and Saint Paul the Hermit***
1563	Council of Trent concludes. Titian, Tintoretto, and Veronese serve as expert witnesses in the dispute over mosaics executed by the Zuccati family.			Finishes the *Wedding Feast at Cana* for the monastery of San Giorgio Maggiore in just over twelve months.
1564	Michelangelo dies.	Titian visits Brescia to negotiate terms for three canvases for the Palazzo Pubblico.	Through devious means, Tintoretto wins the competition for a ceiling painting at the Scuola Grande di San Rocco and donates his *Saint Roch in Glory* to the Scuola, beginning more than two decades of activity there.	
1565		Philip II urges Titian to complete the *Martyrdom of Saint Lawrence*, begun the previous year.	Completes the *Crucifixion* for the Scuola Grande di San Rocco and the *Resurrection of Christ with Saints Cassian and Cecilia* for the high altar of the church of San Cassiano.	
1566	Jacopo Sansovino creates statues for the Scala dei Giganti in the Palazzo Ducale. Work is begun on Palladio's church of San Giorgio Maggiore.	Vasari visits Titian's studio while in Venice. Titian is elected a member of the Accademia del Disegno in Florence, along with Tintoretto, Palladio, and others. ***Christ Carrying the Cross*** (1565–70)	Elected a member of the Accademia del Disegno in Florence.	Living in parish of San Felice, in a house owned by Vincenzo Morosini.
1567		***Saint Catherine of Alexandria at Prayer*** (about 1567)	Receives payment for large paintings in the church of San Rocco.	
1568	El Greco is documented in Venice. Second edition of Vasari's *Lives* is published, with a long biography of Titian and discussions of Tintoretto and Veronese within the biographies of other artists.			

Date	Historical Events	TITIAN	TINTORETTO	VERONESE
1571	Venetian navy and other Christian powers win victory over Turks at Lepanto. Fire in the refectory of Santi Giovanni e Paolo destroys Titian's *Last Supper* of 1555.	In a letter to Philip II, states that he is ninety-five years old. Bordeaux version of ***Tarquin and Lucretia*** (about 1568–71)	Receives payment for a series of *Philosophers* in the Libreria Marciana. ***Sebastiano Venier*** (about 1571–72); ***Saint Jerome in the Wilderness*** (about 1571–72)	***Agostino Barbarigo*** (about 1571–72)
1573	Venice cedes Cyprus to the Ottoman Empire.			After Titian's *Last Supper* is destroyed by fire, Veronese completes a replacement and is called before the Inquisition to defend it; the painting is ultimately retitled the *Feast in the House of Levi*.
1574	Fire at the Palazzo Ducale destroys the Sala del Collegio and the Sala del Senato, including many paintings by Titian; the decision is immediately made to reconstruct the destroyed rooms.		Petitions the Council of Ten to receive a *senseria* at the Fondaco dei Tedeschi.	Starts ceiling decoration for the Sala del Collegio in the Palazzo Ducale.
1576	Devastating plague hits Venice (1575–77).	On August 27, Titian dies in his house in Biri Grande and is buried in Santa Maria Gloriosa dei Frari.	Begins work in the Sala Superiore, Scuola Grande di San Rocco.	Active in decorating the Sala del Collegio in the Palazzo Ducale.
1577	Second fire in the Palazzo Ducale destroys the Sala del Maggior Consiglio and the cycle of paintings by Gentile and Giovanni Bellini, Vivarini, Carpaccio, Veronese, Tintoretto, and Titian. Sebastiano Venier is elected doge.		Agrees to provide further ceiling paintings for the Sala Superiore in the Scuola Grande di San Rocco. ***Temptation of Saint Anthony*** (about 1577)	
1578	Nicolò da Ponte succeeds Sebastiano Venier as doge.		Provveditori al Sal pay Tintoretto 200 ducats for his *Allegories* in the Sala dell'Anticollegio in the Palazzo Ducale. ***Tarquin and Lucretia*** (1578–80)	Along with Palma Giovane, is asked to value four paintings by Tintoretto created for the Palazzo Ducale.
1580			***Baptism of Christ*** (about 1580)	***Saint Jerome in the Wilderness*** (about 1580)
1581			Finishes the canvases for the walls of the Sala Superiore in the Scuola Grande di San Rocco.	***Cupid with Two Dogs*** (about 1581)
1582			At work in the Sala del Collegio and the Sala del Senato in the Palazzo Ducale.	Completes the *Triumph of Venice* for the ceiling of the Sala del Maggior Consiglio. Along with Bassano, wins the competition to paint the *Paradiso* in the Palazzo Ducale.
1585	Pasquale Cicogna succeeds Nicolò da Ponte as doge.			Invited to work for the Spanish court, but declines the invitation.
1588	Construction of the Rialto Bridge is begun under the direction of Antonio Da Ponte.		Obtains the commission for the *Paradiso* after the death of Veronese. ***Self-Portrait*** (about 1588)	On April 19, Veronese dies at his house in San Samuele and is buried in the church of San Sebastiano.
1594			Completes, with much help from his workshop, large paintings for the church of San Giorgio Maggiore. On May 31, Tintoretto dies and is buried in the vault of his father-in-law in the church of Madonna dell'Orto.	

Selected Bibliography

The sources listed in this selected bibliography are those referenced most frequently in the notes or deemed most important for a general knowledge of Venetian Renaissance painting.

Aikema, Bernard, and Beverly Louise Brown, eds. *Renaissance Venice and the North: Crosscurrents in the Time of Bellini, Dürer, and Titian*. Exh. cat. New York: Rizzoli, 1999.

Ajmar-Wollheim, Marta, and Flora Dennis, eds. *At Home in Renaissance Italy*. Exh. cat. London: Victoria and Albert Museum, 2006.

Ames-Lewis, Francis, ed. *New Interpretations of Venetian Renaissance Painting*. London: University of London, Birkbeck College, 1994.

Anderson, Jaynie. *Giorgione: The Painter of "Poetic Brevity."* Paris: Flammarion, 1997.

Avagnina, Maria Elisa, et al. *Pinacoteca civica di Vicenza: Catalogo scientifico delle collezioni*. Milan: Silvana, 2003.

Ballarin, Alessandro. "L'orto del Bassano (a proposito di alcuni quadri e disegni inediti singolari)." *Arte Veneta* 18 (1964): 55–61.

Berenson, Bernard. *Italian Pictures of the Renaissance: A List of the Principal Artists; Venetian School*. 2 vols. London: Phaidon Press, 1957.

Bettagno, Alessandro, ed. *Venezia da stato a mito*. Exh. cat. Venice: Fondazione Giorgio Cini, 1997.

Biadene, Susanna, and Mary Yakush, eds. *Titian: Prince of Painters*. Exh. cat. Venice: Marsilio, 1990.

Borean, Linda. *La quadreria di Agostino e Giovan Donato Correggio nel collezionismo veneziano del Seicento*. Udine, Italy: Forum, 2000.

Borean, Linda, and Stefania Mason, eds. *Il collezionismo d'arte a Venezia: Il Seicento*. Venice: Marsilio, 2007.

———, eds. *Figure di collezionisti a Venezia tra Cinque e Seicento*. Udine, Italy: Forum, 2002.

Borghini, Raffaello. *Il riposo* [Florence, 1584]. Hildesheim: Georg Olms Verlagsbuchhandlung, 1969.

Boschini, Marco. *La carta del navegar pitoresco* [Venice, 1660]. Edited by Anna Pallucchini. Venice: Istituto per la collaborazione culturale, 1966.

———. *Le minere della pittura*. Venice: F. Nicolini, 1664.

Bottari, Stefano, ed. *Tutta la pittura di Giovanni Bellini*. Milan: Rizzoli, 1963.

Branca, Vittore, and Carlo Ossola, eds. *Cultura e società nel Rinascimento tra riforme e manierismi*. Florence: L. S. Olschki, 1984.

Brown, Beverly Louise, and Paola Marini, eds. *Jacopo Bassano, c. 1510–1592*. Exh. cat. Fort Worth, TX: Kimbell Art Museum, 1993.

Brown, David Alan, and Sylvia Ferino-Pagden, eds. *Bellini, Giorgione, Titian and the Renaissance of Venetian Painting*. Exh. cat. Washington, DC: National Gallery of Art, 2006.

Brown, Katherine T. *The Painter's Reflection: Self-Portraiture in Renaissance Venice, 1458–1625*. Florence: L. S. Olschki, 2000.

Brown, Patricia Fortini. *Art and Life in Renaissance Venice*. New York: Harry N. Abrams, 1997.

———. *Private Lives in Renaissance Venice: Art, Architecture, and the Family*. New Haven, CT: Yale University Press, 2004.

———. *Venetian Narrative Painting in the Age of Carpaccio*. New Haven, CT: Yale University Press, 1988.

Campbell, Lorne. *Renaissance Portraits: European Portrait-Painting in the 14th, 15th and 16th Centuries*. New Haven, CT: Yale University Press, 1990.

Chambers, David, and Brian Pullan, eds., with Jennifer Fletcher. *Venice: A Documentary History, 1450–1630*. Cambridge, MA: Blackwell, 1992.

Chong, Alan, Richard Lingner, and Carl Zahn, eds. *Eye of the Beholder: Masterpieces from the Isabella Stewart Gardner Museum*. Boston: Isabella Stewart Gardner Museum, 2003.

Christiansen, Keith. "Giovanni Bellini and the Practice of Devotional Painting." In *Giovanni Bellini and the Art of Devotion*, edited by Ronda Kasl, 7–57. Indianapolis: Indianapolis Museum of Art, 2004.

Cocke, Richard. *Paolo Veronese: Piety and Display in an Age of Religious Reform*. Aldershot, UK: Ashgate, 2001.

———. *Veronese's Drawings*. Ithaca, NY: Cornell University Press, 1984.

Cooper, Tracy E. *Palladio's Venice: Architecture and Society in a Renaissance Republic*. New Haven, CT: Yale University Press, 2005.

Cottrell, Philip. "Corporate Colors: Bonifacio and Tintoretto at the Palazzo dei Camerlenghi in Venice." *Art Bulletin* 82, no. 4 (Dec. 2000): 658–78.

Crowe, J. A., and G. B. Cavalcaselle. *The Life and Times of Titian*. 2nd ed. London: J. Murray, 1881.

———. *Titian: His Life and Times*. London: J. Murray, 1877.

De Maria, Blake. "The Merchants of Venice: A Study in Sixteenth-Century Cittadino Patronage." PhD diss., Princeton University, 2003.

De Vecchi, Pierluigi. *L'opera completa del Tintoretto*. Milan: Rizzoli Editore, 1970.

Dunkerton, Jill, Susan Foister, and Nicholas Penny. *Dürer to Veronese: Sixteenth-Century Painting in the National Gallery*. London: National Gallery, 1999.

Dunkerton, Jill, Susan Foister, Dillian Gordon, and Nicholas Penny. *Giotto to Dürer: Early Renaissance Painting in the National Gallery*. London: National Gallery, 1991.

Echols, Robert. "Cima da Conegliano and the Theme of Saint Jerome in the Wilderness." *Venezia Cinquecento* 4, no. 8 (1994): 47–69.

Echols, Robert, and Frederick Ilchman. "Toward a New Tintoretto Catalogue, with a Checklist of Revised Attributions and a New Chronology." In *Jacopo Tintoretto: Actas del congreso internacional / Proceedings of the International Symposium*, Museo Nacional del Prado, Madrid, February 26–27, 2007. Madrid: Museo Nacional del Prado, forthcoming.

Falomir, Miguel, ed. *Tintoretto*. Exh. cat. Madrid: Museo Nacional del Prado, 2007.

———, ed. *Tiziano*. Exh. cat. Madrid: Museo Nacional del Prado, 2003.

Fehl, Philipp P. *Decorum and Wit: The Poetry of Venetian Painting*. Vienna: IRSA, 1992.

Ferino-Pagden, Sylvia, ed. *Late Titian and the Sensuality of Painting*. Exh. cat. Venice: Marsilio, 2008.

———, ed. *Der späte Tizian und die Sinnlichkeit der Malerei*. Exh. cat. Vienna: Kunsthistorisches Museum, 2007.

Ferino-Pagden, Sylvia, and Giovanna Nepi Scirè, eds. *Giorgione: Myth and Enigma*. Exh. cat. Vienna: Kunsthistorisches Museum, 2004.

Finlay, Robert. *Politics in Renaissance Venice*. New Brunswick, NJ: Rutgers University Press, 1980.

Fischel, Oskar. *Tizian, des Meisters Gemälde in 368 Abbildungen*. Stuttgart: Deutsche verlagsanstalt, 1924.

Fredericksen, Burton B., and Federico Zeri. *Census of Pre-Nineteenth-Century Italian Paintings in North American Public Collections*. Cambridge, MA: Harvard University Press, 1972.

Freedman, Luba. *Titian's Portraits through Aretino's Lens*. University Park, PA: Penn State University Press, 1995.

Garton, John. *Grace and Grandeur: The Portraiture of Paolo Veronese*. London: Brepols Publishers, 2008.

Gemin, Massimo, ed. *Nuovi studi su Paolo Veronese*. Venice: Arsenale Editrice, 1990.

Goffen, Rona. *Renaissance Rivals: Michelangelo, Leonardo, Raphael, Titian*. New Haven, CT: Yale University Press, 2004.

———. *Titian's Women*. New Haven, CT: Yale University Press, 1997.

Goffen, Rona, and Giovanna Nepi Scirè, eds. *Il colore ritrovato: Bellini a Venezia*. Exh. cat. Milan: Electa, 2000.

Goldfarb, Hilliard. *Titian and Rubens: Power, Politics, and Style*. Exh. cat. Boston: Isabella Stewart Gardner Museum, 1998.

Goldner, George R. "A *Baptism of Christ* by Veronese in the Getty Museum." *The J. Paul Getty Museum Journal* 9 (1981): 111–26.

Habert, Jean, ed. *Le Paradis de Tintoret: Un concours pour le palais des Doges*. Exh. cat. Paris: Musée du Louvre Editions, 2006.

Habert, Jean, and Vincent Pomarède, eds. *Tiziano e la Pittura del Cinquecento a Venezia: Capolavori del Louvre*. Exh. cat. Conegliano, Italy: Linea d'ombra, 2004.

Hadley, Rollin, ed. *The Letters of Bernard Berenson and Isabella Stewart Gardner, 1887–1924*. Boston: Northeastern University Press, 1987.

Hall, Marcia. *Color and Meaning: Practice and Theory in Renaissance Painting*. Cambridge: Cambridge University Press, 1992.

Heinemann, Fritz. *Giovanni Bellini e i Belliniani*. 3 vols. Venice: Neri Pozza, 1962.

Hills, Paul. "Piety and Patronage in Cinquecento Venice: Tintoretto and the Scuole del Sacramento." *Art History* 6 (1983): 30–43.

———. *Venetian Colour: Marble, Mosaic, Painting and Glass, 1250–1550*. New Haven, CT: Yale University Press, 1999.

Hochmann, Michel. *Peintres et commanditaires à Venise (1540-1628)*. Rome: Ecole française de Rome, 1992.

Hope, Charles. *Titian*. London: Jupiter Books, 1980.

———. *Titian*. London: Chaucer Press, 2003.

———. "Titian as a Court Painter." *Oxford Art Journal* 2 (1979): 7–10.

Huber, Hans Dieter. *Paolo Veronese: Kunst als soziales System*. Munich: W. Fink, 2005.

Humfrey, Peter, ed. *The Age of Titian: Venetian Renaissance Art from Scottish Collections*. Exh. cat. Edinburgh: National Galleries of Scotland, 2004.

———. *The Altarpiece in Renaissance Venice*. New Haven, CT: Yale University Press, 1993.

———. *Painting in Renaissance Venice*. New Haven, CT: Yale University Press, 1995.

———. *Titian*. New York: Phaidon, 2007.

———. *Titian: The Complete Paintings*. Ghent: Ludion, 2007.

———, ed. *Venice and the Veneto*. Cambridge: Cambridge University Press, 2007.

Humfrey, Peter, and Richard Mackenney. "The Venetian Trade Guilds as Patrons of Art in the Renaissance." *The Burlington Magazine* 128, no. 998 (May 1986): 317–30.

Huse, Norbert, and Wolfgang Wolters. *The Art of Renaissance Venice: Architecture, Sculpture, and Painting, 1460–1590*. Chicago: University of Chicago Press, 1990.

Ilchman, Frederick, and Victoria S. Reed. "*The Birth of Saint John the Baptist* by Tintoretto in the Church of San Zaccaria: Conservation and Iconography." In *Arte nelle Venezie: Scritti di amici per Sandro Sponza*, edited by Chiara Ceschi, Pierluigi Fantelli, and Francesca Flores d'Arcais, 107–14. Saonara, Italy: Il Prato, 2007.

Jaffé, David, ed. *Titian*. Exh. cat. London: National Gallery, 2003.

Joannides, Paul. *Titian to 1518: The Assumption of Genius*. New Haven, CT: Yale University Press, 2001.

Kaftal, George. *Iconography of the Saints in the Painting of North East Italy*. Florence: Sansoni, 1978.

———. *Iconography of the Saints in the Painting of North West Italy*. Florence: Le Lettere, 1985.

———. *Iconography of the Saints in Tuscan Painting*. Florence: Sansoni, 1952.

Kanter, Laurence. *Italian Paintings in the Museum of Fine Arts, Boston*. Vol. 1, *13th–15th Century*. Boston: Museum of Fine Arts, Boston, 1994.

Kennedy, Ian G. *Titian*. Cologne: Taschen, 2006.

Keyes, George, Istvan Bárkóczi, and Jane Satkowski, eds. *Treasures of Venice: Paintings from the Museum of Fine Arts, Budapest*. Exh. cat. New York: Harry N. Abrams, 1995.

Krischel, Roland. *Jacopo Tintoretto, 1519–1594*. Cologne: Könemann, 2000.

Laclotte, Michel, Giovanna Nepi Scirè, et al. *Le siècle de Titien: L'âge d'or de la peinture à Venise*. Exh. cat. Paris: Réunion des musées nationaux, 1993.

Laclotte, Michel, Olivier Le Bihan, Patrick Ramade, and Michel Hochmann. *Splendeur de Venise, 1500–1600*. Exh. cat. Paris: Somogy, 2005.

Lepschy, Anna Laura. *Davanti a Tintoretto: Una storia del gusto attraverso i secoli*. Venice: Marsilio, 1998.

———. *Tintoretto Observed: A Documentary Survey of Critical Reactions from the 16th to the 20th Century*. Ravenna: Longo Editore, 1983.

Manca, Joseph, ed. *Titian 500*. Studies in the History of Art 45. Washington, DC: National Gallery of Art, 1993.

Marinelli, Sergio, ed. *Veronese e Verona*. Exh. cat. Verona: Museo di Castelvecchio, 1988.

Marini, Remigio. *L'opera completa del Veronese*. Milan: Rizzoli, 1968.

Martin, John, and Dennis Romano, eds. *Venice Reconsidered: The History and Civilization of an Italian City-State, 1297–1797*. Baltimore: Johns Hopkins University Press, 2000.

Martineau, Jane, and Charles Hope, eds. *The Genius of Venice, 1500–1600*. Exh. cat. London: Royal Academy of Arts, 1983.

Massimi, Maria Elena. "Jacopo Tintoretto e i confratelli della Scuola Grande di San Rocco: Strategie culturali e committenza artistica." *Venezia Cinquecento* 5 (1995): 5–107.

Matthew, Louisa C. "The Painter's Presence: Signatures in Venetian Renaissance Pictures." *Art Bulletin* 80 (1998): 616–48.

Morale, Giovanni, ed. *La Cena di Tiziano: Immagini del Risorto tra Louvre e Ambrosiana*. Exh. cat. Milan: Pinacoteca Ambrosiana, 2006.

National Gallery of Art. *Retaining the Original: Multiple Originals, Copies, and Reproductions*. Studies in the History of Art 20. Washington, DC: National Gallery of Art, 1989.

Nichols, Tom. *Tintoretto: Tradition and Identity*. London: Reaktion Books, 1999.

Nitti, Patrizia, Tullia Carratù, Morena Costantini, eds. *Titien: Le pouvoir en face*. Exh. cat. Paris: Skira, 2006.

Ost, Hans. *Tizians Kasseler Kavelier: Ein Betrag zum höfischen Porträt unter Karl V.* Cologne: Copy-Star, 1982.

Pallucchini, Rodolfo. *Giovanni Bellini*. Milan: A. Martello 1959.

———. *La giovinezza del Tintoretto*. Milan: D. Guarnati, 1950.

———. *Veronese*. Milan: Mondadori, 1984.

Pallucchini, Rodolfo, and Paola Rossi. *Tintoretto: Le opere sacre e profane*. 2 vols. Venice: Alfieri, 1982.

Panofsky, Erwin. *Problems in Titian, Mostly Iconographic: The Wrightsman Lectures Delivered under the Auspices of the New York University, Institute of Fine Arts*. New York: New York University Press, 1969.

Pedrocco, Filippo. *Titian*. New York: Rizzoli, 2001.

Penny, Nicholas. *National Gallery Catalogues: The Sixteenth Century Italian Paintings*. 2 vols. London: National Gallery, 2004–8.

Pignatti, Terisio. *The Golden Century of Venetian Painting*. Exh. cat. Los Angeles: Los Angeles County Museum of Art, 1979.

———. *Veronese*. 2 vols. Venice: Alfieri, 1976.

Pignatti, Terisio, and Filippo Pedrocco. *Veronese*. 2 vols. Milan: Electa, 1995.

———. *Veronese: Catalogo completo dei dipinti*. Florence: Cantini, 1991.

Pino, Paolo. *Dialogo di pittura* [1548]. Reprinted in vol. 1 of *Trattati d'arte del Cinquecento, fra Manierismo e Controriforma*, edited by Paola Barocchi. Bari: G. Laterza, 1960.

Pliny the Elder. *The Elder Pliny's Chapters on the History of Art*. Translated by K. Jex-Blake. Edited by E. Sellers. London: Macmillan, 1896.

Puttfarken, Thomas. *Titian and Tragic Painting*. New Haven, CT: Yale University Press, 2006.

Rearick, W. R. *The Art of Paolo Veronese, 1528–1588*. Exh. cat. Washington, DC: National Gallery of Art, 1988.

———. *Il disegno veneziano del Cinquecento*. Milan: Electa, 2001.

———. *Paolo Veronese: Disegni e dipinti*. Exh. cat. Venice: Fondazione Giorgio Cini, 1988.

———. "Reflections on Tintoretto as a Portraitist." *Artibus et Historiae* 31 (1995): 51–68.

Rebecchini, Guido. "'Tiziano e Mantova: *La Cena in Emmaus* per Nicola Maffei." *Venezia Cinquecento* 5, no. 10 (1995): 41–68.

Ridolfi, Carlo. *The Life of Tintoretto and of His Children Domenico and Marietta*. Translated by Catherine Enggass and Robert Enggass. University Park, PA: Penn State University Press, 1984.

———. *Le maraviglie dell'arte* [Venice, 1648]. Edited by Detlev von Hadeln. 2 vols. Berlin: Grote'sche Verlagsbuchhandlung, 1914–24.

Ringbom, Sixten. *Icon to Narrative: The Rise of the Dramatic Close-Up in Fifteenth-Century Devotional Painting*. Åbo: Åbo Akademi, 1965.

Romanelli, Giandomenico, and Claudio Strinati. *Veronese: Gods, Heroes, and Allegories*. Exh. cat. Milan: Skira, 2004.

Rosand, David. *Painting in Sixteenth-Century Venice: Titian, Veronese, Tintoretto*. Rev. ed. Cambridge: Cambridge University Press, 1997.

———. "The Stroke of the Brush." In *The Meaning of the Mark: Leonardo and Titian*, 49–89. Lawrence, KS: Spencer Museum of Art, 1988.

———. *Titian*. New York: Harry N. Abrams, 1978.

———. "Titian and the Eloquence of the Brush." *Artibus et Historiae* 2, no. 3 (1981): 85–86.

———, ed. *Titian: His World and His Legacy*. New York: Columbia University Press, 1982.

———. *Veronese and His Studio in North American Collections*. Exh. cat. Birmingham, AL: Birmingham Museum of Art, 1972.

Rosand, David, and Michelangelo Muraro. *Titian and the Venetian Woodcut*. Exh. cat. Washington, DC: International Exhibitions Foundation, 1976.

Roskill, Mark W. *Dolce's "Aretino" and Venetian Art Theory of the Cinquecento*. New York: New York University Press, 1968.

Rossi, Paola. *Jacopo Tintoretto*. Vol. 1, *I ritratti*. Venice: Alfieri, 1974.

———. *Jacopo Tintoretto: Ritratti*. Exh. cat. Milan: Electa, 1994.

———. *Tintoretto: Ritratti*. Milan: Electa, 1994.

Rossi, Paola, and Lionello Puppi, eds. *Jacopo Tintoretto nel quarto centenario della morte: Atti del convegno internazionale di studi. Venezia, 24–26 Novembre, 1994*. Padua: Il Poligrafo, 1996.

Salomon, Xavier F. *Veronese's Allegories: Virtue, Love, and Exploration in Renaissance Venice.* Exh. cat. New York: Frick Collection, 2006.

Sansovino, Francesco. *Venetia, città nobillisima et singolare descritta in XIII libri.* Edited by Giustiniano Martinoni. Venice: S. Curti, 1663.

Schulz, Juergen. *Venetian Painted Ceilings of the Renaissance.* Berkeley: University of California Press, 1968.

Shearman, John. *Only Connect . . . : Art and the Spectator in the Italian Renaissance.* Princeton, NJ: Princeton University Press, 1992.

Sinding-Larsen, Staale. "Christ in the Council Hall: Studies in the Religious Iconography of the Venetian Republic." *Acta ad archaeologiam et artium historiam pertinentia* 5 (1974): 1–262, 269–314.

Sohm, Philip. *The Artist Grows Old: The Aging of Art and Artists in Italy, 1500–1800.* New Haven, CT: Yale University Press, 2007.

———. *Pittoresco: Marco Boschini, His Critics, and Their Critiques of Painterly Brushwork in Seventeenth- and Eighteenth-Century Italy.* Cambridge: Cambridge University Press, 1991.

Spinosa, Nicola, ed. *Tiziano e il ritratto di corte da Raffaello ai Carracci.* Exh. cat. Naples: Museo di Capodimonte, 2006.

Suida, Wilhelm. *Le Titien.* Paris: A. Weber, 1935.

———. *Tiziano.* Zurich: Orell Füssli Verlag, 1933.

Syre, Cornelia, ed. *Tintoretto: The Gonzaga Cycle.* Exh. cat. Ostfildern-Ruit: Hatje Cantz, 2000.

Tietze, Hans. *Tintoretto.* New York: Phaidon, 1948.

Tietze, Hans, and Erika Tietze-Conrat. *The Drawings of the Venetian Painters in the 15th and 16th Centuries.* New York: J. J. Augustin, 1944.

Titian: Prince of Painters. Exh. cat. See Biadene, Susanna, and Mary Yakush, eds.

Tiziano e Venezia: Convegno internazionale di studi, Venezia, 1976. Vicenza: Neri Pozza, 1980.

Tiziano: Téchnicas y restauraciones; Actas del Simposium Internacional celebrado en el Museo Nacional del Prado los días 3, 4 y 5 junio de 1999. Madrid: Museo Nacional del Prado, 1999.

Toscano, Gennaro, and Francesco Valcanover, eds. *Da Bellini a Veronese: Temi di arte Veneta.* Venice: Istituto veneto di scienze, lettere ed arti, 2004.

Valcanover, Francesco. *L'opera completa di Tiziano.* Milan: Rizzoli, 1969.

Valcanover, Francesco, and Terisio Pignatti. *Tintoretto.* New York: Harry N. Abrams, 1985.

Vasari, Giorgio. *Lives of the Painters, Sculptors and Architects.* Translated by Gaston de Vere. 2 vols. New York: Alfred A. Knopf, 1996.

———. *Le vite de' più eccellenti pittori, scultori ed architettori* [1568]. Edited by Gaetano Milanesi. 9 vols. Florence: G. C. Sansoni, 1878–85.

Waagen, Gustav. *Galleries and Cabinets of Art in Great Britain.* London: John Murray, 1857.

———. *Treasures of Art in Great Britain.* 3 vols. London: John Murray, 1854.

Wethey, Harold E. *The Paintings of Titian: Complete Edition.* 3 vols. London: Phaidon, 1969–75.

Whitaker, Lucy, and Martin Clayton. *The Art of Italy in the Royal Collection: Renaissance and Baroque.* Exh. cat. London: Royal Collection Publications, 2007.

Wiel, Maria Agnese Chiari Moretto, ed. *Jacopo Tintoretto e i suoi incisori.* Exh. cat. Milan: Electa, 1994.

Wolters, Wolfgang. *Storia e politica nei dipinti di Palazzo Ducale: Aspetti dell'autocelebrazione della Repubblica di Venezia nel Cinquecento.* Venice: Arsenale Editrice, 1983.

Woods-Marsden, Joanna. *Renaissance Self-Portraiture: The Visual Construction of Identity and the Social Status of the Artist.* New Haven, CT: Yale University Press, 1998.

———, ed. *Titian: Materiality, Likeness, Istoria.* Turnhout, Belgium: Brepols, 2007.

Worthen, Thomas. "Tintoretto's Paintings for the *Banco del Sacramento* in S. Margherita." *Art Bulletin* 78 (1996): 707–32.

Zafran, Eric, ed. *Renaissance to Rococo: Masterpieces from the Wadsworth Atheneum Museum of Art.* New Haven, CT: Wadsworth Atheneum Museum of Art in association with Yale University Press, 2004.

Zanetti, Anton Maria. *Della pittura veneziana.* Venice: Giambatista Albrizzi, 1771.

Zeri, Federico, and Elizabeth E. Gardner. *Italian Paintings: A Catalogue of the Collection of the Metropolitan Museum of Art, Venetian School.* Greenwich, CT: New York Graphic Society, 1973.

Zorzi, Alvise. *Venezia scomparsa.* Milan: Mondadori, 2001.

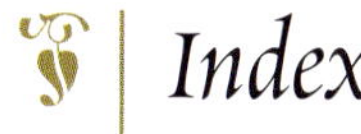

Index

Works by an artist appear at the end of the relevant entry. Churches and other buildings are located in Venice and its environs unless otherwise identified. Page numbers in italics indicate illustrations.